W9-BSD-019

# elevate science

SAVVAS
LEARNING COMPANY

# AUTHORS

## You're an author!

As you write in this science book, your answers and personal discoveries will be recorded for you to keep, making this book unique to you. That is why you are one of the primary authors of this book.

✏️ **In the space below, print your name, school, town, and state. Then write a short autobiography that includes your interests and accomplishments.**

YOUR NAME .......................................................................................

SCHOOL .............................................................................................

TOWN, STATE ....................................................................................

AUTOBIOGRAPHY .............................................................................

...........................................................................................................

...........................................................................................................

...........................................................................................................

Your Photo

**SAVVAS**
LEARNING COMPANY

ISBN-13: 978-0-328-94856-7
ISBN-10: 0-328-94856-X
11  21

# Program Authors

**ZIPPORAH MILLER, EdD**
*Coordinator for K-12 Science Programs, Anne Arundel County Public Schools*
Dr. Zipporah Miller currently serves as the Senior Manager for Organizational Learning with the Anne Arundel County Public School System. Prior to that she served as the K-12 Coordinator for science in Anne Arundel County. She conducts national training to science stakeholders on the Next Generation Science Standards. Dr. Miller also served as the Associate Executive Director for Professional Development Programs and conferences at the National Science Teachers Association (NSTA) and served as a reviewer during the development of Next Generation Science Standards. Dr. Miller holds a doctoral degree from the University of Maryland College Park, a master's degree in school administration and supervision from Bowie State University and a bachelor's degree from Chadron State College.

**MICHAEL J. PADILLA, PhD**
*Professor Emeritus, Eugene P. Moore School of Education, Clemson University, Clemson, South Carolina*
Michael J. Padilla taught science in middle and secondary schools, has more than 30 years of experience educating middle-school science teachers, and served as one of the writers of the 1996 U.S. National Science Education Standards. In recent years Mike has focused on teaching science to English Language Learners. His extensive experience as Principal Investigator on numerous National Science Foundation and U.S. Department of Education grants resulted in more than $35 million in funding to improve science education. He served as president of the National Science Teachers Association, the world's largest science teaching organization, in 2005–6.

**MICHAEL E. WYSESSION, PhD**
*Professor of Earth and Planetary Sciences, Washington University, St. Louis, Missouri*
Author of more than 100 science and science education publications, Dr. Wysession was awarded the prestigious National Science Foundation Presidential Faculty Fellowship and Packard Foundation Fellowship for his research in geophysics, primarily focused on using seismic tomography to determine the forces driving plate tectonics. Dr. Wysession is also a leader in geoscience literacy and education; he is the chair of the Earth Science Literacy Initiative, the author of several popular video lectures on geology in the *Great Courses* series, and a lead writer of the *Next Generation Science Standards**.

---

## Program Consultants

### Carol Baker
**Science Curriculum**

Dr. Carol K. Baker is superintendent for Lyons Elementary K-8 School District in Lyons, Illinois. Prior to this, she was Director of Curriculum for Science and Music in Oak Lawn, Illinois. Before this she taught Physics and Earth Science for 18 years. In the recent past, Dr. Baker also wrote assessment questions for ACT (EXPLORE and PLAN), was elected president of the Illinois Science Teachers Association from 2011–2013, and served as a member of the Museum of Science and Industry (Chicago) advisory board. She is a writer of the Next Generation Science Standards. Dr. Baker received her B.S. in Physics and a science teaching certification. She completed her master's of Educational Administration (K-12) and earned her doctorate in Educational Leadership.

### Jim Cummins
**ELL**

Dr. Cummins's research focuses on literacy development in multilingual schools and the role technology plays in learning across the curriculum. *Elevate Science* incorporates research-based principles for integrating language with the teaching of academic content based on Dr. Cummins's work.

### Elfrieda Hiebert
**Literacy**

Dr. Hiebert, a former primary-school teacher, is President and CEO of TextProject, a non-profit aimed at providing open-access resources for instruction of beginning and struggling readers, She is also a research associate at the University of California Santa Cruz. Her research addresses how fluency, vocabulary, and knowledge can be fostered through appropriate texts, and her contributions have been recognized through awards such as the Oscar Causey Award for Outstanding Contributions to Reading Research (Literacy Research Association, 2015), Research to Practice award (American Educational Research Association, 2013), and the William S. Gray Citation of Merit Award for Outstanding Contributions to Reading Research (International Reading Association, 2008).

## Content Reviewers

**Alex Blom, Ph.D.**
Associate Professor
Department Of Physical Sciences
Alverno College
Milwaukee, Wisconsin

**Joy Branlund, Ph.D.**
Department of Physical Science
Southwestern Illinois College
Granite City, Illinois

**Judy Calhoun**
Associate Professor
Physical Sciences
Alverno College
Milwaukee, Wisconsin

**Stefan Debbert**
Associate Professor of Chemistry
Lawrence University
Appleton, Wisconsin

**Diane Doser**
Professor
Department of Geological Sciences
University of Texas at El Paso
El Paso, Texas

**Rick Duhrkopf, Ph.D.**
Department of Biology
Baylor University
Waco, Texas

**Jennifer Liang**
University of Minnesota Duluth
Duluth, Minnesota

**Heather Mernitz, Ph.D.**
Associate Professor of Physical
 Sciences
Alverno College
Milwaukee, Wisconsin

**Joseph McCullough, Ph.D.**
Cabrillo College
Aptos, California

**Katie M. Nemeth, Ph.D.**
Assistant Professor
College of Science and Engineering
University of Minnesota Duluth
Duluth, Minnesota

**Maik Petermann**
Department of Geology
Western Wyoming Community College
Rock Springs, Wyoming

**Scott Rochette**
Department of the Earth Sciences
The College at Brockport
 State University of New York
Brockport, New York

**David Schuster**
Washington University in St Louis
St. Louis, Missouri

**Shannon Stevenson**
Department of Biology
University of Minnesota Duluth
Duluth, Minnesota

**Paul Stoddard, Ph.D.**
Department of Geology and
 Environmental Geosciences
Northern Illinois University
DeKalb, Illinois

**Nancy Taylor**
American Public University
Charles Town, West Virginia

## Teacher Reviewers

**Jennifer Bennett, M.A.**
Memorial Middle School
Tampa, Florida

**Sonia Blackstone**
Lake County Schools
Howey In the Hills, Florida

**Teresa Bode**
Roosevelt Elementary
Tampa, Florida

**Tyler C. Britt, Ed.S.**
Curriculum & Instructional
  Practice Coordinator
Raytown Quality Schools
Raytown, Missouri

**A. Colleen Campos**
Grandview High School
Aurora, Colorado

**Ronald Davis**
Riverview Elementary
Riverview, Florida

**Coleen Doulk**
Challenger School
Spring Hill, Florida

**Mary D. Dube**
Burnett Middle School
Seffner, Florida

**Sandra Galpin**
Adams Middle School
Tampa, Florida

**Margaret Henry**
Lebanon Junior High School
Lebanon, Ohio

**Christina Hill**
Beth Shields Middle School
Ruskin, Florida

**Judy Johnis**
Gorden Burnett Middle School
Seffner, Florida

**Karen Y. Johnson**
Beth Shields Middle School
Ruskin, Florida

**Jane Kemp**
Lockhart Elementary School
Tampa, Florida

**Denise Kuhling**
Adams Middle School
Tampa, Florida

**Esther Leonard, M.Ed. and L.M.T.**
Gifted and talented Implementation Specialist
San Antonio Independent School District
San Antonio, Texas

**Kelly Maharaj**
Challenger K–8 School of Science
  and Mathematics
Spring Hill, Florida

**Kevin J. Maser, Ed.D.**
H. Frank Carey Jr/Sr High School
Franklin Square, New York

**Angie L. Matamoros, Ph.D.**
ALM Science Consultant
Weston, Florida

**Corey Mayle**
Brogden Middle School
Durham, North Carolina

**Keith McCarthy**
George Washington Middle School
Wayne, New Jersey

**Yolanda O. Peña**
John F. Kennedy Junior High School
West Valley City, Utah

**Kathleen M. Poe**
Jacksonville Beach Elementary School
Jacksonville Beach, Florida

**Wendy Rauld**
Monroe Middle School
Tampa, Florida

**Anne Rice**
Woodland Middle School
Gurnee, Illinois

**Bryna Selig**
Gaithersburg Middle School
Gaithersburg, Maryland

**Pat (Patricia) Shane, Ph.D.**
STEM & ELA Education Consultant
Chapel Hill, North Carolina

**Diana Shelton**
Burnett Middle School
Seffner, Florida

**Nakia Sturrup**
Jennings Middle School
Seffner, Florida

**Melissa Triebwasser**
Walden Lake Elementary
Plant City, Florida

**Michele Bubley Wiehagen**
Science Coach
Miles Elementary School
Tampa, Florida

**Pauline Wilcox**
Instructional Science Coach
Fox Chapel Middle School
Spring Hill, Florida

## Safety Reviewers

**Douglas Mandt, M.S.**
Science Education Consultant
Edgewood, Washington

**Juliana Textley, Ph.D.**
Author, NSTA books on school science safety
Adjunct Professor
Lesley University
Cambridge, Massachusetts

v

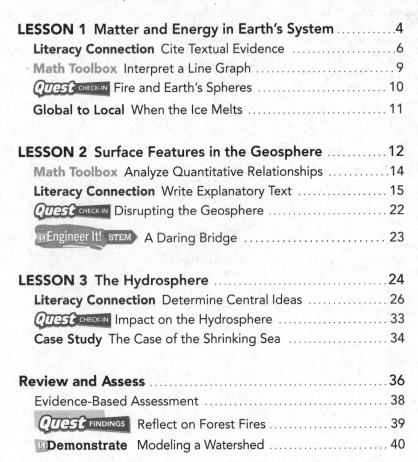

Go to SavvasRealize.com to access your digital course.

**▶ VIDEO**
- Aquaculture Manager

**👆 INTERACTIVITY**
- Describing Systems
- Thermal Energy and the Cycling of Matter
- Maps and Methods
- Constructive and Destructive Forces
- The Water Cycle
- Siting a Fish Farm
- Floridan Aquifer System

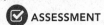

**📖 VIRTUAL LAB**
- Changes in the Water Cycle

**☑ ASSESSMENT**

**📖 eTEXT**

## HANDS-ON LABS

**Connect** What Interactions Occur Within the Earth System?

**Investigate**
- Where Heat Flows
- Surface Features
- Water on Earth

**Demonstrate**
Modeling a Watershed

Go to SavvasRealize.com to access your digital course.

▶ **VIDEO**
• Meteorologist

**INTERACTIVITY**
• Layers in the Atmosphere • Patterns in the Wind • Ways That Water Moves • Water Cycle • Interruptions in the Water Cycle • Clean Drinking Water • When Air Masses Collide • Mapping Out the Weather • Using Air Masses to Predict Weather • Weather Predicting • Not in Kansas Anymore • Tinkering with Technology

**VIRTUAL LAB**
• Hurricane Season

**ASSESSMENT**

**eTEXT**

## HANDS-ON LABS

иConnect Puddle Befuddlement

иInvestigate
• Effects of Altitude on the Atmosphere
• How Clouds and Fog Form
• Weather Fronts
• Tracking Weather
• Predicting Hurricanes

иDemonstrate
Water from Trees

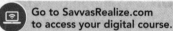
Go to SavvasRealize.com
to access your digital course.

▶ **VIDEO**
- Product Engineer

👆 **INTERACTIVITY**
- Hot on the Inside
- Earth's Layers
- Comparing Earth and the Moon
- Designing Satellites
- So Many, Many Minerals
- Mineral Management
- Don't Take it for Granite
- Is There a Geologist in the House?
- Rocky Changes
- Rock Cycle
- Rocks on the Move

📱 **VIRTUAL LAB**
- Rocks and Minerals: The Story
  of Earth

☑ **ASSESSMENT**

📖 **eTEXT**

HANDS-ON LABS

**Connect** Build a Model of Earth

**Investigate**
- Heat and Motion in a Liquid
- Mineral Mash-Up
- Growing a Crystal Garden
- A Sequined Rock
- Ages of Rocks

**Demonstrate**
The Rock Cycle in Action

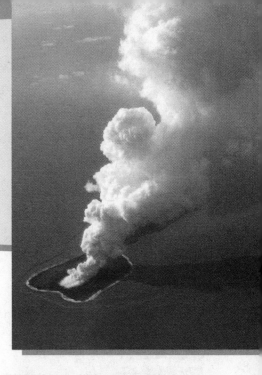

Go to SavvasRealize.com
to access your digital course.

▶ **VIDEO**
• Volcanologist

👆 **INTERACTIVITY**
• Land and Seafloor Patterns
• Slow and Steady
• By No Fault of Their Own
• Relative Plate Motion
• Stressed to a Fault
• Earthquake Engineering
• Locating an Earthquake
• Placing a Bay Area Stadium
• Landforms from Volcanic Activity
• Volcanoes Changing Earth's Surface

📱 **VIRTUAL LAB**
• Geological Processes and Evil Plans

☑ **ASSESSMENT**

📖 **eTEXT**

**uConnect** How Are Earth's Continents
Linked Together?

**uInvestigate**
• Piecing Together a Supercontinent
• Plate Interactions
• Analyze Earthquake Data to Identify
Patterns
• Moving Volcanoes

**uDemonstrate**
Model Sea-Floor Spreading

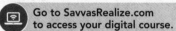
Go to SavvasRealize.com
to access your digital course.

**▶ VIDEO**
• Civil Engineer

**👆 INTERACTIVITY**
• Colors of the Sand
• Dating Using Weathering Rates
• Classify the Force of Weathering
• Predicting Disasters
• Material Slope Angle
• Changing Landscapes
• Karst Topography
• Carving a Canyon
• Mammoth Caves
• Effects of Glaciers
• Glacial Ice
• Coastline Management

**📱 VIRTUAL LAB**
• Save the Town

**☑ ASSESSMENT**

**📖 eTEXT**

# HANDS-ON LABS

**иConnect** How Does Gravity
Affect Materials on a Slope?

**иInvestigate**
• Freezing and Thawing
• Small, Medium, and Large
• Raindrops Falling
• Changing Coastlines

**иDemonstrate**
Materials on a Slope

Go to SavvasRealize.com to access your digital course.

**VIDEO**
- Geophysicist

**INTERACTIVITY**
- Distribution of Fossil Fuels
- Using Renewable Resources
- Biogas Farming
- Distribution of Minerals
- Distribution of Water Resources
- Wetland Restoration
- Water Worth

**VIRTUAL LAB**
- Go With the Flow (Through an Aquifer)

**ASSESSMENT**

**eTEXT**

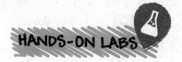
## HANDS-ON LABS

**иConnect** What's in a Piece of Coal?

**иInvestigate**
- Fossil Fuels
- The Power of Wind
- Cool Crystals
- An Artesian Well

**иDemonstrate**
To Drill or Not to Drill

Go to SavvasRealize.com to access your digital course.

▶ **VIDEO**
- Water Engineer

👆 **INTERACTIVITY**
- Modern Life
- Human Population Growth
- Sources of Resources
- Damage From the Skies
- Sources and Solutions of Air Pollution
- Farming Lessons
- Ride the Light Rail
- Water Cycle Interrupted
- Mutation Mystery
- Wetland Restoration
- Research Water Pollution

📱 **VIRTUAL LAB**
- Electricity Usage

☑ **ASSESSMENT**

📖 **eTEXT**

## HANDS-ON LABS

**иConnect** Finding a Solution for Your Pollution

**иInvestigate**
- Doubling Time
- It's All in the Air
- Mining Matters
- Getting Clean

**иDemonstrate**
Washing Away

**TOPIC 8**

# History of Earth ............ 362

**The Essential Question** How can events in Earth's past be organized?

**Quest KICKOFF** The Big Fossil Hunt ............. 364

**µConnect Lab** Dividing History ............365A

MS-ESS1-4

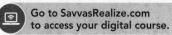

Go to SavvasRealize.com
to access your digital course.

▶ **VIDEO**
• Paleontologist

👆 **INTERACTIVITY**
• Oldest to Youngest
• Radiometric Dating
• Know Your Index Fossils
• On the Clock
• A Very Grand Canyon
• Going Away
• How Old Are These Rocks?
• Observation and Deduction
• Big Changes

**VIRTUAL LAB**
• The Story in the Strata

☑ **ASSESSMENT**

📖 **eTEXT**

**HANDS-ON LABS**

**µConnect** Dividing History

**µInvestigate**
• The Story in Rocks
• Going Back in Time
• Changes in the Water

**µDemonstrate**
Core Sampling Through Time

# Energy in the Atmosphere and Ocean ............................ 402

**The Essential Question** How does energy move throughout Earth's atmosphere and ocean?

**Quest KICKOFF** Crossing the Atlantic ............. 404

uConnect Lab Does a Plastic Bag Trap Heat? ...405A

MS-ESS2-6

Go to SavvasRealize.com to access your digital course.

**VIDEO**
• Ship Captain

**INTERACTIVITY**
• Fluids on the Move
• Patterns in the Wind
• Where the Wind Blows
• Winds Across the Globe
• Currents and Climate
• Ocean Habitats
• Keeping Current on Currents

**VIRTUAL LAB**
• An Adventure at Maui Beach

**ASSESSMENT**

**eTEXT**

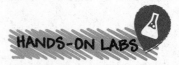

**HANDS-ON LABS**

uConnect Does a Plastic Bag Trap Heat?

uInvestigate
• Heating Earth's Surface
• United States Precipitation
• Modeling Ocean Current Formation

uDemonstrate
Not All Heating Is Equal

 Go to SavvasRealize.com to access your digital course.

▶ **VIDEO**
• Science Writer

👆 **INTERACTIVITY**
• Two Sides of a Mountain
• Olympic Choices
• In the Greenhouse
• Human Impact on Climate Change
• Climate Change Q&A
• Methane Management
• Emission Reduction

📱 **VIRTUAL LAB**
• Frozen in Time

✅ **ASSESSMENT**

📖 **eTEXT**

## HANDS-ON LABS

**uConnect** How Climates Differ

**uInvestigate**
• Classifying Climates
• What is the Greenhouse Effect?
• Thermal Expansion of Water

**uDemonstrate**
An Ocean of a Problem

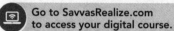

Go to SavvasRealize.com
to access your digital course.

▶ **VIDEO**
• Planetarium Technician

👆 **INTERACTIVITY**
• Discovery of the Solar System
• Interpreting the Night Sky
• Patterns in Earth's Rotation
  and Revolution
• What Keeps Objects in Motion?
• Seasons on Earth
• Our View of the Moon
• Eclipses
• Moon Phases and Eclipses

📱 **VIRTUAL LAB**
• Shadows in Space

☑ **ASSESSMENT**

📖 **eTEXT**

## HANDS-ON LABS

**Connect** What Is at the Center?
**Investigate**
• Watching the Skies
• Lighten Up!
• How Does the Moon Move?

**Demonstrate**
Modeling Lunar Phases

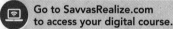

Go to SavvasRealize.com
to access your digital course.

**▶ VIDEO**
• Astrophysicist

**👆 INTERACTIVITY**
• Distance Learning
• Anatomy of the Sun
• Solar System
• How to Make a Solar System
• Space Exploration
• Telescopes
• Launch a Space Probe
• Eyes in Sky
• Star Systems
• Lives of the Stars
• Types of Galaxies
• Model a Galaxy

**📱 VIRTUAL LAB**
• A New Home

**☑ ASSESSMENT**

**📖 eTEXT**

## HANDS-ON LABS

**uConnect** Planetary Measures
**uInvestigate**
• Pulling Planets
• Layers of the Sun
• Space Exploration Vehicle
• How Far Is That Star?
• Model the Milky Way

**uDemonstrate**
Scaling Down the Solar System

# Elevate your thinking!

*Elevate Science* takes science to a whole new level and lets you take ownership of your learning. Explore science in the world around you. Investigate how things work. Think critically and solve problems! *Elevate Science* helps you think like a scientist, so you're ready for a world of discoveries.

## Explore Your World

Explore real-life scenarios with engaging Quests that dig into science topics around the world. You can:

- Solve real-world problems
- Apply skills and knowledge
- Communicate solutions

### Quest KICKOFF

**What do you think is causing Pleasant Pond to turn green?**

In 2016, algal blooms turned bodies of water green and slimy in Florida, Utah, California, and 17 other states. These blooms put people and ecosystems in danger. Scientists, such as limnologists, are working to predict and prevent future algal blooms. In this problem-based Quest activity, you will investigate an algal bloom at a lake and determine its cause. In labs and digital activities, you will apply what you learn in each lesson to help you gather evidence to solve the mystery. With enough evidence, you will be able to identify what you believe is the cause of the algal bloom and present a solution in the Findings activity.

## Make Connections

*Elevate Science* connects science to other subjects and shows you how to better understand the world through:

- Mathematics
- Reading and Writing
- Literacy

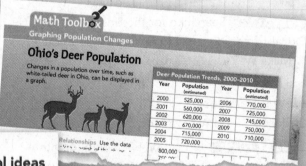

### Math Toolbox
Graphing Population Changes

#### Ohio's Deer Population

Changes in a population over time, such as white-tailed deer in Ohio, can be displayed in a graph.

Deer Population Trends, 2000–2010

| Year | Population (estimated) | Year | Population (estimated) |
|------|------------------------|------|------------------------|
| 2000 | 525,000 | 2006 | 770,000 |
| 2001 | 560,000 | 2007 | 725,000 |
| 2002 | 620,000 | 2008 | 745,000 |
| 2003 | 670,000 | 2009 | 750,000 |
| 2004 | 715,000 | 2010 | 710,000 |
| 2005 | 720,000 | | |

Relationships Use the data

800,000

### READING CHECK  Determine Central ideas
What adaptations might the giraffe have that help it survive in its environment?

### Academic Vocabulary
Relate the term *decomposer* to the verb *compose*. What does it mean to compose something?

# Build Skills for the Future

- Master the Engineering Design Process
- Apply critical thinking and analytical skills
- Learn about STEM careers

# Focus on Inquiry

Case studies put you in the shoes of a scientist to solve real-world mysteries using real data. You will be able to:

- Analyze Data
- Test a hypothesis
- Solve the Case

Case Study

MS-LS2-1

THE CASE OF THE DISAPPEARING

## Cerulean Warbler

The cerulean warbler is a small, migratory songbird named for its blue color. Cerulean warblers breed in eastern North America during the spring and summer. The warblers spend the winter months in the Andes Mountains of Colombia, Venezuela, Ecuador, and Peru in northern part of South America.

# Enter the Lab

Hands-on experiments and virtual labs help you test ideas and show what you know in performance-based assessments. Scaffolded labs include:

- STEM Labs
- Design Your Own
- Open-ended Labs

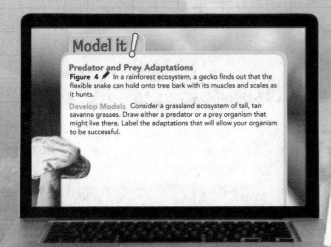

## Model it

**Predator and Prey Adaptations**
**Figure 4** In a rainforest ecosystem, a gecko finds out that the flexible snake can hold onto tree bark with its muscles and scales as it hunts.

Develop Models Consider a grassland ecosystem of tall, tan savanna grasses. Draw either a predator or a prey organism that might live there. Label the adaptations that will allow your organism to be successful.

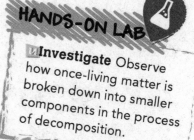

HANDS-ON LAB

**Investigate** Observe how once-living matter is broken down into smaller components in the process of decomposition.

# TOPIC
# 1

# Introduction to Earth's Systems

**NGSS PERFORMANCE EXPECTATIONS**

**MS-ESS2-1** Develop a model to describe the
cycling of Earth's materials and the flow of energy
that drives this process.

**MS-ESS2-4** Develop a model to describe the
cycling of water through Earth's systems driven by
energy from the sun and the force of gravity.

## HANDS-ON LAB

**uConnect** Develop a model to
describe interactions among
Earth's spheres.

GO ONLINE
to access your
digital course

 VIDEO

 INTERACTIVITY

 VIRTUAL LAB

 ASSESSMENT

 eTEXT

 HANDS-ON LAB

HOW do all the things in this photo interact with each other?

## The Essential Question

How do matter and energy cycle through Earth's systems?

**CCC Systems and System Models** How do water, rock, air, and organisms interact to make Earth's surface features and systems?

................................................................

................................................................

................................................................

................................................................

................................................................

................................................................

................................................................

# How can you predict the effects of a forest fire?

**Phenomenon** You just watched a news report about a wildfire that is burning just north of your town. The fire is not under control, and you wonder what will happen to the forest. In this problem-based Quest activity, you will take on the role of a scientist whose task is to educate and inform local residents about the harmful effects of a forest fire. You will consider how all the spheres of the Earth system interact, then use that information to make predictions about the outcome of the fire's damage. Your presentation will take the form of a poster, photo essay, or a multimedia report.

**NBC LEARN** ▶ VIDEO

After watching the Quest Kickoff video, which explores the effects of a forest fire, record ways in which a fire will impact Earth's spheres.

**Organisms:**

.................................................................

.................................................................

**Ground/Earth:**

.................................................................

.................................................................

**Air:**

.................................................................

.................................................................

**Water:**

.................................................................

.................................................................

### 👆 INTERACTIVITY

Forest Fires

**MS-ESS2-1** Develop a model to describe the cycling of Earth's materials and the flow of energy that drives this process.
**MS-ESS2-4** Develop a model to describe the cycling of water through Earth's systems driven by energy from the sun and the force of gravity.

## Quest CHECK-IN

### IN LESSON 1

How can an event in one sphere, such as the atmosphere, have an impact on another sphere? Think about the flow of energy as the fire started, then spread.

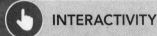

### 👆 INTERACTIVITY

Fire and Earth's Spheres

## Quest CHECK-IN

### IN LESSON 2

How do all of Earth's spheres interact? Consider these interactions as you learn how fire affects the geosphere.

### 👆 INTERACTIVITY

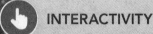

Disrupting the Geosphere

Fires are part of the natural life cycle of a forest. However, when they happen at the wrong time or burn for too long, forest fires have a devastating effect on plant and animal populations. Fires also affect the surrounding air, water, and land.

## Quest CHECK-IN

### IN LESSON 3

How does the hydrosphere interact with the other spheres, and vice versa? Examine the effects of fire on the hydrosphere. Then review all data and finalize your predictions.

👆 **INTERACTIVITY**

Impact on the Hydrosphere

## Quest FINDINGS

## Complete the Quest!

Create an engaging presentation to summarize your findings. Reflect on how the spheres influence each other—and your town.

👆 **INTERACTIVITY**

Reflect on Forest Fires

MS-ESS2-1

# What Interactions Occur Within the Earth System?

How can you **develop and use a model** to describe interactions within the Earth system?

## Materials

**(per group)**

- index cards in green, yellow, blue, and white
- bulletin board
- pushpins
- poster paper
- variety of art and office supplies, such as the following: tape, markers, colored paper, scissors, paper cups, yarn or string, magazines, newspapers, staples, and stapler

Be sure to follow all safety procedures provided by your teacher. The Safety Appendix of your textbook provides more details about the safety icons.

## Background

**Phenomenon** You read in an article that "Scientists classify matter on Earth into four spheres: living things, rocks, water, and air. The spheres interact and form the Earth system." You wonder how the spheres interact. You turn the page, only to find the rest of the article is missing. When you ask your teacher to help you understand the Earth system, he challenges you to complete the article by doing your own analysis of interactions among Earth's spheres.

## Develop a Model

1. Get an index card from your teacher. Join other students with the same color card to form a sphere group. Green is living things, yellow is rocks, blue is water, and white is air.

2. As a group, brainstorm about matter that makes up your sphere. Discuss these questions. Record your ideas in the table.
   - What are some of properties, or characteristics of the matter in your sphere?
   - What are some examples of living things/rocks/water/air in your town, state, or elsewhere? How do they change or move?

3. Read the number on your card. Join other students with the same number to form an Earth system group.

4. Share what you know about your sphere with your group. Then brainstorm how different spheres interact with and affect each other. Discuss these questions. Record your ideas in the table.
   - In what ways does your sphere depend on other spheres?
   - How do parts of your sphere move within or cycle through other spheres?

5. ✂️ **SEP Develop a Model** As a group, build an Earth system model that illustrates the interactions among the spheres. Include specific examples.

**Connect** Go online for a downloadable worksheet of this lab.

HANDS-ON LAB

## Observations

| Ideas About Your Sphere | Ideas About Sphere Interactions |
|---|---|
| | |

## Analyze and Conclude

1. **SEP Use a Model** How did you represent Earth's spheres and the interactions between those spheres in your model?

..................................................................................................................................
..................................................................................................................................
..................................................................................................................................
..................................................................................................................................

2. **CCC Energy and Matter** How might matter represented in your model move from one sphere to another on Earth? Give two examples.

..................................................................................................................................
..................................................................................................................................

3. **SEP Communicate Scientific Information** Complete the magazine article by writing a paragraph that describes at least three interactions between Earth's spheres.

..................................................................................................................................
..................................................................................................................................
..................................................................................................................................

# 1 Matter and Energy in Earth's System

## Guiding Questions

- What are the different components of the Earth system?
- What are the sources of energy for the processes that affect Earth?
- How can you model the cycling of matter in the Earth system?

## Connections

**Literacy** Cite Textual Evidence

**Math** Interpret a Line Graph

MS-ESS2-1

## HANDS-ON LAB

иInvestigate Model how energy flows within Earth.

### Vocabulary

atmosphere
geosphere
hydrosphere
cryosphere
biosphere
energy

### Academic Vocabulary

system
feedback

## Connect It !

✏ **Draw a line on the photo to indicate where the surface of the lake was in the past.**

CCC Cause and Effect What happened to the water in this lake? Why do you think this happened?

......................................................................................................

......................................................................................................

# The Earth System

Lake Mead, shown in **Figure 1**, is part of a large system consisting of the Colorado River, Hoover Dam, and Las Vegas, Nevada. A **system** is a group of parts that work together as a whole. If we zoom way out, the universe is the biggest system of all, and it contains all other systems. Earth is a system, too.

**Water and Rock Cycles** The Earth system involves flows of matter and energy through different components. In the water cycle, water evaporates from the ocean and other bodies of water. Then it rises into the atmosphere and eventually falls back to Earth's surface as precipitation. Rain and meltwater then flow to rivers, lakes, and the ocean. Eventually the water cycles back into the atmosphere. At each step of a cycle of matter, some change in energy occurs to keep the cycle going. Evaporation of water requires heat energy. The heat energy may come from the sun or from within Earth, as in a hot spring.

Rock also cycles through the Earth system. Hot molten material inside Earth, called magma, flows up through cracks in Earth's crust. This new material cools—loses heat energy—to form solid rock. Over time, the rock can be eroded into small pieces. If enough small pieces collect, they may get packed together to form new rock.

☑ READING CHECK **Compare and Contrast** How are the rock and water cycles similar? How are they different?

..............................................................................................................

..............................................................................................................

..............................................................................................................

..............................................................................................................

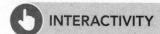

INTERACTIVITY

Explore different types of systems.

**Academic Vocabulary**
Much of science involves identifying components of different systems. List two systems you hear about in everyday life. What are their components?

..............................................................

..............................................................

..............................................................

..............................................................

..............................................................

..............................................................

..............................................................

**The Cycling of Water**
**Figure 1** Drought has had a serious impact on Lake Mead, a reservoir in Nevada.

**VIDEO**

Learn about the main spheres of Earth's system and how they interact.

**Literacy Connection**

**Cite Textual Evidence**
Reread the sections about the atmosphere. Underline the evidence that supports the idea that the atmosphere affects Earth's climate.

**Earth's Spheres** The Earth system is made up of four main spheres, or subsystems, shown in **Figure 2**. Earth's **atmosphere** (AT muh sfeer) is the relatively thin envelope of gases that forms Earth's outermost layer. It is made of air— a mixture of gases including nitrogen, oxygen, water vapor, and carbon dioxide—and dust particles. It contains Earth's weather, and it is the foundation for the different climates around the world. Most of Earth's mass is in the form of rock and metal of the **geosphere** (GEE uh sfeer). The geosphere includes the solid metal inner core, the liquid metal outer core, and the rocky mantle and crust. All of Earth's water, including water that cycles through the atmosphere, is called the **hydrosphere** (HI druh sfeer). The **cryosphere** (CRY uh sfeer) is the frozen component of the hydrosphere. It is made up of all the ice and snow on land, plus sea and lake ice. The parts of Earth that contain all living organisms are collectively known as the **biosphere** (BI uh sfeer).

Earth's outermost layer receives energy in the form of sunlight that passes through it and from heat that rises from Earth's surface, including the ocean. Heat rising from Earth's surface creates wind, which distributes heat as well as water through the atmosphere.

Earth's rock and metal contain an enormous amount of energy. Exposed rock absorbs sunlight and radiates heat into the atmosphere. In some locations, energy and new material make up the rocky outer layer of the geosphere in the form of lava. Major eruptions can affect the atmosphere, which in turn affects the hydrosphere and biosphere.

**Energy Flow** The constant flow, or cycling, of matter through the Earth system requires energy. **Energy** is the ability to do work. The Earth system has two main sources of energy: heat from the sun and heat from Earth's interior. These energy sources drive cycles of matter in the four spheres.

🧪 **HANDS-ON LAB**

☑**Investigate** Model how energy flows within Earth.

☑ READING CHECK **Use Information** Which part of each sphere do you interact with in your daily life? Give one example for each of the main spheres.

.......................................................................................................

.......................................................................................................

.......................................................................................................

## Earth's Spheres

**Figure 2** Earth has four major spheres that cycle matter and energy and shape Earth's surface. Label each box with the correct sphere name. Then, list at least two spheres that show an interaction within the photo.

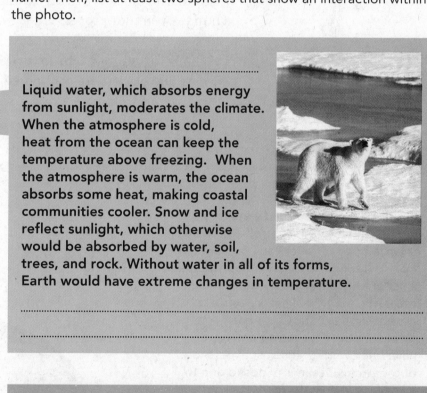

Liquid water, which absorbs energy from sunlight, moderates the climate. When the atmosphere is cold, heat from the ocean can keep the temperature above freezing. When the atmosphere is warm, the ocean absorbs some heat, making coastal communities cooler. Snow and ice reflect sunlight, which otherwise would be absorbed by water, soil, trees, and rock. Without water in all of its forms, Earth would have extreme changes in temperature.

.......................................................................................................

.......................................................................................................

Life has been found in virtually every part of Earth, from deep below the continental ice shelf of Antarctica to high up in the Himalayan Mountains.

.......................................................................................................

.......................................................................................................

## Academic Vocabulary

Feedback involves a loop in which a signal or action triggers another signal or action. This can happen when a microphone picks up sound from a speaker that is amplifying the microphone's signal. The equipment passes the signal back and forth, and it becomes louder and harsher. What is one form of feedback that you encounter in your life?

..............................................

..............................................

..............................................

..............................................

# System Feedback

Glaciers, part of the cryosphere, are large blocks of ancient ice, usually found near mountains and in polar regions. Like a freezer pack in a cooler, a glacier keeps the surrounding air and land cool. But many glaciers are melting around the world. As glaciers melt, they lose mass and volume and turn into liquid water that drains away or evaporates. This allows the land underneath to absorb more sunlight, which causes the surrounding air and land to get warmer. The warmer air makes glaciers melt even faster. This is an example of **feedback**. The system returns, or feeds back, information about itself, and that information results in change.

### Positive and Negative Feedback
Sometimes feedback is negative: it causes a process to slow down, or go in reverse. But some types of feedback are positive: they reinforce, speed up, or enhance the process that's already underway. Feedback may result in stability or it may cause more change. The melting glaciers are an example of positive feedback and change. A similar process is causing change in the Arctic.

**READING CHECK Cite Textual Evidence** Name a reason why melting glaciers are considered positive feedback.

..............................................................................................

..............................................................................................

## Model It !

### Sea Ice and Climate

**Figure 3** Liquid and solid water are important factors in controlling climate. A large body of water can absorb energy from the sun, while snow or ice reflects solar energy back into space. In recent years, the amount of sea ice—frozen water—in the Arctic Circle has been dwindling because the air and water have been warmer than usual. As more of the Arctic Ocean is exposed due to loss of ice, it absorbs more sunlight and gets warmer. This makes it less likely for sea ice to form even when the air is well below freezing.

**CCC Energy and Matter** ✏ On the image provided, draw and label a cycle diagram for the feedback that is occurring in the Arctic among ice, liquid seawater, atmosphere, and solar energy.

Sea Ice

# Math Toolbox

## Arctic Sea Ice

Historically, Arctic winters had long, dark nights and seawater froze. In the warmer summers, much of the sea ice melted. Today, more Arctic ice melts in summer than it has in human history. The total area of Arctic sea ice has changed in recent years as the globe has warmed. The graph shows the amount of sea ice found in the Arctic Ocean for the following years: 1986, 1996, 2006, and 2016.

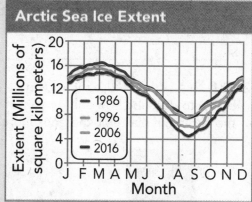

Arctic Sea Ice Extent

1. **CCC Patterns** What is the trend in the data?

.................................................................

2. **Interpret a Line Graph** What was the lowest extent of sea ice in the data, and when did it occur?

.................................................................

3. **CCC Stability and Change** What will happen to the extent of sea ice in the Arctic if temperatures continue to rise? Incorporate what you know about "feedback" into your prediction.

.................................................................

.................................................................

.................................................................

## Interacting Spheres
An event in one sphere can affect another, which in turn can affect another. For example, Greenland is losing about 250 billion tons of ice each year. As the massive ice sheet thins, the weight of the ice decreases. As a result, in some parts of Greenland, the land is rising about 1.0 cm per year. How can this happen? Earth's rocky outer layer is floating on a denser layer of rock below the crust.

A landmass that gets heavier by gaining more water or other material will "sink," while a landmass that gets lighter by losing material will rise. It's like a boat in the water with its cargo off-loaded, as shown in **Figure 4**. As containers are removed, there's less mass on the boat. This causes the boat to sit higher in the water because it is more buoyant.

**INTERACTIVITY**

Examine thermal energy and the cycling of matter in Earth's spheres.

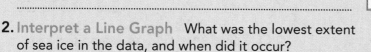
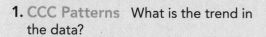

Lighter boat    Heavier boat

Water level    Draft    A boat's **draft** shows how deep it sits in the water.    Water level    Draft

**Buoyancy of Landmasses**
**Figure 4** A landmass can rise and sit higher on Earth's surface if it sheds a lot of mass, just like a boat floating on water.

# ☑ LESSON 1 Check

MS-ESS2-1

**1. Identify** What is the term for the part of the hydrosphere that is frozen?

...............................................................

**2. SEP Use Models** Use the rock cycle diagram below to describe how energy is involved in the cycling of matter in the geosphere.

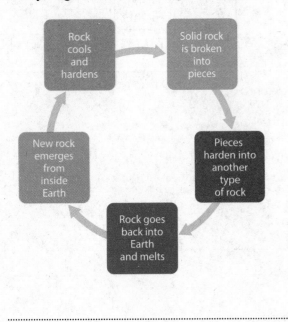

...............................................................
...............................................................
...............................................................
...............................................................

**3. CCC Cause and Effect** During the water cycle, water evaporates, rises into the atmosphere, and eventually falls back to Earth's surface as precipitation. What is the original source of energy that produces these changes?

...............................................................
...............................................................
...............................................................
...............................................................

**4. CCC Systems** Give an example of the hydrosphere interacting with the geosphere.

...............................................................
...............................................................
...............................................................
...............................................................
...............................................................

**5. Connect to the Environment** Give an example of how changes in the cryosphere affect the biosphere.

...............................................................
...............................................................
...............................................................

# Quest CHECK-IN

**In this lesson, you learned about the different spheres that make up Earth. You also learned how these spheres affect and shape each other, and how feedback within or between spheres produces stability or change.**

Evaluate What are three ways in which factors or events in the atmosphere could increase the damage of fire in the biosphere?

...............................................................
...............................................................
...............................................................
...............................................................

 **INTERACTIVITY**

Fire and Earth's Spheres

**Go online** to trace how the forest fire started and discover factors that can start and spread a forest fire. Think about the flow of energy as the fire spreads and how you might use this information in your presentation.

MS-ESS2-1, MS-ESS2-4

# When the ICE MELTS

Florida, a semi-tropical paradise far from the northern latitudes, might seem to have nothing to do with Greenland, the island of ice between the Atlantic and Arctic Oceans. But Florida is a coastal state with one of the largest populations in the United States.

And if you live near the coast, then you'll definitely want to pay attention to what's happening in Greenland. About 82 percent of Greenland is covered by an ice sheet. But in recent years, this ice sheet has been melting at an advanced rate due to warming global temperatures. When ice on land melts and runs into the ocean, it has the potential to raise sea levels around the world.

Sea levels have risen at an average rate of 1.5 cm every decade for the last century. But during the last 25 years, that rate has doubled, mostly as a result of ice melting in Greenland and Antarctica.

Higher sea levels threaten infrastructure, such as roadways or utility lines, as well as lives and property. The higher the sea level, the more vulnerable Florida is to deadly storms and coastal flooding. Government officials and scientists from a variety of fields are working together to create and implement protection measures to deal with potential problems in the future.

## MY COMMUNITY

How would you deal with the problem of rising sea levels? Go online to research what Florida or another coastal state is doing to protect its coastline from the encroaching ocean.

If the entire ice sheet on Greenland melted, sea levels would rise about 7 meters.

# Surface Features in the Geosphere

## Guiding Questions

- What are the different landforms found on Earth?
- What forces and energy make the different landforms?
- What are the various ways to model landforms?

## Connections

**Literacy** Write Explanatory Texts

**Math** Analyze Quantitative Relationships

MS-ESS2-1

## HANDS-ON LAB

ᴎ**Investigate** Model landforms to learn about elevation and relief.

### Vocabulary

topography
landform
mountain
coastline
dune
river
delta
surveying

### Academic Vocabulary

model

## Connect It !

✏️ **Circle the places of high elevation in the Western and Eastern United States. What other features do you notice on the map?**

**SEP Make Observations** What observations can you make about the elevations of the coasts and center of the United States?

..............................................................................................................................

..............................................................................................................................

**SEP Apply Scientific Reasoning** Do you think other countries around the world also have a variety of land elevations? Explain.

..............................................................................................................................

..............................................................................................................................

# Topography of the Geosphere

If you drove across the United States, you would observe many changes in topography, as shown in **Figure 1. Topography** (tuh PAWG ruh fee) is the shape of the land. Land can be described using elevation, relief, and landforms.

The height of a point above sea level on Earth's surface is its elevation. California has the lowest and highest points of elevation in the contiguous United States. The lowest point, found at Badwater Basin in Death Valley, is 86 meters below sea level. The highest elevation is Mount Whitney at 4,418 meters. The difference in elevation between the highest and lowest points of an area is its relief. An area's relief is the result of the different landforms found there. **Landforms** are features such as coastlines, dunes, and mountains. Different landforms have different combinations of elevation and relief.

**✓ READING CHECK Determine Central Ideas** Explain the three ways that land can be described.

...........................................................................................

...........................................................................................

...........................................................................................

...........................................................................................

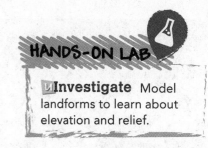

**HANDS-ON LAB**

**Investigate** Model landforms to learn about elevation and relief.

👆 **INTERACTIVITY**

Think about landforms that can be found in Florida.

## Relief Map

**Figure 1** The United States has many different land features such as mountains, rivers, and plains.

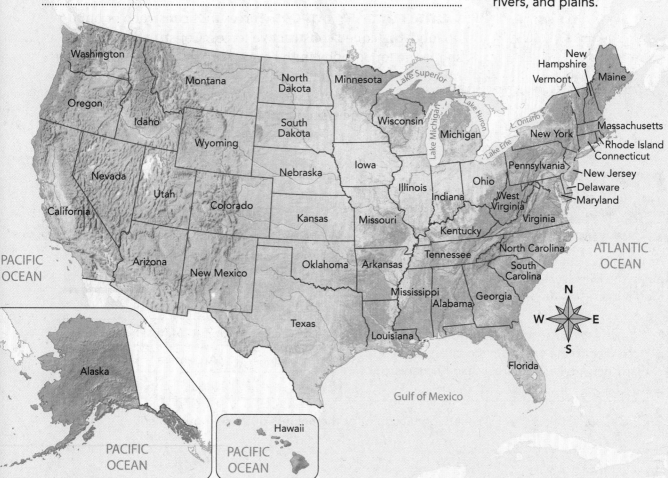

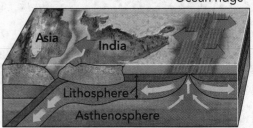

Ocean ridge

Asia
India
Lithosphere
Asthenosphere

Himalayas
Ocean ridge

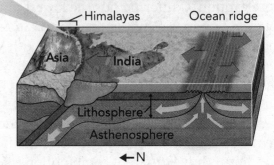

Asia
India
Lithosphere
Asthenosphere
←N

## Plates Collide

**Figure 2** India was pushed against Asia, which caused the formation of the Himalayan mountain range, located mainly in the countries of Nepal, India, and Bhutan.

# Constructive and Destructive Forces in the Geosphere

The topography of the land is constantly being created and destroyed by competing constructive and destructive forces. For example, over time, mountains are built up, but they're also being worn down.

**Constructive Forces** Forces that construct, or build up land, are called constructive forces. Constructive forces shape the topography in the geosphere by creating mountains and other huge landmasses. The Himalayan mountain range in Asia formed over millions of years, as India collided with Asia and pushed up sections of the ocean floor, as shown in **Figure 2**.

## Math Toolbox

### Tallest Mountains

As the plates continue to push against each other, the Himalayas are still rising to new heights. Mount Everest is the world's tallest mountain.

1. **Analyze Quantitative Relationships** According to the data from the table, about how many times taller is Everest than Kilimanjaro?

.................................................................

2. **CCC Cause and Effect** What might account for the heights of these mountains?

.................................................................

| Mountain | Location | Height (meters) |
|----------|----------|-----------------|
| Kilimanjaro | Tanzania | 5,895 |
| Denali | United States | 6,190 |
| Aconcagua | Argentina | 6,962 |
| Everest | Nepal/Tibet | 8,850 |

A volcano erupts.
..........................................

The eruption sends ash and gases into the air.
..........................

Lava and ash flow down into the surrounding habitats.
..........................

Mudflows form when ash and other volcanic material mix with water.
..........................

**Destructive Forces** The Himalayas were formed because land was built up, but there are destructive forces that also change Earth's topography. For example, rain, wind, ice, and fire destroy and wear away landmasses and affect the geosphere.

The geosphere, atmosphere, hydrosphere, and biosphere interact with each other to affect Earth. For example, an event that occurs in the geosphere, such as the volcano in **Figure 3**, will change the other spheres. A volcano releases ash and gases into the atmosphere and volcanic material into the hydrosphere. Initially, the volcanic material and gases may kill organisms in the biosphere. However, ash can enrich the soil and give new plants more nutrients. Hardened lava may cut off old river channels but form a new lake.

☑ READING CHECK **Integrate With Visuals** Refer to the art in **Figure 2** that shows the collision of India with Asia. How did changes in the geosphere cause the Himalayas to form?

..................................................................................

..................................................................................

## A Volcano Changes Everything
**Figure 3** ✏ A volcano causes changes in four spheres. Record which sphere is affected during each step in an eruption.

## Literacy Connection

**Write Explanatory Texts** As you read, number the steps in which an erupting volcano starts the cycle of change. Then, think about a forest fire. Explain how a fire would affect the geosphere, atmosphere, hydrosphere, and biosphere.

15

# Exploring Earth's Surface

There are a variety of landforms on Earth because Earth's surface differs from place to place. In addition, landforms change over time due to constructive and destructive forces. Some landforms are snow-capped mountains, some are giant glaciers, and others are ever-changing sand dunes. **Figure 4** shows some of the landforms found on Earth.

## Many Landforms

**Figure 4** 🖉 There are so many different landforms, but they are all connected. Choose two landforms. Draw a line from one landform to another and tell how they are connected to each other.

...............................................

...............................................

...............................................

...............................................

...............................................

## Mountains
A **mountain** is a landform with both high elevation and high relief. Mountains that are closely related in shape, structure, location, and age are called a mountain range. Different mountain ranges in one region make up a mountain system. The Rocky Mountains are a famous mountain system. Mountain ranges and mountain systems in a long, connected chain form a larger unit called a mountain belt.

## Plateaus and Plains
Landforms that have high elevation and low relief are called plateaus. Streams and rivers may cut into the plateau's surface. Landforms that have low elevation and low relief are called plains. A plain that lies along a seacoast is called a coastal plain. In North America, the Atlantic coastal plain extends from Florida all the way up to Cape Cod in Massachusetts.

Plateau

Lake

Plain

Dune

**Coastlines** The boundary between the land and the ocean or a lake is the **coastline**. Among the 50 states, the mainland of Alaska has the longest coastline at 10,686 kilometers. The mainland of Florida has the second longest coastline, measuring 2,170 kilometers.

**Dunes** The land that extends from a coastline may be rocky cliffs, sandy beaches, or dunes. A **dune** is a hill of sand piled up by the wind. Dunes in the coastal regions are parallel to the coastline and protect the land from ocean waves.

**Rivers and Deltas** A **river** is a natural stream of water that flows into another body of water such as an ocean, lake, or another river. When a river reaches an ocean, the water slows and sand, clay, and sediment in the water sink. When the sediment builds up, it makes a landform called a **delta**. In Florida, the Apalachicola River supplies sand to St. Vincent's Island, a barrier island and wildlife refuge.

✓ READING CHECK **Compare and Contrast** How are dunes and deltas similar and different?

..........................................................................................

..........................................................................................

Mountain

Glacier

River

Plain

Delta

Coastline

17

## Academic Vocabulary

Making a model of something helps you understand how things work. You can make a model using many different materials. Describe a model you have made and the materials you used.

.......................................................

.......................................................

.......................................................

# Modeling Landforms

Before modern technology, scientists and mapmakers studied the land and drew maps by hand. They spent hundreds of hours walking over landforms or sailing along coastlines to **model** what they saw. Then people used a process called surveying. In **surveying**, mapmakers determine distances and elevations using instruments and the principles of geometry. Today, people use computers to create topographic and other maps from aerial photography and satellite imagery.

**Topographic Maps**  Imagine that you are in a plane flying high above the United States. How does it look? A topographic map portrays the surface features of an area as if being viewed from above. Topographic maps provide accurate information on the elevation, relief, and slope of the ground, as shown in **Figure 5**.

**Contour Lines**  Topographic maps have contour lines to show elevation, relief, and slope. A contour line connects points of equal elevation. Contour lines also show how steep or gradual a slope is. Contour lines that are far apart represent flat areas or areas with gradual slopes. Lines that are close together represent areas with steep slopes.

The change in elevation from one contour line to the next is called a contour interval. On a given map, the contour interval is always consistent. Every fifth contour line is known as an index contour. These lines are darker and heavier than the other lines.

## Topographic Map of Mt. Grinnell

**Figure 5**  The contour lines on the map can be used to determine a feature's elevation. Use the contour lines to determine the elevation of Mt. Grinnell.

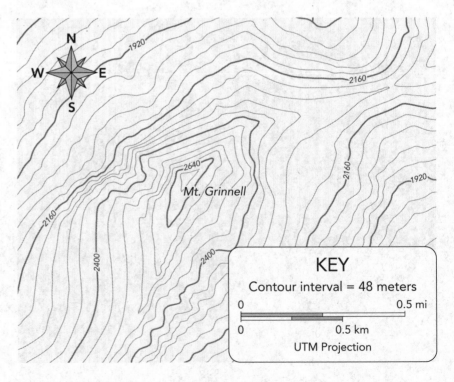

KEY

Contour interval = 48 meters

0 — 0.5 mi

0 — 0.5 km

UTM Projection

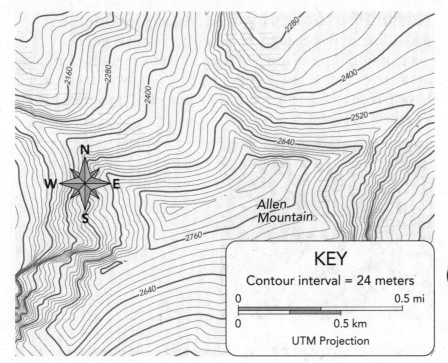

**Shape of Contour Lines**
**Figure 6** 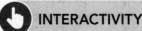 The area around Allen Mountain has many features. Circle the hilltops. Mark the steepest slopes with an X.

KEY

Contour interval = 24 meters

0               0.5 mi

0        0.5 km

UTM Projection

**INTERACTIVITY**

Investigate how constructive and destructive forces affect Earth's landforms.

**Reading a Topographic Map** In the United States, the scale of many topographic maps is 1 centimeter on the map for every 0.24 kilometers on the ground. This scale allows mapmakers to show land features such as rivers and coastlines. Large human-made structures, such as airports and highways, appear as outlines, while small structures, such as houses, are represented with symbols.

To find the elevation of a feature on the map in **Figure 6**, begin at an index contour line and count the number of lines up or down the feature. The shape of contour lines also provides information. V-shaped contour lines pointing away from a summit indicate a ridge line. V-shaped contour lines pointing toward a summit indicate a valley. A contour line that forms a closed loop indicates a hilltop. A closed loop with dashes inside indicates a depression, or hollow in the ground.

## Model It !

A map is a way to model Earth. What features are modeled by the topographic map in **Figure 6**?

SEP Use Mathematics ✏ Use the topographic map to create a drawing of the features it represents. Use the contour lines to help determine whether the area has a steep or gradual elevation. Be sure to label your illustration with the elevation of each feature.

**Aerial Photography** When photographs are taken with cameras mounted in airplanes, it is called aerial photography. As the airplane flies, the camera takes pictures of strips of land. These picture strips are fitted together like a large puzzle to form an accurate picture of a large area of land, as shown in **Figure 7**.

## Aerial Photograph

**Figure 7** ✎ Mapmakers use aerial photographs such as this one to create a map. Use the photo to make a street map of the neighborhood in the photograph. Be sure to add your own street names.

**Satellite Imagery** With the creation of computers, mapping has become easier and more accurate. Mapmakers can make maps of Earth using computers that interpret satellite data. Mapping satellites use electronic devices to collect data about the land surface. Pictures of the surface based on these data are called satellite images. These images are made up of pixels, and each pixel has information about the color and brightness of a part of Earth's surface, as shown in **Figure 8**.

Satellites orbit Earth collecting and storing data. Then, computers use the data to create images. Satellite images show details including plants, soil, rock, water, snow, and ice that cover Earth's surface.

## Satellite Image of North America

**Figure 8** ✎ Scientists and mapmakers identify special features on an image by their color and shape. For example, forests appear green, water may be blue or black, and snow is white. Draw an X to show where your state is.

**Interpret Photos** Write about the features you see in the satellite image.

........................................................
........................................................
........................................................
........................................................

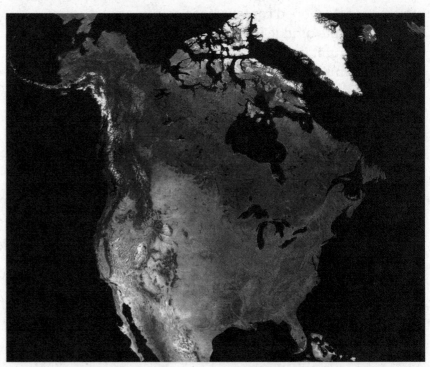

**GPS** The Global Positioning System, or GPS, is a navigational system that uses satellite signals to fix the location of a radio receiver on Earth. GPS helps anyone with a receiver locate his or her position anywhere on or above Earth.

You may have used GPS on a phone or in a car to navigate, but do you know how it works? Twenty-four orbiting satellites continuously send their current location and time to a GPS receiver on Earth. A user's receiver, such as a phone, needs information from at least three satellites to determine its location.

**GIS** A Geographic Information System, or GIS, is a system of computer hardware and software used to produce interactive maps. GIS uses GPS, satellite images, statistics about an area, and other maps to display and analyze geographic data.

The different types of information stored in a GIS are called data layers. The data layers help scientists and city planners to solve problems by understanding patterns, relationships, and trends. **Figure 9** shows how GIS could be used to determine a neighborhood's flood risk by analyzing data layers about the location of a river, its floodplain boundary, and the streets in a neighborhood.

**INTERACTIVITY**

Explore how maps can help solve problems.

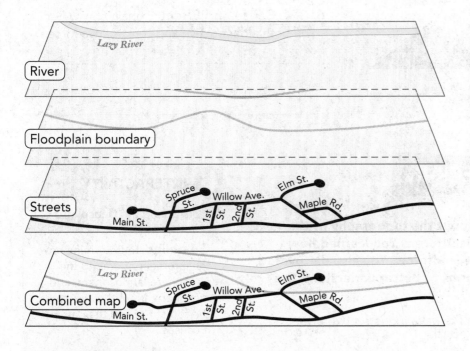

**GIS Map**
**Figure 9** 🖉 A GIS map has many data layers that can be used to analyze how different systems interact. Shade in the floodplain on the combined map. Where should a city planner avoid building houses? Why?

........................................................

........................................................

**READING CHECK** **Write Explanatory Texts** Explain ways in which GPS and GIS are more useful than a topographic map.

.................................................................................

.................................................................................

.................................................................................

MS-ESS2-1

1. **Define** What is topography?

.................................................................

.................................................................

.................................................................

.................................................................

2. **Identify** A mountain is a landform with both

high ............................ and high ............................

3. **SEP Use Models** ✏ Match each set of contour lines to the correct drawing.

4. **Compare and Contrast** Compare and
contrast constructive and destructive forces.

.................................................................

.................................................................

.................................................................

.................................................................

.................................................................

5. **Infer** The owner of a car wash wants to open a
new location in a different neighborhood. How
could the owner use GIS to figure out where to
put the new car wash? Explain what information
should be included in the data layers.

.................................................................

.................................................................

.................................................................

.................................................................

6. **CCC Cause and Effect** Explain how water can
be both a destructive and constructive force.

.................................................................

.................................................................

.................................................................

# Quest CHECK-IN

In this lesson, you learned about the topography of the
geosphere and the various landforms. You learned how
different forces shape these landforms. You also discovered
how scientists model landforms to better understand the
topography.

CCC Systems   How might a fire have a destructive effect on
the geosphere?

.................................................................

.................................................................

.................................................................

.................................................................

## 👆 INTERACTIVITY

Disrupting the Geosphere

**Go online** to determine how
the interactions among the
geosphere, atmosphere, and
biosphere affect the course of
the forest fire and the damage
it causes.

# A DARING BRIDGE

▶ VIDEO

Learn how engineers considered each sphere when building the Bixby Bridge.

**Do you know how** to build a bridge with some tough budget and environmental constraints? You engineer it! Plans for the Bixby Bridge in California show us how.

**The Challenge:** To design a cost-effective bridge across a canyon that withstands the elements.

**Phenomenon** Every winter, people in Big Sur, California, were trapped. Bad weather made the Old Coast Road impossible to travel. That changed in the 1930s when the state built a bridge across the canyon cut by Bixby Creek.

In designing the bridge, engineers weighed its impact on the environment. Then they considered costs and appearance. The country had entered the Great Depression. Funds were scarce, and a steel bridge would be costly. Also, a steel bridge so close to the Pacific Ocean would rust.

Finally, the engineers decided on an uncovered arch bridge 713 feet long and more than 260 feet above the canyon floor. They used concrete—45,000 sacks of it. Its appearance fit better alongside the area's stone cliffs. This design was also much less expensive. The Bixby Bridge reached completion on time and under budget—a success for any building project!

During the 1930s and 1940s, the lack of good roads and bridges could sometimes make traveling by car impossible.

**DESIGN CHALLENGE**

Can you design a bridge? Go to the Engineering Design Notebook to find out!

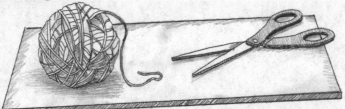

# 3 The Hydrosphere

## Guiding Questions

- Where and in what features is water found on Earth?
- How does water cycle through Earth's systems?

## Connection

**Literacy** Determine Central Ideas

MS-ESS2-4

## HANDS-ON LAB

ᵘ**Investigate** Model the distribution of water on Earth.

### Vocabulary

water cycle
evaporation
transpiration
condensation
precipitation
watershed
aquifer
well

### Academic Vocabulary

process

## Connect It!

✏ **Circle the different areas of water in this photo.**

Infer  Why do human practices depend upon and benefit from water?

.................................................................................................................................

.................................................................................................................................

.................................................................................................................................

SEP Apply Scientific Reasoning  Why is water important to our planet?

.................................................................................................................................

.................................................................................................................................

.................................................................................................................................

# The Water Cycle

Without water, life as we know it would not exist. As shown in **Figure 1**, water is an important characteristic of Earth. All living things require water to live. Fortunately, Earth has its own built-in water recycling system: the water cycle.

The **water cycle** is the continuous process by which water moves from Earth's surface to the atmosphere and back again. This movement is driven by energy from the sun and by gravity. In the water cycle, water moves through the geosphere, the biosphere, the hydrosphere, and the atmosphere.

**Evaporation** The sun heats up the surface of bodies of water and causes water molecules to undergo a change. The process by which molecules at the surface of a liquid absorb enough energy to change to a gas is called **evaporation**. Water constantly evaporates from the surfaces of bodies of water.

Elements of the geosphere and biosphere can also add water vapor to the atmosphere. Water evaporates from soil in the geosphere. Animals in the biosphere release water vapor as they breathe. Water even evaporates from your skin.

Plants also play a role in this step of the water cycle. Plants draw in water from the soil through their roots. Eventually the water vapor is given off through the leaves in a process called **transpiration**.

**Importance of Water**
**Figure 1** Water makes life on Earth possible.

## The Water Cycle

**Figure 2** 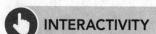 This diagram shows some of the major processes that make up the water cycle. Draw arrows to show the way that water moves through the cycle. Then, in the blank spaces, write the process that is at work.

**INTERACTIVITY**

Review all of the processes of the water cycle.

### Literacy Connection

**Determine Central Ideas** As you read, underline the central idea of each paragraph. Note how this idea is developed through examples and details.

**Condensation** After a water molecule evaporates into the atmosphere, warm air carries the water molecule upward. **Condensation** is the process by which water vapor becomes liquid water. As water vapor rises into the colder air, some water vapor cools and condenses into liquid or solid water. Droplets of liquid water and ice crystals collect around solid particles in the air, forming clouds. Eventually, this results in precipitation.

**Precipitation** As more water vapor condenses, the water droplets and ice crystals grow larger. Eventually, they become so heavy that gravity causes them to fall back to Earth in the form of precipitation. Water that forms in clouds and falls to Earth as rain, snow, hail, or sleet is called **precipitation**. Once it falls, it collects in rivers, lakes, and streams. It is also absorbed by the soil in the geosphere. Precipitation is the source of almost all fresh water on and below Earth's surface.

For millions of years, the total amount of water cycling through the Earth's system has remained fairly constant—the rates of evaporation and precipitation are balanced. That means that the water you use today is the same water that your ancestors used.

☑ READING CHECK **Draw Evidence** The biosphere interacts with the hydrosphere within the water cycle. Cite one example of that interaction.

.............................................................................................

.............................................................................................

.............................................................................................

# Distribution of Earth's Water

Most of the water in the hydrosphere—roughly 97 percent—is salt water found mostly in the ocean. Only 3 percent is fresh water, as shown in **Figure 3**.

**Fresh Water** Of the 3 percent that is fresh water, about two-thirds is frozen in huge masses of ice near the North and South poles. Much of Earth's fresh water is frozen into thickened ice masses called glaciers. Massive glacial ice sheets cover most of Greenland and Antarctica.

About a third of Earth's fresh water is underground. A tiny fraction of fresh water occurs in lakes and rivers. An even tinier fraction is found in the atmosphere, most of it in the form of invisible water vapor, the gaseous form of water.

Most precipitation falls directly into the ocean. Of the precipitation that falls on land, most evaporates. A small amount of the remaining water runs off the surface into streams and lakes in a **process** called runoff, but most of it seeps into the ground. After a long time, this groundwater eventually comes to the surface and evaporates again.

**Salt Water** Atlantic, Indian, Pacific, and Arctic are the names for the different parts of the ocean. The Pacific Ocean is the largest, covering an area greater than all the land on Earth. Smaller saltwater bodies are called seas. Seas are generally inland and landlocked. A small percentage of Earth's salt water is found in some saline lakes.

**Academic Vocabulary**

A process is a series of actions or operations leading toward a particular result. List some processes you are familiar with in your daily life.

..................................................

..................................................

..................................................

..................................................

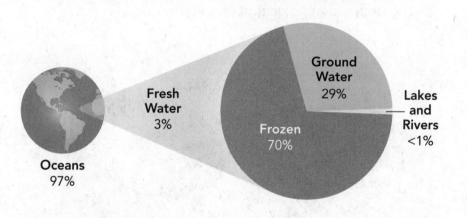

Fresh Water 3%

Ground Water 29%

Frozen 70%

Lakes and Rivers <1%

Oceans 97%

**Water Resources**

**Figure 3** Most of the water on Earth is salt water in the ocean.

**Reflect** NASA satellite data show that the ice sheets are melting at a rate of about 350 billion tons of ice each year, which is far above historic averages. What do you think is causing this to happen? What effect would this increased amount of ice melt have on the ocean?

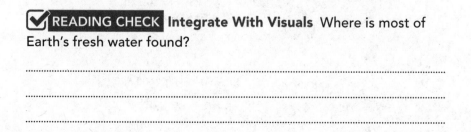

☑ READING CHECK **Integrate With Visuals** Where is most of Earth's fresh water found?

..................................................................

..................................................................

..................................................................

# Surface Water

Surface water includes all the water found on the surface of Earth. The ocean, rivers, lakes, and ponds are all part of the surface water in the hydrosphere.

**Rivers** Even large rivers, such as the Mississippi River or St. Johns River, start as a trickle of water that originates from a source—an underground stream, runoff from rain, or melting snow or ice. Gravity causes these tiny streams to flow downhill. These small streams join others to form a larger stream. Larger streams join others to form a river that flows into the ocean. The streams and smaller rivers that feed into a main river are called tributaries. A river and all the tributaries that flow into it make up a river system, as shown in **Figure 4**.

**Watersheds** The land area that supplies water to a river system is called a **watershed**. When rivers join another river system, the areas they drain become part of the largest river's watershed. **Figure 5** shows the major watersheds that cover the United States.

**Divides** Watersheds stay separated from each other by a ridge of land called a divide. Streams on each side of the divide flow in different directions. The Great Divide, the longest divide in North America, follows the Rocky Mountains. West of this divide, water flows toward the Pacific Ocean. Some water stays in the Great Basin between the Rocky and Sierra Nevada Mountains. East of the divide, water flows toward the Mississippi River and into the Gulf of Mexico, joining rivers flowing from the Appalachian Mountains.

**The Mississippi River**
**Figure 4** Many tributaries contribute to the Mississippi River.

> ▶ **VIDEO**
>
> Discover how an aquaculture manager helps meet the needs of people while protecting the habitats of living things.

**Watersheds**
**Figure 5** ✏ This map shows the watersheds of some large rivers in the United States. Draw a line on the map to represent the Great Divide. Use arrows to show the direction in which the water flows on each side of the divide.

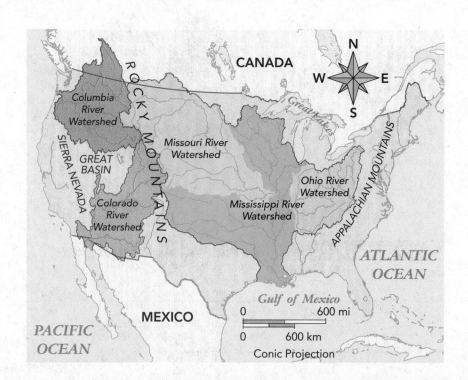

**Ponds and Lakes** Ponds and lakes form when water collects in hollows and low-lying areas of land. Unlike streams and rivers, ponds and lakes contain mostly still water. Ponds are smaller and shallower than lakes. Like other bodies of water, lakes and ponds are supplied by rainfall, melting snow and ice, and runoff. Some are fed by rivers or groundwater.

Lakes, such as the ones in **Figure 6**, form through several natural processes. When a river bends, a new channel may form, cutting off a loop to form an oxbow lake. Some lakes, such as the Great Lakes, formed in depressions created by ice sheets that melted at the end of the Ice Age. Other lakes were created by movements of Earth's crust that formed long, deep valleys called rift valleys. Lakes can also form in the empty craters of volcanoes.

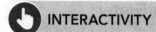
**INTERACTIVITY**

Discover the best site on which to locate a fish farm.

☑ READING CHECK **Summarize** How do river systems, watersheds, and divides interact?

..................................................................................

..................................................................................

..................................................................................

..................................................................................

..................................................................................

..................................................................................

**Lakes in Mountains**
**Figure 6** Lakes are important because they hold some of Earth's fresh water.

## Plan It

### Building a Reservoir

SEP Design Solutions 🖉 In order to increase the benefit from the water cycle, humans alter it by building reservoirs, which store water. Do some research to help you plan how to build a reservoir in your region of the country. Use the space provided to draw a diagram showing the features of your reservoir. Write out the steps of your plan below.

..................................................................................

..................................................................................

..................................................................................

..................................................................................

## Groundwater

**Figure 7** ✏ This diagram shows how water travels underground. Add arrows to identify the paths that water takes.

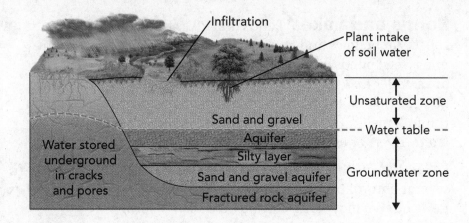

Infiltration

Plant intake of soil water

Unsaturated zone

Water table

Groundwater zone

Sand and gravel

Aquifer

Silty layer

Sand and gravel aquifer

Fractured rock aquifer

Water stored underground in cracks and pores

**INTERACTIVITY**

Explore how the Floridan aquifer formed and describe its importance today.

**VIDEO**

Learn more about the role of groundwater in the water cycle.

# Groundwater

A large portion of fresh water in the hydrosphere is underground, as shown in **Figure 7**. Water that fills the cracks and spaces in soil and rock layers is called groundwater. Far more fresh water is located underground than in all of Earth's rivers and lakes.

**Aquifers** As precipitation falls to Earth, it moves through the soil and the small spaces within underground rock layers. These layers contain air as well as water, so they are not saturated, or filled, with water. This top layer is called the unsaturated zone.

Eventually, the water reaches a level where the openings in the layers are filled with water, or saturated. The upper level of the saturated zone is called the water table. Below the saturated zone there are layers of rock that hold water called **aquifers**.

Aquifers range in size from a small patch to an area the size of several states. Aquifers and other groundwater sources provide 55 percent of the drinking water for the United States. In rural areas, aquifers provide as much as 99 percent of the water used.

**Wells** People can get groundwater from an aquifer by digging a well that reaches below the water table. A **well** is a hole sunk into the earth to reach a supply of water. Long ago, people dug wells by hand and used buckets to bring up the water. Today, most wells are created with drilling equipment and the water is retrieved using mechanical pumps that run on electricity.

✓ **READING CHECK** **Determine Central Ideas** What is an aquifer?

.......................................................................................

.......................................................................................

.......................................................................................

.......................................................................................

# Exploring the Ocean

There are several ways that the ocean is unique in the hydrosphere. The water in Earth's ocean varies in salinity, temperature, and depth.

**Salinity** The total amount of dissolved salts in a sample of water is the salinity. Near the ocean's surface, rain, snow, and melting ice add fresh water, lowering the salinity. Evaporation, on the other hand, increases salinity. Salinity is also higher near the poles because the forming of sea ice leaves some salt behind in the seawater.

Salinity affects ocean water in different ways. For instance, fresh water freezes at 0°C but ocean water freezes at about –1.9°C because the salt interferes with the formation of ice. Salt water also has a higher density than fresh water. Therefore, seawater lifts, or buoys up, less dense objects floating in it.

**Temperature** The broad surface of the ocean absorbs energy from the sun. Temperatures at the surface of the ocean vary with location and the seasons. Near the equator, surface ocean temperatures often reach 25°C, about room temperature. The temperatures drop as you travel away from the equator.

**Depth** The ocean is very deep—3.8 kilometers deep on average. That's more than twice as deep as the Grand Canyon. As you descend through the ocean, the water temperature decreases. Water pressure, the force exerted by the weight of water, increases by 1 bar, the air pressure at sea level, with each 10 meters of depth. Use **Figure 8** to explore temperature, pressure, and depth.

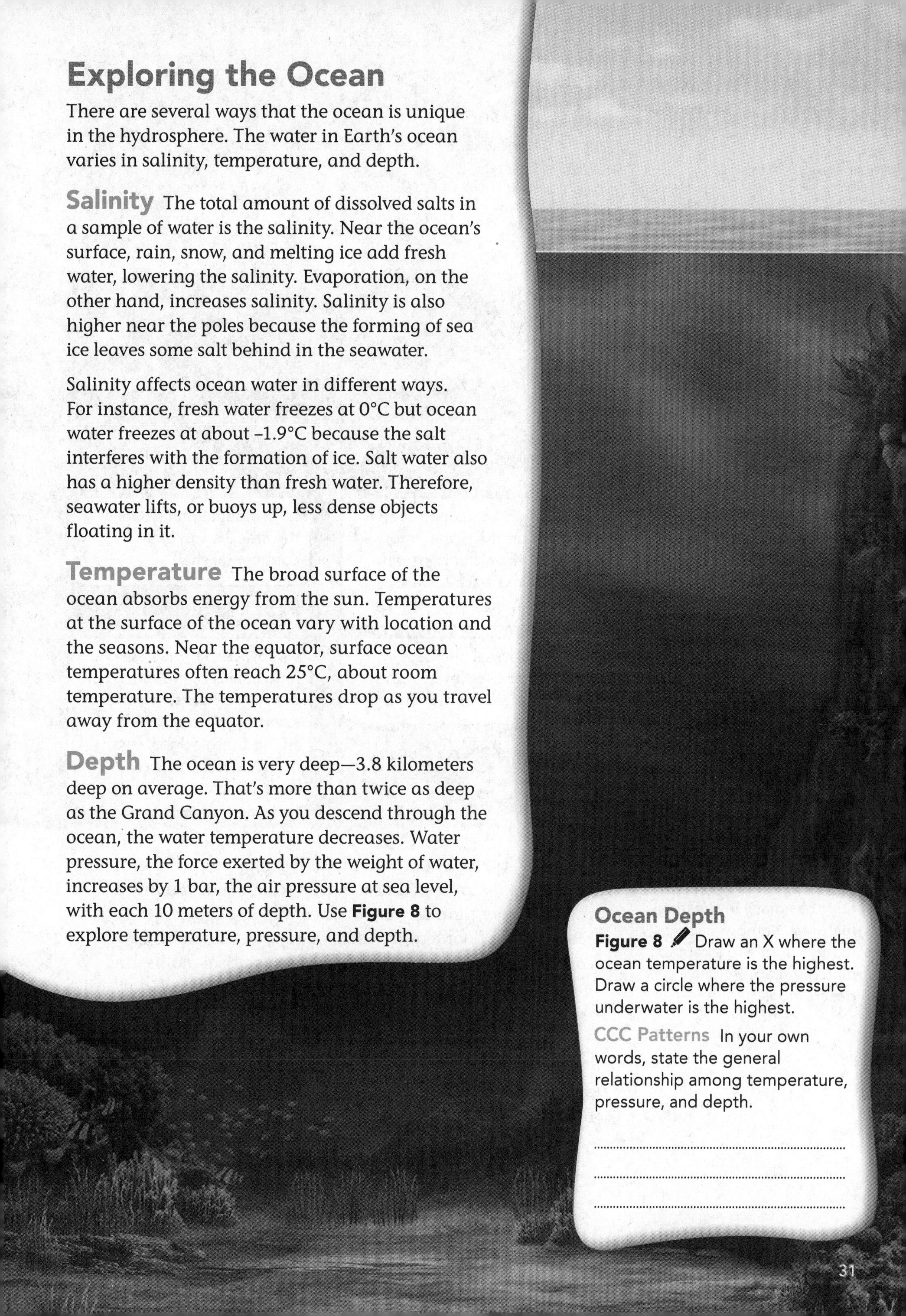

**Ocean Depth**

**Figure 8** 🖊 Draw an X where the ocean temperature is the highest. Draw a circle where the pressure underwater is the highest.

**CCC Patterns** In your own words, state the general relationship among temperature, pressure, and depth.

........................................................................

........................................................................

........................................................................

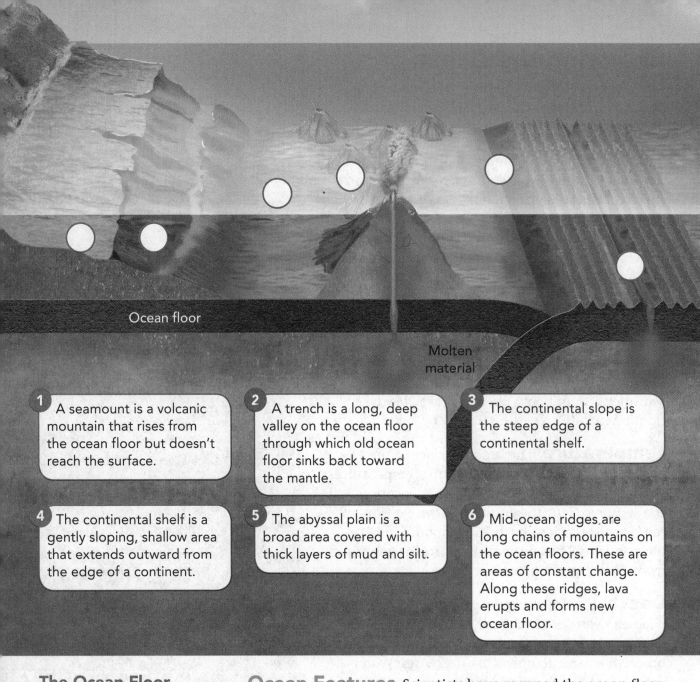

Ocean floor

Molten material

**1** A seamount is a volcanic mountain that rises from the ocean floor but doesn't reach the surface.

**2** A trench is a long, deep valley on the ocean floor through which old ocean floor sinks back toward the mantle.

**3** The continental slope is the steep edge of a continental shelf.

**4** The continental shelf is a gently sloping, shallow area that extends outward from the edge of a continent.

**5** The abyssal plain is a broad area covered with thick layers of mud and silt.

**6** Mid-ocean ridges are long chains of mountains on the ocean floors. These are areas of constant change. Along these ridges, lava erupts and forms new ocean floor.

### The Ocean Floor
**Figure 9** ✏ The ocean floor has many interesting features. Number each feature on the diagram to match the accompanying descriptions.

**Ocean Features** Scientists have mapped the ocean floor. They have discovered that the deep waters hide mountain ranges bigger than any on land, as well as deep canyons. Major ocean floor features include seamounts, trenches, continental shelves, continental slopes, abyssal plains, and mid-ocean ridges. These features, shown in **Figure 9**, have all been formed by the interaction of Earth's plates.

✅ **READING CHECK** **Draw Conclusions** How do the temperature and pressure most likely differ at the top of a seamount and the bottom of a trench?

..................................................................................

..................................................................................

..................................................................................

..................................................................................

MS-ESS2-4

**1. CCC Systems** What are the important processes in the water cycle?

...................................................................

...................................................................

...................................................................

**2. CCC Structure and Function** What are the components of a river system?

...................................................................

...................................................................

...................................................................

...................................................................

**3. Summarize** What are the main features of the ocean floor?

...................................................................

...................................................................

...................................................................

...................................................................

...................................................................

...................................................................

...................................................................

**4. SEP Communicate Information** How does the interaction between the hydrosphere and the geosphere affect the supply of drinking water?

...................................................................

...................................................................

...................................................................

...................................................................

...................................................................

...................................................................

...................................................................

**5. Compare and Contrast** 🖊 Create a Venn diagram comparing fresh water and salt water.

# Quest CHECK-IN

**In this lesson, you learned how the water of the hydrosphere is cycled and how it interacts with the other spheres. You also learned about the characteristics of each portion of the hydrosphere, including surface water, ocean water, and groundwater.**

**CCC Cause and Effect** How might a natural disaster, such as a forest fire, affect the elements of the hydrosphere?

...................................................................

...................................................................

...................................................................

...................................................................

**INTERACTIVITY**

Impact on the Hydrosphere

**Go online** to examine how the hydrosphere interacts with other spheres and the effect of a forest fire on those interactions. Then review the data and finalize your predictions about the fire's damage.

MS-ESS2-4

# The CASE of the
# Shrinking Sea

1989

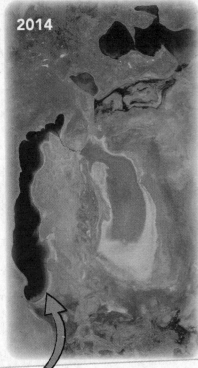

2014

The remaining areas of water now cover only 10 to 25 percent of the former surface area. The volume of water has been reduced by 90 percent.

The Aral Sea in Central Asia was once the fourth largest lake in the world, and it supported many fisheries and shipping lines. Bordered by the countries of Uzbekistan and Kazakhstan, the lake is fed by water from melting glaciers and the rivers of the Aral Sea Basin, which flow from five countries in the region.

But the Aral Sea has been rapidly disappearing since the 1960s. As the population in the area grew to more than 60 million, people diverted major rivers flowing into the lake for agricultural and industrial use. However, up to one quarter of this diverted water was wasted due to poor management and planning. This wasted water was either absorbed by dry desert soil surrounding the lake or flowed into unused run-off ditches. Additionally, the rate of evaporation from the Aral Sea has increased, contributing to its disappearance.

In the past 50 years, the water levels have dropped so rapidly that the lake has fragmented into several smaller bodies of water separated by barren desert in between.

## Effects of a Disappearing Sea

As the lake evaporates and shrinks, its salinity increases. Between the 1960s and the 1980s, the salt concentration of the Aral Sea increased dramatically, killing wildlife and destroying the fishing trade. The concentration of salt is so high in some areas that efforts to reintroduce fish have failed. Concentrated salt, minerals, and pollutants from the now-exposed sea floor are whipped into sandstorms that also threaten the health of the human population in the area.

To improve the conditions in the area, some water management efforts started in the 1990s. Then, in 2005, the Kok-Aral Dam was built to keep water from the northern fragment from flowing to the southern fragment. The dam was a success and the North Aral Sea rose more than 3 meters in the first year. Surveyors hope that in the future the water levels in the north will rise to the point that they can begin to let water flow to the South Aral Sea as well.

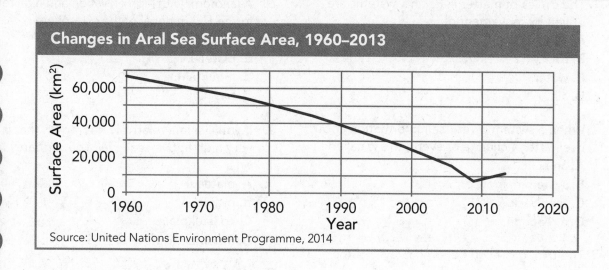

**Changes in Aral Sea Surface Area, 1960–2013**

Source: United Nations Environment Programme, 2014

**Use the graph to answer the following questions.**

1. **CCC Patterns** Describe any patterns you see in the graph.

2. **Predict** What do you think the data for the Aral Sea surface area might look like in 2020? Why?

3. **SEP Construct Explanations** How have human actions and the impact of the water cycle affected the Aral Sea?

4. **SEP Design Solutions** What are some strategies you can think of to conserve water and stabilize the decline of the Aral Sea?

# ☑TOPIC 1 Review and Assess

## 1 Matter and Energy in Earth's System

MS-ESS2-1

1. The cycles of matter in Earth's systems are driven by movement of
   A. heat.
   B. rock.
   C. water.
   D. air.

2. When a system gives itself information about itself after a change or event, this is called
   A. an echo.
   B. system response.
   C. feedback.
   D. a reaction.

3. The thin, gas-filled outermost layer of the Earth system is called the
   A. cryosphere.
   B. atmosphere.
   C. geosphere.
   D. hydrosphere.

4. In the ........................................., water exists in its solid form as ice.

5. **CCC Systems** Give an example of an interaction involving the cycling of matter between two or more spheres.

   ...............................................................

   ...............................................................

   ...............................................................

   ...............................................................

   ...............................................................

   ...............................................................

   ...............................................................

   ...............................................................

## 2 Surface Features in the Geosphere

MS-ESS2-1

6. A landform with high elevation and high relief formed by material of the geosphere is called a
   A. plain.
   B. plateau.
   C. mountain.
   D. basin.

7. If you live in a relatively flat region that is not very high above sea level, you probably live on a
   A. plateau.
   B. prairie.
   C. coastal plain.
   D. mountaintop.

8. Which type of map image would you use if you wanted to represent plant density across the United States?
   A. satellite imagery
   B. aerial photography
   C. topographic map
   D. relief map

9. With ........................................., you can find your precise location on a digital map if your device can receive signals from three satellites. A ........................... map is a low-tech tool for visualizing the contours and elevations of a landform.

10. **SEP Engage in Argument** Write a brief proposal for why GPS technology and surveying should be used to study changes on a low-lying part of the coast.

    ...............................................................

    ...............................................................

    ...............................................................

    ...............................................................

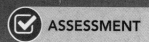
# ③ The Hydrosphere

MS-ESS2-4

**11.** Which is not a part of the hydrosphere?
A. sediment
B. pond
C. rain
D. ice

**12.** When ocean water reaches the poles, some of it turns to ice. Some salt is trapped between ice crystals, but most is left behind in the unfrozen seawater. This causes an increase in
A. evaporation.    B. salinity.
C. pressure.       D. temperature.

**13.** About 97 percent of the hydrosphere is
A. salt water in lakes, seas, and the ocean.
B. water vapor in the atmosphere.
C. fresh water in ice and snow.
D. also part of the cryosphere.

**14.** ................................. from plants and ................................. from bodies of water both add water vapor to the .................................

**15.** In this photo, the ................................. is interacting with the ................................. by wearing down the rocks as the water flows.

**16. CCC Cause and Effect** Describe how groundwater is replenished.

..................................................................
..................................................................
..................................................................
..................................................................
..................................................................

**17. CCC System Models** Suppose you have a teakettle boiling on a hotplate next to a window. It is a cold morning, and as steam from the kettle hits the window, it forms ice. What parts of the water cycle are you modeling?

..................................................................
..................................................................
..................................................................

**18. SEP Develop Models** 🖊 How might water from a lake move through the water cycle and eventually fall as rain? Draw a diagram to model the cycle.

MS-ESS2-4

## Evidence-Based Assessment

Scientists have been monitoring the enormous volumes of ice at Earth's poles with curiosity and concern. In western Antarctica, the ice shelves are deteriorating. An ice shelf acts as a dam between land-based glaciers and the ocean. As a shelf crumbles into the ocean, glacial ice behind the ice shelf can flow more freely from higher elevations. The collapsing ice shelf, which floats on the ocean, does not directly contribute to sea level rise. However, scientists predict that the increased flow of glacial ice and meltwater from land will contribute to a global sea level rise of two meters by 2100.

The graph provides data about the volume of ice lost at four different glacier systems.

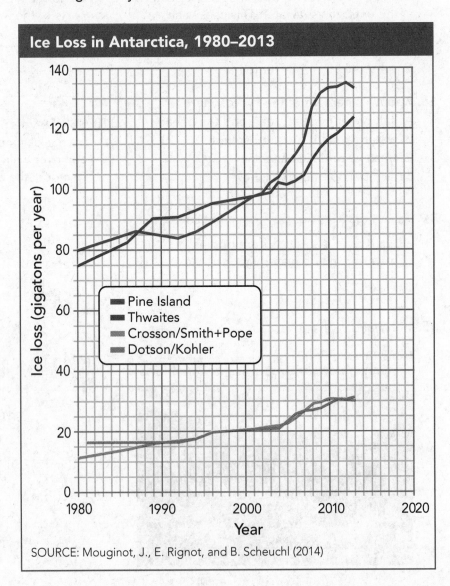

SOURCE: Mouginot, J., E. Rignot, and B. Scheuchl (2014)

1. **CCC Stability and Change** What is the overall trend in ice loss at the four locations?
   - **A.** Ice loss has been increasing at all four locations, but the rate has been getting higher since about 2000.
   - **B.** Ice loss has remained at a steady rate at all four locations.
   - **C.** Ice loss was decreasing at all four locations until 2005, when it began to increase.
   - **D.** Ice loss has been decreasing at a steady rate at all four locations.

2. **SEP Use Mathematics** Which location lost the most ice in 2013? Approximately how much ice was lost from the four locations in 2013? Show your work.

   ..................................................................

   ..................................................................

   ..................................................................

   ..................................................................

   ..................................................................

   ..................................................................

   ..................................................................

   ..................................................................

   ..................................................................

   ..................................................................

3. **CCC Cause and Effect** What role does the sun play in driving the water cycle in Antarctica?

   ..................................................................

   ..................................................................

   ..................................................................

   ..................................................................

   ..................................................................

   ..................................................................

   ..................................................................

   ..................................................................

4. **SEP Engage in Argument** Average temperatures on the Antarctic Peninsula have risen 3°C over the last 50 years. If this trend continues, what effect would it have on the water cycle in Antarctica? In your answer, explain the impact on ice flows.

   ..................................................................

   ..................................................................

   ..................................................................

   ..................................................................

   ..................................................................

   ..................................................................

# Quest FINDINGS

## Complete the Quest!

**Phenomenon** Determine the best medium for presenting your findings, such as a map or a multimedia presentation.

**CCC Systems** How does a forest fire demonstrate how the different spheres of Earth interact with each other?

..................................................................

..................................................................

..................................................................

..................................................................

..................................................................

..................................................................

..................................................................

**INTERACTIVITY**

Reflect on Forest Fires

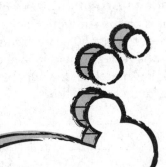

# Modeling a Watershed

How can you **model** the effects of **pollution** on a watershed?

## Background

**Phenomenon** A factory has released pollutants into a nearby river. You discovered dead fish far downstream from the factory. But the factory claims that it can't be responsible because the fish were found so far away. You have been asked to help biologists demonstrate that when contaminated water enters one part of a watershed, it can affect the entire watershed.

In this investigation, you will model the effects of pollution on surface water in a watershed and demonstrate the importance of protecting watershed areas.

## Materials

### (per group)

- small wooden or plastic blocks
- paper or plastic drinking cups
- newspaper
- markers
- craft sticks
- plastic CD cases
- light paper
- aluminum foil
- plastic wrap
- large pan
- water
- red food coloring
- metric ruler
- tape
- digital camera (optional)
- goggles
- apron
- gloves

# Procedure

**HANDS-ON LAB**

**Demonstrate** Go online for a downloadable worksheet of this lab.

1. Use the materials provided by your teacher to design and build a model watershed for your demonstration. Use a camera or drawings to record and analyze information to show how pollution affects an entire watershed.

2. Consider the following questions before you begin planning your model:

   - How can the materials help you to model a watershed?

   - How will you form highlands in your model?

   - How can you include streams and rivers in your model?

   - How can you use food coloring to represent the effects of pollution on surface water in the watershed?

   - What are some ways that a watershed can be polluted?

3. Once you have worked out a design, draw a sketch of your model. Label the objects in your model and identify the materials you are using.

4. Write a short procedure that details the steps you will follow to model how pollution can affect surface water in a watershed.

5. Once your teacher has approved your design and procedure, carry out the investigation. If possible, use a camera to photograph your model during the investigation. Record observations about how your model represents the effects of pollution in a watershed.

## Sketch  Design and sketch your model here.

## Observations

.....................................................................................................................

.....................................................................................................................

.....................................................................................................................

.....................................................................................................................

.....................................................................................................................

.....................................................................................................................

.....................................................................................................................

.....................................................................................................................

.....................................................................................................................

.....................................................................................................................

.....................................................................................................................

.....................................................................................................................

.....................................................................................................................

.....................................................................................................................

# Analyze and Interpret Data

1. **Claim** What other human activity takes place in the watersheds that might lead to pollution?

.................................................................................................................

.................................................................................................................

.................................................................................................................

2. **Evidence** Describe the path that the food coloring took through your model. What does the pattern of the food coloring's path tell you about the effect of pollution on surface water in a watershed? Based on your observations and evidence, could the factory's pollution have caused the fish to die?

.................................................................................................................

.................................................................................................................

.................................................................................................................

.................................................................................................................

3. **Reasoning** Explain the importance of laws that restrict and punish individuals or businesses that pollute healthy watersheds. Include a description of any cause-and-effect relationships that you think scientists might observe when pollutants are introduced into a watershed area. Use your model and your observations in this lab as evidence for your answer.

.................................................................................................................

.................................................................................................................

.................................................................................................................

.................................................................................................................

.................................................................................................................

4. **SEP Identify Limitations** Compare your model to other models. How can you improve your model based on other examples? What parts of a watershed, if any, are missing from your model?

.................................................................................................................

.................................................................................................................

.................................................................................................................

# TOPIC

# 2

# Weather in the Atmosphere

**NGSS PERFORMANCE EXPECTATIONS**

**MS-ESS2-4** Develop a model to describe the cycling of water through Earth's systems driven by energy from the sun and the force of gravity.

**MS-ESS2-5** Collect data to provide evidence for how the motions and complex interactions of air masses results in changes in weather conditions.

**MS-ESS2-6** Develop and use a model to describe how unequal heating and rotation of the Earth cause patterns of atmospheric and oceanic circulation that determine regional climates.

**MS-ESS3-2** Analyze and interpret data on natural hazards to forecast future catastrophic events and inform the development of technologies to mitigate their effects.

**MS-PS1-4** Develop a model that predicts and describes changes in particle motion, temperature, and state of a pure substance when thermal energy is added or removed.

HANDS-ON LAB

**uConnect** Explore what happens to water in a puddle when sunlight acts upon it.

What happened to this house?

**GO ONLINE** to access your digital course

▶ VIDEO

👆 INTERACTIVITY

📱 VIRTUAL LAB

☑ ASSESSMENT

📖 eTEXT

🧪 HANDS-ON LAB

## The Essential Question
## What determines weather on Earth?

**CCC Cause and Effect** One of the first things you might have done this morning was to look out the window to see what the weather was like. It might be warm and sunny, or you might be expecting a severe storm. Is your weather today typical for the climate in which you live? List some ways in which your life depends on weather.

........................................................................................................

........................................................................................................

........................................................................................................

........................................................................................................

# Quest KICKOFF

## How can you prepare for severe weather?

**Phenomenon** Severe weather can put people's lives and property at risk. Part of the job of a meteorologist, or a scientist who studies the weather, is to help keep the public safe by informing them about severe weather events. In this Quest activity, you will explore the factors that cause severe weather and the ways people can protect themselves and reduce damage during these weather events. Applying what you learn in each lesson, you will develop a public service announcement (PSA) to teach people about severe weather and what they can do to prepare for it and stay safe. In the Findings activity, you will present your PSA and reflect on your work.

**INTERACTIVITY**

Preparing a Plan

**MS-ESS2-5** Collect data to provide evidence for how the motions and complex interactions of air masses results in changes in weather conditions.
**MS-ESS3-2** Analyze and interpret data on natural hazards to forecast future catastrophic events and inform the development of technologies to mitigate their effects.

**NBC LEARN** ▶ VIDEO

After watching the video, which explores the tools that meteorologists use to study and predict the weather, complete the 3-2-1 activity.

**3** tools that a meteorologist uses

.............................................

.............................................

.............................................

**2** types of severe weather that a meteorologist might predict

.............................................

.............................................

.............................................

**1** question I have for the meteorologist

.............................................

.............................................

.............................................

## IN LESSON 1
How does the atmosphere affect the weather? Think about conditions in the atmosphere and how they are related to severe weather.

## Quest CHECK-IN

### IN LESSON 2
How is the water cycle involved in severe weather? Consider the information you should include in your PSA.

**INTERACTIVITY**

Weather and Severe Weather

## Quest CHECK-IN

### IN LESSON 3
What happens when different air masses interact? Explore how tornadoes form and decide what information about air masses you will include in your PSA.

**INTERACTIVITY**

All About Air Masses

A tornado is one of the most destructive types of severe weather that occurs in the United States.

## Quest CHECK-IN

### IN LESSON 4

How can forecasts help people to prepare for severe weather? Record ideas about weather predictions that your PSA should address.

 **INTERACTIVITY**

Predicting Severe Weather

## Quest CHECK-IN

### IN LESSON 5

How does examining past data help prepare people for future weather hazards? Analyze historical data about tornadoes in the United States.

**HANDS-ON LAB**

The History of Hazardous Weather

## Quest FINDINGS

## Complete the Quest!

Create your PSA to help people to understand, predict, prepare for, and avoid the dangers of severe weather.

 **INTERACTIVITY**

Reflect on Your PSA

MS-ESS2-4

# Puddle Befuddlement

## Background

**Phenomenon** On a hot sunny day, you and a friend are walking on a paved path next to the ocean. A wave leaves a puddle of ocean water on the hot pavement. When you return to the same spot a little while later, you see a white outline, but the water is gone. Your friend asks: "Where did the water go? Why is there a white outline?" You think that there is a transfer in energy that changed the form of water and decide to develop a model to explain it to your friend. In this investigation, you will model how energy helps change the form of water as it cycles through Earth's atmosphere and on Earth's surface.

How can you **model** what happens to water in puddle?

## Materials

(per group)
- large glass beaker
- tap water
- salt
- plastic spoon
- electric burner
- clock

## Safety

Be sure to follow all safety procedures provided by your teacher. The Safety Appendix of your textbook provides more details about the safety icons.

## Develop a Procedure

☐ 1. **SEP Develop a Model** Use the materials provided by your teacher to develop a model that explains what happened to the ocean water. Identify the parts of your model and which material will represent each part.

..................................................................................
..................................................................................
..................................................................................

☐ 2. **SEP Use a Model** Using your model, write a procedure that shows what happened to the puddle. *Do not use the electric burner for more than 7 minutes.* Show your procedure to your teacher before you begin.

..................................................................................
..................................................................................
..................................................................................
..................................................................................
..................................................................................

## Observations

**HANDS-ON LAB**

**Connect** Go online for a downloadable worksheet of this lab.

## Analyze and Interpret Data

**1. SEP Use a Model** Explain what happened to the materials you used in your model. How did energy play a role in what you observed?

...................................................................................................................

...................................................................................................................

...................................................................................................................

**2. SEP Use a Model** How is what happened to the water in the beaker similar to what happens to a puddle in the sun? How is it different?

...................................................................................................................

...................................................................................................................

...................................................................................................................

...................................................................................................................

**3. SEP Develop a Model** How could you improve your model to describe the mechanism by which a puddle dries up in the sun?

...................................................................................................................

...................................................................................................................

...................................................................................................................

# The Atmosphere Around You

## Guiding Questions

- What is the composition and structure of Earth's atmosphere?
- How does energy from the sun affect Earth's atmosphere?

## Connections

**Literacy** Support Author's Claim

**Math** Represent Quantitative Relationships

MS-ESS2-5, MS-ESS2-6, MS-ESS3-2, MS-PS1-4

## HANDS-ON LAB

**uInvestigate** Observe how changes in altitude affect the atmosphere.

**Vocabulary**

atmosphere
air pressure
altitude
wind

**Academic Vocabulary**

stable

## Connect It!

✏️ **Draw a line on the image showing how far from Earth's surface you think the atmosphere extends. What do you notice about the structure of the atmosphere?**

**Make Observations** Where is most of the gas in the atmosphere found?

.......................................................................................................

.......................................................................................................

**SEP Construct Explanations** How does the atmosphere protect life on Earth?

.......................................................................................................

.......................................................................................................

.......................................................................................................

# Earth's Insulator

The thin envelope of gases that surrounds the planet, shown in **Figure 1**, is called the **atmosphere**. This envelope acts like a coat for Earth. Just as you wear a coat to protect you from the elements and keep warm, the atmosphere protects the planet from harmful solar radiation and keeps the planet's temperature within a range that allows life to exist.

The protection our atmosphere provides is "just right." Too heavy a coat, and you would be too warm. Too light a coat, and you would be too cold. Venus and Mars, our planetary neighbors, are good examples of this. Venus's thick atmosphere traps heat and smothers the planet, while Mars's thin atmosphere retains little heat and results in huge temperature swings on the planet.

Earth's atmosphere includes air, water, and energy all connected within a system. All parts of the system interact with each other to produce the weather and climate around our planet. The atmosphere also interacts with Earth's other systems, such as the biosphere and the ocean, and its motions are driven by energy from the sun.

**Reflect** Many parts of the system that make up the atmosphere cannot be seen, such as the movement of air. In your science notebook, describe how you think evidence of these parts could be observed and measured.

**Earth's Atmosphere**
**Figure 1** Our planet is surrounded by a protective covering of gases.

## Suspended Particles

**Figure 2** During a volcanic eruption, fine particles of ash spew into the atmosphere.

**CCC Cause and Effect** How might suspended particles in the atmosphere affect life on Earth?

........................................................

........................................................

........................................................

## Composition of the Atmosphere

The air that makes up the atmosphere is a mixture of various gases, including water vapor, and other fine particles. The most abundant gases found in the atmosphere are nitrogen and oxygen. These two gases account for 99 percent of the atmosphere.

Nitrogen makes up about 78 percent of the air we breathe. Oxygen is essential for animal life, and makes up about 21 percent of the atmosphere's gases. The remaining one percent of the gases in our atmosphere consists of trace, or very small, amounts of gases such as argon, carbon dioxide, methane, and ozone. Though these gases are far less abundant, they help insulate Earth by trapping solar energy before it escapes into space. Burning fuels can increase the amount of carbon dioxide in the air.

The atmosphere also contains water vapor, which is the gaseous form of water. The amount of water vapor in the atmosphere varies from nearly zero percent in the driest deserts to as high as four percent in the extremely humid tropics. Water vapor cannot be seen, but when it condenses into tiny droplets of liquid water or frozen ice, it forms the clouds we see in the sky. In addition, fine particles of dust, ash, and other chemicals can be suspended in air. These particles can be seen as smog or smoke when they occur in large enough amounts, as shown in **Figure 2**.

# Math Toolbox
## Temperature Scales

1. **Construct Graphs** ✎ Create a circle graph of the gases that make up air. Fill in the circle using percentages from the text. Use a different color for each gas and provide a key.

2. **Hypothesize** If gases like carbon dioxide and methane make up less than 1% of the total atmosphere, why is it important for scientists to monitor changes in percentages of these gases?

........................................................

........................................................

........................................................

........................................................

**Composition of Air**

# Model It!

## Altitude and Air Density

**Figure 3** The density of air decreases at higher altitudes because there is less pressure forcing the air molecules together.

**SEP Develop Models** ✐
Consider the molecules of air at different altitudes. The bottom magnification shows the air molecules near sea level. The center magnification shows the air molecules halfway up the mountain. Draw how you think the air molecules would be arranged at the top of the mountain.

**Air Pressure** The atmosphere is composed of tiny molecules of gases, water vapor, and particles. Each molecule exerts a small amount of force when it collides with other particles or a surface. Imagine the column of air above you that extends all the way into space. This column of air exerts a force on you called **air pressure**.

Earth's gravity pulls the molecules in the atmosphere toward the surface. The weight of the molecules presses down on the molecules below them. As a result, the molecules closest to the surface of Earth are pressed the most closely together. As you move up through the atmosphere, the density, or amount of air particles found within a certain volume, decreases. The molecules are more and more spread out. The distance above sea level is called **altitude**. The higher the altitude, the lower the air pressure because there is less air pushing down on you. Air pressure is measured using a barometer (**Figure 4**).

Gravity is not the only force that affects air pressure. Air pressure is also affected by temperature. When air is warm, heat energy causes the particles to move more rapidly, forcing the particles around them to spread out. Warm air is less dense than cold air, so it exerts less pressure.

☑ **READING CHECK** **Summarize** How does altitude affect air pressure?

..........................................................................

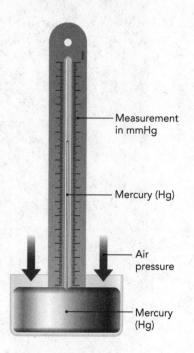

Measurement in mmHg

Mercury (Hg)

Air pressure

Mercury (Hg)

## Measuring Air Pressure

**Figure 4** As the column of air pushes on the mercury in the barometer, it causes the mercury to rise in a tube. The measurements are read as millimeters of mercury, or mmHg.

51

# Identifying the Atmosphere's Layers

**Figure 5** The atmosphere is divided into different layers by how the temperature (the yellow line in the graph) changes with altitude.

**Synthesize Information** 🖊 Read each caption. Draw dotted lines to represent the boundary between each layer of the atmosphere.

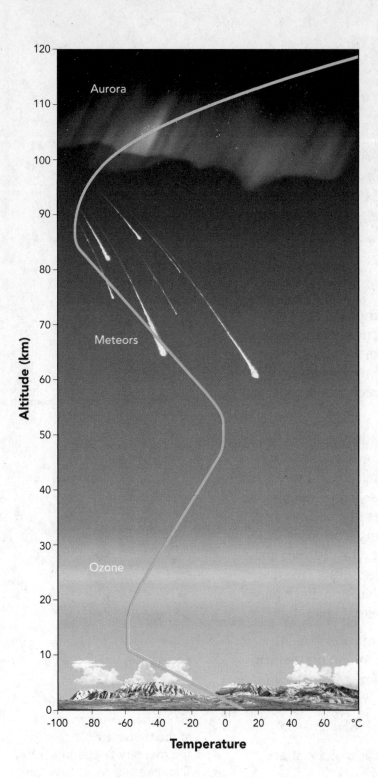

**Thermosphere:** This is the uppermost layer of the atmosphere, with the lowest density of air. The thermosphere is Earth's boundary with space. Radiation from the sun is absorbed by molecules in this layer, causing the temperatures to reach up to 1,800°C. But the molecules are so far apart that it would feel extremely cold.

Altitude Range: 85 km and above

**Mesosphere:** This layer of the atmosphere is directly above the stratosphere. It protects Earth from most meteoroids, which burn up due to friction as they strike the gases in this layer. The temperature in this layer decreases as the altitude increases.

Altitude Range: 50–85 km

**Stratosphere:** This layer of Earth's atmosphere contains the most ozone. As ozone in this layer absorbs ultraviolet radiation from the sun, it heats up the molecules of air. The temperature increases as altitude increases.

Altitude Range: 10–50 km

**Troposphere:** This is the layer where Earth's weather occurs. The troposphere is the closest to Earth's surface and experiences changeable conditions. This layer also contains 80 percent of the atmosphere by weight. The temperature decreases quickly as the altitude increases.

Altitude Range: 0–10 km

## Layers of the Atmosphere

As you have learned, the density of air in the atmosphere decreases the farther up you travel from the surface. In fact, those changes create distinct layers around Earth, which scientists identify based on the temperature characteristics of each layer. There are four main layers of the atmosphere: the troposphere, the stratosphere, the mesosphere, and the thermosphere (see **Figure 5**).

# Energy in the Atmosphere

The sun provides most of the energy that drives Earth's systems, including the atmosphere. Solar energy in the form of light travels through space and reaches Earth. Some is reflected back into space, but most passes through the atmosphere to be trapped by the air or absorbed as heat at the surface. This energy drives the processes in the atmosphere, such as the water cycle and the movement of air.

The solar energy absorbed and stored by the atmosphere causes Earth's surface temperatures to remain relatively **stable**, or constant. Recall that the thin atmosphere of Mars causes huge temperatures changes on the planet, and the thick atmosphere of Venus traps so much heat that the planet is smothered and extremely hot. Earth's atmosphere is unique because it holds just the right amount of solar energy to protect life.

## Heating of Earth

The atmosphere plays an important role in transferring heat to and from Earth's surface. Heat is transferred in three ways: convection, conduction, and radiation.

Energy from the sun warms Earth's atmosphere as it reaches its surface by radiation. Some of the energy that hits Earth's surface is absorbed by land or water, some is reflected back into space, and some warms the air that touches Earth's surface through conduction.

Convection currents are also always moving Earth's air and water to redistribute heat to and from cool and warm places. This constant transfer of energy in the atmosphere and hydrosphere is responsible for the movement and cycling of air and water around Earth.

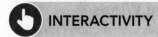

**INTERACTIVITY**

Explore the structure of the atmosphere.

**HANDS-ON LAB**

**Investigate** Observe how changes in altitude affect the atmosphere.

**Academic Vocabulary**

How is the term *stable* used in the text?

........................................................

........................................................

**Literacy Connection**

**Support Author's Claim**
As you read, underline evidence in the text that you think supports the idea that our atmosphere provides stable conditions that support life on Earth.

## Global Winds

**Figure 6** Convection currents caused by the uneven heating of Earth's surface and Earth's rotation interact to create the global wind patterns shown in the diagram.

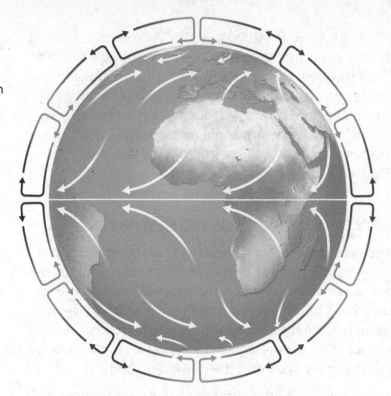

 **INTERACTIVITY**

Learn about patterns in the wind.

**Winds** As the air in the atmosphere is heated by solar energy and Earth's surface, the unequal heating causes changes in air pressure. Warm air expands and becomes less dense. Cool, dense air nearby pushes in underneath, causing the warmer air to rise. This movement of air parallel to Earth's surface is called **wind**. Air moves as wind from areas of higher pressure to areas of lower pressure.

Unequal heating over small areas results in local winds, which are winds that blow over short distances. Two examples of local winds seen along shorelines are sea breezes and land breezes. Unequal heating causes sea breezes to occur during the day, when the land heats up faster than the water. Through conduction, the land heats up the air above it, causing the air to expand and rise. The cooler air over the water moves into the low-pressure area over the land. At night, the reverse happens and land breezes occur. The land cools off faster than the water and the cool, dense air blows from the land to the water, where the air pressure is lower.

Global winds, shown in **Figure 6**, are also caused by unequal heating, but they occur over much larger areas. As solar energy warms the areas near the equator, cold air near the poles moves in global winds to areas of low pressure. Convection currents caused by cool and warm air produce global winds.

☑ **READING CHECK** **Determine Central Ideas** Why is the atmosphere heated unequally by the sun?

........................................................................................

........................................................................................

# ☑ LESSON 1 Check

MS-ESS2-5, MS-ESS2-6, MS-ESS3-2, MS-PS1-4

**1. Identify** What is the relative abundance of oxygen in the atmosphere?

...............................................................................

...............................................................................

...............................................................................

**2. Compare and Contrast** How are the troposphere and the stratosphere different?

...............................................................................

...............................................................................

...............................................................................

...............................................................................

...............................................................................

**3. SEP Communicate Information** Suppose a plane is flying at an altitude of 11,000 meters. Describe how the air pressure and temperature will change as the airplane comes down to land.

...............................................................................

...............................................................................

...............................................................................

...............................................................................

...............................................................................

**4. CCC Cause and Effect** How does the atmosphere affect life on Earth? Include both positive and negative effects in your response.

...............................................................................

...............................................................................

...............................................................................

...............................................................................

...............................................................................

...............................................................................

**5. SEP Construct Explanations** Explain how temperature and air pressure play a role in creating wind.

...............................................................................

...............................................................................

...............................................................................

...............................................................................

**6. SEP Develop Models** ✏ Draw a model of the atmosphere showing the transfer of solar energy through radiation, conduction, and convection.

# 2 Water in the Atmosphere

## Guiding Questions

- What processes make up the water cycle?
- How does energy drive the processes of the water cycle?
- How does the water cycle affect weather?

## Connections

**Literacy** Summarize Text

**Math** Convert Measurements

MS-ESS2-4

## HANDS-ON LAB

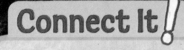

**Investigate** Investigate how clouds and fog form.

### Vocabulary

water cycle
evaporation
condensation
dew point
humidity
relative humidity
precipitation

### Academic Vocabulary

cycle

## Connect It!

✏ Circle the organisms in the photo. Do the organisms have any effect on the water in the stream?

**SEP Construct Explanations** How does the grass in the photo affect the movement of water?

.................................................................................................................

.................................................................................................................

**CCC Cause and Effect** How might the cattle affect the movement of water?

.................................................................................................................

.................................................................................................................

# Water Enters the Atmosphere

During a humid day, the air around you may feel moist and thick. On a clear, cloudless day, the air may feel dry. The difference between these feelings is caused by the amount of water in the air. Water is always moving between the surface of Earth and the atmosphere. This process is known as the **water cycle**. A **cycle** is any series of events that repeat in the same order over and over again.

In one phase of the water cycle, water vapor enters the atmosphere through a number of processes. One of these processes is **evaporation**. During evaporation, molecules of liquid water in oceans, lakes, and other bodies of water are heated by the sun. The energy of the sun causes the water molecules to speed up and collide more often. As the molecules collide, some of them "escape" and enter the surrounding air.

The stream in **Figure 1** is not the only source of water for the atmosphere. Plants and animals also release water vapor into the air. In plants, water enters through the roots, rises to the leaves, and is released into the air as water vapor. This is known as transpiration. Animals (and people!) release water vapor into the air every time they breathe out, or exhale. This is known as respiration.

**HANDS-ON LAB**

Explore the conditions under which water vapor becomes liquid water.

**Academic Vocabulary**

How do the four seasons also represent a cycle?

........................................................

........................................................

........................................................

**Water Enters the Atmosphere**

**Figure 1** Water is released into the atmosphere as water vapor from bodies of water such as this stream and living things, such as grass and cattle.

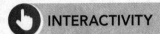

**INTERACTIVITY**

Investigate the stages of the water cycle.

**HANDS-ON LAB**

**Investigate** Investigate how clouds and fog form.

**Forming a Cloud**

**Figure 2** ✏ Complete the diagram to show how clouds form when warm, moist air rises and cools. Use the following terms: *evaporation, cooling air, condensation,* and *particles.*

**Condensation** Recall that water vapor is a gas mixed in with the rest of the air. **Condensation** occurs when water vapor changes into liquid water.

For condensation to occur, tiny particles must be present in the atmosphere so that the water has a surface on which to condense. Most of these particles are salt crystals, dust from soil, bacteria, or particles contained in smoke. During condensation, molecules of water vapor mix with these particles.

Temperature is also a major factor in condensation. Warm air can hold more water vapor than cold air can. Therefore, as warm air cools, the amount of water vapor it can hold decreases, and the water vapor starts to condense. Liquid water that condenses from the air onto a cooler surface is called dew. The temperature at which condensation begins is called the **dew point**. If the dew point is above freezing, the water vapor forms droplets. If the dew point is below freezing, the water vapor may change directly into ice crystals called frost.

One result of condensation of water vapor in the atmosphere is cloud formation. Clouds form when water vapor in the air condenses to form liquid water or ice crystals. When you look at a cloud, such as the one in **Figure 2,** you are seeing millions of these tiny water droplets or ice crystals. When water vapor condenses near ground level, it can take the form of fog. Water can condense as dew on any solid surface, such as a blade of grass or a window pane.

## Relative Humidity
Meteorologists often warn of high or low humidity during their weather forecasts. **Humidity** is a measure of the amount of water vapor in the air.

The ability of air to hold water vapor depends on temperature. Warm air can hold more water than cool air. So, in their weather reports, meteorologists usually refer to the amount of water vapor in the air as relative humidity.

**Relative humidity** is the percent of water vapor in the air compared to the maximum amount of water vapor the air can hold at a particular temperature. For example, suppose that 1 cubic meter of air can hold no more than 8 grams of water vapor at 10°C. If there are 8 grams of water vapor in the air, then the relative humidity is 100 percent and the air would be said to be saturated. Similarly, the relative humidity would be 50 percent if the air had only 4 grams of water vapor per cubic meter.

Relative humidity is a better reflection of how the air feels than humidity. For example, air that holds 4 grams of water vapor per cubic meter can feel moist on a cold day or dry on a hot day. Relative humidity reflects this feeling. It would be near 100 percent on a cold day, and much lower on a hot day.

Relative humidity can be measured using a psychrometer. It is a device made up of two thermometers, a wet-bulb thermometer and a dry-bulb thermometer. As shown in **Figure 3**, a moist cloth covers the wet bulb. When the psychrometer is "slung," or spun around, air flows over both thermometers. The wet-bulb thermometer is cooled by evaporation, causing its temperature reading to fall. If the relative humidity is high, evaporation occurs slowly and the wet-bulb temperature does not change much. If the relative humidity is low, evaporation occurs rapidly and the wet-bulb temperature drops by a large amount. Relative humidity is measured by comparing the temperatures of the two bulbs.

✓ READING CHECK **Determine Conclusions** Suppose the two thermometers on a sling psychrometer show almost identical readings. Was the psychrometer more likely used on a Florida beach or in an Arizona desert? Explain your answer.

.................................................................................

.................................................................................

.................................................................................

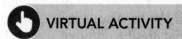
**VIRTUAL ACTIVITY**

Observe how water moves in the water cycle.

## Literacy Connection

**Summarize Text** As you read, underline sentences that contain information you consider important to remember.

**Tools for Measuring Humidity**

**Figure 3** Digital hygrometers and sling psychrometers like the ones shown are used to find relative humidity.

## Write About It

What are the different types of precipitation you encounter in your daily life? In your science notebook, describe how precipitation impacts your life.

# Water Leaves the Atmosphere

Water is continually evaporating and condensing in the atmosphere, and this process forms clouds. When enough condensation occurs within a cloud, water droplets form. At first, the droplets are very small, but they grow larger as condensation continues. Depending on temperature and other conditions in the atmosphere, the droplets may grow heavy enough that gravity pulls them down toward Earth's surface. When this happens, precipitation occurs. **Precipitation** is any form of water that falls from clouds and reaches Earth's surface.

**Types of Precipitation** The most common kind of precipitation is rain. Rain comes in various forms depending on the size of the water droplets that form, as seen in **Figure 4**. Rain starts out as cloud droplets. When cloud droplets grow a bit bigger, they become mist. When droplets reach a size of 0.05 to 0.5 millimeters in diameter, they are known as drizzle. Drops of water are called rain when they are larger than 0.5 millimeters in diameter.

## Water Droplets

**Figure 4** 🖉 On the diagram, label the drops as *mist, rain, drizzle,* or *droplet.*

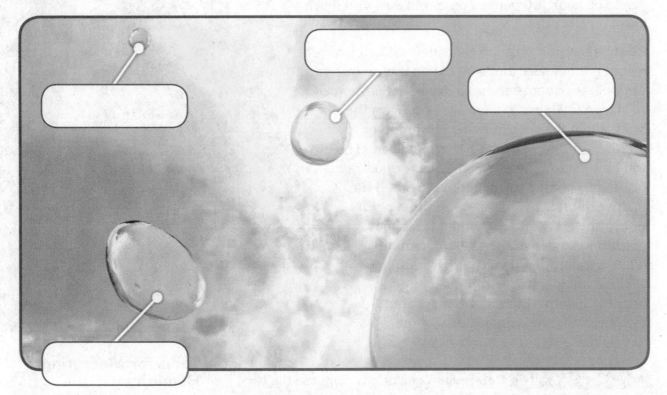

Temperature is a very important factor in determining the type of precipitation an area may get at any given time. In warm climates, precipitation is almost always rain. However, there are many other types of precipitation. In colder regions, precipitation often falls as snow or ice. Besides rain, common types of precipitation include sleet, freezing rain, snow, and hail, as shown in **Figure 5**.

## Freezing Precipitation

**Figure 5** Draw a check mark on the photos showing the precipitation that occurs when the air temperature is above 0°C and the ground temperature is below 0°C. Draw an X on the photos showing the precipitation that occurs when the air temperature is below 0°C and the ground temperature is above 0°C. Draw a triangle on the photos showing the precipitation that occurs when both air and ground temperature are below 0°C.

**Freezing Rain** Raindrops sometimes freeze when they hit a cold surface. This kind of precipitation is called freezing rain.

**Hail** A hailstone is a round pellet of ice at least 5 millimeters in diameter. Hail starts as an ice pellet inside a cold region of a cloud. Strong updrafts of wind carry the hailstone up through the cold region many times, adding ice in layers to the outside of the hailstone. Eventually the hailstone becomes heavy enough for gravity to pull it to the ground.

**Sleet** Raindrops that fall through a layer of air below 0°C freeze into solid particles of ice before they hit the ground. Ice particles smaller than hailstones are called sleet.

**Snow** Snow forms when water vapor in a cloud is converted directly into ice crystals that clump together. The clumps fall in the form of ice crystals called snowflakes.

VIDEO

Watch a single drop of water as it moves through the water cycle.

**Measuring Precipitation** If a town receives a large snowfall, meteorologists need to track how much snow fell to determine how safe it is to travel. Similarly, if a big storm delivers a lot of rain, people would need to know how much rain fell to determine whether flooding might occur.

Rain can be measured by using a rain gauge, which is an open-ended tube that collects rain. The amount of rain is measured either by dipping a ruler into the water in the tube or by reading a scale printed on the tube. Snowfall is usually measured in two ways: by using a simple measuring stick or by melting collected snow and measuring the depth of water it produces. On average, 10 centimeters of snow contain about the same amount of water as 1 centimeter of rain. However, light, fluffy snow contains far less water than heavy, wet snow does.

✓ READING CHECK **Determine Central Ideas** How are snow and rain formation similar? How are they different?

.................................................................................................

.................................................................................................

.................................................................................................

.................................................................................................

# Math Toolbox

## Measuring Precipitation

In late September and early October of 2016, Hurricane Matthew brought a huge amount of rain to the Caribbean and then the southeastern United States, causing major flooding and damage. The table shows approximate rainfall during the hurricane. Use the table to answer the questions about this powerful storm.

1. **SEP Use Mathematics** ✏ Complete the table. Use the fact that 1 inch is equal to 25.4 millimeters.

2. **SEP Interpret Data** Do the data in the table support the conclusion that the rainfall lessened before reaching the United States? Explain.

.................................................................................................

.................................................................................................

| Rainfall During Hurricane Matthew | | |
| --- | --- | --- |
| Location | Rain in mm | Rain in inches |
| Hewanorra, Saint Lucia | | 12.6 |
| Santo Domingo, Dominican Republic | | 9.21 |
| Fayetteville, NC, United States | 355 | |

# The Water Cycle

The water cycle describes the way that water moves through Earth's systems and affects our lives in many ways. As the sun heats the land, ocean, lakes, and other bodies of water, its energy changes the amount of water in the atmosphere. Through evaporation, transpiration, and respiration, water rises up and forms clouds. Rain, snow, and other forms of precipitation fall from the clouds toward Earth's surface. The water then runs off the surface or moves through the ground, back into lakes, streams, and eventually the ocean. As seen in **Figure 6**, gravity and energy from the sun together drive water molecules through this never-ending cycle.

**INTERACTIVITY**

Examine your own role in the water cycle.

☑ READING CHECK **Summarize Text** What role does energy play in the water cycle?

........................................................................

........................................................................

........................................................................

# Model It!

**Figure 6** CCC Patterns ✏ Study this diagram of the water cycle in action. Label the various processes you see in the diagram.

MS-ESS2-4

1. **CCC Energy and Matter** Besides energy from the sun, what force helps move water molecules through the water cycle?

.......................................................

2. **SEP Construct Explanations** What conditions must change for rain to become snow?

.......................................................
.......................................................
.......................................................
.......................................................
.......................................................

3. **SEP Construct Explanations** Suppose you use a sling psychrometer in two different locations. How will you know which location has lower relative humidity?

.......................................................
.......................................................
.......................................................
.......................................................
.......................................................
.......................................................

4. **CCC Systems** Explain how animals affect the water cycle as they breathe.

.......................................................
.......................................................
.......................................................

5. **SEP Use Models** ✏ Create a diagram that shows how water cycles through the environment around your neighborhood.

# Quest CHECK-IN

In this lesson, you learned how water cycles through Earth's systems. You also discovered that the water cycle can influence the weather.

Evaluate How does each part of the water cycle contribute to the weather?

.......................................................
.......................................................
.......................................................
.......................................................
.......................................................
.......................................................

## 👆 INTERACTIVITY

Weather and Severe Weather

**Go online** to analyze how the water cycle is involved in weather, especially severe weather. Then consider possible causes and effects of various weather events, and suggest how people can prepare for those events.

MS-ESS2-4

# CATCHING WATER
# With a Net

**INTERACTIVITY**

Explore the factors affecting the amount of water that a dew catcher can collect.

**How can you** provide safe drinking water for small villages far from any clean water source? By extracting it from the air!

**The Challenge:** To reclaim clean drinking water from humidity in the air.

**Phenomenon** You can get a fresh drink of water almost anywhere in the United States simply by turning on a faucet. However, in many villages and cities around the world, people have to go a long way to find clean water that is safe to drink.

Scientists have taken up the challenge of bringing water to these people through the ancient method of collecting dew. Recall that dew is the moisture that condenses on surfaces as a result of cooling temperatures and the available humidity in the air.

In rural villages across the world, people are putting up nets. Cooler night temperatures cause moisture in the air from higher humidity or fog to condense and cover the nets with water. The water drains into a container, providing a lifeline to thirsty communities. The water is safe for drinking, cooking, bathing, and tending crops.

Members of the Swakopmund People of the Topnaar tribe work on a fog collection system in the Namib Desert in Namibia.

**DESIGN CHALLENGE** Can you build a device to catch dew from the air? Go to the Engineering Design Notebook to find out!

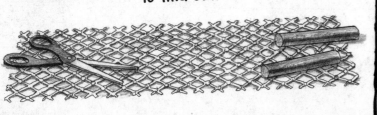

# 3 Air Masses

## Guiding Questions

- How do global patterns, such as the jet stream, affect air masses?
- How do air masses interact to form fronts?
- How do the interactions of air masses result in changes in weather?

## Connections

**Literacy** Read and Comprehend

MS-ESS2-5

## HANDS-ON LAB

**Investigate** Model the behavior of cold and warm fronts.

### Vocabulary

air mass
jet stream
front
cyclone
anticyclone

### Academic Vocabulary

prevailing
stationary

# Connect It !

✎ **Make a checkmark on something in the picture that indicates whether the air is warm or cool. Make an X on something that indicates the relative humidity.**

**Claim** Do you think the air at this beach is humid or dry?

.........................................................................................................................

**Evidence** What evidence is there in the image to support your answer?

.........................................................................................................................

**Reasoning** What facts affect the temperature at this beach?

.........................................................................................................................

.........................................................................................................................

# Major Air Masses

Look outside your window. What is the weather like where you are today? The weather you see is happening due to the influence of air masses. An **air mass** is a huge body of air that has similar temperature, humidity, and air pressure at any given height. Scientists classify air masses based on temperature and humidity.

The characteristics of an air mass depend on the temperature and moisture content of the region over which the air mass forms. Whether an air mass is humid or dry depends on whether it forms over water or dry land. For example, an air mass that forms above the ocean in **Figure 1** would have different characteristics than an air mass that forms over a desert.

**How Air Masses Move** Air masses are always on the move. In the continental United States, air masses are commonly moved by the **prevailing** westerlies and jet streams.

In general, the major wind belts over the continental United States, known as the prevailing westerlies, push air masses from west to east. For example, cool, moist air masses from the Pacific Ocean may be blown onto the West Coast, bringing low clouds and showers. Embedded within the prevailing westerlies are jet streams. A **jet stream** is a band of high-speed winds about 6 to 14 km above Earth's surface. As jet streams blow from west to east, the surface air masses beneath them are carried along. The movement of these air masses, and their interactions have a great impact on weather.

**Air Masses**

**Figure 1** Air masses near this beach have specific temperature and humidity profiles based on conditions where the air masses formed.

**INTERACTIVITY**

Explore the characteristics of air masses.

**Academic Vocabulary**

Think about the meaning of *prevailing* in terms of wind. Keeping this in mind, what might be the prevailing noise at a concert?

......................................................

......................................................

......................................................

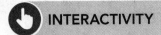

INTERACTIVITY

Describe the properties and characteristics of the different kinds of air masses.

## Types of Air Masses

**Figure 2** These four major types of air masses affect North American weather.

**Integrate with Visuals** ✏ Label each type of air mass with two words that describe its temperature and humidity such as *warm* and *dry*.

## Types of Air Masses

Is it often windy or rainy where you live? Your local weather, and all the weather in North America, is influenced by one of four major types of air masses: maritime tropical, continental tropical, maritime polar, and continental polar. These air masses are shown in **Figure 2**.

Tropical, or warm, air masses form in the tropics and have low air pressure. Polar, or cold, air masses form in the high latitudes and have high air pressure. Maritime air masses form over the ocean and are very humid. Continental air masses have less exposure to large amounts of moisture, and are drier than maritime air masses. The high and low temperatures in continental air masses can be more extreme than the temperatures in maritime air masses. This is because large bodies of water moderate air temperatures.

✓ READING CHECK **Read and Comprehend** What types of air masses affect the weather in North America?

.................................................................................

.................................................................................

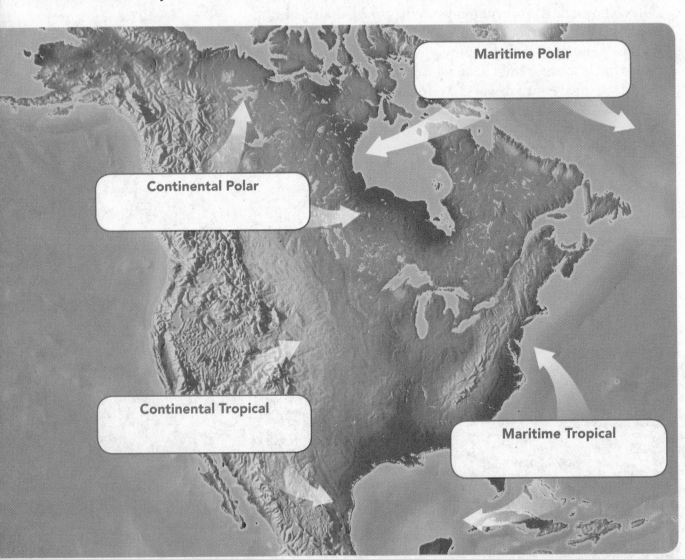

Maritime Polar

Continental Polar

Continental Tropical

Maritime Tropical

# Types of Fronts

Think about a bottle of oil and water. What happens when you shake the bottle? If you try this, you will see that the two substances do not mix—the less-dense oil winds up floating on top of the water. Air masses of different temperatures and humidity act the same way. Although they move across the land and frequently collide with each other, they do not mix easily. Instead, the boundary where the air masses meet becomes a **front**. Storms and changeable weather often develop along fronts like the one in **Figure 3**.

The weather may be different when you leave school this afternoon than it was when you arrived in the morning. The change might be due to a front passing through your area. Colliding air masses can form four types of fronts: cold fronts, warm fronts, stationary fronts, and occluded fronts, as shown on the next two pages in **Figure 4**. The kind of front that develops depends on the characteristics of the air masses and the direction in which they move.

**How a Front Forms**
**Figure 3** A front may be 15 to 600 km wide and extend high into the troposphere.

**CCC Stability and Change** What kind of weather would develop along the front shown in the photo?

............................................................

............................................................

HANDS-ON LAB

**Investigate** Model the behavior of cold and warm fronts.

Cold Front

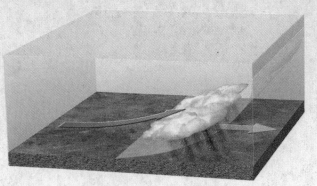

Warm Front

**Cold Fronts** A cold front forms when a cold air mass runs into a warm air mass. Because cold air is denser than warm air, the warm air is pushed up rapidly as the colder air slides beneath it. Cold fronts can result in abrupt and hazardous weather such as heavy rains and winds, thunderstorms, and even tornadoes. After the front passes, the weather usually cools and the skies become clear.

**Warm Fronts** A warm front forms when a fast-moving warm air mass overtakes a slower-moving cold air mass. Because the warm air mass is less dense, it rises above the cold air mass. Along the front, light rain or snow can fall if the warm air is humid. Scattered clouds can form if the warm air mass is dry. These fronts often move slowly, so there may be rain and clouds for a few days. The weather usually is warmer and more humid after a warm front moves by.

**Occluded Fronts** Sometimes, a warm air mass gets caught between two cold air masses, forming an occluded front. Because the cooler air is denser, it moves under the warm air, causing the warm air to rise. When the two cold air masses meet, they mix together. Air temperature drops as the warm air mass becomes occluded, or prevented from reaching the ground. As the warm air mass rises and cools, clouds gather, and rain or snow may fall.

**Stationary Fronts** Sometimes cold and warm air masses meet, but neither one can move the other. This non-moving front is called a **stationary** front. Where the warm and cool air meet, water vapor in the warm air condenses into rain, snow, fog, or clouds. A stationary front may bring many days of clouds and precipitation.

☑ READING CHECK **Determine Central Ideas** What do all of these different types of fronts have in common?

.............................................................................................

.............................................................................................

**Occluded Front**

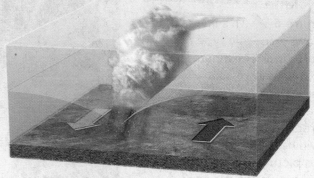

**Stationary Front**

# Model It

SEP Develop Models ✏ Draw a diagram to model what would happen when a cold air mass moving from the south collides with a warm air mass moving from the north.

## Types of Fronts

**Figure 4** Different types of fronts occur, depending on how the different air masses interact.

SEP Evaluate Information How are cold and warm fronts different?

......................................................

......................................................

......................................................

......................................................

 **VIDEO**

Watch how the different fronts could affect the weather.

## Cyclone

**Figure 5** ✏ This image shows a specific type of Northern Hemisphere cyclone known as a hurricane. On the image, draw arrows to show the direction the cyclone is swirling. How do you know this picture is of a cyclone and not an anticyclone?

..............................................

..............................................

..............................................

..............................................

✊ **INTERACTIVITY**

Identify the types of weather that take place in different locations.

📓 **Write About It** Watch water swirl down a drain. In your science notebook, describe how this swirling water is related to a cyclone.

# Cyclones and Anticyclones

When air masses collide, they form fronts that can sometimes become distorted by surface features, such as mountains, or by strong winds, such as a jet stream. When this happens, the air begins to swirl, causing a low-pressure center to form. Areas of relatively low air pressure can also form in other ways.

**Cyclones** As shown in **Figure 5**, a swirling center of low air pressure can form a **cyclone**. As warm air at the center of a cyclone rises, the air pressure decreases. Cooler air blows inward from nearby areas of higher air pressure. Winds spiral inward toward the center. In the Northern Hemisphere, the Coriolis effect deflects these winds towards the right, so the cyclone winds spin counterclockwise when viewed from above. As air rises in a cyclone, the air cools, forming clouds and precipitation.

**Anticyclones** An **anticyclone** is the opposite of a cyclone. It is a high-pressure center of dry air, shown by an H on a weather map. In an anticyclone, winds spiral outward from the center, moving toward areas of lower pressure. The Coriolis effect, which is the deflection of the winds towards the right, causes the winds in an anticyclone to spin clockwise in the Northern Hemisphere. As air moves out from the center, cool air moves downward from higher in the atmosphere. As the cool air warms up, its relative humidity drops, so no clouds form and the weather is clear and dry.

☑ READING CHECK **Read and Comprehend** How do cyclones and anticyclones differ?

..............................................

..............................................

..............................................

# ✓ LESSON 3 Check

MS-ESS2-5

**1. Compare and Contrast** What is the difference between an air mass and a front?

......................................................................

......................................................................

......................................................................

......................................................................

......................................................................

......................................................................

......................................................................

**2. CCC Cause and Effect** A state often has cold, snowy winters and cool, rainy summers. Is this state more likely to be New York or Nebraska? Explain your answer.

......................................................................

......................................................................

......................................................................

......................................................................

......................................................................

......................................................................

......................................................................

......................................................................

......................................................................

**3. Use Tables** ✏ For each description in the table, write the name of the type of front it describes.

| Type | Description |
|------|-------------|
|      | A cold air mass pushes under a warm air mass. |
|      | A warm air mass is trapped by two cold air masses. |
|      | A warm air mass rises over a cold air mass. |
|      | The front does not move. |

**4. SEP Develop Models** ✏ Use the two models to show the air pattern in a cyclone and in an anticyclone. On each sketch, draw arrows that trace the direction of the air and label the cyclone and anticyclone.

# Quest CHECK-IN

**In this lesson, you learned that air masses interact at fronts. You also discovered that interacting air masses can cause severe weather.**

CCC Energy and Matter Why is it important for people to understand how interacting air masses can affect the weather?

......................................................................

......................................................................

......................................................................

......................................................................

## INTERACTIVITY

All About Air Masses

**Go online** to explore what happens when different air masses interact. Then find out how and where tornadoes form.

# LESSON 4 Predicting Weather Changes

## Guiding Questions

- How do meteorologists use the interactions of air masses to forecast changes in weather?
- How does technology aid in collecting and analyzing weather data?
- How do weather maps help to model current weather and predict future weather?

## Connections

**Literacy** Determine Central Ideas

**Math** Analyze Quantitative Relationships

MS-ESS2-5, MS-ESS2-6

## HANDS-ON LAB

**uInvestigate** Consider how barometric pressure is related to weather conditions.

**Vocabulary**

meteorologist

**Academic Vocabulary**

synthesize

## Connect It!

✏ **On two different places in the photo, draw a symbol to indicate the type of weather occurring in that location.**

SEP Evaluate Information What details in the photo support your predictions?

.......................................................................................................

.......................................................................................................

.......................................................................................................

# How To Predict Weather

Whether you're planning on going on a hike, driving to an amusement park, or having a picnic in the park, you'll need to know the day's weather to make your plans. Before you're able to predict the weather, you'll first need to collect data, either through direct observations or by using special instruments, such as a barometer. A barometer measures air pressure. If the reading is falling, meaning the air pressure in the area is decreasing, then you can expect stormy weather.

Making observations is a simple way of predicting how the weather might change. Looking at the sky shown in **Figure 1** might make you wonder how you can use your observations to forecast weather. You might read signs of changing weather in the clouds. On a warm day, you may see clouds that slowly grow larger and taller, which could indicate that a thunderstorm is on the way. If you can see thin, high clouds in the sky, a warm front may be approaching.

Usually, your observations won't tell you everything you need to know. Even careful observers often turn to meteorologists for weather information. A **meteorologist** (mee tee uh RAHL uh jist) is a scientist who studies and predicts weather.

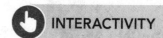

**INTERACTIVITY**

Explore some of the factors that make it difficult to predict the weather.

**Predicting Weather Changes**
**Figure 1** Meteorologists forecast the weather using direct observations about the conditions.

**Investigate** Consider how barometric pressure is related to weather conditions.

## Weather Technology

**Figure 2** Technological improvements in gathering weather data have improved the accuracy of weather forecasts.

**Weather Balloons** Weather balloons carry instruments for collecting weather data high into the atmosphere where human observation is not feasible.

**Automated Weather Stations** Weather stations in many locations can gather real-time weather data.

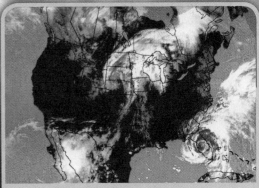

**Computer Forecasts** Computers process weather data quickly, which enables forecasters to make timely predictions.

**Weather Satellites** Satellites orbit high above Earth collecting data as well as images of Earth's surface and atmosphere.

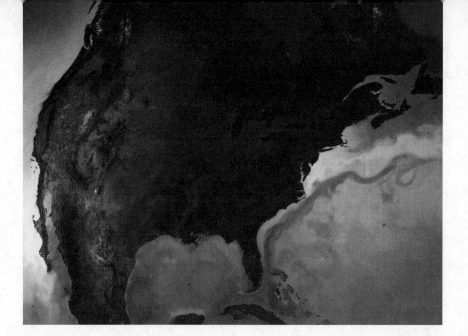

## Weather Technology

In recent years, new technologies have been developed to help meteorologists predict the weather, as shown in **Figure 2**. Short-range forecasts—forecasts for up to five days—are now fairly reliable. Meteorologists can also make somewhat accurate long-range predictions.

## Global Patterns and Local Weather

Recognizing patterns is another component of weather forecasting. A large part of the job of a meteorologist is to determine how global patterns affect the local weather. Meteorologists look at many different factors, including temperature, wind, air pressure, humidity, and precipitation. They closely observe and track the movements of jet streams and ocean currents to help predict future weather changes.

Jet streams help to move air masses and weather systems around the globe. While the weather may be warm and sunny one day, a jet stream can push a cold, moist air mass into the area and change the forecast to cooler, stormy days.

Ocean currents, which move warm and cold water around the world, also affect local weather. Warm ocean currents cause the air masses above them to become warmer, while cold currents lower the temperature of air masses above them. These currents affect local air temperatures and precipitation, and they also cause changes in wind speed and direction. Observe **Figure 3** to see how one ocean current, the Gulf Stream, influences the temperatures on the east coast of North America.

**✓ READING CHECK Determine Conclusions** Based on the image in **Figure 3**, how does the Gulf Stream most likely affect temperatures on the East Coast?

........................................................................................

........................................................................................

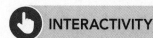

### INTERACTIVITY

Discover how air masses can be used to predict weather.

### VIDEO

Learn how weather satellites are used in meteorology.

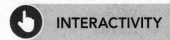

**INTERACTIVITY**

Practice developing your own weather predictions.

## Learning from Weather Maps

Do you ever check the weather on your phone or a tablet? In addition to telling you the temperature and atmospheric conditions, many apps will show you a weather map. A weather map is a model that shows the weather conditions at a particular time over a large area. There are many types of weather maps.

**Reading Weather Maps** Data from many local weather stations all over the country are **synthesized** into weather maps at the National Weather Service. Some weather maps show curved lines. These lines connect places with similar conditions of temperature or air pressure. Isobars are lines joining places on the map that have the same air pressure. Isotherms are lines joining places that have the same temperature.

**Figure 4** shows a typical newspaper weather map. Standard symbols on weather maps show many features, including fronts, areas of high and low pressure (measured in millibars), types of precipitation, and temperatures.

### Academic Vocabulary

What do you think it means to synthesize a chemical?

........................................................

........................................................

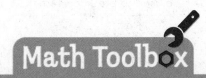

## Math Toolbox

### Isobars

The black lines on this map of the United States are isobars, which connect points of equal air pressure, measured in millibars.

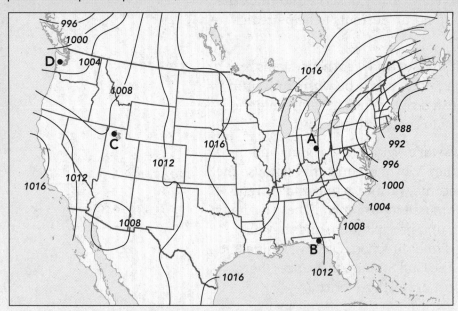

**Analyze Quantitative Relationships** Use the locations A, B, C, and D from the map to answer the questions about air pressure.

1. Which two locations have approximately the same air pressure? _____
2. Which two locations have the greatest difference in air pressure? _____

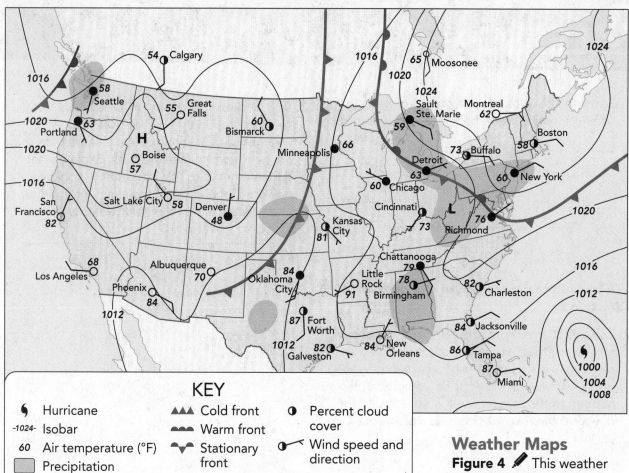

## KEY

- **◖** Hurricane
- **-1024-** Isobar
- **60** Air temperature (°F)
- ▨ Precipitation
- **▲▲▲** Cold front
- **●●●** Warm front
- **▼▼▼** Stationary front
- **▲▲▲** Occluded front
- **◖** Percent cloud cover
- **○—** Wind speed and direction

## The Future of Meteorology

As computers, satellites, and radar technologies become more sophisticated, scientists can make better forecasts. But even with these advanced tools, no forecaster will ever be one hundred percent accurate. This is because the atmosphere works in such a way that a small change in the weather today can mean a larger change in the weather a week later! A tiny event might cause a larger disturbance that could—eventually—grow into a large storm.

☑ **READING CHECK** **Determine Central Ideas** How are isobars and isotherms alike? How are they different?

.....................................................................................

.....................................................................................

.....................................................................................

## Weather Maps

**Figure 4** ✏ This weather map of the United States uses many symbols. Use the key to interpret the symbols. Underline the cities with the highest and lowest temperatures. (Note that the temperatures are given in degrees Fahrenheit.) Then circle the area showing the highest levels of atmospheric pressure.

## Literacy Connection

**Determine Central Ideas** Compare the information you read about weather forecasts in the text with the information you gained about forecasts from looking at the weather map. Use the central idea from the reading and map reading to compare the information.

MS-ESS2-5, MS-ESS2-6

1. **Summarize** What does a meteorologist do? Use information from the lesson to summarize.

........................................................

........................................................

........................................................

........................................................

**Use the information in Figure 4 to answer Question 2.**

2. **CCC Patterns** From the temperatures shown on the weather map and the knowledge that air masses are usually pushed eastward by the prevailing westerlies, what do you predict will happen to the temperature in Kansas City the day after the map was made? Explain your answer.

........................................................

........................................................

........................................................

........................................................

........................................................

3. **SEP Develop Models** ✏ Describe a weather station that will be used to collect weather data. It should collect all the data that are needed to make forecasts. Explain what data are needed, how the station would be powered, and any other relevant information. Then sketch a model of your weather station.

........................................................

........................................................

........................................................

........................................................

# Quest CHECK-IN

**In this lesson, you learned how meteorologists use observations, patterns, and tools to predict the weather.**

**SEP Evaluate Information** How might accurate weather forecasting help people who work as farmers or fishers? How does it help everyone?

........................................................

........................................................

........................................................

........................................................

........................................................

## ☝ INTERACTIVITY

Predicting Severe Weather

**Go online** to determine how weather forecasts help people to prepare for severe weather. Then identify which weather conditions you should address in your PSA.

## Meteorologist

# Watching the CLOUDS GO BY

People have been trying to predict the weather for thousands of years. In ancient times, people observed the clouds, the wind, and the temperature changes. They recognized patterns that helped them to forecast the weather with some accuracy.

Today, forecasting the weather combines data collection with the old skill of pattern recognition. Scientists called meteorologists collect weather data using computers and other tools. They analyze and interpret the data and compare it to their knowledge and experience. This process allows meteorologists to make predictions about the weather days and even weeks in advance.

There are many different types of meteorologists. Broadcast meteorologists report the weather on television. Research meteorologists work at government agencies and study particular issues related to weather and climate. Forensic meteorologists are called upon to research past weather events for court cases or insurance claims.

Meteorologists often have a good background in subjects such as physics, astronomy, and math. It also helps if you like different kinds of weather and if you are observant and curious!

 **VIDEO**

Find out how a meteorologist predicts the weather in an area.

Meteorologists check instruments at an automated weather station in a remote desert location at the Jornada Biosphere Reserve in southern New Mexico.

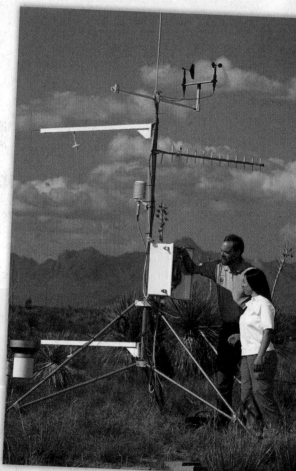

## MY CAREER

Type "meteorologist" into an online search engine to learn more about this career.

# 5 Severe Weather and Floods

## Guiding Questions

- How does severe weather affect human life?
- How do humans protect themselves from severe weather?

## Connections

**Literacy** Cite Textual Evidence

MS-ESS3-2

## HANDS-ON LAB

**ᴜInvestigate** Record and analyze historical hurricane data to predict future events.

### Vocabulary

storm
thunderstorm
hurricane
tornado
storm surge
flood
drought

### Academic Vocabulary

approximate

## Connect It!

✏️ **Label the center, or eye, of this North Atlantic hurricane.**

**SEP Analyze Data** In what direction are the winds swirling around the location you identified?

.............................................................................................................

.............................................................................................................

**Predict** How might this storm affect people living near its path?

.............................................................................................................

.............................................................................................................

# Types of Severe Storms

In October 2016, Hurricane Matthew struck the Caribbean and the southeastern United States with torrential rains and winds that reached **approximate** speeds of 250 km/h. Shown in the satellite image in **Figure 1**, it was one of the most intense storms ever to hit that part of the United States.

The death toll due to Hurricane Matthew surpassed 1000, with most of those deaths occurring in Haiti. In the United States, approximately 40 people died, more than half of these in North Carolina. Florida did not receive the extremely strong winds that some areas did, but the hurricane dropped between 7 and 10 inches of rain in the eastern half of the state.

In addition to casualties, property damage from the hurricane was extreme. Many areas were battered by winds or flooded for days. Many buildings were blown down and roads washed away.

A hurricane is one example of a storm. A **storm** is a violent disturbance in the atmosphere. Storms involve sudden changes in air pressure, which cause rapid air movements and often precipitation. There are several types of severe storms: winter storms, thunderstorms, hurricanes, and tornadoes.

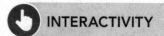
INTERACTIVITY

Write about your experiences with severe weather.

**Academic Vocabulary**

What is the difference between an approximate and an exact number?

.....................................................

.....................................................

.....................................................

**Hurricane Matthew**

**Figure 1** This satellite image shows Hurricane Matthew swirling north of Cuba and beginning to engulf the Florida peninsula.

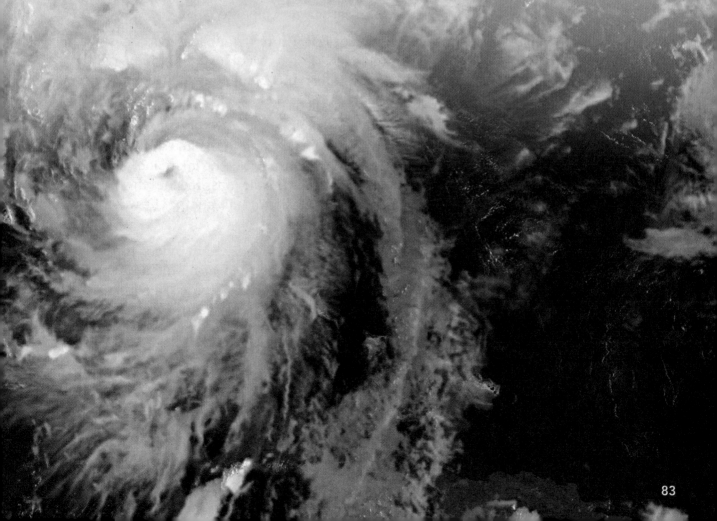

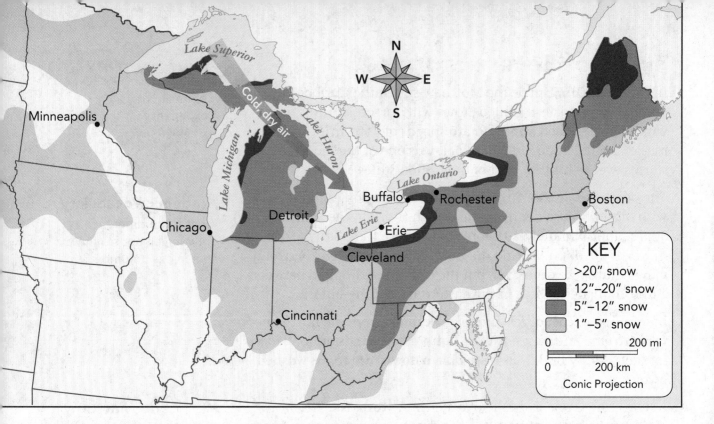

## Lake-Effect Snow

**Figure 2** 🖊 This map shows the snow totals after a certain winter storm. The higher totals are a result of lake-effect snow. Draw arrows on the map to represent the wind blowing across the lakes.

📓 **Write About It** Identify the actions you can take to remain safe during a severe storm of any kind.

**Winter Storms** In the winter in the northern United States, most of the precipitation that occurs is in the form of snow. If the air is colder than 0°C all the way to the ground, the precipitation falls as snow. Heavy snow can block roads, trap people in their homes, and delay emergency vehicles. Extreme cold can cause water pipes to burst.

Some places, such as Erie, Pennsylvania, get more snow than other places relatively close by. In an average winter, nearly 118 inches of snow fall on these cities due to lake-effect snow, as shown in **Figure 2.**

In the fall and winter, the land near the Great Lakes cools much more rapidly than the water in the lakes. When a cold, dry air mass moves southeast across the lakes, it picks up water vapor and heat. As soon as the air mass reaches the other side of the lake, the air rises and cools again. The water vapor condenses and falls as snow.

Some winter storms are more intense than others. In February 1978, a huge blizzard hit the northeastern United States. During this storm, weather stations recorded hurricane-force winds and record-breaking amounts of snow. The storm hovered over New England, and heavy snow fell for almost 33 hours without letting up.

People driving on highways abandoned their cars when the snow became too deep. Rescuers traveled on cross-country skis and snowmobiles to help stranded drivers. It was almost a week until the roads opened again.

**Thunderstorms** Spring and summer are often associated with clear, warm weather, but they are also the times when hazardous thunderstorms can form.

A **thunderstorm** is a localized storm often accompanied by heavy precipitation, frequent thunder, and dangerous lightning. It usually forms when warm air carrying lots of moisture is forced upward along a cold front. The warm, humid air rises rapidly, forming dense thunderheads. Thunderstorms can bring heavy rain and hail.

During a thunderstorm, positive and negative electrical charges build up and discharge in the thunderheads. Lightning occurs as these charges jump between parts of a cloud, between nearby clouds, or between a cloud and the ground, all of which are shown in **Figure 3**.

The loud booms of thunder that can keep us up at night are produced when lightning heats the air near it to as much as 30,000°C. That's hotter than the sun's surface! The rapidly heated air expands explosively, creating the shockwave we call thunder in the surrounding air as it is compressed.

Thunderstorms cause severe damage. Their heavy rains may flood low-lying areas. Large hailstones ruin crops, damage property such as cars and windows, and may even cause fatalities to people and animals out in the open. Lightning strikes start fires and damage structures or sometimes just the electrical equipment within a structure. If lightning strikes a person, it can cause unconsciousness, serious burns, and even death.

**Thunder and Lightning**
**Figure 3** Lightning strikes can cause severe damage during thunderstorms.

# Model It !

### How Thunderstorms Form

SEP Develop Models ✐ Draw a labeled diagram to show the formation of a thunderstorm.

## Hurricanes

When a cyclone's winds exceed 119 km/h, we call it a hurricane. A **hurricane** can stretch more than 600 kilometers across and it may have winds as strong as 320 km/h. In the western Pacific Ocean, these storms are called typhoons. When they occur in the Indian Ocean, they are known simply as cyclones.

A typical hurricane that strikes the United States forms in the Atlantic Ocean north of the equator during the late summer. It begins as a low-pressure area, or tropical disturbance, over ocean water warmed by solar radiation.

A hurricane draws its energy from the warm, humid air near the warm ocean's surface. This air rises, forming clouds and drawing surrounding air into the area, as shown in **Figure 4**. Bands of heavy rains and high winds spiral inward toward the area of lowest pressure at the center. The lower the air pressure at the center of the storm, the faster the winds blow toward it.

Hurricane winds are strongest in a narrow band or ring of clouds at the storm's center called the eyewall, which encloses the storm's "eye." When the eye arrives, the weather changes suddenly, growing calm and clear. After the eye passes, the storm resumes, but the winds blow from the opposite direction.

Hurricanes often result in severe flooding, which in turn contaminates drinking water supplies. Wind damage and severe flooding often mean that travel after the storm will be difficult. Residents of hurricane-prone areas are encouraged to stock a three-day supply of drinking water, ready-to-eat food, and any other necessary items, such as medications or diapers, to help them through the aftermath of a hurricane.

## Literacy Connection

**Cite Textual Evidence**
Textual evidence is information or clues that reinforce or support an idea. Reread the third and fourth paragraphs on this page. Underline the evidence that supports the statement that hurricane winds are strongest around the storm's center.

### Formation of a Hurricane

**Figure 4** ✏ Draw arrows to show how warm, humid air rises to form clouds and how winds spiral toward the area of low pressure.

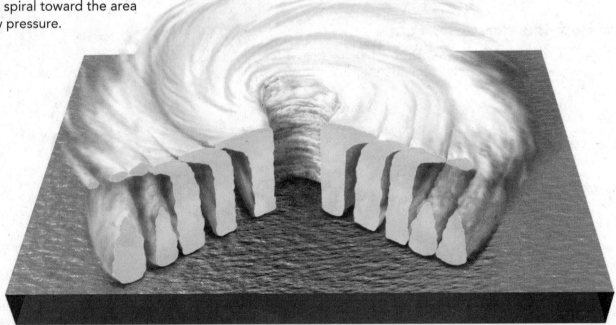

## The Path of Hurricane Sandy

**Figure 5** This map shows the progress of Hurricane Sandy over the course of several days in 2012. As Sandy made landfall, the hurricane lost strength and became a post-tropical cyclone.

**CCC Cause and Effect** What do you think caused the storm to turn back toward land and strike the Northeast?

.........................................................................

.........................................................................

.........................................................................

.........................................................................

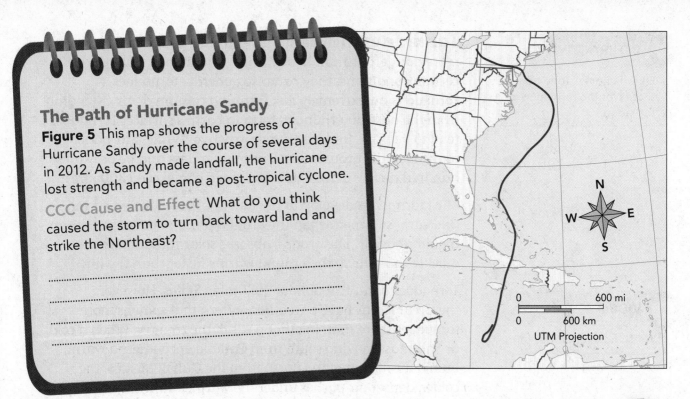

0         600 mi

0      600 km

UTM Projection

## How Hurricanes Move

Hurricanes are long-lasting storms, existing for a week or more. They can travel thousands of kilometers from where they originally formed. Hurricanes that form in the Atlantic Ocean are usually steered by easterly trade winds toward the Caribbean islands and then up toward the southeastern and eastern United States, as was Hurricane Sandy in 2012 (**Figure 5**). Once a hurricane passes over land, it loses its energy source: warm, moist air. If the hurricane doesn't travel over another source of warm, moist air to fuel it, it will gradually weaken.

When a hurricane makes landfall, high waves, severe flooding, and wind damage often accompany it. A hurricane's low pressure and high winds can raise the level of the water in the ocean below it by as much as 6 meters above normal sea level. The result is a **storm surge**, a "dome" of water that sweeps across the coast where the hurricane is traveling. Storm surges can cause great damage, destroying human-made structures as well as coastal ecosystems.

## HANDS-ON LAB

**Investigate** Record and analyze historical hurricane data to predict future events.

## VIRTUAL LAB

Investigate conditions that form hurricanes.

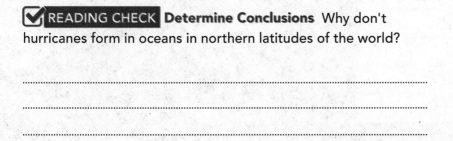

**READING CHECK** **Determine Conclusions** Why don't hurricanes form in oceans in northern latitudes of the world?

.........................................................................

.........................................................................

.........................................................................

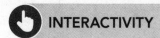

**INTERACTIVITY**

Determine the conditions that favor the formation of tornadoes.

**VIDEO**

Watch how tornadoes form.

**Tornado Damage**

**Figure 6** Use the image to rate the damage shown by circling a rating on the Fujita Scale.

**Tornadoes** Thunderstorms can lead to something even more dangerous than heavy rains, flooding, or hail. Under certain conditions, they can also generate tornadoes. A **tornado** is an extremely fast spinning column of air extending from the base of a thunderstorm to Earth's surface. Tornadoes tend to be brief, intense, and destructive. While a tornado may touch the ground for 15 minutes or less and be only a few hundred meters across, its wind speed can exceed 300 km/h.

Most tornadoes develop in the late afternoon during spring and early summer, when the ground tends to be warmer than the air above it. The ground absorbs solar radiation more quickly than air so the ground warms faster than the air.

Tornadoes occur throughout the United States. However, the Great Plains have a weather pattern that spawns more tornadoes there than in other parts of the country. When a cold, dry air mass moving south from Canada encounters a warm, humid air mass moving north from the Gulf of Mexico, the colder, denser air pushes under the warmer air mass, forcing it to rise. Warm ground can "turbo-charge" this process by releasing some of the heat it absorbed from the sun. This extra heat forces the air above to rise even faster. An area of low pressure develops and rapidly draws surrounding air inward and up. This fast-moving air rotates as it rises and forms a funnel. If the funnel touches Earth's surface, it becomes a tornado.

Tornado damage comes from both strong winds and the flying debris those winds carry. Tornadoes can move large objects and scatter debris many miles away. The Fujita Scale, shown in **Figure 6**, allows meteorologists to categorize tornadoes based on the amount and type of damage they cause. Only about one percent of tornadoes is ranked as F4 or F5. In 2007, the original Fujita Scale was replaced by the Enhanced Fujita Scale to more closely align high wind speeds with the types of damage they typically cause to structures.

| Fujita Scale | Types of Damage |
| --- | --- |
| F0 | Branches broken off trees |
| F1 | Mobile homes overturned |
| F2 | Trees uprooted |
| F3 | Roofs torn off |
| F4 | Houses leveled |
| F5 | Houses carried away |

# Floods and Drought

Storms are not the only type of hazardous severe weather. Floods, droughts, and excessive heat can occur in many different areas in the United States.

**Floods** Flooding is a major danger during severe storms, such as the one shown in **Figure 7**. A **flood** is an overflowing of water in a normally dry area. Some floods occur when excess water from rain or melting snow overflows a stream or river. In urban areas, floods occur when the ground can't absorb any water because it is already saturated.

Dams and levees are used to control flooding near rivers. A dam is a barrier across a river that may redirect the flow of the river or store floodwaters so that they can be released slowly. An embankment built along a river to prevent flooding of the surrounding land is a levee.

**Droughts and Excessive Heat** Having too little water can also cause problems. A long period with little or no rainfall is known as a **drought**. Drought is caused by hot, dry weather systems that stay in one place for weeks or months at a time. Long-term droughts can lead to crop failures and wild-fires. Streams, reservoirs, and wells dry up, causing shortages of water for homes, businesses, plants, and animals. People can help lessen the impacts of drought by conserving water.

The excessive heat caused by heat waves can also be harmful to people. Prolonged exposure to heat and the sun can cause skin damage, heat stroke, and dehydration. To prevent over-exposure to the sun, wear protective clothing, sunglasses, and sunscreen, and avoid direct sunlight between the hours of 10 am and 2 pm.

**Flood Damage**
**Figure 7** In 2012, as Sandy made landfall, the hurricane lost strength and became a post-tropical cyclone, causing heavy damage from flooding.

☑ **READING CHECK** **Cite Textual Evidence** What are two ways to help prevent floods?

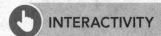

INTERACTIVITY

Examine the technologies used to predict and mitigate the effects of severe weather.

# Storm Safety

When potentially dangerous storms are likely, weather announcements indicate where there is a storm "watch" and where there is a storm "warning." A watch means that conditions are right for producing severe weather, but the severe weather has not yet developed. A warning signifies that severe weather is approaching and people should take shelter. **Figure 8** shows the precautions people should take for each type of severe storm.

## Severe Storm Safety

**Figure 8** Different severe storms require different safety measures.

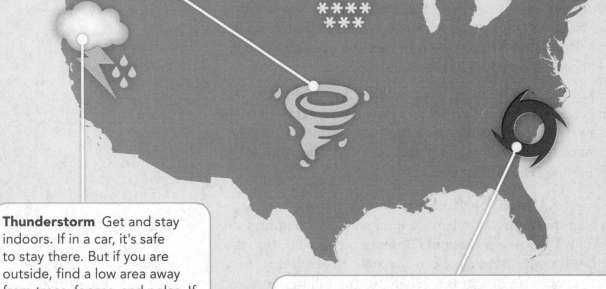

**Tornado** If you hear a tornado warning, go to a safe area quickly. Move to the middle of the ground floor. Stay away from windows and doors.

**Winter Storm** Winter storms can limit your vision and make it easy to get lost. Strong winds cool bodies rapidly. Stay or get indoors and keep a supply of water and food on hand in case of a power outage.

**Thunderstorm** Get and stay indoors. If in a car, it's safe to stay there. But if you are outside, find a low area away from trees, fences, and poles. If you are swimming or in a boat, get to shore and find shelter.

**Hurricane** Today, weather satellites can track and warn people well in advance of an approaching hurricane. You should be prepared to evacuate, or move away temporarily. If you hear a hurricane warning and are told to evacuate, leave the area immediately.

✓ READING CHECK **Determine Central Ideas** What safety precautions are common to all types of severe weather?

......................................................................

......................................................................

MS-ESS3-2

1. **Identify** What are four types of severe storms?

........................................................................

........................................................................

2. **CCC Patterns** A certain severe storm causes much property damage from heavy rain and winds that travel in a straight line. What type of severe storm has these characteristics? Why don't the other types of storms apply to this description?

........................................................................

........................................................................

........................................................................

........................................................................

3. **Draw Conclusions** When hurricanes or thunderstorms strike, damage from the floods they may produce can last much longer than the storms themselves. Why do floods cause damage for longer periods of time?

........................................................................

........................................................................

........................................................................

........................................................................

........................................................................

4. **SEP Develop Models** ✏ Assume a tornado warning has been issued for where you live. Draw a diagram of your home and show where in it you would go to be safe during a tornado. Then, beneath your diagram, explain why that location would be safe.

........................................................................

........................................................................

........................................................................

........................................................................

........................................................................

# Quest CHECK-IN

In this lesson, you studied how storms like thunderstorms, hurricanes, and tornadoes form. You also learned about the damage these storms can cause and how people can protect themselves from severe storms.

**SEP Communicate Information** Choose a severe storm. What information about this storm would you include in a public service announcement about storm safety?

........................................................................

........................................................................

........................................................................

........................................................................

........................................................................

........................................................................

## HANDS-ON LAB

The History of Hazardous Weather

**Do the Hands-On lab** to determine how examining past data help to prepare people for future weather hazards. Then analyze data about tornadoes in the United States.

MS-ESS2-5, MS-ESS3-2

# THE CASE OF THE

# Runaway Hurricane

Have you ever lived through a hurricane? If so, you know how dangerous they can be. Hurricane winds range from 74 to nearly 200 miles per hour. Storm surges can be greater than 8 feet. These major storms can submerge whole neighborhoods and destroy houses.

During a hurricane, downed power lines result in widespread power outages, flooding can reach as high as the second floor of houses, and downed trees and telephone poles make roads dangerous or impassable. Roofs can be torn off buildings and hurled violently through the air, along with other movable property such as lawn chairs. The powerful storm can even cause some buildings to collapse.

Hurricanes generate far out at sea. They may pick up strength and speed over warm water as they move toward the coast, or weaken in cold water before they reach land. Florida's exceptionally long coastline and tropical location make it a prime target for hurricanes. These two factors explain why Florida is hit by more major hurricanes than any other U.S. state.

In 2016, Hurricane Matthew did not hit Florida directly, but it dumped flooding rains on the state. Insurance claims for damage have thus far added up to more than $218 million.

There's no changing the fact that many states lie in the path of hurricanes. Officials in high-risk areas are working hard to find ways to lower the risks, including issuing new rules for storm-resistant structures and spending more money on disaster planning, so that communities will be better prepared for future storms.

Hurricane Matthew caused severe flooding and major property damage in Florida in 2016.

**Use the map to answer questions 1–2.**

**1. SEP Analyze Data**
What general observations can you make about hurricane risk in the U.S.?

........................................................

........................................................

........................................................

........................................................

........................................................

........................................................

**Hurricane and Tropical Storm Frequency, 1851–2012**

**KEY**
- 65–141
- 29–64
- 1–28
- No hurricanes

Source: FEMA

**2. SEP Construct Explanations**
How would you characterize the risk of a hurricane strike where you live? Use evidence from the map to support your explanation.

........................................................

........................................................

........................................................

**3. SEP Design Solutions** Besides the solutions mentioned in the text, what do you think people living in areas where hurricanes are common might do to address the continual threat of major hurricanes?

........................................................

........................................................

........................................................

# ☑TOPIC 2 Review and Assess

## 1 The Atmosphere Around You

MS-ESS2-5, MS-ESS2-6, MS-ESS3-2, MS-PS1-4

1. The atmosphere is mostly made up of the gases ................ and ................ .

2. **Explain Phenomena** In what sense does Earth's atmosphere help to keep Earth "just right"?

................................................................

................................................................

................................................................

................................................................

................................................................

................................................................

3. **SEP Develop Models** In the space below, draw a simple diagram of the layers of Earth's atmosphere.

## 2 Water in the Atmosphere

MS-ESS2-4

4. What is the measure of the amount of water vapor in the air?
   A. dew point     B. evaporation
   C. precipitation   D. humidity

5. What process in the water cycle is driven directly by the sun's energy?
   A. precipitation   B. condensation
   C. evaporation    D. transpiration

6. In the water cycle, water vapor becomes liquid water during

................................................................

7. **SEP Construct an Explanation** Describe how clouds form during the water cycle.

................................................................

................................................................

................................................................

................................................................

................................................................

................................................................

................................................................

................................................................

................................................................

................................................................

................................................................

................................................................

................................................................

................................................................

................................................................

................................................................

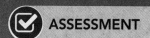 
# 3 Air Masses

MS-ESS2-5

**8.** Which type of front does not move?
   **A.** cold      **B.** occluded
   **C.** stationary      **D.** warm

**9.** Which term describes the boundary where two air masses meet?
   **A.** anticyclone      **B.** cyclone
   **C.** front      **D.** jet stream

**10.** What type of air mass is most likely to form over the Atlantic Ocean near the equator?

..................................................................

# 4 Predicting Weather Changes

MS-ESS2-5, MS-ESS2-6

**11.** What does an isobar show on a weather map?
   **A.** areas of low humidity
   **B.** areas of high wind speeds
   **C.** areas of equal air pressure
   **D.** areas of equal temperature

**12.** A person who collects and analyzes weather data and uses the results to make weather forecasts is a(n)

..................................................................

**13.** CCC System Models How are cold fronts and warm fronts represented on a weather map?

..................................................................

..................................................................

..................................................................

..................................................................

# 5 Severe Weather and Floods

MS-ESS3-2

**14.** Which type of storm always forms over and pulls energy from a large body of warm water?
   **A.** hurricane      **B.** thunderstorm
   **C.** tornado      **D.** winter storm

**15.** Which of the following are <u>not</u> used to prevent flooding during storms?
   **A.** dams      **B.** levees
   **C.** boats      **D.** sandbags

**16.** What type of storm is associated with the term "lake effect"?
   **A.** hurricane      **B.** thunderstorm
   **C.** tornado      **D.** winter storm

**17.** SEP Develop Models Thunderstorms are rainstorms that include thunder and lightning. Draw a diagram that illustrates how thunder and lightning occur during a thunderstorm. Be sure to use labels to explain your diagram.

MS-ESS2-5

## Evidence-Based Assessment

Kamiko is researching local weather patterns in her region. She observes the air pressure each day at noon and records it in millibars, a unit for measuring pressure in the atmosphere. She displays these data in a graph. In addition to recording the air pressure each day, Kamiko records her observations about the general weather, as well as wind direction and speed. The data she records are shown in the table.

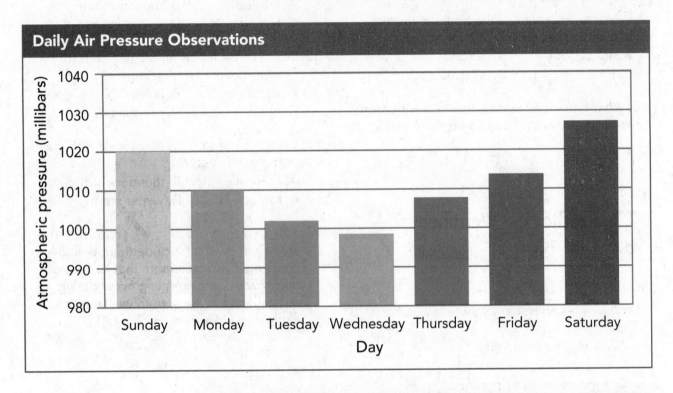

**Daily Air Pressure Observations**

| Day | Weather | Wind (kilometers per hour) |
|---|---|---|
| Sunday | sunny | 11 from south |
| Monday | cloudy | 15 from south |
| Tuesday | rain | 22 from south |
| Wednesday | snow | 22 from northwest |
| Thursday | breezy | 30 from northwest |
| Friday | sunny | 19 from northwest |
| Saturday | sunny | 9 from north |

1. **SEP Analyze Data** Between which two days did Kamiko observe the greatest change in air pressure?

   A. Sunday to Monday
   B. Tuesday to Wednesday
   C. Thursday to Friday
   D. Friday to Saturday

2. **CCC Patterns** What pattern do you notice in the wind speed data? What is responsible for this pattern?

   ......................................................................
   ......................................................................
   ......................................................................
   ......................................................................
   ......................................................................
   ......................................................................
   ......................................................................
   ......................................................................
   ......................................................................
   ......................................................................
   ......................................................................
   ......................................................................
   ......................................................................

3. **Apply Scientific Reasoning** Which of the following statements about Kamiko's observations from Sunday to Monday are true?

   ☐ The increase in wind speed indicated that temperatures would begin to rise.

   ☐ The drop in air pressure indicated that rain was probably on its way.

   ☐ The decrease in wind speed indicated that a high pressure system was moving in.

   ☐ The increase in clouds and wind speed indicated that inclement weather was coming.

4. **SEP Construct Arguments** Use evidence from the graph and data table to explain why Kamiko observed rain on Tuesday, but snow on Wednesday.

   ......................................................................
   ......................................................................
   ......................................................................
   ......................................................................
   ......................................................................
   ......................................................................
   ......................................................................
   ......................................................................

# Quest FINDINGS

## Complete the Quest!

**Phenomenon** Create your PSA to help people understand, predict, prepare for, and avoid the dangers of severe weather.

Apply Concepts Severe storms can harm people and damage property. What climate and weather factors do meteorologists track to help people stay informed about severe weather events? Explain.

......................................................................
......................................................................
......................................................................
......................................................................
......................................................................

👆 **INTERACTIVITY**

Reflect on Your PSA

MS-ESS2-4

# Water From Trees

How can you **gather evidence** that **plants** are part of the **water cycle**?

## Background

**Phenomenon** A local horticultural society that opposes the construction of a new mall in the community has enlisted your help.

The group members believe that cutting down thousands of trees will have a negative impact on the environment. In this lab, you will design an investigation to collect evidence that trees play an important role in the water cycle.

## Materials

(per group)

- balance scale
- 3 plastic sandwich bags
- 3 small pebbles
- 3 twist ties

# Plan Your Investigation

☐ 1. You will use the materials provided by your teacher to design and conduct an investigation to identify the mass of water released by several plant leaves outside over a 7-day period.

**Demonstrate** Go online for a downloadable worksheet of this lab.

☐ 2. Consider the following questions before you begin planning your investigation:

- How can you use the bag, pebble, and twist tie to collect water from several leaves of a tree?

- How many trials will you conduct?

- What data will you collect?

- How can you determine the mass of water released by the plant leaf after 7 days?

☐ 3. In the space provided, write out a procedure that identifies the steps you will follow to conduct your investigation. Include a sketch of your setup.

☐ 4. Create a data table in the space provided to record the data you collect.

☐ 5. After receiving your teacher's approval for your plan, conduct your investigation.

## Procedure and Sketch

## Data Table

# Analyze and Interpret Data

1. **SEP Construct Explanations** What did you observe in the plastic bags after 7 days? Where did the water you observed come from?

......................................................................................................................

......................................................................................................................

......................................................................................................................

2. **SEP Use Mathematics** A large, mature tree can contain as many as 200,000 leaves. Using the data you collected, calculate the mass of water that might transpire from a mature tree in one day.

......................................................................................................................

......................................................................................................................

3. **SEP Plan an Investigation** Review the data table from another group's investigation. How might your group modify your data table?

......................................................................................................................

......................................................................................................................

......................................................................................................................

4. **SEP Engage in Argument** In the space provided, sketch a diagram of Earth's water cycle. Use arrows and labels to indicate water's movement through the cycle. Based on your evidence, include a tree in your diagram to show the role that trees and other plants play in the water cycle.

# TOPIC 3

# Minerals and Rocks in the Geosphere

**NGSS PERFORMANCE EXPECTATION**

**MS-ESS2-1** Develop a model to describe the cycling of Earth's materials and the flow of energy that drives this process.

What caused
this rock to look
like this?

**GO ONLINE**
to access your
digital course

 VIDEO

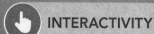 INTERACTIVITY

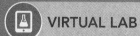 VIRTUAL LAB

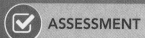 ASSESSMENT

 eTEXT

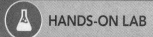 HANDS-ON LAB

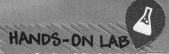

**HANDS-ON LAB**

иConnect Explore and model Earth's
structure.

## The Essential Question

# What events form Earth's rocks?

**SEP Construct Explanations** Shiprock is a rock formation in New
Mexico that stands about 480 meters (about 1,600 feet) tall. How do
you think this rock formed?

..................................................................................................................................

..................................................................................................................................

..................................................................................................................................

..................................................................................................................................

..................................................................................................................................

# Quest KICKOFF

## How can you depict Earth processes in a movie script?

**Phenomenon** A movie producer is working on an exciting new adventure film. Much of the action takes place not in space, not on Earth, but *under* the surface of Earth. The producer wants to present a realistic view of this world, so she hires a science consultant to help get the facts right. In this problem-based Quest activity, you will help evaluate and revise movie scripts whose plots involve action that takes place within Earth. Based on your research and understanding of Earth's structure, you will suggest changes that reflect accurate science. In the Findings activity, you will reflect on how accurately movies depict scientific facts.

👆 **INTERACTIVITY**

Science in the Movies

**MS-ESS2-1** Develop a model to describe the cycling of Earth's materials and the flow of energy that drives this process.

### 🔶NBC LEARN ▶ VIDEO

After watching the Quest Kickoff video and reacting to some movie scenes, think about a scientific falsehood that you have seen in a movie. How do you suggest changing the script to reflect the science accurately?

**The scene and its false science**

........................................................................

........................................................................

........................................................................

........................................................................

**How the scene should be changed**

........................................................................

........................................................................

........................................................................

........................................................................

........................................................................

---

# Quest CHECK-IN

## IN LESSON 1

What is the structure of Earth's mantle and core? How could a movie accurately depict these regions inside Earth?

👆 **INTERACTIVITY**

The Deep Drill

# Quest CHECK-INS

## IN LESSON 2

How do stalactites and stalagmites form? Model the formation of these structures.

⚗️ **HANDS-ON LAB**

Make Your Own Stalactites and Stalagmites

# Quest CHECK-IN

## IN LESSON 3

What are the three types of rocks and how do they form? Consider how different types of rock form and represent that information accurately in a movie script.

👆 **INTERACTIVITY**

Rocky Business

The 1959 movie *Journey to the Center of the Earth* was based on Jules Verne's novel, published in 1864. In the story, a professor and several other characters travel through the center of Earth, entering through a volcano in Iceland and exiting through a volcano in Italy.

## Quest CHECK-IN

### IN LESSON 4

What processes affect rock formation? Understand different rock cycle processes and appropriately depict those processes in a script.

**INTERACTIVITY**

The Rock Cyclers

## Quest FINDINGS

### Complete the Quest!

Now that you have revised movie scripts to be more scientifically accurate, consider how you will view the science in other movies differently.

**INTERACTIVITY**

Reflect on Science in Movies

# Build a Model of Earth

How can you **develop a scale model** of Earth?

## Background

**Phenomenon** As a summer camp counselor, you challenge the campers to show energy cycling inside Earth by making a scale model of Earth. Recalling that Earth has four main layers—inner core, outer core, mantle, and crust—you will instruct the campers to develop and construct a sample scale model of Earth that shows the flow of energy.

## Develop a Model

1. **CCC Energy and Matter** Use the following information to help you develop your model. The temperature inside Earth increases with depth. Earth's mantle is heated by high temperatures near the core, causing it to sink and rise with the constant cycle of convection currents. These convection currents carry hot, solid rock up toward the surface where it cools and sinks.

2. **CCC Scale, Proportion, Quantity** Use the information in the table to determine what scale you will use for your model. Record your scale.

| Component | Actual Thickness | Scaled Thickness |
|---|---|---|
| Earth's Radius | 6,370 km | |
| Inner Core | 1,220 km | |
| Outer Core | 2,260 km | |
| Mantle | 2,880 km | |
| Crust | 30 km | |

### Materials

(per group)
- plastic knife
- different colors of modeling clay
- toothpicks
- colored pencils
- wax paper
- ruler

### Safety

Be sure to follow all safety procedures provided by your teacher. The Safety Appendix of your textbook provides more details about the safety icons.

3. **SEP Develop a Model** Use the provided materials. Decide how to make your model using the information from step 1 and the scale you calculated. Record your plan for your model. Draw a sketch to help you build your model. Include labels for the layers, the thicknesses, and convection currents. Show your plan to your teacher for approval.

4. Build your model on a piece of wax paper.

**HANDS-ON LAB**

**Connect** Go online for a downloadable worksheet of this lab.

## Plan and Sketch

## Analyze and Conclude

1. **SEP Use Models** Using your model as supporting evidence, describe the structure of Earth, including the relative thickness of each layer.

......................................................................................................................

......................................................................................................................

......................................................................................................................

2. **CCC Cause and Effect** Suppose the crust in your model were not solid, but was broken into several large sections. What effect might this movement of material in the mantle have on the crust?

......................................................................................................................

......................................................................................................................

......................................................................................................................

# 1 Earth's Interior

## Guiding Questions

- How do geologists study Earth's layered interior?
- What roles do heat and pressure in Earth's interior play in the cycling of matter?
- What are the patterns and effects of convection in Earth's mantle?

## Connections

**Literacy** Translate Information

**Math** Construct Graphs

MS-ESS2-1

## HANDS-ON LAB

### Investigate Explore how convection works.

### Vocabulary
seismic wave
crust
mantle
outer core
inner core

### Academic Vocabulary
evidence
elements

## Connect It!

**What do you observe about the rock shown in Figure 1?**

**Determine Differences** How do the xenoliths compare to the surrounding rock?

...................................................................................................................

**Apply Scientific Reasoning** How might xenoliths help geologists understand Earth's interior?

...................................................................................................................

...................................................................................................................

# Learning About Earth's Interior

How do we study Earth's interior and connect those interior processes to things we see or experience on Earth's surface? This question is difficult to answer because geologists are unable to see deep inside Earth. However, geologists have found other ways to study the unseen interior of Earth. Their methods focus on two main types of **evidence**: direct evidence from rock samples and indirect evidence from seismic waves.

**Academic Vocabulary**

Suppose you think the air temperature is getting colder. Give two examples of evidence you could use to support your idea.

..............................................................

..............................................................

..............................................................

..............................................................

..............................................................

..............................................................

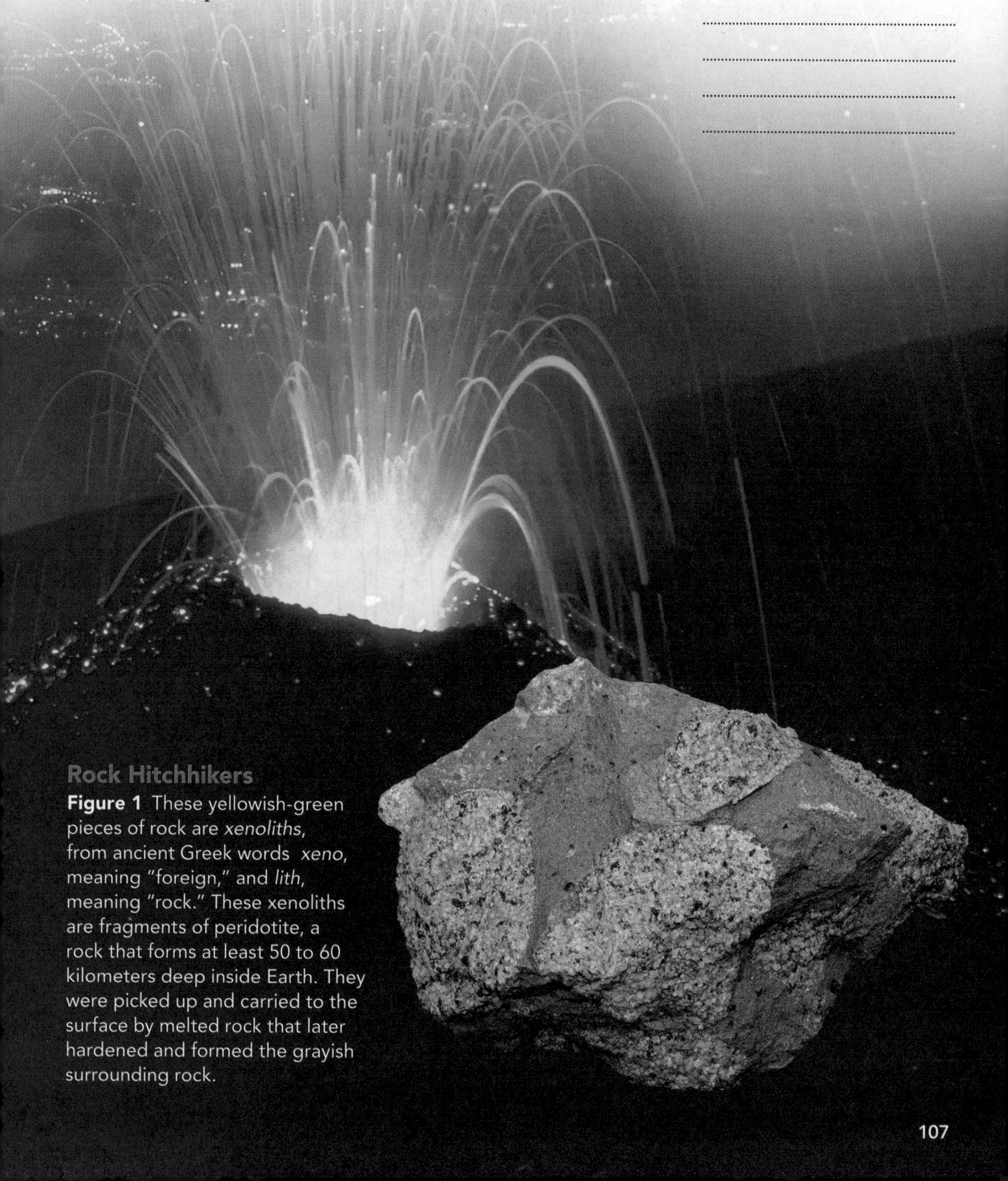

**Rock Hitchhikers**

**Figure 1** These yellowish-green pieces of rock are *xenoliths*, from ancient Greek words *xeno*, meaning "foreign," and *lith*, meaning "rock." These xenoliths are fragments of peridotite, a rock that forms at least 50 to 60 kilometers deep inside Earth. They were picked up and carried to the surface by melted rock that later hardened and formed the grayish surrounding rock.

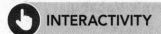

**INTERACTIVITY**

Explore how to investigate something you cannot directly observe.

**Evidence From Rock Samples** Geologists have drilled holes as deep as 12.3 kilometers into Earth. Drilling brings up many samples of rock and gives geologists many clues. They learn about Earth's structure and conditions deep inside Earth where the rocks are formed. In addition, volcanoes sometimes carry rocks to the surface from depths of more than 100 kilometers. These rocks provide more information about Earth's interior, including clues about how matter and energy flow there. Some rocks from mountain ranges show evidence that they formed deep within Earth's crust and later were elevated as mountains formed. Also, in laboratories, geologists have used models to recreate conditions similar to those inside Earth to see how those conditions affect rock.

**Evidence From Seismic Waves** To study Earth's interior, geologists also use an indirect method. When earthquakes occur, they produce **seismic waves** (SIZE mik). Geologists record the seismic waves and study how they travel through Earth. The paths of seismic waves reveal where the makeup or form of the rocks change, as shown in **Figure 2**.

**Waves**

**Figure 2** Earthquakes produce different types of seismic waves that travel through Earth. The speed of these waves and the paths they take give geologists clues about the structure of the planet's interior.

**Make Observations** Compare and contrast the paths that P-waves and S-waves take through Earth. How do you think this information helps geologists understand Earth's interior?

..............................................
..............................................
..............................................
..............................................
..............................................
..............................................

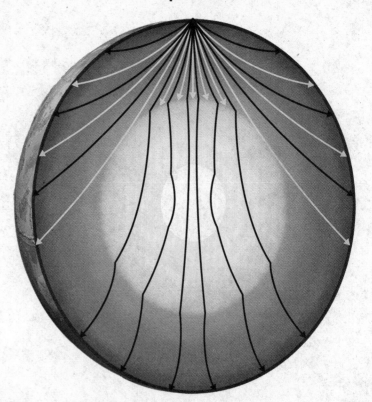

**Earthquake epicenter**

⟶ P-waves travel through solids and liquids.

⟶ S-waves only travel through solids.

# Earth's Layers

After many years of research, scientists today know that Earth's interior is made up of three main layers: crust, mantle, and core. These layers vary greatly in thickness, composition, temperature, and pressure.

Pressure results from a force pressing on an area. Within Earth's interior, the mass of rock that is pressing down from above causes an increase of pressure on the rocks below. The deeper inside Earth's interior, the greater the pressure becomes. Pressure inside Earth increases much like water pressure in the swimming pool increases as you dive down deeper, as in **Figure 3**.

The temperature inside Earth increases as depth increases. Just beneath Earth's surface, the surrounding rock is cool. At about 20 meters down, the rock starts to get warmer. For every 40 meters of depth from that point, the temperature typically rises 1 degree Celsius. The rapid rise in temperature continues for several tens of kilometers. Eventually, the temperature increases more slowly, but steadily. The high temperatures inside Earth are mostly the result of the release of energy from radioactive substances and heat left over from the formation of Earth 4.6 billion years ago.

Pressure Increases

## Pressure and Depth
**Figure 3** The deeper that the swimmer goes, the greater the pressure on the swimmer from the surrounding water.

1. Compare and Contrast  How is the water in the swimming pool similar to Earth's interior? How is it different? (*Hint:* Consider both temperature and pressure in your answer.)

.................................................................

.................................................................

.................................................................

.................................................................

.................................................................

2. CCC Use Proportional Relationships
   At what location in the pool would the water pressure be greatest?

.................................................................

## Earth's Layers

**Figure 4** The crust and uppermost mantle make up the rigid lithosphere. The lithosphere rests on the softer material of the asthenosphere.

**Translate Information** Use the diagram to identify the layers and contrast how rigid they are.

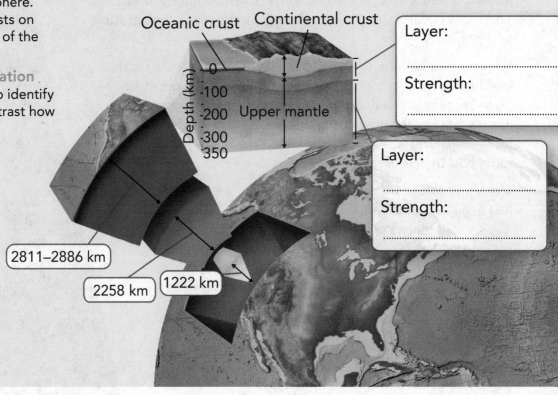

Oceanic crust    Continental crust

Upper mantle

Depth (km)
0
-100
-200
-300
-350

Layer:
.......................................
Strength:
.......................................

Layer:
.......................................
Strength:
.......................................

2811–2886 km

2258 km    1222 km

**The Crust** Have you ever hiked up a mountain, toured a mine, or explored a cave? During each of these activities people interact with Earth's **crust**, the rock that forms Earth's outer layer. The crust is a layer of solid rock that includes both dry land and the ocean floor. The main **elements** of the rocks in the crust are oxygen and silicon.

The crust is much thinner than the layers beneath it. In most places, the crust is between 5 and 40 kilometers thick. It is thickest under high mountains, where it can be as thick as 80 kilometers, and it is thinnest beneath the ocean floor. There are two types of crust: oceanic crust and continental crust.

The crust that lies beneath the ocean is called oceanic crust. The composition of all oceanic crust is nearly the same. Its overall composition is much like basalt, with small amounts of ocean sediment on top. Basalt (buh SAWLT) is a dark, fine-grained rock.

Continental crust forms the continents. It contains many types of rocks. But overall the composition of continental crust is much like granite. Granite is a rock that usually is a light color and has coarse grains.

**The Mantle** Directly below the crust, the rock in Earth's interior changes. Rock here contains more magnesium and iron than does the rock above it. The rock below the crust is the solid material of the **mantle**, a layer of hot rock. Overall, the mantle is nearly 3,000 kilometers thick.

The uppermost part of the mantle is brittle rock, like the rock of the crust. Both the crust and the uppermost part of the mantle are strong, hard, and rigid. Geologists often group the crust and uppermost mantle into a single layer called the lithosphere. As shown in **Figure 4**, Earth's lithosphere is about 100 kilometers thick.

Below the lithosphere, the material is increasingly hotter. As a result, the part of the mantle just beneath the lithosphere is less rigid than the lithosphere itself. Over thousands of years, this part of the mantle may bend like a metal spoon, but it is still solid. This solid yet bendable layer is called the asthenosphere.

Beneath the asthenosphere is the lower mantle, which is hot, rigid, and under intense pressure. The lower mantle extends down to Earth's core.

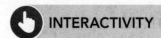

**INTERACTIVITY**

Examine the different layers of Earth.

**Math Toolbox**

## Temperature in Earth's Layers

1. **Construct Graphs** Use the data in the table to complete the line graph.

2. **Interpret Graphs** How does temperature change with depth in Earth's mantle?

.................................................................................

.................................................................................

.................................................................................

.................................................................................

| Depth (km) | Temperature (°C) |
|------------|------------------|
| 500        | 1,600°C          |
| 1,000      | 1,800°C          |
| 1,500      | 2,200°C          |
| 2,000      | 2,500°C          |
| 2,500      | 2,900°C          |

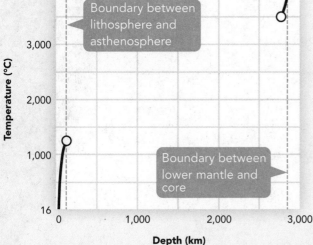

Temperature and Depth

Boundary between lithosphere and asthenosphere

Boundary between lower mantle and core

**The Core** Below the mantle is Earth's dense core. Earth's core occupies the center of the planet. It consists of two parts, a liquid outer core and a solid inner core. The outer core is 2,260 kilometers thick. The inner core is a solid ball with a radius of about 1,220 kilometers. Therefore, the total radius of the entire core is approximately 3,480 kilometers.

The **outer core** is a layer of molten metal surrounding the inner core. Despite enormous pressure, the outer core is liquid. The **inner core** is a dense ball of solid metal. In the inner core, extreme pressure squeezes the atoms of iron and nickel so much that they cannot spread out to become liquid despite the extremely high temperatures.

Currently, most evidence suggests that both parts of the core are mostly made of iron and nickel. Scientists have found data suggesting that the core also contains smaller amounts of oxygen, sulfur, and silicon.

# Model It!

**1. SEP Evaluate Evidence** ✏ Label Earth's layers and use the text on the page to fill in the table with details about the layers.

| | Thickness | Composition | Solid/Liquid |
|---|---|---|---|
| Crust: | | | |
| Mantle: | | | |
| Outer core: | | | |
| Inner core: | | | |
| Total: | 6,370 km | | |

**2. Compare and Contrast** ✏ Pick any two points inside Earth and label them A and B. Record their locations.

My Point A is in the .................................................

My Point B is in the .................................................

Compare and contrast Earth at those two points.

........................................................................................................

........................................................................................................

........................................................................................................

## The Core and Earth's Magnetic Field
Scientists think that movements in the liquid outer core produce Earth's magnetic field. Earth's magnetic field affects the whole planet.

To understand how a magnetic field affects an object, think about a bar magnet. If you place the magnet on a piece of paper and sprinkle iron filings on the paper, the iron filings automatically line up in a pattern matching the bar's magnetic field. If you could surround Earth with iron filings, they would form a similar pattern. This is also what happens when you use a compass. The compass needle aligns with Earth's magnetic field.

**✓ READING CHECK** **Identify Evidence** How can iron filings provide evidence that a bar magnet has a magnetic field?

.......................................................................................................................

.......................................................................................................................

**Modeling Earth's Interior**
**Figure 5** Earth is divided into distinct layers. Each layer has its own characteristics.

# Movement in Earth's Mantle

Recall that Earth's mantle and core are extremely hot. Heat is a form of energy that flows. It transfers from matter at a higher temperature to matter at a lower temperature. The transfer of heat in the mantle drives a process called convection. This process is how matter and energy cycle through Earth's interior as well as its surface.

**Convection Currents** When you heat water on a stove, the water at the bottom of the pot gets hot and expands. As the heated water expands, its density decreases. Less-dense fluids flow up through denser fluids.

## Convection Currents in Hot Springs

**Figure 6** Hot springs are common in Yellowstone National Park. Here, melted snow and rainwater seep far below the crust into the mantle, where a shallow magma chamber heats the rock of Earth's crust. The rock heats the water to more than 200°C and puts it under very high pressure. This superheated groundwater rises to the surface and forms pools of hot water.

1. **Compare and Contrast** The heated water is (more/less) dense than the melted snow and rainwater.

2. **Apply Concepts** What process causes convection currents to form in a hot spring?

...................................................

...................................................

...................................................

Hot spring pool

The warm, less dense water moves upward and floats over the cooler, denser water. Near the surface, the warm water cools, becoming denser again. It sinks back down to the bottom of the pot. Here, the water heats and rises again. The flows shown in **Figure 6** that transfer heat within matter are called convection currents. Heating and cooling of matter, changes in matter's density, and the force of gravity combine and set convection currents in motion. Without heat, convection currents eventually stop.

**✓ READING CHECK** **Cause and Effect** What three processes or forces combine to set convection currents in motion?

....................................................................................

....................................................................................

....................................................................................

## Convection Currents in Earth

Heat from the core and from the mantle itself drives convection currents. These currents carry hot, solid rock of the mantle outward and cooled, solid rock inward in a never-ending cycle.

As the oceanic lithosphere cools and sinks, it drives a pattern of mantle convection. The cold lithosphere moves down into the mantle, where it is heated. An upward return flow of hot rock completes the cycle, as shown in **Figure 7**. Over and over, the cycle of sinking and rising takes place. One full cycle takes millions of years. Convection currents are involved in the production of new rock at Earth's surface. There are also convection currents in the outer core.

**Translate Information** As you look at the visuals depicting convection, come up with an explanation for how the directions of two side-by-side convection currents determine whether material in the mantle rises or descends.

........................................................

........................................................

........................................................

........................................................

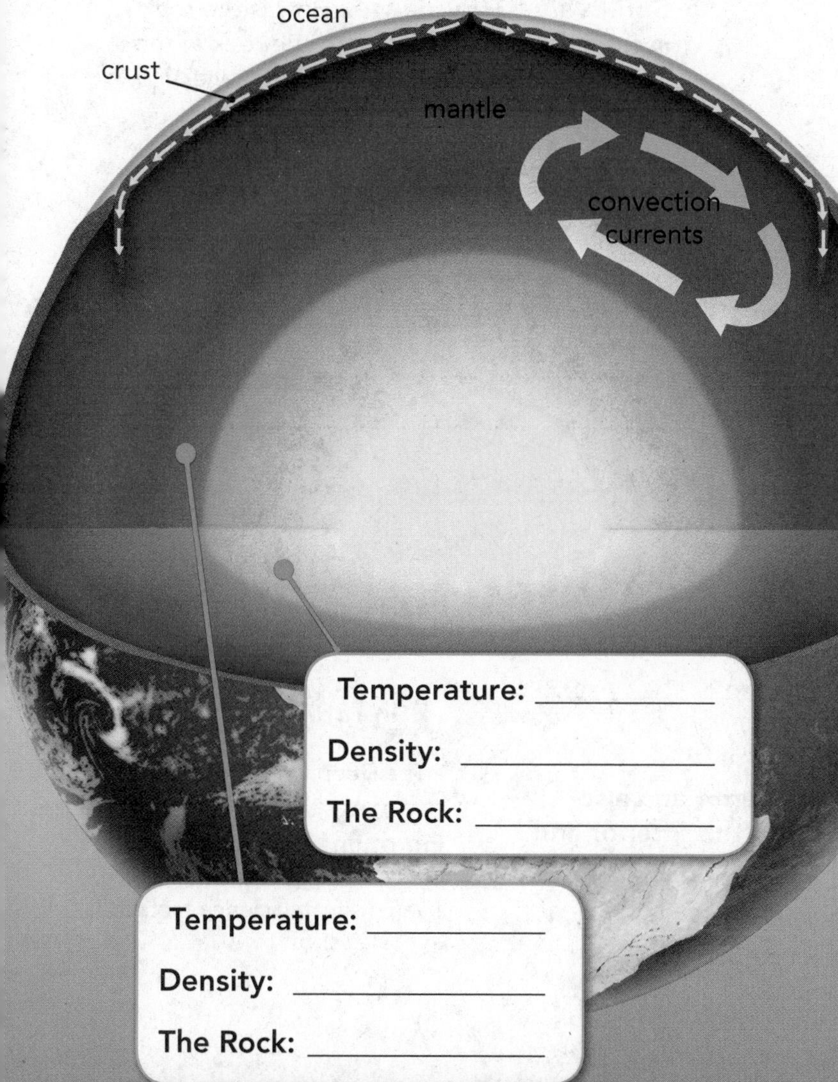

### Mantle Convection

**Figure 7** ✏ Complete the model by drawing the missing convection currents.

**SEP Use Models** Then complete the figure labels by using the terms in the box.

> hotter
>
> colder
>
> less dense
>
> more dense
>
> sinks
>
> rises

ocean

crust

mantle

convection currents

Temperature: _____

Density: _____

The Rock: _____

Temperature: _____

Density: _____

The Rock: _____

📓 **Make Meaning** How can a solid such as mantle rock flow? Think about candle wax. In your science notebook, describe how you can make candle wax flow. What other solids have you observed that can flow?

# ☑ LESSON 1 Check

MS-ESS2-1

1. **Identify** Name each layer of Earth, starting from Earth's center.

.................................................................

.................................................................

.................................................................

.................................................................

2. **Apply Concepts** Give examples of direct evidence and indirect evidence that geologists use to learn about Earth's interior.

.................................................................

.................................................................

.................................................................

.................................................................

.................................................................

.................................................................

3. **CCC Cause and Effect** What would happen to the convection currents in the mantle if Earth's interior cooled down? Why?

.................................................................

.................................................................

.................................................................

.................................................................

4. **SEP Construct Explanations** How does convection cause movement of material and energy in Earth's interior?

.................................................................

.................................................................

.................................................................

.................................................................

.................................................................

.................................................................

.................................................................

5. **SEP Evaluate Evidence** How is the rock in the deep mantle similar to the rock in the parts of the mantle nearest the surface? How are they different?

.................................................................

.................................................................

.................................................................

.................................................................

.................................................................

.................................................................

.................................................................

# Quest CHECK-IN

**In this lesson, you learned about Earth's interior and also how energy and material move between Earth's interior and its surface.**

**SEP Engage in Argument** Explain why you think it is or isn't important for science fiction films to depict natural processes and geological events as accurately as possible.

.................................................................

.................................................................

.................................................................

.................................................................

## ☝ INTERACTIVITY

The Deep Drill

**Go online** to find out more about Earth's interior structure. Then evaluate science facts in a movie script.

# Examining **Earth's Interior** *from* **Space**

**INTERACTIVITY**

Design a satellite that can collect electromagnetic field data.

**How can you** study Earth's interior? You engineer it! Geologist use satellites to help them visualize what they cannot see.

**The Challenge:** To understand how scientists study what they can't observe directly.

**Phenomenon** As Earth rotates, its liquid outer core spins. The flow and movement of Earth's oceans also create electric currents that generate secondary magnetic fields. Scientists call this process "motional induction." The European Space Agency (ESA) has launched three satellites into Earth's orbit that are sensitive to these electric currents.

The satellites also tell us many details about the electrical conductivity inside Earth's core—both the liquid of the outer core and the solid metallic sphere found at the center of the planet. A rock's ability to conduct electricity is related to its temperature, mineral composition, and water content. A satellite cannot directly measure these things. However, scientists can now draw reasonable conclusions about them by studying satellite data about the electric currents that flow through and just below Earth's surface.

**DESIGN CHALLENGE** Can you design your own satellite? Go to the Engineering Design Notebook to find out!

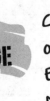

Swarm Satellites launched in November 2013. The ESA's three-satellite Swarm mission is helping to improve our understanding of Earth's interior by taking measurements of its magnetic fields.

# (2) Minerals

## Guiding Questions

- What are the characteristics and properties of minerals?
- What processes result in the formation of minerals?
- What processes explain the distribution of mineral resources on Earth?

## Connections

**Literacy** Integrate With Visuals

**Math** Calculate

MS-ESS2-1, MS-ESS3-1

## HANDS-ON LAB

**uInvestigate** Model mineral crystals and observe how they can change.

## Vocabulary

mineral
crystal
crystallization

## Academic Vocabulary

organic

## Connect It!

✏️ **Circle two crystals in the photo.**

**Relate Change** Do you think these crystals formed in conditions that were stable or that changed often? Explain.

................................................................................

................................................................................

................................................................................

................................................................................

# Defining Minerals

Look at the objects in **Figure 1**. They are solid matter that formed deep beneath Earth's surface. They are beautiful, gigantic crystals of the mineral selenite, which is a form of gypsum. But what is a mineral?

**Characteristics** A **mineral** is a naturally occurring solid that can form by inorganic processes and has a crystal structure and definite chemical composition. For a substance to be a mineral, it must have the following five characteristics.

**Naturally Occurring** All minerals are substances that form by natural processes. Gypsum forms naturally from chemical elements that precipitate from water.

**Solid** A mineral is always a solid, which means it has a definite volume and shape. The particles in a solid are packed tightly together. Gypsum is a solid.

**Forms by Inorganic Processes** All minerals must form by inorganic processes. That is, they can form from materials that were not a part of living things. Gypsum forms naturally as sulfate-rich solutions evaporate. Some minerals, such as calcite, form from both inorganic and organic processes.

**Crystal Structure** The particles of a mineral line up in a pattern that repeats over and over again. The repeating pattern of a mineral's particles forms a solid called a **crystal**. The gypsum in the image has a crystal structure.

**Definite Chemical Composition** A mineral has a definite chemical composition. This means it always contains the same elements in certain proportions. Gypsum always contains calcium, oxygen, sulfur, and hydrogen, in set proportions.

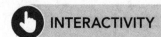

INTERACTIVITY

Explain what the term *mineral* means to you.

**Reflect** Write down where you have heard of minerals before, and the names of any minerals that play a role in your everyday life.

**Mineral Giants**
**Figure 1** Dwarfed by megacrystals of the mineral selenite, miners explore Mexico's Cave of Crystals. Located about 300 meters below Earth's surface, the cave contains some of the largest crystals ever discovered in nature—up to 12 meters long!

**INTERACTIVITY**

Compare and contrast the different properties of minerals.

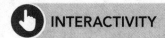

**Mineral Properties** Geologists have identified and named more than 5,000 minerals, though only about 20 make up most of the rocks of Earth's crust. Because there are so many minerals, telling them apart can be challenging. Each mineral has characteristic properties that are used to identify and describe it. **Figure 2** shows some of the properties of the mineral pyrite.

**Luster** Luster is the term that describes how light reflects from a mineral's surface. Terms used to describe luster include *metallic, glassy, earthy, silky, waxy,* and *pearly.*

**Streak** The streak of a mineral is the color of its powder. Although the color of a mineral can vary, its streak does not.

**Color** Minerals come in many colors. Only a few minerals have their own characteristic color.

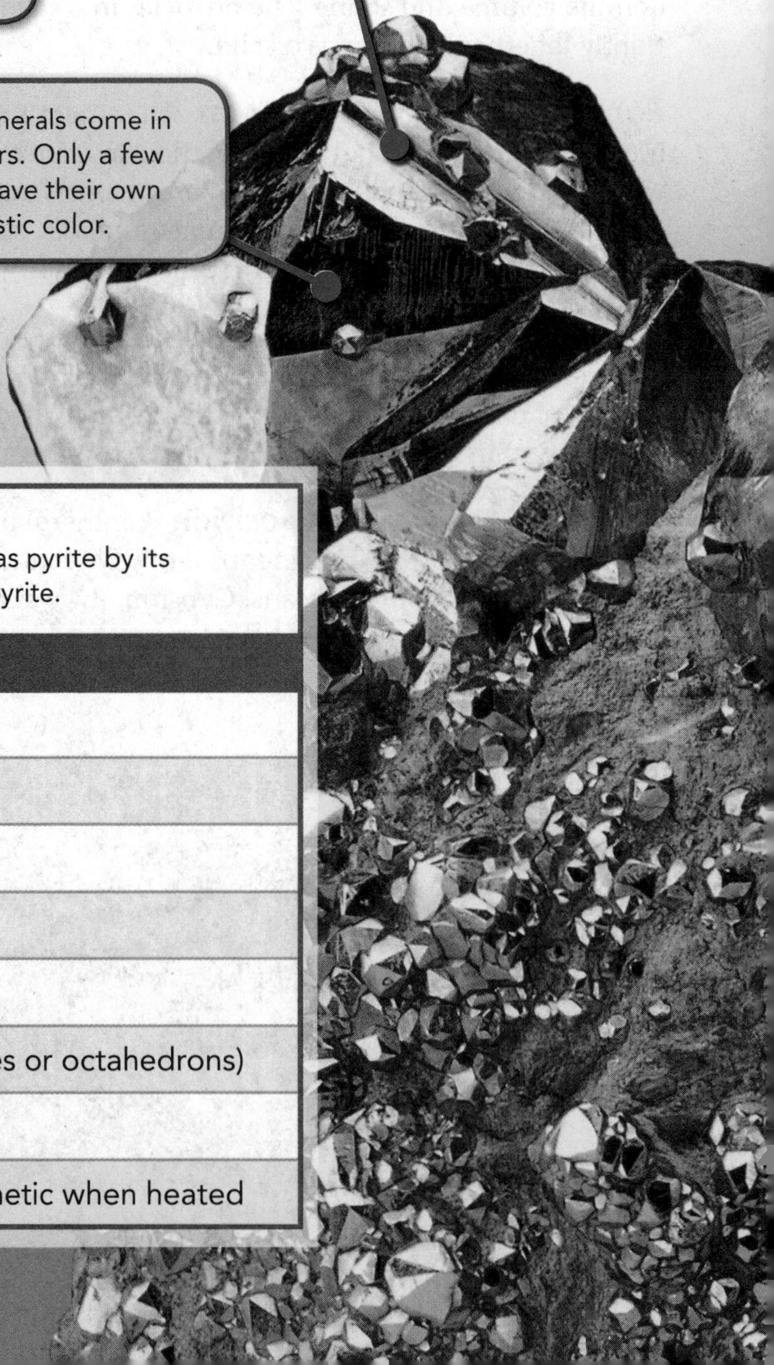

## Identifying Minerals

**Figure 2** ✎ You can identify a mineral such as pyrite by its properties. Describe the color and luster of pyrite.

| Properties of Pyrite | |
|---|---|
| Color | |
| Streak | Greenish black |
| Luster | |
| Hardness | 6–6.5 |
| Density | 5 g/cm$^3$ |
| Crystal structure | Isometric (cubes or octahedrons) |
| Cleavage or fracture | None; uneven |
| Special | Becomes magnetic when heated |

**Density** Each mineral has a characteristic density, or mass in a given volume. To calculate a mineral's density, use this formula:

Density = Mass/Volume

**Cleavage and Fracture** A mineral that splits easily along flat surfaces has the property called cleavage. Whether a mineral has cleavage depends on how the atoms in its crystals are arranged. Most minerals do not split apart evenly. Instead, they have a characteristic type of fracture. Fracture describes how a mineral looks when it breaks apart in an irregular way.

**Special Properties** Some minerals can be identified by special physical properties. For example, calcite bends light to produce double images. Other minerals conduct electricity, glow when placed under ultraviolet light, or are magnetic.

**Crystal Structure** All the crystals of a mineral have the same crystal structure. Different minerals have crystals that are shaped differently. Geologists classify crystals by the number of faces, or sides, on the crystal and the angles at which the faces meet.

**Hardness** The Mohs hardness scale is used to rank the hardness of minerals from 1 being the softest to 10 being the hardest. A mineral can scratch any mineral softer than itself but can be scratched by any mineral that is harder.

# Math Toolbox

## Calculate Density

A sample of the mineral cinnabar has a mass of 251.1 g and a volume of 31.0 cm³.

SEP Use Mathematics What is the density of cinnabar?

..................................................................

..................................................................

..................................................................

..................................................................

## Where Minerals Form

**Figure 3** ✎ Minerals can form by crystallization of magma and lava or precipitation of materials dissolved in water. Circle the area where you might find a cave with crystals similar to the large crystals shown in **Figure 1**.

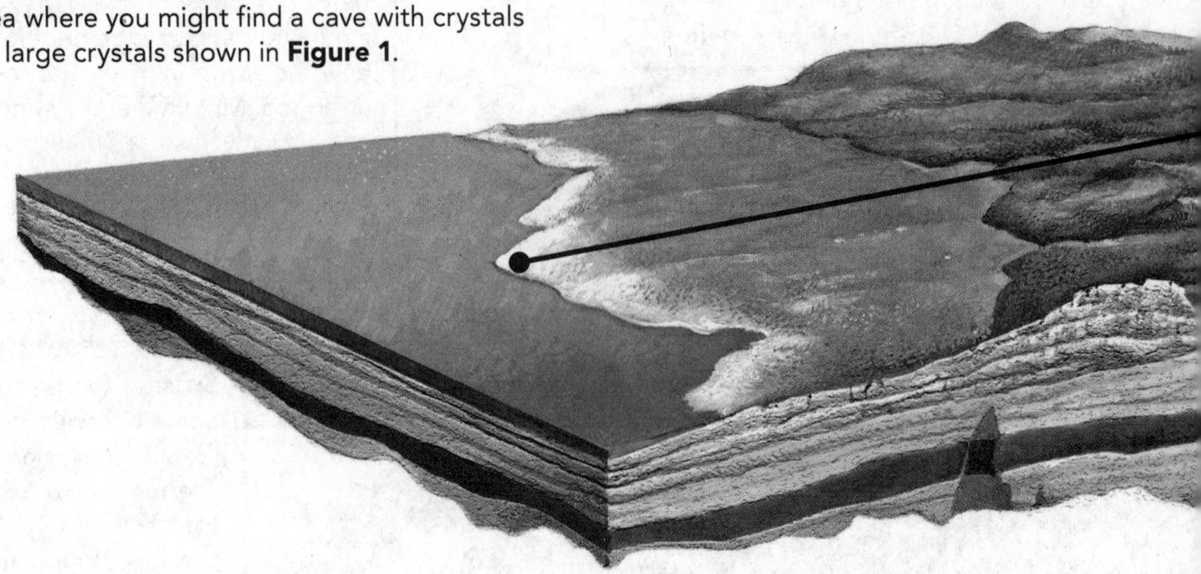

HANDS-ON LAB

**Investigate** Model mineral crystals and observe how they can change.

### Academic Vocabulary

You might be familiar with term *organic food*. How does this meaning of *organic* differ from the scientific meaning?

....................................

....................................

....................................

....................................

....................................

# Mineral Formation

In general, minerals can form in a few different ways and at different locations at or below Earth's surface. Some minerals form from organic processes. Other minerals form from the materials dissolved in evaporating solutions of water. Many minerals form when magma and lava originally heated by the energy of Earth's interior cool and solidify. Finally, some minerals form when other minerals are heated or compressed, which causes the material to deform.

**Organic Minerals** All minerals can form by inorganic processes. However, many **organic** processes can also form minerals. For instance, animals such as cows and humans produce skeletons made of the mineral calcium phosphate. Ultimately, the energy used to drive the processes of mineral formation in most living things can be traced all the way back to the sun and the plants that use its energy.

**Minerals From Solutions** Sometimes the elements and compounds that form minerals dissolve in water and form solutions. On Earth's surface, energy from the sun can cause water to evaporate, leaving behind minerals. Water below Earth's surface, which is under intense pressure and at high temperatures, can pick up elements and compounds from surrounding rock. When these elements and compounds leave the water solution through precipitation, crystallization can occur.

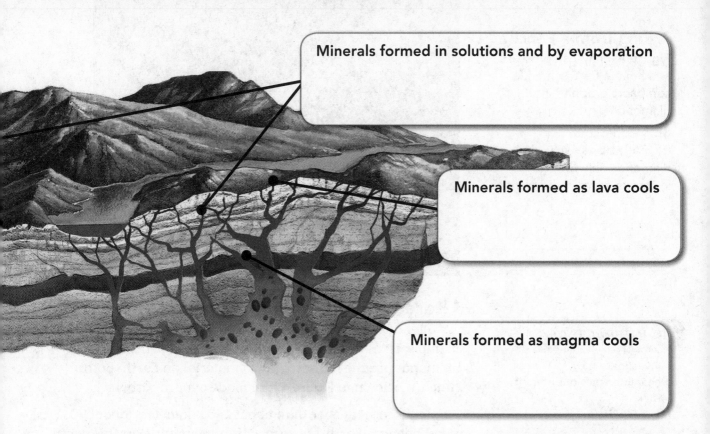

**Minerals formed in solutions and by evaporation**

**Minerals formed as lava cools**

**Minerals formed as magma cools**

**Crystallization** is the process by which atoms are arranged to form a material that has a crystal structure. Minerals such as halite, calcite, and gypsum form through crystallization when bodies of water on Earth's surface evaporate.

In another example, the huge crystals in **Figure 1** formed from a solution of water heated by energy from Earth's interior that eventually cooled underground. But the process was an extremely long one, taking place over millions of years.

## Minerals From Magma and Lava

Many minerals form when hot magma from Earth's interior cools higher up in the crust, or as lava cools and hardens on the surface. When these liquids cool to a solid state, they form crystals.

The size of the crystals depends on several factors, including the rate at which the melted rock cools. Slow cooling leads to the formation of large crystals, such as coarse quartz and feldspar crystals found in granite that slowly cools underground. Fast cooling leaves very little time for crystals to grow. Lava cools quickly on the surface or under water and forms small crystals, such as pyroxene and fine-grained olivine in basalt rock of the oceanic crust.

**READING CHECK** **Summarize Text** What type of minerals might a geologist expect to find near the site of an ancient lava flow? Explain.

..............................................................................................................

..............................................................................................................

**Literacy Connection**

**Integrate With Visuals**
Underline the name of each mineral mentioned on this page. Then, record each mineral in its correct place in **Figure 3**.

123

## A Ring from a Pencil?

**Figure 4** Immense pressure and heat in Earth's mantle compacts graphite into diamond.

**SEP Construct Explanations** Why do diamonds only form in certain spots in the mantle?

...................................................

...................................................

...................................................

graphite

cut diamond

 **INTERACTIVITY**

Investigate the characteristics of different rocks.

## Altered Minerals

A change of temperature or pressure can alter one mineral into a new mineral. Graphite, for example, is a soft mineral commonly used in pencils. Diamonds are the hardest known material on Earth. Both minerals, shown in **Figure 4**, are made of pure carbon.

Diamonds form deeper than about 150 kilometers (about 90 miles) beneath Earth's surface within the mantle. At this depth below continental crust, temperatures reach between 900°C to 1,300°C, and the pressure is about 50,000 times greater than at Earth's surface. The intense pressure and high temperature alter the structure of the carbon atoms in graphite, forming diamond.

These diamond zones may also contain magma. Long ago, the pressure that formed diamonds also caused magma to squeeze toward Earth's surface, where it might erupt. Sometimes, diamonds were carried along for the ride. When the magma cooled in pipe-like formations, the diamonds were embedded in this rock.

## Model It !

### Diamond Formation

**SEP Develop Models** ✏ Use the information in the text and **Figure 3** to draw a diagram that shows how diamonds form. Your model should show and label the following parts of the process:

1. Graphite in the mantle that is under intense pressure becomes diamonds.

2. In the past, magma from the mantle moved quickly toward Earth's surface, forming pipes.

3. The magma cooled with the diamonds trapped within it.

**Mineral Distribution** The common minerals that make up the rocks of Earth's crust are found abundantly throughout Earth's surface. Other minerals are much less common because their formation depends on certain materials and conditions that may be limited. Other minerals may form as the result of processes that take a very long time, which will limit where and how much of the mineral can form. The process by which diamonds are formed is one example.

Geological processes often tied to plate tectonics, such as volcanic eruptions or evaporations in ocean basins, can cause certain minerals to collect in concentrated deposits. These deposits, or ores, are mined for the valuable materials they contain. **Figure 5** shows the distribution of some of Earth's mineral resources.

✓ READING CHECK **Integrate With Visuals** What ideas from the text are illustrated in the map in **Figure 5**?

..................................................................................

..................................................................................

## Mineral Resources

**Figure 5** The map shows the location of some important mineral resources. Many of the minerals represented on the map are not evenly distributed across the planet.

**SEP Construct Explanations** What patterns do you notice in the distributions of different minerals on Earth?

..................................................................................

..................................................................................

..................................................................................

..................................................................................

..................................................................................

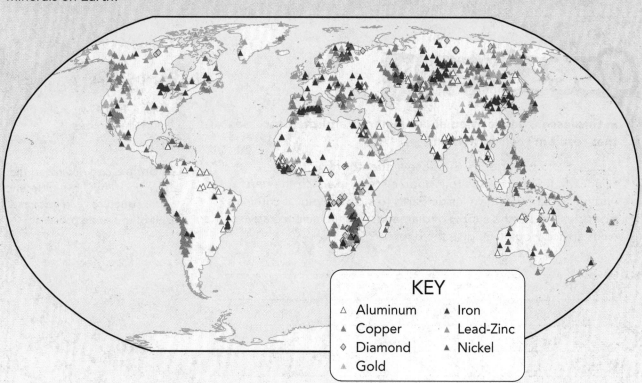

KEY
△ Aluminum    ▲ Iron
▲ Copper      ▲ Lead-Zinc
◇ Diamond     ▲ Nickel
▲ Gold

# ☑ LESSON 2 Check

**1. Analyze Properties** What are some of the properties that geologists use to identify and describe minerals?

...................................................................

...................................................................

...................................................................

**2. SEP Construct Explanations** Why aren't diamonds found evenly distributed on Earth?

...................................................................

...................................................................

...................................................................

...................................................................

...................................................................

**3. Apply Concepts** Amber is a solid material used in jewelry. It forms in nature only by the process of pine tree resin hardening. Explain why you think amber is or is not a mineral.

...................................................................

...................................................................

...................................................................

...................................................................

**4. CCC Cause and Effect** What role does the sun's energy play in the formation of minerals from solutions?

...................................................................

...................................................................

...................................................................

...................................................................

...................................................................

**5. SEP Develop Models** ✏ Draw a flow chart or cycle diagram to show one way a mineral gets recycled in nature and forms a new mineral.

# Quest CHECK-INS

**In this lesson, you learned about minerals and the processes that result in their formation.**

**Construct Arguments** Suppose a director filming a science fiction film wants to include a scene in which the hero and heroine travel down inside Earth to stop a band of criminals from stealing Earth's supply of diamonds. As the science advisor, what advice would you give the director?

...................................................................

...................................................................

...................................................................

...................................................................

## HANDS-ON LAB

Make Your Own Stalactites and Stalagmites

**Go online** and download the lab to model how two different crystal structures can form as a result of the same process.

126  Minerals and Rocks in The Geosphere

MS-ESS2-1

# The Cost of
# TECHNOLOGY

Coltan ore before processing to extract tantalum.

**Y**ou may never have heard of the element tantalum, but you probably use it every day. The electrical properties of tantalum make it a good material to use in capacitors in electronic devices. And it's found in all the smartphones, laptops, and other electronics that billions of people use to stay organized, get work done, and communicate with each other.

Tantalum must be extracted from an ore called coltan. The ore must be mined and refined before the tantalum can be used. By the turn of the 21st century, worldwide demand for electronics reached a peak, which increased demand for tantalum. Prior to 2000, most of the world's tantalum was extracted from coltan mined in Australia and Brazil. These countries have stricter mining regulations, which increases the cost of mining tantalum.

When demand for tantalum exploded, coltan mining increased in the Democratic Republic of Congo (DRC) and neighboring countries in Africa. But the DRC has been torn apart by civil war, which has lured armed coltan miners looking for a fast profit. The government does little to regulate how the coltan is mined. The unregulated, often illegal, mining provides inexpensive tantalum but destroys vital wildlife habitats and helps to fund continued conflict in this war-ravaged country.

## MY COMMUNITY

How would you solve the problem of the need for coltan versus the need to source the coltan responsibly? Work in a small group to identify possible solutions. Conduct internet research to find facts and evidence that support your arguments.

These miners search for coltan, iron ore, and manganese at the Mudere mine in eastern Democratic Republic of Congo.

# ③ Rocks

## Guiding Questions

- What are the three major types of rocks and how do they form?
- How is the formation of rocks the result of the flow of energy and cycling of matter within Earth?

## Connections

**Literacy** Summarize Text

**Math** Analyze Relationships

MS-ESS2-1

## HANDS-ON LAB

**ᴜInvestigate** Examine how pressure can change rock.

## Vocabulary

igneous rock
sedimentary rock
sediment
metamorphic
  rock

## Academic Vocabulary

apply

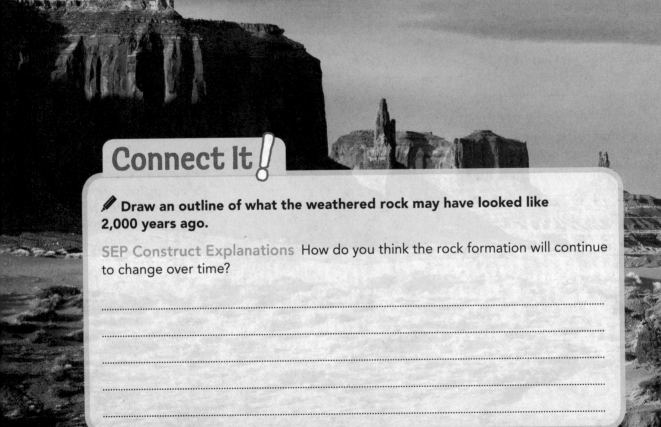

# Connect It!

✏ **Draw an outline of what the weathered rock may have looked like 2,000 years ago.**

SEP Construct Explanations How do you think the rock formation will continue to change over time?

.........................................................................................................................

.........................................................................................................................

.........................................................................................................................

.........................................................................................................................

.........................................................................................................................

# Describing Rocks

In southern Utah, spires and buttes of red sandstone rise up into the sky in Monument Valley (**Figure 1**). To a tourist or other casual observer, these rock formations seem to stand motionless and unchanging. But every moment of every day, forces are at work on these rocks, slowly changing their shapes and sizes. Weathering, erosion, transportation, and deposition all work to wear away and alter the appearance of the rock formations.

Rocks, like the sandstone in Monument Valley, are made of mixtures of minerals and other materials. To describe rocks, geologists observe mineral composition, color, and texture.

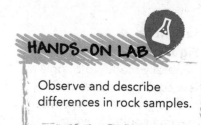

**HANDS-ON LAB**

Observe and describe differences in rock samples.

**Towers of Rock**

**Figure 1** The striking red color of Monument Valley is the result of iron oxide minerals exposed within the rock.

## Granite

**Figure 2** Granite is generally made up of only a few common minerals. This coarse granite formed when magma cooled slowly.

Mica

Quartz

Granite

Feldspar

Hornblende

**1. Claim** ✏ Circle the best word to complete each sentence.

Granite is generally (dark/ light) in color.

Granite has a (high/low) silica content.

The grains in granite are (fine/coarse).

**2. Evidence** What evidence did you use to make your claim?

.......................................................

.......................................................

**3. Reasoning** Explain how your evidence supported your claim.

.......................................................

.......................................................

.......................................................

.......................................................

.......................................................

.......................................................

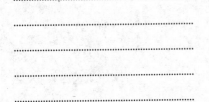

**INTERACTIVITY**

Identify and evaluate the characteristics of different rocks.

**Mineral Composition and Color** Some rocks contain only a single mineral. Other rocks contain several minerals. About 20 minerals make up most of the rocks of Earth's crust. These minerals are known as rock-forming minerals.

A rock's color provides clues to the rock's mineral composition. Granite, as shown in **Figure 2**, is generally a light-colored rock that has high silica content, meaning it is rich in the elements silicon and oxygen.

**Texture** Most rocks are made up of particles of minerals or other rocks, which geologists call grains. To describe the texture of a rock, geologists use terms that are based on the size, shape, and pattern of the grains. For example, rocks with grains that are large and easy to see are coarse-grained. In fine-grained rocks, grains can be seen only with a microscope.

**Origin** Using mineral composition, color, and texture, geologists classify a rock's origin—how the rock formed. Geologists have classified rocks into three major groups based on origin: igneous rock, sedimentary rock, and metamorphic rock.

✓ READING CHECK **Determine Meaning** *Ignis* means "fire" in Latin. What is "fiery" about igneous rocks?

.......................................................

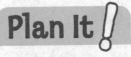

**Plan It**

**Rocky Observations**

As part of a geological investigation you are conducting, you observe three rock samples.

**SEP Analyze Data** What characteristics would you examine to help you distinguish among the three rocks?

.......................................................

.......................................................

# How Rocks Form

Each type of rock, whether its igneous, sedimentary, or metamorphic, forms in a different way.

**Igneous Rock** Rock that forms from cooled magma or lava is **igneous rock** (IG nee us). Igneous rocks can look very different from each other. The temperature and composition of the molten rock determine the kind of igneous rock that is formed.

Igneous rock may form on or beneath Earth's surface from molten material that cools and hardens. Extrusive rock is igneous rock formed from lava that erupted onto Earth's surface. Basalt is the most common extrusive rock, making up a large part of oceanic crust. Igneous rock that formed when magma hardened beneath the surface of Earth is called intrusive rock. The most abundant type of intrusive rock in the continental crust is granite. Granite forms tens of kilometers below Earth's surface and over hundreds of thousands of years or longer. When granite ends up close to the surface, it may be mined for use as road-building material, in a crushed state, or as a building material, in large polished slabs.

The texture of most igneous rock depends on the size and shape of its mineral crystals (**Figure 3**). Rapidly cooling lava found at or near Earth's surface forms fine-grained igneous rocks with small crystals or no minerals at all. Slowly cooling magma below Earth's surface forms coarse-grained rocks, such as granite and diorite, with large crystals. Intrusive rocks have larger grains than extrusive rocks. Extrusive rocks that cool too quickly to form any minerals are called glass.

**HANDS-ON LAB**

**Investigate** Examine how pressure can change rock.

## Igneous Rock Formation

**Figure 3** The texture of igneous rock varies according to how it forms.

**SEP Evaluate Evidence** Did the rocks in the photographs form at A or B? Write your answers in the spaces provided.

**Diorite**
A very coarse-grained, intrusive igneous rock. ..............

**Rhyolite**
Rhyolite is a fine-grained, extrusive igneous rock with a composition that is similar to granite. ..............

**Sedimentary Rock** Most **sedimentary rock** (sed uh MEN tur ee) forms when small particles of rocks or the remains of plants and animals are pressed and cemented together. The raw material is **sediment**—small, solid pieces of material that come from rocks or living things. As shown in **Figure 4**, sediment forms and becomes sedimentary rock through a sequence of processes: weathering and erosion, transportation, deposition, compaction, and cementation. Examples of sedimentary rock include sandstone, shale, and limestone.

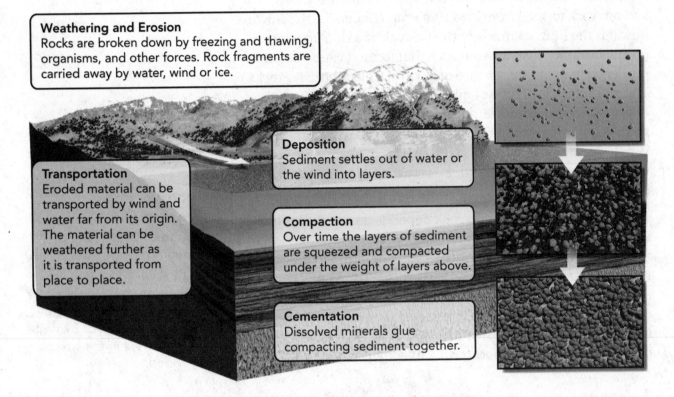

**Weathering and Erosion**
Rocks are broken down by freezing and thawing, organisms, and other forces. Rock fragments are carried away by water, wind or ice.

**Deposition**
Sediment settles out of water or the wind into layers.

**Transportation**
Eroded material can be transported by wind and water far from its origin. The material can be weathered further as it is transported from place to place.

**Compaction**
Over time the layers of sediment are squeezed and compacted under the weight of layers above.

**Cementation**
Dissolved minerals glue compacting sediment together.

## Sequencing Sedimentary Rock Formation

**Figure 4** Sedimentary rock forms in layers that are then buried below the surface. Formation occurs through a series of processes over millions of years.

1. CCC Patterns ✏ Summarize how sedimentary rock forms by using the flow chart to sequence the following processes correctly: *transportation, compaction, cementation, weathering and erosion,* and *deposition*.

2. Synthesize Information Which two processes turn layers of loose sediment into hard sedimentary rock?

........................................................................................................

........................................................................................................

## Metamorphic Rock

**Metamorphic rock** (met uh MOR fik) forms when a rock is changed by heat or pressure or by chemical reactions. When high heat and pressure are **applied** to rock, the rock's shape, texture, or composition can change, as shown in **Figure 5**.

Most metamorphic rock forms deep inside Earth, where both heat and pressure are much greater than at Earth's surface. Collisions between Earth's plates can push rock down toward the deeper, hotter mantle, altering the rock. The heat that changes rock into metamorphic rock can also come from very hot magma that rises up into colder rock. The high heat of this magma changes surrounding rock into metamorphic rock.

Very high pressure can also change rock into metamorphic rock. When plates collide, or when rock is buried deep beneath millions of tons of rock, the pressure can be enough to chemically change the rock's minerals to other types. The physical appearance, texture, and crystal structure of the minerals changes as a result.

Metamorphic rocks whose grains are arranged in parallel layers or bands are said to be foliated. For example, the crystals in granite can be flattened to form the foliated texture of gneiss. Some metamorphic rocks, such as marble, are nonfoliated. Their mineral grains are arranged randomly.

✓ **READING CHECK** **Summarize Text** Explain the basic difference between igneous and metamorphic rock.

.................................................................................................

.................................................................................................

**Academic Vocabulary**
*Applied* is the past tense of the verb *apply*. What is applied to rock that causes the rock to change shape and composition? Underline your answer in the text.

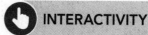

**INTERACTIVITY**

Explore different regions' rocks.

Granite

...........................................

...........................................

Gneiss

...........................................

...........................................

Marble

...........................................

...........................................

Limestone

...........................................

...........................................

**Metamorphic Changes**
**Figure 5** ✏ Heat and pressure can change one type of rock into another. Label each rock *sedimentary, igneous,* or *metamorphic.* Indicate whether the metamorphic rocks are foliated. Then shade the correct arrowhead to show which rock can form from the other rock.

## Eruption!

**Figure 6** A volcanic eruption brings up magma that will be subject to weathering and erosion when it cools.

**Evaluate Change** Would you describe the processes that change the rocks making up this volcano as fast or slow? Explain.

.............................................................

.............................................................

.............................................................

.............................................................

**The Flow of Energy** No matter what type of rock is formed, it formed as a result of the energy that flows through the Earth system. The energy that drives forces affecting the formation of sedimentary rock, such as weathering, erosion, transportation, and deposition, comes in the form of heat from the sun. Heat from Earth's interior drives the processes that control the formation of igneous and metamorphic rocks.

✓ READING CHECK **Summarize Text** What are the sources of energy that drive volcanic processes?

.............................................................................

.............................................................................

.............................................................................

# Math Toolbox
## Pressure and Depth

Pressure increases inside Earth as depth increases.

1. **SEP Interpret Data** About how far must one travel to experience the greatest pressure inside Earth?

.............................................................

.............................................................

2. **Analyze Relationships** How is pressure related to depth?

.............................................................

.............................................................

.............................................................

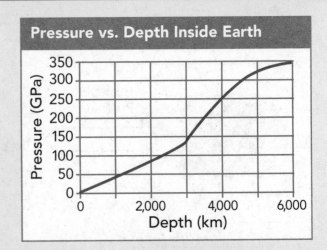

**Pressure vs. Depth Inside Earth**

MS-ESS2-1

1. **Identify** What are the three major kinds of rocks?

....................................................................

....................................................................

2. **CCC Cause and Effect** What is the source of energy that drives the weathering and erosion of sedimentary rock? Explain.

....................................................................

....................................................................

....................................................................

....................................................................

....................................................................

3. **SEP Evaluate Evidence** High heat melts a deposit of sedimentary rock, which then hardens into new rock. What kind of rock forms? Explain your answer.

....................................................................

....................................................................

....................................................................

....................................................................

....................................................................

....................................................................

4. **Analyze Properties** You are examining a sample of igneous rock. What factors affect the kind of igneous rock found in the sample?

....................................................................

....................................................................

....................................................................

....................................................................

....................................................................

5. **SEP Construct Explanations** If rocks, such as the sandstone formations in **Figure 1**, are constantly changing as a result of weathering and erosion, then why do they appear to be stable and unchanging to us?

....................................................................

....................................................................

....................................................................

....................................................................

....................................................................

....................................................................

....................................................................

## Quest CHECK-IN

In this lesson, you learned about rocks and how energy from the sun and Earth's interior drives their formation.

**SEP Use Models** How could the formation of metamorphic rock be modeled in a science fiction film through special effects?

....................................................................

....................................................................

....................................................................

....................................................................

### ☝ INTERACTIVITY

Rocky Business

**Go online** to evaluate the science facts in a movie script and the ways they are presented, revising the script as necessary.

# (4) Cycling of Rocks

## Guiding Questions

- How are Earth's materials cycled in the rock cycle?
- How does the flow of energy drive the processes of the rock cycle?

## Connection

**Literacy** Translate Information

MS-ESS2-1

## HANDS-ON LAB

**uInvestigate** Determine the relative ages of rocks.

**Vocabulary**

rock cycle

**Academic Vocabulary**

process
source

## Connect It !

🖉 **Look closely at the desert photograph in Figure 1. Circle a change that you can observe in the image.**

**Examine Change** What change did you observe? What agent is causing the change?

............................................................................................................

............................................................................................................

**Relate Change** What rock-forming processes are taking place?

............................................................................................................

............................................................................................................

# The Cycling of Earth's Materials

The rock in Earth's crust is always changing. Forces deep inside Earth and at the surface build, destroy, and change the rocks in the crust. The **rock cycle** is the series of processes that occur on Earth's surface and in the crust and mantle that slowly change rocks from one kind to another. For example, the **process** of weathering breaks down granite into sediment that gets carried away and dropped by the wind. Some of that sediment can later form sandstone.

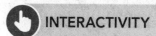
**INTERACTIVITY**

Explore the different phases of the rock cycle.

**Academic Vocabulary**

Circle the name of a process in the text. Then name two processes you go through in your daily life.

.........................................................

**Rock Cycle in Action**

**Figure 1** In Death Valley, California, and other locations on Earth's surface, processes of the rock cycle continuously move and change sediment and rocks.

HANDS-ON LAB

**Investigate** Determine the relative ages of rocks.

**Translate Information**
Review the sequence of events described in the text. Then number the materials from Granite Mountain in the order in which they move through the rock cycle.

**Sandstone** ......................................

**Granite** ......................................

**Quartzite** ......................................

**Sediment** ......................................

## Granite Mountain

**Figure 2** Processes in the rock cycle change the granite in Granite Mountain.

**SEP Evidence** Circle the words that best complete the sentences.

The (leaves/roots) of the trees on the mountain cause (weathering/erosion) of the granite. (Erosion/Deposition) by streams transports sediment away.

**Reason Quantitatively**
How long will it most likely take for processes in the rock cycle to change most of Granite Mountain into sediment? Check the box next to the correct answer.

☐ less than 1 million years
☐ 1 million years
☐ 10 million years or more

**The Flow of Energy in the Rock Cycle** There are many pathways by which rocks move through the rock cycle. These pathways and the processes and events they include are patterns that repeat again and again. For example, **Figure 2** shows Granite Mountain in Arizona. The granite in Granite Mountain formed millions of years ago below Earth's surface as magma cooled.

After the granite formed, the forces of mountain building slowly pushed the granite up to the surface. Since then, weathering and erosion have been breaking down and carrying away the granite. Transportation by streams carries some of the pieces of granite, called sediment, to rivers and eventually to the ocean. What might happen next?

Over millions of years, layers of sediment build up on the ocean floor. Slowly, the weight of the layers would physically compact the sediment. Then calcite that is dissolved in the ocean water could cement the particles together, causing a chemical change in the material. Over time, the material that once formed the igneous rock granite of Granite Mountain could become the sedimentary rock sandstone.

Sediment could keep piling up and burying the sandstone. The motion of Earth's plates could move the sandstone even deeper below the surface. Eventually, extreme pressure could deform the rocks by compacting them and causing physical and chemical changes in the rock particles. Some of the particles might crystallize. Silica, the main ingredient in quartz, would replace the calcite cement. The rock's physical texture would change from gritty to smooth. After millions of years, the sandstone could change into the metamorphic rock quartzite. Or, the heat below Earth's surface could melt the sandstone and form magma, starting the cycle over again. **Figure 3** shows this process.

## The Rock Cycle

**Figure 3** Patterns of repeating events in the rock cycle, including melting, weathering, erosion, and the application of heat and pressure, constantly change rocks from one type into another type. Through these events, Earth's materials get recycled.

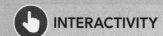

1. **SEP Develop Models** ✏ Study the photographs of the Earth materials. Fill in each blank box in the rock cycle diagram with the correct material.

2. **SEP Use Models** ✏ Study the diagram. Then label each arrow with the correct term: *melting, weathering and erosion, heat and pressure, volcanic activity,* or *deposition*. (*Hint:* To fit your answers, abbreviate "weathering and erosion" as "w & e.")

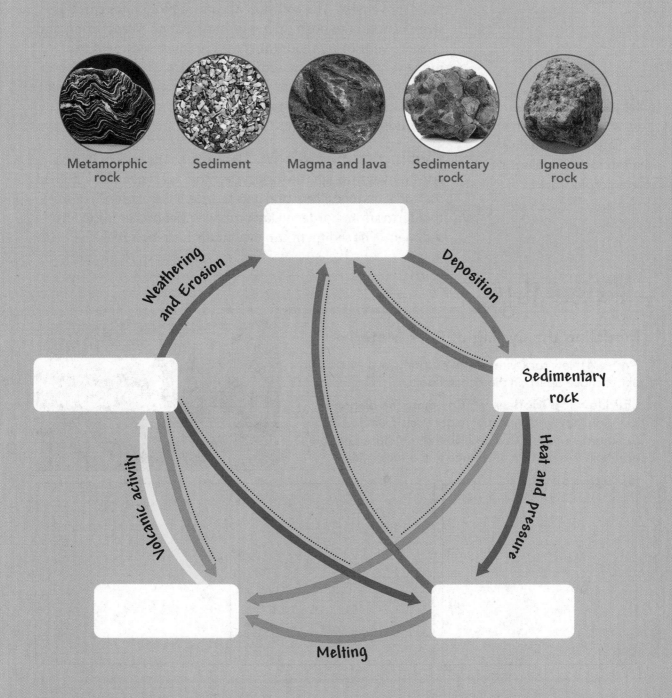

139

## Academic Vocabulary

Fill in the blanks to describe two sources.

.................... is the source of igneous rocks.

.................... is the source of the energy my body needs.

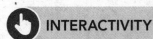

### INTERACTIVITY

Track Earth materials as they move through the rock cycle.

### ✓ READING CHECK

**Cause and Effect** Underline the plate motion that can lead to rock changing into metamorphic rock.

## Plate Tectonics and the Rock Cycle

The rock cycle is driven in part by plate tectonics. Recall that Earth's lithosphere is made up of huge plates that slowly move over Earth's surface due to convection currents in the mantle. As the plates move, they carry the continents and ocean floors with them. Plate movements help drive the rock cycle by helping to form magma, the **source** of igneous rock.

Where oceanic plates move apart, magma moves upward and fills the gap with new igneous rock. Where an oceanic plate moves beneath a continental plate, magma forms and rises. The result is a volcano where lava flows onto the overlying plate, forming igneous rock. Sedimentary rock can also result from plate movement. The collision of continental plates can be strong enough to push up a mountain range. Weathering and erosion wear away mountains and produce sediment that may eventually become sedimentary rock. Finally, a collision between continental plates can push rocks down deep beneath the surface. Here, heat and pressure could change the rocks to metamorphic rock.

## Cycling of Earth's Materials

As the rock in Earth's crust moves through the rock cycle, material is not lost or gained. Instead it changes form and gets recycled. For example, basalt that forms from hardened lava can weather and erode to form sediment. The sediment can eventually form new rock.

## Model It

### Modeling the Cycling of Rock Material

**Figure 4** New rock forms from erupting lava where two plates move apart on the ocean floor.

**SEP Develop Models** ✏ Complete the diagram to model how rock material might cycle from lava to sedimentary rock. Draw and label three more possible events in this pattern of change in the rock cycle.

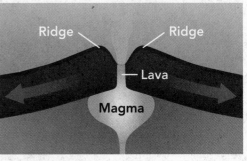

MS-ESS2-1

1. **Relate Change** What processes can recycle sedimentary rock into sediment?

........................................................................

........................................................................

........................................................................

2. **CCC Describe Patterns** Describe a process that happens again and again in the rock cycle.

........................................................................

........................................................................

........................................................................

........................................................................

3. **SEP Construct Explanations** Explain why the change from metamorphic rock to magma almost always occurs below Earth's surface.

........................................................................

........................................................................

........................................................................

........................................................................

........................................................................

........................................................................

4. **SEP Evaluate Evidence** Do you think that plate tectonics plays a major or minor role in the rock cycle? Explain your answer.

........................................................................

........................................................................

........................................................................

........................................................................

........................................................................

**Use the rock cycle diagram in Figure 3 to help you answer Question 5.**

5. **SEP Use Models** Describe two different ways that sedimentary rock can become igneous rock.

........................................................................

........................................................................

........................................................................

........................................................................

........................................................................

........................................................................

# Quest CHECK-IN

**In this lesson, you learned how Earth's materials move through the rock cycle. You also learned about the flow of energy that drives the processes of the rock cycle.**

**SEP Ask Questions** Suppose you could meet with a science consultant for movies and scripts. What questions would you have for the consultant about reviewing, evaluating, and revising scripts to make them more scientifically accurate?

........................................................................

........................................................................

........................................................................

........................................................................

👆 **INTERACTIVITY**

The Rock Cyclers

**Go online** to identify and evaluate scientific facts of the rock cycle in a movie script, and then revise the script to make it more accurate.

MS-ESS2-1

# Mighty Mauna Loa

The high summit of Mauna Loa is often surrounded by tropical rain clouds. The large volcano, outlined in red on the satellite image below, makes up a majority of the area of the main island of Hawaii.

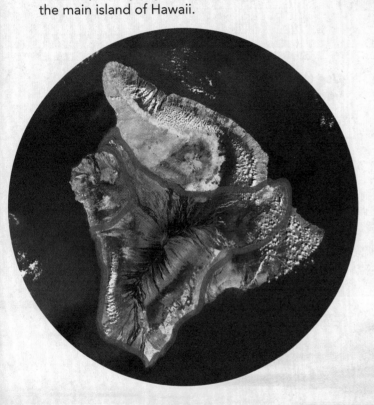

**M**auna Loa is one of Hawaii's most active volcanoes, located on the largest of the islands. The volcano sits on an active hotspot. For more than 80 million years, the Hawaiian Islands and seamounts have formed as the Pacific Plate has been sliding northwest over a hotspot—a plume of magma that causes eruptions through the overlying plate.

Mauna Loa illustrates the rock cycle in action. Over time, rock will continue to be buried as more lava flows and more sediment is carried down the volcano. Under high temperatures and pressure, some of the sedimentary rock will become metamorphic rock.

When Mauna Loa erupts, magma from inside Earth pours out of the volcano as lava. The lava flows down the slopes of the volcano.

Lava cools to form igneous rock. Some lava cools on the slopes of the volcano. Other lava flows to the ocean, where the lava cools and slowly increases the size of the island.

Weathering and erosion break down some of the igneous rock. Through the process of deposition, some of this sediment is carried down the volcano. As the sediment becomes compacted, it forms sedimentary rock.

1. **SEP Develop Models** ✏️ Complete the diagram using arrows, labels, and captions to describe the processes that drive the rock cycle on Mauna Loa.

2. **CCC Patterns** The last few eruptions of Mauna Loa happened in 1942, 1949, 1950, 1975, and 1984. The volcano has erupted 33 times since 1843. When do you think the next eruption will occur, and why do you think so?

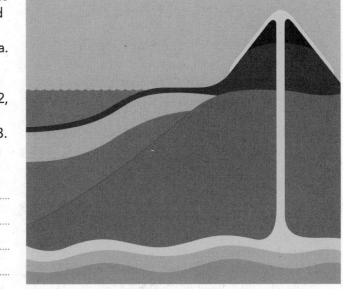

3. **SEP Construct Explanations** Why do you think Mauna Loa erupts periodically instead of steadily?

143

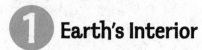 

## 1 Earth's Interior

MS-ESS2-1

**1.** Which part(s) of Earth's interior has two distinct layers?
- **A.** crust
- **B.** mantle
- **C.** core
- **D.** crust and core

**2.** Which is Earth's thinnest layer?
- **A.** crust
- **B.** inner core
- **C.** mantle
- **D.** outer core

**3.** Which of the following is an example of indirect evidence about Earth's layers?
- **A.** rock samples obtained by drilling
- **B.** mantle rocks produced by volcanoes
- **C.** changes observed in seismic wave data
- **D.** data gathered from high–pressure lab experiments

**4.** Heat in the core and the ................................. cause

.............................................., which help to cycle

material on Earth.

**5. SEP Develop Models** ✏ Draw a model to show the flow of energy and rock material through convection currents in Earth's interior. Be sure to show movement, label the layers involved, and give your model a title.

## 2 Minerals

MS-ESS2-1

**6.** Which statement best identifies the substance whose characteristics are listed in the table?

| Characteristic | Observation |
|---|---|
| Naturally occurring | Yes |
| Can form by inorganic processes | No |
| Solid | Yes |
| Crystal structure | No |
| Definite chemical composition | No |

- **A.** It is not a mineral because it is a solid.
- **B.** It is a mineral because it occurs naturally.
- **C.** It is not a mineral because it doesn't have a crystal structure.
- **D.** It is a mineral because it forms only organically.

**7.** What causes the crystals in gneiss to line up in bands?
- **A.** deposition
- **B.** erosion
- **C.** pressure
- **D.** weathering

**8.** *Metallic, glassy, earthy,* and *pearly* are words that describe a mineral's .................................................

**9. SEP Analyze Data** Mineral A has a hardness of 5. Mineral B has a hardness of 7. Mineral C can scratch Mineral A, but it can be scratched by Mineral B. What ranking on the Mohs hardness scale should Mineral C be assigned? Explain.

.................................................................................

.................................................................................

.................................................................................

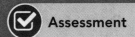
 **Rocks**

MS-ESS2-1

**10.** Which process acts on Earth's surface to break rocks into pieces?
A. compaction        B. deposition
C. erosion           D. weathering

**11.** Metamorphic rock forms as a result of

changes in .............................................. and

...............................................in Earth's interior.

**12. SEP Evaluate Evidence** An igneous rock contains large crystals of quartz, feldspar, and hornblende. How did the rock most likely form?

...............................................................................

...............................................................................

**13. CCC Identify Patterns** A rock sample contains tiny pieces of other rocks that are cemented together. Is it an igneous, sedimentary, or metamorphic rock? Explain your answer.

...............................................................................

...............................................................................

...............................................................................

**14. Apply Concepts** ✏ Create a model that represents the formation of sedimentary rock.

**4 Cycling of Rocks**

MS-ESS2-1

**15.** Which of the following leads most directly to the production of igneous rock?
A. formation of magma
B. cementation of rocks
C. weathering of rocks
D. deposition of sediment

**Use the model of the rock cycle to answer questions 16 and 17.**

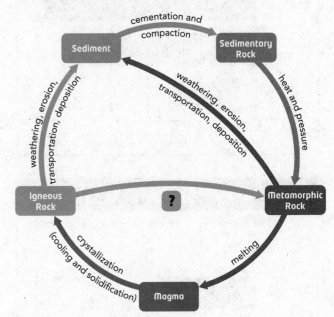

**16.** Which is the **best** way to complete this model of the rock cycle?
A. crystallization
B. solidification
C. heat and pressure
D. melting

**17.** What is a step in the process of a rock changing from sedimentary to igneous?
A. crystallization
B. deposition
C. erosion
D. melting

MS-ESS2-1

## Evidence-Based Assessment

Earth's layers vary in thickness, temperature, pressure, density, state of matter, and composition. The infographic below compares some of these characteristics of Earth's layers.

**Analyze the infographic to answer the questions.**

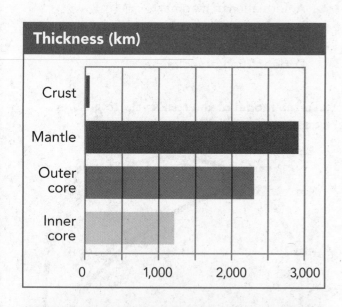

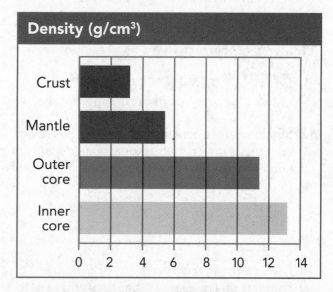

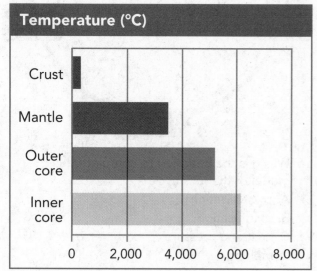

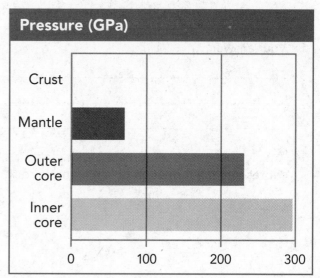

1. **SEP Analyze Data** Which of the following correctly lists Earth's layers from thickest to thinnest?
   A. crust, mantle, outer core, inner core
   B. mantle, outer core, inner core, crust
   C. inner core, outer core, mantle, crust
   D. mantle, crust, outer core, inner core

2. **SEP Analyze Data** About how many times denser is the liquid outer core than the solid crust?
   A. 6          B. 4
   C. 2          D. 3

3. **CCC Cause and Effect** Suppose the mantle were thicker than it is. What effect would this have on the pressure in the outer core? Explain.

   ........................................................
   ........................................................
   ........................................................
   ........................................................
   ........................................................

4. **CCC Patterns** What is the relationship among density, pressure, and temperature across the different layers of Earth? What explains this relationship?

   ........................................................
   ........................................................
   ........................................................
   ........................................................
   ........................................................
   ........................................................
   ........................................................
   ........................................................
   ........................................................
   ........................................................
   ........................................................

5. **Synthesize Information** Both the inner and outer core are made of iron and nickel. The inner core is hotter and denser than the outer core, yet the outer core is in a liquid state and the inner core is solid. Why is this the case? Use evidence from the data tables to support your response.

   ........................................................
   ........................................................
   ........................................................
   ........................................................
   ........................................................
   ........................................................

# Quest FINDINGS

## Complete the Quest!

**Phenomenon Review and revise the movie scripts. Consider how you can stage readings of the scripts.**

Defend Your Claim Do you think producers of fictional films that depict scientific processes should be required to hire a science consultant? Support your opinion with facts and details.

........................................................
........................................................
........................................................
........................................................
........................................................
........................................................

👆 **INTERACTIVITY**

Reflect on Science in the Movies

MS-ESS2-1

# The Rock Cycle in Action

Can you make **models** that show **third-grade students** how sedimentary, igneous, and metamorphic **rocks** form?

## Background

**Phenomenon** At first glance, rock formations—such as the Vasquez Rocks in California shown here—don't seem to do much other than sit motionless. But rocks are constantly being cycled through processes that can take just a few minutes or thousands of years.

Your task is to work with a partner to design and build models that could be used to show how the rock cycle works to someone who has never heard of it. Your teacher will assign you a specific type of rock—sedimentary, metamorphic, or igneous—and you will design a model of its formation.

## Materials

(per group)

- crayons or crayon rocks of a few different colors
- plastic knife
- paper plates
- aluminum foil
- books or other heavy objects
- hot water or hot plate
- tongs or oven mitts
- beaker

## Safety

Be sure to follow all safety guidelines provided by your teacher. Appendix B of your textbook provides more details about the safety icons.

# Plan Your Investigation

☐ You will create a plan and design a procedure to model the processes that form the type of rock that has been assigned to you. You must consider:

- the roles that weathering and erosion, deposition, and cementation play in forming sedimentary rock
- the role that high amounts of pressure and energy play in forming metamorphic rock
- the role that high amounts of heat and energy play in forming igneous rock

☐ As you design your model, consider these questions:

- What will the different crayons represent in your model?
- How can you use the available materials to represent specific processes such as weathering and erosion, or melting and cementation?
- How can you use the available materials to simulate the processes and flow of energy, such as heat and pressure, that result in the formation of sedimentary, metamorphic, and igneous rocks?

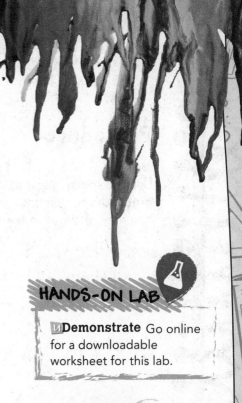

## HANDS-ON LAB

и**Demonstrate** Go online for a downloadable worksheet for this lab.

☐ Organize your ideas in the table. Then plan your procedure.

| Processes | Materials | Notes |
|---|---|---|
| 1. Weathering and erosion to form sediment | | |
| 2. Formation of sedimentary rock | | |
| 3. Formation of metamorphic rock | | |
| 4. Formation of igneous rock | | |

## Procedure

Use the space below to describe your model(s) and list steps in a procedure to demonstrate the formation of your assigned rock type. You may wish to use sketches to show some steps.

# Analyze and Interpret Data

1. **SEP Develop Models** Work with other pairs to develop a complete model of the rock cycle. Draw your model in the space provided. Include labels to explain what each part of the model represents.

2. **Relate Change** Describe the flow of energy and cycling of matter represented by your pair's model. How does your model help you to understand processes that can last thousands of years?

......................................................................................................................

......................................................................................................................

......................................................................................................................

......................................................................................................................

3. **Identify Limitations** How does your model differ from the actual rock cycle on Earth? How could you make your model more accurate?

......................................................................................................................

......................................................................................................................

......................................................................................................................

......................................................................................................................

......................................................................................................................

......................................................................................................................

# TOPIC 4

# Plate Tectonics

### NGSS PERFORMANCE EXPECTATIONS

**MS-ESS2-2** Construct an explanation based on evidence for how geoscience processes have changed Earth's surface at varying time and spatial scales.

**MS-ESS2-3** Analyze and interpret data on the distribution of fossils and rocks, continental shapes, and seafloor structures to provide evidence of the past plate motions.

**MS-ESS3-2** Analyze and interpret data on natural hazards to forecast future catastrophic events and inform the development of technologies to mitigate their effects.

How did this island get here?

**HANDS-ON LAB**

uConnect Explore how Earth's continents can be linked together.

VIDEO

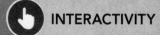 INTERACTIVITY

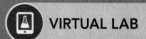 VIRTUAL LAB

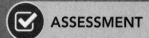 ASSESSMENT

 eTEXT

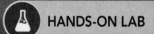 HANDS-ON LAB

**The Essential Question**

# How do geological processes change Earth's surface?

**CCC Cause and Effect** This island in the South Pacific formed as the result of a violent eruption of material from deep inside Earth. What role does this kind of event play in shaping Earth's surface?

....................................................................................................

....................................................................................................

....................................................................................................

....................................................................................................

....................................................................................................

....................................................................................................

# How safe is it to hike around Mount Rainier?

**STEM** **Phenomenon** Camping and hiking in the mountains are popular pastimes for people all over the world. But what if the mountain is actually an active volcano? It hasn't erupted for thousands of years—but it *could*. Would volcanologists say it is safe to hike? What kinds of data do they collect to predict eruptions? In this problem-based Quest activity, you will determine whether it is safe to take an extended camping and hiking trip on Mount Rainier. Through hands-on labs and digital activities, you'll gather evidence about Rainier's history and look into current research on the mountain's volcanic activity. You will use this information to create a presentation that supports your claim and synthesizes your findings.

## 🦚 NBC LEARN ▶ VIDEO

After watching the Quest Kickoff video, which explains volcanic processes, think about the pros and cons of hiking on Mount Rainier. Record your ideas.

**PROS**

.................................................................................

.................................................................................

.................................................................................

**CONS**

.................................................................................

.................................................................................

.................................................................................

👆 **INTERACTIVITY**

To Hike or Not to Hike

**MS-ESS2-2** Construct an explanation based on evidence for how geoscience processes have changed Earth's surface at varying time and spatial scales.

**MS-ESS3-2** Analyze and interpret data on natural hazards to forecast future catastrophic events and inform the development of technologies to mitigate their effects.

## Quest CHECK-IN

### IN LESSON 1
**STEM** What is Mount Rainier's history of eruption? Investigate the mountain range's history and draw conclusions about the likelihood of an eruption.

🧪 **HANDS-ON LAB**

Patterns in the Cascade Range

## Quest CHECK-IN

### IN LESSON 2
How is volcanic activity related to tectonic plate movements? Explore the science behind the connection.

👆 **INTERACTIVITY**

Mount Rainier's Threat

## Quest CHECK-IN

### IN LESSON 3
What processes cause earthquakes and tsunamis to form? Think about the possible risks caused by movements of the ground beneath your feet.

👆 **INTERACTIVITY**

Monitoring a Volcano

The Cascade Range stretches from northern California all the way up through British Columbia, Canada. Mount Rainier is just one of many volcanoes that lie within the range and are considered "active."

## Quest CHECK-IN

### STEM IN LESSON 4

What kinds of data can be used to predict an eruption? Investigate the tools and methods that volcanologists use to study volcanoes. Then analyze some data to determine the likelihood of an eruption.

### HANDS-ON LAB

Signs of Eruption?

## Quest FINDINGS

### Complete the Quest!

Present information on Mount Rainier's history and current geological research, along with your evidence-based argument about whether it is safe to hike and camp there.

### 👆 INTERACTIVITY

Reflect on Mount Rainier's Safety

# How Are Earth's Continents Linked Together?

How can you **interpret data** to infer evidence of moving continents?

## Background

**Phenomenon** Your science classroom most likely has a globe sitting on a shelf. Have you ever examined it closely? Are there any features that you find interesting? In this activity, you will make observations of a globe and look for evidence of moving continents.

## Materials

**(per group)**

- globe that shows physical features
- colored markers or crayons
- paper (optional)
- scissors (optional)

## Develop a Model

1. Search the globe for two of Earth's features that occur frequently. List them.

.....................................................................................................

2. ✂ **SEP Develop a Model** Use the materials to help you make a model of Earth. As you develop your model think about features that will help provide evidence. You may want to develop a legend.

3. **SEP Use a Model** Use your model to find evidence of moving continents.

4. Record your observations.

# Observations

**HANDS-ON LAB**

**Connect** Go online for a downloadable worksheet of this lab.

## Analyze and Conclude

1. **SEP Use Models** About how much of Earth's surface is covered by the Pacific Ocean? Identify at least two major mountain chains that extend over more than one continent.

   ......................................................................................................................................

   ......................................................................................................................................

   ......................................................................................................................................

2. **CCC Patterns** Did you notice any patterns in the shape of the continents? Give an example.

   ......................................................................................................................................

   ......................................................................................................................................

   ......................................................................................................................................

3. **SEP Cite Evidence** What evidence did you observe that indicates that the continents might have moved over time?

   ......................................................................................................................................

   ......................................................................................................................................

   ......................................................................................................................................

# ① Evidence of Plate Motions

## Guiding Questions

- What evidence supported the hypothesis of continental drift?
- What roles do mid-ocean ridges and ocean trenches play in the movement of plates?

## Connection

**Literacy** Cite Textual Evidence

MS-ESS2-3

## HANDS-ON LAB

**ᴜInvestigate** Piece Pangaea together.

### Vocabulary

mid-ocean ridge
sea-floor
  spreading
subduction
ocean trench

### Academic Vocabulary

hypothesis

## Connect It !

✎ **Draw lines between South America and Africa to show how the contours of the two continents could fit together.**

CCC Stability and Change What might you infer about South America and Africa if you thought the continents were movable objects?

........................................................................

# Hypothesis of Continental Drift

For many centuries, scientists and map-makers had been curious about why some continents look as though they could fit together like the pieces of a jigsaw puzzle. The continents on the east and west sides of the South Atlantic Ocean, for example, looked like they would fit together perfectly (**Figure 1**). In the mid 1800s, scientists began to gather clues that suggested the slow movement, or drift, of continents. In 1912, German meteorologist Alfred Wegener (VAY guh nur) further developed the **hypothesis** that all of of the continents had once been fused together, and that over time they had drifted apart. This hypothesis became known as "continental drift."

In 1915, after gathering evidence that supported the hypothesis, Wegener published *The Origin of Continents and Oceans*. The book connected clues from studies of land features, fossils, and climate to make a compelling case for the hypothesis that a supercontinent called Pangaea (pan JEE uh) had broken up into the continents we know today.

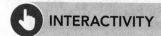

## INTERACTIVITY

Try your hand at piecing together puzzles.

## Academic Vocabulary

In science, a hypothesis is an idea that can be tested by experimentation or investigation. It is an evidence-based idea that serves as a starting point, whereas a scientific theory is what science produces when a hypothesis has been shown to be true through a broad range of studies. As you read this lesson, highlight or underline the key components of the hypothesis of continental drift.

## Pieces of the Puzzle

**Figure 1** Scientists wondered whether the continents' coastlines seemed to fit like jigsaw puzzle pieces because they had once been joined together.

**Cite Textual Evidence** Use your science notebook to organize the evidence that supports the hypothesis of continental drift. Identify a common theme among the different pieces of evidence.

## Evidence From Land Features

There were other pieces of evidence to support the hypothesis of continental drift. Mountain ranges near those continents' coasts seemed to line up, as though they had been made in the same place and at the same time. Coal deposits, made of the remains of plants that thrived in warm locations millions of years ago, were found on multiple continents and in regions that no longer supported that kind of plant life. The separate, scattered locations of these features (**Figure 2**) suggested that they hadn't always been separate.

## Evidence From Fossils

Geologists noticed that evidence from the fossil record supported continental drift. (**Figure 2**). Fossils are traces of organisms preserved in rock. Geologist Edward Suess noted that fossils of *Glossopteris* (glaw SAHP tuh ris), a fernlike plant from 250 million years ago, were found on five continents. This suggested that those landmasses had once been connected, as part of Pangaea. Fossils of animals told a similar story. *Mesosaurus* was a reptile that lived in fresh-water habitats millions of years ago, yet *Mesosaurus* fossils were found in both South America and Africa.

### Evidence for Continental Drift

**Figure 2** Study the map key to see how Wegener pieced together similar pieces of evidence from separate sites to support his hypothesis.

**Interpret Visuals** Present-day India is in South Asia, at the northern end of the Indian Ocean. What evidence found in India matches that of other locations?

........................................................

........................................................

........................................................

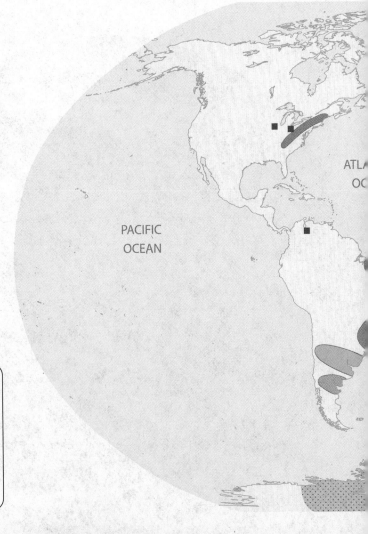

ATLANTIC OCEAN

PACIFIC OCEAN

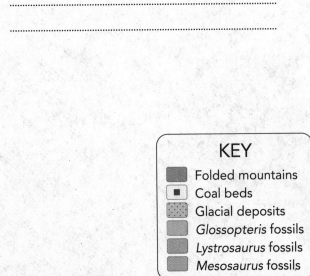

**KEY**

- Folded mountains
- ■ Coal beds
- Glacial deposits
- *Glossopteris* fossils
- *Lystrosaurus* fossils
- *Mesosaurus* fossils

**Evidence From Climate** Wegener, whose own expertise was in the study of weather and climate and not geology, also gathered evidence that showed Earth's continents had experienced different climates than the ones they have today. For example, Spitsbergen, an island in the Arctic Ocean, has fossils of plants that could have survived only in a tropical climate. This doesn't mean that the Arctic Ocean once had a tropical climate. That isn't possible, because the poles do not receive enough sunlight to produce tropical weather or support tropical plants. Instead, this evidence means Spitsbergen used to be at the equator, part of a supercontinent. The supercontinent slowly broke apart, and the island now known as Spitsbergen drifted far to the north over the course of millions of years.

**HANDS-ON LAB**

☑**Investigate** Piece Pangaea together.

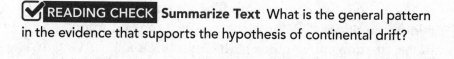

✓ READING CHECK **Summarize Text** What is the general pattern in the evidence that supports the hypothesis of continental drift?

...........................................................................................

...........................................................................................

**Reflect** Think of some organic item (such as a flower or type of fruit) that you've found in at least two places that are many miles apart. Do the items have a common origin? Why do you think so? What conclusions can you draw from the item's presence in widely-different locations?

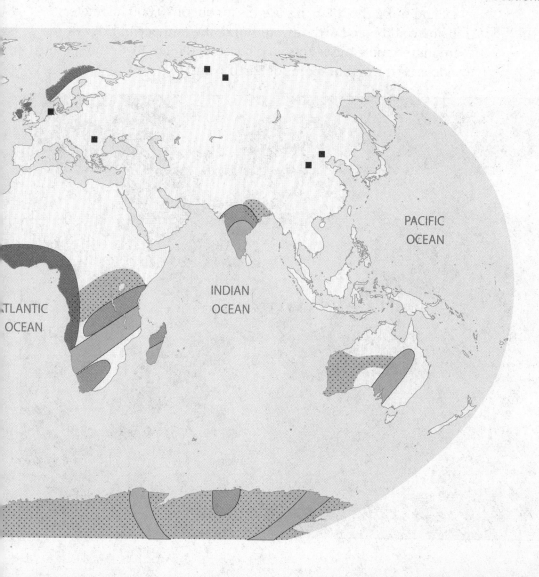

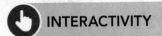
# Mid-Ocean Ridges

The hypothesis of continental drift included evidence from different areas of science, but it had a major flaw. It lacked a good explanation for *how* the continents could have broken up and moved apart. Many scientists rejected the hypothesis for that reason. By the middle of the twentieth century, advances in oceanography—the study of Earth's oceans—allowed a mapping of the ocean floor that renewed interest in continental drift. Undersea exploration provided evidence that Earth's surface was composed of moving plates—large pieces of the lithosphere.

By measuring distances from the sea surface to its floor, scientists now had a clear visual of what Earth's surface looked like under the oceans. What surprised many was the presence of long, zipper-like chains of undersea mountains called **mid-ocean ridges**. One such chain, called the Mid-Atlantic Ridge, ran down the middle of the Atlantic Ocean, curving in a pattern that seemed to mirror the contours of the surrounding continental coastlines. Further modeling and mapping of the ocean floor in the 1990s showed that these mid-ocean ridges extend throughout Earth's oceans for about 70,000 kilometers. If you could hold Earth in your hand, the mid-ocean ridges might resemble the seams on a baseball (**Figure 3**). Could these ridges be the actual seams of Earth's crust?

## Mid-Ocean Ridges

**Figure 3** Mapping of mid-ocean ridges in the mid-twentieth century provided supporting evidence that Earth's surface was composed of moving plates.

**Interpret Visuals** Do any of the mid-ocean ridges appear to extend into continents? Which ones?

..................................................

..................................................

..................................................

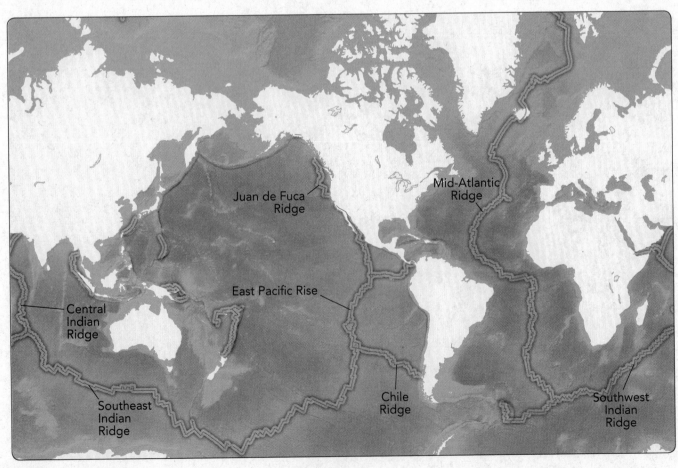

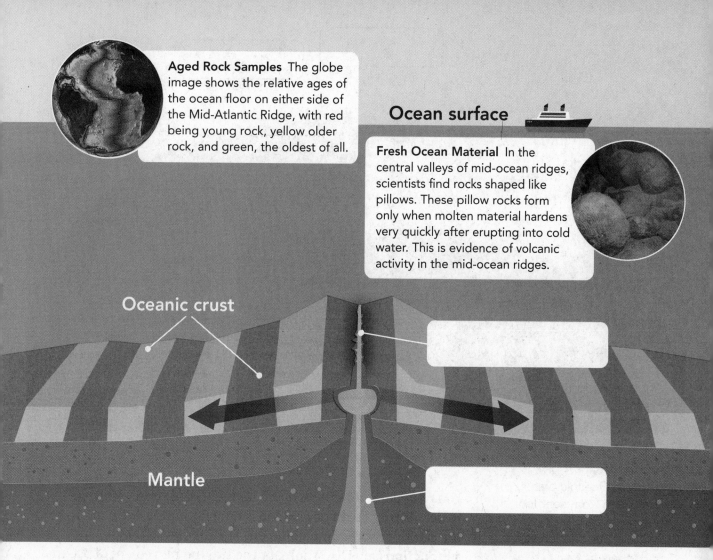

**Aged Rock Samples** The globe image shows the relative ages of the ocean floor on either side of the Mid-Atlantic Ridge, with red being young rock, yellow older rock, and green, the oldest of all.

**Ocean surface**

**Fresh Ocean Material** In the central valleys of mid-ocean ridges, scientists find rocks shaped like pillows. These pillow rocks form only when molten material hardens very quickly after erupting into cold water. This is evidence of volcanic activity in the mid-ocean ridges.

Oceanic crust

Mantle

# Sea-Floor Spreading

While ocean-floor mapping was underway, geologists began to gather samples of rock from the ocean floor. They learned that mid-ocean ridges are the sources of new spans of the ocean floor. In a process called **sea-floor spreading**, molten rock flows up through a crack in Earth's crust and hardens into solid strips of new rock on both sides of the crack. The entire floor on either side of the ridge moves away when this occurs, meaning the older strips of rock move farther from the ridge over time. It's like a two-way conveyer belt with new material appearing at the ridge while older material is carried farther away. **Figure 4** shows a model and describes some specific evidence of sea-floor spreading.

✓ READING CHECK **Cite Textual Evidence** Why was undersea exploration important for developing the theory of plate tectonics?

**Sea-Floor Spreading**
**Figure 4** Sea-floor spreading continually adds material to the ocean floor on both sides of the ridge.

SEP Develop Models ✏
Label the different features that play a role in sea-floor spreading.

Subduction

[empty label box]

[empty label box]

[empty label box]

### Subduction

**Figure 5** Oceanic plates, which form from sea-floor spreading, sink back into the mantle at subduction zones.

**CCC System Models** ✏
Label the mantle, mid-ocean ridge, and ocean trench.

 **VIDEO**

Watch what happens at ocean ridges and trenches.

# Ocean Trenches

You may be wondering why all of the oceans aren't getting wider, or why Earth as a whole is not expanding, with all of the sea-floor spreading going on. The answer to that is **subduction** (sub DUC shun), or the sinking movement of ocean floor back into the mantle. Subduction occurs where a dense plate of oceanic crust goes under an adjacent section of Earth's crust. This occurs at **ocean trenches**, which are undersea valleys that are the deepest parts of the ocean (**Figure 5**).

**The Process of Subduction** New oceanic crust is relatively warm. As the rock cools and moves away from a mid-ocean ridge, it gets denser. At some point, the dense slab of oceanic crust may meet another section of ocean floor, or a continent. What happens? Because the oceanic crust is cooler than the mantle underneath, it is denser and will sink into the mantle if given the chance. At an ocean trench, it has that chance, and the oceanic crust will sink under the edge of a continent or a younger, less-dense slab of oceanic crust. The oceanic plate that sinks back into the mantle gets recycled. This process can produce volcanic eruptions at the surface. If the oceanic crust meets continental crust, then a chain of volcanoes will form. If it meets more oceanic crust, then there will likely be a chain of volcanic islands.

**Subduction and the Oceans** An ocean basin can have a spreading ridge, subduction zones, or both, depending on its age. An ocean basin starts with just a spreading ridge. The Atlantic Ocean, for example, has the Mid-Atlantic Ridge running down its full length, but no subduction zones. This means that the Atlantic Ocean is still getting wider—by about 2 to 5 centimeters per year. At some point, part of the oceanic plate will begin to sink back into the mantle and a subduction zone will form.

The Pacific Ocean is a more mature ocean basin. While it still has a spreading ridge, the Pacific basin is surrounded by subduction zones. The oceanic crust in the Pacific is being recycled back into the mantle faster than it is being created. This means that the Pacific Ocean basin is getting smaller.

Eventually, hundreds of millions of years from now, as Africa collides into Europe and the Pacific Ocean closes up, a new supercontinent may appear.

**☑ READING CHECK Cite Textual Evidence** What features are evidence of the Pacific Ocean's maturity?

**👆 INTERACTIVITY**

Learn about the slow and steady movement on Earth.

# Model It !

## Predict North America's Movement

**Figure 6** The map shows the layout of some of Earth's landmasses, the mid-ocean ridges where plates are made, and ocean trenches where plates are recycled.

**CCC Stability and Change** 🖊 Draw a line to indicate where you think the west coast of North America will eventually be located.

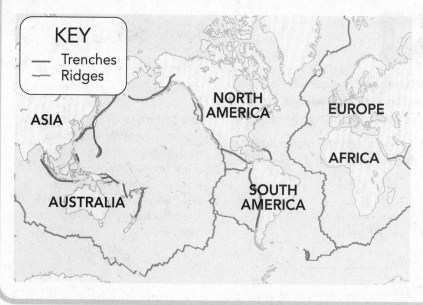

KEY
— Trenches
— Ridges

ASIA
NORTH AMERICA
EUROPE
AFRICA
AUSTRALIA
SOUTH AMERICA

# ☑ LESSON 1 Check

1. **SEP Communicate Information** Describe the hypothesis of continental drift.

.......................................................................

.......................................................................

.......................................................................

.......................................................................

2. **SEP Analyze Data** How did the study of fossils provide support for the ideas behind the existence of Pangaea?

.......................................................................

.......................................................................

.......................................................................

.......................................................................

.......................................................................

.......................................................................

.......................................................................

.......................................................................

.......................................................................

3. **SEP Interpret Data** How did the discovery of mid-ocean ridges support the hypothesis of continental drift?

.......................................................................

.......................................................................

.......................................................................

4. **CCC Cause and Effect** A large oceanic crust collides with the edge of a continent. What will happen?

.......................................................................

.......................................................................

.......................................................................

5. **Infer** A remotely-operated vehicle is sent to the deepest part of the Mariana Trench. It returns with a sample of rock from the ocean floor. Would this rock be old or young? Explain.

.......................................................................

.......................................................................

.......................................................................

.......................................................................

.......................................................................

.......................................................................

.......................................................................

## Quest CHECK-IN

In this lesson you learned about Wegener's hypothesis of continental drift and how he pieced together evidence from different areas of natural history to support his hypothesis.

**Connect to the Nature of Science** How can the history of Mount Rainier's eruptions help you decide whether hiking around Mount Rainier is safe?

.......................................................................

.......................................................................

.......................................................................

.......................................................................

## HANDS-ON LAB

Patterns in the Cascade Range

**Go online** to download the lab worksheet. Analyze data to determine whether there is a pattern to Mount Rainier's eruptions and those of other nearby volcanoes in the Cascade Range of the Pacific Northwest.

# The Slow Acceptance of
# Continental Drift

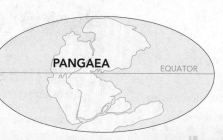

PANGAEA          EQUATOR

"Utter rot," a "fairy tale," and "delirious ravings." These statements are how some scientists in the early 1900s responded to Alfred Wegener's book describing the hypothesis continental drift.

This case demonstrates that scientific thought doesn't always advance neatly or without controversy. Long-held scientific attitudes can be slow to change when new evidence or interpretations are encountered.

The hypothesis of continental drift faced a number of challenges. Though there was evidence to support it, there was not a convincing explanation of how continental drift actually occurred. Scientists who were already skeptical of the idea only heaped additional ridicule on Wegener.

In addition, Wegener was a trained meteorologist, but the hypothesis crossed multiple scientific disciplines. Many experts in their respective fields felt threatened because Wegener—viewed as an outsider—challenged their authority and expertise. After his death in 1930, continental drift was virtually ignored.

Over the next few decades, advances in technology led to a better understanding of the geological forces that shape Earth's surface. By the early 1960s, younger geologists were able to explain the mechanism by which the continents moved. The ideas behind continental drift re-emerged as the theory of plate tectonics.

Wegener often took research trips to Greenland to study its climate. By taking core samples of ice, climatologists can learn about the climate of the past.

**CONNECT TO YOU**

Do you think skepticism is an important quality for a scientist to have? Why or why not? Discuss your ideas with a partner.

# Plate Tectonics and Earth's Surface

## Guiding Questions

- How do Earth's plates move?
- How do Earth's surface features support the theory of plate tectonics?
- What are the products of plate movement at different scales?

## Connections

**Literacy** Integrate With Visuals

**Math** Reason Quantitatively

MS-ESS2-2

## HANDS-ON LAB

µ**Investigate** Explore different plate interactions.

## Vocabulary

divergent boundary

convergent boundary

transform boundary

## Academic Vocabulary

theory

## Connect It !

✎ **Identify where the Himalayan Mountains are and circle them.**

**CCC Stability and Change** Scientists are measuring Mount Everest to determine whether its height has changed. Why would the Himalayas be getting taller?

.................................................................................

.................................................................................

.................................................................................

# The Theory of Plate Tectonics

With observations of many geologists in the 1950s and 1960s, particularly of the features of the ocean floor, the ideas behind continental drift re-emerged as the **theory** of plate tectonics. This theory states that Earth's lithosphere—the crust and upper part of the mantle—is broken up into distinct plates. The plates are puzzle-like pieces that are in slow, constant motion relative to each other due to forces within the mantle. The theory explains the specific patterns of motion among the plates, including the different types of boundaries where they meet and the events and features that occur at their boundaries (**Figure 1**). The term *tectonic* refers to Earth's crust and to the large-scale processes that occur within it.

## Academic Vocabulary

In science, the term *theory* is applied only to ideas that are supported by a vast, diverse array of evidence. How is the term used in everyday life?

.................................................................

.................................................................

.................................................................

.................................................................

.................................................................

### Plate Tectonics Give Rise to the Himalayas

**Figure 1** The tallest mountains on Earth, K2 and Mount Everest, are part of the Himalayas. When the landmass that is now known as India collided with Asia, these mountains began to form.

## Convection Currents

**Figure 2** In a pot of boiling water, warmer water rises and cooler water sinks to fill the void. This movement creates convection currents in the pot of water.

**Convection Drives Plate Motions** The tectonic plates move because they are part of convection currents in the mantle. You may recall that convection is a cyclical movement of fluid driven by temperature differences at the top and bottom, such as cold water sinking from the surface and warm water rising from below (**Figure 2**). Convection occurs in the mantle where solid rock flows in slow-moving currents. These currents are responsible for moving the continents great distances across Earth's surface, even if they move at speeds too slow to be noticed.

## Types of Crust

Plates consist of one or two types of crust. Oceanic crust is the dense type of crust that is found at the bottom of the ocean (**Figure 3**). Some plates, such as the Pacific Plate, consist entirely of oceanic crust. The other type of crust is called continental crust. It is less dense than oceanic crust and is almost always thicker. As a result, the surfaces of continents are above sea level.

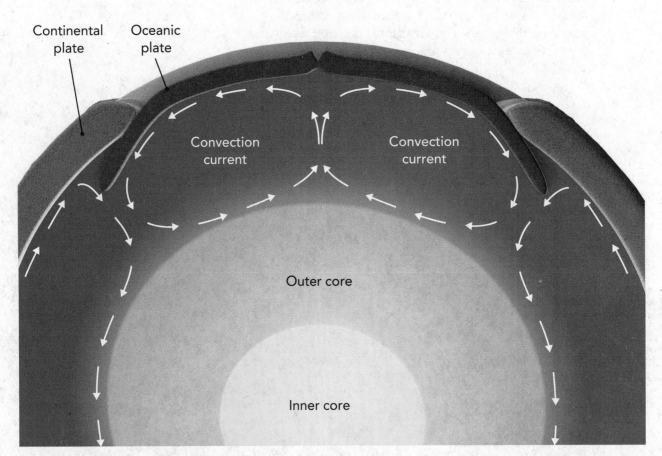

Continental plate

Oceanic plate

Convection current

Convection current

Outer core

Inner core

## Oceanic and Continental Crust

**Figure 3** The very dense crust of the ocean floor is oceanic crust. Crust that is less dense can be thick enough that it's above sea level. Continental crust gets its name from the fact that the surfaces of continents are mostly above sea level.

**Interpret Visuals** ✏ Use the directions in which the convection currents are moving in the figure to draw in arrows indicating the direction of the oceanic plates.

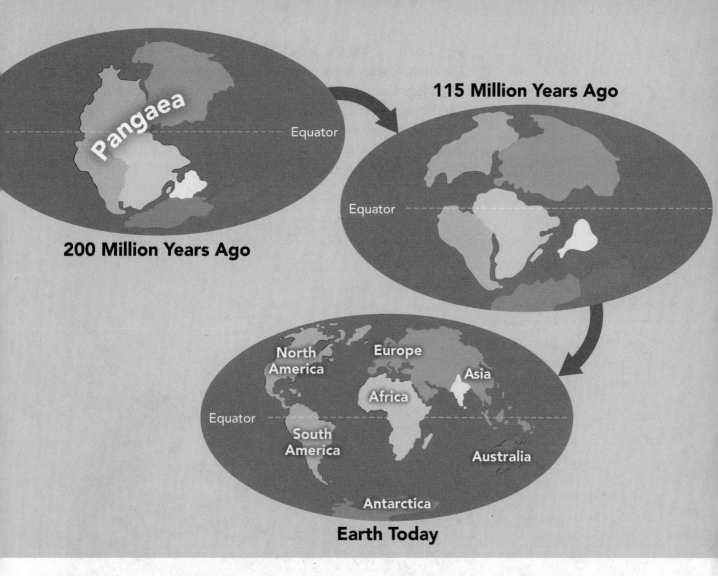

**200 Million Years Ago** Pangaea

Equator

**115 Million Years Ago**

Equator

**Earth Today**

North America

Europe

Asia

Africa

Equator

South America

Australia

Antarctica

**Plate Motions Over Time** Scientists use satellites to measure plate motions precisely. The plates move very slowly— about 1 to 10 centimeters per year. The North American and Eurasian plates, named for the continents they carry, move apart at a rate of 1 to 2 centimeters per year, or about as fast as your fingernails grow. Because the plates have been moving for billions of years, they have moved great distances.

Over time, the movement of Earth's plates has greatly changed the locations of the continents and the size and shape of the ocean basins. Long before Pangaea existed, over billions of years, other supercontinents had formed and split apart. Pangaea itself formed when Earth's landmasses moved together about 350 to 250 million years ago. Then, about 200 million years ago, Pangaea began to break apart (**Figure 4**).

☑ READING CHECK **Draw Conclusions** When might the continents we know today form a new supercontinent?

..................................................................................

**200 Million Years of Plate Motions**

**Figure 4** It has taken the continents about 200 million years to move to their present locations, since the breakup of Pangaea.

**Interpret Visuals** 🖊

Label the landmasses from 115 million years ago with the present-day names of landmasses, as shown on the "Earth Today" map.

 **INTERACTIVITY**

Compare the relative rates of motion of different plates.

## Tectonic Plates and the "Ring of Fire"

The theory of plate tectonics predicts that earthquakes and volcanoes should occur at plate boundaries, and that some landforms, such as mountain ranges, should mark the plate boundaries. For example, many volcanic eruptions and earthquakes occur at the edges of the Pacific Plate (**Figure 5**), that lies under the Pacific Ocean.

## Model It

### Ring of Fire

**Figure 5** Because the region around the Pacific Ocean is prone to volcanic activity and earthquakes, it is known as the "Ring of Fire."

1. **Claim** Why do so many volcanoes seem to occur on coastlines of the Pacific Ocean?

...............................................

...............................................

...............................................

...............................................

...............................................

...............................................

▲ Volcanoes

2. **Evidence** 🖊 According to the theory of plate tectonics, how do the locations of volcanoes compare with plate boundaries? On **Figure 5,** draw the edges of the different plates, including the Pacific Plate. Use **Figure 6** to help you.

3. **Reasoning** Describe how the symbols on the map guided your mark-up of the map.

...............................................................................

...............................................................................

## Plate Map

**Figure 6** ✏ Earth scientists have identified the different tectonic plates, many of which are named for the continents they carry. The boundaries have been identified as convergent, divergent, or transform. Relative plate movements at some of the boundaries are indicated with red arrows.

**SEP Develop Models** ✏ Using the map key as a reference, add the arrows that are missing in the circles provided.

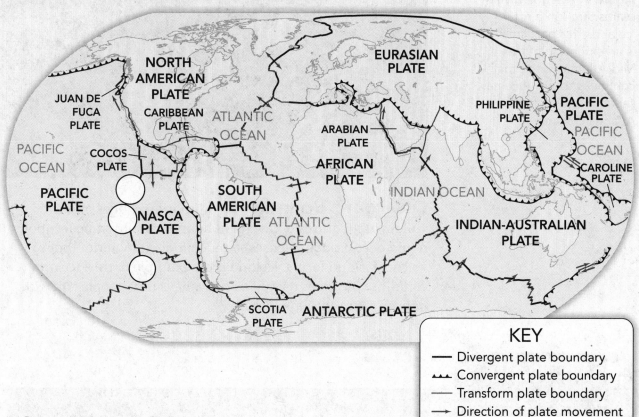

**KEY**
— Divergent plate boundary
⌃⌃⌃ Convergent plate boundary
— Transform plate boundary
→ Direction of plate movement

# Plate Boundaries

Earth's plates meet and interact at boundaries. Along each boundary, plates move in one of three ways. Plates move apart, or diverge, from each other at a **divergent boundary** (dy VUR junt). Plates come together, or converge, at a **convergent boundary** (kun VER junt). Plates slip past each other along a **transform boundary**. The interactions of plates at boundaries produce great changes on land and on the ocean floor. These changes include the formation of volcanoes, mountain ranges, and deep-ocean trenches. Earthquakes and the triggering of tsunamis are also more common at or near plate boundaries. **Figure 6** depicts the major tectonic plates and the types of boundaries between them.

✓ **READING CHECK Integrate With Visuals** Which of the plates from the map would be a good starting point for a diagram that summarizes the different boundaries? Why?

......................................................................

......................................................................

## Literacy Connection

**Integrate With Visuals**
In your science notebook, draw sketches of the different interactions at plate boundaries. Work toward a visual presentation that summarizes the plate boundaries in a single diagram.

👆 **INTERACTIVITY**

Explore surface features associated with plate movement at different locations around the world.

**VIDEO**

Learn about the tectonic plate boundary types.

## Iceland

**Figure 7** A scuba diver swims through a rift in Iceland. This particular rift is an extension of the Mid-Atlantic Ridge that continues to produce new seafloor and widen the Atlantic Ocean.

**Divergent Boundaries** Mid-ocean ridges and rift valleys are features of divergent boundaries. In some locations, a mid-ocean ridge releases so much molten material that a volcanic island forms. Iceland is an example of this. Iceland contains volcanoes as well as rift valleys that people can walk or even swim through (**Figure 7**).

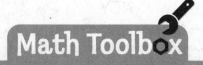

# Math Toolbox

## Rates of Plate Movement

Earth scientists measure plate movement by using the Global Positioning System (GPS) of satellites. Receivers anchored in Earth's surface receive signals from satellites, and calculate their positions using the time it takes for signals to be received. Over time, changes in those signal times indicate plate movement.

**1. Reason Quantitatively** Evidence from GPS readings suggests that the Mid-Atlantic Ridge spreads about 2.5 cm per year. How fast is the North American Plate moving away from the ridge? Explain your answer.

.................................................................

.................................................................

.................................................................

.................................................................

.................................................................

.................................................................

**2. SEP Use Mathematics** The Pacific Plate moves to the northwest at an average rate of 10 cm per year. Hawaii is in the middle of the Pacific Plate, 6,600 kilometers southeast of Japan, which is on the edge of several adjacent plates. If the Pacific Plate continues to move at the same rate and in the same direction, when will Hawaii collide with Japan? Show your work.

.................................................................

.................................................................

.................................................................

.................................................................

## Convergent Boundaries

**Convergent Boundaries** A boundary where two plates collide, or move toward each other, is called a convergent boundary. If two continents collide, then a mountain range is pushed up. This is how the Himalayas formed, and are still being pushed up. What is now India used to be a separate continent that broke away from Antarctica and headed north. It began colliding with Asia more than 60 million years ago, and the edges of the two plates folded like the hoods of two cars in a head-on collision (**Figure 8**). Mount Everest and the rest of the Himalayas are the result.

If one or both plates are oceanic, then subduction occurs. The ocean plate always subducts if it collides with a continent. If two oceanic plates collide, the older, colder, and denser plate usually subducts beneath the younger plate, with an ocean trench marking the plate boundary. As the subducting plate sinks back into the mantle, water that was in the ocean crust rises into the overlying mantle, lowering its melting point. Magma forms and rises up through the overlying plate, producing volcanoes. On land, this results in the formation of volcanic mountains. Mountains can also form as ocean seafloor sediments are scraped onto the edge of the overlying plate, forming a large wedge of rock.

Under the sea, subduction produces undersea volcanoes, also known as seamounts. If they grow tall enough, these volcanoes form a volcanic island chain. This is why there are often chains of volcanic islands where convergent boundaries exist in the ocean.

HANDS-ON LAB

☑**Investigate** Explore different plate interactions.

### Collision at a Convergent Boundary

**Figure 8** When two continental plates collide, their collision can have a crumpling effect on the crust that produces tall mountains, just as when two cars crash in a head-on collision. If one plate is denser, such as a plate of oceanic crust, that denser plate will dive under the other. This can also produce mountains as the overlying plate edge is nudged upward.

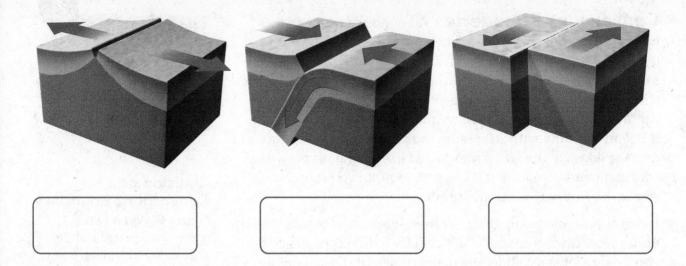

```
┌─────────────────┐   ┌─────────────────┐   ┌─────────────────┐
│                 │   │                 │   │                 │
└─────────────────┘   └─────────────────┘   └─────────────────┘
```

## Types of Plate Boundaries

**Figure 9** 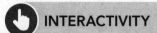 The three types of plate boundaries are modeled here. Label each illustration with the term that describes the boundary.

### ☞ INTERACTIVITY

Investigate how stress is built up and released at faults.

**Transform Boundaries** Plates slide past each other at a transform boundary. Earthquakes occur here on faults called transform faults. Bending across a fault occurs when the two sides remain locked together. When enough stress builds up, the fault ruptures and an earthquake occurs. This is what causes earthquakes along transform faults such as the San Andreas Fault in California. In some cases a surface feature (such as a stream or road) that crossed a fault is visibly offset after a major slippage of the plates. Depending on how the plate edges match up, a vertical offset can exist across the fault.

Keep in mind that the tectonic plates of Earth's lithosphere are three-dimensional objects that are moving around a sphere. The shapes of the plates are irregular. This means every plate has some mixture of the different types of boundaries, and at some point the boundaries may change as the plates shrink, grow, collide, slip past each other, subduct, and so on. Interactions among tectonic plates continue to reshape Earth's surface features.

☑ READING CHECK **Summarize Text** What happens at divergent, convergent, and transform boundaries?

.........................................................................................................................

.........................................................................................................................

.........................................................................................................................

MS-ESS2-2

1. **Compare and Contrast** At what type of plate boundary would you find a rift valley that is growing wider?

........................................................................

2. **SEP Interpret Data** Describe what is going on in this diagram.

........................................................................

........................................................................

........................................................................

........................................................................

........................................................................

3. **CCC Cause and Effect** What other surface feature that is not shown in the diagram could be produced as a result of the process shown?

........................................................................

4. **SEP Use Mathematics** It takes 100,000 years for a plate to move about 2 kilometers. What is that plate's rate of motion in centimeters per year?

........................................................................

5. **Connect to Nature of Science** What does the theory of plate tectonics have that Wegener's hypothesis of continental drift did not have?

........................................................................

........................................................................

........................................................................

........................................................................

........................................................................

........................................................................

........................................................................

........................................................................

## Quest CHECK-IN

**In this lesson, you learned about the specific mechanisms by which plates move and how interactions of tectonic plates affect Earth's surface.**

**SEP Construct Explanations** What's the connection between Mount Rainier and the plate boundaries along the coast of the Pacific Northwest?

........................................................................

........................................................................

........................................................................

........................................................................

### ☞ INTERACTIVITY

Mount Rainier's Threat

**Go online** to learn how Mount Rainier and other volcanic mountains in the Cascade Range formed as a result of geologic activity at tectonic plate boundaries.

175

# AUSTRALIA on the Move

Located on one of the world's fastest moving tectonic plates—the Australian Plate—Australia is moving about 7 centimeters north, and slightly east, each year.

## A Kangaroo's Length
The movement of Australia requires updates to its official location on maps. In 2017, it moved 1.5 meters north. This is about the length of a gray kangaroo.

Australia's plate, of course, is not the only moving plate on Earth. But each of the planet's plates moves at a different rate. Most move at a rate of a few centimeters a year. At 7 centimeters a year, Australia is one of the fastest.

In the 1960s, geologists confirmed that tectonic plates move along Earth's mantle. But only recently, with the help of computer modeling, have they come to understand why the plates move at different speeds. As a plate sinks into the mantle at a subduction zone, it pulls along the rest of the plate. It's similar to what happens to all the dishes and glasses on a dinner table when you pull the tablecloth down on one side. The size and structure of the subduction zone influence the strength of this pull. A large plate edge that is descending into the mantle at a large subduction zone would exert more force on the rest of the plate.

## Measuring Movement
No one can feel the plates moving. They move only about as fast as your fingernails grow. But the movement adds up. In 50 million years, the Australian Plate could collide with Southeast Asia.

Over time, the continent's movement means that Australia's latitude and longitude on older maps no longer match the actual location of the continent. Maps require corrections to compensate for Australia's movement.

Australia has officially changed its location four times in the last 50 years. At the beginning of 2017, Australia changed its location once again, this time moving it another 1.5 meters (about 5 feet) north.

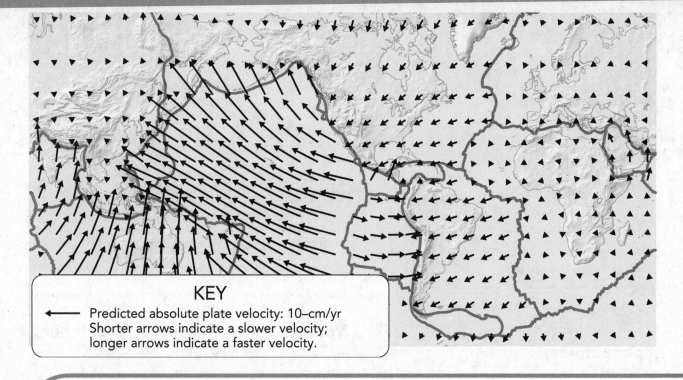

**KEY**

← Predicted absolute plate velocity: 10–cm/yr
Shorter arrows indicate a slower velocity;
longer arrows indicate a faster velocity.

**Use this map and Figure 6 in Lesson 2 to answer the following questions.**

1. **Summarize** What factors affect the speed at which a tectonic plate moves?

2. **Interpret Data** Which plate is moving fastest? Cite evidence to justify your answer.

3. **Apply Concepts** Would you expect a largely oceanic plate to move faster than a largely continental plate? Explain.

4. **Construct Explanations** The Australian and Pacific plates are among the fastest-moving plates. What conclusions can you draw about the subduction zone where the Australian Plate meets the Pacific Plate? Use evidence from the text and the map to support your explanation.

# Earthquakes and Tsunami Hazards

## Guiding Questions

- How do plate movement and stress produce new landforms?
- What are earthquakes and tsunamis, and why do they occur?
- How can the effects of earthquakes and tsunamis be mitigated?

## Connections

**Literacy** Evaluate Media

**Math** Analyze Graphs

MS-ESS2-2, MS-ESS3-2

## HANDS-ON LAB

**ʜInvestigate** Analyze data and interpret patterns to predict future earthquakes.

## Vocabulary

stress
tension
compression
shearing
fault
earthquake
magnitude
tsunami

## Academic Vocabulary

scale

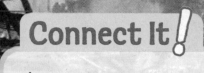

## Connect It!

✎ **Circle and label evidence that a tsunami occurred.**

CCC Cause and Effect How did the ship come to rest on land?

............................................................................................................

............................................................................................................

............................................................................................................

# Stress and Earth's Crust

The movement of Earth's massive tectonic plates generates tremendous force. This force can bend and break the rock of Earth's crust. The force that acts on rock to change its shape or volume is called **stress**. There are three kinds of stress. **Tension** pulls on Earth's crust, stretching the rock to make it thinner, especially at the point halfway between the two pulling forces. **Compression** squeezes rock until it bends or breaks. When compression occurs at a large scale, rock can be folded into mountains. **Shearing** occurs when rock is being pushed in two opposite directions, to the point that it bends or breaks. These types of stress can produce both folds and faults. Movement of Earth's crust around faults can produce destructive earthquakes and, in some cases, tsunamis **(Figure 1)**.

**Make Meaning** As you go through the lesson, keep notes in your science notebook about how the physical stresses described here are involved in processes that produce earthquakes and tsunamis.

**Tsunami Damage**
**Figure 1** In 2011, a major tsunami engulfed parts of Japan, killing thousands and destroying property.

## Death Valley

**Figure 2** Tension can result in peaks around a sunken valley, such as Death Valley in California.

## Types of Faults

**Figure 3** ✏ SEP Develop Models The three types of faults are shown here. Complete diagrams A and B by labeling the hanging walls and footwalls. In Diagram C, draw arrows to indicate the direction of shearing force and the movement along the fault.

### Normal Fault

A **fault** is a break in the rock of Earth's crust or mantle. Most faults occur along plate boundaries, where stress of one or more types is deforming the rock, leading to changes at Earth's surface (**Figure 2**). The two sides of a fault are referred to as walls. The wall whose rock is over the other is called the hanging wall, and the other is called the footwall. In a normal fault, the hanging wall slips down relative to the footwall (**Figure 3A**). This usually occurs at a divergent plate boundary, where tension is pulling the plates away from each other. If there is a series of normal faults, a slab of crust that falls away can become a valley while the adjacent slabs can become mountains.

### Reverse Fault

Compression can produce a reverse fault, in which the hanging wall slides up and over the footwall (**Figure 3B**). The northern Rocky Mountains were gradually lifted by the action at several reverse faults. Reverse faults are common at convergent boundaries.

### Strike-Slip Fault

California's San Andreas Fault is a product of shearing. Walls of rock grind past each other in opposite directions, making a strike-slip fault (**Figure 3C**). Transform boundaries are home to strike-slip faults.

☑ **READING CHECK** **Determine Central Ideas** Pair each fault type with the type of stress that produces it.

.................................................................................

.................................................................................

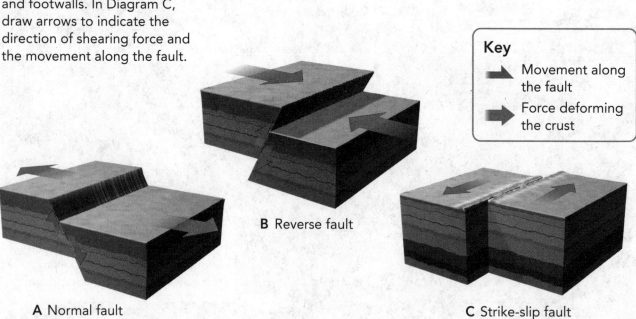

**Key**
→ Movement along the fault
→ Force deforming the crust

**A** Normal fault

**B** Reverse fault

**C** Strike-slip fault

## Valleys and Mountains

**Figure 4** As tension pulls rock apart along normal faults, some blocks fall, leaving others elevated. Over time, the resulting mountains weather.

Rift valley

Fault-block mountains

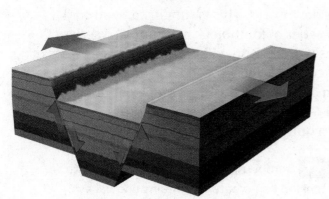

# New Landforms From Plate Movement

Over millions of years, the forces of plate movement can change a flat plain into folded mountains, fault-block mountains, and other dramatic features of Earth's surface.

**Tension and Normal Faults** To see how tension and normal faults produce mountains, we need to zoom out and look at a series of at least two normal faults. Where two plates move away from each other, tension forms numerous faults that run parallel to each other over a wide area. A wedge of rock that has hanging walls at both faults drops down as tension pulls the adjacent footwalls away to form a rift valley (**Figure 4**). This leaves the other blocks higher up, as mountains. Mountains built this way are called fault-block mountains.

**Folding** Compression within a plate causes the crust to deform without breaking. Folds are bends in rock that form when compression shortens and thickens Earth's crust. Folds may be centimeters across or they may span many kilometers. The folds are often most visible and obvious when the rock is layered. When folding occurs on a large **scale,** folds that bend upward become mountains and folds that bend downward become valleys.

**Academic Vocabulary**

The processes of plate tectonics occur at different scales of time and space. List some different terms that are used to describe distance and time at vastly different scales.

....................................................

....................................................

....................................................

## Folded Mountain

**Figure 5** Formations at the Hong Kong UNESCO Global Geopark reveal distinct folding patterns.

## Anticlines and Synclines

A fold in rock that bends upward into an arch is called an anticline (AN tih klyn). This may resemble the crest of a wave, as seen in **Figure 5**. Weathering and erosion have shaped many large-scale anticlines into mountains. The height of an anticline is exaggerated by the valley-like syncline (SIN klyn), which is a fold that bends downward. This is similar to the trough of a wave. Like a series of fault-block mountains, a series of folded mountains is often marked by valleys between rows of mountains. Viewed at a large scale, a wide area of compressed crust may have mountains and valleys made of anticlines and synclines (**Figure 6**), while the large-scale folds may themselves contain their own anticlines and synclines.

☑ **READING CHECK** **Summarize Text** Describe how both compression and tension can create mountains and valleys.

.............................................................................................................

.............................................................................................................

.............................................................................................................

.............................................................................................................

## Anticlines and Synclines as Mountains and Valleys

**Figure 6** ✐ Label the anticlines and synclines in the diagram.

**SEP Evaluate Information** How does this figure oversimplify how compression produces folds in Earth's crust?

.............................................................................................................

.............................................................................................................

.............................................................................................................

# Earthquakes

Some plate interactions are gradual, quiet, and almost imperceptible. Others can be sudden, violent, loud, and destructive. At some faults, the plates may grind to a halt and remain stuck in place for years. Stress builds up until the plates lurch into motion, releasing a great amount of energy. The shaking and trembling that results from this plate movement is an **earthquake**. Some of the energy released in an earthquake is in the form of seismic waves.

HANDS-ON LAB

**Investigate** Analyze data and interpret patterns to predict future earthquakes.

**Seismic Waves** Similar to sound waves, seismic waves are vibrations that travel through Earth carrying energy released by various processes, such as earthquakes, ocean storms, and volcanic eruptions. There are three types of seismic waves, as shown in **Figure 7.** The waves begin at the earthquake's focus, where rock that was under stress begins to break or move. Waves may strike quickest and with the most energy at the point on Earth's surface directly above the earthquake's focus, called the epicenter. But seismic waves also move in all directions, through and across Earth's interior and surface. When seismic waves pass from one material to another, they can change speeds and directions.

## P and S Waves
**Figure 7** 🖉 SEP Develop Models The motion of particles in Earth's surface is shown for P waves and S waves. Draw the particle motion for the surface waves.

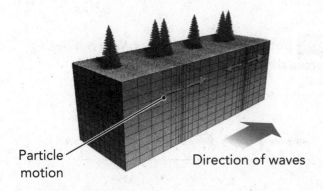

Particle motion        Direction of waves

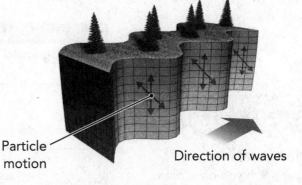

Particle motion        Direction of waves

P waves, short for primary waves, travel the fastest. They are the first to arrive at a location on Earth's surface. P waves compress and expand the ground.

S waves, short for secondary waves, travel more slowly so they arrive after P waves. S waves can move the ground side to side or up and down, relative to the direction in which they travel.

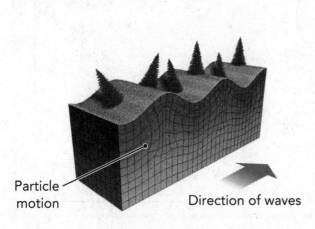

Particle motion        Direction of waves

Surface waves can form when P waves and S waves reach Earth's surface. The result can be a kind of rolling motion, like ocean waves, where particles move in a pattern that is almost circular. Surface waves damage structures on the surface.

## Seismogram

**Figure 8** The surface waves that travel along Earth's surface usually have the largest amplitudes and therefore cause the most damage.

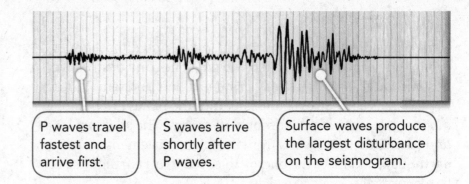

P waves travel fastest and arrive first.

S waves arrive shortly after P waves.

Surface waves produce the largest disturbance on the seismogram.

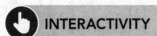

**INTERACTIVITY**

Analyze seismic waves to locate an earthquake.

**Seismographs** Seismic waves produced by earthquakes are measured by a device called a seismograph, or seismometer. This device converts the energy in the different waves to a visual called a seismogram **(Figure 8)**. The seismogram shows the timing of the different seismic waves, with the relatively gentle P and S waves arriving first, followed by surface waves with larger amplitudes. The amplitudes, or heights, of the waves on a seismogram are used to quantify the size of the earthquake.

When an earthquake occurs, geologists use data from seismograph stations in different locations to pinpoint the earthquake's epicenter **(Figure 9)**. Locating the epicenter helps geologists to identify areas where earthquakes may occur in the future.

**READING CHECK** **Determine Central Ideas** Why is it helpful for geologists to locate the epicenters of earthquakes?

....................................................................................................................

....................................................................................................................

## Model It

### Triangulation

**Figure 9** If you have data from three seismograph stations, you can locate the precise location of an earthquake's epicenter. The center of each circle is the location of a station. The radius of each circle is the distance from the epicenter. The point where the three circles overlap is the location of the epicenter.

**SEP Analyze Data** ✎ Draw an X on the map to indicate the epicenter of the earthquake.

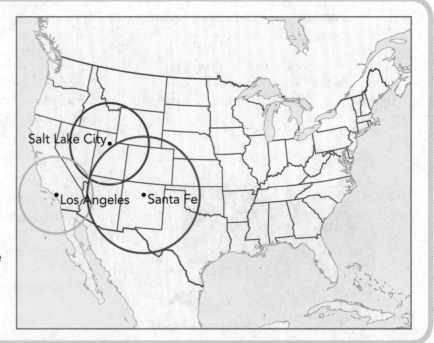

# Math Toolbox

## Finding an Epicenter

Geologists are trying to locate the epicenter of an earthquake. The data table below shows the arrival times of seismic waves at three different stations across Earth's surface. Use the graph to answer the questions.

| Station | P Wave Arrival Time | S Wave Arrival Time | Distance from Epicenter (km) |
|---------|---------------------|---------------------|------------------------------|
| A | 4 mins, 6 s | 7 mins, 25 s | |
| B | 6 mins, 58 s | 12 mins, 36 s | |
| C | 9 mins, 21 s | 16 mins, 56 s | |

1. **Analyze Graphs** Use the graph to determine the distance of each station from the epicenter. Record the distances in the table.

2. **SEP Interpret Data** If another station is 5,000 km from the epicenter of the earthquake, about how long after the start of the earthquake would the S waves have arrived at this station?

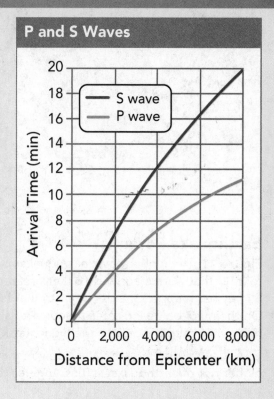

**P and S Waves**

Legend: — S wave, — P wave

Y-axis: Arrival Time (min)
X-axis: Distance from Epicenter (km)

---

## Magnitude
An earthquake's **magnitude** is a single number that geologists use to assign to an earthquake based on the earthquake's size. The size of an earthquake is usually measured using the moment magnitude scale, which is a measure of the energy released. Each whole-number increase in this scale represents a roughly 32-fold increase in energy. So, the seismic waves of a magnitude-9 earthquake are 10 times larger than for a magnitude-8 earthquake. The energy released, however, is 32 times greater **(Figure 10)**.

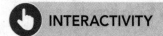

**INTERACTIVITY**

Explore technologies that help make buildings earthquake resistant.

| Magnitude | Location | Date |
|-----------|----------|------|
| 9.2 | Sumatra | 2004 |
| 9.0 | Japan | 2011 |
| 7.9 | China | 2008 |
| 7.9 | Nepal | 2015 |
| 7.0 | Haiti | 2010 |

**Earthquake Magnitude**

**Figure 10** The table shows the moment magnitudes of some large earthquakes.

CCC Scale, Proportion, and Quantity How much more energy was released by the earthquake in China than the one in Haiti?

185

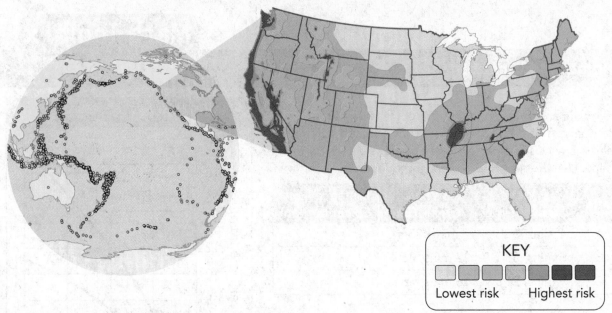

## Earthquake Potential

**Figure 11** The globe shows earthquakes occurring from 2007 to 2017 that were magnitude 6.0 or greater. The U.S. Geological Survey has mapped the risk of earthquakes in the United States. On the map, beige indicates the lowest risk of earthquakes occurring, while purple indicates the highest risk.

**KEY**

Lowest risk    Highest risk

**CCC Cause and Effect** What do you think accounts for the higher risk of earthquakes in Los Angeles than in Chicago?

.............................................................................................

.............................................................................................

**Connect to Society** What societal need would wider use of technology for forecasting earthquakes address?

.............................................................................................

### Literacy Connection

**Evaluate Media** ✎
Identify an area of the U.S. earthquake risk map in **Figure 11** that does not fit the pattern of earthquake occurrences described on this page. Circle the area.

**INTERACTIVITY**

Help determine the best location for a new stadium in an earthquake zone.

# Earthquake Risks and Tsunamis

The "Ring of Fire" around the Pacific Ocean is where many of the world's earthquakes occur. There are many plate boundaries around the Pacific, including convergent and transform boundaries where stress builds up. Because the west coast of the United States, including Alaska, is on the edge of several boundaries, the western states have a much higher risk of experiencing an earthquake than other regions of the U.S., as shown in **Figure 11**. Earthquakes themselves can cause tremendous damage, but if they occur near or below the ocean floor they can produce another type of disaster.

**Ocean Floor Uplift** When an area of Earth's crust moves during an earthquake, it can force anything above it to move as well. For example, an area of off-shore ocean floor that has been stressed for years at a convergent plate boundary can suddenly pop up, thrusting up the ocean water above it. Depending on how the water is moved, a tsunami may form.

A **tsunami** is a wave or series of waves produced by an earthquake or landslide. Unlike typical ocean waves formed by the wind, tsunami waves can involve the entire water column—every drop between the surface and the ocean floor—and this means they can carry tremendous energy and can be highly destructive **(Figure 12)**. In 2004, hundreds of thousands of people lost their lives due to a tsunami that struck Indonesia, Thailand, Sri Lanka, and other coastal nations around the Indian Ocean. That tsunami travelled across the Indian Ocean at a speed of 800 kilometers per hour.

**Landslides** Ocean floor uplift is one cause of tsunamis. Landslides are another. In both cases, some kind of displacement of water occurs, setting the tsunami in motion. In 1958, an earthquake triggered a landslide on a mountainside on the shore of Lituya Bay, Alaska. About 30 million cubic meters of rock tumbled into the water at one end of the bay, producing a tsunami that swept across the bay and splashed as high as 524 meters up along the steep shoreline **(Figure 13)**.

☑ READING CHECK How can an earthquake or landslide produce a tsunami?

................................................................................

................................................................................

................................................................................

**A Wall of Water**
**Figure 12** A tsunami does not always look like a wave. In some cases it is more like a sudden, massive rise in sea level, which simply floods low-lying areas.

**Tsunami Hazards**
**Figure 13** The site of the rockslide that produced the tsunami in Lituya Bay is marked by the circle.

SEP Cite Evidence 🖉
Draw lines to indicate where the water splashed up and tore away plants and sediment from the bay's shore.

# ☑ LESSON 3 Check

**1. Identify** Which type of stress on Earth's crust can make a slab of rock shorter and thicker?

...................................................................

**2. SEP Construct Explanations** How do mountains and valleys form through folding?

...................................................................

...................................................................

...................................................................

...................................................................

...................................................................

**3. SEP Explain Phenomena** You hear about a magnitude 8.0 earthquake on the news. Someone says "That doesn't sound too bad. An 8.0 is just one more than the 7.0 we had here last year." Explain why that's not the right way to think about the moment magnitude scale.

...................................................................

...................................................................

...................................................................

...................................................................

**4. CCC Cause and Effect** A news bulletin reports a powerful earthquake 200 kilometers off the coast of California. Hours later, there's no sign of any tsunami anywhere on the West Coast. Why not?

...................................................................

...................................................................

...................................................................

...................................................................

**5. CCC Stability and Change** Describe the roll that stress plays in the production of earthquakes and tsunamis.

...................................................................

...................................................................

...................................................................

...................................................................

...................................................................

...................................................................

...................................................................

...................................................................

...................................................................

## Quest CHECK-INS

**In this lesson, you learned about the connection between plate tectonics and features and events at Earth's surface, including mountains and earthquakes.**

Evaluate How can monitoring Earth for seismic activity near plate boundaries be useful in monitoring volcanoes?

...................................................................

...................................................................

...................................................................

...................................................................

...................................................................

...................................................................

👆 **INTERACTIVITY**

Monitoring a Volcano

**Go online** to practice several data collection and analysis techniques to monitor a volcano and predict an eruption.

MS-ESS3-2

# DESIGNING TO PREVENT
# Destruction

▶ VIDEO

Watch how underwater earthquakes displace water.

**How do you design** buildings that can withstand the forceful waves of a tsunami? You engineer it!

**The Challenge:** To construct tsunami-safe buildings.

**Phenomenon** A seafloor earthquake can displace water above it, causing a tsunami to form. When the tsunami reaches land, giant waves cause widespread destruction.

Because parts of the United States are at risk for tsunamis, U.S. engineers have developed new building standards to save lives. They studied new design concepts. Strong columns enable buildings to stand, even when battered by tons of water and debris. Exits on upper floors allow people to get out when lower floors are flooded.

To develop standards, engineers visited Japan, where an earthquake and tsunami in 2011 caused terrible losses of life and property. The engineers also used wave research to model tsunamis and their impact on buildings.

These engineers hope that hospitals, schools, and police stations, if built to the new standards, can then provide shelter for people fleeing danger.

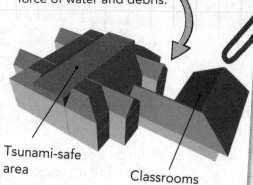

It is a challenge to design and engineer structures that can withstand the force of a tsunami. Under the new standards, schools would be built to withstand the force of water and debris.

Tsunami-safe area

Classrooms

**DESIGN CHALLENGE** Can you design a structure that will withstand the force of a tsunami? Go to the Engineering Design Notebook to find out!

# Volcanoes and Earth's Surface

## Guiding Questions

- How is plate tectonics connected to volcanic eruptions and landforms?
- What role does volcanic activity play in shaping Earth's surface?
- What hazards do different types of volcanoes pose?

## Connections

**Literacy** Integrate With Visuals

**Math** Analyze Proportional Relationships

MS-ESS2-2, MS-ESS3-2

## HANDS-ON LAB

**uInvestigate** Explore moving volcanoes.

### Vocabulary

volcano
magma
lava
hot spot
extinct
dormant

### Academic Vocabulary

active
composite

## Connect It!

✏ Circle and label effects that the volcano in the photo is having on Earth's surface and atmosphere.

CCC Systems List the effects that you identified in the photo, and categorize them by the Earth system that is affected—hydrosphere, atmosphere, geosphere, biosphere.

........................................................................................

........................................................................................

........................................................................................

# Volcanoes

While active volcanoes are found in a relatively small number of states in the U.S., they have a profound impact on Earth's surface—especially at plate boundaries. Volcanoes add new material to Earth's surface, release gases into the atmosphere, build new islands in the ocean, and shape habitats for organisms. A **volcano** is a structure that forms in Earth's crust when molten material, or magma, reaches Earth's surface. This can occur on land or on the ocean floor. **Magma** is a molten mixture of rock-forming substances, gases, and water from the mantle. Once magma reaches the surface, it is known as **lava**. When lava cools, it forms solid rock.

As with earthquakes, there is a pattern to where volcanoes occur on Earth. Most are found at convergent or divergent plate boundaries, but they can also occur at seemingly random places far from plate boundaries.

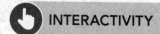

**INTERACTIVITY**

Explore how an erupting volcano might change Earth's surface.

**Volcanism**

**Figure 1** The activity of volcanoes is called volcanism. Eruptions that release lava and other matter from Earth's interior can pose hazards to organisms, including humans.

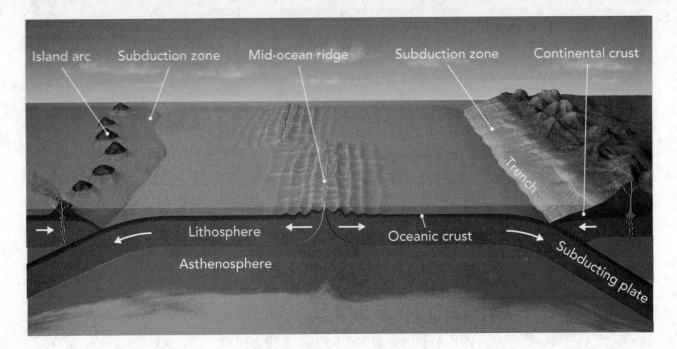

Island arc  Subduction zone  Mid-ocean ridge  Subduction zone  Continental crust

Trench

Lithosphere

Asthenosphere

Oceanic crust

Subducting plate

**HANDS-ON LAB**

**Investigate** Explore
moving volcanoes.

# Volcanoes and Plate Boundaries

At convergent boundaries, the subduction of an oceanic plate
under a continental plate can produce volcanoes along the
edge of the continent. Subduction of an oceanic plate under an
adjacent oceanic plate can result in a volcanic island arc. At
divergent boundaries, molten magma comes through the crust
as lava, which quickly hardens into rock, but if the volume of
magma is especially large, then a volcanic cone may form.
**Figure 2** summarizes these processes.

**At Divergent Boundaries** Volcanoes form at
divergent boundaries when plates move apart and rock
rises to fill the vacant space. Most volcanoes at divergent
boundaries occur in the ocean at mid-ocean ridges, so they
are never seen. Only in places such as Iceland can you see
ocean-ridge volcanoes. Less common are volcanoes like Mt.
Kilimanjaro that occur at continental divergent boundaries
such as the East African Rift.

**At Convergent Boundaries** When a plate dives into
the mantle in the process of subduction, trapped water leaves
the sinking plate and mixes with the material of the overlying
mantle, causing it to melt. The buoyant magma starts to rise
toward the surface. If the magma reaches the surface before
cooling, a volcano forms. If the overlying plate is part of
the ocean floor, the resulting volcano begins to form on the
seafloor as a seamount. If it grows large enough to break the
ocean surface, it becomes a volcanic island. A whole chain
of islands may form when volcanism occurs at multiple spots
along the edge of an oceanic plate. This is called a volcanic
island arc.

## Hot Spot Volcanism

**Hot Spot Volcanism** In addition to divergent and convergent plate boundaries, there is a third source of volcanoes: hot spots. A **hot spot** is an area where lava frequently erupts at the surface, independent of plate boundary processes. Most hot spots sit atop mantle plumes of hot rock. Hot spot plumes are fixed within the deep mantle. As a plate moves over the plume, a chain of volcanoes is created because older volcanoes keep being carried away from the hot spot. The many islands and seamounts of Hawaii have formed from the westward motion of the Pacific Plate, as is illustrated in **Figure 3**. Another hot spot is found at Yellowstone National Park in Wyoming. The "supervolcano" beneath the park may erupt again someday. During past giant eruptions of Yellowstone, the last one being 640,000 years ago, most of North America was covered with volcanic ash.

 **VIDEO**

Learn more about volcanology.

✔️ **READING CHECK** **Determine Conclusions** The Aleutian Islands of Alaska occur in a chain near a plate boundary. What type of boundary is it?

....................................................................................................

## Model It

### Hot Spot Modeling

**Figure 3** The Hawaiian Islands have formed from the movement of the Pacific Plate over a hot spot plume.

**Integrate With Visuals**
🖊️ Using the diagram as inspiration, design a functioning physical model of how a hot spot makes volcanoes on the ocean crust of a moving plate. Sketch or describe your model in the space here, including details on how it would work.

## Composite Volcano

**Figure 4** ✏ A composite volcano has alternating layers of hardened lava and ash.

**SEP Develop Models** Complete the diagram by reading the description of the volcano's parts and writing in the missing labels.

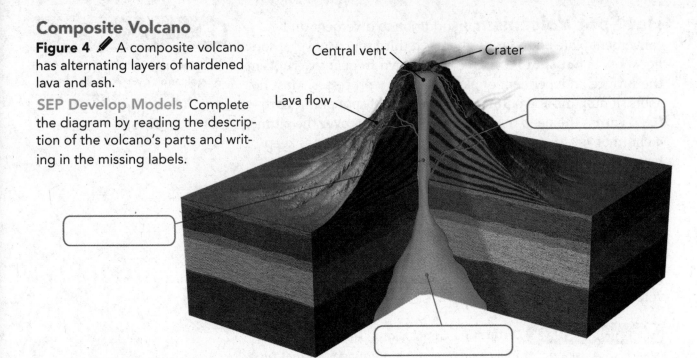

Central vent    Crater

Lava flow

## Literacy Connection

**Integrate With Visuals**
Use the diagram of the volcano to help you understand the text on this page.

## Academic Vocabulary

*Composite* refers to something made of a mixture of different parts or elements. Many manufactured objects are made of composites—blends of different raw materials. How does this help you to understand what a composite volcano is?

........................................................

........................................................

........................................................

........................................................

# Volcano Landforms

Magma usually forms in the layer of hot rock in the upper mantle. Because magma is less dense than the rock around it, it cracks on its way up to the surface. Once the magma exits a volcano and is exposed to air or water, it is called lava.

**Volcano Parts** Inside a volcano (**Figure 4**) is a system of passageways through which magma travels. Below the volcano is a magma chamber, where magma collects before an eruption. The volcano and surrounding landscape may swell slightly as the magma chamber fills. Magma moves up from the chamber through a pipe, which leads to the central vent—an opening at the top, which may be in a bowl-shaped crater. Some volcanoes have side vents, too. When lava flows out from a vent, it begins to cool and harden as it is pulled by gravity down the slope of the volcano. If lava is thrown explosively into the air, it hardens and falls to Earth in different forms. Bombs are large chunks of hardened lava. Cinders are the size of pebbles. The finest particles are called ash. The type of lava-based material that emerges from a new volcano defines the type of volcano that is built.

**Volcano Types** The volcano in **Figure 4** is a **composite** volcano. Also called a stratovolcano, it is made of alternating layers of lava flows and ash falls. These tend to be cone-shaped and tall. Mount Fuji in Japan is an example of a composite volcano. Other types of volcanic formations are shown in **Figure 5**.

# Volcanic Formations

**Figure 5** Volcanic activity can result in different landforms.

1. **Compare and Contrast** How are shield volcanoes and lava plateaus similar? How are they different?

........................................................

........................................................

........................................................

2. **SEP Develop Models** ✏️ Review the three steps of caldera formation. Finish the sentence to describe the second phase of caldera formation.

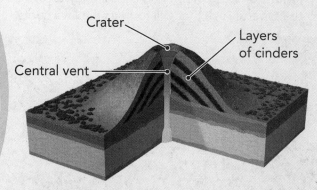

Crater

Layers of cinders

Central vent

**Cinder Cone Volcano** If lava emerges from a new vent in Earth's crust as a mix of bombs, ash, and cinders, these materials build up into a cinder cone volcano. The loose, ashy material tends to erode quickly.

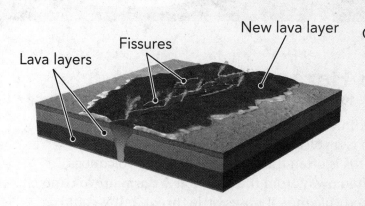

Lava layers

Fissures

New lava layer

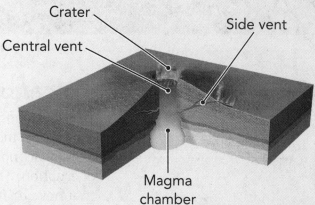

Crater

Side vent

Central vent

Magma chamber

**Lava Plateau** Lava can flow out of several long cracks in Earth's crust and flood an area repeatedly over many years. Over time, these relatively flat layers of hardened lava build up into a lava plateau.

**Shield Volcano** Some volcanoes have slow, steady eruptions in which lava flows out and builds up over a broad area. Hot spot volcanoes tend to be shield volcanoes, and they can be massive.

**Caldera** A caldera forms when a volcano collapses on itself.

❶   ❷   ❸

Large eruptions empty the main vent and magma chamber of the volcano.

Lacking support,

.........................................................

.........................................................

A lake fills the caldera. Later eruptions form a small cone.

## Lava from Quiet Eruptions

**Figure 6** The content and consistency of lava determines the type of rock that will form as the lava cools.

**INTERACTIVITY**

Explore different volcanic landforms.

**Academic Vocabulary**

What does it mean if you have an active lifestyle?

........................................................

........................................................

........................................................

# Volcano Hazards

Volcanoes pose different hazards to humans and other organisms, mainly through eruptions. An **extinct**, or dead, volcano is a volcano that poses very little threat of eruption. This is often the case with hot-spot volcanoes that have drifted away from the hot spot. A **dormant** volcano is like a sleeping volcano—it poses little threat, but it could reawaken someday. **Active** volcanoes are the more immediate threat. Volcanologists classify eruptions as quiet or explosive. Whether an eruption is quiet or explosive depends in part on the magma's silica content and whether the magma is thin and runny or thick and sticky. Temperature helps determine how runny magma is.

**Quiet Eruptions** If the magma in a volcano's magma chamber is hot or low in silica, it will erupt quietly. The lava will be thin and runny, and trapped gases will bubble out gently. The consistency of the lava that emerges during a quiet eruption will affect how it looks and feels when it cools, as shown in **Figure 6**.

The Hawaiian Islands continue to be produced mostly by quiet eruptions. Quiet eruptions are not necessarily safe. For example, the Hawaii Volcanoes National Park's visitors center was threatened in 1989 by a lava flow from Mount Kilauea.

**Explosive Eruptions** Magma that has a lot of silica will erupt more than magma containing little or no silica. High-silica magma is thick and sticky, causing it to build up in a pipe until pressure is so great that it bursts out over the surface. Trapped gases explode out instead of bubbling out gently. An explosion with that much force can hurl lava, ash, cinders, and bombs high into the atmosphere.

Krakatau, a volcano in a large volcanic arc in Indonesia, erupted in 1883. The eruption, depicted in **Figure 7**, was so violent that much of the the visible part of the island collapsed into the sea, producing a tsunami that killed 36,000 people. Gas and debris billowed more than 25 kilometers into the sky, and the sound from the explosion was heard 4,500 kilometers away. So much ash and sulfur dioxide was emitted into the atmosphere by the eruption that global temperatures were cooler for the following five years.

**Krakatau Explodes**

**Figure 7** The eruption of Krakatau was a major disaster in Indonesia, but it affected the entire world as ash and sulfur dioxide entered the atmosphere.

# Math Toolbox

## Magma Composition

Magma is classified according to the amount of silica it contains. The less silica the magma contains, the more easily it flows. More silica makes magma stickier and thicker. Trapped gases can't emerge easily, so eruptions are explosive.

1. **Analyze Proportional Relationships**
   How do the two magma types compare in terms of silica content?

   ........................................................................

   ........................................................................

2. **SEP Construct Explanations** Which of the magma types would erupt more explosively? How would knowing the type of magma a volcano produces help nearby communities prepare for eruptions?

   ........................................................................

   ........................................................................

   ........................................................................

   ........................................................................

**Types of Magma**

Low-Silica
Silica 50%
Other oxides 47.5%
All other solids 2.5%

High-Silica
Silica 70%
Other oxides 27.5%
All other solids 2.5%

## Measuring Gas Concentration

**Figure 8** This device, called a spectrometer, can measure concentrations of volcanic gases by measuring how light passes through them. A high concentration of sulfur dioxide may mean an eruption is likely to occur.

 **INTERACTIVITY**

Analyze how volcanic activity can change Earth's surface.

**Predicting Volcano Hazards** Volcanologists use different tools to monitor volcanoes and predict eruptions. The gas emissions from volcanoes can be monitored to check for increases in sulfur dioxide, which may indicate that an eruption is coming **(Figure 8)**. Seismographs can detect rumblings deep inside a volcano that precede an eruption.

Volcanologists can also use devices to measure whether a volcano is swelling as its magma chamber fills up. These devices, called tiltmeters, are like carpenters' levels but much more sensitive. They can detect very slight changes in the tilt of a volcano's slopes. If the tilt increases, it means the volcano is swelling and likely to erupt. Telecommunications technology can transmit the data from these devices to scientists, who can then interpret the data and look for patterns associated with eruptions. They can then notify the public if an eruption is predicted.

☑ **READING CHECK** **Summarize Text** If the concentration of sulfur dioxide emitted from a volcano increases from less than one part per million (ppm) to 4 ppm, is the volcano more or less likely to erupt soon?

........................................................................................

........................................................................................

........................................................................................

# Question It!

## Building on a Volcano

In some parts of the world, building on a volcano is a necessity because most of the land is volcanic. Suppose you had to build a home on a volcanic island.

**SEP Ask Questions** What questions would you want to answer before choosing a specific site for construction?

........................................................................................

........................................................................................

........................................................................................

........................................................................................

........................................................................................

........................................................................................

........................................................................................

MS-ESS2-2, MS-ESS3-2

1. **Identify Phenomena** Runny lava oozes from the vent of a broad, gently-sloping shield volcano. What type of eruption is this?

................................................................

2. **SEP Construct Explanations** Why do volcanoes form at divergent and convergent boundaries?

................................................................
................................................................
................................................................
................................................................
................................................................
................................................................

3. **CCC Patterns** The Hawaiian Islands formed as the Pacific Plate has moved west-northwest over a hot spot. In which part of the islands would you expect to find the most active volcanoes? What about dormant and extinct volcanoes? Explain.

................................................................
................................................................
................................................................
................................................................
................................................................
................................................................

4. **SEP Interpret Data** You are sailing in the South Pacific Ocean, far from any plate boundary. Looming on the horizon is a dark, broad, rounded island with sparse vegetation. A few thin flows of orange lava drip into the sea. Some smoky vapor unfurls from the center of the island. What kind of volcano is this? Explain.

................................................................
................................................................
................................................................
................................................................
................................................................
................................................................

5. **CCC Structure and Function** How are volcanic island arcs formed?

................................................................
................................................................
................................................................
................................................................
................................................................
................................................................

# Quest CHECK-INS

**In this lesson, you learned about the connection between plate tectonics and volcanoes.**

SEP Analyze Data Why is it important to understand the type of volcano Mount Rainier is and the patterns of activity at the nearest plate boundary?

................................................................
................................................................
................................................................

## HANDS-ON LAB

Signs of Eruption

**Go online** to download the lab and identify signs of a volcanic eruption.

## 1 Evidence of Plate Motions

MS-ESS2-3

1. Wegener developed the hypothesis that Earth's landmasses had once been fused together, and then slowly broke apart in a process called
   A. continental drift.
   B. subduction.
   C. Pangaea.
   D. divergence.

2. Evidence that supported the hypothesis of continental drift included fossils, land features, and
   A. ocean currents.
   B. solar activity.
   C. climate data.
   D. presence of bacteria.

3. The zipper-like mountain ranges that run across the floors of the ocean are called
   A. tectonic plates.
   B. mid-ocean ridges.
   C. subduction zones.
   D. convergent boundaries.

4. **SEP Develop Models** ✏ In the space below, sketch one of the types of stress that affect Earth's crust.

## 2 Plate Tectonics and Earth's Surface

MS-ESS2-2

5. Which of the following explains how Mount Everest formed?
   A. The mountain formed from volcanic activity at a divergent boundary.
   B. The mountain formed when two tectonic plates collided at a convergent boundary.
   C. The mountain formed from volcanic activity at a convergent boundary.
   D. The mountain formed as a result of an earthquake when two plates slipped past each other.

6. The circular movement of material in the mantle that drives plate movement is called
   A. conduction.
   B. subduction.
   C. compression.
   D. convection.

7. Plates move apart from each other at a
   A. divergent boundary.
   B. convergent boundary.
   C. transform boundary.
   D. subduction boundary.

8. Earthquakes often occur along
   ...................................... as a result of the buildup of stress.

9. **SEP Construct Explanations** A local official pledges to have a new highway built over a transform boundary. Explain why this may be a bad idea.

   ..................................................................
   ..................................................................
   ..................................................................
   ..................................................................
   ..................................................................

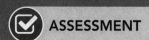
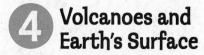

## 3 Earthquakes and Tsunami Hazards

MS-ESS2-2, MS-ESS3-2

10. The type of stress that pulls on and thins an area of Earth's crust is called
    A. torsion.
    B. tension.
    C. shearing.
    D. diverging.

11. When a plate is compressed, it can create anticlines and synclines that can become
    A. mountains and valleys.
    B. folds and breaks.
    C. plateaus and canyons.
    D. landmasses and oceans.

12. How much more energy is released by an earthquake with a magnitude of 8.0 on the moment magnitude scale than one with a 6.0 magnitude?
    A. 32 times more
    B. 64 times more
    C. 2 times more
    D. 20 times more

13. **SEP Explain Phenomena** Describe how ocean floor uplift and landslides can cause tsunamis.

    ...................................................................

    ...................................................................

    ...................................................................

    ...................................................................

    ...................................................................

    ...................................................................

    ...................................................................

    ...................................................................

## 4 Volcanoes and Earth's Surface

MS-ESS2-2, MS-ESS3-2

14. Volcanoes may emerge at long cracks in Earth's crust at ........................................... ridges, on continents near convergent .........................................., and at random locations away from plate boundaries called ..............................................

15. **SEP Construct Explanations** What causes volcanoes to form along a mid-ocean ridge?

    ...................................................................

    ...................................................................

    ...................................................................

    ...................................................................

    ...................................................................

16. **CCC Cause and Effect** Why are volcanoes often found along both convergent and divergent plate boundaries?

    ...................................................................

    ...................................................................

    ...................................................................

    ...................................................................

    ...................................................................

    ...................................................................

    ...................................................................

MS-ESS2-2, MS-ESS3-2

## Evidence-Based Assessment

In 2011, a magnitude 9.0 earthquake occurred in the ocean floor off the east coast of Japan. Tsunameter buoys and tide gauges recorded tsunami waves as they crossed the Pacific Ocean. Scientists used the data to predict how large the waves would be and when they would arrive at different locations. The map shown represents the tsunami forecast model for the event, which was used by coastal communities around the Pacific to prepare for local impacts of the tsunami.

**Analyze the map of the 2011 tsunami wave forecast. Keep in mind the following information:**

- The triangles symbolize specific tsunameter buoys, which measure wave height, or amplitude.

- The numbered contour lines represent how many hours after the earthquake the tsunami waves were forecasted to reach those areas of the ocean.

- Major plate boundaries are are indicated on the map.

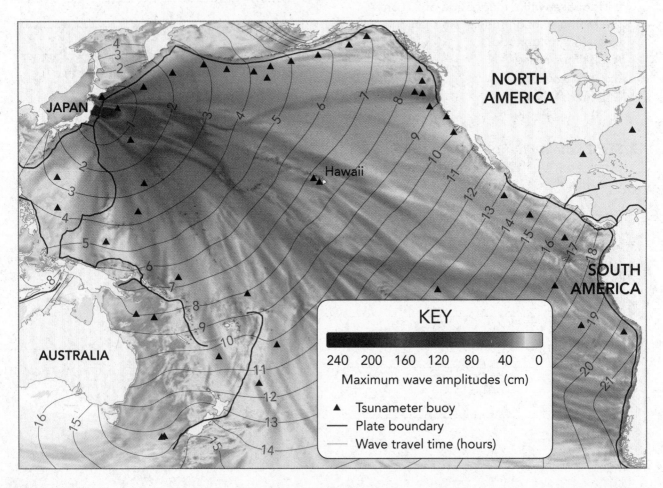

**KEY**

240  200  160  120  80  40  0

Maximum wave amplitudes (cm)

▲  Tsunameter buoy
—  Plate boundary
·····  Wave travel time (hours)

1. **SEP Analyze Data** According to the data, where was tsunami wave height expected to be greatest?
   A. Australia      B. Japan
   C. North America      D. South America

2. **SEP Interpret Data** How many hours after the earthquake were the tsunami waves expected to reach South America?
   A. 9      B. 23
   C. 7      D. 19

3. **Model Phenomena** When was a tsunami wave expected to reach Hawaii, and what was the expected wave height?

4. **CCC Cause and Effect** Describe how the motion of tectonic plates can result in a tsunami.

5. **SEP Construct Explanations** In terms of their usefulness in protecting human lives, why are so many tsunameters placed along coastlines of the Pacific Ocean? Provide two explanations.

## Quest FINDINGS

## Complete the Quest!

**Phenomenon Present information on Mount Rainier's history and current geological research, along with your evidence-based argument about whether it is safe to hike and camp there.**

**SEP Reason Quantitatively** What data will help you to predict that Mount Rainier could erupt while you are on a two-week camping trip nearby? Explain.

👆 **INTERACTIVITY**

Reflect on Mount Rainier's Safety

MS-ESS2-2, MS-ESS3-2

# Modeling Sea-Floor Spreading

How can you prevent a major oil spill by **designing** and building a model that **demonstrates** sea-floor spreading?

## Background

**Phenomenon** Imagine you are a marine geologist reviewing a plan to construct a gas pipeline attached to the ocean floor. You notice that part of the pipeline will cross a mid-ocean ridge zone. In this investigation, you will design and build a model that demonstrates sea-floor spreading to show why this plan is not a good idea.

## Materials

(per group)
• scissors
• transparent tape
• colored marker
• metric ruler
• 2 sheets of unlined letter-sized paper
• manila folder or file
• crayons or colored pencils

## Safety

Be sure to follow all safety guidelines provided by your teacher. The Safety Appendix of your textbook provides more details about the safety icons.

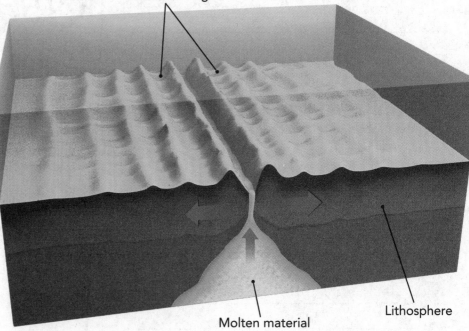

New rock added to each side of the mid-ocean ridge

Molten material

Lithosphere

# Design Your Model and Investigation

Discuss with your group why building a pipeline that spans the mid-ocean ridge is a bad idea. Over time, what will happen to the pipeline?

With your group, take a look at the materials. How can you use the materials to construct a model that demonstrates why the pipeline plan is a problem?

**HANDS-ON LAB**

☑ **Demonstrate** Go online for a downloadable worksheet of this lab.

## Consider the following questions:

- How can you use the manila folder to represent the mantle?

- How can you use the two pieces of plain letter-sized paper to create matching strips of striped sea floor?

- How can you represent the mid-ocean ridge and the subduction zones on either side of the ridge?

Use the space provided to sketch your group's model and write notes for guiding its construction. Have your teacher approve your group's plan, and then construct and demonstrate the model.

## Sketch of Model

## Design Notes

_____
_____
_____
_____
_____
_____
_____
_____
_____
_____
_____
_____
_____
_____

# Analyze and Interpret Data

1. **SEP Develop Models** Why is it important that your model have identical patterns of stripes on both sides of the center slit?

........................................................................

........................................................................

........................................................................

........................................................................

2. **SEP Construct Explanations** Use evidence from your model to support the claim that sea-floor spreading builds two different tectonic plates.

........................................................................

........................................................................

........................................................................

........................................................................

3. **SEP Refine Your Solution** Look at the models created by other groups. How are the other solutions different? How might you revise your group's model to better demonstrate sea-floor spreading?

........................................................................

........................................................................

........................................................................

........................................................................

4. **SEP Use Models** How could your group revise the model to reinforce the idea that the amount of crust that forms at the mid-ocean ridge is equal to the amount of crust recycled back into the mantle at subduction zones?

........................................................................

........................................................................

........................................................................

........................................................................

5. **CCC Stability and Change** How does your model support the claim that building an oil pipeline across a divergent boundary would be a bad idea?

........................................................................

........................................................................

........................................................................

# Earth's Surface Systems

How did this rock get its strange shape?

**NGSS PERFORMANCE EXPECTATIONS**

**MS-ESS2-2** Construct an explanation based on evidence for how geoscience processes have changed Earth's surface at varying time and spatial scales.

**MS-ESS3-2** Analyze and interpret data on natural hazards to forecast future catastrophic events and inform the development of technologies to mitigate their effects.

HANDS-ON LAB

**uConnect** Explore how the height and width of a hill affects mass movement.

**GO ONLINE**
to access your
digital course

 ▶ VIDEO

 👆 INTERACTIVITY

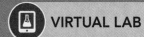 🌡 VIRTUAL LAB

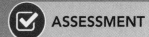 ☑ ASSESSMENT

 📖 eTEXT

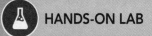 ⚗ HANDS-ON LAB

## The Essential Question

# What processes change Earth's surface?

**SEP Construct Explanations** Known as Thor's Hammer, this towering column of rock is a favorite sight at Bryce Canyon National Park in Utah. Hoodoos, or the tall, sedimentary rock spires, are commonly found in high plateau areas and regions of the northern Great Plains, but they are most abundant in Bryce Canyon. How do you think this feature formed?

........................................................................

........................................................................

........................................................................

# Quest KICKOFF

## How can I design and build an artificial island?

**STEM** **Phenomenon** One way to expand a city surrounded by water is to make more land. In New York City, the area of lower Manhattan known as Battery Park City was created by civil engineers using soil and rock excavated during the construction of new skyscrapers. But what factors do engineers need to consider when they create new land in water? In this problem-based Quest activity, you will design an artificial island that can withstand nature's forces and that has minimal environmental impact.

**INTERACTIVITY**

Ingenious Island

**MS-ESS2-2** Construct an explanation based on evidence for how geoscience processes have changed Earth's surface at varying time and spatial scales.
**MS-ESS3-2** Analyze and interpret data on natural hazards to forecast future catastrophic events and inform the development of technologies to mitigate their effects.

**NBC LEARN** ▶ **VIDEO**

After watching the Quest Kickoff video about how coastal engineers study and reduce coastal erosion, complete the 3-2-1 activity.

**3** ways that water changes land

..........................................................

..........................................................

..........................................................

**2** ways that wind changes land

..........................................................

..........................................................

**1** way that those changes could be prevented or minimized

..........................................................

..........................................................

# Quest CHECK-IN

## IN LESSON 1

How does weathering affect various materials? Consider the benefits and drawbacks of using different materials for an artificial island.

**HANDS-ON LAB**

Breaking It Down

# Quest CHECK-INS

## IN LESSON 2

**STEM** What criteria and constraints need to be considered when designing your island model to resist erosion over periods of time? Design and build your island model.

**HANDS-ON LAB**

Ingenious Island: Part I

**INTERACTIVITY**

Changing Landscapes

# Quest CHECK-IN

## IN LESSON 3

**STEM** How resistant is your island model to erosion? Test the effects of the agents of erosion on your model and make improvements.

**HANDS-ON LAB**

Ingenious Island: Part II

Beachfront properties line one of the "branches" of the Palm Jumeirah in the United Arab Emirates. The palm-shaped artificial island extends into the Persian Gulf off the coast of Dubai. It provides miles of additional shoreline for homes and elaborate hotels.

 Quest CHECK-IN

### IN LESSON 4

How can wave erosion impact the location of your artificial island? Adjust your design as needed to account for wave erosion.

 **INTERACTIVITY**

Breaking Waves

Quest FINDINGS

## Complete the Quest!

Present your island model and explain how your design decisions relate to the forces that change Earth's surface.

**INTERACTIVITY**

Reflect on Your Ingenious Island

# How Does Gravity Affect Materials On A Slope?

How can you collect and **analyze data** to help determine if earth material will move downslope and pose a hazard?

## Background

**Phenomenon** You are a park ranger at Yellowstone National Park and have been asked to scout the park for high-risk areas where debris may move down a slope due to gravity. Identifying these areas can help limit damage to structures and prevent injuries to people. Before you identify high-risk areas, you want to collect and analyze data on different types of ground materials and how steep an incline made of that material can be before it starts to slide down a slope. The angle of the slope just before material starts to move is known as the angle of repose.

## Materials

### (per group)

- large plastic cup
- cardboard
- beaker
- piece of paper on clipboard
- dry sand
- dry pea gravel
- dry potting soil
- protractor
- paper
- empty container for materials

## Safety

Be sure to follow all safety procedures provided by your teacher. The Safety Appendix of your textbook provides more details about the safety icons.

## Plan an Investigation

1. **Plan an Investigation** Use the materials provided to plan an investigation to determine the angle of repose of dry gravel, soil, and sand.

2. Consider the following questions before you begin:
   - What variables do you need to control?
   - What data will you collect?
   - How many trials will you conduct?

3. On a piece of paper write your procedure. Have your teacher approve your plan before you begin.

# Observations

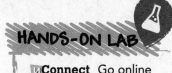

## Analyze and Interpret Data

1. **SEP Analyze Data** Which material had the highest angle of repose? Which had the lowest?

   ......................................................................................................

   ......................................................................................................

2. **CCC Cause and Effect** Observe the list of slopes around Yellowstone National Park. On which slopes should signs be placed warning of landslide danger?

   |  | Angle | Type of Material | Should a Sign be Placed? |
   |---|---|---|---|
   | **Slope A** | 45 degrees | sand | |
   | **Slope B** | 20 degrees | soil | |
   | **Slope C** | 50 degrees | gravel | |

3. **SEP Explain Phenomena** Antlions are a type of insect that build a cone-shaped hole in sandy soil and lie beneath it in the center. When ants or other insects walk into the cone, they slide down and into the grasp of the waiting antlion. Use what you learned in the lab to explain how antlions capture prey.

   ......................................................................................................

   ......................................................................................................

   ......................................................................................................

# Weathering and Soil

## Guiding Questions

- How does erosion change Earth's surface?
- How does weathering change Earth's surface?
- How does soil form?

## Connections

**Literacy** Write Explanatory Texts

**Math** Reason Quantitatively

MS-ESS2-2

**HANDS-ON LAB**

и**Investigate** Look at how ice helps to break down rock.

## Vocabulary

uniformitarianism
erosion
mechanical
   weathering
chemical
   weathering
soil
humus

## Academic Vocabulary

principle
component

## Connect It !

✎ **The Wave is a stunning dip in Earth's surface. Draw an arrow showing where the material originally covering the Wave would have begun.**

SEP Construct Explanations What processes have broken apart and carried off the many layers of solid rock that covered the Wave for millions of years?

..................................................................................................................................

..................................................................................................................................

# Breaking Down Earth's Surface

Even the hardest rocks wear down over time on Earth's surface. Natural processes, such as the one that produced the Wave in **Figure 1**, break down rocks and carry the pieces away. Geologists make inferences about what processes shaped Earth's surface in the past based on the **principle** of **uniformitarianism** (yoon uh form uh TAYR ee un iz um). This principle states that the geologic processes that operate today also operated in the past. Scientists infer that ancient landforms and features formed through the same processes they observe today and will continue to do so in the future.

**Academic Vocabulary**

Describe another principle you follow in science or in your everyday life.

........................................................

........................................................

........................................................

The processes of weathering and **erosion** (ee ROH zhun) work together to change Earth's surface by wearing down and carrying away rock particles. The process of weathering breaks down rock and other substances. Heat, cold, water, ice, and gases all contribute to weathering. Erosion involves the removal of rock particles by wind, water, ice, or gravity.

**Determine Meaning**

How has weathering or erosion affected you? In your science notebook, describe an example of weathering or erosion you observed and any impact it had on you or your community.

Weathering and erosion work continuously to reshape Earth's surface. The same processes that wear down mountains also cause bicycles to rust, paint to peel, and sidewalks to crack. Weathering and erosion can take millions of years to break down and wear away huge mountains, or they can take seconds to carry rock away in an avalanche. These processes started changing Earth's surface billions of years ago and they continue to do so.

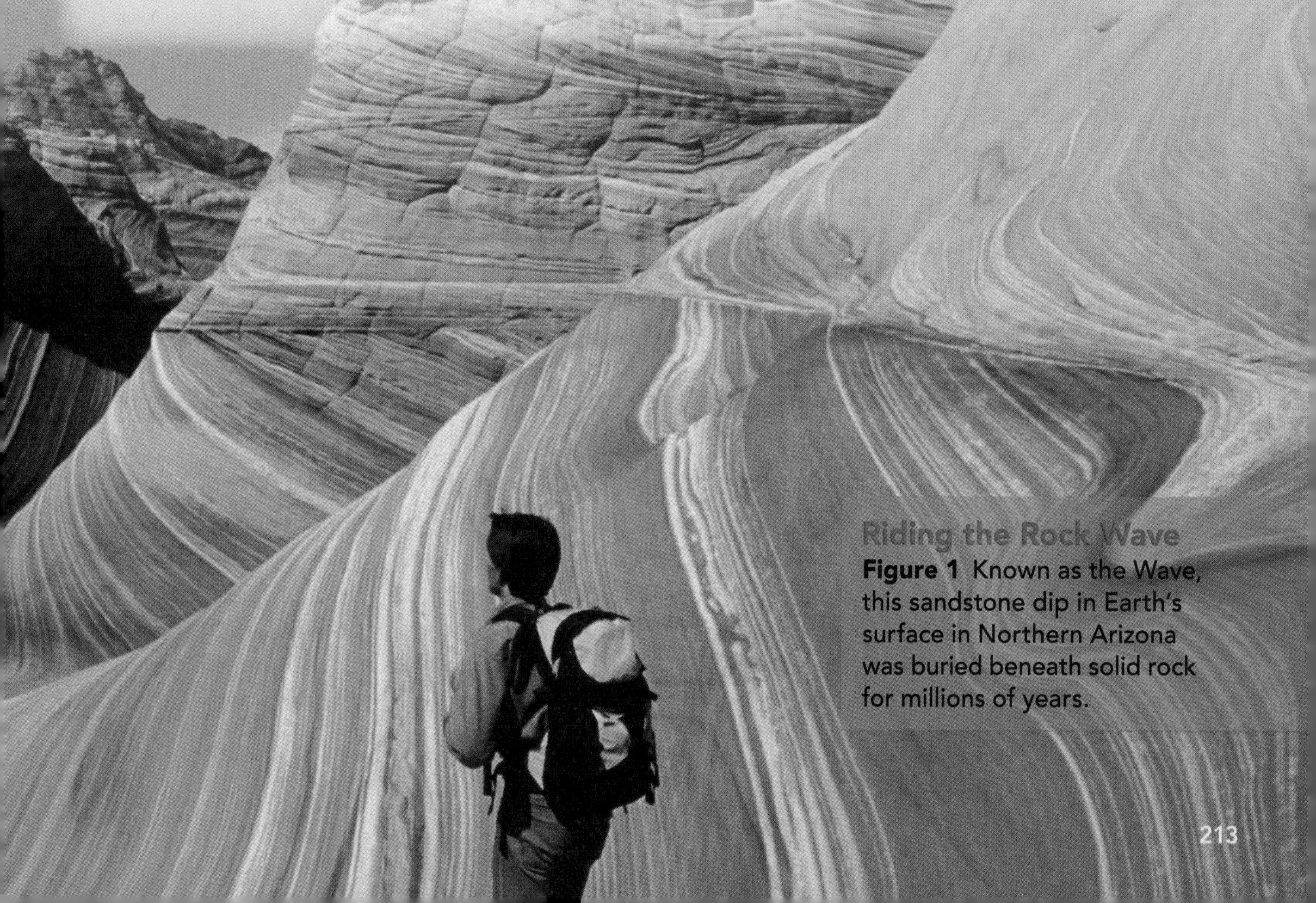

**Riding the Rock Wave**

**Figure 1** Known as the Wave, this sandstone dip in Earth's surface in Northern Arizona was buried beneath solid rock for millions of years.

## Mechanical Weathering

**Figure 2** Label each photo with an agent of mechanical weathering.

**CCC Stability and Change** How might more than one agent of mechanical weathering operate in the same place?

....................................................

....................................................

....................................................

....................................................

**HANDS-ON LAB**

**Investigate** Look at how ice helps to break down rock.

# Weathering Earth's Surface

The type of weathering in which rock is physically broken into smaller pieces is called **mechanical weathering**. A second type of weathering, called chemical weathering, also breaks down rock. **Chemical weathering** is the process that breaks down rock through chemical changes.

**Mechanical Weathering** Rocks that are cracked or split in layers have undergone mechanical weathering. Mechanical weathering usually happens gradually, over very long periods of time. Mechanical weathering, as part of erosion, can eventually wear away whole mountains.

The natural agents of mechanical weathering include freezing and thawing, release of pressure, plant growth, actions of animals, and abrasion, as shown in **Figure 2**. Abrasion (uh BRAY zhun) refers to the wearing away of rock by rock particles carried by water, ice, wind, or gravity. Human activities, such as mining and farming, also cause mechanical weathering.

Through mechanical weathering, Earth systems interact and shape the surface. For example, the geosphere (rocks) interacts with the hydrosphere (water, ice) during frost wedging. Frost wedging occurs when water seeps into cracks in rocks and expands as it freezes. Wedges of ice in rocks widen and deepen cracks. When the ice melts, water seeps deeper into the cracks. With repeated freezing and thawing, the cracks slowly expand until pieces of rock break off.

## Chemical Weathering

Chemical weathering often produces new minerals as it breaks down rock. For example, granite is made up of several minerals, including feldspars. Chemical weathering causes the feldspar to eventually change to clay minerals.

Water, oxygen, carbon dioxide, living organisms, and acid rain cause chemical weathering. Water weathers some rock by dissolving it. Water also carries other substances, including oxygen, carbon dioxide, and other chemicals, that dissolve or break down rock.

The oxygen and carbon dioxide gases in the atmosphere cause chemical weathering. Rust forms when iron combines with oxygen in the presence of water. Rusting makes rock soft and crumbly and gives it a red or brown color. When carbon dioxide dissolves in water, carbonic acid forms. This weak acid easily weathers certain types of rock, such as marble and limestone.

As a plant's roots grow, they produce weak acids that gradually dissolve rock. Lichens—plantlike organisms that grow on rocks—also produce weak acids.

Humans escalate chemical weathering by burning fossil fuels. This pollutes the air and results in rainwater that is more strongly acidic. Acid rain causes very rapid chemical weathering of rock.

☑ **READING CHECK** **Summarize Text** How are the agents of weathering similar and different?

...........................................................................................................

...........................................................................................................

## Literacy Connection

**Write Explanatory Texts**
An ancient marble statue is moved from a rural location to a highly polluted city. Explain how the move might affect the statue and why you think so.

......................................................

......................................................

......................................................

......................................................

......................................................

......................................................

......................................................

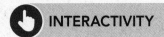

**Rate of Weathering** In historic cemeteries, slate tombstones from the 1700s are less weathered than marble tombstones from the 1800s. Why? Some kinds of rocks weather more rapidly than others. The rate at which weathering occurs is determined by the type of rock and the climate.

**Type of Rock** Rocks wear down slowly if they are made of minerals that do not dissolve easily. Rocks weather faster if they are made of minerals that dissolve easily.

Some rocks weather more easily because they are permeable. A permeable (PUR mee uh bul) material is full of tiny air spaces. The spaces increase the surface area. As water seeps through the spaces in the rock, it carries chemicals that dissolve the rock and removes material broken down by weathering.

**Climate** Climate is the average weather conditions in an area. Weathering occurs faster in wet climates. Rainfall causes chemical changes. Freezing and thawing cause mechanical changes in cold and wet climates.

Chemical reactions occur faster at higher temperatures. That is why chemical weathering occurs more quickly where the climate is both hot and wet. Human activities, such as those that produce acid rain, also increase the rate of weathering.

# Math Toolbox

## Comparing Weathered Limestone

The data table shows how much rock was broken down by weathering for two identical pieces of limestone in two different locations.

1. **Construct Graphs**  Use the data to make a double-line graph. Decide how to make each line look different. Be sure to provide a title and label the axes and each graph line.

2. **SEP Use Mathematics** Compare the slopes of each line

........................................................................

........................................................................

3. **Reason Quantitatively** As time increases, the limestone thickness (increases/decreases).

4. **Analyze Data** Limestone A weathered at a (slower/faster) rate than Limestone B.

### Weathering Rates of Limestone

| Time (years) | Thickness of Limestone Lost (mm) | |
| --- | --- | --- |
| | Limestone A | Limestone B |
| 200 | 1.75 | 0.80 |
| 400 | 3.50 | 1.60 |
| 600 | 5.25 | 2.40 |
| 800 | 7.00 | 3.20 |
| 1,000 | 8.75 | 4.00 |

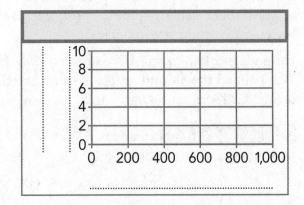

| Gravel | Sand | Silt | Clay |
|--------|------|------|------|
| 2 mm & larger | Less than 2 mm | Less than 0.05 mm | Less than 0.002 mm |

Source: Michigan Technological University

# Forming Soil

Have you ever wondered how plants grow on rocks? Plants can grow only when soil begins to form in the cracks. **Soil** is the loose, weathered material on Earth's surface in which plants grow.

**Soil Composition** Soil is a mixture of rock particles, minerals, decayed organic material, water, and air. The main **components** of soil come from bedrock. Bedrock is the solid layer of rock beneath the soil. Once bedrock is exposed to air, water, and living things, it gradually weathers into smaller and smaller particles.

The particles of rock in soil are classified by size as gravel, sand, silt, and clay. **Figure 3** shows the relative sizes of these particles. A soil's texture depends on the size of the soil particles.

The decayed organic material in soil is called humus. **Humus** (HYOO mus) is a dark-colored substance that forms as plant and animal remains decay. Humus helps to create spaces in soil that are then filled by air and water. It contains nutrients that plants need.

☑ READING CHECK **Write Explanatory Texts** Explain how you might determine the rate of weathering on a sample of rock.

...............................................................................

...............................................................................

...............................................................................

...............................................................................

## Soil Particle Size

**Figure 3** ✎ The rock particles shown here have been enlarged. On the graph, mark the size of a 1.5-mm particle with an X.

Classify Explain how you would classify that size particle and why.

...............................................................

...............................................................

...............................................................

## Academic Vocabulary

What are the similarities between components of a computer and the components of soil?

...............................................................

...............................................................

...............................................................

...............................................................

👆 **INTERACTIVITY**

Learn how minerals affect the colors of sand.

217

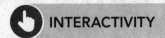
## Soil Formation

Soil forms as rock is broken down by weathering and mixes with other materials on the surface. Soil forms constantly wherever bedrock weathers. Soil formation continues over a long period of time, taking hundreds to thousands of years. The same process that forms soil today was also taking place billions of years ago and will continue to form soil in the future.

Gradually, soil develops layers called horizons. A soil horizon is a layer of soil that differs in color, texture, and composition from the layers above or below it. **Figure 4** shows the sequence in which soil horizons form.

## Soil and Organisms

Recall that organisms are part of Earth's biosphere. Many organisms live in soil and interact with the geosphere. Some soil organisms aid in the formation of humus, which makes soil rich in the nutrients that plants need. Other soil organisms mix the soil and make spaces in it for air and water.

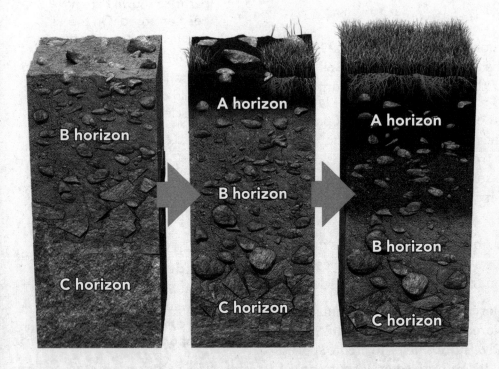

**A horizon**
The A horizon is made up of topsoil, a crumbly, dark brown soil that is a mixture of humus, clay, and minerals. Topsoil forms as plants add organic material to the soil, and plant roots weather pieces of rock.

**B horizon**
The B horizon, often called subsoil, usually consists of clay and other particles of rock, but little humus. It forms as rainwater washes these materials down from the A horizon.

**C horizon**
The C horizon forms as bedrock begins to weather. The rock breaks up into small particles.

### Soil Horizons

**Figure 4** Soil horizons form in three main steps.

1. **SEP Use Models** ✏️ Underline the soil horizon that contains the most organic matter.

2. **SEP Construct Explanations** In what climates would you expect soil to form fastest? Why?

..................................................................................................................

..................................................................................................................

**Forming Humus** Dead leaves, roots, and other plant materials contribute most of the organic remains that form humus. Humus forms in a process called decomposition carried out by a combination of decomposers including fungi, bacteria, worms, and other organisms. Decomposers break down the remains of dead organisms into smaller pieces through the process of chemical digestion. This material then mixes with the soil as nutrient-rich humus where it can be used by living plants.

**Mixing the Soil** Earthworms and burrowing mammals mix humus with air and other materials in soil, as shown in **Figure 5**. As earthworms eat their way through the soil, they carry humus down to the subsoil and from the subsoil up to the surface. These organisms increase the soil's fertility by dispersing organic matter throughout the soil. Mammals such as mice, moles, and prairie dogs break up hard, compacted soil and mix humus with it. Animal wastes contribute nutrients to the soil as well.

✅ **READING CHECK** **Integrate With Visuals** Review the information and illustrations in **Figure 4**. How is weathering related to soil formation?

........................................................................................

........................................................................................

........................................................................................

**Organisms Impact Soil**
**Figure 5** Earthworms and chipmunks break up hard, compacted soil, making it easier for air and water to enter the soil.

1. **SEP Synthesize Information** Besides breaking up and mixing soil, the (earthworm/chipmunk) is also a decomposer.

2. **CCC Systems** As these organisms change the soil, which Earth systems are interacting?

........................................

........................................

# Model It !

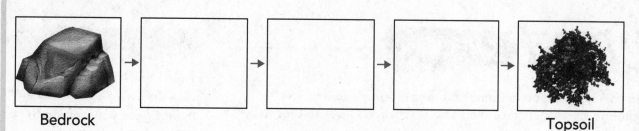

Bedrock ................................ Topsoil

**From Rock to Soil**

**Figure 6** The illustrations show bedrock and topsoil rich in humus.

1. **SEP Develop Models** 🖉 In the empty boxes, draw the processes that help to change the bedrock into soil. Label the processes in each drawing. Include at least two processes that involve organisms.

2. **SEP Use Models** The topsoil represents the (A/B/C) horizon.

1. **CCC Cause and Effect** How does erosion affect Earth's surface?

..................................................................

..................................................................

..................................................................

..................................................................

2. **SEP Construct Explanations** Explain how water can wear down Earth's surface at scales that are large and small in size, or short and long in duration.

..................................................................

..................................................................

..................................................................

..................................................................

..................................................................

3. **Compare and Contrast** Compare and contrast mechanical weathering and chemical weathering.

..................................................................

..................................................................

..................................................................

..................................................................

..................................................................

4. **SEP Evaluate Information** A community group needs advice on choosing rock for a city park monument that will last a long time. Explain the factors that would likely affect how long the monument lasts.

..................................................................

..................................................................

..................................................................

..................................................................

..................................................................

..................................................................

..................................................................

..................................................................

..................................................................

5. **CCC Stability and Change** How did organisms change the soil in North America over millions of years? Cite evidence to support your answer.

..................................................................

..................................................................

..................................................................

..................................................................

..................................................................

# Quest CHECK-IN

**In this lesson, you learned how weathering and erosion change Earth's surface. You also discovered how soil forms.**

**SEP Use Models** How can modeling the effects of weathering on different materials help you to design your island?

..................................................................

..................................................................

..................................................................

..................................................................

..................................................................

## HANDS-ON LAB

Breaking It Down

**Investigate** what constraints need to be considered when designing an island to resist long-term erosion.

MS-ESS2-2, MS-ESS3-2

# GROUND SHIFTING ADVANCES:
# Maps Help Predict

**INTERACTIVITY**

Learn about the causes of landslides and predict where they might occur.

**Do you know what** happens after heavy rains or earthquakes in California? There are landslides. Engineers look for patterns to determine how and where they can happen.

**The Challenge:** To protect highways and towns from landslides.

**Phenomenon** Evaluating hazards is one way to prepare for natural disasters. In the early 1970s, the California Geological Survey (CGS) began drawing up "Geology for Planning" maps. Its goal was to create maps showing areas all over the state where natural hazards, such as wildfires and landslides, were most likely to occur. Engineers and city planners could then use the maps to prepare for, or possibly prevent, natural disasters.

In 1997, the Caltrans Highway Corridor Mapping project began. Caltrans stands for California Department of Transportation. Caltrans engineers set out to map all known sites of landslides, as well as unstable slopes along the major interstate highways. Most of the landslide sites were along highways that wind through California's mountains. Using these maps, engineers have installed sensitive monitoring equipment to help predict future landslides.

Landslides destroy roadways, cut people off from access to vital services, and disrupt local economies.

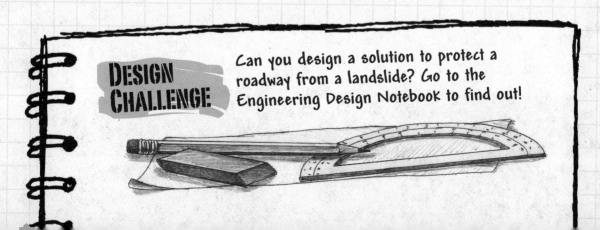

**DESIGN CHALLENGE**

Can you design a solution to protect a roadway from a landslide? Go to the Engineering Design Notebook to find out!

# Erosion and Deposition

## Guiding Questions

- What processes change Earth's surface?
- How does mass movement change Earth's surface?
- How does wind change Earth's surface?

## Connections

Literacy  Integrate With Visuals

Math  Analyze Quantitative Relationships

MS-ESS2-2, MS-ESS3-2

## HANDS-ON LAB

**ᴜInvestigate**  Examine how particle size affects erosion and deposition.

## Vocabulary

sediment
deposition
mass movement
deflation
sand dune
loess

## Academic Vocabulary

similar
significant

## Connect It !

✏️ **Circle the change shown in the photo, then draw an arrow to show the direction of the rocks' movement.**

CCC Stability and Change  How has Earth's surface changed in this photo?

..............................................................................................................................

..............................................................................................................................

CCC Cause and Effect  What natural processes do you think caused the change you observe?

..............................................................................................................................

..............................................................................................................................

# Changing Earth's Surface

Have you ever watched water carry away bits of gravel and soil during a rainstorm? If so, you observed erosion. Recall that erosion is a process that moves weathered rock from its original location. Gravity, water, ice, and wind are all agents of erosion.

The process of erosion moves material called **sediment**. Sediment may consist of pieces of rock or soil, or the remains of plants and animals.

**Deposition** occurs where the agents of erosion deposit, or lay down, sediment. Like erosion, deposition changes the shape of Earth's surface. You may have watched an ant carry away bits of soil and then put the soil down in a different location to build an ant hill. The ant's activity is **similar** to erosion and deposition, which involves picking up, carrying away, and putting down sediment in a different place.

Weathering, erosion, transportation, and deposition act together in a continuous cycle that wears down and builds up Earth's surface. As erosion wears down a mountain in one place, deposition builds up a new landform in another place. Some changes happen over a large area, while others occur in a small space. Some happen slowly over thousands or millions of years, and others take only a few minutes or seconds, such as the rockslide shown in **Figure 1**. No matter how large or fast the changes, the cycle of erosion and deposition is continuous. The same changes that shaped Earth's surface in the past still shape it today and will continue to shape it in the future.

## Moving Rock
**Figure 1** The sudden change in the appearance of this hillside was caused by the natural movement of rock.

# Mass Movement

If you place a ball at the top of a hill, with a slight push the ball will roll down the hill. Gravity pulls the ball downward. Gravity is also the force that moves rock and other materials downhill.

Gravity causes **mass movement**, one of several processes that move sediment downhill. Mass movement can be rapid or slow. Erosion and deposition both take place during a mass movement event. The different types of mass movement include landslides, mudflows, slumps, and creep (**Figure 2**).

A mass movement may be caused by a natural disaster, such as a flood, earthquake, or hurricane. Natural disasters can dramatically and suddenly change Earth's surface. Scientists make maps of past mass movements in a region to better understand their hazards. Such maps help scientists to identify patterns and predict where future mass movement is likely to occur in order to prevent human casualties.

☑ READING CHECK **Integrate With Visuals** Read and think about the information relating to different kinds of mass movement. Which type of mass movement do you think is least dangerous? Why?

....................................................................................................................................................

....................................................................................................................................................

**Mass Movement**

**Figure 2** Different types of mass movement have different characteristics.

1. SEP Develop Models ✏️ Draw arrows on each image of mass movement to show the direction that material moves.

2. CCC Patterns What pattern(s) can you identify among the types of mass movement?

....................................................................................................................................................

....................................................................................................................................................

**Landslides**

A landslide occurs when rock and soil slide quickly down a steep slope. Some landslides contain huge masses of rock, while others contain only small amounts of rock and soil. Often caused by earthquakes, landslides occur where road builders have cut highways through hills or mountains, leaving behind unstable slopes.

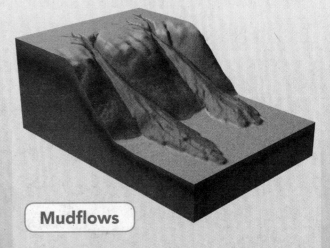

**Mudflows**

A mudflow is the rapid downhill movement of a mixture of water, rock, and soil. Mudflows often occur after heavy rains in a normally dry area. In clay-rich soils with a high water content, mudflows may occur even on very gentle slopes. Under certain conditions, clay-rich soil suddenly behaves as a liquid and begins to flow.

## Major Landslides and Mudflows

Landslides and mudflows are a problem in all 50 states and all around the world. Annually in the United States, landslides cause $1 billion to $2 billion in damage and about 25 deaths. But some catastrophic mass movements in other countries have killed more than 100,000 people.

**1. CCC Scale, Proportion, and Quantity** What proportion of the landslides were caused by earthquakes?

...................................................................................

**2. Analyze Quantitative Relationships** Which process caused the most landslides? Which caused the fewest landslides?

...................................................................................

### Major Landslides and Mudflows of the 20th Century

| Year | Location | Cause |
|------|----------|-------|
| 1919 | Java, Indonesia | volcanic eruption |
| 1920 | Ningxia, China | earthquake |
| 1933 | Sichuan, China | earthquake |
| 1949 | Tadzhikistan | earthquake |
| 1958 | Japan | heavy rains |
| 1970 | Peru | earthquake |
| 1980 | Washington, USA | earthquakes |
| 1983 | Utah, USA | heavy rain and snowmelt |
| 1985 | Colombia | volcano |
| 1998 | Central America | hurricane rains |

### Slumps

In a slump, a mass of rock and soil suddenly slips down a slope. Unlike a landslide, the material in a slump moves down in one large mass. It looks as if someone pulled the bottom out from under part of the slope. A slump often occurs when water soaks the bottom of clay-rich soil.

### Creep

Creep is the very slow downhill movement of rock and soil. It can even occur on gentle slopes. Creep often results from the freezing and thawing of water in cracked layers of rock beneath the soil. Even though it occurs slowly, you can see the effects of creep in vertical objects such as telephone poles and tree trunks. Creep may tilt these objects at unusual angles.

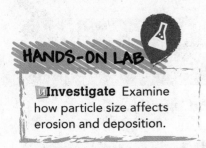
**Investigate** Examine how particle size affects erosion and deposition.

## Academic Vocabulary

Describe a significant change in weather from the winter to the summer.

.................................................

.................................................

.................................................

# Erosion and Deposition by Wind

Recall that wind, or moving air, is an agent of erosion and deposition. Through these processes, wind wears down and builds up Earth's surface.

**Wind Erosion** Wind can be a **significant** agent in shaping the land in areas where there are few plants to hold the soil in place. In a sandstorm, strong winds pick up large amounts of sediment and loose soil and transport it to new locations.

**Deflation** Wind causes erosion mainly by **deflation**, the process by which wind removes surface materials. You can see the process of deflation in **Figure 3**. When wind blows over the land, it picks up the smallest particles of sediment, such as clay and silt. Stronger, faster winds pick up larger particles. Slightly larger particles, such as sand, might skip or bounce for a short distance. Strong winds can roll even larger and heavier sediment particles. In deserts, deflation can create an area called desert pavement where smaller sediments are blown away, and larger rock fragments are left behind.

**Abrasion** Wind, water, and ice carry particles that rub or scrape against exposed rock. As particles move against the rock, friction wears away the rock by the process of abrasion.

## Wind Erosion and Deflation

**Figure 3** Wind causes deflation by moving surface particles in three ways.

1. **Claim** ✏ In each circle, draw the size of particles that would be moved by the wind.

2. **Evidence** How does a particle's size affect how high and far it travels?

.................................................

.................................................

.................................................

3. **Reasoning** Complete each sentence to the right with one of the following words: Fine, Medium, Large.

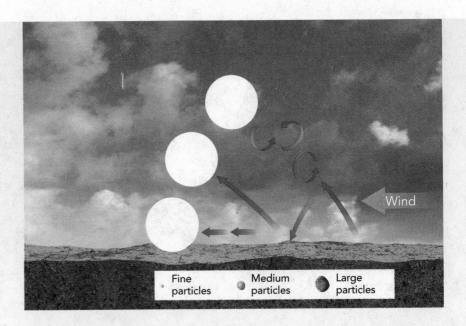

Fine particles   Medium particles   Large particles

........................... particles are carried through the air.

........................... particles skip or bounce.

........................... particles slide or roll.

**Wind Deposition** All the sediment picked up by wind eventually falls to the ground. This happens when the wind slows down or encounters an obstacle. Wind deposition may form sand dunes and loess deposits.

**Sand Dunes** When wind meets an obstacle, such as a clump of grass, the result is usually a deposit of windblown sand called a **sand dune**. **Figure 4** shows how wind direction can form different dunes. The shape and size of sand dunes is determined by the direction of the wind, the amount of sand, and the presence of plants. This same process changed Earth's surface billions of years ago, just as it does today. You can predict how wind deposition will affect the surface in the future. You can see sand dunes on beaches and in deserts where wind-blown sediment builds up. Sand dunes also move over time because the sand shifts with the wind from one side of the dune to the other. Sometimes plants begin growing on a dune, and the roots help to anchor the dune in one place.

**Loess Deposits** The wind drops sediment that is finer than sand but coarser than clay far from its source. This fine, wind-deposited sediment is **loess** (LOH es). There are large loess deposits in central China and in states such as Nebraska, South Dakota, Iowa, Missouri, and Illinois. Loess helps to form soil rich in nutrients. Many areas with thick loess deposits are valuable farmlands.

✅ **READING CHECK** **Cite Textual Evidence** What factors affect wind erosion and deposition?

......................................................................................................................

......................................................................................................................

# Question It!

**Moving Sand Dunes**

Sand dunes keep drifting and covering a nearby, busy parking lot.

**SEP Define Problems** State the problem that needs to be solved in the form of a question.

......................................................................................................................

......................................................................................................................

**SEP Design Solutions** Describe two possible solutions to the problem. Explain why each would solve the problem.

......................................................................................................................

......................................................................................................................

......................................................................................................................

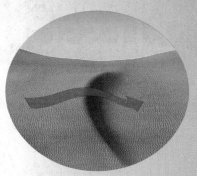

Crescent-shaped dune

Wind direction

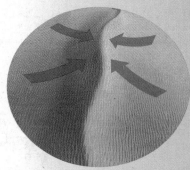

Star-shaped dune

**Dune Formation**

**Figure 4** Sand dunes form and change shape as the wind deposits sand.

1. **Predict** ✏ Draw a line to show how the ridge of the crescent-shaped dune will likely shift over time.

2. **CCC Cause and Effect** Why do these dunes have different shapes?

......................................................................

......................................................................

......................................................................

 **INTERACTIVITY**

Explore fast and slow changes to Earth's surface.

# ☑ LESSON 2 Check

1. **Classify** Which kinds of mass movement happen quickly?

.......................................................

.......................................................

2. **CCC Stability and Change** Describe a way in which deposition by gravity slowly changes Earth's surface.

.......................................................

.......................................................

.......................................................

3. **CCC Patterns** Explain how the wind both builds up and wears down Earth's surface in a desert. Give examples of features that result from these processes.

.......................................................

.......................................................

.......................................................

.......................................................

4. **SEP Construct Explanations** Explain why a scientist may make a map of the location of landslides in a certain area.

.......................................................

.......................................................

.......................................................

.......................................................

.......................................................

5. **SEP Interpret Data** Two towns are located in the same dry region. Town X has steeper slopes than Town Y. Town Y gets heavier than normal rain for several days while Town X remains dry. Which town is more likely to experience mass movement in the near future? Explain your answer.

.......................................................

.......................................................

.......................................................

.......................................................

.......................................................

## Quest CHECK-INS

In this lesson, you learned how gravity causes erosion and deposition. You also learned how wind causes erosion and deposition.

**CCC System Models** What are some ways that the effects of erosion can be mitigated in your design for the artificial island?

.......................................................

.......................................................

.......................................................

.......................................................

### HANDS-ON LAB

Ingenious Island, Part I

### 👆 INTERACTIVITY

Changing Landscapes

**Do the hands-on lab** to test your island's resistance to erosion by surface water.

**Go online** to explore how landscapes can be changed.

**228** Earth's Surface Systems

CAREERS
Civil Engineer

# Civil Engineers
## SAVE THE DAY!

Who put the civil in civilization? Engineers! Civil engineers are responsible for all the works that benefit the citizens of a society. After a natural disaster, civil engineers get involved in reconstruction efforts.

Think of the networks and systems we rely on every day—roadways, train tracks, cell phone towers, the electrical grid, and gas lines. Consider the cities built on filled-in swamp or a town built over rough terrain. Think of all the bridges connecting two sides of a river—even one as wide as the Mississippi. Civil engineers and the construction workers they guided made all of this possible.

Whether planning a new road or bridge, civil engineers must take into account the forces that change Earth's surface. Water and wind erosion, for example, have serious effects on roadways and can cause costly damage. A civil engineer's job is to determine how to build the road in a way that minimizes nature's potentially damaging effects.

If you want to be a civil engineer, you'll need to study science and math. You'll also need to develop your imagination, because solutions require creativity as well as analytical thinking.

▶ **VIDEO**

Watch what's involved in being a civil engineer.

**MY CAREER**

Type "civil engineer" into an online search engine to learn more about this career.

Civil engineers survey and measure the surface of Earth. The data they collect are used to plan construction projects such as this bridge.

## Guiding Questions

- How does moving water change Earth's surface?
- What landforms form from water erosion and deposition?
- How does groundwater change Earth?

## Connection

**Literacy** Cite Textual Evidence

MS-ESS2-2

**HANDS-ON LAB**

**Investigate** Trace the paths raindrops can follow after hitting the ground.

### Vocabulary

runoff
stream
tributary
flood plain
delta
alluvial fan
groundwater

### Academic Vocabulary

develop
suggest

## Connect It!

✏️ **Draw a line showing where Niagara Falls may have been in the past.**

**SEP Construct Explanations** How do you think Niagara Falls formed?

........................................................................................................

........................................................................................................

........................................................................................................

**SEP Apply Scientific Reasoning** What do you think this waterfall and all other waterfalls have in common?

........................................................................................................

# How Water Causes Erosion

Erosion by water doesn't start with a giant waterfall, such as the one in **Figure 1**. It begins with a little splash of rain. Some rainfall sinks into the ground, where it is absorbed by plant roots. Some water evaporates, while the rest of the water runs off over the land surface. Moving water of the hydrosphere is the primary agent of the erosion that shaped Earth's land surface, the geosphere, for billions of years. It continues to shape the surface today in small and large ways.

**Runoff** As water moves over the land, it picks up and carries sediment. This moving water is called **runoff**. When runoff flows over the land, it may cause a type of erosion called sheet erosion, where thin layers of soil are removed. The amount of runoff in an area depends on five main factors. The first factor is the amount of rain an area gets. A heavy or lengthy rainfall can add water to the surface more quickly than the surface can absorb it. A second factor is vegetation. Grasses, shrubs, and trees reduce runoff by absorbing water and holding soil in place. A third factor is the type of soil. Different types of soils absorb different amounts of water. A fourth factor is the shape of the land. Runoff is more likely to occur on steeply sloped land than on flatter land. Finally, a fifth factor is how people use land. For example, pavement does not absorb water. All the rain that falls on it becomes runoff. Runoff also increases when trees or crops are cut down, because this removes vegetation from the land.

Factors that reduce runoff also reduce erosion. Even though deserts have little rainfall, they often have high runoff and erosion because they have few plants and thin, sandy soil. In wet areas, such as rain forests and wetlands, runoff and erosion may be low because there are more plants to protect the soil.

**INTERACTIVITY**

Locate evidence of water erosion and determine why it happened.

## Literacy Connection

**Cite Textual Evidence** As you read the second paragraph, number the factors that affect runoff.

## Taking the Plunge
**Figure 1** The powerful Niagara River plunges more than 50 meters from the highest point of Niagara Falls. Here, the hydrosphere (river) interacts with the geosphere (land) and shapes Earth's surface.

HANDS-ON LAB

☑Investigate Trace the paths raindrops can follow after hitting the ground.

**Stream Formation** Gravity causes runoff and the sediment it carries to flow downhill. As runoff moves across the land, it flows together to form rills, gullies, and streams, as shown in **Figure 2**.

**Rills and Gullies** As runoff travels, it forms tiny grooves in the soil called rills. Many rills flow into one another to form a gully. A gully is a large groove, or channel, in the soil that carries runoff after a rainstorm. As water flows through gullies, it picks up and moves sediment with it, thus enlarging the gullies through erosion.

**Streams and Rivers** Gullies join to form a stream. A **stream** is a channel along which water is continually flowing down a slope. Unlike gullies, streams rarely dry up. Small streams are also known as creeks or brooks. As streams flow together, they form larger bodies of flowing water called rivers.

**Tributaries** A **tributary** is a stream or river that flows into a larger river. For example, the Missouri and Ohio rivers are tributaries of the Mississippi River. A drainage basin, or watershed, is the area from which a river and its tributaries collect their water.

☑READING CHECK **Integrate With Visuals** Review the information in paragraph 2 and in **Figure 2**. How does the amount of water change as it moves from rills and gullies to streams?

.................................................................................................................................

.................................................................................................................................

**Stream Formation**

**Figure 2** 🖉 In the diagram, shade only the arrows that indicate the direction of runoff flow that causes erosion.

CCC Cause and Effect How will the depth of the channel likely change with further erosion?

.............................................................................................

.............................................................................................

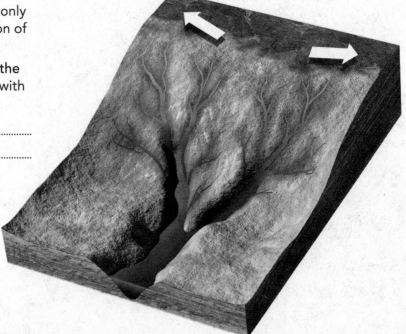

**Waterfalls**
**Figure 3** Waterfalls form where rivers erode hard and soft rock layers at different rates.

1. SEP Use Models The rock at the top of the waterfall erodes at a (slower/faster) rate than the rock below it.

2. Predict How do you think erosion will change this waterfall in the next 100 years?

......................................................

......................................................

......................................................

......................................................

# Water Erosion and Deposition Change Earth's Surface

Some landforms result from erosion by rivers and streams, while others result from deposition. Still other landforms are created from a combination of these processes. Erosion by water removes particles on Earth's surface, while deposition by water builds it up.

**Water Erosion** Many rivers begin on steep mountain slopes as flowing rain water or melted snow. This running water starts out fast-flowing and generally follows a straight, narrow course. The steep slopes along the river erode rapidly, resulting in a deep, V-shaped valley. As a river flows to the sea, it forms other features such as waterfalls, flood plains, meanders, and oxbow lakes.

**Waterfalls** Waterfalls, as shown in **Figure 3,** erode soft rock, leaving a ledge made up of hard, slowly eroding rock. Eventually a waterfall develops along the ledge where the softer rock has worn away. Rushing water and sediment can cause further erosion at the base of the waterfall. Rough water rapids also occur where a river tumbles over hard rock, wearing away the supporting rock base and leaving the rock above it unsupported.

**Flood Plains** Lower down on its course, a river usually flows over more gently sloping land. The river spreads out and erodes the land along its side, forming a wide river valley. The flat, wide area of land along a river is a **flood plain**. During a flood or a rainy season, a river overflows its banks and flows onto the flood plain. As the flood water retreats, it deposits sediment. This gradually makes the soil of a flood plain rich in nutrients.

## Academic Vocabulary

What things did you develop in science class this year? Name two examples.

........................................................

........................................................

........................................................

### ▶ VIDEO

Explore landforms caused by water erosion.

**Meanders** A river often **develops** meanders where it flows through easily eroded rock or sediment. A meander is a loop-like bend in the course of a river. A meandering river erodes sediment from the outer bank and deposits the sediment on the inner bank farther downstream. The water flows faster in the deeper, outer section of each bend, causing more erosion. Over time, a meander becomes more curved.

Flood plains also follow the meander as sediment erodes more of the land to the side of the river. Here, the river's channel is often deep and wide. For example, the southern stretch of the Mississippi River meanders on a wide, gently sloping flood plain.

**Oxbow Lakes** Sometimes a meandering river forms a feature called an oxbow lake. An oxbow lake occurs when a meander develops such a large loop that the bends of the river join together. Sediment deposits block the ends of the bends, cutting off the river flow. Oxbow lakes are the remains of the river's former bend, seen in **Figure 4**.

✓ READING CHECK **Cite Textual Evidence** What evidence supports the idea that a floodplain is formed by erosion and deposition?

........................................................................

........................................................................

........................................................................

## Model It !

### Oxbow Lakes

**Figure 4** A meander may gradually form an oxbow lake.

SEP Develop Models ✏ Draw steps 2 and 4 to show how an oxbow lake forms. Then describe step 4.

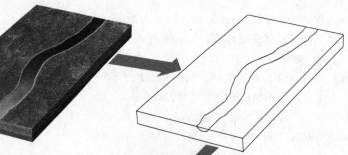

**1.** A small obstacle creates a slight bend in the river.

**2.** As water erodes the outer edge, the bend becomes bigger, forming a meander. Deposition occurs along the inside bend of the river.

**3.** Gradually, the meander becomes more curved. The river breaks through and takes a new course.

**4.** ........................................................................

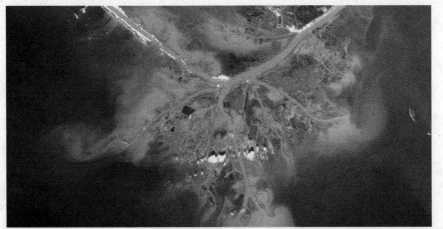

**Delta and Alluvial Fan**
**Figure 5** ✎ Draw arrows to show the direction in which water carries sediment to each landform.

**Interpret Photos** Record your observations about deltas and alluvial fans.

.................................................
.................................................
.................................................
.................................................
.................................................
.................................................
.................................................

**Water Deposition** Any time moving water slows, it deposits some of the sediment it carries. First, larger rocks stop rolling and sliding as fast-moving water starts to slow down. Then, finer and finer particles fall to the river's bed as the water flows even more slowly. In this way, water deposition builds up Earth's surface and produces landforms such as deltas and alluvial fans.

**Deltas** Eventually, a river flows into a body of water, such as an ocean or a lake. Because the river water no longer flows downhill, the water slows down. At this point, the sediment in the water drops to the bottom. Sediment deposited where a river flows into an ocean or lake builds up a landform called a **delta**. Some deltas are arc-shaped, while others are triangular. The delta of the Mississippi River, shown in **Figure 5**, is an example of a type of delta called a "bird's foot" delta.

**Alluvial Fans** When a stream flows out of a steep, narrow mountain valley, it suddenly becomes wider and shallower. The water slows down and deposits sediments in an **alluvial fan**. An alluvial fan is a wide, sloping deposit of sediment formed where a stream leaves a mountain range. As its name **suggests**, this deposit is shaped like a fan.

**Academic Vocabulary**
*Suggest* means "to mention as a possibility." Use *suggest* in a sentence.

.................................................
.................................................
.................................................
.................................................

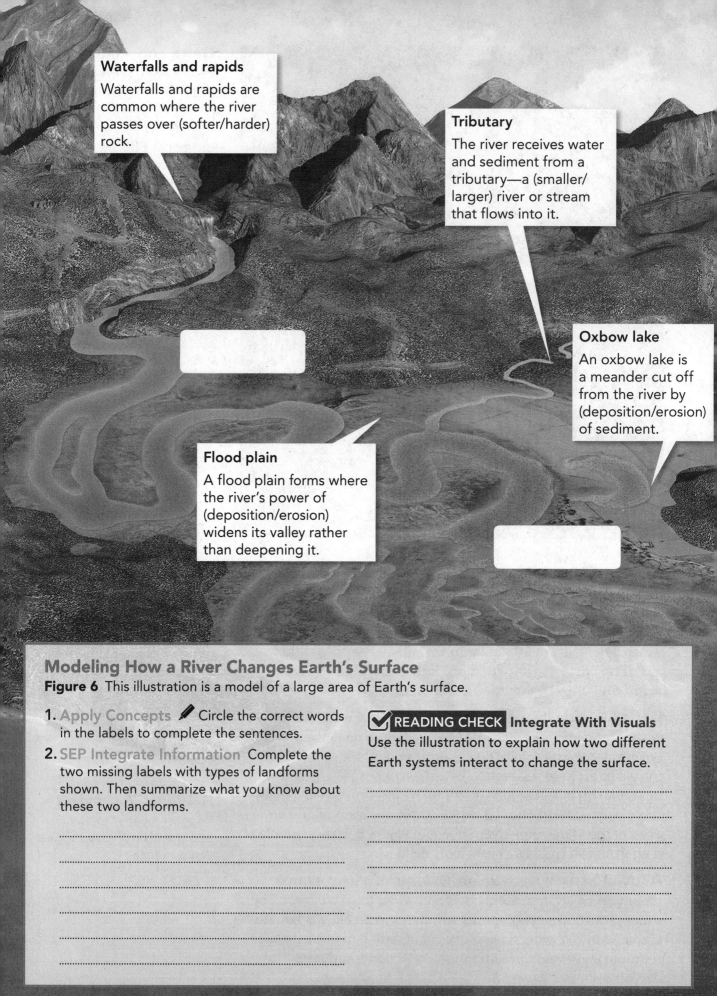

**Waterfalls and rapids**
Waterfalls and rapids are common where the river passes over (softer/harder) rock.

**Tributary**
The river receives water and sediment from a tributary—a (smaller/larger) river or stream that flows into it.

**Oxbow lake**
An oxbow lake is a meander cut off from the river by (deposition/erosion) of sediment.

**Flood plain**
A flood plain forms where the river's power of (deposition/erosion) widens its valley rather than deepening it.

## Modeling How a River Changes Earth's Surface

**Figure 6** This illustration is a model of a large area of Earth's surface.

1. **Apply Concepts** ✏️ Circle the correct words in the labels to complete the sentences.

2. **SEP Integrate Information** Complete the two missing labels with types of landforms shown. Then summarize what you know about these two landforms.

..........................................................................
..........................................................................
..........................................................................
..........................................................................
..........................................................................
..........................................................................

☑ **READING CHECK** **Integrate With Visuals**
Use the illustration to explain how two different Earth systems interact to change the surface.

..........................................................................
..........................................................................
..........................................................................
..........................................................................
..........................................................................
..........................................................................

# Groundwater Changes Earth's Surface

When rain falls and snow melts, some water soaks into the ground. It trickles into cracks and spaces in layers of soil and rock. **Groundwater** is the term geologists use for this underground water. Like moving water, groundwater changes the shape of Earth's surface.

**Groundwater Erosion** Groundwater causes erosion by chemical weathering. In the atmosphere, rain water combines with carbon dioxide to form a weak acid called carbonic acid, which can break down limestone. Groundwater may also become more acidic as it flows through leaf debris at the surface. When groundwater flows into cracks in limestone, some of the limestone dissolves and gets carried away. This process gradually hollows out pockets in the rock. Over time, large underground holes, called caves or caverns, develop.

**Groundwater Deposition** The action of carbonic acid on limestone can also result in deposition. Water containing carbonic acid and calcium drips from a cave's roof. Carbon dioxide escapes from the solution, leaving behind a deposit of calcite. A deposit that hangs like an icicle from the roof of a cave is known as a stalactite (stuh LAK tyt). On the floor of the cave, a cone-shaped stalagmite (stuh LAG myt) builds up as water drops from the cave roof (**Figure 7**).

**Write About It** How does groundwater form caves? In your science notebook, write entries for a tourist brochure for a cave, explaining to visitors how the cave and its features formed through erosion and deposition.

## INTERACTIVITY

Explore erosion caused by groundwater.

**Groundwater Erosion and Deposition**
**Figure 7** On the photo, draw a line from each label to the formation it names.

SEP Construct Explanations How do deposition and erosion shape caves? Outline your ideas in the table.

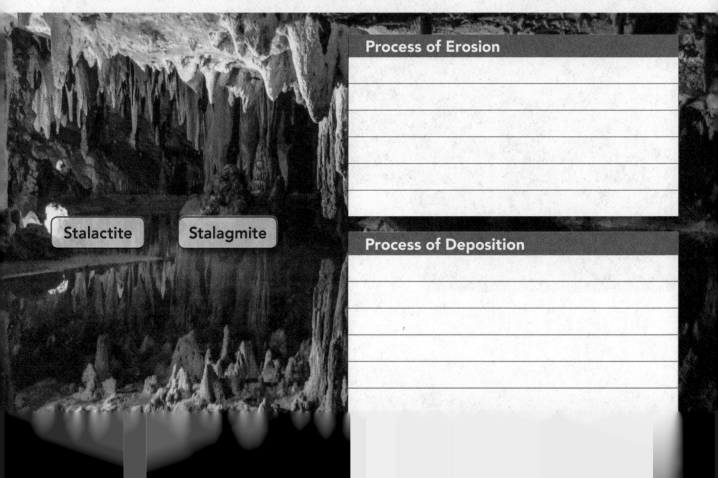

Stalactite     Stalagmite

| Process of Erosion |
|---|
|  |
|  |
|  |
|  |
|  |

| Process of Deposition |
|---|
|  |
|  |
|  |
|  |
|  |

## Karst Topography

**Figure 8** This sinkhole formed in a day in Winter Park, Florida, in 1981. What was the cause of the sinkhole?

........................................................

1. **SEP Use Models** ✎ Circle the state that has the most karst topography.

2. **Identify** Identify two states that have very little karst topography.

........................................................

........................................................

**Karst Topography** In rainy regions such as Florida where there is a layer of limestone near the surface, groundwater erosion can significantly change the shape of Earth's surface. Deep valleys and caverns commonly form. If the roof of a cave collapses because of limestone erosion, the result is a depression called a sinkhole. This type of landscape is called karst topography.

The formation of karst topography happens over small to large areas and over short to very long time periods. Groundwater erosion starts with a single drop of water that dissolves a microscopic amount of limestone in seconds. After 100 years, groundwater might deposit 1 or 2 cm of calcite on the roof of a cave. Erosion might take thousands to millions of years to form a deep valley or huge cave system hundreds of kilometers long. The roof of a cave may very slowly erode over hundreds of years, but collapse within minutes to form a small or large sinkhole, as shown in **Figure 8**.

✓ **READING CHECK** **Summarize** How does groundwater cause karst topography?

........................................................

........................................................

........................................................

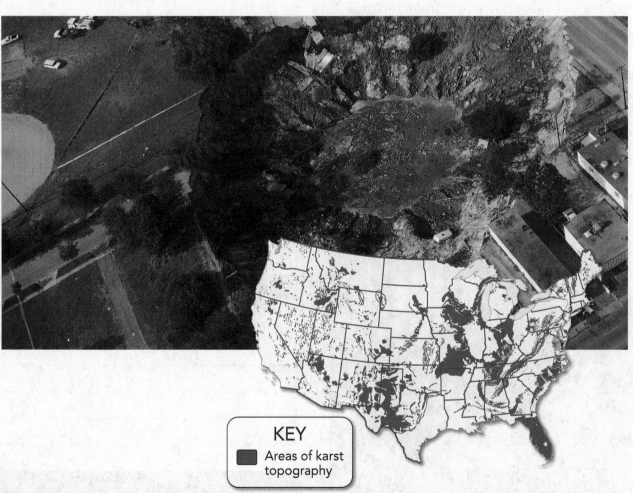

KEY

■ Areas of karst topography

1. **Identify** What are two features that result from deposition by groundwater?

.......................................................................

.......................................................................

2. **CCC Cause and Effect** How does a meander form by erosion and deposition?

.......................................................................

.......................................................................

.......................................................................

.......................................................................

.......................................................................

3. **CCC Stability and Change** Identify and describe a landform that results from water wearing down Earth's surface.

.......................................................................

.......................................................................

.......................................................................

.......................................................................

.......................................................................

4. **CCC Patterns** How will Niagara Falls most likely change naturally in the future?

.......................................................................

.......................................................................

.......................................................................

.......................................................................

.......................................................................

.......................................................................

5. **SEP Evaluate Information** Suggest two things a property owner could do to reduce water erosion on soil-covered land that has a steep slope.

.......................................................................

.......................................................................

.......................................................................

.......................................................................

.......................................................................

.......................................................................

.......................................................................

## Quest CHECK-IN

**In this lesson, you learned how water on Earth's surface causes erosion and deposition. You also found out how groundwater causes erosion and deposition.**

SEP Evaluate Your Solution Why is it important to take different types of erosion and deposition into account when designing an artificial island?

.......................................................................

.......................................................................

.......................................................................

.......................................................................

.......................................................................

.......................................................................

### HANDS-ON LAB

Ingenious Island: Part II

**Investigate** how you can use a model to test the effects of the agents of erosion on your artificial island.

When a cavity forms in limestone below the ground, a sinkhole can form when the ground eventually collapses into the cavity.

# Buyer Beware!

It may sound like something out of a science fiction movie, but the United States is home to monsters that can destroy a roadway or swallow an entire house in a single gulp. They're known as sinkholes.

## Geologic Hazards

Sinkholes come in all sizes—from an area the size of a small carpet and 30 centimeters deep to an area spreading over hundreds of acres and several hundreds of meters deep. The size of a sinkhole depends on the surrounding land features. Collapse sinkholes, for example, tend to happen in regions with clay sediments on top of limestone bedrock. As their name suggests, collapse sinkholes form quickly. The ceiling of an underground cavity suddenly gives way, and everything on the surface above that cavity collapses down into it.

In addition to the natural processes, such as heavy rainfall or extreme drought, that form sinkholes, human activities can have an impact. As we turn more of the countryside into housing developments, more people are living in areas prone to sinkholes. As we develop land, we use more water. Overuse of the groundwater, digging new water wells, or creating artificial ponds of surface water can all increase the chances of sinkhole formation.

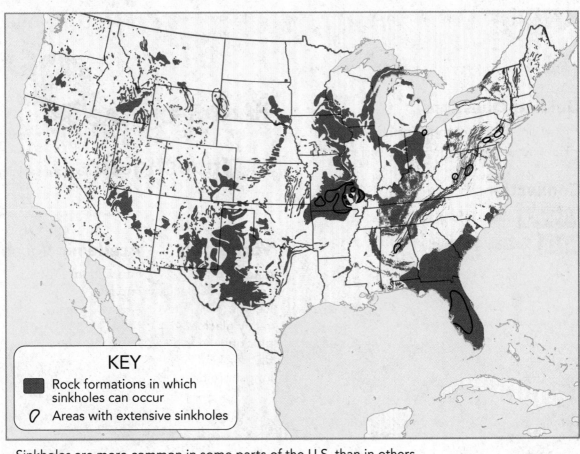

**KEY**

- ■ Rock formations in which sinkholes can occur
- ⟨⟩ Areas with extensive sinkholes

Sinkholes are more common in some parts of the U.S. than in others.

1. **Patterns** What patterns do you observe in the map? What might account for these patterns?

......................................................................................

......................................................................................

......................................................................................

2. **Interpret Diagrams** Based on the map, why do you think that the overuse of groundwater can cause a sinkhole to form?

......................................................................................

......................................................................................

......................................................................................

3. **Form an Opinion** How might communities prevent the damage and destruction caused by sinkholes?

......................................................................................

......................................................................................

# Glacial and Wave Erosion

## Guiding Questions

• How do glaciers change Earth's surface?
• How do waves change Earth's surface?

## Connections

**Literacy** Write Informative Texts

**Math** Reason Abstractly

MS-ESS2-2

## HANDS-ON LAB

**ɥInvestigate** Explore coastline erosion.

### Vocabulary

glacier
continental glacier
ice age
valley glacier
plucking
till
longshore drift

### Academic Vocabulary

interaction
impact

## Connect It!

✎ **Look closely at the image of the glacier. Draw an arrow showing the direction in which the glacier is flowing.**

CCC Stability and Change How do you think this giant mass of ice changes Earth's surface?

.......................................................................................................................

.......................................................................................................................

# Glaciers Change Earth's Surface

If you were to fly over Alaska, you would see snowcapped mountains and evergreen forests. Between the mountains and the Gulf of Alaska, you would also see a thick, winding mass of ice. This river of ice in **Figure 1** is a glacier. Geologists define a **glacier** (GLAY shur) as any large mass of ice that moves slowly over land.

Glaciers occur in the coldest places on Earth. That's because they can form only in an area where more snow falls than melts. Layers of snow pile on top of more layers of snow. Over time, the weight of the layers presses the particles of snow so tightly together that they form a solid block of ice.

Glaciers are part of the cryosphere (KRI oh sfear), which includes all the frozen water on Earth. As glaciers move slowly over land, the cryosphere interacts with the rocky upper layer of the geosphere that is known as the lithosphere. This **interaction** changes Earth's surface through weathering, erosion, and deposition. When the ice of the cryosphere melts, it becomes part of the hydrosphere.

## HANDS-ON LAB

Examine how glaciers move across Earth's surface.

### Academic Vocabulary

Describe an interaction you observed and one you took part in. Be sure to identify the people and things involved in the interaction.

........................................................

........................................................

........................................................

........................................................

........................................................

### Giant Bulldozer of Ice

**Figure 1** Like a slow-moving bulldozer, Alaska's Bering Glacier, the largest glacier in North America, plows across Earth's surface.

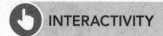

**INTERACTIVITY**

Learn about the effects of glaciers.

**Continental Glaciers** A **continental glacier** is a glacier that covers much of a continent or large island. It can spread out over millions of square kilometers and flow in all directions. Today, continental glaciers cover about 10 percent of Earth's land, including Antarctica and most of Greenland.

During **ice ages**, continental glaciers covered larger parts of Earth's surface. The glaciers gradually advanced and retreated several times, changing the shape of Earth's surface each time.

**Valley Glaciers** A **valley glacier** is a long, narrow glacier that forms when snow and ice build up in a mountain valley. High mountains keep these glaciers from spreading out in all directions, and gravity pulls the glacier downhill. Valley glaciers usually move slowly down valleys that have already been cut by rivers. Sometimes a valley glacier can experience a surge, or a quick slide, and move about 6 kilometers in one year. Alaska's Bering Glacier, shown in **Figure 1**, is a valley glacier.

## Math Toolbox

### Comparing Glacier Thickness

The graph shows the cumulative mass balance of a set of glaciers observed by scientists from 1945 to 2015. The cumulative mass balance is the total amount of ice the glaciers have gained or lost since 1945. The curve is always negative, so the glaciers have lost ice since 1945. The slope of the curve (how steep it is) shows how fast or slow the glaciers are losing ice.

1. **Reason Abstractly** What does a flat slope indicate? What does a steep slope indicate?

   .................................................

   .................................................

   .................................................

   .................................................

2. **SEP Use Models** According to the data, the reference glaciers have melted and lost ice in every decade. In which decade did the glaciers lose ice slowest? In which decade did they lose ice quickest?

   .................................................

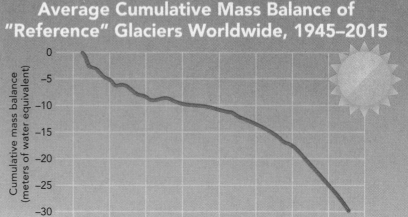

**Average Cumulative Mass Balance of "Reference" Glaciers Worldwide, 1945–2015**

Source: World Glacier Monitoring Service, 2016

## Glacial Erosion

The movement of a glacier slowly changes the land beneath it. The two processes by which glaciers erode the land are plucking and abrasion.

As a glacier flows over the land, it picks up rocks in a process called **plucking**. The weight of the ice breaks rocks into fragments that freeze to the bottom of the glacier. Then the rock fragments get carried with the glacier, as shown in **Figure 2**. Plucking leaves behind a jagged landscape.

Many rocks remain embedded on the bottom and sides of the glacier, and the glacier drags them across the land much like sandpaper in a process called abrasion. Land is worn away and deep gouges and scratches form in the bedrock.

For most glaciers, advancing, retreating, and eroding the land are very slow events. It can take years for scientists to observe any change in a glacier or its effects. Sometimes, however, glaciers move unusually fast. In 2012, scientists determined that a glacier in Greenland advanced up to 46 meters per day, faster than any other glacier recorded.

Although glaciers move and work slowly, they are a major force of erosion. They can take years to carve tiny scratches in bedrock. They can also carve out huge valleys hundreds of kilometers long over thousands of years. Through slow movement and erosion, glaciers dramatically change the shape of large areas of Earth's surface.

## Glacial Erosion

**Figure 2** Glaciers wear down Earth's surface by plucking and abrasion.

1. Interpret Diagrams 🖊
   Draw an arrow in the diagram to show the direction in which the ice is moving. Draw an X where you think abrasion is occurring. Draw a circle where plucking is happening.

2. SEP Construct Explanations In your own words, describe the glacial erosion taking place in the diagram.

   ..................................................

   ..................................................

   ..................................................

   ..................................................

   ..................................................

   ..................................................

   ..................................................

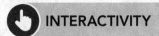
**INTERACTIVITY**

Examine water's effect on glaciers.

## Glacial Deposition

A glacier carries large amounts of rock and soil as it erodes the land in its path. As the glacier melts, it deposits the sediment it eroded from the land, creating various landforms, detailed in **Figure 3**. These landforms remain for thousands of years after the glacier has melted. The mixture of sediments that a glacier deposits directly on the surface is called **till**, which includes clay, silt, sand, gravel, boulders, and even rock ground so finely it is called rock flour.

**Moraine** The till deposited at the edges of a glacier forms a ridge called a moraine. Lateral moraines are deposits of sediment along the sides of a glacier. A terminal moraine is the ridge of till that is dropped at the farthest point reached by a glacier.

## Landforms of Glacial Erosion and Deposition

**Figure 3** Glacial erosion and deposition wear down and build up Earth's surface, producing landforms.

Classify ✏ In the model of a landscape shaped by glaciers, identify the features of erosion and deposition. In the circles, write *E* for erosion and *D* for deposition.

**Horn** When glaciers carve away the sides of a mountain, the result is a sharpened peak called a horn.

**Cirque** A cirque is a bowl-shaped hollow eroded by a glacier.

**Moraine** A moraine is a ridge that forms where a glacier deposits till.

**Fjord** A fjord forms when the level of the sea rises, filling a valley once cut by a glacier.

**Arête** An arête is a sharp ridge separating two cirques.

**Kettle** Retreating, or melting, glaciers also create features called kettles. A kettle is a steep-sided depression that forms when a chunk of ice is left in glacial till. When the ice melts, the kettle remains. The continental glacier of the last ice age left behind many kettles. Kettles often fill with water, forming small ponds or lakes called kettle lakes. Such lakes are common in areas such as Wisconsin that were once covered with glaciers.

✓ READING CHECK **Write Informative Texts** What are the effects of glacial deposition?

..............................................................................................................

..............................................................................................................

..............................................................................................................

..............................................................................................................

**U-Shaped valley** A flowing glacier scoops out a U-shaped valley.

**Kettle lake** A kettle lake forms when a depression left in till by melting ice fills with water.

## Model It!

**SEP Develop Models** ✏ In the space provided, draw part of the same landscape to show what the surface looked like before glacial erosion and deposition.

## Waves Change Earth's Surface

Like glaciers, waves change Earth's surface. The energy in most waves comes from the wind. Stronger winds cause larger waves. The friction between the wave and the ocean floor slows the wave. Then the water breaks powerfully on the shore. This forward-moving water provides the force that changes the land along the shoreline.

**Wave Erosion** Waves shape the coast through weathering and erosion by breaking down rock and moving sand and other sediments. Large waves can hit rocks along the shore with great force, or **impact**. Over time, waves can enlarge small cracks in rocks and cause pieces of rock to break off. Waves also break apart rocks by abrasion. As a wave approaches shallow water, it picks up and carries sediment, including sand and gravel. When the wave hits land, the sediment wears away rock like sandpaper slowly wearing away wood.

Waves approaching the shore gradually change direction as different parts of the waves drag on the bottom, as shown in **Figure 4**. The energy of these waves is concentrated on headlands. A headland is a part of the shore that extends into the ocean. Gradually, soft rock erodes, leaving behind the harder rock that is resistant to wave erosion. But over time, waves erode the headlands and even out the shoreline.

### Academic Vocabulary

How might you use the word *impact* in everyday life? Write a sentence using the word.

.............................................................

.............................................................

.............................................................

.............................................................

.............................................................

### Headland Erosion

**Figure 4** Wave erosion wears away rock to form headlands.

1. SEP Develop Models 🖊 Shade in the arrows that indicate where waves concentrate the greatest amount of energy.

2. CCC Cause and Effect 🖊 Draw a line to show how continued erosion will change the shoreline.

3. CCC Stability and Change How does this model help you understand a system or process of change?

.............................................................

.............................................................

.............................................................

.............................................................

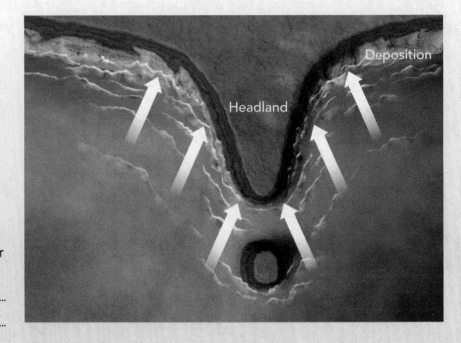

Deposition

Headland

## Landforms Formed by Wave Erosion

When an ax strikes the base of a tree trunk, the cut gets bigger and deeper with each strike. Similarly, when ocean waves hit a steep, rocky coast, they erode the base of the land. Waves erode the softer rock first. Over time, the waves may erode a hollow notch in the rock called a sea cave. Eventually, waves may erode the base of a cliff so much that the cliff collapses. The rubble is washed out by wave action and the result is a wave-cut platform at the cliff's base, which is all that remains of the eroded cliff. A sea arch is another feature of wave erosion that forms when waves erode a layer of softer rock that underlies a layer of harder rock. If an arch collapses, a pillar of rock called a sea stack may result.

Wave erosion changes Earth's surface at different rates. Sometimes it changes the land quickly. During a single powerful storm with strong winds that form high-energy waves, part of a cliff or sea stack may crumble. Waves may pick up and carry away large amounts of sediment along a shore. In general, waves erode rock slowly, cutting cliffs and headlands back centimeters to meters in a year. Waves may take hundreds to thousands of years to wear away headlands and even out shorelines.

☑ **READING CHECK** **Write Explanatory Texts** Reread the text. Then explain how you think a sea cave might become a sea arch.

.....................................................................................

.....................................................................................

**Landforms Formed by Wave Erosion**
**Figure 5** 🖊 Identify and label the landforms in the photo.

---

### Literacy Connection

**Write Informative Texts** As you read, think about how you could help another student understand the concepts. Then, in your own words, describe how waves cause erosion.

.............................................................

.............................................................

.............................................................

.............................................................

.............................................................

.............................................................

.............................................................

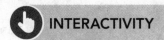

**INTERACTIVITY**

Investigate wind and water erosion in Florida.

**Wave Deposition** Deposition occurs when waves lose energy and slow down, causing the water to drop the sediment it carries. Waves change the shape of a coast when they deposit sediment and form landforms.

## Landforms Formed by Wave Deposition

A beach is an area of wave-washed sediment along a coast. The sediment deposited on beaches is usually sand. Some beaches are made of coral or seashell fragments piled up by wave action. Florida has many such beaches.

Waves usually hit the beach at an angle, creating a current that runs parallel to the coastline. As waves repeatedly hit the beach, some of the sediment gets carried along the beach with the current, in a process called **longshore drift**.

Longshore drift also builds up sandbars and creates barrier islands. Sandbars are long ridges of sand parallel to the shore. A spit is an extended part of a beach that is connected by one end to the mainland. A barrier island forms when waves pile up large amounts of sand above sea level, forming a long, narrow island parallel to the coast. Barrier islands are found in Florida and numerous other places along the Atlantic coast of the United States. Barrier islands are constantly changing from wave erosion and deposition that occur during hurricanes and other storms.

✓ **READING CHECK** **Translate Information** Use the information in the text and **Figure 6** to determine how the coastline might change if large amounts of sand built up higher than sea level as a result of storm deposition.

**Landforms Formed by Wave Deposition**

**Figure 6** ✎ On the diagram, draw arrows and label them to show the direction of longshore drift and the flow of sediment from the river to the sea.

Beach

Spit

Sandbar

**1. Identify** What are three landforms formed by wave deposition?

........................................................................

........................................................................

........................................................................

........................................................................

........................................................................

**2. CCC Stability and Change** How are the ways in which glaciers and waves wear down Earth's surface similar?

........................................................................

........................................................................

........................................................................

........................................................................

........................................................................

........................................................................

........................................................................

**3. CCC Cause and Effect** A valley in the Rocky Mountains contains a glacier. How might the glacier change this valley in the future?

........................................................................

........................................................................

........................................................................

........................................................................

........................................................................

........................................................................

........................................................................

........................................................................

**4. SEP Develop Models** 🖋 Draw and label diagrams to show how a sea arch might form from a headland.

# Quest CHECK-IN

**In this lesson, you discovered how erosion and deposition by glaciers change Earth's surface. You also learned how erosion and deposition by waves change Earth's surface.**

CCC System Models Why is it important to consider the effects of wave erosion and deposition when designing an artificial island?

........................................................................

........................................................................

........................................................................

........................................................................

## 👆 INTERACTIVITY

Breaking Waves

**Go online** to examine how wave erosion might impact the location of your island, and adjust your design as needed.

# ☑ TOPIC 5 Review and Assess

## 1 Weathering and Soil

MS-ESS2-2

1. How does acid rain cause weathering?
   A. through abrasion
   B. through oxidation
   C. by dissolving rock
   D. by carrying rock away

2. Mechanical weathering breaks some limestone into pieces. What effect would this have on chemical weathering of the limestone?
   A. Chemical weathering would stop occurring.
   B. Chemical weathering would remain the same.
   C. Chemical weathering would occur at a slower rate.
   D. Chemical weathering would occur at a faster rate.

3. The process of ................................................. is an example of ................................................. weathering in which rock splits through repeated freezing and thawing.

4. SEP Develop Models ✏ Draw a diagram of the A, B, and C horizons of soil. Label the horizons and describe the processes that formed each layer. Include examples of weathering in your description.

.................................................................

.................................................................

.................................................................

.................................................................

.................................................................

## 2 Erosion and Deposition

MS-ESS2-2, MS-ESS3-2

5. Which change occurs as a result of wind slowing down?
   A. erosion
   B. deposition
   C. chemical weathering
   D. mechanical weathering

6. How are erosion and deposition alike?
   A. Both change Earth's surface over time.
   B. Both build up Earth's surface quickly.
   C. Both wear down Earth's surface slowly.
   D. Neither changes Earth's surface.

7. Which type of mass movement occurs rapidly when a single mass of soil and rock suddenly slip downhill?
   A. creep
   B. landslide
   C. mudslide
   D. slump

8. Deposition by ................................................. causes sand ................................................. to form.

9. CCC Stability and Change  A scientist observes that over several decades, fence posts placed in soil on a slope became tilted. Have erosion, deposition, or both occurred in this area? Use evidence to explain how you know.

.................................................................

.................................................................

.................................................................

.................................................................

.................................................................

.................................................................

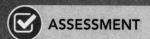 
# ③ Water Erosion

MS-ESS2-2

**10.** Which landform develops as a result of river deposition?
A. cave
B. delta
C. stalactite
D. waterfall

**11.** Which of the following processes causes sinkholes to form?
A. erosion of sediment by runoff
B. deposition of sediment by a river
C. deposition of calcite by groundwater
D. erosion of limestone by groundwater

**12.** Sediments get deposited in an alluvial fan because ..................................................................
.............................................................................

**13. SEP Develop Models** 🖉 Complete the flow chart to model a process that changes Earth's surface. Be sure to give the model a title.

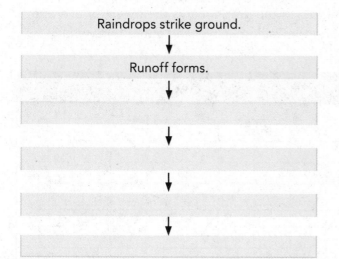

Raindrops strike ground.

↓

Runoff forms.

↓

↓

↓

# ④ Glacial and Wave Erosion

MS-ESS2-2

**14.** Which term describes sediment of mixed sizes deposited directly by a glacier?
A. kettle
B. loess
C. slump
D. till

**15.** How does longshore drift affect Earth's surface?
A. Rivers carry sediment to the ocean.
B. Rock cliffs break apart from impact.
C. Sediment moves down a beach with the current.
D. Waves concentrate their energy on headlands.

**16.** Which landform is created as a direct result of waves slowly eroding rocks?
A. beach
B. sandbar
C. sea stack
D. spit

**17.** Glaciers erode Earth's surface through the processes of ...........................................
and ...........................................

**18. CCC Cause and Effect** You are in a mountain valley studying a glacier. How could you use local landforms to tell whether the glacier is advancing or retreating?

.............................................................................
.............................................................................
.............................................................................
.............................................................................
.............................................................................

MS-ESS2-2, MS-ESS3-2

## Evidence-Based Assessment

A team of researchers is studying a massive landslide that occurred on the scenic stretch of California's coast known as Big Sur on May 20, 2017. Millions of tons of rock and dirt collapsed down a seaside slope onto the highway and spilled into the sea.

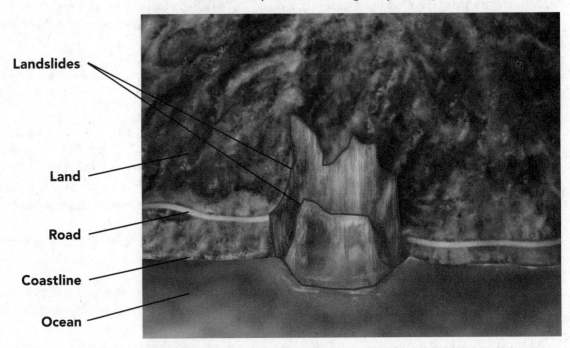

Landslides

Land

Road

Coastline

Ocean

To understand what happened in Big Sur, researchers are analyzing average winter precipitation data collected over a thirty-year period. The data is displayed in the graph. The solid line across the middle of the graph marks the mean, or average, winter precipitation for California over the entire thirty-year period.

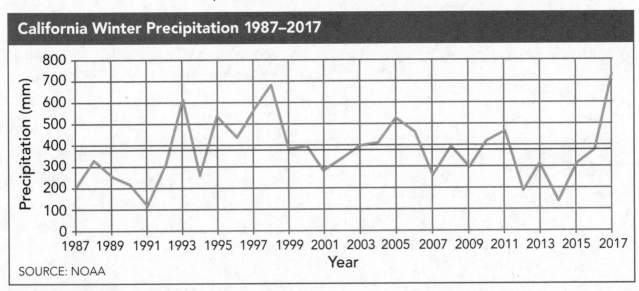

**California Winter Precipitation 1987–2017**

SOURCE: NOAA

1. **SEP Analyze Data** How much precipitation did California receive in the winter prior to the May 20 landslide of 2017?

   **A.** 710 mm      **B.** 390 mm

   **C.** 520 mm      **D.** 800 mm

2. **SEP Interpret Data** How would you describe California's precipitation in the five winters prior to 2017? Select all the statements that apply.

   ☐ It was above average for the five winters.

   ☐ It was below average for four winters, and average for one.

   ☐ It was below average for the five winters.

   ☐ It was mostly above average.

   ☐ It was mostly below average.

   ☐ It was above average for four winters, and below average for one.

3. **CCC Stability and Change** In the image of the coast at Big Sur, what are three visible indications that a large landslide occurred?

   ...........................................................................

   ...........................................................................

   ...........................................................................

   ...........................................................................

   ...........................................................................

   ...........................................................................

   ...........................................................................

4. **CCC Cause and Effect** How do you think weathering and erosion will affect the base of the deposited sediment, which is in the ocean? How will this affect the coastline in the future?

   ...........................................................................

   ...........................................................................

   ...........................................................................

   ...........................................................................

   ...........................................................................

   ...........................................................................

   ...........................................................................

5. **SEP Construct Explanations** What do you think is the connection between the precipitation in the winter of 2017 and the landslide?

   ...........................................................................

   ...........................................................................

   ...........................................................................

   ...........................................................................

   ...........................................................................

   ...........................................................................

   ...........................................................................

# Quest FINDINGS

## Complete the Quest!

**Phenomenon Reflect on how changes to Earth's surface will impact an artificial island. Then, prepare and deliver an oral or written presentation explaining your island design and your model.**

**CCC System Models** What are three things you learned about the processes that shape Earth's surface that helped you to design your artificial island?

...........................................................................

...........................................................................

...........................................................................

...........................................................................

...........................................................................

...........................................................................

👆 **INTERACTIVITY**

Reflect on Your Ingenious Island

# Materials on a Slope

How can you use a **model** to determine the likelihood of **mass movement**?

## Background

**Phenomenon** Geoscience processes such as rapid mass movement result in large amounts of sediment moving down hillsides.

In this investigation, you will work as part of a landslide monitoring team. You will develop and use a model to explore the relationship between the height and width of a hill. You will gain understanding about how these factors affect the hill's stability and the likelihood that mass movement will occur.

## Safety

Be sure to follow all safety guidelines provided by your teacher. The Safety Appendix of your textbook provides more details about the safety icons.

## Materials

(per group)

- tray (about 15 cm × 45 cm × 60 cm)
- several sheets of white paper
- masking tape
- cardboard tube
- spoon or paper cup

- dry sand (500 mL) in container
- wooden skewer
- metric ruler
- pencil or crayon
- graph paper

Landslides are destructive events that not only damage roadways and buildings, but also result in the loss of life.

# Plan Your Investigation

HANDS-ON LAB

и**Demonstrate** Go online for a downloadable worksheet of this lab.

☐ Use the metric ruler to mark off centimeters across the length of the paper. Take the tray provided by your teacher and use the paper to cover its interior surface. Secure the paper with tape. In the middle of the tray, stand the cardboard tube upright. Use a spoon or cup to fill the tube with sand.

☐ When the tube is nearly full, slowly and steadily pull the tube straight up so that the sand falls out of the bottom and forms a cone-shaped hill. Use different quantities of sand and observe the shapes and sizes of the sand hills created.

☐ Using the materials provided by your teacher, design an investigation to explore the relationship between the height and width of a sand hill. Determine how many sand hills you will create in your investigation.

☐ Then use the space provided to outline your procedure. Have your teacher review and approve your procedure, and then conduct your investigation. Create a data table to record your data about the heights and widths of the sand hills your group models.

## Design Your Procedure

## Data Table

# Analyze and Interpret Data

1. **SEP Analyze Data** Study your data table. What patterns do you notice in your data?

....................................................................................................

....................................................................................................

2. **SEP Evaluate Information** What do your data suggest about the relationship between the height and width of a sand hill?

....................................................................................................

....................................................................................................

....................................................................................................

3. **SEP Identify Limitations** What are the advantages of using the sand hill model in this investigation? What are the limitations of using the model?

....................................................................................................

....................................................................................................

....................................................................................................

....................................................................................................

....................................................................................................

....................................................................................................

4. **CCC Scale, Proportion, and Quantity** How is your sand hill model similar to and different from a natural hill that undergoes mass movement?

....................................................................................................

....................................................................................................

....................................................................................................

....................................................................................................

5. **CCC Stability and Change** How could you apply the results of your investigation to help assess the likelihood of and forecast future mass movement events such as landslides? Use evidence from your investigation to support your explanation.

....................................................................................................

....................................................................................................

....................................................................................................

....................................................................................................

# Distribution of Natural Resources

**NGSS PERFORMANCE EXPECTATIONS**

**MS-ESS3-1** Construct a scientific explanation based on evidence for how the uneven distributions of Earth's mineral, energy, and groundwater resources are the result of past and current geoscience processes.

**MS-ESS3-3** Apply scientific principles to design a method for monitoring and minimizing a human impact on the environment.

**MS-ESS3-4** Construct an argument supported by evidence for how increases in human population and per-capita consumption of natural resources impact Earth's systems.

What is responsible
for these colorful
rock formations?

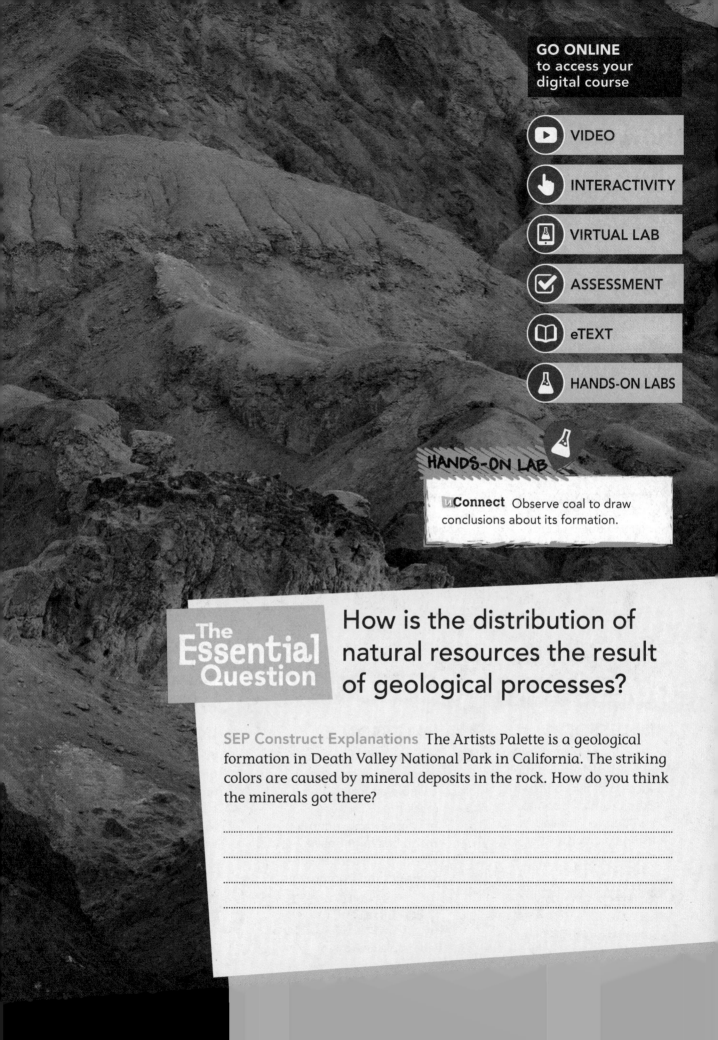

**GO ONLINE**
to access your
digital course

▶ VIDEO

👆 INTERACTIVITY

🧪 VIRTUAL LAB

☑ ASSESSMENT

📖 eTEXT

⚗ HANDS-ON LABS

**HANDS-ON LAB**

u**Connect** Observe coal to draw conclusions about its formation.

**The Essential Question**

How is the distribution of natural resources the result of geological processes?

SEP Construct Explanations The Artists Palette is a geological formation in Death Valley National Park in California. The striking colors are caused by mineral deposits in the rock. How do you think the minerals got there?

.............................................................................................

.............................................................................................

.............................................................................................

.............................................................................................

# Quest KICKOFF

## How could natural resources have saved a ghost town?

**Phenomenon** In the past, the discovery of valuable or rare natural resources often led to the quick development of towns as people rushed to strike it rich. But many of these boomtowns, as they came to be known, died as quickly as they began. In this problem-based Quest activity, you will investigate how resource availability affected the longevity and success of boomtowns. By applying what you learn in each lesson, you will gather key Quest information and evidence. In the Findings activity, you will choose a boomtown to explore in more detail and explain the role that resource availability played in the fate of the town.

### NBC LEARN ▶ VIDEO

After watching the Quest Kickoff video, which explores how resource availability affected the success or failure of boomtowns, think about what made your town or city a desirable location for people to settle in the past.

........................................................

........................................................

........................................................

........................................................

........................................................

........................................................

........................................................

........................................................

........................................................

 **INTERACTIVITY**

Predicting Boom or Bust

**MS-ESS3-1** Construct a scientific explanation based on evidence for how the uneven distributions of Earth's mineral, energy, and groundwater resources are the result of past and current geoscience processes.

---

## Quest CHECK-IN

### IN LESSON 1

How does the availability of fossil fuels affect the success of a boomtown? Predict which boomtowns could have survived by using coal, oil, and/or natural gas.

 **INTERACTIVITY**

Surviving on Fossil Fuels

## Quest CHECK-IN

### IN LESSON 2

What conditions make renewable resources a viable alternative to fossil fuels? Explore how renewable energy resources might have affected the success or failure of the boomtowns.

 **INTERACTIVITY**

Renewable Energy

## Quest CHECK-IN

### IN LESSON 3

What effect does the distribution of minerals have on the success of a boomtown? Analyze the distribution of gold, copper, and salt to help you determine the fates of the boomtowns.

 **INTERACTIVITY**

Surviving on Minerals

Many towns like the one shown here did not have the resources required to sustain growth and development.

BLACKSMITH

## Quest CHECK-IN

### IN LESSON 4

How does access to water affect the fate of a boomtown? Predict which boomtowns might have survived based on the availability of water resources.

**INTERACTIVITY**

Surviving on Water

## Quest FINDINGS

## Complete the Quest!

Find out what happened to each boomtown and then create a travel brochure for one of the boomtowns to explain how resource availability affected the fate of that town.

**INTERACTIVITY**

Reflect on Boomtowns

# What's in a Piece of Coal?

What evidence can you gather to **explain** what coal is made of?

## Background

**Phenomenon** Coal is the most abundant fossil fuel in the world. About 40% the world's electricity is generated by coal, and it is also used in many industries such as steel production. Coal-fired electrical power plants use the heat given off by burning coal to make steam. Different kinds of coal release different amounts of energy when they are burned. To understand where the energy stored in coal comes from, you need to know what coal is made of and how it forms. In this activity, you will use observations of a piece of coal to try to explain its composition and formation.

## Materials

**(per group)**
- lignite coal
- hand lens
- ruler
- paper

## Safety

Be sure to follow all safety procedures provided by your teacher. The Safety Appendix of your textbook provides more details about the safety icons.

## Design a Procedure

1. Observe the piece of coal. Make a table of properties of coal that you can investigate and record your observations in the table in as much detail as possible.

2. **SEP Plan an Investigation** Using the tools provided, write a procedure to test the properties you added to your table. Show your plan to your teacher before you begin. Record your observations.

.............................................................................

.............................................................................

.............................................................................

.............................................................................

.............................................................................

# Observations

## Analyze and Interpret Data

**HANDS-ON LAB**

**Connect** Go online for a downloadable worksheet of this lab.

1. **CCC Scale, Proportion, and Quantity** Compare your initial observations to those you made using the hand lens. What did you notice?

..............................................................................................................

..............................................................................................................

..............................................................................................................

..............................................................................................................

2. **SEP Construct Explanations** Based on your observations, what do you think coal is made of?

..............................................................................................................

..............................................................................................................

..............................................................................................................

3. **SEP Construct Explanations** Based on your observations, how do you think coal is formed?

..............................................................................................................

..............................................................................................................

..............................................................................................................

# Nonrenewable Energy Resources

## Guiding Questions

- What are nonrenewable resources?
- What factors affect the distribution of nonrenewable energy resources?
- How has human activity impacted the distribution of fossil fuels?

## Connections

**Literacy** Cite Textual Evidence

**Math** Analyze Relationships

MS-ESS3-1, MS-ESS3-4

## HANDS-ON LAB

**uInvestigate** Explore why fossil fuels are considered nonrenewable resources.

## Vocabulary

natural resource
nonrenewable
  resource
fossil fuels
nuclear fission

## Academic Vocabulary

renew

## Connect It !

✏️ **Identify and label some the materials that are being used in this construction project.**

Classify Pick one of the materials you identified in the photo and explain whether you think the resource is limited or unlimited.

.....................................................................................................................................

.....................................................................................................................................

# Natural Resources

We all rely on natural resources to survive. A **natural resource** is anything occuring naturally in the environment that humans use. We need air to breathe, water to drink, soil in which to grow plants to eat, sunlight to make those plants grow, and other natural resources. Some of these resources are essentially unlimited and renewable regardless of what we do. For example, sunlight and wind are available daily at most places on Earth. Other renewable resources can be reused or replenished, but it may require some care or planning. For example, wood from trees is a renewable resource as long as some trees are spared to reproduce and make the next generation of trees.

Other resources are **nonrenewable resources,** which cannot be replaced. This may be because there is a finite amount of the resource on Earth and we don't have a way to make more of it. The element silver, for example, cannot be made from other substances. The amount of silver on Earth is set. Other resources are considered nonrenewable because it takes very long periods of time for them to form.

☑ READING CHECK **Cite Evidence** Why is wood considered to be a renewable resource?

........................................................................................

........................................................................................

........................................................................................

HANDS-ON LAB

Classify resources that you use in a typical day.

📖 **Reflect** In your science notebook, describe how a natural resource could shift from being renewable to nonrenewable.

**Resource Use**
**Figure 1** This construction project relies on a number of natural resources.

Lignite

Bituminous Coal

Anthracite

## Types of Coal

**Figure 2** Brittle, lustrous anthracite has more energy than crumbly, dull lignite.

**Determine Differences** Why might one type of coal contain more energy than another type of coal?

.............................................

.............................................

.............................................

.............................................

# Fossil Fuels

The sources of energy commonly called fossil fuels include coal, petroleum, and natural gas. **Fossil fuels** are the energy-rich substances made from the preserved remains of organisms. The chemical energy in fossil fuels can be converted to other forms by burning them.

The energy stored in these compounds originally arrived on Earth as sunlight. Photosynthetic organisms such as algae, moss, grasses, and trees converted sunlight into carbon-based compounds. When animals ate the plants, they absorbed some of those compounds. Under certain conditions involving high temperatures and pressures, the remains of these organisms were transformed into new materials, including solid coal, liquid petroleum, and methane gas.

**Coal** Coal is formed from the remains of plants that died long ago in and around swampy areas. There are different grades, or types, of coal (**Figure 2**). Each grade forms under different conditions, as shown in **Figure 3**. In addition to being a source of energy, coal is used in a wide array of applications. Coal is used in water and air purification systems, as well as medical equipment such as kidney dialysis devices. Coal is used to make steel from iron ore. Coal is also an essential ingredient in carbon fiber, an extremely durable and lightweight material used to construct everything from bicycles to buildings.

Burning coal in coal-fired power plants accounts for about 30 percent of the electricity produced in the United States. Coal has long been used as a fuel because it has twice as much energy per unit of mass as wood. So, when coal can be mined at a large scale, it can be an efficient source of energy.

Unfortunately, burning coal produces pollutants and causes millions of deaths each year from health problems. Coal mining also requires large mines to be dug into the ground, or the removal of mountaintops or other surface layers to access coal beds. Removing coal causes great damage to the surrounding environment.

✓ READING CHECK **Determine Central Ideas** What is the original source of the energy contained in coal? Explain.

.................................................................................................

.................................................................................................

.................................................................................................

## Coal Formation and Distribution

**Figure 3** Coal only forms under the right conditions. The map shows major deposits of coal around the world.

1. **SEP Use Models** 🖊 Circle the three continents that have the most coal resources.

2. **SEP Construct Explanations** Why is coal not found evenly distributed around the world?

.................................................................................

.................................................................................

.................................................................................

.................................................................................

KEY

■ Coal deposit

Swamp Environment

**PEAT**
(Partially altered plant material; very smoky when burned, low energy)

Burial

**LIGNITE**
(Soft, brown coal; moderate energy)

Compaction

Greater burial

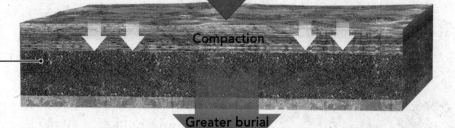

**BITUMINOUS COAL**
(Soft, black coal; major coal used in power generation and industry; high energy)

Compaction

Metamorphism

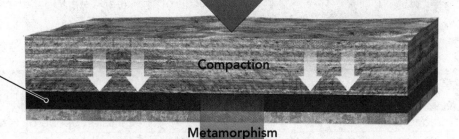

**ANTHRACITE**
(Hard, black coal; used in industry; highest energy)

Stress

**Oil** What we commonly refer to as oil is scientifically known as **petroleum**, from the Latin terms *petra* (rock) and *oleum* (oil). Petroleum is made of the remains of small animals, algae, and other organisms that lived in marine environments hundreds of millions of years ago. Oil deposits form when these remains become trapped underground and are subject to high pressure and temperature.

Because it is a liquid and can be processed into different fuels, petroleum is especially useful for powering engines in automobiles, ships, trains, and airplanes. Petroleum also has many important industrial uses, such as making plastics, lubricants, and fertilizers. Petroleum is also the basis for synthetic fibers, such as rayon and nylon. Many cosmetic and pharmaceutical products such as petroleum jelly and tar shampoos that treat dandruff, contain forms of petroleum.

As with coal, burning oil and natural gas emits carbon dioxide. Oil can also be spilled, which can be disastrous for wildlife and water quality (**Figure 4**). Natural gas leaks contribute to global warming, and can result in explosions if the concentration of gas is high and a spark ignites it.

## Oil Impacts

**Figure 4** Oil is often drilled from the ocean floor and transported by ship. Major oil spills can harm or kill wildlife, as well as damaging habitats and water quality.

1. SEP Interpret Data What are the two major causes of accidental oil spills?

......................................................................

2. SEP Use Mathematics About how much more oil was spilled as a result of the *Deepwater Horizon* explosion than the *Valdez* running aground?

......................................................................

| Location and Date | Amount Spilled (gallons) | Cause |
|---|---|---|
| Trinidad and Tobago, 1979 | 90 million | Collision of two oil tanker ships |
| Gulf of Mexico, 1979 | 140 million | Blown-out *Ixtoc 1* oil well on ocean floor, fire, collapse of drilling platform |
| Persian Gulf, 1983 | 80 million | Collision of ship with oil-drilling platform during Iraq-Iran war |
| Prince William Sound, Alaska, 1989 | 11 million | *Exxon Valdez* oil tanker ship runs aground, puncturing hull |
| Angola, 1991 | 80 million | Oil tanker ship explodes and sinks |
| Gulf of Mexico, 2010 | 181 million | Blown-out *Deepwater Horizon* oil well, explosion of platform |

## Petroleum Formation and Distribution

**Figure 5** Petroleum has been drilled for all over the world. Wells or rigs are constructed to tap "fields" of oil hundreds or thousands of meters below Earth's surface, both on land and water.

**SEP Engage in Argument** A large sea once existed in the United States. Shade the area of the country where you think the sea likely existed. Then explain your choice.

........................................................................

........................................................................

........................................................................

**KEY**

☐ Onshore basins
☐ Offshore basins

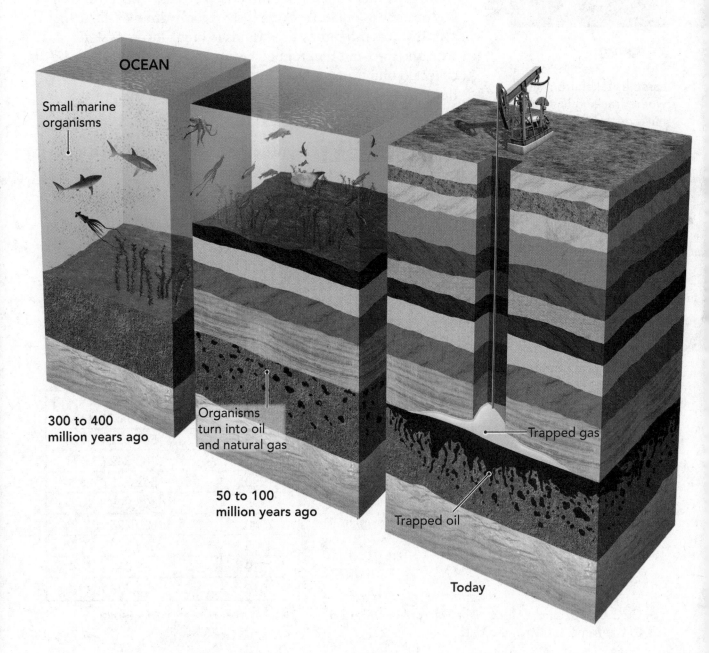

OCEAN

Small marine organisms

300 to 400 million years ago

Organisms turn into oil and natural gas

50 to 100 million years ago

Trapped gas

Trapped oil

Today

## Fracking

**Figure 6** Groundwater samples taken from sites where fracking has occurred have tested positive for methane and other hydrocarbons.

**Natural Gas** Formed from the same processes that produce oil and found in the same locations, natural gas is trapped in pockets within layers of rock deep below Earth's surface. A drill can tap the trapped gas, and then pipelines carry the gas for processing and transport. Burning petroleum and coal releases more carbon dioxide than burning natural gas. This is one reason many countries have encouraged more use of natural gas and are surveying underground basins of gas for further exploitation. On the other hand, the gas itself is a powerful greenhouse gas that contributes to global warming. This means any leaks of natural gas from wells, pipelines, and other structures pose a pollution problem.

To meet the demand for natural gas, a process called fracking has become popular. Fracking is short for hydraulic fracturing. This involves using pressured fluids to break layers of shale rock and force out the trapped natural gas, which can then be collected and transported. There are concerns that the fracking fluids are contaminating vital stores of groundwater that humans rely on (**Figure 6**).

**READING CHECK** **Cite Textual Evidence** Natural gas burns cleaner than coal, yet it is considered a pollutant. Why?

........................................................................................

........................................................................................

# Math Toolbox

## Natural Gas Consumption in the U.S.

In recent years, consumption patterns of natural gas have changed.

1. **SEP Use Mathematics** What was the percent increase in gas usage from 1980 to 2015? Show your work.

........................................................................................

........................................................................................

2. **Analyze Relationships** What trend is shown in the data?

........................................................................................

........................................................................................

3. **CCC Cause and Effect** What factors contributed to the trend shown in the data?

........................................................................................

........................................................................................

| Year | Volume (Million Cubic Meters) |
|------|-------------------------------|
| 1980 | 562,862 |
| 1985 | 489,342 |
| 1990 | 542,935 |
| 1995 | 628,829 |
| 2000 | 660,720 |
| 2005 | 623,379 |
| 2010 | 682,062 |
| 2015 | 773,228 |

**U.S. Annual Natural Gas Consumption**

Source: U.S. Energy Information Administration

# Nuclear Energy

Nuclear power is another nonrenewable energy resource used to generate much of the world's electricity. Nuclear energy provides 20 percent of the electricity in the United States. Inside a nuclear power plant, controlled nuclear fission reactions occur. **Nuclear fission** is the splitting of an atom's nucleus into two nuclei. Fission releases a great deal of energy. This energy is used to heat water, turning it into steam. The steam is then used to turn the blades of a turbine to produce electricity.

Uranium is the fuel used for nuclear fission inside nuclear reactors. It is a heavy metal that occurs in most rocks and is usually extracted through mining. The uranium found on Earth was part of the original cloud of dust and gas from which our solar system formed. Uranium is found throughout Earth's crust. But large ores of the material are formed from geological processes that only occur in certain locations on Earth (**Figure 7**).

**Literacy Connection**

**Cite Textual Evidence** As you read, underline text that supports the idea that uranium is a limited resource with finite amounts on Earth.

Source: World Nuclear Association

### Distribution of Uranium

**Figure 7** According to the World Nuclear Association, almost 70 percent of accessible uranium is found in only 5 countries.

1. SEP Use Models ✏ Circle the two countries with the greatest percentage of uranium resources.

2. CCC Patterns What patterns do you observe in the distribution of uranium?

.................................................................................

.................................................................................

.................................................................................

**INTERACTIVITY**

Learn more about the progression of living matter to petroleum.

# Using Energy Resources

Fossil fuels are among the most important nonrenewable resources for humans. As the human population has grown, these resources have become less abundant. Geologists estimate that we have already used about half the petroleum that fossilization, pressure, heat, and time have produced over hundreds of millions of years—and all in just a few centuries.

**Pollution** Humans are burning fossil fuels at a faster rate than the resulting carbon emissions can be absorbed by natural processes, such as photosynthesis. This is why the concentration of carbon dioxide in the atmosphere is now 45 percent higher than it was just over 200 years ago. Scientists have concluded that this is fueling global warming and climate change.

**World Politics** The uneven distribution of fossil fuel resources has led to political problems, including war. In 1990, Iraq invaded neighboring Kuwait in part because of disagreements over how oil fields at a shared border should be used. When the United States and other nations came to Kuwait's defense and drove out the Iraqi forces, oil fields and wells were set on fire. This resulted in hundreds of millions of gallons of oil being burned or spilled, and untreated emissions billowing into the atmosphere (**Figure 8**).

**Gulf War Oil Fires**
**Figure 8** The oil fields that were set on fire during the first Gulf War in 1991 caused significant damage to the land and living things.

☑ **READING CHECK** **Determine Conclusions** How have human activities affected the distribution of fossil fuels on Earth?

.......................................................................................................................................

.......................................................................................................................................

.......................................................................................................................................

## Plan It!

**Household Energy Use**
**SEP Plan an Investigation** Use the space to describe how you could determine how much fossil fuel is used in your home and then make recommendations about how to reduce your usage.

.......................................................................................................................................

.......................................................................................................................................

.......................................................................................................................................

.......................................................................................................................................

.......................................................................................................................................

1. **Identify** Which fossil fuel is produced from the remains of peat?

.................................................................................

2. **CCC Cause and Effect** A friend argues that the location of a petroleum deposit is a sign that marine organisms once lived there. Is your friend correct? Explain.

.................................................................................

.................................................................................

.................................................................................

.................................................................................

3. **Apply Scientific Reasoning** How does the abundance of a resource, and whether it is renewable or nonrenewable, affect how much it is used?

.................................................................................

.................................................................................

.................................................................................

.................................................................................

.................................................................................

.................................................................................

.................................................................................

4. **SEP Engage in Argument** What advantage does coal have over wood as an energy source? What is the major disadvantage of using coal for energy?

.................................................................................

.................................................................................

.................................................................................

.................................................................................

.................................................................................

.................................................................................

5. **SEP Construct Explanations** Why are oil, coal, and natural gas not found evenly distributed on Earth?

.................................................................................

.................................................................................

.................................................................................

.................................................................................

.................................................................................

.................................................................................

.................................................................................

.................................................................................

.................................................................................

# Quest CHECK-IN

**In this lesson, you learned about different types of nonrenewable energy resources called fossil fuels and the impacts of human activities related to extracting and using these resources.**

**Evaluate** Why is access to energy resources such as fossil fuels important to the economic and social development of a town?

.................................................................................

.................................................................................

.................................................................................

.................................................................................

👆 **INTERACTIVITY**

Surviving on Fossil Fuels

**Go online** to examine four different towns in the United States and determine the distribution pattern of the resources and the processes that may have resulted in the resource formation.

# 2 Renewable Energy Resources

## Guiding Questions

- What are renewable energy resources?
- How do renewable energy resources reduce human reliance on other natural resources?

## Connections

**Literacy** Draw Evidence

**Math** Represent Quantitative Relationships

MS-ESS3-1, MS-ESS3-3

## HANDS-ON LAB

**иInvestigate** Design, build, and test a model of wind power technology.

**Vocabulary**

renewable resource

**Academic Vocabulary**

cost

## Connect It!

✏ **Draw arrows to indicate how the mirrors in this thermal energy plant direct the sun's rays to a small point on the tower.**

CCC Cause and Effect How do you think this thermal energy plant helps reduce reliance on fossil fuels?

....................................................................................................

....................................................................................................

# Reducing Fossil Fuel Usage

The abundance of energy-rich fossil fuels has made it easy for humankind to justify using petroleum, coal, and natural gas. However, there are both benefits and costs in terms of the short-term and long-term effects. Even though they are nonrenewable and impact Earth's systems, it was easier and less expensive in the past to mine and drill for coal, oil, and gas than to harness other sources of energy. Due to increased awareness of the consequences of mining and burning fossil fuels, as well as advances in technology, things are beginning to change in favor of alternative sources of energy.

Alternative energy resources, such as the solar power tower in **Figure 1**, are considered **renewable resources** because we cannot run out of them. They are replaced by nature, or with a little help from us.

✓ READING CHECK **Determine Meaning** Why are some energy resources referred to as "renewable"?

...................................................................................

...................................................................................

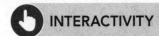

**INTERACTIVITY**

Identify renewable resources that are most suitable for use in your community.

**Thermal Power**
**Figure 1** This thermal energy plant uses energy from the sun to heat water and produce electricity using steam.

**VIDEO**

Learn more about the sun's role in providing energy that cycles through different processes on Earth.

# Alternative Sources of Energy

Using renewable energy resources can reduce our dependence on nonrenewables and avoid some of the problems associated with them.

**Solar Energy** One of the most basic types of solar energy is passive solar power. It involves letting sunlight pass through glass to heat a room or building to maximize its exposure to sunlight and retain that heat. A greenhouse is a good example of passive solar power.

In an active solar power system, sunlight is captured by solar cells, which can power things as small as wristwatches or as large as entire cities. As shown in **Figure 2**, a solar (or photovoltaic) cell converts the energy from sunlight directly into electrical energy. Solar cells are not a new technology, but they are now much more efficient and less expensive than they were years ago.

Though the sunlight is free, the **costs** of the initial investment can be high. Another drawback is the inconsistency of sunlight. More solar energy is available near the equator and in drier climates that do not experience many cloudy days. Additional technology must be used to store the electrical energy for use at night. Finally, not all places on Earth receive the same amount of sunlight throughout the year.

**Academic Vocabulary**

What are two different meanings of the term *cost*?

...............................................

...............................................

...............................................

...............................................

☑ READING CHECK **Summarize** What is the difference between passive solar power and active solar power?

...............................................

...............................................

## Model It!

### Solar Cells

**Figure 2** When sunlight hits it, each solar cell in a panel generates a small amount of electricity.

SEP Develop Models ✐ Trace the path of a negative particle from the top layer to the bottom layer to indicate how electrical energy is generated.

1. Sunlight hits the solar cell, which is made up of two layers separated by a barrier.

2. Energy from the sun excites the material in each layer. One layer ends up with negative particles and the other layer with positive particles.

2. The negative particles are attracted to the positive particles, but the barrier keeps the particles apart. Instead, the negative particles are guided along a path of wiring to the other layer. This creates electrical energy that can be used to power equipment.

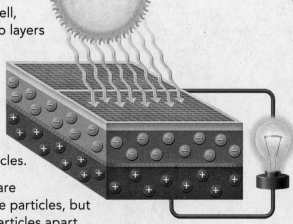

## Hydroelectric Resources

The sun's energy drives the water cycle, which moves large volumes of water to higher elevations from lower elevations in the form of rain and snow. Gravity pulls water downhill, giving rivers, streams, waterfalls, and tides their movement. Turbines can convert the energy of moving water into electricity.

Hydroelectric dams restrict the natural flow of a river by controlling how much water passes through turbines, as shown in **Figure 3**. Hydroelectric dams can generate a great deal of power, but they disrupt natural processes such as migrations of fish. Dams also alter habitats by creating reservoirs above the dam and reducing the width and flow of the river below. Most importantly, a dam must be close to a source of moving water.

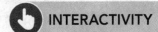

**INTERACTIVITY**

Learn about renewable resources, their global distributions, and the processes necessary for them to be viable.

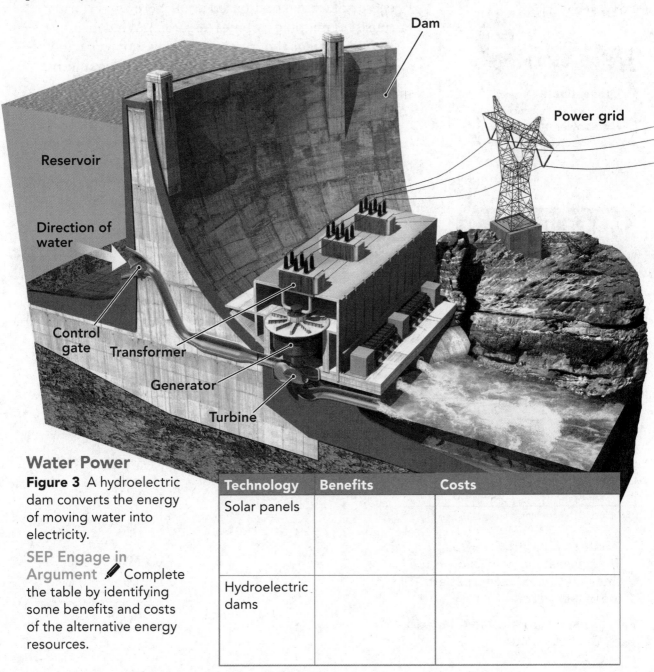

### Water Power

**Figure 3** A hydroelectric dam converts the energy of moving water into electricity.

**SEP Engage in Argument** ✏ Complete the table by identifying some benefits and costs of the alternative energy resources.

| Technology | Benefits | Costs |
|---|---|---|
| Solar panels | | |
| Hydroelectric dams | | |

## Offshore Wind Farm

**Figure 3** Wind is plentiful on the water, but turbines introduce obstacles to both boats and wildlife.

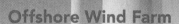

## HANDS-ON LAB

**Investigate** Design, build, and test a model of wind power technology.

# Math Toolbox

### Wind Power

**Wind Energy** Like the water cycle, wind is powered by energy from sunlight. An area of Earth's surface warms as sunlight is converted to thermal energy. Warm air rises and expands, allowing cooler, denser air to flow in to fill the void. We know this movement of air masses as wind. Just as turbines can be used to harness the energy in moving water, they can be used to harness the energy of wind. Land-based or offshore wind "farms" consist of multiple turbines (**Figure 3**). Wind farms do best in areas that receive a steady supply of wind. Some farms are found in valleys between mountains that channel and concentrate the wind. Others are found in the ocean, where land and sea breezes provide strong winds. The costs of constructing wind farms are considerable, and some people are concerned that large turbines threaten birds and spoil natural scenery. But wind power is already less expensive than coal power in many parts of the country, and it is the fastest-growing energy source in the world.

The table shows the projected production of industrial wind farms in the U.S. over the coming decades.

| Year | Production (gigawatts) |
|------|------------------------|
| 2000 | 2.5 |
| 2010 | 40.2 |
| 2020 | 113.4 |
| 2030 | 224.1 |
| 2040 | |
| 2050 | 404.3 |

Source: U.S Department of Energy

1. **Analyze Quantitative Relationships** Predict what the production in 2040 should be, based on the pattern. Fill in the empty cell of the table.

2. **Represent Quantitative Relationships** Graph the data.

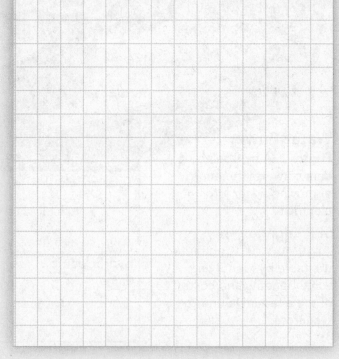

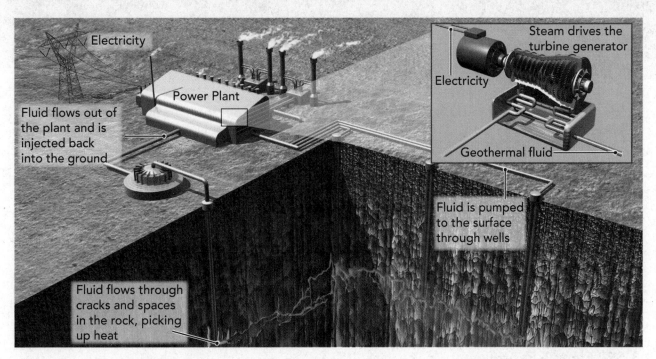

Electricity

Power Plant

Fluid flows out of the plant and is injected back into the ground

Fluid flows through cracks and spaces in the rock, picking up heat

Steam drives the turbine generator

Electricity

Geothermal fluid

Fluid is pumped to the surface through wells

## Geothermal Energy

One renewable energy source not originating with the sun is geothermal energy. Deep below Earth's surface, the rock of Earth's crust is hot. In some places on Earth's surface, this heat can be used on a small scale to warm homes. On a larger scale, geothermal energy plants (**Figure 4**) use this heat to generate electricity. One of the biggest drawbacks is that geothermal reservoirs are not easy to find. The site must be located over a geothermal hot spot, where the rock is hot enough to continuously reheat pumped water. The best sites are near volcanic areas. While initial costs to construct the plant and drill the pipes are expensive, the power it can provide in the long run makes up for it.

## Bioenergy Resources

Biomass such as wood, grasses, coconut husks, and other plant-based materials have been burned to produce light and heat for thousands of years. These resources are only limited by where they can grow. Scientists have developed ways to turn these resources into biofuels such as ethanol, which is usually made from corn or sugar cane, and biodiesel, which can be made from used cooking oil. Unfortunately, the energy that goes into producing these biofuels is often equal to or greater than the energy they yield. Also, burning biofuels is not much better for the atmosphere than burning fossil fuels.

✓ **READING CHECK** **Summarize** In the long run, why might it be less expensive to construct 100 geothermal power plants than to farm the same area for corn to make ethanol?

.................................................................................................................

.................................................................................................................

.................................................................................................................

### Geothermal Power Plant

**Figure 4** 🖉 Draw arrows to indicate the flow of water through the geothermal power plant. Use the information in the text to help you.

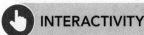 **INTERACTIVITY**

Set up a dairy farm and investigate how much electricity you can generate from biogas.

### Literacy Connection

**Draw Evidence** Underline the text that supports the idea that geothermal energy is a cost-effective solution in the long run.

# ☑ LESSON 2 Check

MSS-ESS3-1

**1. Identify** Name five renewable energy resources.

.......................................................................

.......................................................................

**2. CCC Cause and Effect** Is wind power a practical source of renewable energy everywhere on Earth? Explain.

.......................................................................

.......................................................................

.......................................................................

**3. SEP Engage in Argument** Do you think the benefits of using water resources to generate electricity outweight the costs and drawbacks? Explan.

.......................................................................

.......................................................................

.......................................................................

.......................................................................

.......................................................................

.......................................................................

**4. SEP Obtain Information** Suppose your local government wants to encourage the use of renewable energy resources by investing in a power plant fueled by a renewable energy source. Describe how you would investigate which renewable source would be most suitable for your area.

.......................................................................

.......................................................................

.......................................................................

.......................................................................

.......................................................................

.......................................................................

.......................................................................

.......................................................................

.......................................................................

.......................................................................

.......................................................................

.......................................................................

.......................................................................

.......................................................................

## Quest CHECK-IN

**In this lesson, you learned about different renewable energy resources, or renewables, and the costs and benefits of using them.**

**SEP Engage in Argument** What impact might the availability of renewable energy resources, such as water or wind, have on the success of a town?

.......................................................................

.......................................................................

.......................................................................

.......................................................................

### 👆 INTERACTIVITY

Renewable Energy

**Go online** to apply what you have learned about renewable energy to supplying energy to a boomtown.

# Micro-Hydro
# POWER

▶ VIDEO

Examine how hydroelectric power plants and wind farms generate clean energy.

**How can people without** access to electricity use moving water to generate power? You engineer it!

**The Challenge:** To generate power from moving water.

Earth's water system is an excellent source of power. Centuries ago, people realized that moving water, properly channeled, can turn wheels that make machinery move. More recently, engineers designed large-scale dams to harness the energy of moving water. Water power's great advantage is that the water is always moving, so electricity can be generated 24 hours a day.

Now engineers have developed hydropower on a small scale, known as micro-hydro power. If there is a small river or stream running through your property, then you need only a few basic things: a turbine, pipes to channel the water to the turbine, and a generator that will transform the energy into electricity.

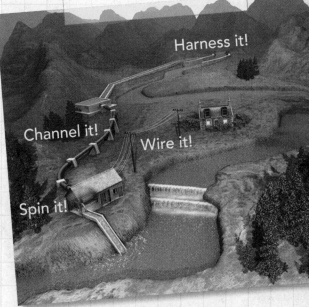

Harness it!

Channel it!

Wire it!

Spin it!

In this micro-hydro system, water from the river is channeled to the generator, which transforms the energy of the moving water into electrical energy.

**DESIGN CHALLENGE**

Can you design a micro-hydro system? Go to the Engineering Design Notebook to find out!

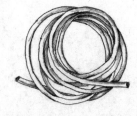
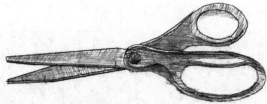

# LESSON
# 3 Mineral Resources

## Guiding Questions
- What are mineral resources?
- What factors affect the distribution of minerals on Earth?

## Connection
**Literacy** Determine Meaning

MS-ESS3-1, MS-ESS3-4

## HANDS-ON LAB

**uInvestigate** Explore the geological processes that form minerals.

**Vocabulary**
ore
crystallize

**Academic Vocabulary**
distribution

## Connect It!

✏️ **Circle some of the objects in the photo that you think contain minerals.**

SEP Construct Explanations  How do you think these minerals formed?

........................................................................................

........................................................................................

........................................................................................

# Minerals and Ores

You may think that minerals are only found in rocks. It's true that rocks are made from minerals, but if you look around, you will probably see several other things that are made from minerals. Metals are made from one or more minerals. The graphite in a pencil is a type of mineral. Computers, smartphones, and other electronic devices are made with metals and other minerals, too. Even you contain minerals, such as the calcium-bearing minerals that make up your bones and teeth.

But what is a mineral? A mineral is a solid substance that is non-living and made from a particular combination of elements. There are over 5,000 named minerals on Earth. Gold, quartz, and talc are just a few examples. When a mineral deposit is large enough and valuable enough for it to be extracted from the ground, it is known as **ore**. People remove ore from the ground so they can use it or sell it to make money.

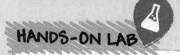

## HANDS-ON LAB

**Investigate** Explore the geological processes that form minerals.

**Reflect** Throughout the day, list some of the things you see and use that are made from minerals. Then, at the end of the day, write a paragraph explaining why minerals are important and describing some of their most important uses.

## Stalactite Formation

**Figure 1** These stalactites in Carlsbad Caverns National Park in New Mexico formed as minerals deposited by a dripping mineral-rich solution built up over long periods of time.

**Determine Meaning**
As you read, circle or underline an unknown word in the text and use context clues to help you determine the meaning. Revisit the unknown word at the end of the lesson and use a resource if you still cannot determine the meaning.

**How Minerals Form** Minerals form in different ways. They can form from organic materials, from mineral-rich solutions, and from cooling magma and lava.

**Organic Material** Corals like the ones in **Figure 2** create a hard outer skeleton that provides the coral with shape and protection. This skeleton is made from thin layers of calcium carbonate (also called calcite), a chemical compound similar to the shells of other sea animals. Once the coral is dead, the calcium carbonate skeleton is left behind. It may get buried and broken down into smaller fragments.

**Minerals from Living Things**
**Figure 2** These corals produce a hard outer skeleton made from the mineral calcite. The skeleton will be around for a long time after the coral dies.

**Apply Concepts** Why wouldn't other body parts of living things, such as skin, become minerals after an organism's death?

.................................................................................................

**Solutions** When water contains dissolved substances it is called a solution. In some cases, the elements in these solutions will **crystallize** to form a new mineral. This can happen within bodies of water and underground. One way this happens on Earth's surface involves the process of evaporation. When the water evaporates, the elements and compounds that are left behind crystallize into new minerals such as salts. This is how the mineral formations in **Figure 3** formed.

Another way that minerals form from solutions is through a process in which a warm solution flows through a crack in existing rock. Elements and compounds leave the solution as it cools and crystallize as minerals in the crack. These form veins of ores that are different from the surrounding rock.

**Magma and Lava** The molten and semi-molten rock mixture found beneath Earth's surface is known as magma. In its molten, or melted state, magma is very hot. But when it cools, it hardens into solid rock. This rock is made from crystallized minerals. It may form beneath Earth's surface or above Earth's surface when magma (which is known as lava when it breaks the surface) erupts from the ground and then cools and hardens as is shown in **Figure 4**.

The types of minerals that form from magma and lava vary based on the materials and gases in the magma, as well as the rate at which it cools.

**✔READING CHECK Analyze Text Structure** Examine the way the text on these two pages has been organized. Describe how the author has organized the text so that it supports the reader's comprehension.

...................................................................

...................................................................

...................................................................

...................................................................

...................................................................

**Minerals from Solutions**
**Figure 3** These mineral deposits in Mammoth Hot Springs in Yellowstone National Park formed from a solution.

SEP Analyze Data ✎ Draw an X on the solution the minerals formed from. Circle some of the mineral deposits.

**Minerals from Magma**
**Figure 4** As this lava cools, it will harden and crystallize into minerals.

CCC Cause and Effect Where would you expect to find minerals that have formed in this way?

...................................................................

...................................................................

...................................................................

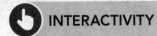

## Academic Vocabulary

Explain what *distributed* means and give one or two examples of something that is distributed.

........................................................

........................................................

........................................................

........................................................

........................................................

**Distribution of Minerals** The distribution of mineral resources on Earth depends on how and when the minerals form. Common minerals, such as the ones that make up most of the rocks in Earth's crust, are found roughly evenly distributed around the planet. Other minerals are rare because they only form as a result of tremendous heat and pressure near volcanic systems. Therefore, these minerals will only be found near subduction zones or other regions associated with volcanic activity. Other minerals may form from evaporation in the ocean or on land, such as in basins called playas. The map in **Figure 5** shows how some minerals are **distributed** around the world.

Gold, for example, is a heavy metal that formed, along with all other atoms other than hydrogen and helium, from stars that went supernova preceding the formation of our solar system. Gold is rare at the surface because most of it sank into the core when the early Earth was molten. Gold gets concentrated when hot fluids pass through the crust and pick up the gold, which doesn't fit well in the crystals of most rocks.

✓ **READING CHECK Determine Meaning** Locate the term concentrated in the second paragraph. Using context clues, what do you think this word means? Explain your thinking.

........................................................

........................................................

........................................................

# Question It!

## Minerals for Dinner?

Minerals are used in many ways in our everyday lives. We even need minerals in our diets to stay healthy. Humans need minerals that contain calcium, potassium, and magnesium to grow, fight illness, and carry out everyday functions.

### Apply Scientific Reasoning

Write two or three questions you would like to have answered about the importance of minerals in your diet.

........................................................

........................................................

........................................................

........................................................

........................................................

........................................................

........................................................

........................................................

........................................................

........................................................

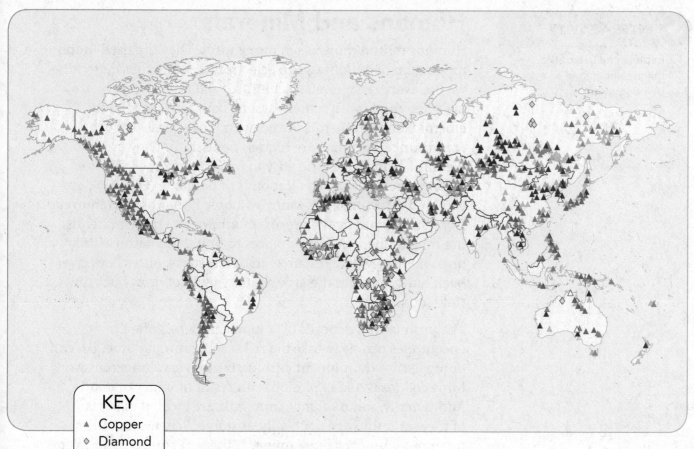

**KEY**
- ▲ Copper
- ◇ Diamond
- ▲ Gold
- ▲ Iron
- ▲ Lead-Zinc
- ▲ Silver
- △ Uranium

## Mineral Distribution

**Figure 5** Minerals are distributed unevenly on Earth.

1. **Claim** Which part of the United States is the richest in gold and other mineral resources?

   ........................................................................................

   ........................................................................................

2. **Evidence** ✏ Circle the area on the map that provides evidence to support your claim.

3. **Reasoning** Suppose you were to draw the boundaries of tectonic plates and locations of volcanic activity on the map. What patterns would you notice among plate boundaries, volcanic activity, and the distribution of different mineral resources? Explain.

   ........................................................................................
   ........................................................................................
   ........................................................................................
   ........................................................................................
   ........................................................................................
   ........................................................................................
   ........................................................................................
   ........................................................................................

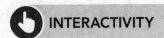
INTERACTIVITY

Explore the use of the mineral limestone as a building material.

# Humans and Minerals

Humans rely on minerals in many ways. They are used in the production of buildings, cars, electronics, and other materials we use every day. Jewelry, sculpture, and other works of art are often made with minerals, such as marble, jade, and emerald. Some minerals are easy and inexpensive to get. For instance, bananas are high in potassium. They are also plentiful, affordable, and easy to find in any grocery store. Other minerals, such as diamonds or benitoite (**Figure 6**), are rare and difficult to get. Many valuable minerals are removed from the ground by the process of mining. As more minerals are mined, there are fewer places to find them because they are a nonrenewable resource. In other words, once they have been removed from the ground, they will not grow back any time soon.

The push to find deposits of valuable minerals often encourages people to take big risks. Some mining practices can damage the environment. Mining is also very dangerous work. Mine collapses and explosions can result in injury or death. Additionally, some valuable minerals are located in parts of the world that are politically unstable. When companies attempt to mine for these minerals there, it can cause problems and danger for everyone involved.

✓ READING CHECK **Summarize Text** How do humans rely on minerals?

...................................................................................................

...................................................................................................

...................................................................................................

## Rare Mineral

**Figure 6** Benitoite is a very rare blue mineral that forms as a result of hydrothermal processes in Earth's crust. It has been discovered in a few locations on Earth. But gemstone-quality benitoite can be found in only one place in California.

**Connect to Society**

Do you think a benitoite ring would be costly or inexpensive? Explain your reasoning.

...............................................

...............................................

...............................................

...............................................

...............................................

...............................................

MS-ESS3-1

1. **Define** What are minerals? List examples.

..................................................................

..................................................................

..................................................................

..................................................................

2. **SEP Construct Explanations** Explain the relationship between minerals and ores.

..................................................................

..................................................................

..................................................................

..................................................................

..................................................................

3. **CCC Cause and Effect** What causes minerals to be unevenly distributed on Earth?

..................................................................

..................................................................

..................................................................

..................................................................

..................................................................

4. **CCC Patterns** 🖊 Use drawings to show one of the ways that minerals can form.

# Quest CHECK-IN

**In this lesson, you learned why minerals are important resources and about how they form. You also learned that the different ways that minerals form leads to uneven distribution of different types of minerals around the world.**

**SEP Evaluate Information** Why should you consider mineral resources when trying to determine whether a town will boom or become a ghost town?

..................................................................

..................................................................

..................................................................

..................................................................

..................................................................

## ✋ INTERACTIVITY

Surviving on Minerals

**Go online** to find out more about how some mineral resources in the United States are distributed. Then, apply this information to your analysis of the town you are researching.

# Phosphorus Fiasco

**W**ithout phosphorus, living things would not exist on Earth. All animals and plants need phosphorus to produce the energy that keeps them alive. Unfortunately, like all minerals, phosphorus is not a renewable resource. Only a certain amount exists in nature, where it moves in a natural cycle. In recent years, however, that cycle has been broken, and we run the risk of using up Earth's supply of phosphorus.

In the phosphorus cycle, animals and people eat phosphorus-rich plants. The excess phosphorus leaves the bodies of organisms as waste. The waste returns to the soil to enrich the plants, starting the cycle again.

Phosphorus mining has altered the natural phosphorus cycle.

For many centuries, farmers used manure, which is rich in phosphorus, to fertilize their crops. About 175 years ago, as the population grew, farmers looked for new sources of fertilizer to keep up with the demand for food. Engineers and geologists realized that phosphorus might be mined from underground and used to manufacture fertilizers. Most of the world's phosphorus reserves are in the United States, China, Russia, and northern Africa.

The "phosphorus fiasco" is a result of improved technology that has interrupted the natural phosphorus cycle. Because most human waste now ends up in sewer and water treatment systems, phosphorus ends up in the ocean. More manufactured fertilizer is used to fertilize plants and crops. We still get our required phosphorus, but we are using up the natural supply in the process.

## World Phosphate Mine Production and Reserves

| Country | Mine Production (tons) | | Reserves |
| --- | --- | --- | --- |
| | 2015 | 2016 | |
| China | 120,000 | 138,000 | 3,100,000 |
| Jordan | 8,340 | 8,300 | 1,200,000 |
| Morocco/Western Sahara | 29,000 | 30,000 | 50,000,000 |
| Russia | 11,600 | 11,600 | 1,300,000 |
| United States | 27,400 | 27,800 | 1,100,000 |

Source: U.S. Geological Survey, 2017

**Use the text and the data table to answer the following questions.**

1. CCC Scale, Proportion, and Quantity  Which country saw the greatest increase in phosphorus production between 2015 and 2016? Describe the amount of the increase as a fraction or percentage.

.................................................................................

.................................................................................

2. CCC Cause and Effect  How have technological developments affected the natural phosphorus cycle? What do you think can be done to address this problem?

.................................................................................

.................................................................................

.................................................................................

.................................................................................

3. SEP Analyze Data  Based on its current rate of production, in how many years will the United States use up its known reserves of phosphate?

.................................................................................

.................................................................................

.................................................................................

4. SEP Construct Explanations  Morocco/Western Sahara has by far the greatest reserves of phosphorus, but it is not the largest producer. Why do you think this is the case? Do you think the situation might change? Explain.

.................................................................................

.................................................................................

.................................................................................

.................................................................................

.................................................................................

## Guiding Questions

- How do geological processes affect the distribution of groundwater on Earth?
- How is water used as a resource?

## Connections

**Literacy** Support Author's Claim

**Math** Draw Comparative Inferences

MS-ESS3-1, MS-ESS3-4

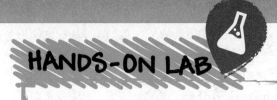

## HANDS-ON LAB

**uInvestigate** Model how an artesian well accesses groundwater.

**Vocabulary**

desalination

**Academic Vocabulary**

component

obtain

## Connect It !

✏ **The drop of water on Earth represents all the water on the planet. Draw a circle inside the drop of water to represent the amount of freshwater you think exists on Earth.**

CCC Systems and System Models  How does water's role in Earth systems make it an important natural resource?

.........................................................................................................................

.........................................................................................................................

.........................................................................................................................

# Water on Earth

Although Earth is known as the water planet, the water that living things rely on represents only a fraction of the planet's total water supply **(Figure 1)**. Most water on Earth is salt water. Freshwater is only found on the surface of our planet as surface ice or water, or within Earth's crust as groundwater.

Water is a limited resource, which means there is a finite amount of it on Earth. In addition, it is not evenly distributed around the planet as a result of meteorological and geological forces. The water cycle circulates water through Earth's ocean and other bodies of water, on and below its surface, and in the atmosphere. A tiny amount of the freshwater on Earth is in the atmosphere, and a fair amount of water is contained underground as groundwater. But most freshwater is locked up as ice at the poles and in glaciers. A very small amount of the water on the surface of the planet is immediately available for human use in lakes and rivers.

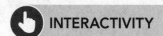

**INTERACTIVITY**

Predict how much water on Earth is drinkable.

**Reflect** How is water used in your local environment? In your science notebook, describe some ways your local environment would be affected if there were suddenly less water available.

## A Drop to Drink

**Figure 1** If all of the water on Earth were collected, it would form a sphere about 1,380 kilometers (860 miles) across.

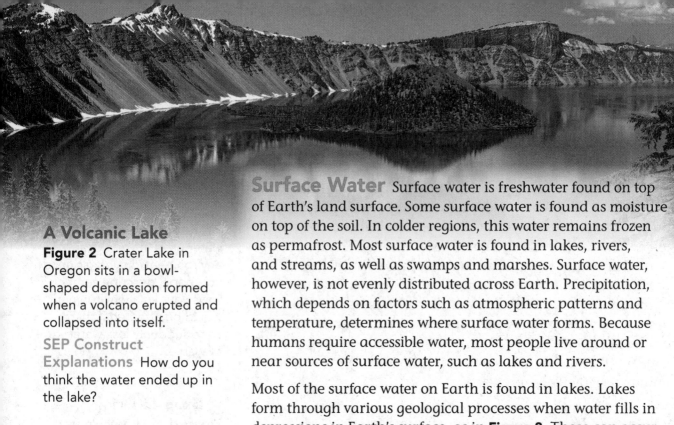

## A Volcanic Lake

**Figure 2** Crater Lake in Oregon sits in a bowl-shaped depression formed when a volcano erupted and collapsed into itself.

**SEP Construct Explanations** How do you think the water ended up in the lake?

......................................................

......................................................

......................................................

......................................................

**Surface Water** Surface water is freshwater found on top of Earth's land surface. Some surface water is found as moisture on top of the soil. In colder regions, this water remains frozen as permafrost. Most surface water is found in lakes, rivers, and streams, as well as swamps and marshes. Surface water, however, is not evenly distributed across Earth. Precipitation, which depends on factors such as atmospheric patterns and temperature, determines where surface water forms. Because humans require accessible water, most people live around or near sources of surface water, such as lakes and rivers.

Most of the surface water on Earth is found in lakes. Lakes form through various geological processes when water fills in depressions in Earth's surface, as in **Figure 2.** These can occur as a result of erosion, the movement of tectonic plates, and retreating glaciers. Some lakes form when a river's path erodes away an area or a dam blocks a river's flow. All rivers begin as a small flow of water caused by gravity. Runoff from rain or melting ice collects and flows downhill following the least resistant path. These small flows of water form streams, which combine and grow to form larger rivers and river systems.

# Math Toolbox

## Distribution of Water Resources

While most of the planet is covered in water, only a small amount of it is available to humans for cooking, drinking, and bathing.

1. **SEP Develop Models** Use the data in the graphs to complete the missing values.

2. **Draw Comparative Inferences** About how much more accessible surface freshwater is found in lakes than in the atmosphere as water vapor?

......................................................

......................................................

......................................................

......................................................

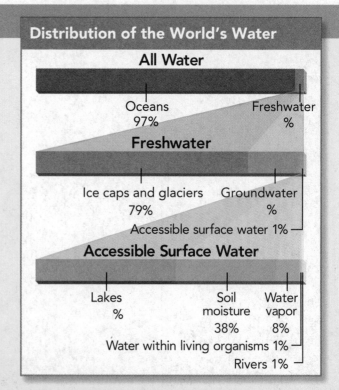

**Distribution of the World's Water**

**All Water**

Oceans 97%          Freshwater %

**Freshwater**

Ice caps and glaciers 79%     Groundwater %

Accessible surface water 1%

**Accessible Surface Water**

Lakes %          Soil moisture 38%     Water vapor 8%

Water within living organisms 1%

Rivers 1%

## Groundwater

As with surface water, groundwater is not evenly distributed across Earth (Figure 3). The presence of groundwater depends on the type of rock layers in Earth's crust. Groundwater forms when gravity causes water from precipitation and runoff to seep into the ground and fill the empty spaces between these rocks. Some rocks are more porous, or have more empty spaces in which water can collect. The volume of porous rock that can contain groundwater is called an aquifer. Wells are drilled into aquifers to access the water.

Deep groundwater reservoirs can take hundreds or thousands of years to accumulate, especially in arid regions where there is little rainfall or surface water to supply the aquifer. New studies of Earth's mantle reveal there may be many oceans' worth of water locked hundreds of kilometers below the surface in mineral formations. This groundwater may take millions of years to exchange with surface water through the movement of tectonic plates and mantle convection.

☑ READING CHECK **Summarize** How does the type of rock in Earth's crust affect the distribution of groundwater?

.........................................................................................................

.........................................................................................................

.........................................................................................................

**INTERACTIVITY**

Explore how groundwater is distributed around Earth.

**HANDS-ON LAB**

ɥ**Investigate** Model how an artesian well accesses groundwater.

### Distribution of Groundwater

**Figure 3** Groundwater is especially important in areas that do not have immediate access to rivers or lakes for sources of freshwater.

SEP Use Models ✏

Indicate the areas on the map with the greatest groundwater resources with a circle. Indicate the areas with the least groundwater resources with an X.

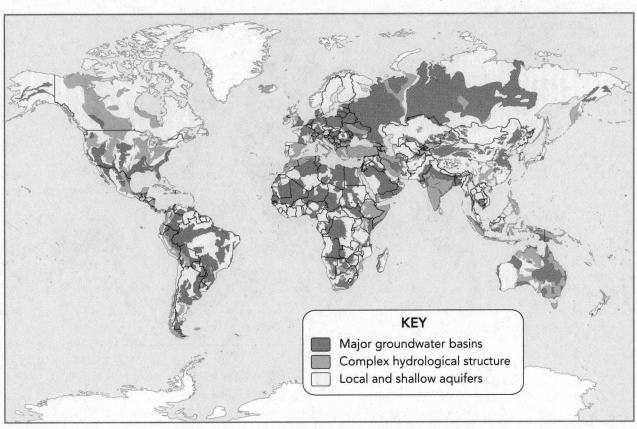

KEY

▨ Major groundwater basins
▨ Complex hydrological structure
☐ Local and shallow aquifers

## Literacy Connection

**Support Author's Claim** Underline the text that support the claim that human activity can cause water shortages.

### Water Scarcity

**Figure 4** Many people and regions will be affected by water scarcity in the future.

**CCC Cause and Effect** How might water scarcity affect economic development in an area?

.........................................................

.........................................................

.........................................................

.........................................................

# Human Impacts

Humans rely on water not only to live and grow, but also for agriculture and industry. Water is needed to produce our food, manufacture products, and carry out many chemical reactions. The distribution of water resources is a result of past and current geologic processes such as the water cycle, plate tectonics, and the formation of rock. These processes take time, and in some areas humans are depleting water resources faster than they can be replenished. The human impact on water distribution is already a cause of social and economic conflict in some areas.

**Using Water** Humans use surface water, which often involves changing its natural path, such as with dams. This affects the amount of water that continues to flow and the ecology of the area. Humans access groundwater resources by digging wells in aquifers. But if more water is removed from an aquifer or other groundwater source than is replenished through the water cycle, water shortages can occur. As with surface water, pollution can enter groundwater supplies and impact the quality of the water. Study the effects of water scarcity in **Figure 4**.

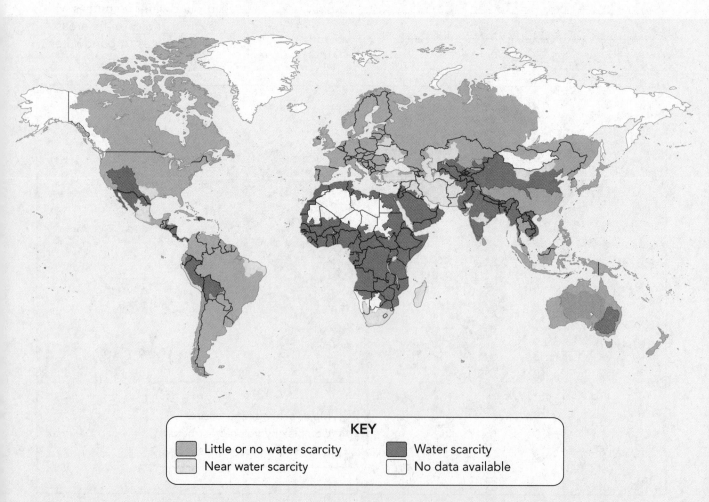

**KEY**

| | | | |
|---|---|---|---|
| ▢ | Little or no water scarcity | ▢ | Water scarcity |
| ▢ | Near water scarcity | ▢ | No data available |

**Using Ocean Resources**

**Figure 5** If too many of these fish are caught, then fewer will survive to produce new generations.

**Desalination** In the future, humans may look to technology and the ocean to meet their water needs. The process of **desalination** removes salt and minerals from saltwater to make freshwater. Today, desalination plants around the world are costly and require a lot of energy to distill saltwater. We may eventually use solar energy to convert ocean water into freshwater.

**Other Water Resources** Humans rely on the ocean to provide a number of other important resources besides water, such as sea organisms for food and other products **(Figure 5)**. The ocean also provides salt, minerals, and fuels.

Living resources like fish are replenished through a natural cycle. However, overfishing can result in severe reductions or complete collapses of ocean ecosystems and the resources they provide. In addition, pollution and global climate change can have serious impacts on the living resources we rely on from the ocean.

**INTERACTIVITY**

Examine the factors that affect water availability on Earth.

**READING CHECK**

**Identify** What are some other ocean resources humans use besides water?

................................................................

................................................................

................................................................

................................................................

................................................................

................................................................

## Design It!

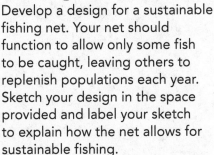

### Sustainable Fishing

Fish populations are replenished only if sufficient numbers are allowed to live and reproduce in their ecosystems.

**SEP Design Solutions**
Develop a design for a sustainable fishing net. Your net should function to allow only some fish to be caught, leaving others to replenish populations each year. Sketch your design in the space provided and label your sketch to explain how the net allows for sustainable fishing.

1. **Identify** What are the different sources of freshwater on Earth?

.................................................................

.................................................................

.................................................................

2. **SEP Construct Explanations** What factors account for the uneven distribution of groundwater on Earth?

.................................................................

.................................................................

.................................................................

.................................................................

.................................................................

3. **Infer** Are humans more likely to use surface water or groundwater as a freshwater source? Explain your answer.

.................................................................

.................................................................

.................................................................

.................................................................

.................................................................

4. **CCC Cause and Effect** Explain why some regions are more extremely affected by water scarcity than others.

.................................................................

.................................................................

.................................................................

.................................................................

.................................................................

.................................................................

.................................................................

.................................................................

5. **Connect to Society** In what way does water scarcity harm the economic development of an area?

.................................................................

.................................................................

.................................................................

.................................................................

.................................................................

.................................................................

# Quest CHECK-IN

**In this lesson, you learned how water is distributed on Earth and what effects geologic processes have on water resources. You also discovered how human activities are affected by water availability and limit its distribution.**

**SEP Define Problems** Why is it important to consider how water is distributed when considering the availability of resources in a new town?

.................................................................

.................................................................

.................................................................

.................................................................

.................................................................

## ☞ INTERACTIVITY

Surviving on Water

**Go online** to use what you have learned about water resources and relate it to the available resources for a ghost town.

# The Pseudoscience of
# Water Dowsing

It's the early 1800s and you're moving westward across America. When you arrive at your land, you see that there's no nearby river or lake. As you look out, you wonder how to decide where to dig the well that will provide your freshwater. This is where someone known as a water dowser comes in.

Water dowsers claim to be able to use a simple tool to locate underground water. The two arms of a Y-shaped stick are held in the hands, with the end of the stick pointing upward. As the dowser walks around the property, he keeps an eye on the stick. When the stick pulls toward the ground, he claims that water is somewhere below.

Dowsers still work today, usually in areas where there are no easily accessible sources of groundwater. Some people believe the dowsing stick responds to the presence of water. Scientifically, though, the explanation is much simpler. In many places, groundwater is abundant enough that, in a temperate climate, you have an excellent chance of striking water no matter where you dig a well.

Geologists searching for underground water use much sounder methods. In a desert, for example, growing plants indicate there might be water present. Technology like sonar can also reveal if water lies below the ground.

## CONNECT TO YOU

Do you think it's important for people to understand the difference between science and pseudoscience? Why? Discuss your ideas with a partner.

# ☑TOPIC 6 Review and Assess

## 1 Nonrenewable Energy Resources

MS-ESS3-1, MS-ESS3-4

**1.** Which of the following is considered a nonrenewable resource?
A. sunlight     B. wood
C. water     D. natural gas

**2.** Which of the following is *not* an effect of our growing population's use of fossil fuels?
A. The distribution of these resources is changing.
B. The amount of carbon dioxide in the atmosphere is increasing.
C. The resources are now being replaced faster than they are being used.
D. Political conflicts occur over control of these resources.

**3.** Which of the following is directly involved in transforming the remains of organisms into fossil fuels?
A. pressure     B. wind
C. sunlight     D. precipitation

**4.** Fossil fuels are ................................................ resources that are ................................................ distributed on Earth.

**5. SEP Construct Explanations** Why are coal and petroleum resources not commonly found across the planet?

..........................................................................
..........................................................................
..........................................................................
..........................................................................
..........................................................................
..........................................................................
..........................................................................
..........................................................................

## 2 Renewable Energy Resources

MS-ESS3-1, MS-ESS3-4

**6.** Which of the following renewable energy resources comes from underground?
A. geothermal energy     B. hydropower
C. wind power     D. solar power

**7.** Which of the following is a drawback of biofuels such as ethanol?
A. The energy ethanol can provide is about the same as the energy required to make it.
B. It is much more expensive than gasoline.
C. There are few places where plants used to make ethanol can be grown.
D. When it is burned, ethanol produces even more emissions than coal.

**8. SEP Define Problems** What areas on Earth are worst suited for using solar energy to generate electricity?

..........................................................................
..........................................................................
..........................................................................

**9. SEP Develop Models** ✏ Draw a diagram that shows how the sun is responsible for the production of wind energy.

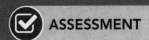 
# 3 Mineral Resources

MS-ESS3-1, MS-ESS3-4

**10.** Which of the following is an essential
characteristic of a mineral?
A. crystal structure
B. artificially manufactured
C. liquid
D. formed from organic processes

**11.** Which of the following statements about
minerals and ores is true?
A. Minerals are deposits of valuable ores.
B. Minerals are products that are made
from ores.
C. Minerals form from solutions, but ores
form from volcanoes.
D. All ores are minerals, but not all minerals
are ores.

**12.** Many minerals are formed from ...................
as water ...................... .

**13. SEP Construct Explanations** Gold is a
valuable mineral that is found underground.
It is brought closer to the surface, where it
can be mined, by volcanic activity. Why do
you think gold is not evenly distributed on
Earth?

...............................................................................

...............................................................................

...............................................................................

...............................................................................

...............................................................................

...............................................................................

...............................................................................

...............................................................................

...............................................................................

# 4 Water Resources

MS-ESS3-1, MS-ESS3-4

**14.** The most abundant water resource on
Earth is
A. salt water       B. fresh water
C. groundwater      D. surface water

**15.** Most fresh water on Earth is
A. in the atmosphere as water vapor.
B. found on the surface in lakes and rivers.
C. locked up in ice.
D. located underground.

**16.** Factors such as precipitation, ......................
and surface features determine where
surface water can form on Earth.

**17. SEP Engage in Argument** How could
groundwater sources become depleted if
water is constantly being cycled?

...............................................................................

...............................................................................

...............................................................................

...............................................................................

...............................................................................

**18. Draw Conclusions** Why is the distribution
of water resources a concern for the
economic and social welfare of people
around the world?

...............................................................................

...............................................................................

...............................................................................

...............................................................................

...............................................................................

...............................................................................

MS-ESS3-1

## Evidence-Based Assessment

Van is researching information about the mineral copper and its distribution on Earth. Copper is used in electrical systems and even found in very small amounts in living things. Here is some of the other information Van finds, along with two maps that he finds during his research:

- copper ore can form from different geological processes

- one type of copper, called porphyry copper, is found in large deposits in certain types of rock

- most porphyry copper deposits are 340 million years old or younger

- porphyry copper forms at relatively shallow depths of about 4,500 to 9,000 meters (15,000 to 30,000 feet) in Earth's crust

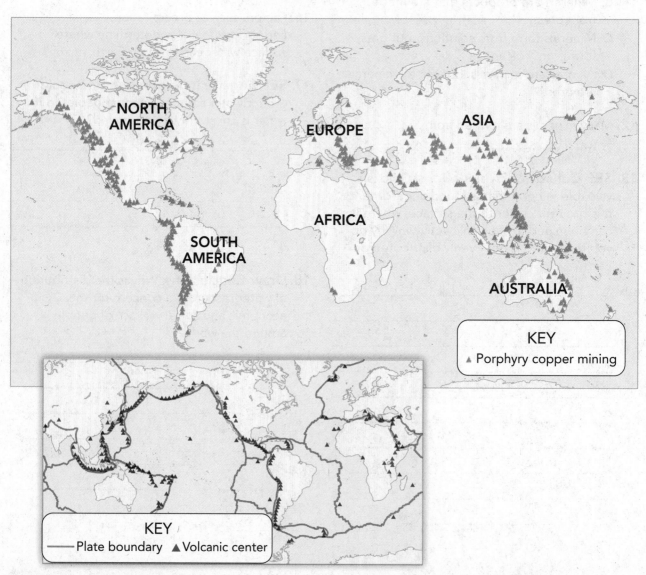

NORTH AMERICA

EUROPE

ASIA

AFRICA

SOUTH AMERICA

AUSTRALIA

KEY
▲ Porphyry copper mining

KEY
—— Plate boundary ▲ Volcanic center

**1. SEP Analyze Data** Which of these regions seems to have the greatest concentration of porphyry copper mining?
A. Africa  B. Australia
C. Europe  D. South America

**2. CCC Cause and Effect** Why are there so many volcanoes around the Pacific Ocean? Support your answer with evidence from the volcanic activity map.

..............................................................................
..............................................................................
..............................................................................
..............................................................................
..............................................................................
..............................................................................
..............................................................................
..............................................................................
..............................................................................
..............................................................................
..............................................................................
..............................................................................
..............................................................................
..............................................................................

**3. CCC Patterns** Based on the map of porphyry copper mining, which of the following statements about the distribution of copper is correct? Select all that apply.
- ☐ Porphyry copper is distributed relatively evenly across most of the continents.
- ☐ Very little porphyry copper is found in Africa.
- ☐ A concentration of porphyry copper runs from Europe eastward through Asia and then south into Australia.
- ☐ Porphyry copper is widely distributed across South America.
- ☐ A majority of porphyry copper is found on continents that border the Pacific Ocean.
- ☐ There are fewer sources of porphyry copper in North America than in Asia.

**4. SEP Construct Explanations** Use evidence from the maps to explain why porphyry copper is generally found near areas where volcanic activity, often associated with plate collisions, has occurred in the past.

..............................................................................
..............................................................................
..............................................................................
..............................................................................
..............................................................................
..............................................................................
..............................................................................
..............................................................................
..............................................................................
..............................................................................

## Quest FINDINGS

## Complete the Quest!

**Phenomenon** Choose one of the boomtowns you studied and develop a travel brochure to describe what the town was like when it was settled and what it is like now.

**CCC Cause and Effect** In what ways can proximity to a valuable natural resource affect the success of a town or city?

..............................................................................
..............................................................................
..............................................................................
..............................................................................
..............................................................................
..............................................................................

**INTERACTIVITY**

Reflect on Boomtowns

# To Drill or Not to Drill

How can you **use a model** to confirm the location of a **petroleum** deposit?

## Background

**Phenomenon** An energy company wants to drill for oil on the outskirts of a small town. The owners of the energy company have provided evidence that the town is located near an area that was a large sea millions of years ago. Based on that evidence, they believe there is a large deposit of petroleum under the town. Town officials have hired you as an expert to look for evidence of oil under the town.

In this investigation, you will develop a model that you can use to predict whether or not the company will locate any oil below the town.

## Materials

(per group)

- aquarium gravel
- glass baking dish
- wax crayons or candles
- plastic knife
- small weight or heavy book
- hot plate

## Safety

Be sure to follow all safety guidelines provided by your teacher. The Safety Appendix of your textbook provides more details about the safety icons.

# Develop Your Model

1. Using the available materials, your group must develop a model that meets the following criteria:

   - It must show how oil forms from ancient marine plants.

   - It must demonstrate the geological forces involved in the formation of oil.

   - It must indicate whether or not oil can form below the town.

2. Work with your group to develop ideas for a model that meets the criteria. Consider the following questions as you develop and design your model:

   - What materials can you use to represent the buried organic material that eventually forms oil?

   - How can your model demonstrate the geological forces that form oil?

   - What observations will you make?

3. After agreeing on a plan, write out the steps that your group will follow to develop and use the model. Include a sketch of the model that labels the materials you will be using and what they represent.

4. After getting your teacher's approval, construct your model and use it to demonstrate how oil forms. Record your observations and data in the space provided.

## Plan and Sketch

## Observations

..............................................................................................................
..............................................................................................................
..............................................................................................................
..............................................................................................................
..............................................................................................................
..............................................................................................................
..............................................................................................................
..............................................................................................................
..............................................................................................................
..............................................................................................................
..............................................................................................................
..............................................................................................................
..............................................................................................................
..............................................................................................................
..............................................................................................................

# Analyze and Interpret Data

1. **SEP Use Models** Use your model to explain why oil is a nonrenewable resource.

   ................................................................................

   ................................................................................

   ................................................................................

   ................................................................................

2. **CCC Cause and Effect** What geological forces are involved in the formation of oil? How did you incorporate these forces into your model?

   ................................................................................

   ................................................................................

   ................................................................................

   ................................................................................

   ................................................................................

3. **SEP Construct Explanations** Explain whether or not oil will be found under the town. Use evidence from your model to support your explanation.

   ................................................................................

   ................................................................................

   ................................................................................

   ................................................................................

   ................................................................................

   ................................................................................

4. **Identify Limitations** In what ways is your model not reflective of the actual conditions that lead to the formation of oil? How could your group improve the model?

   ................................................................................

   ................................................................................

   ................................................................................

   ................................................................................

   ................................................................................

**NGSS PERFORMANCE EXPECTATIONS**

**MS-ESS3-4** Construct an argument supported by evidence for how increases in human population and per-capita consumption of natural resources impact Earth's systems.

HANDS-ON LAB

uConnect Explore ways that you can reduce the pollution you create.

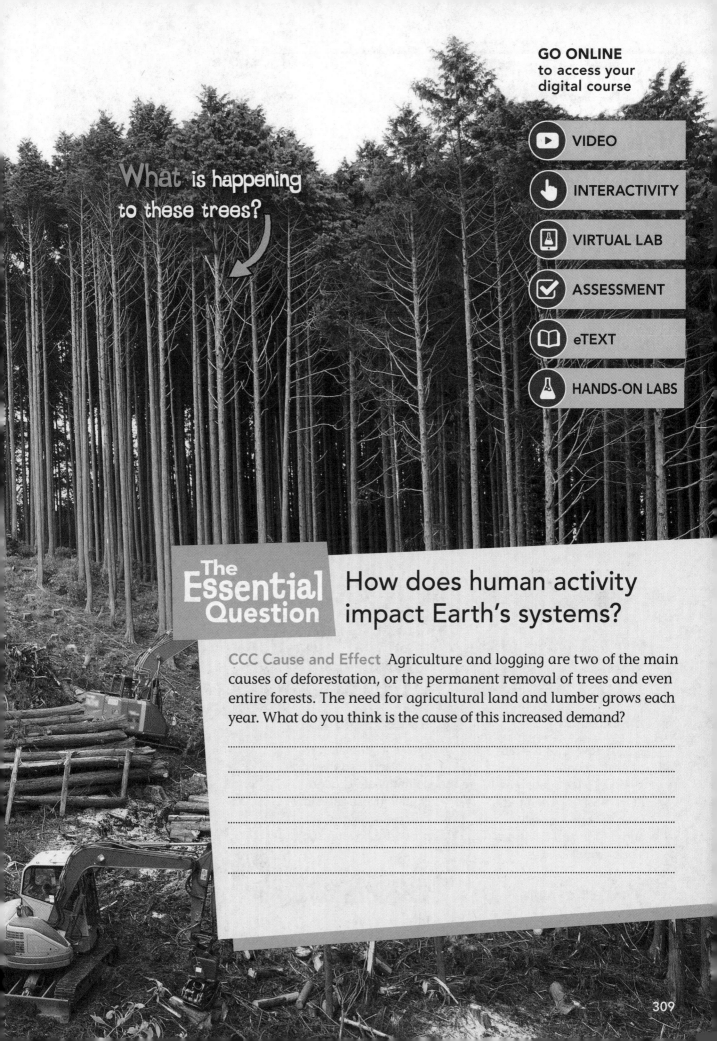

What is happening to these trees?

**GO ONLINE**
to access your
digital course

▶ VIDEO

👆 INTERACTIVITY

🧪 VIRTUAL LAB

☑ ASSESSMENT

📖 eTEXT

⚗ HANDS-ON LABS

## The Essential Question

# How does human activity impact Earth's systems?

**CCC Cause and Effect** Agriculture and logging are two of the main causes of deforestation, or the permanent removal of trees and even entire forests. The need for agricultural land and lumber grows each year. What do you think is the cause of this increased demand?

.............................................................................................

.............................................................................................

.............................................................................................

.............................................................................................

.............................................................................................

.............................................................................................

# Quest KICKOFF

## How can you help your school reduce its impact on Earth's systems?

**NBC LEARN** ▶ VIDEO

**STEM** | **Phenomenon** The landfill used by your community is running out of space. The community must expand it or find other ways to deal with the trash. Your principal has decided to help the community by finding ways to reduce the school's trash output. In this problem-based Quest activity, you will evaluate the trash output at your school. You will then develop a plan to decrease that output through a combination of reducing, reusing, and recycling. As you work, you should anticipate objections to your plan. Finally, you will present your plan and work to implement it at your school.

After watching the Quest Kickoff video, which explores the plastic items that end up in the ocean, think about the trash you generate. How can you reduce, recycle, or reuse your trash?

Reduce:

.................................................................

.................................................................

Recycle:

.................................................................

.................................................................

Reuse:

.................................................................

.................................................................

 **INTERACTIVITY**

Trash Backlash

**MS-ESS3-4** Construct an argument supported by evidence for how increases in human population and per-capita consumption of natural resources impact Earth's systems.

---

## Quest CHECK-IN

### IN LESSON 1

**STEM** How does the rate of trash generation affect landfills? Investigate how much trash is generated in an area of your school, and design and construct landfill models.

👆 **INTERACTIVITY**

More Trash, Less Space

## Quest CHECK-IN

### IN LESSON 2

How can landfills be constructed so they don't contaminate ground-water? Investigate how different designs will protect the water supply.

**HANDS-ON LAB**

Trash vs. Water

## Quest CHECK-IN

### IN LESSON 3

How is a landfill site chosen, and what laws regulate landfill use? Explore the stages of a landfill's life, and conduct research about laws that affect landfills.

👆 **INTERACTIVITY**

Life of a Landfill

According to the U.S. Environmental Protection Agency, Americans recycled only about 35 percent of their waste in 2014. Much of the rest of the waste ended up in landfills such as this one.

## Quest CHECK-IN

### IN LESSON 4

How can everyone contribute to reducing waste at your school? Develop a plan to reduce trash output in at least one area of your school.

### HANDS-ON LAB

Reducing Waste

## Quest FINDINGS

### Complete the Quest!

Refine and present your plan to reduce trash output at your school.

👆 **INTERACTIVITY**

Reflect on Trash Backlash

How can you **design a solution** that decreases the amount of garbage you throw away?

# Finding a Solution for Your Pollution

## Background

**Phenomenon** Imagine it is lunchtime at school, and you have just finished eating. As you toss your trash into one of the garbage cans, you notice that the can is filled with plastic bottles and paper trays. "We would have a lot less garbage to throw away if we could recycle these bottles and trays," you say to your friend. "You're right. We should start a recycling program," your friend replies. Time to do some research, you think to yourself as you walk out of the cafeteria. In this activity, you will design a school lunch environment that generates zero waste.

## Materials

**(per class)**
- garbage can full of cafeteria garbage
- containers
- scale

## Safety

Be sure to follow all safety procedures provided by your teacher. The Safety Appendix of your textbook provides more details about the safety icons.

## Design a Procedure

1. **Plan an Investigation** As a class, design a procedure to gather evidence that supports the need for a zero-waste school lunch environment.

...............................................................................

...............................................................................

...............................................................................

...............................................................................

...............................................................................

...............................................................................

2.  Show your procedure to your teacher. Then, use your materials to carry out your investigation. Be sure to wear gloves when handling the garbage.

3. Draw a table to record your observations and to collect evidence.

# Observations

HANDS-ON LAB

Connect Go online for a downloadable worksheet of this lab.

## Analyze and Conclude

1. **CCC Cause and Effect** According to the Duke Center of Sustainability and Commerce, the average person generates 4.3 pounds of waste per day. Describe the impacts all of this waste has on Earth's systems.

.............................................................................................................

.............................................................................................................

.............................................................................................................

.............................................................................................................

.............................................................................................................

2. **SEP Construct an Argument** Should recycling be mandatory? Make an argument using evidence from your observations.

.............................................................................................................

.............................................................................................................

.............................................................................................................

.............................................................................................................

.............................................................................................................

3. **SEP Design a Solution** Work with a partner to design a school lunch with zero waste.

.............................................................................................................

.............................................................................................................

.............................................................................................................

.............................................................................................................

#  Population Growth and Resource Consumption

## Guiding Questions

- How has the human population changed over time?
- How is the consumption of natural resources by humans affected by changes in population size?

## Connections

**Literacy** Determine Conclusions

**Math** Draw Comparative Inferences

MS-ESS3-4

## HANDS-ON LAB

и**Investigate** Examine how population growth affects the availability of natural resources.

### Vocabulary

birth rate
death rate
exponential
 growth
pollution
overpopulation
conservation
sustainable use

### Academic Vocabulary

estimate
constraints

## Connect It !

✎ **Draw a line to indicate where you think the city limits of Los Angeles were about 100 years ago.**

**Apply Scientific Reasoning** How do you think the amount of resources used by the human population of Los Angeles has changed in the past 100 years?

........................................................................................................

........................................................................................................

........................................................................................................

# The Human Population

There are more humans living on Earth today than any time in our history. Human populations have fluctuated in the past, mostly due to environmental or climate conditions. Around 60,000 years ago, the human population was generally stable at around 600,000 individuals. A warming climate and improvements in hunting and fishing techniques resulted in a rapid increase to about 6 million humans over a few thousand years.

This population remained fairly constant until about 10,000 years ago, when agriculture and livestock breeding gave rise to steady, long-term population growth. This growth dropped occasionally during war, epidemics, or invasions, but maintained a steady climb until the 1700s. Since then, unprecedented population growth has occurred, with the human population reaching 1 billion by the early 1800s. In the last 300 years, the world population has increased tenfold. As of 2017, there were 7.5 billion people on Earth.

**HANDS-ON LAB**

Explore how food becomes a limiting factor when population size increases.

**Reflect** How has the population of your community changed in your lifetime? In your science notebook, describe some ways your community would be affected if the population were to suddenly increase or decrease.

### Growth of a City

**Figure 1** A little over 4 million people call the city of Los Angeles home. The population has grown a great deal since the first Native American tribes settled there thousands of years ago.

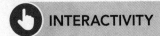
## Academic Vocabulary

What other kinds of information might scientists need to estimate?

..............................................................

..............................................................

..............................................................

..............................................................

..............................................................

# Population Changes

Population growth, whether in a town, a country, or the world, is determined by calculating the number of individuals who are born, die, or move into or out of an area. The number of births per 1,000 individuals for a certain time period is called the **birth rate**. On the other hand, the number of deaths per 1,000 individuals for a certain time period is called the **death rate**. When the rates of births and people moving into an area are greater than the rates of deaths and people moving out of an area, the population increases. Otherwise, the population decreases. In 2016, scientists **estimate** there were 280 births and 109 deaths every minute.

In early human history, birth rates and death rates were fairly balanced, which resulted in little change in the size of the human population. For most of human history, birth rates were only slightly higher than death rates, resulting in a slow, steady increase in population.

The graph in **Figure 2** shows human population growth beginning in 1750, around the start of the Industrial Revolution. Human population grew rapidly after the Industrial Revolution because the death rate began to decline. Advances in technology resulted in new farming and transportation methods that increased the availability of resources, such as food and clean water. Improvements in public health and general living standards also played a role in decreasing the death rate.

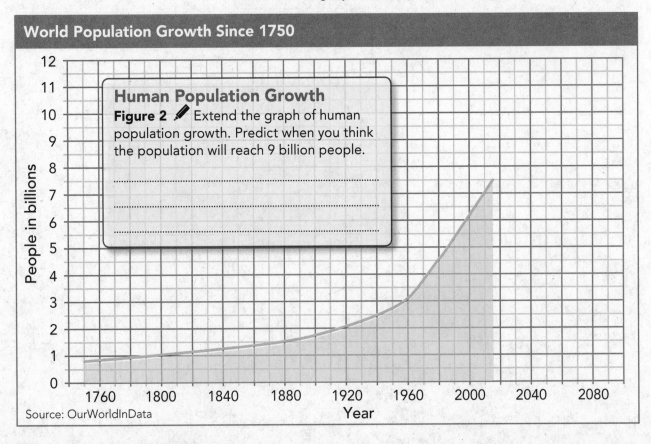

**World Population Growth Since 1750**

**Human Population Growth**

**Figure 2** Extend the graph of human population growth. Predict when you think the population will reach 9 billion people.

..............................................................

..............................................................

..............................................................

Source: OurWorldInData

# Population Growth Rate

Human population changes do not represent a straight line of increase on a graph. Instead the population increases more and more rapidly over time. This rate of change is called **exponential growth**—a growth pattern in which individuals in a population reproduce at a constant rate, so that the larger population gets, the faster it grows.

However, no living population can experience such extreme exponential growth for very long. Populations are limited by space and resources. Exponential growth will cease when a population reaches the upper limit of organisms its environment can support. At that point, the population will stabilize or possibly decline. Throughout history, human populations have experienced periods of growth and decline, depending on the conditions and resources available.

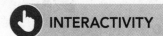
**INTERACTIVITY**

Learn about how human population growth affects Earth's systems.

✓ READING CHECK **Determine Conclusions** What would happen if the population growth rate reached zero?

..........................................................................

..........................................................................

## Math Toolbox

## Projected Growth Rates

The rate of human population growth is not the same all around the world. Experts use existing data to predict growth rates in different countries. Some areas may experience rapid growth, while others may have no growth or a decline.

1. **SEP Interpret Data** Which country represented has the highest population growth rate? Lowest?

.......................................................

.......................................................

2. **SEP Evaluate Evidence** What conclusions can you draw from the growth rates of Angola and Germany?

.......................................................

.......................................................

.......................................................

.......................................................

| Country | Population Growth Rate (%) |
|---|---|
| Angola | 1.9 |
| Australia | 1.0 |
| Canada | 0.7 |
| Germany | –0.2 |
| Haiti | 1.3 |
| Japan | –0.2 |
| South Korea | 0.5 |
| United States | 0.8 |
| Venezuela | 1.2 |

Source: CIA World Factbook, 2017 estimates

315

**☑Investigate** Examine how population growth affects the availability of natural resources.

**Academic Vocabulary**

What are some other words that have the same meaning as *constraint*?

..................................................

..................................................

..................................................

# Using Natural Resources

Earth provides many resources that humans rely on to live, such as energy sources, minerals, water, trees, and plants. These resources are needed by all organisms on Earth. Some resources, such as water, are part of systems that affect our planet's climate and other natural cycles.

**Human Activity** Industries and families alike rely on energy sources such as fossil fuels to provide electricity to power our lives. We use fuel to keep us warm in the winter and cool in the summer, to travel from place to place, and to grow and transport the food we eat. We use wood from trees and minerals that are mined from the ground to build everything from the tiniest computer chips to the tallest skyscrapers. Every human being relies on fresh, clean water to survive.

As the world's population grows, so does our demand for resources. Like the human population, many resources are not evenly distributed around Earth. For example, the availability of fresh, usable water varies in different locations on Earth. It is one of the factors that may act as a **constraint** on human activities in the near future. Currently, more than 700 million people do not have access to safe, clean water. This lack of clean water forces many individuals to consume unsafe water. Experts estimate that by 2025, nearly 1.8 billion people could be suffering from water scarcity.

# Question It!

**Mining Salt**

Salt is not only a necessary part of the human diet, it is used in numerous industrial and agricultural applications. Most of the salt used today is mined from underground deposits.

**SEP Ask Questions** Develop a list of questions you would ask to help determine the relationship between human population growth and salt mining.

..................................................
..................................................
..................................................
..................................................
..................................................
..................................................
..................................................
..................................................
..................................................
..................................................

**Impact of Agriculture**
**Figure 3** In order to grow food for people to eat, farmers use fertilizers and other chemicals. These chemicals often run off the land and pollute lakes, rivers, and the ocean.

**CCC Cause and Effect** What effect does farming food for a growing population have on the environment?

.................................................

.................................................

.................................................

.................................................

.................................................

.................................................

.................................................

## Impact on the Earth System

Using resources reduces their amounts, which is a problem for nonrenewable resources like fossil fuels. The way in which we obtain many of these resources involves drilling, mining, or clearing Earth's surface, which damages the land. As some resources such as minerals or fossil fuels become scarce, humans dig deeper and disturb more areas to keep up with our growing population. When we remove resources, it increases the potential to release harmful substances into the environment. For example, using resources creates waste. If left untreated, waste can harm the environment. Motorized vehicles, such as the one shown in **Figure 3,** burn petroleum and release gases and chemicals that can cause **pollution**, which is the contamination of Earth's land, water, or air.

Human activities also affect other life on Earth. When we mine for a mineral or divert water for our use we often destroy valuable habitats. Pollution in land and water habitats endangers the organisms that live there. Also, many organisms are over-exploited as food for growing human numbers. When the number of humans grows beyond what the available resources can support, we reach the point of **overpopulation**. Human overpopulation is a driving force of many environmental and social issues, including climate change, habitat loss, and human conflict. There may come a point at which Earth cannot adequately meet human needs at our current rate of resource use. In some parts of the world, this is already the case.

**READING CHECK Determine Conclusions** How does a growing population impact land, air, and water resources?

.................................................................................................

.................................................................................................

**Literacy Connection**

**Determine Conclusions** As you read, underline evidence in the text that supports your conclusions about how growing populations impact the environment.

INTERACTIVITY

Examine the different types of resources available on Earth.

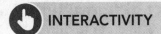

## Balancing Needs

Science can identify problems and offer possible solutions, but it is up to individuals, governments, and international organizations to decide how to manage the impacts of a growing population. There are economic, social, and environmental costs and benefits which all must be weighed against one another (**Figure 4**). For example, humans use a variety of resources to produce electricity, from burning fossil fuels to building dams. No single method works in every situation, and there are benefits and costs to each.

The practice of using less of a resource so that it can last longer is called **conservation**. To ensure that future generations have access to the same resources we enjoy now, we need to use resources in ways that maintain them at a certain quality for a certain period of time. This practice is known as **sustainable use** of living resources. It gives resources time to recover and replenish themselves.

Addressing human impacts on the environment also requires engineering new solutions to our problems. These might include using desalination to counter water shortages, or advances in solar power, wind power, and other forms of renewable energy. As human populations continue to rise, the need for new ideas and solutions will increase.

READING CHECK **Develop an Argument** Why is it important to conserve natural resources?

..............................................................................................................

..............................................................................................................

..............................................................................................................

**Harvesting Timber**

**Figure 4** We use timber, but there is an impact of our use on the environment. In the table, list the benefits and costs of logging.

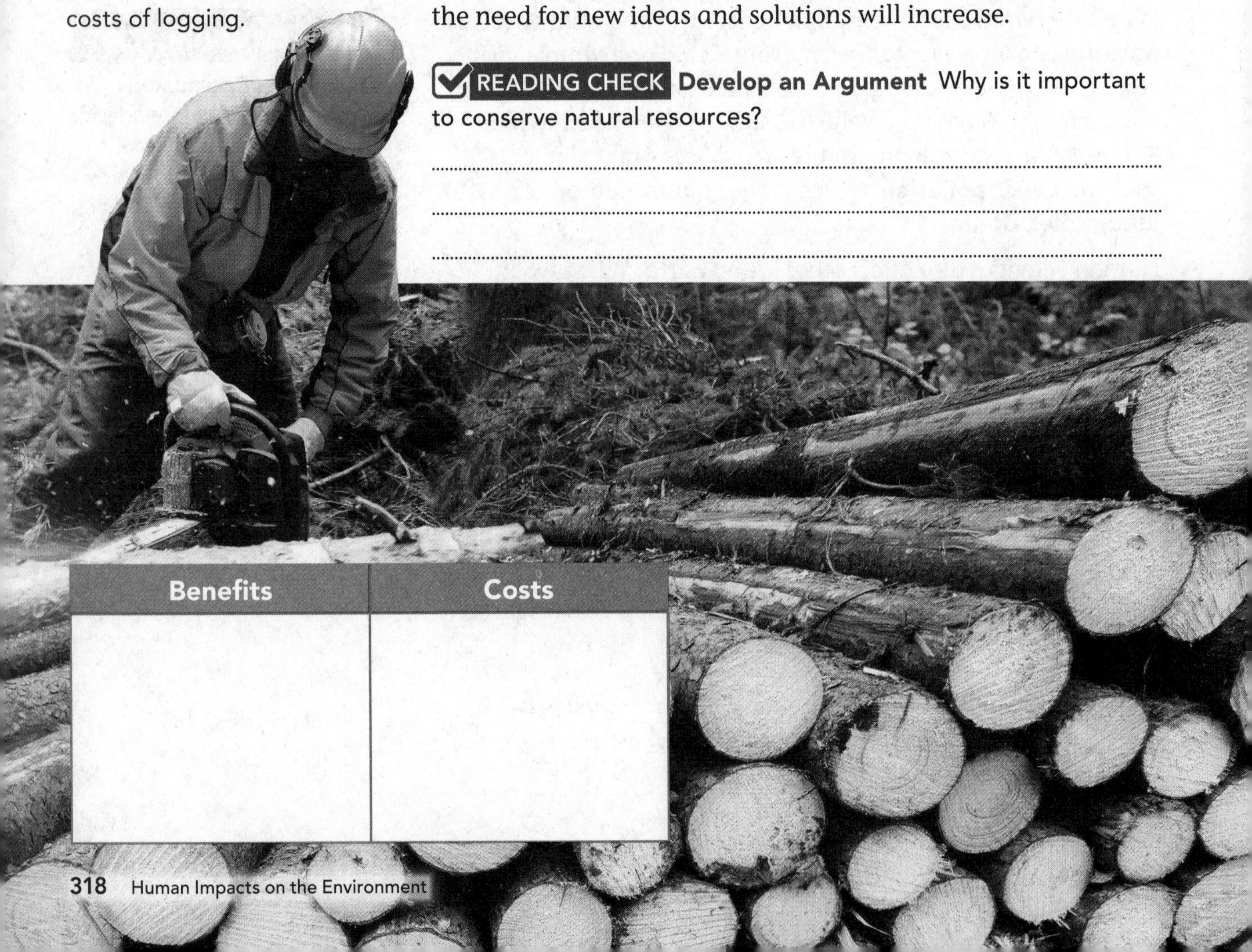

| Benefits | Costs |
| --- | --- |
| | |

# ☑ LESSON 1 Check

1. **SEP Cite Evidence** What factors limited human population growth in the past?

..................................................................

..................................................................

..................................................................

..................................................................

2. **CCC Cause and Effect** How did the Industrial Revolution affect human population growth?

..................................................................

..................................................................

..................................................................

..................................................................

..................................................................

3. **CCC Engage in Argument** What actions should humans take to conserve natural resources?

..................................................................

..................................................................

..................................................................

..................................................................

..................................................................

**Use the graph to answer questions 4 and 5.**

**Human Population 1750–2020**

4. **CCC Evaluate Proportions** What was the approximate population growth per year from 1800 to 1925? What was the approximate growth rate from 1925 to 2000? What is the ratio between the two rates?

..................................................................

..................................................................

..................................................................

5. **Use Ratios** Suggest two explanations for the ratio relationship you described in question 4.

..................................................................

..................................................................

..................................................................

..................................................................

---

# Quest CHECK-IN

In this lesson, you learned how human population has changed over time and how human population growth impacts Earth's systems.

**Connect to the Environment** Why is it important to consider human population growth when developing strategies for dealing with pollution?

..................................................................

..................................................................

..................................................................

..................................................................

👆 **INTERACTIVITY**

More Trash, Less Space

**Go online** to learn about the total volume of trash generated in the United States and to determine how much trash is generated at your school.

# (2) Air Pollution

## Guiding Questions

- What are the causes of air pollution?
- What are the long-term negative impacts of air pollution?
- What efforts are being made to decrease the levels of air pollution around the world?

## Connections

**Literacy** Cite Textual Evidence

**Math** Analyze Quantitative Relationships

MS-ESS3-4

**HANDS-ON LAB**

**uInvestigate** Evaluate how different types of pollution affect air and water clarity.

## Vocabulary

point source
nonpoint source
emissions
ozone
acid rain

## Academic Vocabulary

primary

## Connect It!

✎ Circle each mode of transportation that causes air pollution.

**SEP Construct Explanations** How do these different forms of transportation pollute the air?

......................................................................................................

......................................................................................................

**Make Predictions** What is the benefit of walking or riding a bike?

......................................................................................................

......................................................................................................

# Causes of Pollution

You are surrounded by air. Air is a mixture of nitrogen, oxygen, carbon dioxide, water vapor, and other gases. Almost all living things depend on these gases to survive. These gases cycle between the biosphere and the atmosphere. The cycles guarantee that the air supply will not run out, but they don't ensure that the air will be clean.

**Pollution** The contamination of Earth's land, water, or air is called pollution. Pollution is caused by liquids, chemicals, heat, light, and noise. Pollution can have dramatic negative effects on the environment and on living organisms.

Humans affect the levels of pollution by using natural resources and manufactured products. For example, **Figure 1** shows how the burning of gasoline pollutes the air. In addition, when coal and oil-based fuels are burned to generate electricity, carbon dioxide and sulfur dioxide are released into the air.

**Types of Pollution** A specific, identifiable pollution source is called a **point source**. A sewer that drains untreated wastewater into a river is an example of a point source.

A **nonpoint source** of pollution is widely spread and cannot be tied to a specific origin. For example, the polluted air around big cities is caused by vehicles, factories, and other sources. Because it is difficult to identify the exact source of the pollution, that pollution has a nonpoint source.

✓ **READING CHECK** **Determine Central Ideas** What is the difference between point and nonpoint sources of pollution?

....................................................................................................

....................................................................................................

....................................................................................................

**HANDS-ON LAB**

Explore how particles move through the air.

📓 **Write About It** What are the large-scale impacts of breathing polluted air?

**Different Sources of Pollution**
**Figure 1** Pollution can occur naturally or through human activities. Sometimes the level of pollution is so great that it harms people.

321

Forest fires

Industrial emissions

Motor vehicle emissions

Livestock

## Sources of Air Pollution

**Figure 2** ✐ Circle the natural sources of pollution. Mark an X on the human-made causes of pollution.

### HANDS-ON LAB

**Investigate** Evaluate how different types of pollution affect air and water clarity.

# Outdoor Air Pollution

The air you are breathing is a combination of different gases. If you are in the mountains, the air might feel fresh and crisp. If you are at the shore, you might smell the salt water. In large cities, however, the air might not be as refreshing. Air pollution can be a big problem in areas where there are a lot of factories or a lot of people.

**Emissions** Many years ago, the main source of air pollution was the smoke being pumped out of factories. You have probably seen images of these **emissions**, or pollutants that are released into the air, as the dark smoke coming out of a factory's tall chimneys. This smoke is loaded with chemicals that mix with the gases in the air. However, today, most air pollution is released from coal-fired power plants and from motor vehicles, as shown in **Figure 2.** Emissions often contain carbon dioxide, which is also a pollutant. The increasing level of carbon dioxide is the primary contributor to the rise in average global temperatures over the past century.

Not all air pollution is caused by people. There are also some natural causes of air pollution, such as forest fires and volcanic eruptions. For example, the Hawaiian volcano Kilauea releases nearly 1,500–2,000 tons of harmful sulfur dioxide into the atmosphere each day during eruptions. However, human activities emit more than ten times as much sulfur dioxide and more than one hundred times as much carbon dioxide as all volcanoes combined.

**Smog** If you live in a large city, chances are you have heard the term "smog alert." This is a warning to alert you that the amount of air pollution may make it difficult to breathe outdoors. Smog forms when certain gases and chemicals react with sunlight. This results in a thick, brownish haze that hovers over a city. Smog can cause breathing problems and diseases of the eyes and throat.

The **primary** source of smog is the emissions of cars and trucks. Among these emissions are chemicals called hydrocarbons and nitrogen oxides. These gases react in the sunlight to produce a form of oxygen called **ozone**. Ozone is toxic to humans, and it causes lung infections and harms the body's immune system.

Under normal conditions, air near the ground is heated by Earth's surface and rises up and away from the surface. Pollutants in the air are carried up into the atmosphere by the rising air. However, under certain weather conditions called temperature inversions, the normal circulation of air is blocked. As **Figure 3** shows, cool air becomes trapped below a layer of warm air during an inversion. This keeps the pollutants trapped near Earth's surface and causes them to become more concentrated and dangerous.

☑ READING CHECK **Cite Textual Evidence** What are the main sources of air pollution and how do they cause smog?

..........................................................................................................

..........................................................................................................

..........................................................................................................

**Academic Vocabulary**
Write a sentence using the word *primary*.

..............................................................

..............................................................

..............................................................

**Temperature Inversion**
**Figure 3** ✏ Complete the image on the right by shading in the air pollutants to show how they are trapped during a temperature inversion.

Normal conditions

Cold Air

Cool Air

Warm Air

Temperature inversion

Cold Air

Warm Air

Cool Air

323

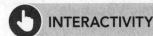
## Literacy Connection

**Cite Textual Evidence**
As you read, underline the statements that support the idea that acid rain causes damage to living and nonliving things.

**Acid Rain** Precipitation that is more acidic than normal because of air pollution is called **acid rain**. When coal and oil are burned, they produce nitrogen oxide and sulfur dioxide gases. These gases are then released as emissions and react with the water vapor in the air to produce nitric and sulfuric acids. These acids become part of rain, snow, sleet, or fog.

When acidic precipitation falls to Earth's surface, it has damaging effects, as shown in **Figure 4**. As water and soil become more acidic, organisms will die off. Acid rain can also remove nutrients and minerals from the soil, affecting plant growth. Sometimes the effects of acid rain can be reversed by adding chemicals that neutralize the acid, but this is very expensive.

Acid rain also causes damage to nonliving things. The acid reacts with metal and stone of buildings, cars, and statues. It can cause metal to rust at a faster rate and causes the chemical weathering of stone. The effects of acid rain on these materials are irreversible.

✓ READING CHECK **Write Arguments** Suppose your state government does not think that outdoor air pollution is a problem. What evidence could you use to convince your government that air pollution is harmful to people and the environment?

.........................................................................................................

.........................................................................................................

.........................................................................................................

.........................................................................................................

.........................................................................................................

### Effects of Acid Rain

**Figure 4** Acid rain can damage nonliving things as well as living things. Explain how acid rain might affect the trees in a forest.

.............................................................

.............................................................

.............................................................

.............................................................

.............................................................

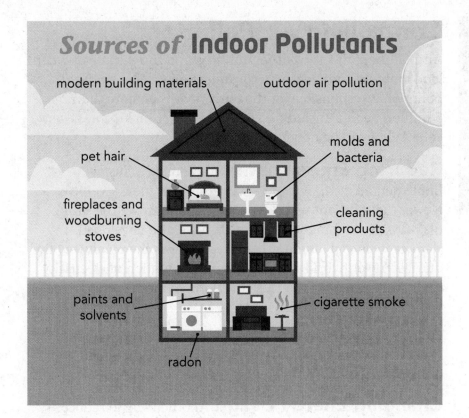

**Sources of Indoor Pollutants**

modern building materials

outdoor air pollution

pet hair

molds and bacteria

fireplaces and woodburning stoves

cleaning products

paints and solvents

cigarette smoke

radon

**Indoor Air Pollution**
**Figure 5** ✏ Underline the indoor pollutants that are human-made. Circle the pollutants that occur naturally.

# Indoor Air Pollution

Sometimes the quality of the air inside a building can be just as bad as the air outside. There are several things that can contribute to indoor air pollution, as shown in **Figure 5**. Some of these can be human-made, while others occur naturally.

**Allergens** Obvious sources of indoor air pollution include dust, mold, and pet hair. These factors, while quite common, usually affect only people who are sensitive to them. Other sources of indoor air pollution include fumes from glues, paints, and cleaning supplies and tobacco smoke from cigarettes or cigars. These can affect everyone in the home.

**Indoor Gases** Radon and carbon monoxide are two harmful pollutants often found in homes or other buildings. Radon is a colorless, odorless gas that is radioactive. It forms underground from the decay of certain rocks. Radon enters a home through cracks in the foundation. Breathing this gas over long periods of time can cause lung cancer and other health issues.

Carbon monoxide forms when fuels such as oil, gas, or wood are burned. Breathing carbon monoxide causes respiratory issues, nausea, headaches, and even death.

The best way to protect against carbon monoxide is to install detectors near sleeping areas. These devices alert homeowners if concentrations get too high.

**▶ VIDEO**

Explore the misconception that indoor spaces do not suffer from air pollution.

**☑ READING CHECK**
**Integrate With Visuals**
What are some ways to reduce the amount of indoor pollution in your home?

.................................................
.................................................
.................................................
.................................................
.................................................
.................................................
.................................................
.................................................
.................................................

## Bike Sharing

**Figure 6** Bike-sharing programs provide a clean-energy alternative to driving a car or taking a bus. What actions can you take to reduce air pollution in your community?

............................................

............................................

............................................

# Controlling Air Pollution

Air pollution affects weather patterns and the climate and can lead to illness and death. According to one recent study, air pollution is responsible for the early deaths of more than 5 million people, including 200,000 in the United States every year. What can be done?

**Reducing Emissions** The automobile industry implemented technology to lower emissions in new vehicles. Newer fuel-efficient vehicles use less fuel to travel the same distance as older models. Scientists have also developed cleaner fuels and biofuels that release fewer chemicals into the air. Electric or hybrid vehicles use a combination of electricity and gasoline, which reduces emissions. Some all-electric vehicles produce zero emissions.

Other ways to reduce emissions include carpooling, biking, or walking. You can also avoid using gas-powered lawn and garden tools and buy only energy-efficient appliances.

**Changing Energy Usage** Another way to reduce emissions is to transition away from fossil fuels, such as coal, oil, and natural gas. Solar, wind, hydroelectric, and geothermal energy produce only a small fraction of the harmful emissions that the burning of fossil fuels generates.

# Math Toolbox

## Energy Usage

The graphs show how energy consumption has changed in the United States over the past century.

1. **Use Ratios** How many times greater was energy consumption in 1908 than in 2015?

............................................

2. **Analyze Quantitative Relationships** Describe any patterns you observe in the graph showing the share of consumption for each energy source. What do you think might explain these patterns?

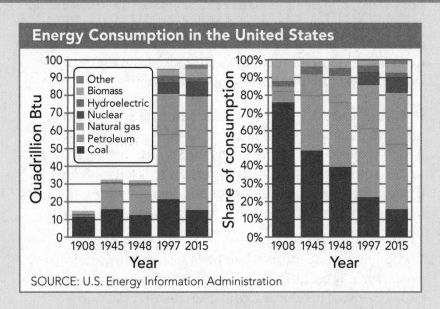

Energy Consumption in the United States

SOURCE: U.S. Energy Information Administration

............................................

............................................

**Protecting the Ozone Layer** If you have ever been sunburned, then you have experienced the effects of the sun's ultraviolet, or UV, radiation. The ozone layer, situated about 15 to 30 km above Earth's surface, works like a shield to protect living things from too much UV radiation.

**The Ozone Cycle** In the ozone layer, ozone is constantly being made and destroyed in a cycle. An ozone molecule has three oxygen atoms. When sunlight hits a molecule, the ozone absorbs UV radiation. The energy causes the ozone to break apart into an oxygen gas molecule (which has two oxygen atoms) and a single oxygen atom. The oxygen atom hits an oxygen molecule and attaches itself to form a new ozone molecule.

**The Ozone Hole** In the late 1970s, scientists discovered an area of severe ozone depletion, or a "hole," in the ozone layer over the southern polar region, shown in **Figure 7**. The main cause of the hole was a group of gases called chlorofluorocarbons (CFCs)—human-made gases that destroy ozone molecules. As a result, more UV radiation reached Earth's surface. Nations around the world worked together to ban CFCs to help restore the amount of ozone in the atmosphere.

☑ READING CHECK **Determine Conclusions** Why did countries work together to ban CFCs to help restore the ozone layer?

..................................................................................................

..................................................................................................

..................................................................................................

..................................................................................................

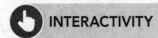
**INTERACTIVITY**

Explore how to reduce your carbon footprint.

**Ozone Hole**
**Figure 7** A hole in the ozone layer (in blue) allows more harmful UV radiation to reach Earth's surface in the Southern Hemisphere.

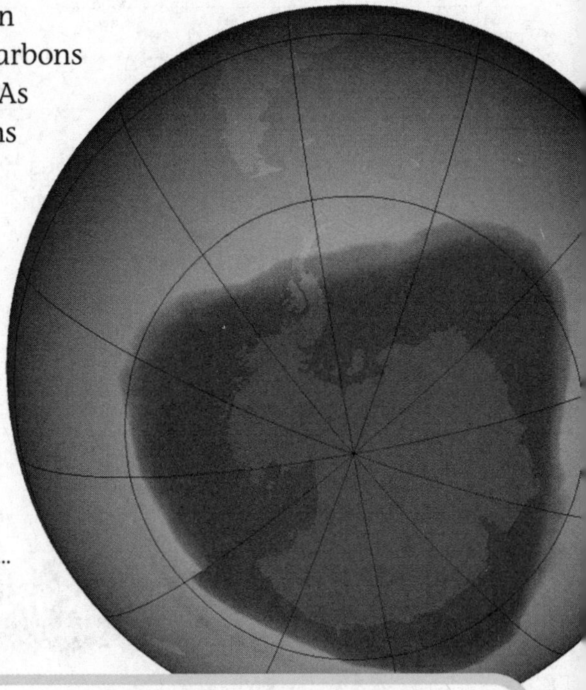

# Model It !

**Ozone Model**
Re-read the paragraph about the ozone cycle.

SEP Develop Models ✏ Use the information in the text to create and label a model of an ozone molecule and how it changes during its life cycle. Explain each stage of the cycle.

..............................................................................

..............................................................................

..............................................................................

..............................................................................

..............................................................................

# ☑ LESSON 2 Check

1. **Determine Differences** What is the difference between "helpful" and "harmful" ozone?

.................................................................

.................................................................

.................................................................

.................................................................

2. **Evaluate Reasoning** Why is the use of fertilizers on lawns in residential areas an example of a nonpoint source of pollution?

.................................................................

.................................................................

.................................................................

3. **SEP Provide Evidence** How does burning fossil fuels affect indoor air pollution?

.................................................................

.................................................................

.................................................................

.................................................................

.................................................................

4. **CCC Cause and Effect** What effect does burning fossil fuels during manufacturing and energy production have on outdoor air pollution?

.................................................................

.................................................................

.................................................................

.................................................................

.................................................................

.................................................................

.................................................................

5. **Construct an Argument** What evidence supports the claim that walking and biking to work would have a positive effect on air pollution?

.................................................................

.................................................................

.................................................................

.................................................................

.................................................................

## Quest CHECK-IN

**In this lesson, you learned how humans affect Earth's systems by producing different forms of air pollution. You also learned how we are working to reduce the impact of air pollution.**

**SEP Evaluate Evidence** Why is it important to work toward reducing activities that contribute to air pollution?

.................................................................

.................................................................

.................................................................

.................................................................

.................................................................

.................................................................

### HANDS-ON LAB

Trash vs. Water

Download the lab to design and construct a model of a landfill.

# Working Together to Reduce Air Pollution

Air pollution knows no borders. For instance, winds can carry pollution from factories in China nearly 10,000 kilometers to California. Many countries are reducing their own pollution, but they still suffer from the effects of air pollution from other countries. The only way to fight this global problem is by working together across borders.

In 2015, 196 countries came together to make a plan to reduce air pollution around the world. The Paris Agreement, as it is known, sets targets to reduce levels of carbon emissions. Carbon dioxide traps heat in the atmosphere, causing global warming. So, reducing pollution will help mitigate global warming.

It took many years to reach the Paris Agreement. Every country has different needs, industries, and laws. Some groups worry that the agreement doesn't go far enough. Others fear that environmental regulations will damage their national economies. Still, most nations believe that the Paris Agreement is necessary to reduce air pollution and protect Earth.

## MY COMMUNITY

What are communities in Florida doing to reduce air pollution? Explore the Florida Climate Center website to find out.

Carbon dioxide, a by-product of burning fossil fuels, is a type of air pollution. It traps heat in Earth's atmosphere, causing global temperatures to rise. Even slight temperature increases can upset the delicate balance of life on Earth.

# 3 Impacts on Land

## Guiding Questions

- What natural resources are obtained from Earth's geosphere?
- Why are natural resources on land so important to Earth's systems?
- How do human activities positively and negatively affect land resources?

## Connections

**Literacy** Cite Textual Evidence

**Math** Analyze Proportional Relationships

MS-ESS3-4

## HANDS-ON LAB

**иInvestigate** Examine the impacts of mining.

### Vocabulary

natural resource
renewable
  resource
nonrenewable
  resource
deforestation
erosion
desertification
sustainable

### Academic Vocabulary

resource

## Connect It!

✏ **Identify and label one unlimited resource and one limited resource shown in the image.**

**CCC Cause and Effect** What impact do you think the overuse of certain resources might have on Earth's ecosystems?

.................................................................................................................

.................................................................................................................

# Land as a Resource

Did you drink water, turn on a light, or ride in a bus today? All of these activities, and many more, depend on Earth's **resources**. Anything we use that occurs naturally in the environment is called a **natural resource**. As **Figure 1** shows, natural resources include organisms, water, sunlight, minerals, and soil.

A **renewable resource** is either always available or is naturally replaced in a relatively short time. Some renewable resources, such as wind and sunlight, are almost always available. Other renewable resources, such as water and trees, are renewable only if they are replaced as fast as they are used.

**Nonrenewable resources** are resources that are not replaced within a relatively short time frame. Metals and most minerals are nonrenewable. Oil and coal are also nonrenewable resources. They were formed over millions of years from the remains of long-dead organisms. Humans use these resources faster than they can be replaced. Over time, they will be used up.

While it does not cover as much of the planet's surface as water, land is also a vital resource. Humans use its many resources to survive. As **Figure 2** will show, it is used to grow food, obtain raw materials, and provide shelter.

### Academic Vocabulary

A resource is not limited to a material, such as water or trees. What other kinds of resources do you rely on in your life?

.................................................................

.................................................................

.................................................................

.................................................................

**Reflect** What are some renewable and nonrenewable resources that you use? In your science notebook, describe these resources.

## Natural Resources

**Figure 1** Humans use many different types of resources. Some of these are in limited supply, while others are essentially limitless.

**Agriculture** Land provides most of the food people eat. The use of land to produce food is called agriculture. Many areas of the world are not suitable for farming. New farmland is often made by draining wetlands, irrigating deserts, or deforestation. **Deforestation** is the removal of forests to use the land for other reasons. This process destroys the habitats of organisms living in these places.

**Mining** The metals and plastics used to make items such as televisions, cellular phones, building materials, and cars are mined from below Earth's surface. Metals and other resources are obtained through one type of mining called strip mining. Strip mining removes the top layer of dirt, exposing the minerals or ore underneath. When heavy winds and rains come, they can wash soil and land away. With it go all the nutrients it contains. It can take thousands of years for soil to be replaced.

**Development** Where do you live? It is a good bet that you live in a structure somewhere on the land. Whether it is a house, a camper, or an apartment building, the space your home takes up was once used as a habitat for other organisms. As the human population grows, more and more land is developed and built up with human structures, leaving no room for the living organisms of the original habitat.

✓READING CHECK

**Cite Textual Evidence**
Which statements from the text support the idea that land is an important resource? Underline them.

clear-cutting

strip mining

development

**Land Use**

**Figure 2** Humans use land is many different ways. How do these activities impact Earth's systems?

..................................................................

..................................................................

..................................................................

..................................................................

# Importance of Soil Management

Healthy, fertile soil is essential for the success of agriculture because it contains the minerals and nutrients that plants require. Soil absorbs, stores, and filters water, which is also necessary for plant growth. Organisms living in soil, such as bacteria, fungi, and earthworms, break down the wastes and remains of living things and return them to the soil as nutrients.

**Structure of Soil** If you take a shovel and dig a hole in the ground, you will encounter several layers of soil, such as those shown in **Figure 3**. The first layer is called the litter. This top layer is where dead leaves and grass are found.

The next layer is called the topsoil. Topsoil is a mixture of nutrients, water, air, rock fragments, and dead and decaying organisms. Moving further down, the shovel will hit the subsoil. This layer contains the same water and air as the topsoil, but there are more rock fragments and fewer plant and animal remains here.

Underneath the subsoil is the layer of bedrock. This is the layer that makes up Earth's crust and is the basis for new soil. As time passes, water dissolves the rock, and its freezing and thawing action cracks and breaks apart the bedrock. Plant roots also help to break the bedrock by growing into cracks and then expanding. Animals such as earthworms and moles also help in the process. And as dead organisms break down, their remains contribute to the mixture of new soil.

## Soil Layers

**Figure 3** 🖊 Fertile soil is made up of several layers. Label each layer of soil in the photo: *bedrock, litter, subsoil, topsoil.*

## Plan It!

### Community Considerations

CCC Cause and Effect Suppose you are part of a group that is converting an abandoned lot into a community garden. You need to plan the garden to avoid damaging the local environment further. What harmful effects should you consider and how can you minimize them?

.....................................................................................................................................................

.....................................................................................................................................................

.....................................................................................................................................................

.....................................................................................................................................................

**Erosion** Without soil, life on land could not exist. Soil takes hundreds of years to form. Therefore, every effort must be made to protect Earth's soil. Sometimes, natural forces cause soil loss. Forces such as wind, water, and ice move particles of rocks or soil through a process called **erosion**.

Usually, plant roots growing deep into the soil help to hold it in place. Human activities such as mining, logging, construction, and farming increase erosion by taking away these plants and exposing the soil to wind and precipitation. With nothing to anchor them in place, soil particles easily move. Human activities cause erosion to happen at a much faster rate than naturally-ocurring processes do. **Figure 4** shows some examples of natural and human-caused erosion.

**Erosion**

**Figure 4** ✏ Check the image that shows naturally-occurring erosion.
**CCC Cause and Effect** How did different events cause these areas to form?

..........................................

..........................................

..........................................

..........................................

..........................................

..........................................

..........................................

**Nutrient Depletion** Plants make their own food through photosynthesis, but they need to take in nutrients such as nitrogen and phosphorus. Decomposers in the soil break down dead organisms, which add these and other nutrients to the soil. If a farmer plants the same crops in a field every year, the crops may use more nutrients than decomposers can supply. This leads to nutrient depletion; the soil is not adequately fertile. Nutrient depletion can directly affect humans. Crops grown in nutrient-poor soil often have less nutritional value.

Farmers add fertilizers to the soil to provide the needed nutrients. This can produce abundant, nutritious crops, but can also cause damage when rain carries the fertilizers into nearby bodies of water. Farmers often manage the soil by allowing it to sit for a season or two in between plantings. This allows the remnant crops to decompose, which replenishes the soil with nutrients.

**Desertification** When the soil in a once-fertile area loses its moisture and nutrients, the area can become a desert. The advance of desert-like conditions into areas that were previously fertile is called **desertification**.

One cause of moisture loss is drought. During these prolonged periods of low precipitation, plants, including crops, will dry up or not grow at all. Allowing livestock to overgraze grasslands and cutting down trees without replanting the area can also result in desertification. Without plant roots to hold the soil together, erosion of fertile topsoil will occur. Plant roots also carry water deeper into the soil, so it doesn't dry out as quickly.

From 2010 to 2016, the state of California experienced a severe drought. The people of California took preventive actions to avoid desertification. The state introduced mandatory water restrictions and regulations on the use of groundwater. Farmers also reduced the growing of certain crops to lessen the need for extensive irrigation.

✔️ READING CHECK **Translate Information** What most likely occurred to cause the conditions in **Figure 5**?

....................................................................................................

....................................................................................................

....................................................................................................

**Desertification**

**Figure 5** Crops cannot grow in arid soil. As a result, many people are unable to grow their own food and must move to a town or city where food is available.

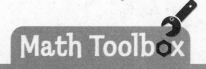

# Math Toolbox

## Causes of Land Degradation

Scientists estimate that there are at least 79.5 million hectares of degraded land in North America. The graph shows the causes of land degradation by percentage.

**Analyze Proportional Relationships** How many more hectares were degraded by agricultural activities than by deforestation? Show your work.

.......................................................................

.......................................................................

.......................................................................

.......................................................................

.......................................................................

.......................................................................

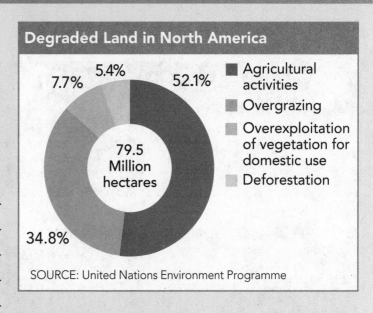

**Degraded Land in North America**

7.7%    5.4%    52.1%

79.5 Million hectares

34.8%

- Agricultural activities
- Overgrazing
- Overexploitation of vegetation for domestic use
- Deforestation

SOURCE: United Nations Environment Programme

**VIDEO**

Learn more about what happens when you throw something "away."

## Land Reclamation

**Figure 6** 🖉 These pictures show an area that was reclaimed to include a stream. Add numbers to put these pictures in chronological order.

**SEP Construct Explanations** Explain what happened to the land in these pictures.

.............................................................

.............................................................

.............................................................

.............................................................

**Landfills** When you are asked to take out the garbage, where does it go once it leaves your curb? Today much of the solid waste, construction debris, and agricultural and industrial waste we produce is buried in holes called landfills. These areas are designed to protect the surrounding areas from soil and water pollution. If landfills are not managed correctly, they can harm the environment. Materials from waste can leak into the groundwater, making it toxic to drink.

Once a landfill is full, it is covered with soil heavy in clay to keep rainwater from entering the waste. These "capped" landfills can be reclaimed as locations for parks and sports arenas, but they cannot be used for housing or agriculture.

**Land Reclamation** It is sometimes possible to restore soil that has been lost to erosion, mining, or waste disposal. This process of restoring land to a more productive state is called land reclamation. Land reclamation could involve trucking in soil from another area. Sometimes mine operations reclaim land by storing the soil that they remove from a site, then putting it back after mining operations cease. Land reclamation can restore farming areas as well as wildlife habitats (see **Figure 6**).

Land reclamation is very expensive and difficult. It is much harder to bring back damaged land than it is to protect and conserve those resources before they become damaged.

✅ **READING CHECK** **Draw Evidence** How do human actions impact land? Give one positive and one negative impact.

.............................................................

.............................................................

.............................................................

.............................................................

# Wetlands

A wetland is an area in which water covers the soil for all or most of the year. They are found in all climates and on all continents except Antarctica. Other terms you may have heard for wetland include bog, marsh, and swamp.

**Figure 7** shows how wetlands support both land and aquatic ecosystems. They serve as breeding and nursery grounds for many organisms, provide habitats to many species of plants, and are feeding sites for many birds, mammals, and fish.

Human activities have greatly impacted wetlands. The development of homes, businesses, and roads requires controlling the flow of water through these areas. But altering the flow of water in a wetland changes the ecosystem and destroys unique habitats. It can also lead to increases in erosion, flooding, and the pollution of water and soil. Wetland soil acts as a natural "sponge" to collect water. Without wetlands, the large amounts of rain produced by severe storms, such as hurricanes, would flow directly into rivers or populated areas. Wetlands help to protect the quality of water by trapping excess sediments and pollutants before they reach the groundwater or waterways.

☑ **READING CHECK** **Integrate With Visuals** How would filling in a wetland to create a field affect the surrounding environment?

......................................................................................................................................

......................................................................................................................................

......................................................................................................................................

## Literacy Connection

**Cite Textual Evidence**
When you write an argument, it should be based on factual evidence, not opinions. As you read, underline the evidence that supports the idea that human activities negatively affect the land.

## How Wetlands Work
**Figure 7** 🖋 Wetland plants, soil, and bacteria protect surrounding aspects. Circle the aspects of the wetland that provide benefits to humans.

plants filter out pollutants and sediments

dissipates stream energy

provides critical wildlife habitat

groundwater flow

bacteria break down pollutants

specialized roots stabilize soil

saturated soil stores water

**Figure 8** Examine the forest closely. Notice the amount of deforestation.

SEP Engage in Argument Do you think these trees are being managed in a way that maintains the overall health of the forest? Explain.

...............................................

...............................................

...............................................

...............................................

...............................................

...............................................

# Sustainable Forest Management

Trees and other plants, like the ones in **Figure 8**, are important land resources. They provide food and shelter for many organisms. Through photosynthesis, they release oxygen into the air. They also absorb carbon dioxide and other pollutants from the air. Their roots absorb rainwater and hold the soil together, which helps to prevent erosion and flooding.

Many products are made from the fruit, seeds, and other parts of forest plants. The wood from some trees is used for making paper, and other trees are used to build homes and furniture. Fruits and seeds from trees provide food for people and animals.

All trees, whether cultivated by farmers or growing in the wild, need to be protected and managed sustainably. Because we can plant trees to replace trees that are cut down, forests can be renewable resources. How long a resource lasts depends on how people use it. **Sustainable** use of a resource means using it in ways that maintain the resource for all future generations. Replacing and reserving trees are important ways to sustain a forest. These practices ensure that the ecosystem remains healthy and that people can still depend on forests for the resources they need.

**Logging Methods** There are two main methods of logging, or cutting down trees: clear-cutting and selective cutting, illustrated in **Figure 9**. Clear-cutting is the process of cutting down all the trees in an area at once. Selective cutting is the process of cutting down only some trees in a forest and leaving a mix of tree sizes and species behind.

Clear-cutting is usually faster and less expensive than selective cutting. However, selective cutting is less damaging to the forest ecosystem than clear-cutting. When a forest is cleared, all the animals' habitats are suddenly gone. Without the protection of the trees, the soil is more easily eroded by wind and rain. The soil can then be blown or washed away and into nearby streams, harming aquatic ecosystems.

Selective cutting takes much longer, as the loggers need to actively choose which trees will come down and which will remain. It is more dangerous for loggers to selectively cut trees because they have to move heavy equipment and logs around the remaining trees.

**Logging Methods**

**Figure 9** ✏ Clear-cutting and selective cutting are two methods of tree harvesting. Label each method shown as clear-cutting or selective cutting.

**Original Forest**

INTERACTIVITY

Create a solution for a controversial use of land.

**Sustainable Forestry** Forests can be managed to provide a sustainable yield. A sustainable yield is the amount of a renewable resource that can be harvested regularly without reducing the future supply. Planting one tree to replace each one that is cut down ensures that the overall yield remains constant.

In sustainable forestry, after trees are harvested, young trees are planted, as shown in **Figure 10**. Trees must be planted frequently enough to maintain a constant supply. Forests containing fast-growing tree species, such as pines, can be harvested and replanted every 20 to 30 years. Forests containing slower-growing species, such as hickory, oak, and cherry, may be harvested only every 40 to 100 years. One sustainable approach is to log small patches within a forest, so different sections can be harvested every year.

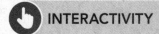

**Write About It** Collect information about how trees in your state are managed. In your science notebook, write an argument from the position of a conservation organization that says the yield is too high and needs to be reduced.

READING CHECK **Draw Evidence** Why is it important to manage forests so that their yield is sustainable?

**Replanting**

**Figure 10** Planting another generation of trees is one technique of sustainable forestry.

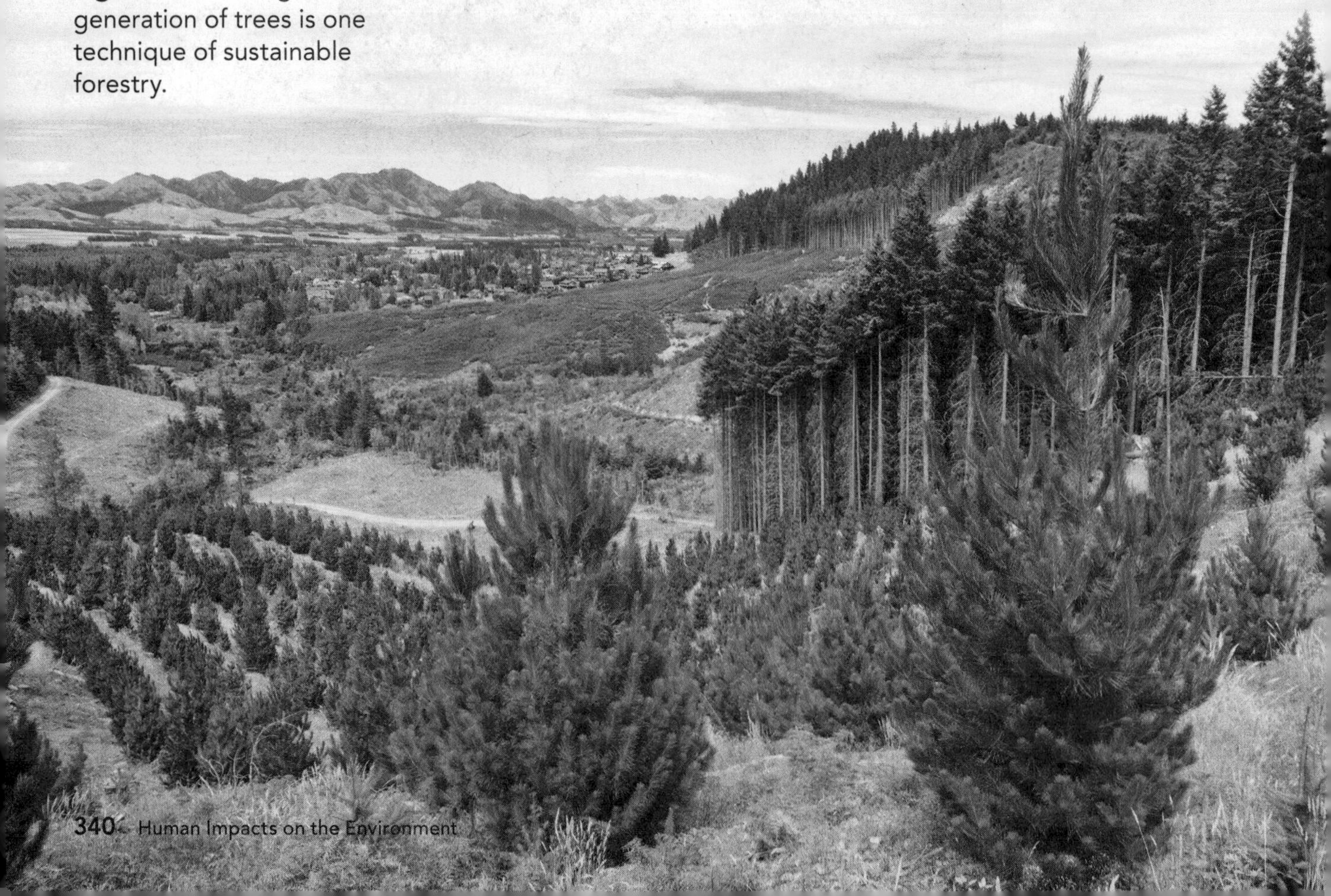

1. **Communicate** What are three different ways land is used as a resource?

   ................................................................

   ................................................................

2. **SEP Cite Evidence** Why are trees considered a renewable resource?

   ................................................................

   ................................................................

   ................................................................

3. **Construct Arguments** How do poor farming methods impact Earth?

   ................................................................

   ................................................................

   ................................................................

   ................................................................

   ................................................................

   ................................................................

   ................................................................

   ................................................................

4. **SEP Evaluate Evidence** Give evidence to defend the claim that it is environmentally unsound to change the flow of water in a wetland.

   ................................................................

   ................................................................

   ................................................................

   ................................................................

   ................................................................

   ................................................................

   ................................................................

   ................................................................

5. **CCC Cause and Effect** How does the presence of trees maintain the stability of land resources?

   ................................................................

   ................................................................

   ................................................................

   ................................................................

   ................................................................

   ................................................................

# Quest CHECK-IN

In this lesson, you learned about natural resources found on land and their importance to Earth's systems. You also learned how humans positively and negatively affect these resources.

**SEP Evaluate Evidence** Why is it important to conserve resources and not simply use them in the most convenient way?

................................................................

................................................................

................................................................

................................................................

................................................................

## INTERACTIVITY

Life of a Landfill

**Go online** to learn about where to site a landfill and how a landfill is constructed.

MS-ESS3-4

# Nothing Goes TO WASTE

One city in Texas is making sure nothing in its sewers goes to waste. The Hornsby Bend Biosolids Management Plant in Austin, Texas, recycles sewage into biosolids. Biosolids are rich in nutrients, so they make great soil and fertilizer.

Every day, Hornsby Bend receives about a million gallons of sewage solids from Austin's water treatment plants, where the sewage is separated from the wastewater. The sewage is screened, and then flows into tanks where bacteria get to work feeding on it. The bacteria break the sewage down, killing most disease organisms as they go. This process is actually not that different from how the human digestive system works. After about 60 days, the sewage is converted into biosolids.

Hornsby Bend is also a bird sanctuary with more than 350 types of birds.

Hornsby Bend also collects Austin's yard trimmings and mixes these with the biosolids to make nutrient-rich soil. The plant sends some soil to nearby farmers who enhance their existing soil with the mix. The rest is used to supplement the soil of Austin's public lawns, gardens, parks, and golf courses. Instead of going to an expensive landfill, the biosolids are put to good use.

All of the water used at the treatment plant is recycled, too. Some of it goes to irrigate the nearby farmland, and the rest goes to ponds at the treatment plant. The nutrient-rich pond water has still another benefit: the treatment plant is also a bird sanctuary. Hornsby Bend is one of the best birding sites in the state. Thanks to the Hornsby Bend Biosolids Management Plant, Austin's waste doesn't go to waste.

**Use the table to answer the following questions.**

1. **CCC Scale, Proportion, and Quantity** One sample of biosolids contains 18.2 mg/kg mercury, 22.5 mg/kg arsenic, and 29.7 mg/kg cadmium. Are these biosolids safe to use? Why or why not?

   ...................................................................

   ...................................................................

2. **SEP Use Mathematics** A biosolids plant is picking up waste from a new factory. The level of lead in the plant's biosolids had been 121 mg/kg. With the waste from the new factory, the lead has increased 12 percent. Calculate the new lead level to determine if the biosolid is still safe to use on farmland.

   ...................................................................

   ...................................................................

   ...................................................................

| Safe Levels of Pollutants in Soil on Farms Fertilized with Biosolids | |
|---|---|
| Pollutant | Risk Assessment Acceptable Soil Concentration (mg/kg-soil) |
| Arsenic | 23.5 |
| Cadmium | 19.7 |
| Copper | 769.0 |
| Lead | 161.0 |
| Mercury | 8.6 |
| Nickel | 228.0 |
| Selenium | 50.21 |
| Zinc | 1,454.0 |

SOURCE: Evironmental Protection Agency

3. **Connect to Society** Why is a chart like this important?

   ...................................................................

   ...................................................................

   ...................................................................

4. **SEP Engage in Argument** Are biosolids safe to use in agriculture? Make an argument to support your answer.

   ...................................................................

   ...................................................................

   ...................................................................

   ...................................................................

# 4 Water Pollution

## Guiding Questions

- Why is fresh water such a limited resource within Earth's systems?
- How do certain human activities cause freshwater and ocean pollution?
- What methods have humans developed to reduce freshwater and ocean pollution?

## Connections

**Literacy** Draw Evidence

**Math** Analyze Proportional Relationships

MS-ESS3-4

## HANDS-ON LAB

**ᴎInvestigate** Practice different techniques for cleaning up oil spills.

### Vocabulary

sewage
sediment
thermal pollution

### Academic Vocabulary

distributed

## Connect It!

✏ **Circle the areas in the photo that contain fresh water.**

SEP Provide Evidence  Why is water an important resource?

......................................................................................................

......................................................................................................

# Water as a Resource

Water is essential for life on Earth. Most of Earth's surface is covered by some form of water, as shown in **Figure 1**. It serves as a habitat for many species. Approximately 97 percent of the water on Earth is undrinkable because it contains salt. Of the remaining 3 percent, most is frozen solid in the polar ice sheets. That leaves less than 1 percent of all the water on the planet as drinkable.

Earth's water is a renewable resource, but fresh water is a limited resource. Recall that water continually moves between the atmosphere and Earth's surface in the water cycle. However, there is not always enough water in a given place at a given time. When water usage is poorly managed, it can lead to water shortages.

The limited supply of fresh water is not evenly **distributed** around the world. Some areas have an abundant supply, while in others it is quite scarce. Water scarcity occurs when there is not enough water to meet demand. It can be caused by droughts, low levels of groundwater, unequal water distribution, or environmental factors such as water pollution. An area faces water scarcity when the water supply is less than 1,000 cubic meters per person.

✅ **READING CHECK** **Draw Evidence** Why is water a limited resource even though it is renewable?

........................................................................................

........................................................................................

📓 **Write About It** What do you think the world's freshwater supply will look like in another 100 years? In your science notebook, describe how and why our water supply might change.

**Academic Vocabulary**

What are some items that might get distributed? Can you think of any examples from your school?

........................................................................................

........................................................................................

**Where is the Fresh Water?**

**Figure 1** Drinkable fresh water makes up less than one percent of the water on Earth.

## Water Pollution

**Figure 2** 🖊 Most sources of freshwater pollution come from human activities.

1. **Claim** 🖊 Mark any examples of nonpoint sources of pollution with a check mark. Mark any examples of point sources of pollution with an X.

2. **Evidence** What evidence did you use to identify your claims?

........................................................

........................................................

3. **Reasoning** Explain how your evidence supports your claim.

........................................................

........................................................

........................................................

........................................................

........................................................

........................................................

# Sources of Freshwater Pollution

With fresh water being so limited, any form of pollution entering the water supply can have drastic results. Most water pollution is directly linked to human activities, as shown in **Figure 2**. Wastes from farming, households, industry, and mining can end up in the water supply. Water pollutants may be point or nonpoint sources, depending on how they enter the water. A point source for water pollution could be a factory output pipe or a leaking landfill. Nonpoint pollution sources could be farm pesticides, farm animal wastes, or runoff of salt and chemicals from roads.

**Farming Wastes** Animal wastes, fertilizers, and pesticides are sources of pollution. When it rains, animal wastes, fertilizers, and pesticides can wash away into nearby water sources and eventually the ocean. These pollutants can cause overgrowths of algae. The algae block light and deplete the water of oxygen, killing everything else in the water.

**Household Pollutants** The water and human wastes that are washed down sinks, showers, and toilets are called **sewage**. Sometimes, the sewage can leak into groundwater before it is treated. Because sewage contains many disease-causing bacteria, people will become ill if they drink or swim in water containing them.

**Industrial Wastes** The waste products of factories and mines may also pollute the water. Many manufacturing processes use or produce toxic chemicals that need to be disposed of properly. During this disposal, chemicals sometimes leak into the groundwater. Some chemicals, such as heavy metals, build up in the bodies of aquatic organisms, making them and the animals that eat them ill.

## Sediment

Erosion carries small particles of rocks and sand from the land into the water. These particles are called **sediment**. Sediment can cover up sources of food, nests, and eggs of aquatic organisms. Sediment also blocks sunlight, which prevents photosynthesis in plants.

## Heat

When heat negatively affects bodies of water, it is known as **thermal pollution**. Factories and power plants use water to cool their machinery. This heated water is often discharged back into the environment. Because it is so hot, the water can kill organisms.

## Oil and Gasoline

Oil and gasoline are often transported in long pipelines, either underground or above ground. Sometimes these pipelines leak into rivers, streams, or groundwater. When oil and gasoline pollute the water, it can take many years for the ecosystem to recover. Oil is difficult to collect and penetrates much of the soil in the area. It also affects the plants that grow along the water's edge. Spilled oil also has both direct and indirect effects on wildlife. It coats their fur or feathers and causes skin irritation, at the least. It kills their food sources as well.

Oil and gasoline leaks from underground storage tanks are also sources of water pollution. These leaks can seep into the groundwater, making it unfit to drink.

☑ **READING CHECK** **Draw Evidence** Does most water pollution happen as a result of human activities? Explain.

...................................................................................................

...................................................................................................

...................................................................................................

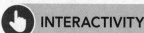 **INTERACTIVITY**

Examine how pollution affects the water cycle.

## Literacy Connection

**Draw Evidence** Sometimes you need to draw evidence to support your analysis of a certain topic. Reread the previous page and the current page. As you read, underline any pieces of evidence that support the idea that most water pollution is directly linked to human activities.

**INTERACTIVITY**

Investigate whether or not human activity is responsible for odd mutations found in frogs.

# Sources of Ocean Pollution

It was once thought that "the solution to pollution is dilution." This meant that whatever was dumped into the ocean would just spread out and eventually go away. Today, we know that isn't true. Dumping large amounts of wastes into the ocean threatens marine organisms and the overall functioning of Earth's systems.

**Natural Occurrences** There are some pollutants that occur naturally. These include freshwater runoff from land after heavy rains. When this freshwater enters the ocean, the salinity drops. Some organisms cannot tolerate this, so they either move to saltier waters or die.

**Human Activities** Most ocean pollution is related to human activities. The chemicals, sewage, and other wastes that are dumped into the ocean come from human sources. Fertilizers and pesticides from farms run off and eventually make it to the ocean. When enough of these build up, they can create an ocean dead zone—an area where nothing can live because there is not enough oxygen in the water.

## Effects of Pollution

**Figure 3** This plastic and trash was recovered from the ocean, where it can harm organisms.

SEP Design Solutions What are some ways humans can reduce the amount of plastic that ends up in the ocean?

........................................................

........................................................

........................................................

**Trash** Trash and plastic, as shown in **Figure 3**, are hazardous to marine animals. For example, sea turtles often mistake plastic bags floating in the water for jellyfish. Once consumed, the bags clog up the intestines of the turtles. Fishing line and nets can catch swimming animals and entangle them. One area in the Pacific Ocean contains about 2 million bits of plastic per square mile. When sea creatures consume these tiny pieces, they can become ill and die. The plastic bits can also cause health problems for animals higher up in the food chain that eat small animals with plastic inside of them.

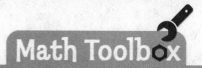

## Sources of Oil Pollution

**There are different ways for oil to pollute the ocean.**

1. **Construct Graphs** ✏ Create a bar graph of the data.

2. **Analyze Proportional Relationships** How many times greater is the amount of pollution caused by runoff than that caused by oil spills?

......................................................................

......................................................................

......................................................................

| Source of Oil Pollution | Oil Pollution (millions of liters) |
| --- | --- |
| Offshore drilling | 80 |
| Land runoff | 1,375 |
| Natural seeps | 240 |
| Ship repair | 510 |
| Oil spills | 125 |

**Oil Spills** Oil that is accidentally spilled into the ocean is also a large source of pollution. Oil rigs that drill for oil sometimes leak into the ocean. This oil coats the feathers of birds, reducing their ability to stay warm. Oil also harms animals if they swallow it. Pollutants can build up in organisms' bodies and poison people or other marine life that feed on them.

 **VIDEO**

Explore the misconception that the ocean cannot be harmed because it is so vast.

**Aquaculture** The practice of raising fish and other water-dwelling organisms for food is called aquaculture. Fish are often raised in artificial ponds and bays that replace and destroy natural habitats, such as salt marshes. The farms can cause pollution and spread diseases into wild fish populations.

✓ **READING CHECK** **Determine Conclusions** How can you help to reduce the amount of pollution that ends up in the ocean?

......................................................................

......................................................................

......................................................................

......................................................................

HANDS-ON LAB

**Investigate** Practice different techniques for cleaning up oil spills.

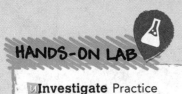

INTERACTIVITY

Take a closer look at water pollution and solutions.

# Reducing Water Pollution

Everyone needs clean water. But how can the pollution that currently enters the water be reduced, and what efforts can be made to prevent future pollution?

The United States and other countries have laws that regulate water-polluting substances. These laws mandate the types and amounts of substances that can be dumped into the water. While these laws help, the keys to keeping water clean are the prevention of oil and gasoline spills, effective cleanup of spills, proper sewage treatment, and reduction of pollutants.

**Protecting the Ocean** The ocean is a continuous body of water. Because no one country owns the ocean, it is every nation's responsibility to do whatever it can to ensure the water stays clean. To help protect the ocean, the United Nations set up regulations that say the first 22 kilometers from the coast are controlled by the nation that owns that coast. That nation also controls any resources, such as oil, natural gas, and fish, that are found out to 370 km.

Many nations are helping to protect the ocean by limiting how much can be taken from it and by establishing marine protected areas (MPAs). They also are working to reduce the amount of pollution in their coastal waters.

**Cleaning Oil Spills** Oil spills, such as the one in **Figure 4**, are one of the worst environmental hazards that can occur. While nature can clean small amounts of oil from the water, large spills such as the Deepwater Horizon oil spill are too much to handle. The bacteria that are able to digest oil cannot keep up with the volume of oil that is released in such a spill. Boats deploy skimming devices to collect floating oil, and barriers are set up to absorb or block oil before it reaches the shore. Chemical dispersants are also sprayed into the water to break up the oil. Cleanup of a major oil spill in the ocean can take many years.

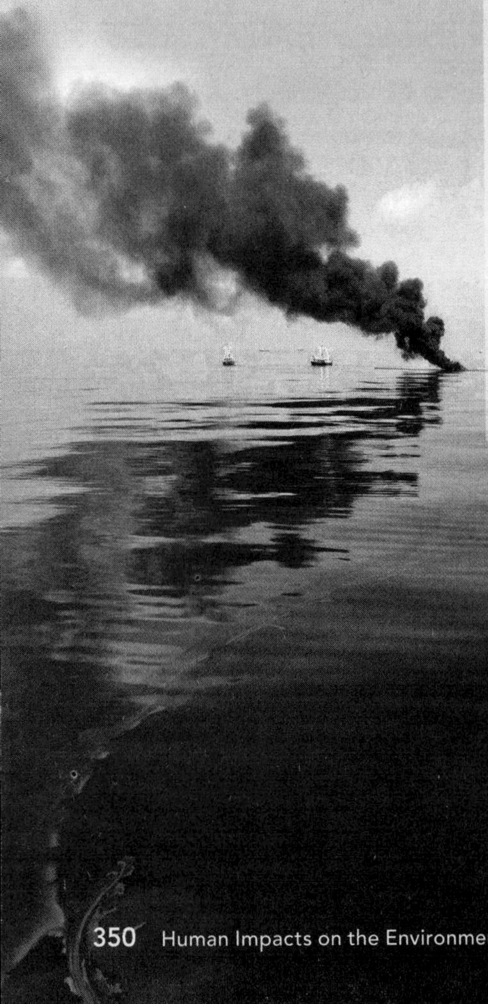

**Deepwater Horizon Disaster**

**Figure 4** In 2010, an oil rig in the Gulf of Mexico exploded, leaving an oil well wide open on the ocean floor. In the following days, 210 million gallons of crude oil spilled into the Gulf.

**Improved Farming Methods** Modern farming practices reduce water pollution. Formerly, farmers would leave fields bare in winter, allowing soil and fertilizers to wash into streams. It was also common to use large amounts of pesticides, herbicides, and fungicides. These chemicals would run off into streams, polluting the water and killing organisms. Today, farmers can reduce erosion and pollution by leaving stalks in the field or planting winter grasses that hold the soil and nutrients in place. Farmers also treat their land with a smaller amount of chemicals, and find natural predators to combat pests.

**Reducing Pollutants** Another way to protect Earth's waters is to reduce the amount of pollution that is created. Instead of dumping waste products directly into the environment, manufacturers can recycle them. By turning waste products into new things, the companies may even save money. Another method to reduce waste is to change the way materials are produced. Factories can eliminate the use of non-recyclable materials. By figuring out more environmentally-friendly manufacturing methods, they may make less total waste or less hazardous waste.

You can help to prevent water pollution in your home. Common household water pollutants include paints, paint thinner, motor oil, and garden chemicals. Instead of dumping these into the environment, save these materials for your community's hazardous waste collection day (**Figure 5**), or take them to a specialized facility for such wastes.

**Hazardous Waste**
**Figure 5** Many towns and cities have special recycling centers that provide safe and proper disposal of household chemicals, such as paint and cleaning supplies.

☑ READING CHECK **Write Explanatory Texts** What can your community do to reduce water pollution?

........................................................................................................

........................................................................................................

........................................................................................................

## Plan It

### Reducing Waste in Factories
Many factories are "going green" and changing the way they manufacture products to create less waste. Suppose there is a manufacturing company in your community that is not reducing its waste.

**Construct Arguments** Come up with a solution to your community's problem. Plan a presentation to convince the factory owners to "go green." How might changing their policy benefit both the community and the factory? How will making these changes impact the environment?

# ☑ LESSON 4 Check

1. **SEP Construct Explanations** Why is it so important for sources of fresh water to be protected?

........................................................

........................................................

........................................................

........................................................

2. **CCC Cause and Effect** How do farming methods cause water pollution?

........................................................

........................................................

........................................................

........................................................

3. **SEP Provide Evidence** What evidence suggests that factories sometimes cause water pollution?

........................................................

........................................................

........................................................

........................................................

........................................................

........................................................

4. **CCC Analyze Systems** How does water pollution in one area affect water and organisms elsewhere?

........................................................

........................................................

........................................................

........................................................

........................................................

........................................................

........................................................

5. **Construct Arguments** Write an argument to defend the idea that oil spills are the worst environmental hazard.

........................................................

........................................................

........................................................

........................................................

........................................................

........................................................

........................................................

........................................................

........................................................

## Quest CHECK-IN

**In this lesson, you learned why fresh water is a limited resource within Earth's systems. You also discovered how human activities lead to water pollution and how humans can reduce freshwater and ocean pollution.**

**CCC Analyze Systems** Why is it important to consider the effects of waste disposal on water sources?

........................................................

........................................................

........................................................

........................................................

## ☞ INTERACTIVITY

Reducing Waste

**Go online** to determine how everyone at your school can work together to reduce wastes and help the environment. Then make a plan to reduce the trash output at your school.

# FROM WASTEWATER TO
# Tap Water

▶ **VIDEO**

Walk through the water treatment process.

Fresh water is a precious resource on Earth, so we reuse every drop we can. Wastewater from homes and businesses ends up being recycled for irrigation, manufacturing, and replenishing aquatic ecosystems. But how do you recycle wastewater into drinking water? You engineer it!

**The Challenge:** To treat wastewater so it can return to the water supply.

**Phenomenon** In San Diego, California, the Point Loma Wastewater Treatment plant treats wastewater and makes it safe to drink, but it takes several steps. First, water from the sewer system passes through screens that filter out large particles. Next, the water flows into tanks where gravity separates solid waste from the water. Heavy solids sink to the bottom.

The water then flows to a second set of tanks where bacteria digest waste that's still in the water. Then the water is left to settle one more time and the last sediments are removed.

Following that, the water goes through a series of filters to get rid of any small solids or harmful microorganisms. The last step is disinfection using chlorine and UV light. Finally, this water will spend about six months in storage before it arrives at a tap.

## DESIGN CHALLENGE

Can you design a model for recycling wastewater or rainwater from your home or school? Go to the Engineering Design Notebook to find out!

A typical wastewater plant has many, many tanks.

| Primary Treatment | | | Secondary Treatment | | Disinfection | | |
|---|---|---|---|---|---|---|---|
| Pumping station | Primary screening | Primary sedimentation | Bacteria treatment | Secondary sedimentation | Filtration for micro-organisms | Cleaning with chlorine and UV | Clean water |

Wastewater

# ☑TOPIC 7 Review and Assess

## 1 Population Growth and Resource Consumption

MS-ESS3-4

**1.** Rather than increasing at a constant rate, human population growth in recent decades has increased more and more rapidly over time. This rate of change is called

A. excessive growth.

B. exponential growth.

C. reverse growth.

D. zero growth.

**2.** For the global population growth rate to reach zero, the number of births would have to be

...............................................................

...............................................................

**3. Connect to Society** Beginning around 1750, the global human population began to grow at a much faster rate than it had in the years before this time. What caused this change in the population growth rate?

...............................................................

...............................................................

...............................................................

...............................................................

**4. CCC Cause and Effect** How does a growing human population affect Earth's resources?

...............................................................

...............................................................

...............................................................

...............................................................

...............................................................

...............................................................

## 2 Air Pollution

MS-ESS3-4

**5. Evaluate Reasoning** A classmate tells you that the good thing about renewable resources like trees is that you can use them and use them and they will never run out. What is your classmate misunderstanding about renewable resources?

...............................................................

...............................................................

...............................................................

...............................................................

...............................................................

...............................................................

**6.** Which is a natural source of air pollution?

A. volcanoes

B. carbon monoxide

C. smog

D. ozone layer

**7.** Automobiles contribute to air pollution by

A. increasing methane.

B. decreasing oxygen.

C. decreasing carbon dioxide.

D. increasing carbon dioxide.

**8.** As human populations continue to increase, the demand for natural resources

.......................................... .

**9. SEP Construct Explanations** Why did it take international efforts to reduce the impact of air pollution on the ozone layer?

...............................................................

...............................................................

...............................................................

...............................................................

...............................................................

...............................................................

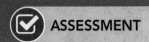 
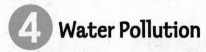

## 3 Impacts on Land

MS-ESS3-4

10. What is the difference between point and nonpoint sources of water pollution?
    A. Point sources can be directly identified, and nonpoint cannot.
    B. Point sources involve solid wastes, and nonpoint sources are liquids.
    C. Point sources contain animal wastes, while nonpoint sources are human-made chemicals.
    D. Point sources break down easily, while nonpoint sources break down over a long time.

11. Which of these changes can lead to desertification?
    A. reduced air quality
    B. increased plant life
    C. reduced moisture
    D. increased nutrient levels

12. What impact does logging have on the land?
    A. increased nutrients
    B. increased erosion
    C. accelerated recycling of organic matter
    D. accelerated soil deposition

13. Changing the flow of water, such as filling in a wetland for development, impacts the environment by
    A. increasing desertification.
    B. increasing flooding and pollution.
    C. decreasing erosion.
    D. decreasing nutrient depletion.

14. As human populations increase, there is a higher demand for ......................., the use of land to produce food.

15. When natural forces such as wind, water, and ice move particles of rocks or soil, the process is called ........................ .

## 4 Water Pollution

MS-ESS3-4

16. **Construct Arguments** What evidence could be used in an argument against planting the same crop in the same field year after year?

...............................................................
...............................................................
...............................................................
...............................................................
...............................................................
...............................................................
...............................................................

17. Which of these is a source of human-made ocean pollution?
    A. fresh water
    B. ozone
    C. plastics
    D. sediment

18. **Construct an Argument** What evidence supports the idea that construction companies should implement protocols that reduce the amount of sediment that runs off from land into the water?

...............................................................
...............................................................
...............................................................
...............................................................
...............................................................
...............................................................

MS-ESS3-4

Lange's metalmark butterfly

## Evidence-Based Assessment

In 1976, ecologists made a disturbing discovery in the Antioch Dunes along the banks of the San Joaquin River in San Francisco. A butterfly, formally observed first in 1939 and only found in the dunes, was going extinct. Known as Lange's metalmark butterfly, it became one of the first insects protected as an endangered species by federal law.

Here are some important facts about the butterfly and its habitat.

- Lange's metalmark butterfly produces one crop of offspring each year, and females only lay their eggs on one species of plant, the naked-stem buckwheat plant.

- The dunes where the butterfly lives formed thousands of years ago, when sand deposited by ancient glaciers was moved and shaped by water and wind.

- When the first American settlers arrived in the early 1800s, the dunes ran along the river for about 3 kilometers (2 miles) and reached over 30 meters (100 feet) high in some places.

- As the population of San Francisco grew, parts of the dunes were leveled and developed for industry. Sand from the dunes was mined to produce bricks and other building materials. The data table shows changes in the population of San Francisco from 1850 to 2000.

| San Francisco County Population, 1850–2000 | | | |
|---|---|---|---|
| Year | Population | Year | Population |
| 1850 | 21,000 | 1930 | 634,394 |
| 1860 | 56,802 | 1940 | 634,536 |
| 1870 | 149,473 | 1950 | 775,357 |
| 1880 | 233,959 | 1960 | 740,316 |
| 1890 | 298,997 | 1970 | 715,674 |
| 1900 | 342,782 | 1980 | 678,974 |
| 1910 | 416,912 | 1990 | 723,959 |
| 1920 | 506,676 | 2000 | 776,733 |

1. **SEP Analyze Data** Which statement about the trends in San Francisco's population growth is valid?
   A. It dropped for a few decades after 1890, but has grown almost every year since then.
   B. It grew slowly each year until 1930, when the population quickly increased.
   C. It increased steadily each year since 1850.
   D. It grew rapidly in the mid to late 1800s and then again in the 1940s.

2. **CCC Cause and Effect** How would mining and extracting sand affect plants that live in the dunes, like the naked-stem buckwheat? Based on the population data, when you do think the most sand was removed from the dunes? Explain.

   ..........................................................................
   ..........................................................................
   ..........................................................................
   ..........................................................................
   ..........................................................................
   ..........................................................................
   ..........................................................................
   ..........................................................................
   ..........................................................................
   ..........................................................................
   ..........................................................................
   ..........................................................................

3. **Apply Scientific Reasoning** The remaining sand dunes became a national wildlife refuge in 1980. A few years later, researchers began an annual count of the butterflies. Between 1999 and 2008, the number of butterflies fell steadily. What might account for this continued drop?

   ..........................................................................
   ..........................................................................
   ..........................................................................
   ..........................................................................
   ..........................................................................

4. **SEP Engage in Argument** How could an increase in the human population of San Francisco have impacted the Lange's metalmark butterflies that lived there? Use evidence from the text to support your answer.

   ..........................................................................
   ..........................................................................
   ..........................................................................
   ..........................................................................
   ..........................................................................
   ..........................................................................
   ..........................................................................
   ..........................................................................
   ..........................................................................
   ..........................................................................
   ..........................................................................
   ..........................................................................
   ..........................................................................
   ..........................................................................

## Quest FINDINGS

## Complete the Quest!

**Phenomenon** Refine your plan to reduce trash at your school and present the plan.

**CCC Cause and Effect** We produce a lot of trash that is disposed of in landfills. How would decreasing the trash we generate affect Earth's systems?

   ..........................................................................
   ..........................................................................
   ..........................................................................
   ..........................................................................

👆 **INTERACTIVITY**

Reflect on Trash Backlash

# Washing Away

How can you demonstrate the impact of **human activity** on **soil erosion?**

## Background

**Phenomenon** A nearby town is considering a developer's plan to turn riverfront property into shops, restaurants, and apartments. The area is now an undisturbed habitat consisting of trees, bushes, and grasses. Almost all of the natural vegetation will be removed during construction. You will be part of a team tasked with providing an environmental impact report to the town board.

In this lab, you will design and conduct an investigation into the impact of vegetation and ground cover on soil erosion. You will test how quickly water runs off soil in different conditions and how much soil is carried away by the water.

## Materials

(per group)
- two 2-liter beverage bottles, cut lengthwise to form troughs
- about 4 cups of potting soil, divided in half
- grass or radish seedlings
- 2 large plastic cups
- 1 liter of water
- watering can with rain spout
- stopwatch

# Plan Your Investigation

☐ 1. Work with your partner to design an experimental setup using the materials provided by your teacher. Your experiment must test how fast water runs off the soil and how much soil is carried away in the runoff. As you design your setup, consider the following questions:

- How would you describe the condition of the riverbank before the proposed construction?

- How would you describe the condition of the riverbank during the construction?

- How can you use the materials to model the condition of the riverbank before and during construction?

- How can you design your setup so that you will be able to measure how fast the water runs off the soil and how much soil is contained in the runoff?

- What are your dependent variable and independent variable, and the factors you hold constant?

- How many tests will you run?

- What observations will you make and what data will you collect?

☐ 2. Write a detailed procedure describing how you will investigate the effects of removing vegetation and ground cover on soil erosion. Include any sketches of your setup.

☐ 3. After getting teacher approval for your procedure, conduct your investigation.

☐ 4. Record your observations and data in the table provided.

# uDemonstrate Lab

## Procedure and Sketches

## Data Table

| Bottle | Water Poured (mL) | Water Captured (mL) | Time (sec) | Observations of Water Collected |
|---|---|---|---|---|
| Grass and soil | | | | |
| Soil only | | | | |

# Analyze and Interpret Data

1. **Compare Data**  Review the data you collected and the observations you recorded. How do the results of your tests compare?

   ..............................................................................................................

   ..............................................................................................................

   ..............................................................................................................

   ..............................................................................................................

2. **Write an Expression**  Suppose you were going to graph the results of your investigation. How would you express the independent variable *Water Poured* as a variable? How would you express the results of your dependent variable *Water Captured* as a variable?.

   ..............................................................................................................

   ..............................................................................................................

3. **Apply Scientific Reasoning**  Based on the results of your investigation, describe how soil erosion might affect the ecology of rivers, lakes, and other bodies of water.

   ..............................................................................................................

   ..............................................................................................................

   ..............................................................................................................

   ..............................................................................................................

4. **Refine Your Plan**  Examine and evaluate the procedures of other teams. Based on what you learned, how might you modify your own procedure to improve the results of your investigation?

   ..............................................................................................................

   ..............................................................................................................

   ..............................................................................................................

   ..............................................................................................................

5. **SEP Engage in Argument**  What would you recommend to the town board? Use the data from your investigation as evidence to justify your claim.

   ..............................................................................................................

   ..............................................................................................................

   ..............................................................................................................

   ..............................................................................................................

   ..............................................................................................................

   ..............................................................................................................

**NGSS PERFORMANCE EXPECTATION**

**MS-ESS1-4** Construct a scientific explanation based on evidence from rock strata for how the geologic time scale is used to organize Earth's 4.6-billion-year-old history.

## HANDS-ON LAB

**uConnect** Develop a timeline of the major events in the life of a family member.

What do these fossils reveal about Earth's past?

GO ONLINE
to access your digital course

▶ VIDEO

👆 INTERACTIVITY

🧪 VIRTUAL LAB

☑ ASSESSMENT

📖 eTEXT

🧪 HANDS-ON LABS

# The Essential Question

## How can events in Earth's past be organized?

CCC Stability and Change  Earth has changed a lot since these ammonites swam the ocean. Our planet has changed even more since it first formed. How do scientists find out about events in Earth's history? Identify several things that you think scientists study to find out how Earth has changed over time.

......................................................................................................

......................................................................................................

......................................................................................................

......................................................................................................

......................................................................................................

# Quest KICKOFF

## How do paleontologists know where to look for fossils?

**Phenomenon** Dr. Digg is the head paleontologist at a museum. She has hired you to help the museum set up a new exhibit on an extinct genus of ancient animal called *Dimetrodon*. Where in the world can you find *Dimetrodon* fossils to form the centerpiece of the exhibit? Fossils are found all over Earth, and you can't dig up the entire planet. In this problem-based Quest activity, you will choose a dig site that is likely to produce fossils of *Dimetrodon*. You will evaluate information about four sites, using information about rock layers and other fossils found at those sites to narrow the choices down. In a final report, you will share your evaluations of each site and give reasons for choosing one site and rejecting the other three.

### NBC LEARN ▶ VIDEO

After viewing the Quest Kickoff video and watching a paleontologist at work, complete the concept map by recording four things that you should consider when exploring for fossils.

How to Find Fossils

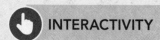

### 👆 INTERACTIVITY

The Big Fossil Hunt

**MS-ESS1-4** Construct a scientific explanation based on evidence from rock strata for how the geologic time scale is used to organize Earth's 4.6-billion-year-old history.

---

# Quest CHECK-INS

## IN LESSON 1

What do paleontologists learn from layers of rock and the organisms found within those layers? Gather clues to find the best dig site.

### 👆 INTERACTIVITY

Clues in the Rock Layers

### 👆 INTERACTIVITY

Fossils Around the World

# Quest CHECK-IN

## IN LESSON 2

How do paleontologists use the geologic time scale to help find fossils? Explore how scientists use information from already-discovered fossils to predict where other fossils might be.

### HANDS-ON LAB

A Matter of Time

The Carnegie Dinosaur Quarry is a dig site within the Dinosaur National Monument in Utah. Paleontologists excavate and preserve dinosaur fossils that range from 148 to 155 million years old.

## Quest CHECK-IN

### IN LESSON 3

How do paleontologists use information about ancient organisms to determine where to search for fossils? Conduct research and make a final selection of a dig site for *Dimetrodon*.

 **INTERACTIVITY**

Time to Choose the Dig Site

## Quest FINDINGS

## Complete the Quest!

Prepare a report in which you evaluate each site and give reasons for choosing or rejecting that site.

 **INTERACTIVITY**

Reflect on the Big Fossil Hunt

# Dividing History

## Background

**Phenomenon** A person's life can be divided into segments based on achievements or other notable events. In this activity, you will divide a family member's life into blocks of time and compare this to how geologic time is divided.

How can you use a timeline of a person's life as a **model** of Earth's history?

## Develop a Model

1. Choose a member of your family or another important person in your life.

2. Interview the person you chose. Select what information you will record in the Observations section, such as his or her career, family life, personal achievements, and so on. As you record your data, be sure to note dates and important names, such as the names of spouses and children.

3. Divide the person's life into at least three separate segments based on criteria that you choose.

4. Use the materials to make a timeline of the person's life. Record important events and accomplishments during each of the segments of time.

5. Exchange your timeline with another student. Discuss the timelines and how they were constructed.

## Materials

**(per individual)**
- sheet of plain white paper (or your lab journal or science notebook)
- metric ruler

# Observations

**HANDS-ON LAB**

**ⓘConnect** Go online for a downloadable worksheet of this lab.

## Analyze and Conclude

1. **SEP Develop Models** Who did you choose, and what types of criteria did you use to divide his or her life into blocks of time?

.......................................................................................................

.......................................................................................................

.......................................................................................................

.......................................................................................................

2. **Determine Differences** Do you agree or disagree with how the timeline you received from the other student is divided? Explain.

.......................................................................................................

.......................................................................................................

3. **SEP Use Models** Why is it important to establish the criteria on which a time scale will be based?

.......................................................................................................

.......................................................................................................

.......................................................................................................

4. **CCC Evaluate Scale** What might a timeline of the history of Earth look like and how could it be divided into sections? Consider the timeline you constructed. What are the advantages and limitations of your timeline as a model for Earth's history? Make sure to account for the time scale of your model.

.......................................................................................................

.......................................................................................................

.......................................................................................................

.......................................................................................................

.......................................................................................................

# Determining Ages of Rocks

## Guiding Questions

- How do geologists describe the ages of rocks?
- How do geologists determine the relative ages of rocks?
- How do geologists determine the absolute ages of rocks?

## Connections

**Literacy** Write Explanatory Texts

**Math** Write an Expression

MS-ESS1-4

## HANDS-ON LAB

**uInvestigate** Model changes in rocks.

### Vocabulary

relative age
absolute age
law of
  superposition
fossil
unconformity
radioactive decay
radioactive dating

### Academic Vocabulary

relative
infer

## Connect It!

🖊 **How many rock layers do you see? Draw an arrow pointing from the youngest rock to the oldest rock.**

**SEP Construct Explanations** How did you decide which rocks are the youngest and oldest?

.......................................................................................................

.......................................................................................................

.......................................................................................................

**SEP Plan and Carry Out Investigations** Suppose you were the first person to study the canyon. How could you find out exactly how old the oldest rock is?

.......................................................................................................

.......................................................................................................

.......................................................................................................

# Describing the Ages of Rocks

If you visit the Painted Desert in Arizona, you will find rock layers that look grey, red, green, blue, and even purple. If you're curious, you might start by asking "How did these colorful rocks form?" Your next question would probably be "How old are these rocks?" In other words, you would want to describe the ages of the rocks. Geologists have two ways to describe the age of a rock: age **relative** to another rock and age in number of years since the rock formed.

## Relative Age
The **relative age** of a rock is its age compared to the ages of other rocks. You probably use the idea of relative age when you compare your age with someone else's. For example, if you say that you are older than your brother but younger than your sister, you describe your relative age.

## Absolute Age
The relative age of a rock does not provide its absolute age. The **absolute age** of a rock is the number of years that have passed since the rock formed. It may be impossible to know the exact absolute age of some rocks, so geologists often use both absolute and relative ages.

Why do geologists want to analyze and describe the ages of rocks? Evidence of past events occurs in rocks. That evidence shows that Earth has changed and evolved over time due to natural processes. Rock layers like those in **Figure 1** form a record of Earth's history of change, known as the geologic record. By studying clues in Earth's rocks and determining their ages, geologist can organize past events in sequence to better understand Earth's history.

✓ **READING CHECK** **Summarize** What is the difference between relative age and absolute age?

.................................................................................................

.................................................................................................

.................................................................................................

**Academic Vocabulary**
Describe your location relative to an object or another person in the room.

.................................................................................

.................................................................................

.................................................................................

## Rainbow of Rock Layers
**Figure 1** Many colorful rock layers make up the hills of Arizona's Painted Desert. These rock layers represent many millions of years of Earth's history.

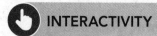 INTERACTIVITY

Examine a sequence of rock layers to learn their relative ages.

# Determining Relative Ages of Rocks

Geologists use many methods to determine the age of Earth's rocks. To find a rock's relative age, they analyze the position of rock layers. They also look for a variety of clues in rocks, such as fossils. These methods provide ways to find relative ages, but not absolute ages, of rocks.

## Clues Within Rocks

**Figure 2** Intrusions and faults can help to determine a sequence of events within rock layers.

1. **Identify Knowns**
   ✏ Draw an X over the igneous intrusion.
   Draw a line along a fault.

2. **CCC Patterns** ✏
   The rock layers are ( older / younger ) than any faults or intrusions that run through them.

3. **Synthesize Information** The San Andreas fault runs for hundreds of miles through California. What occurs when rocks on either side of the fault move?

........................................................

**Position of Rock Layers** Sedimentary rock usually forms in horizontal layers, or strata. Geologists use the **law of superposition** to determine the relative ages of sedimentary rock layers. According to the law of superposition, in undisturbed horizontal sedimentary rock layers, the oldest layer is at the bottom and the youngest layer is at the top. The higher you go, the younger the rocks are. The lower or deeper you go, the older the rocks are.

**Clues from Igneous Rocks** Magma is molten material beneath Earth's surface. Lava (magma that reaches the surface) can harden on the surface to form an igneous extrusion. Magma can also push into layers of rock below the surface. The magma can harden and form an igneous intrusion, like the one shown in **Figure 2**. An extrusion is younger than the rock it covers. An intrusion is younger than the rock around it.

**Clues from Faults** More clues come from the study of faults. A fault, like the one shown in **Figure 2**, is a break in Earth's crust. Forces inside Earth cause movement of the rock on opposite sides of a fault. A fault is always younger than the rock it cuts through. To determine the relative age of a fault, geologists find the relative age of the youngest layer cut by the fault.

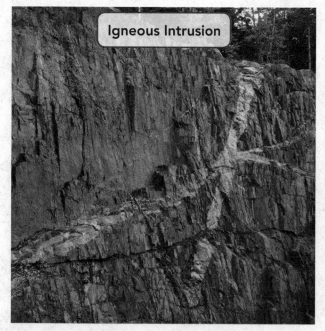
Igneous Intrusion

Faults

**Using Fossils** The preserved remains or traces of living things are called **fossils**. They most often occur in layers of sedimentary rock. Fossils preserved in rock layers provide physical evidence about the history of life on Earth and how Earth has changed over time.

Certain fossils, called index fossils, help geologists to match and date rock layers, even if those layers are far apart or in different locations. An index fossil is a fossil of an organism that was widely distributed and existed for a geologically short period of time. Fossils from organisms that lived for a long geologic time might show up in multiple rock layers, but index fossils show up in only a few layers. Index fossils are useful because they tell the relative ages of the rock layers in which they occur. Geologists **infer** that layers with matching index fossils are the same age.

You can use index fossils to match rock layers and find their relative age. Look at the diagram in **Figure 3,** which shows rock layers from four different locations. Notice that two of the fossils are found in only one rock layer. These are index fossils.

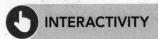

**INTERACTIVITY**

Use index fossils to decode Earth's history.

**Academic Vocabulary**

Think about a pet you saw recently. What can you infer about the animal's age? Explain your answer.

........................................................

........................................................

........................................................

........................................................

# Model It

## Using Fossils to Match Rock Layers

**Figure 3** You can model how scientists use index fossils to match rock layers separated by distance.

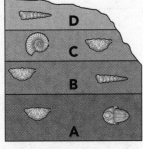

Location 1

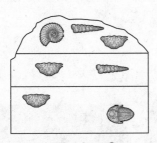

Location 2

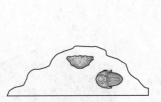

Location 3

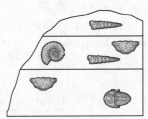

Location 4

1. **Interpret Diagrams** ✏ At Location 1, circle the fossils that you can use as index fossils.

2. **SEP Use Models** ✏ Use the index fossils at Location 1 to label the matching layers at Locations 2–4. Then, draw a line to connect each matching layer across all locations and shade them the same color.

3. **CCC Patterns** At Location 4, what can you infer about the ages of rocks and history? Cite evidence to support your inference.

........................................................

........................................................

## Changes in Rocks

The geologic record of sedimentary rock layers is not complete. In fact, erosion destroyed most of Earth's geologic record over billions of years. Gaps in the geologic record and folding can change the position in which rock layers appear. As was shown in **Figure 2**, motion along faults can also change how rock layers line up. These changes make it harder for scientists to reconstruct Earth's history. **Figure 4** shows how the order of rock layers may change.

### Gaps in the Geologic Record

When rock layers erode, an older rock surface may be exposed. Then deposition begins again, building new rock layers. The surface where new rock layers meet a much older rock surface beneath them is called an unconformity. An **unconformity** is a gap in the geologic record. It shows where rock layers have been lost due to erosion.

### Folding

Sometimes, forces inside Earth fold rock layers so much that the layers are turned over completely. In this case, the youngest rock layers may be on the bottom!

Samples from many different areas are needed to give a complete geologic record. Geologists compare rock layers in many places to understand a complete sequence.

☑ **READING CHECK** **Write Explanatory Texts** In you own words, explain one of the methods that geologists use to find the relative ages of rocks.

........................................................................................................................................

........................................................................................................................................

........................................................................................................................................

## Literacy Connection

**Write Explanatory Texts** Underline the sentences in the text that explain how the rock layers in **Figure 4** changed.

## Unconformity and Folding

**Figure 4** 🖊 Shade the oldest and youngest layers in the last two diagrams. Label the unconformity. Circle the part of the fold that is overturned.

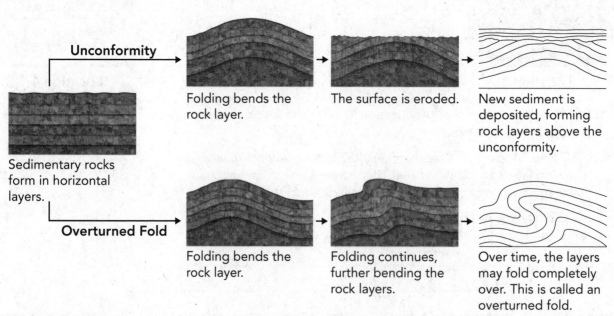

Sedimentary rocks form in horizontal layers.

**Unconformity**

Folding bends the rock layer.

The surface is eroded.

New sediment is deposited, forming rock layers above the unconformity.

**Overturned Fold**

Folding bends the rock layer.

Folding continues, further bending the rock layers.

Over time, the layers may fold completely over. This is called an overturned fold.

# Determining Absolute Ages of Rocks

Geologist use different methods to determine the absolute age of Earth's rocks. To find a rock's absolute age, they use certain elements in rocks that change over time.

**Radioactive Decay** An element is said to be radioactive when its particles become unstable and release energy in the form of radiation. This process is called radioactive decay. During **radioactive decay**, the atoms of one element break down to form atoms of another element.

Radioactive elements occur naturally in some igneous rocks. As an unstable radioactive element decays, it slowly changes into a stable element. The amount of the radioactive element decreases, but the amount of the new element increases, causing the overall composition of elements in the rock to change.

Each radioactive element decays at its own constant rate, represented by its half-life. The half-life of a radioactive element measures the time it takes for half of the radioactive atoms to decay. You can see in **Figure 5** how a radioactive element decays over time. Scientists use the half-life ratio to calculate the age of the rock in which a radioactive element is found.

📓 **Reflect** Think about rocks you have collected, or buildings, statues, or landforms made of rock that you have seen. For which rock would you like to find the absolute age? Record this in your science notebook.

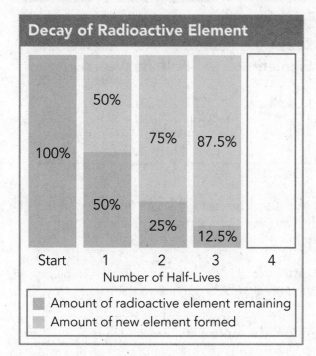

**Decay of Radioactive Element**

100% — Start
50% / 50% — 1
75% / 25% — 2
87.5% / 12.5% — 3
— 4

Number of Half-Lives

■ Amount of radioactive element remaining
■ Amount of new element formed

## Radioactive Decay and Half-Life

**Figure 5** This is a sample element that illustrates radioactive decay.

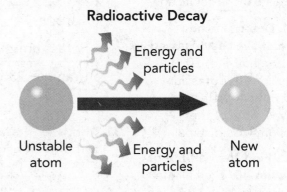

**Radioactive Decay**

Energy and particles

Unstable atom → New atom

Energy and particles

1. **CCC Patterns** ✏️ What pattern do you see in the graph? Use the pattern to complete the last bar.

2. **CCC Scale, Proportion, and Quantity** ✏️ The graph shows that as the amount of the old radioactive element (increases/decreases), the amount of the new stable element (increases/decreases).

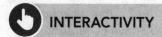

**INTERACTIVITY**

Use radioactive dating to determine the absolute age of different objects.

✓ READING CHECK

**Determine Central Ideas**
Underline the main idea in the first paragraph.

**Radioactive Dating** Geologists use **radioactive dating**, or radiometric dating, to determine the absolute ages of rocks. In radioactive dating, scientists first determine the amount of a radioactive element in a rock sample. Then they compare that with the amount of the stable element into which the radioactive element decays. They use this information and the half-life of the element to calculate the age of the rock.

**Potassium-Argon Dating** Scientists often date rocks using potassium-40. This form of potassium decays to stable argon-40 and has a half-life of 1.3 billion years. Potassium-40 is useful in dating the most ancient rocks because of its long half-life.

**Carbon-14 Dating** Scientists can date plant and animal remains using carbon-14. All organisms contain carbon, including this radioactive form. Carbon-14 decays to stable nitrogen-14 and has a half-life of only 5,730 years. Therefore, this method can't be used to date remains older than about 50,000 years because the amount of carbon-14 left would be too small to measure accurately.

# Math Toolbox

## Using Radioactive Dating to Calculate Absolute Age

A rock contains 25 percent of the potassium-40 it started with. Use radioactive dating to calculate the absolute age.

**Step 1. Determine how many half-lives have passed.** After one half-life, 50 percent of the potassium would remain. After two half-lives, 25% of the potassium would remain.

**Step 2. Find the half-life of potassium-40.** The half-life of potassium-40 is 1.3 billion years.

**Step 3. Multiply the half-life by the number of half-lives that have passed to calculate the rock's age.** 1.3 billion years × 2 half-lives = 2.6 billion years old.

**Elements Used in Radioactive Dating**

| Radioactive Element | Half-life (years) |
| --- | --- |
| Carbon-14 | 5,730 |
| Potassium-40 | 1.3 billion |
| Uranium-235 | 713 million |

1. **SEP Use Mathematics** A bone contains 12.5 percent of the carbon-14 it began with. How old is the bone?

.................................................................................

2. **SEP Interpret Data** A rock is determined to be 1.426 billion years old. How much uranium-235 remains in the rock?

.................................................................................

3. **Write an Expression** If X represents the half-life of potassium–40 and Y represents the half-life of carbon-14, write an expression that correctly compares the two half-lives.

.................................................................................

# ☑ LESSON 1 Check

1. **Identify** What method do geologists use to find the absolute ages of rocks?

..................................................................

2. **Explain** How could a geologist match the rock layers in one area to rock layers found in another area?

..................................................................

..................................................................

..................................................................

..................................................................

3. **CCC Patterns** A layer of sandstone sits above two other layers of rock. A fault cuts through the two lower layers of rock. How does the age of the fault compare with the ages of all three rock layers?

..................................................................

..................................................................

..................................................................

..................................................................

4. **SEP Construct Explanations** A geologist observes rock layers that are folded. She determines that a layer of siltstone is younger than the layer of limestone above it. How can you explain the geologist's findings?

..................................................................

..................................................................

..................................................................

..................................................................

..................................................................

5. **Apply Scientific Reasoning** A scientist finds tools made of rock in the ruins of an ancient home. He also finds burned wood likely cut by the tools in the home's fire pit. How could the scientist estimate when the tools were made?

..................................................................

..................................................................

..................................................................

..................................................................

## Quest CHECK-INS

**In this lesson, you learned how geologists find the ages of rocks and how events and fossil histories are recorded within the rock layers.**

Explain How can information from rock layers give you clues about where to look for additional fossils?

..................................................................

..................................................................

..................................................................

..................................................................

..................................................................

### 👆 INTERACTIVITIES

- Clues in the Rock Layers
- Fossils Around the World

**Go online** to think about the layers of rock at the dig sites and to consider how knowing more about the ages of rocks and fossils can help you to choose where to look for another fossil.

MS-ESS1-4

# REWRiTiNG THE HiSTORY OF

# Your Food

Modern tomatillos

If you have ever eaten salsa verde with your tacos, then you have likely eaten a tomatillo (toh mah TEE yoh). Related to husk tomatoes and ground cherries, modern tomatillos have a paper-thin husk covering their berry-shaped fruit.

Tomatillos are members of the plant genus *Physalis*, a small part of the nightshade family. This family includes many plants that we eat, including peppers, eggplants, and potatoes, and some too dangerous to eat, such as the poisonous belladonna plant.

Until recently, the evolution of these plants was poorly understood. Because many parts of the plants decompose easily, the fossil record is limited. Based on those limited fossils, scientists inferred that plants similar to tomatillos and ground cherries evolved fairly recently, about 9 to 11 million years ago.

However, scientist rewrote the tomatillo's history with a recent discovery from Patagonia, a region that covers southern Argentina and Chile. An international team collected thousands of fossils to study the evolutionary relationship between extinct and living organisms. Among the samples, they found two fossils of husked fruit, ancestors of the modern tomatillo.

The fossils were preserved in sediment deposited in an ancient lake near a volcano. Based on radioactive, or radiometric, dating of volcanic rocks found with the fossils, scientists concluded that ancestral tomatillos are actually more than 50 million years old! These plants existed in southern South America when the region was close to Antarctica and had a warm and wet climate—very different from its modern dry, cool climate. So enjoy some salsa verde and appreciate just how long the ancestors of those tomatillos have been growing on Earth!

**Fossil Location in South America**

fossil location

Patagonia

| Tomatillo Group Fossil Record | | |
|---|---|---|
| | Previously-Discovered Fossils | Newly-Discovered Fossils |
| Plant Parts Preserved | Tiny seeds and wood | Husks and fruit |
| Approximate Age | 9 to 11 million years old | 52 million years old |
| Dating Method Used | Molecular dating (uses rates of change and DNA to determine when organisms evolved) based on modern plants and fossils | Argon-argon dating (a newer variation of potassium-argon dating) of volcanic rocks found with the fossils |

**Use the text and table to answer the following questions.**

1. CCC Scale, Proportion, and Quantity  Based on new data, what conclusion did scientists draw about the tomatillo and nightshade plant family?

2. SEP Use Mathematics  About how much older are the newly-discovered plant fossils compared to the age of previously discovered fossils?

3. SEP Evaluate Information  What evidence supports the scientists' conclusion about the age of the husk fruits and the nightshade family overall?

4. SEP Construct Explanations  How has radioactive dating helped to change our understanding of Earth's history? Use evidence from the fossil discovery to support your answer.

# ② Geologic Time Scale

## Guiding Questions

- What is the purpose of the geologic time scale?
- How do events help geologists define and divide geologic time?

## Connection

**Literacy** Write Informative Texts

MS-ESS1-4

## HANDS-ON LAB

ᵤ**Investigate** Model the geologic time scale.

## Vocabulary

geologic time
  scale
era
period

## Academic Vocabulary

organize
refine

## Connect It!

✎ **Circle the unconformity. What does it tell you about the history of this location?**

SEP Analyze and Interpret Data What can you infer about the history based on these rocks?

....................................................................................................................

....................................................................................................................

....................................................................................................................

Explain How could you use the information in these rocks to organize events in Earth's history?

....................................................................................................................

....................................................................................................................

# The Geologic Time Scale

When you speak of the past, what names do you use for different spans of time? You probably use names such as century, decade, year, month, week, and day. But these units aren't very helpful for thinking about much longer periods of time—such as the 4.6 billion years of Earth's history.

To **organize** this vast number of years into manageable periods, scientists created the geologic time scale. The **geologic time scale** is a record of the geologic events and the evolution of life forms as shown in the rock and fossil records. Notice that it is a timeline—a model of the relative order of events over a long period of time that might otherwise be difficult to study.

Scientists first developed the geologic time scale by studying rock layers and index fossils worldwide. They gathered evidence using methods of determining the relative ages of rocks, such as evidence from unconformities as in **Figure 1**. With this evidence, scientists placed Earth's rocks in order by relative age. Later, they used radioactive dating to help them determine the absolute age of the divisions in the geologic time scale.

✓ READING CHECK **Summarize Text** How do scientists organize Earth's history and what evidence do they use?

....................................................................................................

....................................................................................................

....................................................................................................

**VIDEO**

Consider the best way to represent the geologic time scale.

**Academic Vocabulary**
Describe how you organize something in your life. Compare the state of that thing before and after you organized it.

....................................................................

....................................................................

....................................................................

....................................................................

....................................................................

**A Gap in Time**
**Figure 1** This unconformity represents a gap in geologic time of about 65 million years. The remaining rocks tell the story of how Earth evolved over geologic time.

# The Geologic Time Scale

**Figure 2** The geologic time scale is based on physical evidence from rock and fossil records that show how Earth has evolved over geologic time. The divisions of the geologic time scale are used to organize events in Earth's history.

1. **Calculate** 🖊 After you read the rest of the lesson, calculate and fill in the duration of each period.

2. **Evaluate Scale** 🖊 Use the time scale to identify the period in which each organism pictured below lived.

3. **SEP Develop Models** 🖊 Draw lines from each fossil or rock pictured on the right to the part of the time scale that represents when it formed.

## Precambrian Time

## Paleozoic Era

| Period | | Cambrian | Ordovician | Silurian | Devonian | Carboniferous |
|---|---|---|---|---|---|---|
| **Began** (Millions of Years Ago) | 4,600 | 541 | 485 | 444 | 419 | 359 |
| **Duration** (Millions of Years) | 4,059 | | 41 | 25 | 60 | |

**Organism:** *Velociraptor*

**Age:** about 80 million years

**Period:** ....................................

**Organism:** *Wiwaxia*

**Age:** about 500 million years

**Period:** ....................................

▶ Limestone and shale containing fossil coral from Kentucky and Indiana provide evidence that a shallow sea covered much of North America during the Silurian period.

▼ Geologic evidence such as these deposits from an ancient glacial lake in Washington suggest that a period of major global cooling began about 2.6 million years ago.

◀ Fossilized cyanobacteria that date to about 3.5 billion years ago provide evidence that single-celled organisms actually appeared during the Precambrian.

## Mesozoic Era

## Cenozoic Era

| Permian | Triassic | Jurassic | Cretaceous | Paleogene | Neogene | Quarternary |
|---------|----------|----------|------------|-----------|---------|-------------|
| 299 | 252 | 201 | 145 | 66 | 23 | 2.6 |
| | | 56 | 79 | | 20.4 | 2.6 |

**Organism:** *Smilodon*

**Age:** between about 2.5 million and 10,000 years

**Period:** ...............................

379

## Microscopic Fossil Evidence

**Figure 3** This image, produced by a scanning electron microscope, shows the microscopic shells of fossil foraminifera. Information recorded in the shells of these ancient single-celled ocean organisms provides evidence with which scientists track past changes in Earth's climate and refine the geologic time scale.

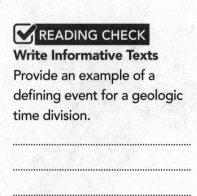

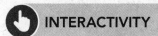

**INTERACTIVITY**

Review how geologists learn about Earth's history.

**HANDS-ON LAB**

Investigate Model the geologic time scale.

**READING CHECK**

**Write Informative Texts** Provide an example of a defining event for a geologic time division.

..............................................................

..............................................................

..............................................................

# Dividing Geologic Time

As geologists studied the rock and fossil records, they found major changes in life forms at certain times. Fossils are widely distributed in Earth's rocks. They occur in rocks in a definite order, with new species appearing and old species disappearing. In this way, fossils provided evidence of change on Earth. Geologists used these changes to help identify major events in Earth's history and mark where one unit of geologic time ends and the next begins. Therefore, most divisions of the geologic time scale depend on events in the history of life on Earth. **Figure 2** shows the major divisions of the geologic time scale.

**Precambrian Time** Geologic time begins with a long span of time called Precambrian (pree KAM bree un) time. Precambrian time covers about 88 percent of Earth's history, from 4.6 billion years ago to 541 million years ago. Few fossils survive from this time period.

**Eras** Geologists divide the time between the Precambrian and the present into three long units of time called **eras**. During the Paleozoic era, life increased in complexity and Pangaea formed. The Mesozoic era is defined by the dominance of dinosaurs and Pangaea breaking apart. During the Cenozoic era, mammals evolved to become the dominant land animals and the continents moved to their present-day positions.

**Periods** Eras are subdivided into units of geologic time called **periods**. You can see in **Figure 2** that the Mesozoic era includes three periods: the Triassic period, the Jurassic period, and the Cretaceous period. Each period is defined by certain events. For example, at the end of the Cretaceous period, major volcanic eruptions coincided with the impact on Earth of a huge asteroid. These events significantly changed the global environment.

## Refining Earth's History

Our understanding of Earth's history changes with each newly-discovered fossil (see **Figure 3**) or rock. Our understanding also changes as the technology used to analyze rocks and fossils advances. That's why geologists continually **refine** the geologic time scale. For example, geologists use the start of a period of major global cooling to mark the beginning of the Quaternary period. Recently, evidence from ocean floor sediments and other sources led scientists to move that boundary from 1.8 to 2.6 million years ago. The new boundary, based on new physical evidence, more accurately reflects a major change in Earth's climate.

## Question It!

**Modeling Geologic Time**
Suppose your friend makes his own model of the geologic time scale. He decided to use a scale of 1 m = 1 million years. Would your friend's model work?

**1.** CCC Scale, Proportion, and Quantity  How would your friend's model differ from the geologic time scale shown in **Figure 2**?

.........................................................................

.........................................................................

**2.** SEP Develop Models  What would be one advantage and one disadvantage of your friend's model?

.........................................................................

.........................................................................

.........................................................................

.........................................................................

MS-ESS1-4

**1. Summarize** What is the geologic time scale?

...................................................................................

...................................................................................

...................................................................................

...................................................................................

**Use Figure 2 in the lesson to help you answer Questions 2 and 3.**

**2. Determine Differences** How is Precambrian Time different from the other divisions of the geologic time scale?

...................................................................................

...................................................................................

...................................................................................

**3. CCC Scale, Proportion, and Quantity** How is the geologic time scale divided?

...................................................................................

...................................................................................

...................................................................................

...................................................................................

**4. CCC Stability and Change** Explain why you think the geologic time scale will or will not change over the next 20 years.

...................................................................................

...................................................................................

...................................................................................

...................................................................................

...................................................................................

...................................................................................

...................................................................................

**5. SEP Construct Explanations** Give an example of physical evidence used to organize Earth's history on the geologic time scale.

...................................................................................

...................................................................................

...................................................................................

...................................................................................

...................................................................................

...................................................................................

...................................................................................

# Quest CHECK-IN

**In this lesson, you learned about the purpose of the geologic time scale and how the segments of the geologic time scale are defined.**

**SEP Evaluate Evidence** How could you organize the fossils of potential dig sites using the geologic time scale?

...................................................................................

...................................................................................

...................................................................................

...................................................................................

**◉ INTERACTIVITY**

A Matter of Time

**Go online** to learn about fossils found at each potential dig site and plot them on the geologic time scale.

MS-ESS1-4

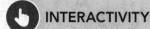

**INTERACTIVITY**

Determine which absolute dating method will return the most accurate result.

# Tiny Fossil,
# BIG ACCURACY

**How can you** determine the age of a small geologic sample with the greatest precision? You engineer it! An accelerator mass spectrometer is designed for accurate dating with less material.

**The Challenge:** To develop ways to determine more precisely the absolute age of a geologic event using smaller samples.

**Phenomenon** Representing a technological leap in absolute dating methods, the accelerator mass spectrometer (AMS) is one of the most important tools scientists use when dating events in Earth's past. Whereas traditional radioactive dating methods might require a 100-gram sample of material, an AMS can help to determine the absolute ages of samples with as little as 20 milligrams. These sensitive devices are also more accurate and can return results in less time than traditional radioactive dating methods. These improvements help geologists organize events in the geologic time scale more accurately and faster. The AMS is particularly helpful when dating more recent events of the Quaternary period, from which only small samples of organic remains may be available for carbon-14 dating.

The accelerator mass spectrometer helps scientists to refine the geologic time scale.

**DESIGN CHALLENGE** Can you make a model of the geologic time scale? Go to the Engineering Design Notebook to find out!

# LESSON 3 Major Events in Earth's History

## Guiding Questions

- How did Earth change in the Paleozoic era?
- How did Earth change in the Mesozoic era?
- How did Earth change in the Cenozoic era?

## Connections

**Literacy** Cite Textual Evidence

**Math** Represent Quantitative Relationships

MS-ESS1-4

**HANDS-ON LAB**

**ʊInvestigate** Analyze changes in biodiversity over time.

## Vocabulary

invertebrate
vertebrate
amphibian
reptile
mass extinction
mammal

## Academic Vocabulary

factors
hypothesize

## Connect It!

🖊 **Circle any organisms you recognize in this Carboniferous swamp.**

**CCC Patterns** How was life during the Carboniferous period similar to life today?

.................................................................................................

.................................................................................................

.................................................................................................

**SEP Engaging in Argument from Evidence** What do you think conditions were like in this Carboniferous period dragonfly's habitat?

.................................................................................................

.................................................................................................

.................................................................................................

# Major Events in the Paleozoic Era

Earth has a long history of change, starting 4.6 billion years ago when the planet formed. The geologic time scale, interpreted from the rock and fossil records, provides a way to organize that long history of change. The development and evolution of organisms is just one example of the changes that have taken place. For example, **Figure 1** shows how different life was on Earth 300 million years ago.

Through most of Earth's history, during Precambrian time, the only living things were single-celled organisms. Near the end of the Precambrian, more complex living things evolved. Feathery, plantlike organisms anchored themselves to the seafloor. Jellyfish-like organisms floated in the oceans. Then, a much greater variety of living things evolved during the next phase of geologic time—the Paleozoic era.

**The Cambrian Explosion** During the first part of the Paleozoic era, known as the Cambrian period, life took a big leap forward. Many different kinds of organisms evolved, including some that had hard parts such as shells and outer skeletons. This evolutionary event is called the Cambrian explosion because so many new life forms appeared within a relatively short time. To date these changes, scientists use the law of superposition and other methods to find relative ages and radioactive dating to find absolute ages in the geologic record.

At this time, all animals lived in the sea. Many were animals without backbones, or **invertebrates**. Common invertebrates included jellyfish, worms, sponges, clam-like brachiopods, and trilobites.

HANDS-ON LAB

Investigate Analyze changes in biodiversity over time.

**Ancient Swamp Life**
**Figure 1** This artist's drawing shows life in a swampy forest during the Carboniferous period, which occurred about 200 million years after the Cambrian period.

## Early Organisms

**Figure 2** ✏ These fossils provide evidence of the evolution of organisms during the Paleozoic era. Write the period during which the organism appeared in the fossil record.

Jawless Fish ........................................

**First Vertebrates and Land Plants** The Ordovician period is the second segment of the Paleozoic era. The first vertebrates, including jawless fish, evolved during the Ordovician. A **vertebrate** is an animal with a backbone. The first insects may have evolved at this time, along with land plants.

Plants grew abundantly during the next period, the Silurian. These simple plants grew low to the ground in damp areas. By the Devonian period that followed, plants evolved that could grow in drier areas. Among these plants were the earliest ferns.

Both invertebrates and vertebrates lived in the Devonian seas. Even though the invertebrates were more numerous, the Devonian is often called the Age of Fish. Every main group of fish, including sharks, was present in the oceans. Most fish had jaws, bony skeletons, and scales on their bodies.

**Animals Reach Land** The Devonian period was also when vertebrates began to live on land. The first land vertebrates were lungfish with strong, muscular fins. The first amphibians evolved from these lungfish. An **amphibian** (am FIB ee un) is an animal that lives part of its life on land and part of its life in water.

**Animals and Plants Evolve Further** The Carboniferous period followed the Devonian in the late Paleozoic era. During this period, the amniote egg (an egg filled with special fluids) evolved. This important adaptation allowed animals to lay eggs on land without the eggs drying out. This adaptation coincides with the appearance of reptiles in the fossil record. **Reptiles** have scaly skin and lay eggs that have tough, leathery shells.

During the Carboniferous, winged insects evolved into many new forms, including huge dragonflies and cockroaches. Giant ferns, mosses, and cone-bearing plants formed vast swampy forests. These plants resembled plants that live in tropical and temperate areas today.

### Literacy Connection

**Cite Textual Evidence**
Underline the evidence that supports the statement "Animals and plants evolved further during the Carboniferous Period."

Lungfish ..........................................

Dragonfly ..........................................

**Pangaea** Over the course of the Paleozoic era, Earth's continents slowly moved together to form a great landmass, or supercontinent, called Pangaea (pan JEE uh). The formation of Pangaea caused deserts to expand in the tropics and sheets of ice to cover land closer to the South Pole.

**Mass Extinction** The organisms in **Figure 2** represent the huge diversity of life that evolved during the Paleozoic era. However, during the Permian period at the end of the Paleozoic, a major change occurred and most species of life on Earth died out during the worst extinction event in Earth's history. This was a **mass extinction**, an event during which many types of living things became extinct at the same time. Scientists estimate that about 90 percent of all ocean species and 70 percent of species on land died out. Even widespread organisms such as trilobites became extinct.

Scientists aren't sure what caused this extinction. Some scientists think multiple volcanoes erupted so much dust and debris that the energy from the sun was blocked. This would have prevented plants from performing photosynthesis. Other scientists think a rise in global temperatures was to blame. Scientists have also found that the amount of carbon dioxide in the oceans increased and the amount of oxygen declined. It would have been difficult for organisms to quickly adjust to these changes. All of these **factors** likely contributed to the mass extinction.

✓ READING CHECK **Cite Textual Evidence** According to the text, what impact did the amniote egg have on lifeforms on Earth?

..........................................................................................

..........................................................................................

..........................................................................................

..........................................................................................

👆 **INTERACTIVITY**

Observe fossils to make deductions about the organisms and their environments.

**Academic Vocabulary**
What two factors determined what you did over the weekend?

..........................................................................

..........................................................................

..........................................................................

..........................................................................

..........................................................................

..........................................................................

## Mesozoic Winged Animals

**Figure 3** This illustration shows an artist's idea of what a *Dimorphodon* (a type of pterosaur) and an *Archaeopteryx* looked like.

1. **Claim** Did these winged animals evolve from a recent common ancestor?

...............................................
...............................................

2. **Evidence** List the evidence that supports your claim

...............................................
...............................................
...............................................
...............................................
...............................................

3. **Reasoning** Explain how your evidence supports your claim.

...............................................
...............................................
...............................................
...............................................
...............................................
...............................................
...............................................

# Major Events in the Mesozoic Era

Mass extinctions are followed by increases in evolution and variation. The mass extinction at the end of the Paleozoic era became an opportunity for many new life forms, including dinosaurs, to develop in the Mesozoic era.

## Age of Reptiles
Some living things managed to survive the Permian mass extinction. Plants and animals that survived included fish, insects, reptiles, and cone-bearing plants called conifers. Reptiles were so successful during the Mesozoic era that this time is often called the Age of Reptiles. The first dinosaurs appeared during the first period of the Mesozoic era, called the Triassic period.

## First Mammals
Mammals also first appeared during the Triassic period. A **mammal** is a vertebrate that controls its own body temperature and feeds milk to its young. Mammals in the Triassic period were very small—about the size of a mouse.

## Reptiles and Birds
During the Jurassic period, the second segment of the Mesozoic era, dinosaurs were the dominant land animals. Scientists have identified several hundred different kinds of dinosaurs, including some that ate plants and some that were predators. One plant-eating dinosaur, *Brachiosaurus*, was 26 meters long!

The ocean and seas during this period were also filled with diverse life forms, including sharks, rays, giant marine crocodiles, and plesiosaurs. Plesiosaurs had long necks and paddle-like fins.

Late in the Jurassic, the first known birds appeared in the skies. *Archaeopteryx*, which means "ancient winged one," is thought to have evolved from a dinosaur. The sky also had flying reptiles, called pterosaurs, and many varieties of insects. Use **Figure 3** to compare *Archaeopteryx* and a type of pterosaur called *Dimorphodon*.

Dimorphodon

Archaeopteryx

**Flowering Plants** The Cretaceous period is the final and longest segment of the Mesozoic era. Reptiles, including dinosaurs, were still widespread throughout the Cretaceous. Ancient birds evolved better adaptations for flying and began to replace flying reptiles.

One of the most important events of the Cretaceous period was the evolution of flowering plants, or angiosperms. Unlike conifers, flowering plants produce seeds that are inside a fruit. Many flowering plants you may recognize today first appeared during this time, such as magnolias, figs, and willows.

**Another Mass Extinction** At the end of the Cretaceous, another mass extinction occurred. Scientists **hypothesize** that this mass extinction occurred when an asteroid struck Earth at a time when extreme volcanic activity in the area that is now India had weakened environments. This mass extinction wiped out more than half of all plant and animal groups, including the dinosaurs. Use **Figure 4** to illustrate the event.

**☑ READING CHECK** **Use Information** How did organisms from the Mesozoic era differ from organisms of the Paleozoic?

.......................................................................................................

.......................................................................................................

.......................................................................................................

**INTERACTIVITY**

Examine evidence that shows major changes over time.

**📓 Reflect** Which major event or time in Earth's history would you most like to witness? In your science notebook, describe the event or time period and why you would like to experience it.

**Academic Vocabulary**

Use *hypothesize* in a sentence about a subject other than science.

.................................................................

.................................................................

.................................................................

.................................................................

# Model It !

## The End of the Dinosaurs

**Figure 4** Scientists hypothesize that an asteroid hit Earth near present-day southeastern Mexico. Show how this event, combined with the environment at the time, contributed to the mass extinction.

**SEP Develop Models** ✏ Complete the comic strip. Draw events that led to the extinction of the dinosaurs. Label each stage. Add a title.

**Title:** ...........................................................................................................

Many giant mammals evolved in the Cenozoic era. The *Megatherium* is related to the modern sloth but is much taller.

1. **Measure** Use the ruler to measure the height of each sloth.

   *Megatherium* height: about ......................

   Modern sloth height: about ......................

2. **Represent Quantitative Relationships** About how many times taller was *Megatherium* than a modern sloth? Complete the equation below, in which *m* is the height of *Megatherium* and *s* is the height of the modern sloth.

   $m = s \times$ ......................

Modern Sloth

Megatherium

# Major Events in the Cenozoic Era

During the Mesozoic era, small mammals had to compete with dinosaurs and other animals for food and places to live. The mass extinction at the end of that era created an opportunity for the species that did survive, including some mammals. During the Cenozoic era that followed, mammals evolved to live in many different environments—on land, in water, and even in the air. Geologists have found evidence for the spread of mammals in the fossils, rocks, and sediment of the early Cenozoic era.

**Mammals Thrive** The Cenozoic begins with the Paleogene and Neogene periods. During these periods, Earth's climate became gradually cooler over time. As the continents drifted apart, ocean basins widened and mammals such as whales and dolphins evolved. On land, mammals flourished. Some birds and mammals became very large. Forests thinned, making space for flowering plants and grasses to become more dominant.

**Ice Ages** At the start of the Quaternary period, large sheets of ice began to appear on Earth's surface. Earth's climate continued to cool and warm in cycles, causing a series of ice ages followed by warmer periods. During an ice age, about 30 percent of Earth's surface was covered in thick glaciers. The latest warm period began between 10,000 and 20,000 years ago. During that time, sea levels rose and most of the glaciers melted.

**Humans** The Quaternary period is sometimes referred to as the "Age of Humans." *Homo erectus*, an ancestor of modern humans, appears in the fossil record near the start of the period, while modern humans appeared about 190,000 years ago. By about 12,000 to 15,000 years ago, humans had migrated to every continent except Antarctica.

## How Scientists Organize Earth's History

**Figure 5** 🖊 This timeline shows major events in Earth's history. It is a model that you can use to study events that occur over geologic time. (Note that, to make the timeline easier to read, periods are not drawn to scale.) Circle the periods during which mass extinctions occurred.

| Events | Period | Began (Millions of Years Ago) | |
|---|---|---|---|
| Earth forms. First single-celled and multi-celled organisms evolve. | | 4,600 | **PRECAMBRIAN TIME** |
| "Explosion" of new forms of life occurs. Invertebrates such as trilobites are common. | Cambrian | 541 | **PALEOZOIC ERA** |
| First vertebrates, insects, and land plants evolve. | Ordovician | 485 | |
| Early fish are common in seas. | Silurian | 444 | |
| "Age of Fish" occurs, with many different kinds of fish. Lungfish and amphibians first reach land. | Devonian | 419 | |
| Appalachian Mountains form. Reptiles and giant insects evolve. Ferns and cone-bearing plants form forests. | Carboniferous | 359 | |
| Pangaea forms. Mass extinction kills most species. | Permian | 299 | |
| Reptiles flourish, including the first dinosaurs. First mammals evolve. | Triassic | 252 | **MESOZOIC ERA** |
| Dinosaurs become common. First birds evolve. | Jurassic | 201 | |
| Dinosaurs are widespread. Birds begin to replace flying reptiles. Flowering plants appear. Mass extinction occurs. | Cretaceous | 145 | |
| Mammals flourish. Grasses first spread widely. | Paleogene | 66 | **CENOZOIC ERA** |
| The Andes and Himalayas form. Some mammals and birds become very large. | Neogene | 23 | |
| Ice ages occur. Many kinds of animals thrive. First modern humans evolve. | Quarternary | 2.6 | |

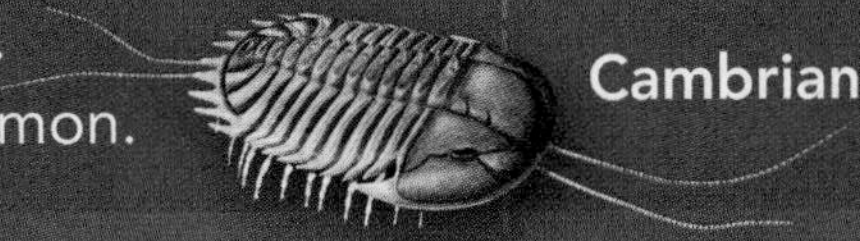

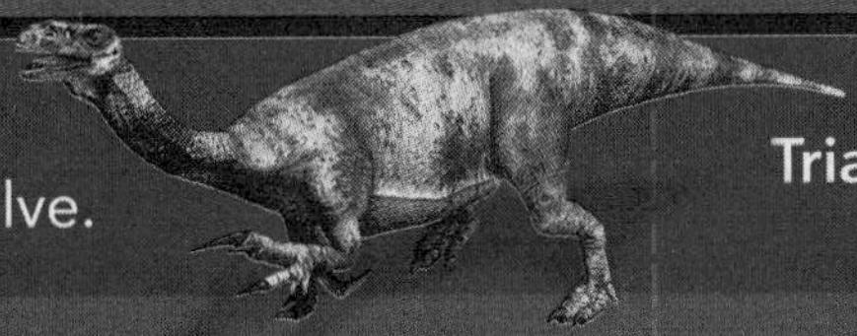

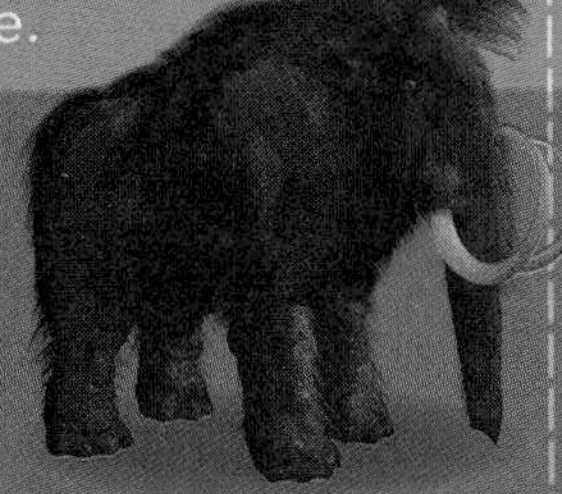

MS-ESS1-4

**1. Identify** During which era was the "Age of Reptiles"?

...........................................................................

**2. Sequence** Arrange the following organisms in order from earliest to latest appearance: amphibians, jawless fish, trilobites, bony fish.

...........................................................................

...........................................................................

**3. CCC Cause and Effect** Name two possible causes of the mass extinction at the end of the Paleozoic.

...........................................................................

...........................................................................

**4. SEP Construct Explanations** What factors allowed new organisms to evolve and thrive during the Cenozoic era?

...........................................................................

...........................................................................

...........................................................................

...........................................................................

...........................................................................

**5. Synthesize Information** Why do you think scientists use mass extinctions to separate one era from another?

...........................................................................

...........................................................................

...........................................................................

...........................................................................

...........................................................................

...........................................................................

...........................................................................

**6. SEP Cite Evidence** Identify a major event in Earth's past and describe the supporting evidence for that event you would expect to observe in the fossil record.

...........................................................................

...........................................................................

...........................................................................

...........................................................................

## Quest CHECK-IN

**In this lesson, you learned about major events that help to define and organize Earth's history.**

**Evaluate Reasoning** How can knowing about Earth's history help you to choose your dig site?

...........................................................................

...........................................................................

...........................................................................

...........................................................................

### 👆 INTERACTIVITY

Time to Choose the Dig Site

**Go online** to conduct research about *Dimetrodon* to make the final site selection.

MS-ESS1-4

# A New Mass Extinction?

When a species dies out, we say it is extinct. When large numbers of species die out at the same time, scientists use the term *mass extinction*. Scientists know of multiple mass extinctions in Earth's history. Some suggest that another mass extinction is approaching.

One factor that can lead to extinctions is the introduction of plant and animal species into new environments. Some of this is due to species migration. Animals and plants can move into new areas where temperature and climate patterns have become more favorable due to global warming. However, most species are brought to new areas by humans. In many cases, this leads to the disappearance of native species.

Habitat loss is another factor that leads to extinctions. When habitats are lost, the species that live within them no longer have the space or resources to live. As the human population increases, so has the human need for resources, such as fuel, land, and food. Habitats are cleared or changed to meet those needs, and the organisms that lived there may die off. For example, burning and clearing tropical forests threatens many endangered primates.

Climate change caused by global warming may also lead to extinctions. Our increased use of fossil fuels and the accompanying rise in carbon dioxide in the atmosphere has led to a steady increase in global temperatures. As temperatures rise, environments change. Species that cannot adapt to the changes may die out.

Most scientists agree that there is a real threat of another mass extinction. However, there are still steps people can take to prevent or minimize the loss of our biodiversity.

Urban development to accommodate a growing human population leads to habitat loss.

## MY COMMUNITY

What steps can you take in your community to change our path away from mass extinction? Use the library and the Internet to find facts and evidence that will support your ideas.

## 1 Determining Ages of Rocks

MS-ESS1-4

**1.** Which term describes a gap in the geologic record that occurs when sedimentary rocks cover an eroded surface?
A. extrusion
B. fault
C. intrusion
D. unconformity

**2.** Which term describes the time it takes for half of a radioactive element's atoms to decay?
A. absolute age
B. half-life
C. radioactive decay
D. relative age

**3.** Which statement **best** describes one rule for determining the relative age of a rock layer?
A. A fault is always younger than the rock it cuts through.
B. An extrusion is always older than the rocks below it.
C. An index fossil is always younger than the rock layer it occurs in.
D. An intrusion is always older than the rock layers around it.

**4.** Which of the following conclusions can geologists draw about a limestone rock layer based on the law of superposition?
A. The limestone layer is 2 million years old.
B. The limestone layer contains 2 million fossils.
C. The limestone layer is younger than the sandstone layer below it.
D. The limestone layer is the same age as another layer 100 hundred kilometers away.

**5.** A geologist finds an area of undisturbed sedimentary rock. The ................................. layer is most likely the oldest.

**6.** Radioactive dating is a method used by geologists to determine the ................................. age of rocks.

**7. SEP Construct Explanations** A geologist finds identical index fossils in a rock layer in the Grand Canyon in Arizona and in a rock layer 675 kilometers away in Utah. What can she infer about the ages of the two rock layers?

.................................................................................

.................................................................................

.................................................................................

**8. Sequence** Using the numbers and letters, list the rock layers and formations in the diagram in order from oldest to youngest. Cite evidence from the diagram to explain your answer.

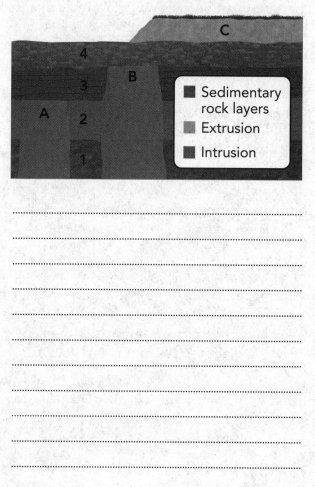

.................................................................................

.................................................................................

.................................................................................

.................................................................................

.................................................................................

.................................................................................

.................................................................................

.................................................................................

.................................................................................

.................................................................................

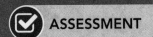
## ② Geologic Time Scale

MS-ESS1-4

**9.** Into which units is the geologic time scale subdivided?
   A. relative ages
   B. absolute ages
   C. months and days
   D. eras and periods

**10.** What do geologists **mostly** study to develop the geologic time scale?
   A. Earth's rotation
   B. tectonic plate motions
   C. volcanoes and earthquakes
   D. rock layers and index fossils

**11.** How do geologists use radioactive dating in developing the geologic time scale?
   A. to identify index fossils
   B. to identify types of rocks
   C. to place rocks in order by relative age
   D. to determine the absolute age of rocks

**12.** The geologic time scale is a record of
   ........................................ and ........................... .

**13. SEP Construct Explanations** Why do geologists need the geologic time scale? Give two reasons.

   ................................................................................
   ................................................................................
   ................................................................................
   ................................................................................
   ................................................................................
   ................................................................................
   ................................................................................
   ................................................................................

## ③ Major Events in Earth's History

MS-ESS1-4

**14.** Which event occurred in the Cenozoic era?
   A. first mammals
   B. spread of mammals
   C. first flowering plants
   D. spread of ferns and conifers

**15.** What were Earth's earliest multicellular organisms?
   A. bacteria
   B. land plants
   C. vertebrates
   D. invertebrates

**16.** The first birds evolved during the
   ........................................ era.

**17. SEP Develop Models** Draw what the Devonian period of the Paleozoic era might have looked like. Think about the events that define the Devonian period when making your model.

MS-ESS1-4

## Evidence-Based Assessment

A team of geologists explores an area of land that was once an ancient sea. They dig for fossils of marine organisms at three locations. The geologists collect and record information about the fossils they have discovered and the rock layers that the fossils were found in. The data are summarized in the diagram.

The geologists attempt to identify an index fossil to help them analyze the relative ages of the rock layers and to determine how the layers at the three sites correspond to each other. The researchers attempt to determine the relative ages of the layers and the marine organisms whose fossils they have dug up.

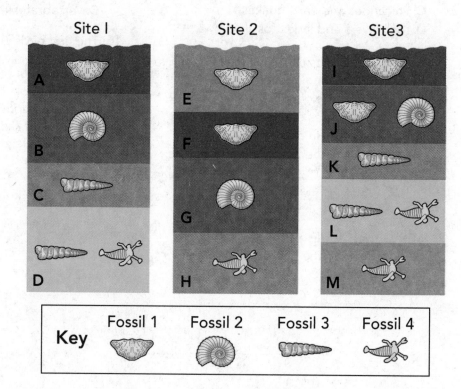

1. **SEP Interpret Data** Which of the following is an index fossil?

   **A.** Fossil 1      **C.** Fossil 3
   **B.** Fossil 2      **D.** Fossil 4

2. **Evaluate Quantity** Which statements about the relative ages of the rock layers is true? Select all that apply.
   - ☐ Layers B, G, and J are the same age.
   - ☐ Layer E is the youngest layer.
   - ☐ Layers D, H, and J are the same age.
   - ☐ Layer M is the oldest layer.
   - ☐ Layer A is the youngest layer.
   - ☐ Layers D and H are the oldest layers.

3. **Apply Scientific Reasoning** Based on the data, what can you conclude about the relative ages of Fossils 1 and 2? What scientific law can you use to support your response?

   ................................................................

   ................................................................

   ................................................................

   ................................................................

   ................................................................

   ................................................................

   ................................................................

   ................................................................

4. **SEP Engage in Argument** A peer claims that Fossil 2 is older than Fossil 3. Using evidence from the rock layers, explain why the evidence does not support their claim.

   ................................................................

   ................................................................

   ................................................................

   ................................................................

   ................................................................

   ................................................................

   ................................................................

5. **SEP Construct Explanations** Fossil 2 is about 300 million years old. Testing reveals that Layer M is about 400 million years old. The geologists conclude that Fossil 3 is an organism that likely lived about 350 million years ago. Do you agree? Support your answer using evidence from the diagram.

   ................................................................

   ................................................................

   ................................................................

   ................................................................

   ................................................................

   ................................................................

   ................................................................

   ................................................................

## Quest FINDINGS

## Complete the Quest!

**Phenomenon** Present your choice of dig site in a report to the head of the science museum that is sponsoring the *Dimetrodon* exhibit. In your report, include evidence and scientific reasoning that supports your choice.

**Evaluate Your Plan** What roles did the rock and fossil record play in determining your choice of dig site?

................................................................

................................................................

................................................................

................................................................

👆 **INTERACTIVITY**

Reflect on the Big Fossil Hunt

# Core Sampling Through Time

## Background

**Phenomenon** Visitors to a local state park see a variety of rocks and fossils on the surface in different locations. They often ask: Are the rocks here the same age as those over there? In your role as volunteer park ranger, how will you answer? You will need to find out how the ages of the rocks throughout the park compare.

You know that you can learn about the order of events in Earth's history by studying rocks. However, geologists cannot simply flip through layers of sedimentary rock like the pages in a magazine to study them. Instead, they must analyze samples taken from deep below the surface. In a process called coring, hollow tubes are driven into sedimentary rock layers. When the tubes are pulled out, they contain samples of each layer.

In this activity, you will illustrate the geologic history of the park using the data you gather through core sampling.

> How can you **determine** the **relative ages of rock layers** in different locations?

## Materials

(per group)

- four models positioned around the classroom representing rock layers
- plastic gloves
- metric ruler
- large-diameter drinking straw
- long dowel or rod that fits into the straw
- several sheets of paper
- colored pencils

## Safety

Be sure to follow all safety guidelines provided by your teacher. The Safety Appendix of your textbook provides more details about the safety icons.

## Plan Your Investigation

**HANDS-ON LAB**

ꓴ**Demonstrate** Go online for a downloadable worksheet of this lab.

1. Your teacher positioned four models around the classroom. The models represent sedimentary rock layers, some with index fossils, in different locations throughout the park.

2. Design an investigation to discover the geologic history of the park by drilling and analyzing core samples. Think about the following questions as you form your plan:

   • In which locations should you drill to get a complete picture of the rocks throughout the park so you can compare their ages?

   • How many core samples will you drill in each location?

   • How will you record what you observe in the core samples?

   • How will you compare the locations of sediment layers and index fossils?

   • How will you present your findings?

3. Use the space provided to summarize your investigation. Show your plan to your teacher for approval.

4. Conduct your investigation, record your observations, and report your findings according to your plan.

## Procedure

_____
_____
_____
_____
_____
_____
_____
_____
_____
_____
_____

## Evidence Gathered from Core Samples

# Analyze and Interpret Data

1. **SEP Develop Models** Use your observations and analysis to make a diagram of the complete geologic history of the park.

2. **SEP Use Models** Compare the geologic record at the different locations represented by your model core samples. Explain any differences you observe.

......................................................................................................................................

......................................................................................................................................

3. **CCC Patterns** Which rock layers at the different locations do you think are the same age? Explain your answer using evidence.

......................................................................................................................................

......................................................................................................................................

4. **Apply Scientific Reasoning** Choose two core samples that represent different locations in the park. Compare the ages of the rocks on the surface. Explain how you determined their relative ages.

......................................................................................................................................

......................................................................................................................................

......................................................................................................................................

......................................................................................................................................

......................................................................................................................................

# TOPIC
# 9

# Energy in the Atmosphere and Ocean

**NGSS PERFORMANCE EXPECTATION**

**MS-ESS2-6** Develop and use a model to describe how unequal heating and rotation of the Earth cause patterns of atmospheric and oceanic circulation that determine regional climates.

GO ONLINE
to access your
digital course

▶ VIDEO

👆 INTERACTIVITY

🧪 VIRTUAL LAB

☑ ASSESSMENT

📖 eTEXT

🧪 HANDS-ON LABS

How does this tree survive in Scotland?

HANDS-ON LAB

**ʋConnect** Explore how Earth's atmosphere traps heat.

## The Essential Question

# How does energy move throughout Earth's atmosphere and ocean?

**CCC Cause and Effect** Plockton, Scotland is located about as far north of the equator as Juneau, Alaska. Yet cabbage trees, which are similar to palm trees, can grow there. How can these warm-weather trees survive so close to the Arctic?

........................................................................................

........................................................................................

........................................................................................

........................................................................................

# Quest KICKOFF

## What is the most efficient way for a container ship to cross the Atlantic?

**Phenomenon** Shipping is a very cost-effective mode of transporting goods. But trips across the ocean can be dangerous, and it is up to the ship's captain and its officers to plan and follow safe navigation routes. In this problem-based Quest activity, you will plot a round-trip ocean journey across the Atlantic Ocean for a container ship. In digital activities and labs, you will evaluate data on fuel consumption and the effects of wind patterns and ocean currents. Finally, you will develop and present a recommended route.

**INTERACTIVITY**

Crossing the Atlantic

**MS-ESS2-6** Develop and use a model to describe how unequal heating and rotation of the Earth cause patterns of atmospheric and oceanic circulation that determine regional climates.

## NBC LEARN ▶ VIDEO

After watching the Quest Kickoff video about the work involved in navigating a ship, identify three dangers a container ship might face at sea.

**1**
..................................................................
..................................................................
..................................................................

**2**
..................................................................
..................................................................
..................................................................

**3**
..................................................................
..................................................................
..................................................................

## Quest CHECK-IN

### IN LESSON 1

How does the speed of a ship affect the cost of the trip? Determine the most cost-effective speed for a ship traveling across the Atlantic.

**HANDS-ON LAB**

## Quest CHECK-IN

### IN LESSON 2

How does wind affect a ship's speed? Consider how using wind can help to decrease the time of the ship's journey.

**INTERACTIVITY**

Wind at Your Back

Each container on this ship is equivalent to the back of a semi-trailer truck.

## Quest FINDINGS

### Complete the Quest!

Present your recommended route and explain the factors that you considered when planning the route.

 **INTERACTIVITY**

Reflect on Crossing the Atlantic

## Quest CHECK-IN

### IN LESSON 3

How do global ocean currents affect navigation routes? Analyze the patterns of currents in the northern Atlantic Ocean, and then finalize your route.

 **INTERACTIVITY**

Find Your Advantage

# Does a Plastic Bag Trap Heat?

How can you **use a model** to investigate how Earth's atmosphere traps heat?

## Background

**Phenomenon** According to the World Meteorological Organization, the hottest temperature recorded on Earth's surface was 56.7°C (135°F) and the coldest recorded surface temperature was -89°C (-129°F). But on the surface of the moon, the temperature ranges from 127°C (261°F) in full sun to -173°C (-279°F) away from the sun. Why are these temperatures so different, when the Earth and its moon are about the same distance from the sun? The sun's energy travels in the form of electromagnetic radiation. Earth absorbs about half of the radiation that arrives at its surface and re-emits it as infrared radiation that heats matter on or near the surface. In this activity, you will use a plastic bag to investigate how the sun's energy is kept near Earth's surface.

## Materials

**(per group)**
- 2 thermometers
- plastic bag
- paper (optional)
- scissors (optional)
- Tape
- Stopwatch
- lamp (optional)

## Safety

Be sure to follow all safety procedures provided by your teacher. The Safety Appendix of your textbook provides more details about the safety icons.

## Design a Procedure

1. **SEP Plan an Investigation** Use the materials to design a procedure to measure whether a plastic bag can trap heat. Be sure to consider variables that you can control. Describe your plan. Show your plan to your teacher for approval.

.................................................................

.................................................................

.................................................................

.................................................................

.................................................................

.................................................................

2. **SEP Carry out an Investigation** Perform your investigation. Record your observations.

# Observations

**HANDS-ON LAB**

**Connect** Go online for a downloadable worksheet of this lab.

## Analyze and Interpret Data

1. **SEP Analyze and Interpret Data** Did your investigation result in evidence that heat can be contained by a plastic bag? What observations provide this evidence?

   .................................................................................................................

   .................................................................................................................

   .................................................................................................................

2. **SEP Use Models** How might your investigation be used to model how energy from the sun stays near Earth's surface? Explain.

   .................................................................................................................

   .................................................................................................................

   .................................................................................................................

   .................................................................................................................

   .................................................................................................................

   .................................................................................................................

# Energy in Earth's Atmosphere

## Guiding Questions

- How does the sun's energy reach and move through Earth's atmosphere?
- How is heat transferred in Earth's atmosphere?
- What role does the atmosphere play in allowing life to thrive on Earth?

## Connections

**Literacy** Determine Central Ideas

**Math** Convert Measurement Units

MS-ESS2-6

## HANDS-ON LAB

**ᵘInvestigate** Develop and test a hypothesis about the heating and cooling rates of land and water.

## Vocabulary

electromagnetic
  wave
greenhouse
  effect
thermal energy
convection
conduction
radiation

## Academic Vocabulary

absorb

## Connect It!

✏ **Circle the correct terms to complete the statement in the box.**

**CCC Energy and Matter** Suppose you observe puddles on the ground after a brief rainstorm. A few hours after the sun comes out, the puddles are no longer there. What has happened to them?

.................................................................................................................................

.................................................................................................................................

.................................................................................................................................

# Energy from the Sun

Most of the energy that is moving within Earth's atmosphere and across Earth's surface comes from the sun. The sun's energy travels to Earth as electromagnetic radiation, a form of energy that can move through the vacuum of space. **Electromagnetic waves** consist of an electric field and a magnetic field.

When you use a microwave oven or watch television, you are using the energy created by electromagnetic waves. The waves are classified according to wavelength, or distance between wave peaks. Most of the electromagnetic waves that travel from the sun and reach Earth are in the form of visible light, which you can see in **Figure 1,** and infrared radiation. A smaller amount arrives as ultraviolet (UV) radiation.

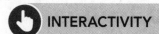 **INTERACTIVITY**

Investigate how sand and water absorb light energy.

**Electromagnetic Waves**

**Figure 1** Energy from the sun travels to Earth in the form of radiation.

Sunlight (warms / cools) the ice, causing it to (freeze / melt).

407

**Academic Vocabulary**
What other things can be absorbed?

................................................

................................................

................................................

................................................

................................................

**Literacy Connection**

**Determine Central Ideas**
As you proceed through the lesson, keep track of how energy moves and changes by underlining relevant sentences or passages.

## Sunlight and the Atmosphere

In order for the sun's energy to reach Earth's surface and sustain life, it must first get through the atmosphere. Earth's atmosphere is divided into layers based on temperature. Some sunlight is **absorbed** or reflected by the different levels of the atmosphere before it can reach the surface, as shown in **Figure 2**.

Some UV wavelengths are absorbed by the topmost layer of the atmosphere, called the thermosphere. More UV energy, along with some infrared energy, is absorbed in the next layer, the mesosphere. Below that, in the stratosphere, ozone absorbs more infrared and UV energy. Without the ozone layer, too much UV radiation would reach Earth's surface and threaten the health of organisms. However, the amount of UV radiation that reaches Earth's surface can still be damaging, which is why humans benefit from wearing clothing, sunscreen, and sunglasses.

By the time sunlight reaches the troposphere, there is some infrared radiation, some UV radiation, and visible light. Some light has been reflected into space by clouds. The daytime sky on a cloudless day appears blue because gas molecules scatter short wavelengths of visible light, which are blue and violet, more than the longer red and orange wavelengths.

**Layers of Atmosphere**
**Figure 2** Much of the energy in sunlight that reaches the atmosphere does not reach Earth's surface.

**CCC Cause and Effect**
What would happen if all of the sun's energy were to reach Earth?

................................................

................................................

................................................

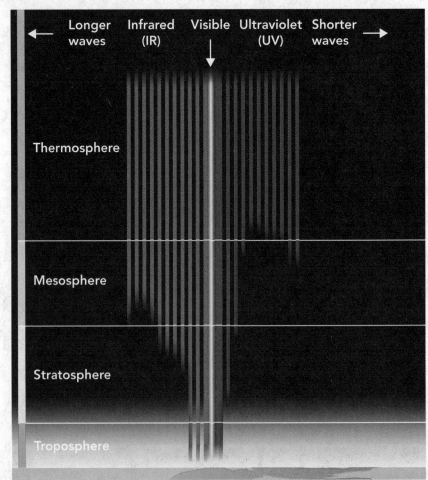

**Earth's Energy Budget** Of the radiation that travels from the sun to the troposphere, only about 50 percent is absorbed by land and water and converted, or transformed, to heat. The rest, as shown in **Figure 3**, is reflected by clouds and other particles in the atmosphere (25%), absorbed by gases and particles (20%), or reflected by the surface itself (5%). Snow, ice, and liquid water reflect some sunlight back into the atmosphere, where some will be absorbed by clouds and particles that the energy missed on the way down.

Only a tiny fraction of the visible light that reaches Earth's surface is transformed to chemical energy in plants and other photosynthetic organisms. The rest is absorbed by Earth and re-emitted into the atmosphere as infrared radiation. Earth's surface absorbs and re-emits equal amounts of energy so that its energy remains in balance over time.

✓READING CHECK **Determine Central Ideas** Describe the atmosphere's role in moderating the amount of electromagnetic radiation necessary to sustain life on Earth.

..................................................................................................

..................................................................................................

**The Sun's Energy**
**Figure 3** 🖊 Label the different percentages of energy that are absorbed or reflected.

When the sun goes down, a real-world greenhouse may need an alternative source of light or heat to keep the plants alive. How is this similar to Earth's surface at night?

## Earth as a Greenhouse

**Figure 4** ✏ Fill in the boxes in the diagram to describe how the atmosphere, Earth's surface, sunlight, and space interact.

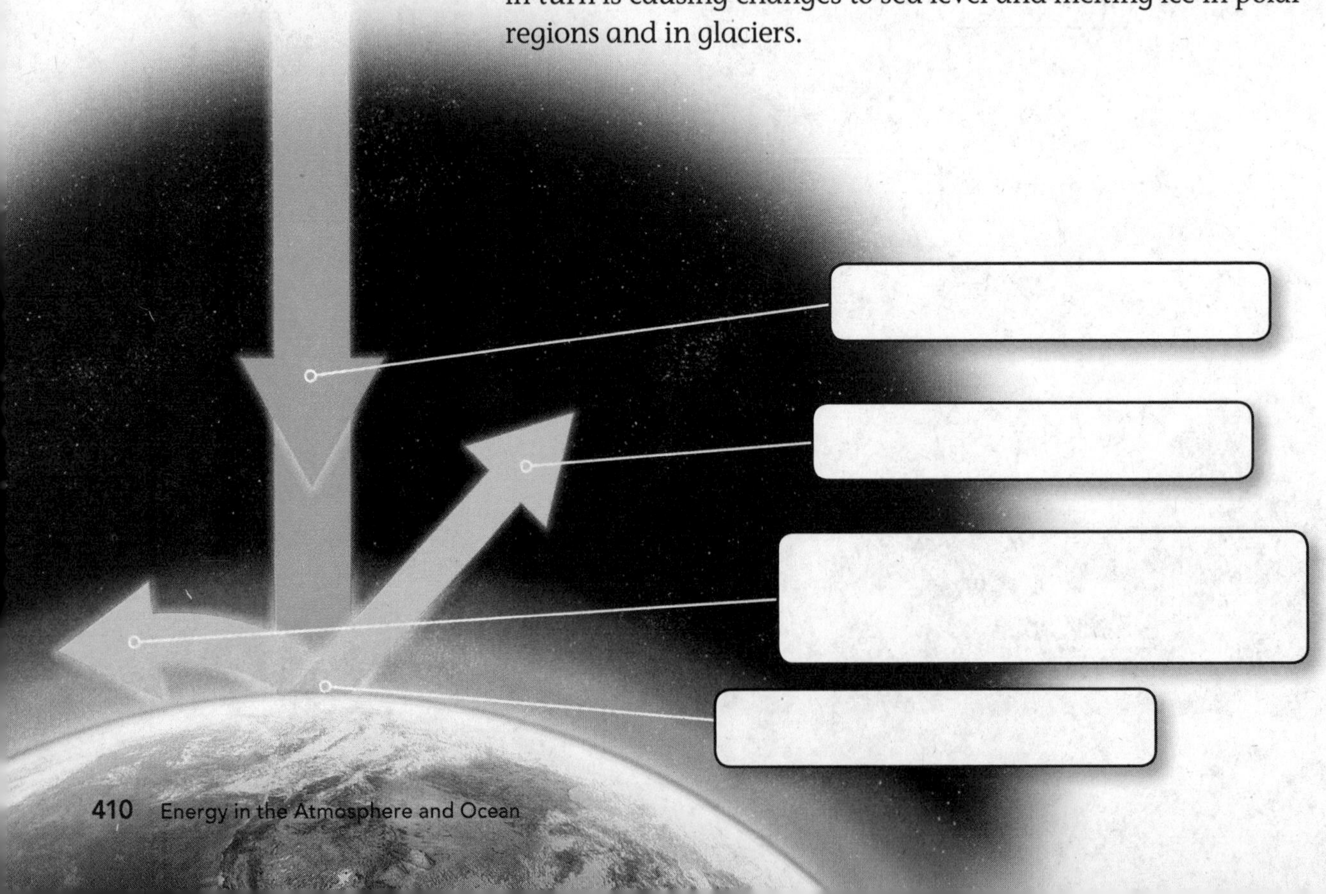

**The Greenhouse Effect** Have you ever been to a greenhouse to buy plants? The glass walls and roof of a greenhouse allow sunlight inside. Some sunlight is absorbed by plants and transformed into chemical energy. Most of the sunlight is converted to heat. Much of the heat is contained by the glass panes of the greenhouse, keeping the interior at an acceptable temperature for plant growth.

Earth's atmosphere plays a similar role. Sunlight is absorbed and transformed into heat within the atmosphere and in the materials at Earth's surface, such as rock and water. The surface reradiates all of that energy, and Earth's total energy remains in balance over time. (Otherwise, Earth would continually heat up and turn into molten rock.) Gases in the atmosphere trap some of the heat near Earth's surface, while some heat escapes into space. This **greenhouse effect** is shown in **Figure 4**.

Overall, Earth's atmosphere keeps our planet at a temperature that is adequate to support life. Organisms are adapted to specific ranges of temperatures. Surface features such as the sea level and the amounts of trapped ice have been relatively constant for thousands of years. However, changes to the composition of the atmosphere—those gases that absorb the infrared energy radiated from Earth's surface—can result in changes in temperature. Most scientists who study the atmosphere and the climate think that humans have been enhancing the greenhouse effect by increasing the amounts of carbon dioxide and methane in the atmosphere. This has caused an increase in the average temperature of Earth, which in turn is causing changes to sea level and melting ice in polar regions and in glaciers.

## Daily Air Temperature

Convert Measurement Units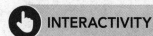
Grace records the air temperature throughout the day in a table. Convert Grace's measurements from degrees Fahrenheit (°F) to degrees Celsius (°C) using the formula shown below.

$$(\text{Temp °F} - 32) \times \frac{5}{9} = \text{Temp °C}$$

| Time | Temperature | |
| --- | --- | --- |
| | °F | °C |
| 8:00 AM | 52 | |
| 11:00 PM | 56 | |
| 2:00 PM | 60 | |
| 5:00 PM | 55 | |
| 8:00 PM | 50 | |

# Heat Transfer in the Atmosphere

All matter is made up of particles that are constantly moving. The faster the particles move, the more energy they have. Temperature is the *average* amount of energy of motion of each particle of a substance. **Thermal energy** is the total energy of motion in the particles of a substance.

It may seem odd to think that particles in solids are moving, but they are vibrating in place. Even the water molecules in a block of ice, or the atoms of iron and carbon in a steel beam, are moving ever so slightly.

When a substance reaches its melting point, the substance has enough energy of motion to reach a new state—liquid. And when the substance reaches its boiling point, it changes into a gas, which has even more energy of motion. The energy that first reaches Earth as sunlight drives many processes on Earth, including the freezing, melting, and evaporation of water.

✓READING CHECK **Determine Conclusions** Which has more thermal energy: a 1-kilogram block of ice or a 1-kilogram volume of water vapor? Why?

....................................................................................................

....................................................................................................

### INTERACTIVITY

Find out how convection currents form in the atmosphere.

### HANDS-ON LAB

☑**Investigate** Develop and test a hypothesis about the heating and cooling rates of land and water.

**Methods of Heat Transfer** We often talk about heat as though it is the same as thermal energy. Heat is actually energy that transfers into an object's thermal energy. Heat only flows from a hotter object to a cooler one. Heat transfers in three ways: **convection**, **conduction**, and **radiation**, as shown in **Figure 5**.

**Things Are Heating Up**
**Figure 5** A campfire can illustrate all three types of heat transfer.

## Convection

In fluids such as a hot campfire's smoke, particles move easily from one place to another, taking energy with them. Convection is the transfer of heat by the movement of a fluid.

## Radiation

The transfer of energy by electromagnetic waves is called radiation. The energy that is transferred from the sun to Earth is radiation. Likewise, the light and heat that are emitted by a campfire to toast a marshmallow or cook a hot dog is radiation.

## Conduction

The transfer of heat between two substances that are in direct contact, such a between a hot metal prong and a hot dog or your hand, is called conduction. The closer together the molecules are in a substance, the better they conduct heat. This is why conduction works well in some solids, such as metals, but not as well in liquids and gases whose particles are farther apart.

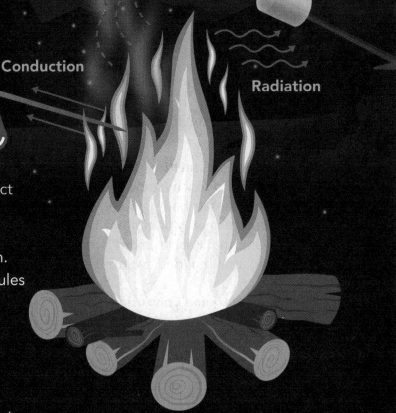

## Heat Transfer at Earth's Surface

The sun's radiation is transformed at Earth's surface into thermal energy. The surface may get warmer than the air above it. Air doesn't conduct heat well. So only the first few centimeters of the troposphere are heated by conduction from Earth's surface to the air. When ground-level air warms up, its molecules move more rapidly. As they bump into each other, they move farther apart, making the air less dense. The warmer, less-dense air rises, and cooler, denser air from above sinks toward the surface.

The cool air then gets warmed by the surface, and the cycle continues. If the source of heat is isolated in one place, a convection current can develop. This occurs in Earth's atmosphere as a result of radiation, conduction, and convection working together. The horizontal movement of the convection current in the atmosphere is what we call wind. Convection currents are especially powerful if Earth's radiant surface is much warmer than the air above it. This is related to why storms can arise much more suddenly and be more severe in warmer regions of Earth. For example, hurricanes tend to form in tropical areas where the sea is very warm and the air above it is relatively cool.

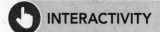

**INTERACTIVITY**

Discover patterns in the wind and how they relate to energy transfer in the atmosphere.

**READING CHECK** **Translate Information** Explain how a pot of heated water could demonstrate convection.

.........................................................................................................................

.........................................................................................................................

.........................................................................................................................

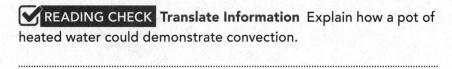

## Model It

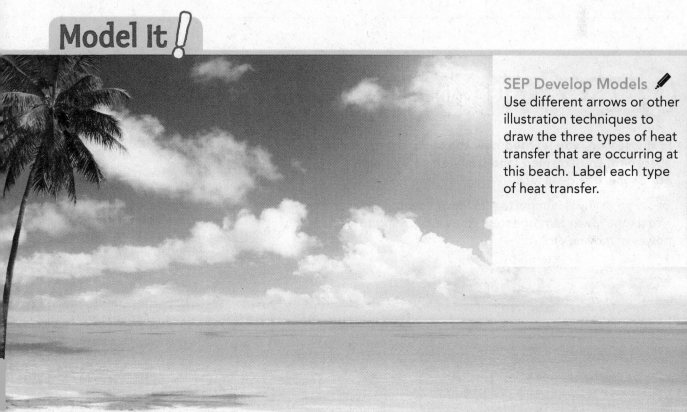

**SEP Develop Models** ✏

Use different arrows or other illustration techniques to draw the three types of heat transfer that are occurring at this beach. Label each type of heat transfer.

**1. Identify** What are the three types of heat transfer that occur on Earth?

......................................................................

......................................................................

**2. Predict** If the amounts of greenhouse gases such as carbon dioxide and methane continue to increase in the atmosphere, what will happen to the average temperature of Earth? Explain.

......................................................................

......................................................................

......................................................................

......................................................................

**3. Summarize** How is the amount of sunlight absorbed by Earth's surface and the amount of energy released by Earth kept in balance?

......................................................................

......................................................................

......................................................................

......................................................................

......................................................................

**4. SEP Construct Explanations** You place a metal spoon in a pot of soup. After a few minutes, you touch the end of the spoon and notice that it is hot. Which type of heat transfer caused this to happen? Explain.

......................................................................

......................................................................

......................................................................

......................................................................

......................................................................

**5. CCC Cause and Effect** What causes sunburn? Why do we have difficulty perceiving the energy that causes it?

......................................................................

......................................................................

......................................................................

......................................................................

......................................................................

......................................................................

......................................................................

# Quest CHECK-IN

**In this lesson, you learned how the sun's energy is reflected, absorbed, transformed, and transferred by Earth's atmosphere and surface.**

**Evaluate** Why is it important to know how the sun's energy affects the lower atmosphere if you are planning to harness the power of moving air?

......................................................................

......................................................................

......................................................................

......................................................................

## HANDS-ON LAB

Choose Your Speed

**Do the Hands-On Lab** to determine the most cost-effective speed for a ship traveling across the Atlantic and how the sun's energy affects moving air.

MS-ESS2-6

# Measure Radiation with a Cube

**Phenonmenon** This RAVAN can measure incoming energy from the sun and outgoing energy from Earth in the form of radiation. A difference in the amounts, called Earth's radiation imbalance, can affect the planet's climate.

**R**ight now, satellites the size of toasters are circling Earth. Each one is collecting data about the planet's atmosphere. These small cube satellites, or CubeSats, give scientists a new way to measure changes in Earth's climate. Different teams have built their own CubeSats, even students.

One team launched a CubeSat called RAVAN to measure the amount of radiation energy leaving Earth's atmosphere. Data from the satellite will allow the team to compare the amount of energy coming in from the sun with the amount of energy leaving Earth. This energy balance reveals a lot about Earth's climate. So tracking the energy balance will help scientists to predict future climate changes.

RAVAN is only the beginning. The team hopes to launch 30 to 40 cubes that will collect data from every part of Earth's atmosphere.

## MY DISCOVERY

Anyone can submit an idea for a CubeSat to NASA. Elementary students at St. Thomas More Cathedral School in Arlington, Virginia, built, tested, and launched their own CubeSat. Everyone in the entire school participated for more than three years to launch it. Search the Internet to learn more about the St. Thomas More CubeSat. Can you think of a school project where a CubeSat would come in handy?

CubeSats are so small that most of their scientific instruments are about the size of a deck of cards.

# Patterns of Circulation in the Atmosphere

## Guiding Questions

- What causes winds?
- How does the sun's energy affect wind characteristics?
- How do winds redistribute energy around Earth?

## Connections

**Literacy** Translate Information

**Math** Analyze Relationships Using Tables

MS-ESS2-6

**HANDS-ON LAB**

μInvestigate Explore precipitation in the United States.

## Vocabulary

wind
sea breeze
land breeze
Coriolis effect
jet stream

## Academic Vocabulary

area
model

## Connect It !

✏ **Without wind, there wouldn't be any kite surfing. Draw an arrow to show the direction you think the wind is blowing.**

SEP Construct Explanations What are some ways that you rely on the wind?

..............................................................................................................

..............................................................................................................

..............................................................................................................

# Winds

The surfer in **Figure 1** is moving over the top of a fluid, water. But the surfer is also moving through another fluid, called air. Air, like water, flows from place to place and does not have a fixed shape. But what causes air to flow?

**Causes of Winds** Air, like most things, moves away from high pressure **areas** to low pressure areas. When there is a difference in air pressure, air moves and wind is created. **Wind** is the movement of air parallel to Earth's surface.

Higher and lower pressure areas are results of the unequal heating of the atmosphere. Air over the heated surface expands, becomes less dense, and rises. As the warm air rises, its air pressure decreases. Meanwhile, if another area is not heated as much, then the air in that area is cooler and denser. The denser air sinks and air pressure increases. The cool, dense air with a higher pressure flows underneath the warm, less dense air. This difference in pressure forces the warm air to rise.

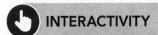

**INTERACTIVITY**

Explore how Earth's rotation affects wind.

## Academic Vocabulary

The word *area* is used in mathematics and in everyday life. How are the two ways to use the word *area* related?

...............................................................

...............................................................

...............................................................

...............................................................

**Catching the Wind**

**Figure 1** Kite surfers need wind to move across the water.

**Anemometer**

**Figure 2** The higher the wind speed, the faster the cups spin around on the anemometer, shown in the top left side of the image.

**Measuring Wind** Wind is a valuable resource, and understanding wind can put this resource to work for us. To identify winds, they are named using the direction from which they originate and their speed. A wind vane is helpful in seeing which way the wind is blowing. The arrow on the wind vane points in the direction from which the wind is blowing. Winds can blow from any of the four directions: north, south, east, and west, and they are named by the direction from which they are blowing. For example, a north wind blows from the north to the south.

Wind speed and pressure can be measured with an anemometer like the one in **Figure 2**. An anemometer has three or four cups mounted at the ends of horizontal spokes that spin on an axle. The force of the wind against the cups turns the axle. The anemometer tracks the number of rotations, and that number is used to calculate wind speed.

✓ **READING CHECK Summarize Text** What causes wind?

......................................................................................

......................................................................................

# Math Toolbox

## Windchill Factor

The wind blowing over your skin removes body heat. The increased cooling that a wind causes is called the windchill factor.

**1. Analyze Relationships Using Tables** A weather reporter says, "It is 20 degrees Fahrenheit. But with a wind speed of 30 miles per hour, the windchill factor makes it feel much colder." Use the table to determine how cold the air will feel with the windchill factor accounted for.

......................................................................................

**2. SEP Construct Explanations** Will it feel colder with an air temperature of 15°F with wind speeds of 40 mph or with an air temperature of 10°F with wind speeds of 25 mph? Explain.

......................................................................................

### Windchill Factor

| Wind (mph) | 35 | 30 | 25 | 20 | 15 | 10 | 5 | 0 | −5 |
|---|---|---|---|---|---|---|---|---|---|
| 5 | 31 | 25 | 19 | 13 | 7 | 1 | −5 | −11 | −16 |
| 10 | 27 | 21 | 15 | 9 | 3 | −4 | −10 | −16 | −22 |
| 15 | 25 | 19 | 13 | 6 | 0 | −7 | −13 | −19 | −26 |
| 20 | 24 | 17 | 11 | 4 | −2 | −9 | −15 | −22 | −29 |
| 25 | 23 | 16 | 9 | 3 | −4 | −11 | −17 | −24 | −31 |
| 30 | 22 | 15 | 8 | 1 | −5 | −12 | −19 | −26 | −33 |
| 35 | 21 | 14 | 7 | 0 | −7 | −14 | −21 | −27 | −34 |
| 40 | 20 | 13 | 6 | −1 | −8 | −15 | −22 | −29 | −36 |
| 45 | 19 | 12 | 5 | −2 | −9 | −16 | −23 | −30 | −37 |

Temperature (°F)

# Local Winds and Global Winds

Because of Earth's shape, surfaces, and tilt, the sun cannot evenly warm all of Earth at the same time. Different parts of Earth are warmed at different times and rates. This unequal heating and Earth's rotation affect wind and weather conditions on land, both in local areas and over global regions. Scientists use this understanding to make a **model**, such as a diagram or a map, to describe and predict wind patterns and their effects.

**Local Winds** Have you ever noticed a breeze at the beach on a hot summer day? Even if there is no wind inland, there may be a cool breeze blowing in from the water. Winds that blow over short distances and affect local weather are called local winds. The unequal heating of Earth's surface within a local area causes local winds. These winds form only when the global winds in an area are weak.

Two types of local winds are sea breezes and land breezes, which are illustrated in **Figure 3** below. When sunlight reaches the surface of Earth, land warms up faster than water. The air over the land gets warmer than the air over the water. As you know, warm air is less dense, and it rises, creating a low-pressure area. Cool air blows inland from over the water and moves underneath the warm air, causing a sea breeze. A **sea breeze** or a lake breeze is a local wind that blows from an ocean or lake.

At night, the land cools faster than water. The air above the land begins to cool and move under the warm air rising off the water. The flow of air from land to a body of water forms a **land breeze**.

## Academic Vocabulary

*Model* can be a noun that means "a picture or other representation of a complex object or process." Or it can be a verb that means "to represent something." Write sentences using the term first as a noun and then as a verb.

.....................................................

.....................................................

.....................................................

.....................................................

.....................................................

## Sea Breeze and Land Breeze

**Figure 3** 🖊 Fill in the labels to indicate how a sea breeze and a land breeze develop.

The ............... air rises.

The ............... air moves to take ............... air's place.

The ............... air rises.

At night, the ............... air moves off land.

INTERACTIVITY

Construct a model to show atmospheric cirulation.

VIDEO

Learn about general circulation and wind belts.

## Global Winds

The patterns of winds moving around the globe are called global winds. Like local winds, global winds are created by the unequal heating of Earth's surface. However, unlike local winds, global winds occur over a large area. **Figure 4** models how the sun's radiation strikes Earth. Direct rays from the sun heat Earth's surface intensely near the equator at midday. Near the poles, the sun's rays strike Earth's surface less directly. The sun's energy is spread out over a larger area, so it heats the surface less. As a result, temperatures near the poles are much lower than they are near the equator.

Global winds form from temperature differences between the equator and the poles. These differences produce giant convection currents in the atmosphere. Warm air rises at the equator, and cold air sinks at the poles. Therefore, air pressure tends to be lower near the equator and greater near the poles. This difference in pressure causes winds at Earth's surface to blow from the poles toward the equator. Away from Earth's surface, the opposite is true. Higher in the atmosphere, air flows away from the equator toward the poles. Those air movements produce global winds.

## Model It

### Earth Is Heating Up

**Figure 4** Depending on where you are on Earth's surface, the sun's rays may be stronger or weaker and you may be hotter or colder. These temperature differences produce convection currents in the atmosphere.

1. **Identify** ✏️ Label the areas where the sun hits Earth most directly (M) and least directly (L).

2. **CCC Patterns** Describe how cool and warm air moves in the atmosphere.

   ........................................................................

   ........................................................................

3. **SEP Develop Models** ✏️ Draw a convection current in the atmosphere north of the equator. Use arrows to show the direction of air movement.

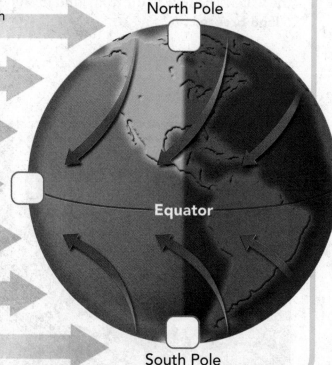

# The Coriolis Effect

If Earth did not rotate on its axis, global winds would blow in straight lines. Instead, global winds get deflected or shifted by Earth's rotation. As the winds blow, Earth rotates from west to east underneath them, making it seem as if the winds curve. The way Earth's rotation makes winds curve is called the **Coriolis effect** (kawr ee OH lis ih FEKT) as shown in **Figure 5**. Because of the Coriolis effect, global winds in the Northern Hemisphere gradually turn toward the right. A wind blowing toward the south gradually turns toward the southwest. In the Southern Hemisphere, winds curve toward the left.

**INTERACTIVITY**

Explain how local wind patterns form.

✓ READING CHECK **Translate Information** How do **Figure 5** and the text support the concept that winds do not follow a straight path due to the Coriolis effect?

......................................................................................................

......................................................................................................

......................................................................................................

......................................................................................................

No rotation

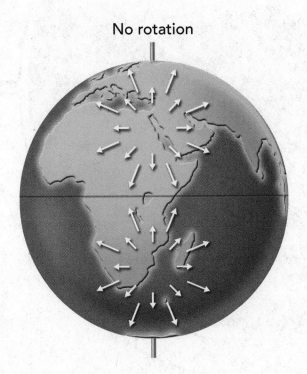

## Modeling the Coriolis Effect

**Figure 5** The Coriolis effect is the result of Earth's rotation. Without it, global winds would travel in straight lines away from their sources. With it, global winds turn to the right in the Northern Hemisphere and to the left in the Southern Hemisphere.

With rotation

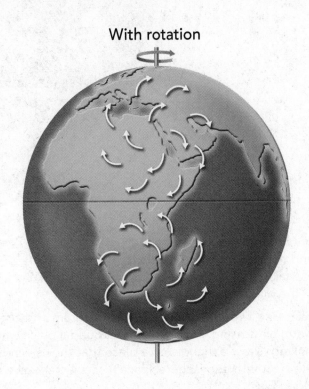

# Global Wind Patterns

The Coriolis effect, global convection currents, and other factors combine to produce a pattern of calm areas and global wind belts around Earth, as shown in **Figure 6**. The calm areas where air rises or sinks include the doldrums and the horse latitudes. The major global wind belts are the trade winds, the polar easterlies, and the prevailing westerlies. These wind belts are not stationary and can shift about from month to month.

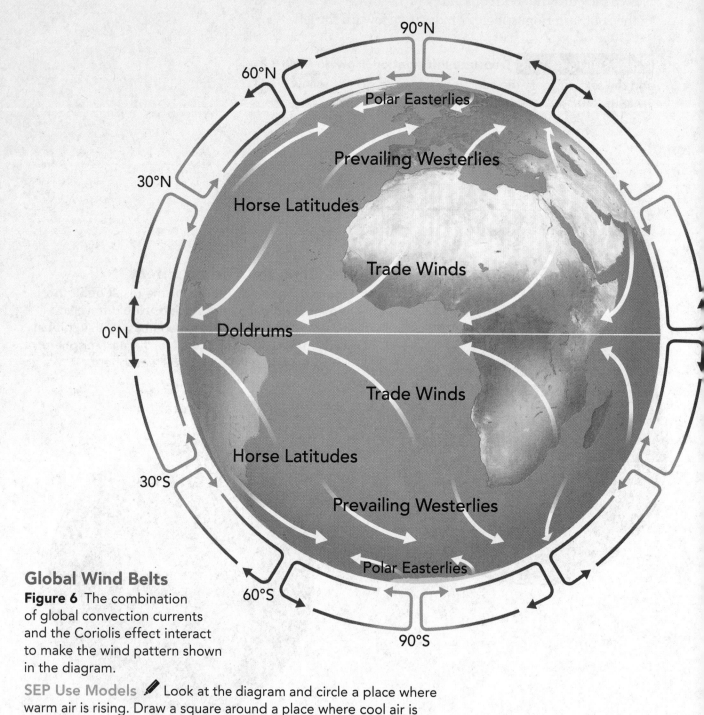

90°N

60°N

Polar Easterlies

Prevailing Westerlies

30°N

Horse Latitudes

Trade Winds

0°N    Doldrums

Trade Winds

Horse Latitudes

30°S

Prevailing Westerlies

Polar Easterlies

60°S

90°S

## Global Wind Belts

**Figure 6** The combination of global convection currents and the Coriolis effect interact to make the wind pattern shown in the diagram.

**SEP Use Models** 🖉 Look at the diagram and circle a place where warm air is rising. Draw a square around a place where cool air is sinking. Draw a triangle on a place that shows winds turning right in the Northern hemisphere. Place a check mark on a place where winds along Earth's surface are calm.

**Effects of Global Wind Belts** Global winds affect local weather by moving masses of air from one place to another. The air masses affect the temperature, rainfall, and air pressure. Overall, the global wind belts move energy away from the equator and toward the poles. This helps to equalize the temperature, allowing life to survive in a larger range of latitudes on Earth.

**Jet Streams** About 10 kilometers above Earth's surface are bands of high-speed winds called **jet streams**. They generally blow from west to east at speeds of 200 to 400 kilometers per hour. As jet streams travel around Earth, they wander north and south along wavy paths that vary over time.

The jet streams greatly affect local weather. As shown in **Figure 7**, the jet streams traveling over North America bring a variety of weather conditions. Weather forecasters track the jet streams to predict temperature and precipitation. If the polar jet stream wanders farther south than usual in winter, it could mean colder temperatures and snowy conditions for areas north of the jet stream. If the jet stream wanders farther north than usual, then warmer air moves up from the south and warmer temperatures are predicted for areas south of the jet stream.

**HANDS-ON LAB**

**Investigate** Explore precipitation in the United States.

**Literacy Connection**

**Translate Information** As you read, underline the text that describes how the jet stream pictured in **Figure 7** can be used to predict weather.

**Jet Streams**

**Figure 7** ✎ The changing positions of the jet streams over the United States influence local weather, particularly in winter. The map shows the position of the polar jet stream on a winter day.

1. **SEP Use Models** The weather in Boise, Idaho, is most likely (colder/warmer) than usual.

2. **SEP Use Models** The weather in Cheyenne, Wyoming, is most likely (colder/warmer) than usual.

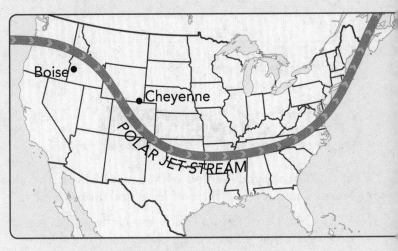

Boise
Cheyenne
POLAR JET STREAM

☑ **READING CHECK** **Integrate With Visuals** How does the map help you to understand the path of the jet stream?

......................................................................................

......................................................................................

MS-ESS2-6

**1. SEP Communicate Information** What is wind?

.......................................................................

.......................................................................

.......................................................................

**2. CCC Patterns** What pattern occurs in the prevailing westerlies and polar easterlies of the Northern Hemisphere because of the Coriolis effect?

.......................................................................

.......................................................................

.......................................................................

**3. SEP Construct Explanations** How is the sun's energy related to winds?

.......................................................................

.......................................................................

.......................................................................

.......................................................................

.......................................................................

.......................................................................

**4. SEP Develop Models** Describe how you could use a globe and your hand to model the path of a global convection current in the atmosphere.

.......................................................................

.......................................................................

.......................................................................

.......................................................................

.......................................................................

.......................................................................

.......................................................................

.......................................................................

**5. CCC Cause and Effect** How might the jet stream affect the weather in your town this winter? Explain your prediction.

.......................................................................

.......................................................................

.......................................................................

.......................................................................

.......................................................................

.......................................................................

## Quest CHECK-IN

**In this lesson, you learned what causes winds. You also learned about the effects of local and global winds.**

**CCC Cause and Effect** Think about how global winds move. How might they affect a large object such as a ship?

.......................................................................

.......................................................................

.......................................................................

.......................................................................

.......................................................................

### ☞ INTERACTIVITY

Wind at Your Back

**Go online** to explain why a container ship's captain might want to travel in the direction the wind is blowing rather than against the wind.

MS-ESS2-6

# Windmills
## of the Future

▶ **VIDEO**

Visualize the inner workings of a turbine.

**Windmills** are great when winds are steady and strong. But how can you capture energy from swirling winds? You engineer it!

**The Challenge:** To make a wind turbine that produces electricity from swirling winds.

**Phenomenon** A company in Spain has come up with a way to capture swirling winds. As wind moves around a tall, slim mast, it vibrates. Magnets located inside a cone at the top of the mast amplify this movement. When wind pushes the mast one way, the magnets push it in the opposite direction so that the whole turbine swirls. The energy of this movement is then converted to electricity. The turbine works no matter the wind direction or speed.

This new turbine needs only a mast, which means no spinning blades, so it doesn't pose a danger to birds and is totally silent. It also costs less, because there are fewer parts to make and maintain. And many more bladeless turbines can fit in one area, so they won't take up as much space. One day soon, forests of these windmills of the future may capture wind energy in a location near you!

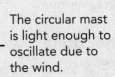

The circular mast is light enough to oscillate due to the wind.

The carbon-fiber rod is strong, but also flexible.

The generator housed inside the bottom of the mast converts the mast's motion into electricity.

**DESIGN CHALLENGE** Can you design and build a wind turbine? Go to the Engineering Design Notebook to find out!

# 3 Patterns of Circulation in the Ocean

## Guiding Questions

• What causes ocean currents?
• How do ocean currents redistribute Earth's energy?

## Connections

**Literacy**  Integrate With Visuals

**Math**  Analyze Quantitative Relationships

MS-ESS2-6

## HANDS-ON LAB

**Investigate Lab**  Model how surface and deep ocean currents form.

### Vocabulary

current
El Niño
La Niña

### Academic Vocabulary

gradually

## Connect It !

✏ **In the space provided, identify how you think ocean currents, water temperature, and weather might affect a sea turtle.**

CCC Cause and Effect  How do factors such as ocean currents, water temperature, and weather affect you in your daily life?

..................................................................................................

..................................................................................................

..................................................................................................

# Surface Currents

You probably know that ocean water moves as waves. It also flows as currents. A **current** is a large stream of moving water that flows through the ocean. Both waves and currents can affect ocean ecosystems, such as the one shown in **Figure 1**. Unlike waves, currents carry water from one place to another. Some currents move water deep in the ocean. Other currents, called surface currents, move water at the surface of the ocean.

Surface currents are driven mainly by global winds and affect water to a depth of several hundred meters. They follow Earth's global wind patterns. Surface currents move in circular patterns in the five major ocean basins.

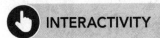

## INTERACTIVITY

Describe what it would be like to swim against a current.

## Riding the Currents

**Figure 1** Sea turtles travel long distances by riding ocean currents.

weather

ocean currents

water temperature

**Factors Affecting Surface Currents** Global wind belts affect surface currents. Unequal heating and the rotation of Earth combine to produce global wind belts. Because global winds drive surface currents, unequal heating and Earth's rotation also drive patterns of ocean circulation. Warm currents moving away from the equator redistribute energy to keep temperatures moderate. Cold currents move toward the equator to complete the circle, as shown in **Figure 2**.

You learned that as Earth rotates, the paths of global winds curve. This effect, known as the Coriolis effect, also applies to surface currents. In the Northern Hemisphere, the Coriolis effect causes the currents to curve to the right. In the Southern Hemisphere, the Coriolis effect causes the currents to curve to the left.

As ocean currents are moved by the winds, the continents stop the movements and redirect the currents. Winds push currents, but once the currents meet land, they have to find a new path.

📖 **Reflect** Along which surface current in **Figure 2** would you most like to float in a boat? In your science notebook, explain why.

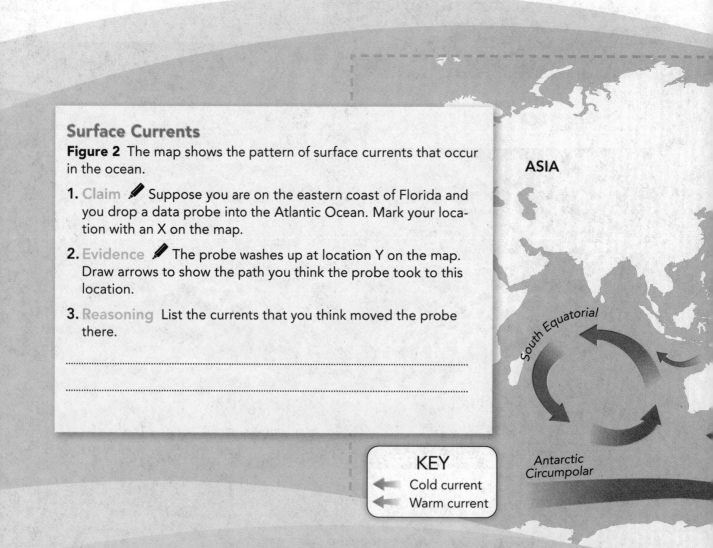

**Surface Currents**

**Figure 2** The map shows the pattern of surface currents that occur in the ocean.

1. Claim 🖊 Suppose you are on the eastern coast of Florida and you drop a data probe into the Atlantic Ocean. Mark your location with an X on the map.

2. Evidence 🖊 The probe washes up at location Y on the map. Draw arrows to show the path you think the probe took to this location.

3. Reasoning List the currents that you think moved the probe there.

...................................................................................

...................................................................................

ASIA

South Equatorial

Antarctic Circumpolar

KEY
⬅ Cold current
⬅ Warm current

**Effects on Climate** The Gulf Stream is the largest and most powerful surface current in the North Atlantic Ocean. It originates from the Gulf of Mexico and brings warm water up the east coast of North America and across the Atlantic. This large, warm current is caused by powerful winds from the west and is more than 30 kilometers wide and 300 meters deep. When the Gulf Stream crosses the Atlantic, it becomes the North Atlantic Drift.

The Gulf Stream and other surface currents redistribute heat from the equator to the poles. These currents have a great impact on local weather and climates. Climate is the temperature and precipitation typical of an area over a long period of time. For example, the North Atlantic Drift brings warm water to Northern Europe. The warm water radiates heat and brings warm temperatures and wet weather. This is why England is warmer and wetter than other countries at the same latitude, such as Canada and Russia. In a similar way, when cold surface currents bring cold water, they cool the air above them. Because cold air holds less moisture than warm air, it results in a cool and dry climate for the land areas.

## Literacy Connection
**Integrate With Visuals**
Use information from **Figure 2** and the text to explain the effects of warm and cold surface currents on climate.

.................................
.................................
.................................
.................................
.................................
.................................
.................................
.................................
.................................

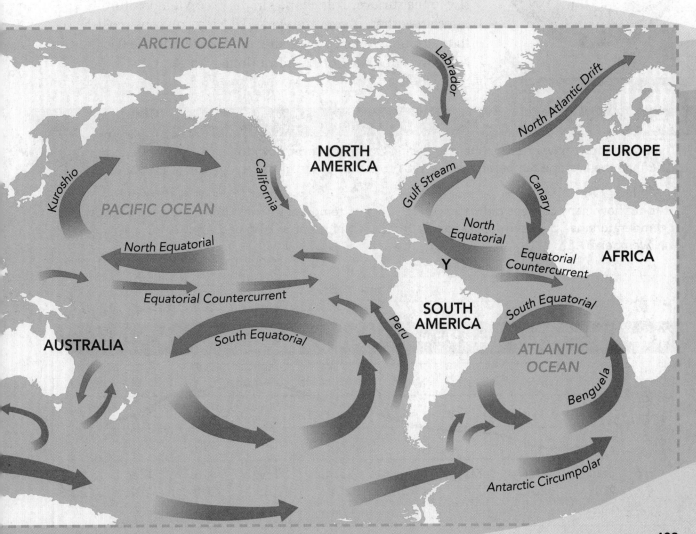

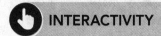
## El Niño

**Figure 3** The image shows
the surface temperatures of
water in the Pacific Ocean
during the 2015–2016 El
Niño. Red indicates the
warmest temperatures and
blue the coolest.

**El Niño and La Niña** Changes in wind patterns and
ocean currents can have major impacts on weather conditions
on nearby land. One example is **El Niño**, a climate event that
occurs every two to seven years in the Pacific Ocean.

Near the equator, winds usually blow east to west. During El
Niño, the winds along the equator weaken and reverse direction.
This change allows warm, tropical water from the Pacific Ocean
to flow east toward the South American coast and prevents the
cold, deep water from moving to the surface. El Niño conditions
can last for one to two years.

El Niño's effects on the atmosphere and ocean cause shifts in
weather patterns. The most recent El Niño in 2015 and 2016,
shown in **Figure 3**, was one of the three strongest on record.
It increased rainfall and snowfall in California and caused
flooding in California and Texas.

When surface waters in the eastern Pacific are colder than
normal, a climate event known as **La Niña** occurs. A La Niña
event is the opposite of an El Niño event. During a La Niña,
stronger winds blow above the Pacific Ocean, causing more
warm water to move west. This allows lots of cold water to
rise to the surface. This change in the ocean temperature
affects weather all over the world. La Niña can cause colder
than normal winters and greater precipitation in the Pacific
Northwest and the north central United States.

## Math Toolbox

### Analyzing El Niño Data

The graph shows how much warmer the Pacific Ocean was from 2015 to
2016 than the average temperature from 1981 to 2010.

**1. Analyze Quantitative Relationships**
About how many degrees did water
temperature rise between January and
November 2015?

.................................................................................

.................................................................................

**2. SEP Interpret Data** Why does the
temperature most likely decrease between
November 2015 and April 2016?

.................................................................................

.................................................................................

.................................................................................

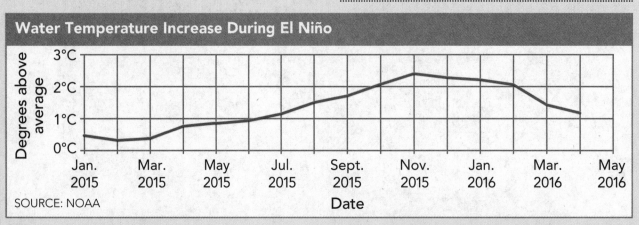

**Water Temperature Increase During El Niño**

SOURCE: NOAA

# Deep Ocean Currents

Deep below the ocean surface, another type of current causes the movement of cold waters across the ocean floor. Deep currents are caused by differences in the density of ocean water.

**Temperature, Salinity, and Density** The density of ocean water varies with its temperature and salinity. Water is dense if it is cold or salty. Dense water sinks, which drives deep ocean currents. When a warm surface current moves from the equator toward one of the poles, it **gradually** gets denser because it both cools and becomes saltier as water evaporates. As ice forms near the poles (see **Figure 4**), the salinity of the water increases even further. This is because the ice contains only fresh water, leaving the salts in the water. The cold salty water sinks and flows along the ocean floor as a deep current. Like surface currents, deep currents are affected by the Coriolis effect, which causes them to curve.

Deep currents move and mix water around the world. They carry cold water from the poles toward the equator. Deep currents flow slowly. They may take longer than 1,000 years to make one full trip around their ocean basins.

**INTERACTIVITY**

Explore ocean habitats.

**Academic Vocabulary**
Use the term *gradually* in a sentence describing Earth's movements.

........................................................

........................................................

........................................................

........................................................

**Sea Ice**
**Figure 4** Sea ice forms different shapes. This ice is called pancake ice.

## Plan It !

### Sea Ice and Salinity

**SEP Plan Your Investigation** How can you use the set up below to investigate how ice formation affects the salinity of ocean water? Summarize your plan.

........................................................

........................................................

**SEP Evaluate Information** 🖊 Each glass of water contains the same amount of salt. Circle the glass that contains water with the greatest salinity.

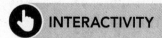
## Global Ocean Conveyor

The ocean currents move in a loop around Earth's bodies of water. The movement looks like a conveyor belt, as shown in **Figure 5**, and results from density differences due to variations in temperature and salinity. The movement of the currents circulates oxygen that is essential for marine life.

The ocean's deep currents mostly start as cold water in the North Atlantic Ocean. This is the same water, called the North Atlantic Deep Water, that moved north across the Atlantic as part of the Gulf Stream. It sinks and flows southward toward Antarctica. From there it flows northward into both the Indian and Pacific oceans. There, deep cold water rises to the surface, warms, and eventually flows back along the surface into the Atlantic.

This system circulates water and transfers heat throughout the interconnected ocean basins and thus around Earth from the equator to the poles and back again.

✓ **READING CHECK** **Integrate With Visuals** How does the map in **Figure 5** relate to the text on this page?

........................................................................................

........................................................................................

## Global Conveyor Belt

**Figure 5** Deep currents and surface currents form a global system of heat distribution through Earth's interconnected ocean basins.

1. **SEP Develop Models** 🖊 Draw arrows on the conveyor to indicate the direction of both cold and warm water movement.

2. **Predict** What might happen if the global conveyor stopped?

........................................................................................

........................................................................................

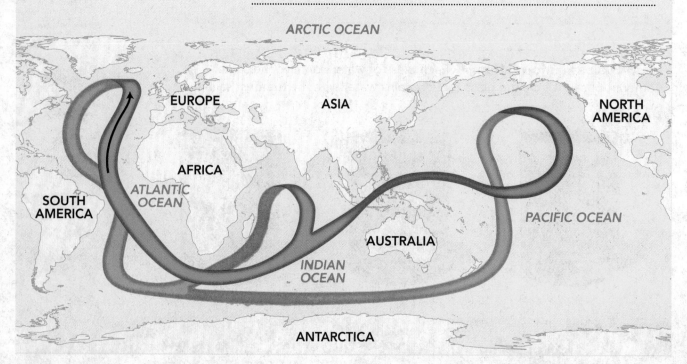

1. **CCC Cause and Effect** What causes surface currents?

..................................................................

2. **CCC Patterns** What pattern of movement do both warm and cold surface currents share?

..................................................................

..................................................................

..................................................................

..................................................................

3. **SEP Construct Explanations** Explain why cities located on the western coast of Norway in northern Europe near the cold Artic Circle have a milder climate compared to other places located farther inland at the lower latitudes.

..................................................................

..................................................................

..................................................................

..................................................................

..................................................................

4. **SEP Develop Models** ✏ Draw a diagram or flow chart to show how variations in ocean water properties result in a deep ocean current forming.

# Quest CHECK-IN

**In this lesson, you learned about how surface currents and deep ocean currents form. You also discovered how they affect weather and climate.**

**Apply Concepts** Which ocean currents are most likely to affect your container ship? Why?

..................................................................

..................................................................

..................................................................

..................................................................

..................................................................

## ✋ INTERACTIVITY

Find Your Advantage

**Go online** to analyze the path of the Gulf Stream.

# HURRICANES in the Making

**Y**ou've probably seen images of enormous hurricanes swirling over the Atlantic Ocean. Where will the next one strike? Thankfully, these giant storms often follow predictable patterns. That's because the development and movement of hurricanes is affected by air and ocean currents.

## How Hurricanes Form

Hurricanes form over the North Atlantic Ocean where the water temperature is at least 80°F. As the warm ocean air rises, it leaves an area of low air pressure in its place. Air rushes in to fill the low pressure area, and then it heats up and rises, too, which makes the air begin to swirl and spin.

Hurricanes move with Earth's air currents. Most hurricanes form in a current of westward-flowing air near the equator called the trade winds. If a low pressure area forms off the coast of Africa, it can then catch a ride on the trade winds. As the low pressure area moves westward across the warm ocean waters, it grows in strength. By the time it reaches the southern United States, the low pressure area has become a hurricane.

## Tracking Hurricanes

A hurricane may take different paths. A hurricane moving northward might run into westerly winds that blow across the United States. These winds will cause the hurricane to turn eastward, back out to sea. Sometimes a northward hurricane also lines up with the Gulf Stream, the warm ocean current running northward up the coast. When that happens, a hurricane can travel up to New England.

Other hurricanes may take a path westward across Florida. Some travel into the Gulf of Mexico, where westerly winds may turn a hurricane back eastward, across Louisiana, Alabama, or Florida.

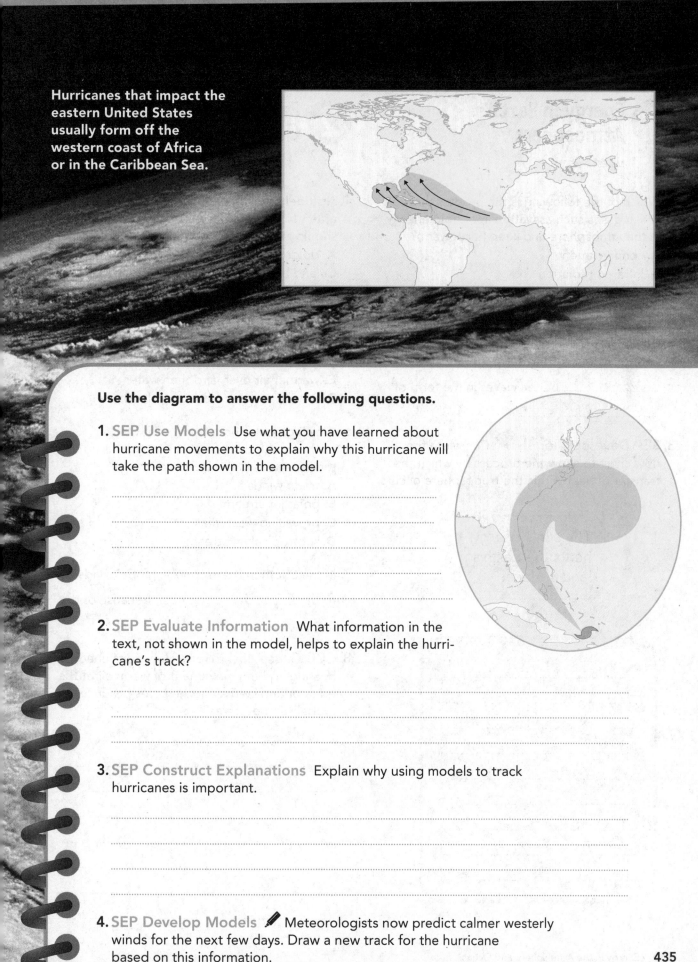

Hurricanes that impact the eastern United States usually form off the western coast of Africa or in the Caribbean Sea.

**Use the diagram to answer the following questions.**

1. **SEP Use Models** Use what you have learned about hurricane movements to explain why this hurricane will take the path shown in the model.

2. **SEP Evaluate Information** What information in the text, not shown in the model, helps to explain the hurricane's track?

3. **SEP Construct Explanations** Explain why using models to track hurricanes is important.

4. **SEP Develop Models** ✏ Meteorologists now predict calmer westerly winds for the next few days. Draw a new track for the hurricane based on this information.

435

# ☑TOPIC 9 Review and Assess

## ① Energy in Earth's Atmosphere

MS-ESS2-6

**1.** Which of the following is the process through which gases such as water vapor hold energy in the atmosphere and keep Earth warm?
A. condensation
B. infrared radiation
C. ultraviolet radiation
D. the greenhouse effect

**2.** When land absorbs sunlight, some energy is directly transferred to the air by

.................................................... waves in the form of

....................................................

**3. SEP Develop Models** ✏ Complete the flow chart to show the process by which the transfer of heat within the troposphere occurs.

The sun's energy heats the Earth's land surface.

....................................................
....................................................
....................................................
....................................................
....................................................
....................................................
....................................................
....................................................
....................................................

## ② Patterns of Circulation in the Atmosphere

MS-ESS2-6

**4.** A student makes a model of global winds that affect North America. Which of the following should the student's model include?
A. doldrums          B. sea breezes
C. land breezes      D. polar easterlies

**5.** Which unequal condition causes a sea breeze to develop?
A. dryer air over land than water
B. dryer air over water than land
C. warmer air over land than water
D. warmer air over water than land

**6.** Which global wind pattern can wander farther south than usual in winter causing temperatures in the U.S. to decrease?
A. trade winds
B. polar jet stream
C. prevailing westerlies
D. subtropical jet stream

**7.** In the Southern Hemisphere, global winds turn

to the .................................................... because of the

....................................................

**8. CCC Cause and Effect** How does unequal heating and the movement of warm air at the equator and cold air at the poles produce global wind patterns?

....................................................
....................................................
....................................................
....................................................
....................................................
....................................................
....................................................
....................................................
....................................................

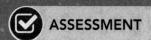
## ③ Patterns of Circulation in the Ocean

MS-ESS2-6

**9.** What makes ocean currents move in a curved path?
A. Earth's rotation    B. unequal density
C. unequal heating    D. Earth's revolution

**10.** What causes deep ocean currents to flow?
A. local winds
B. global winds
C. unequal heating
D. density differences

**11.** Which of the following can bring heavy rains and flooding to California and an especially warm winter in the northeastern United States?
A. El Niño
B. La Niña
C. Coriolis effect
D. North Atlantic Drift

**12.** Which effect does the Gulf Stream have on the climates of nearby land?
A. calming
B. drying
C. freezing
D. warming

**13.** Deep ocean currents slowly carry cold water from the ..................................................... to the

.................................................

**14. CCC Analyze Systems** What is the role of the global conveyor system?

...............................................................................

...............................................................................

...............................................................................

**15. SEP Develop Models** 🖊 Draw a diagram of a major warm ocean surface current flowing along a coastal area. Label the current and type of climate you would most likely find in the area. Show how the current influences the area's climate.

MS-ESS2-1, MS-ESS2-4

## Evidence-Based Assessment

An oceanographic research team is investigating patterns in surface ocean currents around the globe. After collecting the data, they develop a map to record information about major surface currents in the ocean.

Their map shows both the directions of the surface currents and the temperature of the water carried by the currents.

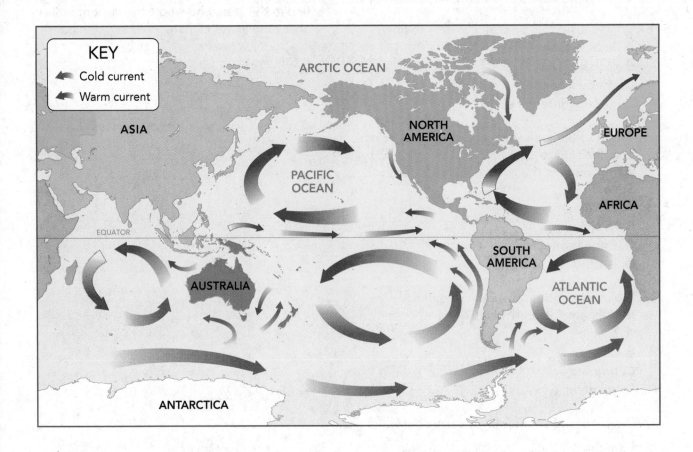

1. **Analyze Systems** According to the research team's map, the longest cold surface currents
   A. travel around the South Pole.
   B. are found in the Atlantic Ocean.
   C. do not interact with warm surface currents.
   D. travel down the eastern coasts of South America and Africa.

2. **SEP Analyze Data** Which continent is mostly surrounded by surface currents carrying cold water?
   A. Africa
   B. Antarctica
   C. Asia
   D. Europe

3. **SEP Develop Models** Suppose the team decides to add arrows to indicate the circulation of winds in the atmosphere. How would these wind circulations compare to the ocean currents? What explains this relationship?

......................................................................
......................................................................
......................................................................
......................................................................
......................................................................
......................................................................
......................................................................
......................................................................
......................................................................
......................................................................
......................................................................
......................................................................
......................................................................
......................................................................
......................................................................
......................................................................
......................................................................

4. **CCC Patterns** Which of the following patterns of ocean circulation are supported by data in the map? Check all that apply.

☐ Warm water is carried by currents from the equator to the poles, where it cools.

☐ Currents move in large circles between continents and landmasses.

☐ Cool water is carried from the west coast of Africa to the north coast of South America, where it is warmed.

☐ Cool water travels from the poles to the equator, where it is warmed.

☐ Ocean currents move in a clockwise direction in the Northern Hemisphere and counterclockwise in the Southern Hemisphere.

☐ Warm water moves from the poles to the equator, where it cools.

5. **CCC Cause and Effect** Explain how Earth's rotation and the sun's uneven heating of the planet are responsible for the patterns of ocean circulation detailed on the map.

......................................................................
......................................................................
......................................................................
......................................................................
......................................................................
......................................................................
......................................................................
......................................................................
......................................................................
......................................................................
......................................................................

## Quest FINDINGS

## Complete the Quest!

**Phenomenon Write a report that recommends a speed and route for the container ship crossing the Atlantic Ocean. Be sure to include evidence that justifies your recommendations and explain the factors that affect your recommendations.**

**SEP Construct Explanations** Explain why you think your recommendations will or will not still be valid in a year.

......................................................................
......................................................................
......................................................................
......................................................................

👆 **INTERACTIVITY**

Reflect on Crossing the Atlantic

MS-ESS2-6

# Not All Heating Is Equal

How can you use a model to **demonstrate** the amount of **solar energy** that different places on **Earth** receive?

## Background

**Phenomenon** As an engineer at a solar energy company, you must help choose a location for a new solar farm. The company has identified three possible sites: near Yellowknife, Canada; La Paz, Mexico; or Quito, Ecuador. In this investigation, you will model how sunlight hits Earth to determine the best location for the solar farm.

## Materials

(per group)

- black construction paper
- polystyrene ball
- scissors
- clear tape
- 3 thermometers
- lamp
- stopwatch or clock

## Safety

Be sure to follow all safety guidelines provided by your teacher. The Safety Appendix of your textbook provides more details about the safety icons.

# Design and Plan Your Investigation

HANDS-ON LAB

□ **Demonstrate** Go online for a downloadable worksheet of this lab.

☐ 1. Look at the diagram. Then predict how you think the amount of solar energy received at each of the three spots is related to its location. Which of the three locations do you think is best suited for a solar farm? Record your prediction in the space provided.

☐ 2. Design your model to test your predictions. Sketch your model and identify the materials you will use. Use your model to measure the temperature of surfaces that face a light source at different angles. (Hint: Assume that the temperature of black construction paper will increase after about 15 minutes when a light shines on it from 30 cm away.) Consider the following questions as you design and plan your investigation:

- How will you represent the sun and Earth in your model?

- What two variables will you investigate?

- How will you make sure that you test only one variable?

- How will you measure the amount of solar energy each location receives?

☐ 3. Write a detailed procedure describing how you will use your model to test your predictions about how the amount of solar energy received at each of the three spots is related to its location. (Hint: Plan to use some of the available materials to determine how the temperature of the black paper is affected by its position on your model.) Record your procedure in the space provided.

☐ 4. Have your teacher approve your procedure. Then make your model and conduct the investigation to test your prediction. Use the data table to record your data.

## Prediction

.......................................................................................................
.......................................................................................................

## Sketch of Model

## Procedure

.......................................................................................................
.......................................................................................................
.......................................................................................................
.......................................................................................................
.......................................................................................................

## Data Table

| Location | Temperature after 15 minutes (°C) |
|---|---|
| A (Yellowknife) | |
| B (La Paz) | |
| C (Quito) | |

# Analyze and Interpret Data

1. **SEP Develop Models** Summarize how you developed your model to test your prediction.

.................................................................................................................
.................................................................................................................
.................................................................................................................
.................................................................................................................

2. **SEP Interpret Data** In which locations did you observe the highest and lowest temperatures?

.................................................................................................................
.................................................................................................................
.................................................................................................................
.................................................................................................................

3. **CCC Cause and Effect** How does the temperature of each location relate to the amount of solar energy it receives? Explain.

.................................................................................................................
.................................................................................................................
.................................................................................................................
.................................................................................................................

4. **CCC Patterns** Based on your results, explain how the location of an area on Earth affects the amount of solar energy it receives. Then describe how your results compare to your prediction.

.................................................................................................................
.................................................................................................................
.................................................................................................................
.................................................................................................................

5. **SEP Construct Explanations** Based on your results, which of the three locations is the best site for the new solar farm? Use evidence from your observations to support your answer.

.................................................................................................................
.................................................................................................................
.................................................................................................................
.................................................................................................................

**NGSS PERFORMANCE EXPECTATIONS**

**MS-ESS2-6** Develop and use a model to describe
how unequal heating and rotation of the Earth
cause patterns of atmospheric and oceanic
circulation that determine regional climates.

**MS-ESS3-5** Ask questions to clarify evidence of
the factors that have caused the rise in global
temperatures over the past century.

HANDS-ON LAB

**uConnect** Make observations about
the factors that determine climate
regions.

What is happening to this glacier?

GO ONLINE to access your digital course

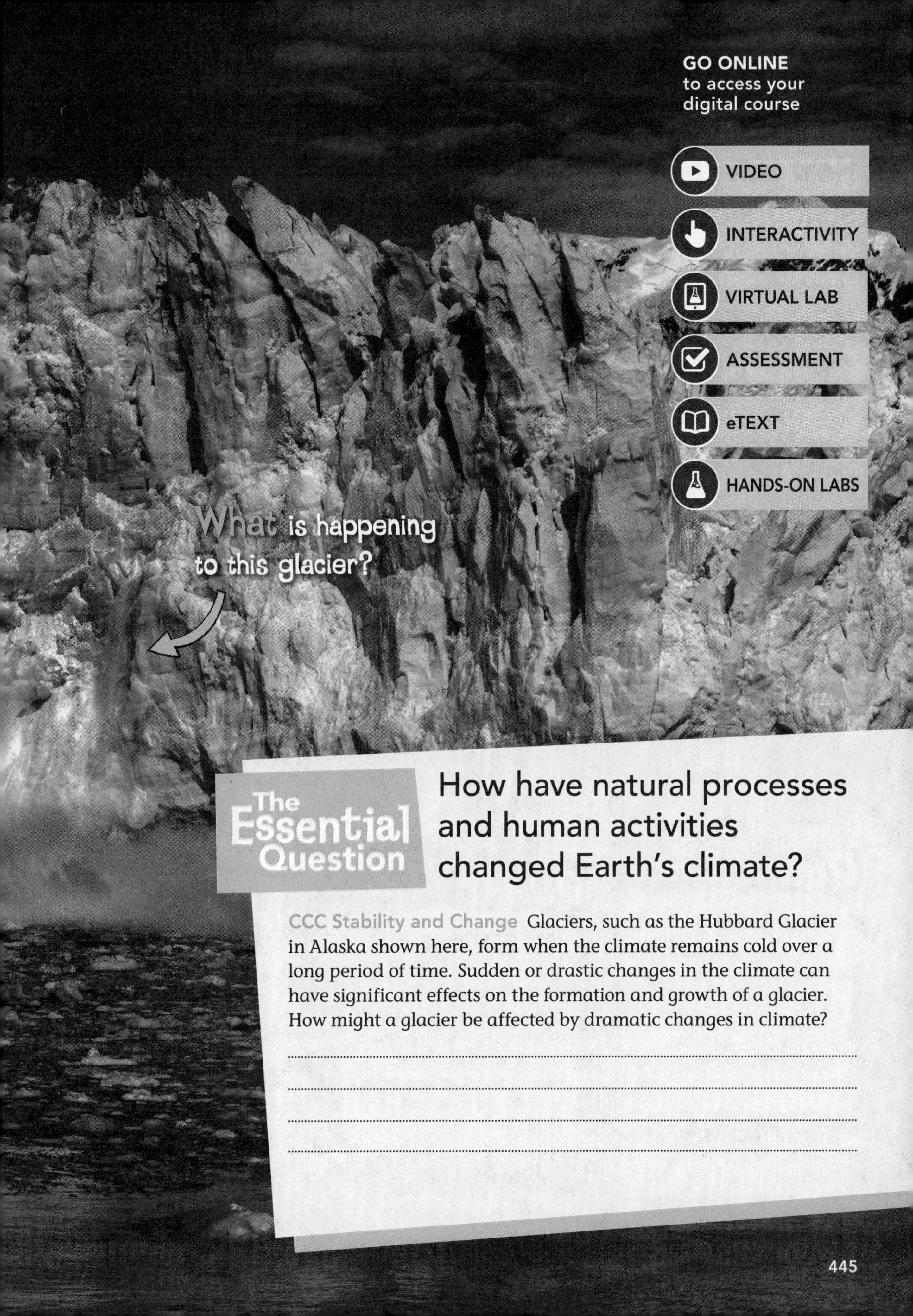

- VIDEO
- INTERACTIVITY
- VIRTUAL LAB
- ASSESSMENT
- eTEXT
- HANDS-ON LABS

## The Essential Question

## How have natural processes and human activities changed Earth's climate?

**CCC Stability and Change** Glaciers, such as the Hubbard Glacier in Alaska shown here, form when the climate remains cold over a long period of time. Sudden or drastic changes in the climate can have significant effects on the formation and growth of a glacier. How might a glacier be affected by dramatic changes in climate?

................................................................................................

................................................................................................

................................................................................................

................................................................................................

# Quest KICKOFF

## How can I help reduce my school's carbon footprint?

**Phenomenon** The construction of new schools often involves the work of energy engineers. These specialists review architectural plans to improve the energy efficiency of buildings. They also recommend equipment that helps to reduce energy usage.

In this Quest activity, you will explore how the climate of your region affects energy usage at your school. In digital activities and labs, you will investigate ways to increase the efficiency of energy usage at your school. By applying what you have learned, you will develop a plan to reduce your school's carbon footprint.

 **INTERACTIVITY**

Shrinking Your Carbon Footprint

**MS-ESS3-5** Ask questions to clarify evidence of the factors that have caused the rise in global temperatures over the past century.

### NBC LEARN ▶ VIDEO

After watching the video, which examines how to make homes more energy efficient, think about ways you use energy sources, such as gas and electricity, in your daily life. List three activities you do each day that use the greatest amount of energy.

**1**
................................................................
................................................................

**2**
................................................................
................................................................

**3**
................................................................
................................................................

---

## Quest CHECK-IN

### IN LESSON 1

How does the climate of a region affect the people who live there? Think about how the climate in your region impacts the energy needs of your school.

**INTERACTIVITY**

Footprint Steps

## Quest CHECK-IN

### IN LESSON 2

How can small changes result in significant cutbacks in energy usage? Analyze the data you have gathered to estimate potential reductions to your school's carbon footprint.

**HANDS-ON LAB**

Energy Savings at School

## Quest CHECK-IN

### IN LESSON 3

How can your school effectively reduce its energy usage? Develop a school-wide plan for reducing your school's carbon footprint.

**INTERACTIVITY**

Make a Difference

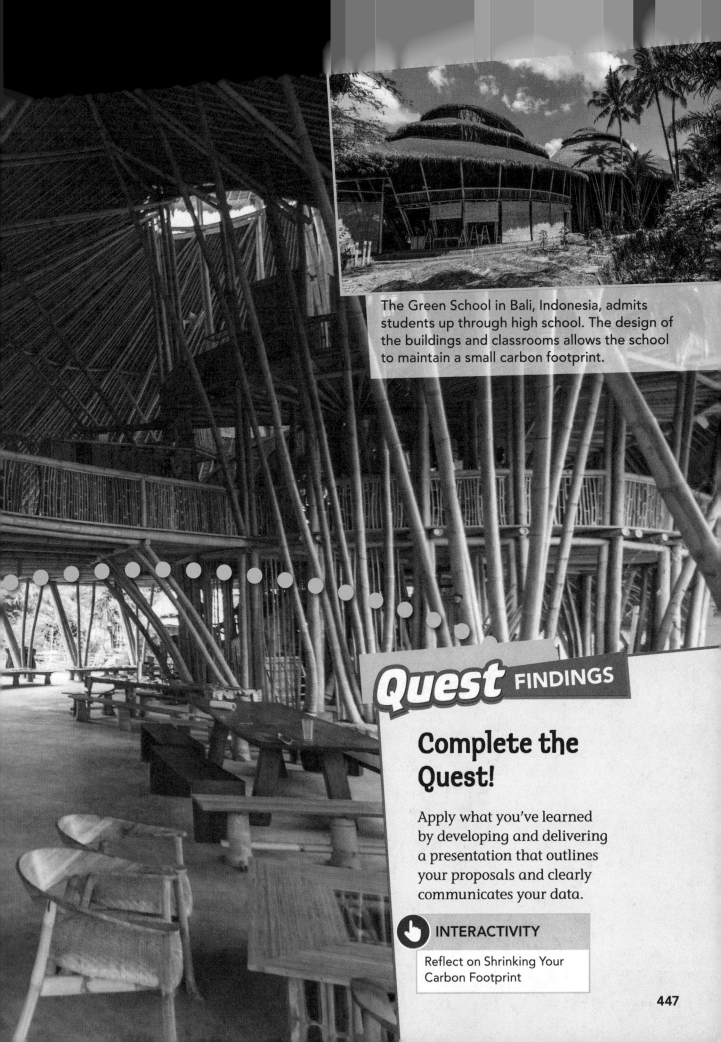

The Green School in Bali, Indonesia, admits students up through high school. The design of the buildings and classrooms allows the school to maintain a small carbon footprint.

## Quest FINDINGS

### Complete the Quest!

Apply what you've learned by developing and delivering a presentation that outlines your proposals and clearly communicates your data.

**INTERACTIVITY**

Reflect on Shrinking Your Carbon Footprint

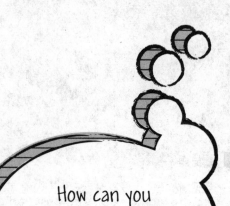

How can you **characterize** the climate of a region?

# How Do Climates Differ?

## Background

**Phenomenon** You call your grandfather in Texas. He tells you that it is a warm sunny day. You look out the window and see snow falling. As you discuss the weather outside, you wonder if the climate in Texas and your climate are similar. In this investigation, you will determine how to classify different climates.

## Materials

**(per group)**
• set of magazine photos

## Design a Procedure

☐ **1.** Obtain a set of photographs from your teacher.

☐ **2.** Think about what you know about different climates. What general characteristics will you use to classify climates? What will you look for in the photographs? Think of at least two characteristics.

.........................................................................................

.........................................................................................

.........................................................................................

.........................................................................................

.........................................................................................

☐ **3.** Sort the photographs into climate categories according to the characteristics you observe.

☐ **4. SEP Develop a Model** Make a table. For each climate category you create, write several words that describe it.

# Observations

**HANDS-ON LAB**

**Connect** Go online for a downloadable worksheet of this lab.

## Analyze and Interpret Data

1. **SEP Use Models** Use the descriptive words you have chosen to write an operational definition for each type of climate you have identified in the photos.

.........................................................................................................

.........................................................................................................

.........................................................................................................

.........................................................................................................

2. **SEP Interpret Data** What are the main characteristics that determine how climates differ?

.........................................................................................................

.........................................................................................................

.........................................................................................................

3. **Apply Concepts** Use your operational definitions to determine the type of climate in which you live.

.........................................................................................................

.........................................................................................................

# ① Climate Factors

## Guiding Questions

- How does climate differ from weather?
- How do latitude, altitude, and land distribution affect patterns of circulation in the atmosphere and ocean?
- How do patterns of circulation in the atmosphere and ocean determine regional climates?

## Connections

**Literacy** Integrate With Visuals

**Math** Analyze Proportional Relationships

MS-ESS2-6

## HANDS-ON LAB

**uInvestigate** Use graphs to classify locations into climate regions.

**Vocabulary**
climate

**Academic Vocabulary**
describe

## Connect It!

✏ **Label the parts on the image that indicate what kind of temperature and precipitation are present in Antarctica.**

**Make Generalizations** From what you see in the image, how would you describe conditions in Antarctica?

.................................................................................

**SEP Design Solutions** How do you think humans would adapt to this climate?

.................................................................................

.................................................................................

.................................................................................

# Factors That Affect Climate

No matter where you live, the weather changes every day. In some areas, the temperature might change just one degree from one day to the next. In other areas, a cold, rainy day might be followed by a warm, sunny one.

While weather describes the short-term conditions in an area, **climate** is the long-term weather pattern in an area. Specifically, climate refers to the average, year-after-year conditions of temperature, precipitation, wind, and clouds. So, while "it's snowing" **describes** the current weather, you need more information to describe the climate.

How water cycles in different areas determines climate patterns. For example, year-round freezing temperatures in Antarctica prevent snow from melting and limit evaporation from the ocean. **Figure 1** shows that Antarctica has a cold, dry climate.

Another example is California's Mojave Desert, where the limited precipitation evaporates rapidly. The climate there is hot and dry. But, if you move west from the Mojave Desert toward California's coast, you would notice a cooler, more humid climate. Why does this happen?

An area's climate is affected by its latitude, altitude, distance from large bodies of water, ocean currents, and global prevailing winds. These factors are continuously changing, but an area's climate does remain relatively stable. However, if these factors change too quickly or drastically, then the area's climate can change as well.

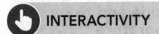
**INTERACTIVITY**

Explore how moving north or south on Earth affects the climate of the region.

**Academic Vocabulary**

How might you describe your favorite food?

..............................................

..............................................

..............................................

..............................................

**Temperature and Climate**

**Figure 1** Polar climates have certain patterns of temperature and precipitation, as shown in this image of Antarctica.

## Latitude and Temperature

**Figure 2** ✎ Label the temperature zones *polar*, *temperate*, or *tropical*, based on the latitudes shown. In which temperature zone is most of the United States located?

.............................................................

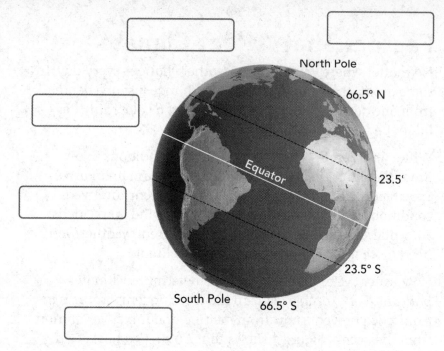

North Pole

66.5° N

Equator

23.5'

23.5° S

South Pole    66.5° S

**Latitude** Towns and cities in the northern United States tend to have snowy winters, while those in the south have mild, warm winters. This is because areas closer to the equator have warmer climates. The sun's rays hit Earth's surface more directly at the equator than at the poles. At the poles, the same amount of solar radiation hits at a greater angle, which brings less warmth. Based on latitude, Earth's surface is divided into three types of temperature zones **(Figure 2)**.

The tropical zone includes all of the locations on Earth that can possibly see the sun directly overhead. The polar zones extend from about 66.5° to 90°N and 66.5° to 90°S latitudes. Between them are the temperate zones. In summer, the sun's rays strike the temperate zones quite directly. In winter, the sun's rays strike at a lower angle.

**Altitude** In the case of high mountains, altitude is a more important climate factor than latitude. Near Earth's surface, temperature decreases as altitude increases. Thus, many mountainous areas have cooler climates than the lower areas around them.

# Math Toolbox

## Temperature and Altitude

For every 1-kilometer increase in altitude in the lower atmosphere, temperature decreases about 6.5°C.

**Analyze Proportional Relationships** A researcher releases a weather balloon to study the atmosphere. The air temperature at the ground is 27°C. If the sensors read an air temperature of 17°C, then about how far up has the balloon traveled?

.............................................................

**Distance from Large Bodies of Water** The ocean and other large bodies of water, such as lakes, can affect the weather and climate of nearby land by moderating local air temperatures. Water heats up and cools down about five times more slowly than land. As a result, the air above water heats up and cools down more slowly than air over land. When winds blow across oceans onto land, they moderate temperatures in coastal areas, bringing mild winters and cool summers. The centers of most continents, however, are too far from the ocean to be warmed or cooled by it. These areas have continental climates, with colder winters and warmer summers.

**Ocean Currents** Marine climates are strongly influenced by the temperature of nearby ocean currents—streams of water within the ocean that move in regular patterns caused by different amounts of solar energy striking Earth at different latitudes. As shown in **Figure 3**, most warm ocean currents move toward the poles. Conversely, cold water currents tend to move toward the equator. Cold currents affect climate by carrying cold water from the polar zones toward the equator, cooling local air masses.

READING CHECK **Determine Conclusions** How does the North Atlantic Drift most likely affect the climate in Europe?

..............................................................................

## Literacy Connection

**Integrate With Visuals**
Underline the text that relates to **Figure 3.** How does the image add to the information in the text?

..............................................

..............................................

### Major Ocean Currents

**Figure 3** Major currents circulate warm and cold ocean water between the poles and the equator. Compare and contrast the major ocean currents north and south of the equator.

..............................................

..............................................

..............................................

..............................................

..............................................

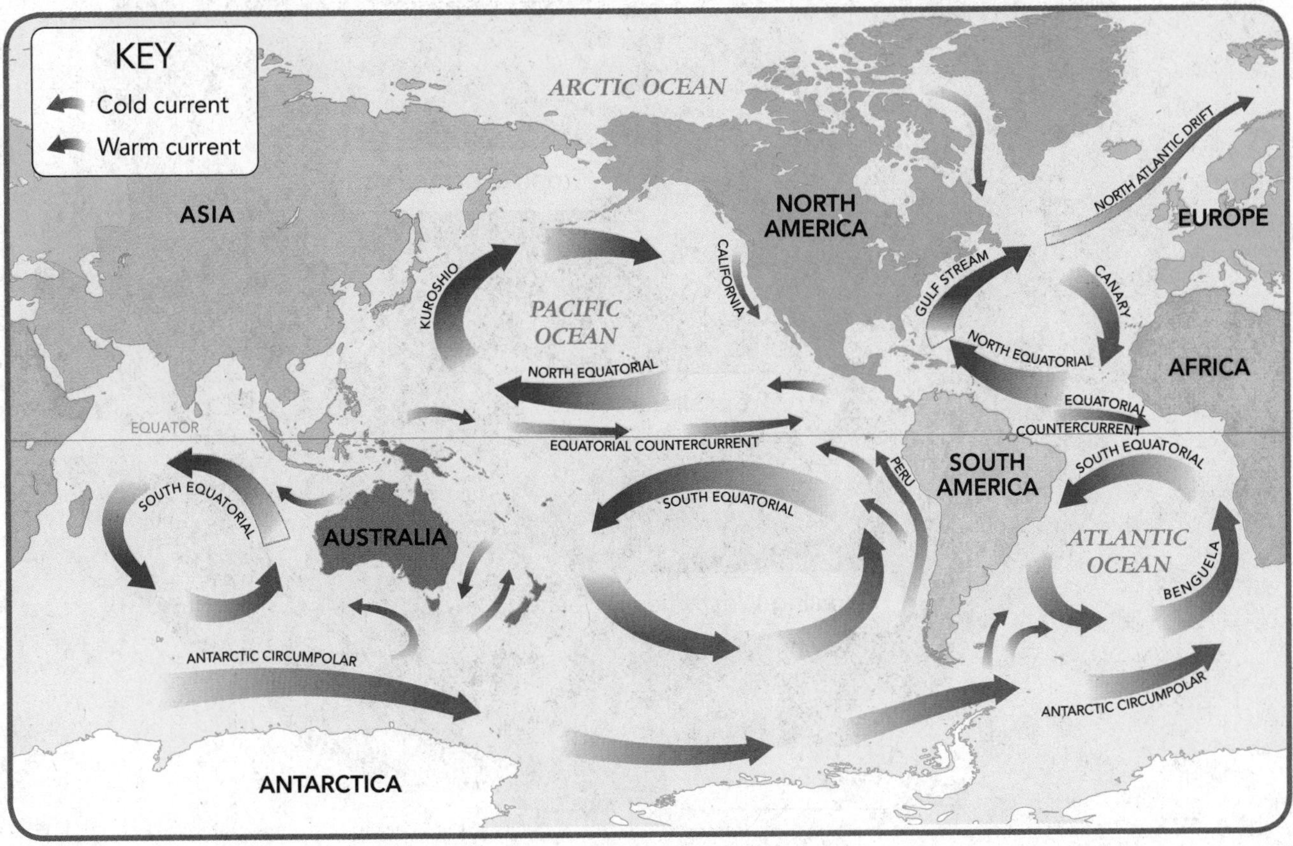
KEY
Cold current
Warm current
ARCTIC OCEAN
ASIA
NORTH AMERICA
EUROPE
AFRICA
SOUTH AMERICA
AUSTRALIA
ANTARCTICA
PACIFIC OCEAN
ATLANTIC OCEAN
EQUATOR
KUROSHIO
CALIFORNIA
NORTH ATLANTIC DRIFT
GULF STREAM
CANARY
NORTH EQUATORIAL
NORTH EQUATORIAL
EQUATORIAL COUNTERCURRENT
EQUATORIAL COUNTERCURRENT
SOUTH EQUATORIAL
SOUTH EQUATORIAL
SOUTH EQUATORIAL
PERU
BENGUELA
ANTARCTIC CIRCUMPOLAR
ANTARCTIC CIRCUMPOLAR

# INTERACTIVITY

Learn how topography affects precipitation in an area.

# VIDEO

Watch how ocean currents help to regulate the climate.

# Factors That Affect Precipitation

The amount of precipitation a particular area experiences from month to month and year to year can vary greatly. By analyzing the amount of precipitation an area has received over many years, meteorologists determine the average yearly precipitation for that area. The main factors that affect the amount of precipitation an area receives are prevailing winds, presence of mountains, and seasonal winds.

**Prevailing Winds** Prevailing winds are winds that usually blow in one direction over large distances on Earth. As shown in **Figure 4,** these winds are organized into belts that can move air masses with different temperatures and humidities over long distances. The amount of water vapor an air mass carries affects how much rain or snow it can produce.

## Prevailing Winds

**Figure 4** ✏ The globe shows Earth's prevailing global winds. Circle the name of the wind belt that most affects Europe.

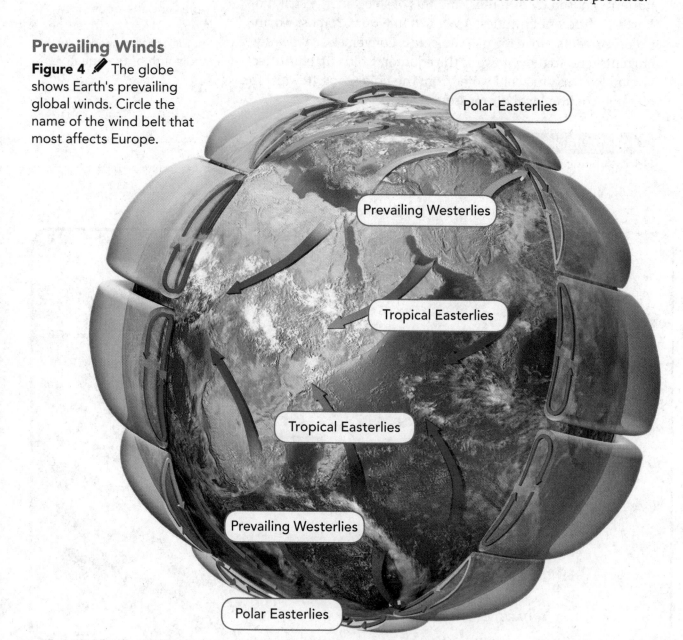

Polar Easterlies

Prevailing Westerlies

Tropical Easterlies

Tropical Easterlies

Prevailing Westerlies

Polar Easterlies

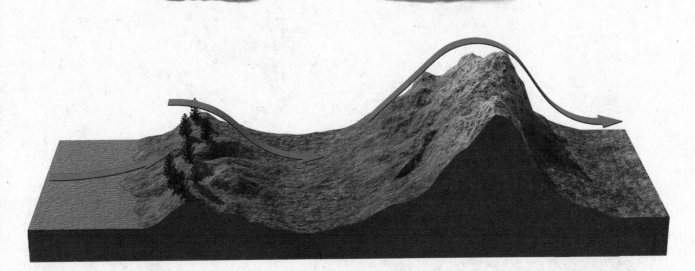

1. Warm, moist air is carried from the Pacific Ocean by the prevailing Westerlies.

2. Somewhat drier air continues to move eastward, rising along with the slope of the land.

3. Now dry air continues to move East after passing the mountains.

**Mountain Ranges** The presence of a mountain range can affect the type and location of precipitation any air masses may produce as they pass over the area **(Figure 5)**. Humid air masses blown in from the ocean are forced to rise as they encounter coastal mountains, producing clouds and precipitation on the side of the mountain facing the wind. After passing over the mountains, the air mass is drier, having lost much of its water vapor. This leaves the side of the mountain facing away from the wind in a rain shadow, where little precipitation falls.

**Seasonal Winds** A seasonal change in wind patterns and precipitation, called a monsoon, occurs in some parts of the world. Monsoons are caused by different rates of heating and cooling between the ocean and nearby land. During the summer in southern Asia, when the land gradually gets warmer than the ocean, warm and humid winds constantly blow in from the ocean, producing heavy rains. In winter, the opposite occurs as the land becomes colder than the ocean. Cool, dry winds constantly blow out to sea from the land.

**Mountains and Precipitation**

**Figure 5** 🖉 This image shows what happens when a mountain range is in the path of a prevailing wind. Draw rain and snow where they are most likely to occur. Add a redwood tree and a cactus in the locations that you think favor the growth of these plants.

 **INTERACTIVITY**

Demonstrate how the atmosphere and ocean circulations affect climate.

✅ READING CHECK **Integrate With Visuals** If the area shown in Figure 5 were located in a region where monsoons occur, would the figure represent a summer monsoon or a winter monsoon? Explain.

.........................................................................................................................

.........................................................................................................................

.........................................................................................................................

## Major Climates

**Figure 6** ✏ The locations of major climate regions covering Earth's surface are influenced by many factors. Draw a circle around the area on the map where you live. What type of climate exists where you live?

..............................................

..............................................

..............................................

..............................................

..............................................

..............................................

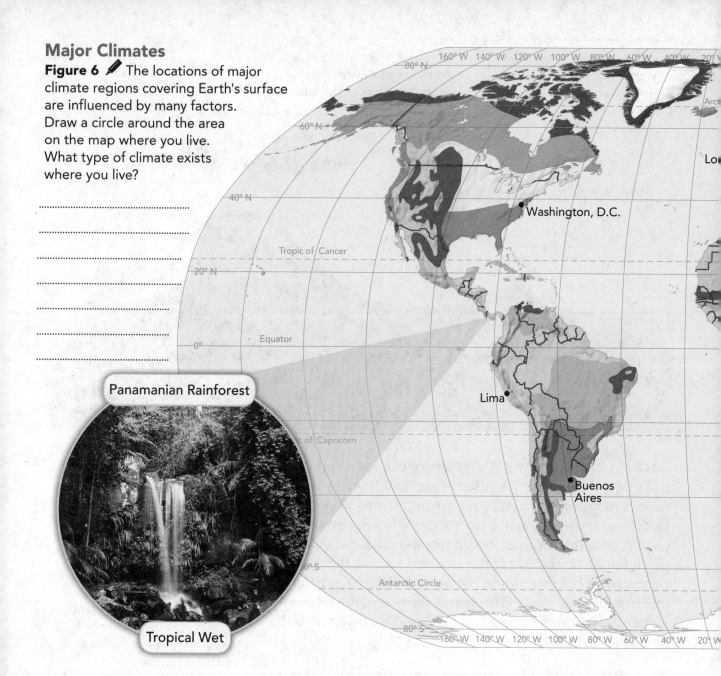

Panamanian Rainforest

Tropical Wet

Washington, D.C.

Lima

Buenos Aires

## HANDS-ON LAB

▸**Investigate** Use graphs to classify locations by their climate regions.

# World Climates

Imagine winning a vacation to the Australian Outback! The Outback is a region near the central area of Australia. What type of clothes should you take on the trip? The best way to find out is to learn more about your destination's climate.

**Classifying Climates** Scientists classify climates by taking into account an area's average temperature, average annual precipitation, and the vegetation found growing there. The major climate regions of Earth each have their own smaller subdivisions **(Figure 6)**. Recall that local climates can be affected by changes in natural climate factors, such as ocean currents and winds. Human activities that affect the atmosphere and ocean can also impact local climates. So Earth's climate regions can change over time.

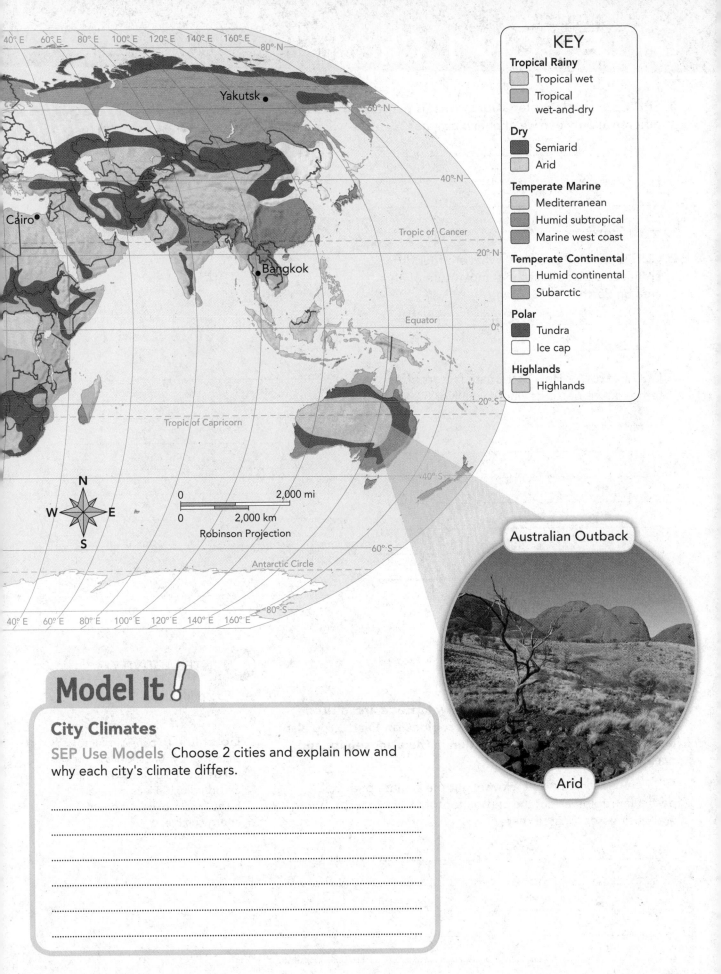

## KEY

**Tropical Rainy**
- Tropical wet
- Tropical wet-and-dry

**Dry**
- Semiarid
- Arid

**Temperate Marine**
- Mediterranean
- Humid subtropical
- Marine west coast

**Temperate Continental**
- Humid continental
- Subarctic

**Polar**
- Tundra
- Ice cap

**Highlands**
- Highlands

Australian Outback

Arid

# Model It

## City Climates

SEP Use Models Choose 2 cities and explain how and why each city's climate differs.

MS-ESS2-6

**1. SEP Construct Explanations** What is the difference between weather and climate?

........................................................

........................................................

........................................................

........................................................

**2. CCC Cause and Effect** What are four different factors that affect the temperature of an area on Earth?

........................................................

........................................................

**3. CCC Patterns** How do climate factors affect temperature patterns where you live?

........................................................

........................................................

........................................................

........................................................

........................................................

........................................................

........................................................

**4. SEP Use Models** How do you think the Gulf Stream influences the climate of northern Europe?

Gulf Stream

........................................................

........................................................

........................................................

........................................................

........................................................

........................................................

........................................................

........................................................

........................................................

# Quest CHECK-IN

**In this lesson, you learned about how latitude and altitude can affect the climate of different regions on Earth. You also learned how patterns of circulation in the atmosphere and ocean affect climate.**

CCC Cause and Effect How might the climate of a particular region affect the carbon footprint of homes, schools, and businesses located there?

........................................................

........................................................

........................................................

........................................................

## INTERACTIVITY

Footprint Steps

**Go online** to consider factors that affect your school's energy usage and calculate how much carbon dioxide was released by your school based on its energy usage.

# Urban Heat Islands

For years, people have observed that cities are often much warmer than less-developed surrounding areas—even at night. Scientists can now precisely measure this phenomenon, which they call the urban heat island effect.

Many of the materials used to build cities absorb a great deal of sunlight, which causes them to become warmer. This makes surface temperatures in many cities higher than they would be if the environment consisted of trees and soil instead of asphalt, granite, and glass. For example, surface temperatures in Providence, Rhode Island, are about 12°C (22°F) warmer than in surrounding towns that are less developed.

As you have probably noticed when walking across a parking lot on a sunny day, the hot surface warms the air above it. This is why the heat island effect can make a city's downtown air feel as hot at night as it was during the day. All the thermal energy absorbed by the streets and buildings during the day is radiated back out into the air at night.

## MY DISCOVERY

Search *urban heat island* in an online search engine and find out about the ways that cities are attempting to reduce the effects of this phenomenon.

**Phenomenon** Satellite images showing temperatures in Providence and the surrounding area (top) and land development (bottom). In the top image, the lighter color indicates warmer areas, while the darker color indicates colder areas.

457

# (2) Climate Change

## Guiding Questions

- What effects do greenhouse gases in the atmosphere have on global temperatures?
- How do natural processes and human activities affect patterns of change in global temperatures?

## Connections

**Literacy** Cite Textual Evidence

**Math** Reason Quantitatively

MS-ESS3-5

## HANDS-ON LAB

**uInvestigate** Model and observe the greenhouse effect in action.

## Vocabulary

greenhouse gas
greenhouse
  effect
climate change
global warming
fossil fuel

## Academic Vocabulary

impact

## Connect It!

✏️ **Label the image with a "W" where you predict the air would be warmer and a "C" where you predict the air would be cooler.**

SEP Construct Explanations Why do these areas have different air temperatures?

........................................................................................

........................................................................................

........................................................................................

# Studying Earth's Climate

Earth has an amazing variety of climates, from the dry, cold polar regions to the wet, hot tropics. Scientists study climates to better understand how the atmosphere, water, land masses, and solar energy all interact within a climate. They look at causes of changes in climates in the past and predict how climates may change in the future.

**Greenhouse Effect** While the differences between climates may seem extreme, Earth's overall climate patterns remain fairly stable compared to conditions in space. This is because of gases in the atmosphere, which help to regulate energy in the system.

The greenhouse in **Figure 1** absorbs thermal energy from the sun to warm the air inside. Gardeners add water and soil to create the special climate conditions the plants inside the greenhouse need to survive. Certain gases in the atmosphere, called **greenhouse gases**, such as water vapor, carbon dioxide, methane, and nitrous oxide, absorb much of the heat leaving Earth's surface. The **greenhouse effect** is the process by which these gases trap heat, keeping Earth warm. Without greenhouse gases, thermal energy would radiate from Earth's surface and escape directly into space, making our planet too cold to support life.

**INTERACTIVITY**

Investigate the different greenhouse gases in Earth's atmosphere.

**Reflect** Does the climate in which you live remain relatively stable? In your science notebook, describe the how patterns in your climate stay the same or change over time.

## Trapping the Sun's Energy

**Figure 1** The glass of this greenhouse in Brazil lets sunlight in and keeps the warmed air from escaping.

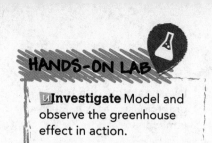

## Earth's Climate History

By studying the data from yearly climate patterns in an area, scientists can observe that some years are cooler and wetter, while others are hotter and drier. However, how do scientists study the climate of the distant past? Scientists use a wide variety of methods to gather data about past conditions.

Fossils found in an area not only indicate organisms living in the past, but what conditions were like. Fossils of warm-weather plants found in Antarctica suggest that, at some time earlier, Antarctica's climate was much warmer. Rock deposits from glaciers in now-warm regions suggest colder conditions.

Scientists collect ice cores by drilling down through layers of ice, sometimes kilometers thick. The ice cores, which look like glass rods, contain air bubbles and particles such as volcanic ash, sea salt, and dust. By analyzing these materials, scientists can reconstruct climate factors in Earth's past and how they have changed. Similarly, the growth rings of trees record climate conditions as the tree lived and grew each year. The tree rings shown in **Figure 2** show how events and climate conditions in the past shaped the tree's growth.

**Climate change** is a sudden or gradual change in Earth's climate. By studying Earth's climate history in the past, scientists can better understand how conditions change over time, and the effects of gradual or sudden climate changes.

## Model It!

### Climate History in Tree Rings

**Figure 2** The growth rings of trees record data about climate conditions during the tree's life.

**SEP Develop Models** Consider the growth of a tree during a period of time when the climate conditions were cold and dry over several years, and then conditions changed and the climate became warmer and wetter. Draw a model of the tree rings to represent these conditions. Label the rings representing the different climate conditions.

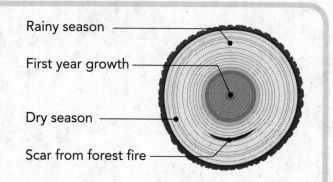

Rainy season

First year growth

Dry season

Scar from forest fire

## Natural Processes
Evidence shows that the overall climate of Earth has changed in the past, both gradually and suddenly. Natural processes that affect climate and may cause climate change include the movements of continents, fluctuations in solar radiation, and volcanic eruptions that disturb the atmosphere.

Recall that landmasses and bodies of water are factors that regulate climate. Earth's continents gradually shift and move. As the size and position of continents and oceans have changed, so too has the climate. This process occurs very slowly, and continues to this day.

Significant climate changes in the past resulted from fluctuations in solar radiation. Like all stars, our sun goes through cycles of energy production. The energy output of the sun varies, as does Earth's tilt and orbit around the sun. Small changes over large periods of time can have big impacts on the climate.

Volcanic eruptions may cause sudden changes in climate by disturbing the atmosphere. In the past, major eruptions have caused short-term global cooling when ash and aerosol particles, or tiny particles suspended in gas, temporarily blocked solar energy. Some scientists theorize that large-scale volcanic eruptions could cause long-term warming by releasing massive amounts of greenhouse gases into the atmosphere.

### Volcanic Eruptions
**Figure 3** The eruption of Mount Pinatubo in 1991 caused the global temperature to drop 1°F for nearly two years.

CCC Cause and Effect ✏️
Label the picture with different substances released by the volcano that could impact climate change.

**Ice Ages** The most researched examples of dramatic climate change in Earth's past are ice ages. During these periods, Earth's climate was 5 to 15 degrees Celsius cooler, causing huge glaciers to extend well beyond the ice caps. Scientists have used evidence from cores of ice and the ocean floor to estimate that there have been about 40 cooling cycles in the past 2.5 million years.

Variations in the tilt of Earth's axis and orbit around the sun occur at regular intervals, and this can **impact** climate. A mathematician named Milutin Milankovitch discovered the pattern. Every 40,000 to 100,000 years, variations in Earth's tilt and orbit result in a period of unusually cool summers in the Northern Hemisphere. Milankovitch theorized the lack of snow melt in the cool summer caused a build-up of reflective ice and snow. This, in turn reflected solar energy even more, causing the cooling trend to escalate. The most recent ice age, which ended about 10,000 years ago, coincided with one of these intervals in which Earth received and retained less energy from sunlight.

### Academic Vocabulary

What are some familiar words that are similar in meaning to *impact*?

..............................................

..............................................

..............................................

☑ READING CHECK **Cite Textual Evidence** How do scientists gather information about climate conditions millions of years ago?

.........................................................................................

.........................................................................................

# Math Toolbox

## Ice Age Cooling Cycles

The graph shows cooling and warming cycles that have occurred during the past 425,000 years on Earth.

**1. Reason Quantitatively** 🖉
Circle areas on the graph where you think the ice ages occurred.

**2. CCC Stability and Change** What do the data in the graph indicate about the stability of Earth's climate?

..............................................

..............................................

..............................................

..............................................

..............................................

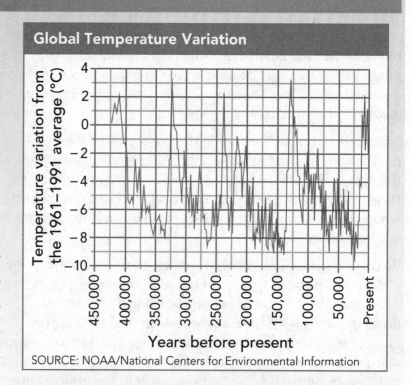

**Global Temperature Variation**

SOURCE: NOAA/National Centers for Environmental Information

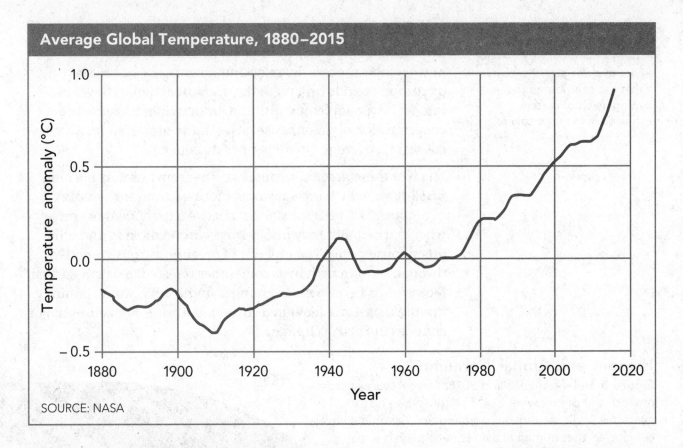

**Average Global Temperature, 1880–2015**

Temperature anomaly (°C) vs Year

SOURCE: NASA

# Recent Climate Change

Evidence of Earth's past suggests that most climate change takes place over long periods of time—thousands or even tens of thousands of years. However, over the past century, scientists studying the climate have observed a clear and alarming trend in the data. Global surface temperature measurements from the past 140 years indicate that the average global temperature has been rising. This gradual increase in temperature is called **global warming**.

In addition to measuring average temperature changes, scientists also gather data about the concentration of greenhouse gases, such as carbon dioxide and methane, in the atmosphere. They also measure changes in annual Arctic sea ice coverage and overall sea levels around the world. All of these data suggest that global warming is occurring at a surprisingly fast rate.

In the Earth's overall geologic timescale, massive climate changes that happen over millions of years have different causes and different impacts on the planet. Even small changes can have a huge impact on Earth when they happen in such a short amount of time. The graph in **Figure 4** measures temperature changes in only the past 140 years. By studying Earth's climate past, scientists hope to predict some of the impacts of the current climate change.

**Global Temperature Change**

**Figure 4** ✏ The graph represents how the average global temperature each year has deviated from a historical norm (shown as 0.0 on the y-axis). Circle the 20-year interval on the graph that shows the most rapid increase in temperature.

**Literacy Connection**

**Cite Textual Evidence** As you read, underline evidence in the text that you think supports the central idea that recent data show a rapid rise in global temperatures.

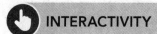
INTERACTIVITY

Examine one human activity that has contributed to the rising levels of carbon dioxide in the atmosphere.

**Human Activities** Human activities, some of which are shown in **Figure 5**, change Earth's surface faster than any geologic process. By releasing greenhouse gases, such as carbon dioxide and methane, human activities have an impact on global temperatures. Our activities increase the concentration of greenhouse gases in the atmosphere, which causes the average global temperature to rise.

Much of these greenhouse gases come from humans burning **fossil fuels**, which are substances formed from the remains of organisms. These substances release a great deal of energy when burned. But they also release carbon dioxide and other greenhouse gases. The amount of greenhouse gases emitted through human activity is sometimes referred to as our carbon footprint. When we make changes to the land, water, or air around us, we are leaving a carbon footprint that causes major changes in Earth's climate.

## Humans and Global Warming

**Figure 5** Between 2012 and 2016, temperatures across most of the planet were 2–4°F warmer than historical averages (indicated by red on the map). Scientists have concluded that human activities have played a major role in these temperature changes.

**SEP Engage in Argument** As you read, identify examples of evidence to support the claims made about the human causes of global warming.

**Agriculture** Raising livestock, producing feed for them, and managing waste produced from agriculture contribute to greenhouse gas emissions, such as nitrous oxide and methane. It is estimated nearly 9 percent of all greenhouse gas emissions in the United States come from agricultural activities.

Evidence

....................................................................

....................................................................

....................................................................

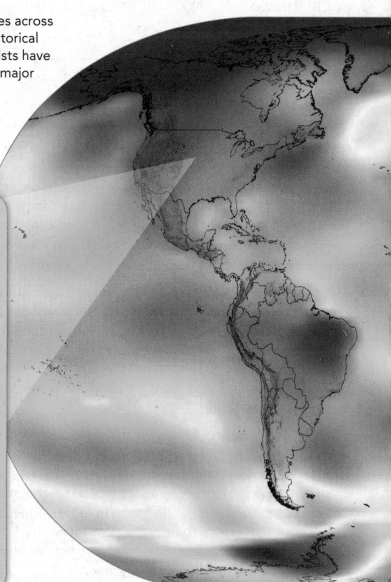

**Mining and Burning Fossil Fuels** For years, fossil fuels, such as coal and petroleum, have powered factories, automobiles, and trains. Chemists have used petroleum to develop revolutionary plastics. However, the mining and burning of fossil fuels have released more greenhouse gases into the atmosphere in the past 150 years than in any other time in human history.

Evidence
.......................................................
.......................................................
.......................................................

**Industry** Industries do not only burn fossil fuels to manufacture and transport goods. They also produce some materials that result in greenhouse gas emissions. Manufacturing processes, such as making cement, produce carbon dioxide from certain chemical reactions that are used to process raw materials.

Evidence
.......................................................
.......................................................
.......................................................

**Deforestation** Trees play an important role in regulating climate by naturally absorbing carbon dioxide from the air for photosynthesis. Removing trees for logging, agriculture, or development results in more carbon dioxide in the atmosphere.

Evidence
.......................................................
.......................................................
.......................................................

Temperature Difference (Fahrenheit)

–4 –3 –2 –1 0 1 2 3 4

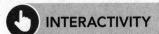

**INTERACTIVITY**

Determine if natural causes can explain the climate change occurring in Antarctica.

## Carbon Dioxide Concentrations

Carbon, like other forms of matter such as water, moves through the land and ocean in a natural cycle. Photosynthetic organisms absorb carbon dioxide from the atmosphere. That carbon is stored and used through life processes until it is released again as carbon dioxide into the atmosphere. Because carbon dioxide is a greenhouse gas, its levels in the atmosphere regulate Earth's global temperature. If there is very little carbon dioxide in the atmosphere, then Earth will not retain enough solar energy to have a stable climate. When carbon dioxide levels are high, global temperatures can rise.

Carbon dioxide concentrations in the atmosphere are constantly being exchanged through natural processes, absorbed by Earth's oceans and locked up in the biosphere in substances such as fossil fuels. Human activities in the past century have upset the balance of these processes. As a result, they have directly impacted the rising concentrations of carbon dioxide in the atmosphere, as shown in **Figure 6**.

## Carbon Dioxide Concentrations

**Figure 6** The graph shows levels of carbon dioxide in the atmosphere during the last 400,000 years.

SEP Develop Models ✎ Draw a line across the graph at 300 ppm. What does this line represent?

.............................................................

.............................................................

.............................................................

.............................................................

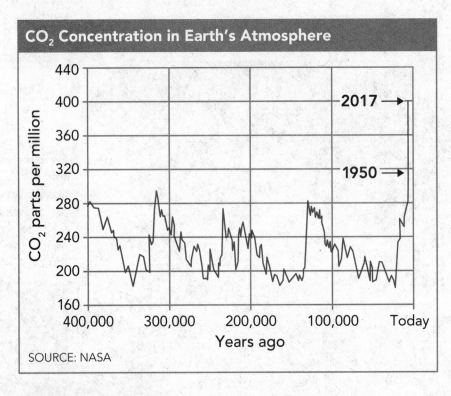

**READING CHECK** **Integrate with Visuals** Study the graph in **Figure 6**. How have human activities affected concentrations of carbon dioxide in the atmosphere?

.............................................................

.............................................................

.............................................................

.............................................................

# ☑LESSON 2 Check

1. **CCC Communicate Information** What are greenhouse gases? List examples.

.......................................................................
.......................................................................
.......................................................................
.......................................................................
.......................................................................

2. **CCC Cause and Effect** How have variations in Earth's tilt and orbit affected its climate conditions in the past?

.......................................................................
.......................................................................
.......................................................................
.......................................................................
.......................................................................

3. **CCC Patterns** What patterns of climate change have scientists observed in the past?

.......................................................................
.......................................................................
.......................................................................
.......................................................................

4. **SEP Interpret Data** How do scientists use changes in carbon dioxide concentrations as evidence that human activities affect Earth's climate?

.......................................................................
.......................................................................
.......................................................................

5. **SEP Ask Questions** How could scientists collect data about the impact of deforestation on global warming?

.......................................................................
.......................................................................
.......................................................................
.......................................................................

6. **CCC Stability and Change** Why has the concentration of carbon dioxide been increasing so rapidly since the 1950s?

.......................................................................
.......................................................................
.......................................................................
.......................................................................

# Quest CHECK-IN

In this lesson, you learned how different natural and human factors interact with one another to affect climate change. You observed data showing how human activities release greenhouse gases that have caused the rise in global temperatures.

**SEP Evaluate Information** Why is it important to consider your school's carbon footprint when making day-to-day decisions about energy use and waste production?

.......................................................................
.......................................................................
.......................................................................

## HANDS-ON LAB

Energy Savings at School

**Do the hands-on lab** to conduct a school energy audit and identify ways for your school to save energy.

MS-LS2-5

# THE CARBON CYCLE

Every year, 120 gigatons of carbon are taken up by plants and other photosynthetic organisms on land. In turn, 60 gigatons are released into the atmosphere by those organisms through respiration. The other 60 gigatons are released by microbes through decomposition. This cycle is detailed in the diagram. Numbers in parentheses represent estimated stores of carbon. These include trees and other plants, seafloor sediments, and carbon in the atmosphere that does not cycle through the biosphere or hydrosphere. It also includes carbon that is locked underground in coal, petroleum, and natural gas. These stores do not enter the carbon cycle until humans mine and burn them.

Human activities that add carbon to the cycle are represented by red numbers. For example, land-use, burning fossil fuels, and cement production add a total of 9 gigatons of carbon to the atmosphere every year.

Like the terrestrial part of the carbon cycle, the marine part is relatively balanced. Ninety gigatons of carbon are exchanged between the ocean and atmosphere through photosynthesis, respiration, and the decomposition of marine organisms. Two of the 9 gigatons of carbon that humans add to the atmosphere are taken up by the ocean.

The 6,000 gigatons of carbon in sediments stored in the ocean floor are made up of substances that contain frozen methane. These solids, called methane hydrates, can melt into methane gas and water if the temperature of the ocean floor rises. Microbes then convert the methane into carbon dioxide. The carbon dioxide will dissolve into the water and eventually move into the atmosphere.

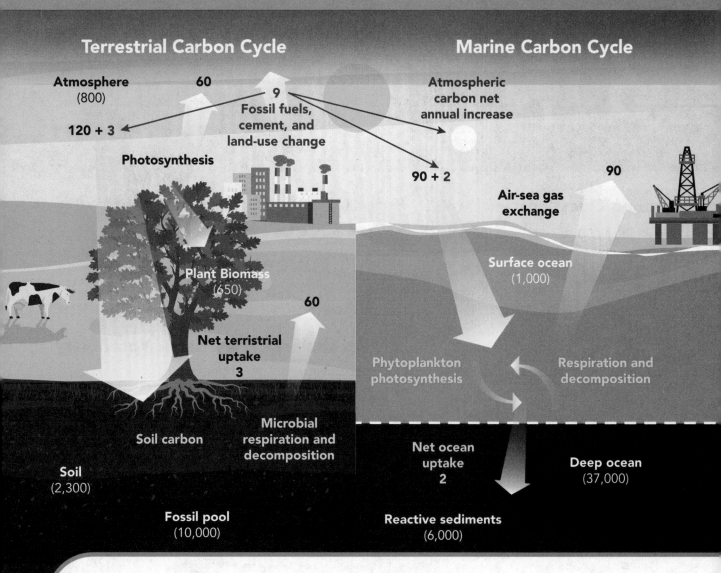

## Terrestrial Carbon Cycle

Atmosphere
(800)

60

9
Fossil fuels,
cement, and
land-use change

120 + 3

Photosynthesis

Plant Biomass
(650)

60

Net terristrial
uptake
3

Soil carbon

Microbial
respiration and
decomposition

Soil
(2,300)

Fossil pool
(10,000)

## Marine Carbon Cycle

Atmospheric
carbon net
annual increase

90 + 2

90

Air-sea gas
exchange

Surface ocean
(1,000)

Phytoplankton
photosynthesis

Respiration and
decomposition

Net ocean
uptake
2

Deep ocean
(37,000)

Reactive sediments
(6,000)

**Study the diagram to answer the following questions.**

1. **SEP Use Mathematics** What is the net annual increase in atmospheric
   carbon dioxide? To calculate the answer, follow the movement
   of the 9 gigatons of carbon released by human activity.
   Fill in the empty circle on the diagram.

2. **CCC System Models** How much of the carbon released
   by human activity ends up being taken up by photosynthesis
   on land?

   ...................................................................................................................

3. **SEP Construct Explanations** What do you think will happen to
   ocean floor sediments if the atmosphere and ocean continue
   to warm?

   ...................................................................................................................
   ...................................................................................................................
   ...................................................................................................................
   ...................................................................................................................

# LESSON 3

# Effects of a Changing Climate

## Guiding Questions

- How do changes in global temperatures impact natural systems on Earth?
- What can be done to mitigate climate change and its effects?

## Connections

**Literacy** Support Author's Claim

**Math** Represent Quantitative Relationships

MS-ESS3-5

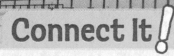

## HANDS-ON LAB

**Investigate** Model the effects of thermal expansion on water.

### Vocabulary

cascade effect
alternative
energy

### Academic Vocabulary

argument

## Connect It!

✎ **Look closely at the city's coastline. Imagine if the level of the water rose by three meters. Draw a line where the new water level would be.**

CCC Cause and Effect How would the lives of the people in this city be affected if the water level rose?

...................................................................................................................

...................................................................................................................

...................................................................................................................

# Impact of Rising Temperatures

Earth's climate is a complex system, acting in ways that scientists can't always predict. There is some **argument** among scientists about how much human activities have impacted global temperatures. However, scientists are certain that global warming will affect our planet in a number of significant ways. Warming temperatures result in changing weather patterns and new environmental conditions in which organisms must adapt quickly or perish.

Humans are vulnerable to the changes that are occurring and will continue to occur as a result of global warming. Millions of people across the United States live in coastal communities, such as downtown Miami in **Figure 1.** Rising sea levels around the world threaten people's homes, businesses, and lives.

Humans have played a role in causing climate change. Some climate models predict global temperatures will continue to rise several more degrees over the next century. We can play an important role in Earth's climate history by trying to reduce our impact on climate change and to minimize its effects.

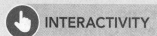

**INTERACTIVITY**

Identify an everyday action you can take to reduce your impact on climate change.

**Academic Vocabulary**

How is a scientific argument different from a fight or disagreement?

......................................

......................................

......................................

......................................

**Rising Sea Levels**

**Figure 1** Downtown Miami, Florida, stands right where land and water meet.

**Figure 2** By 2100, sea levels are expected to rise by about 1 meter. In the next 600 years, sea levels are predicted to rise at least 6 meters.

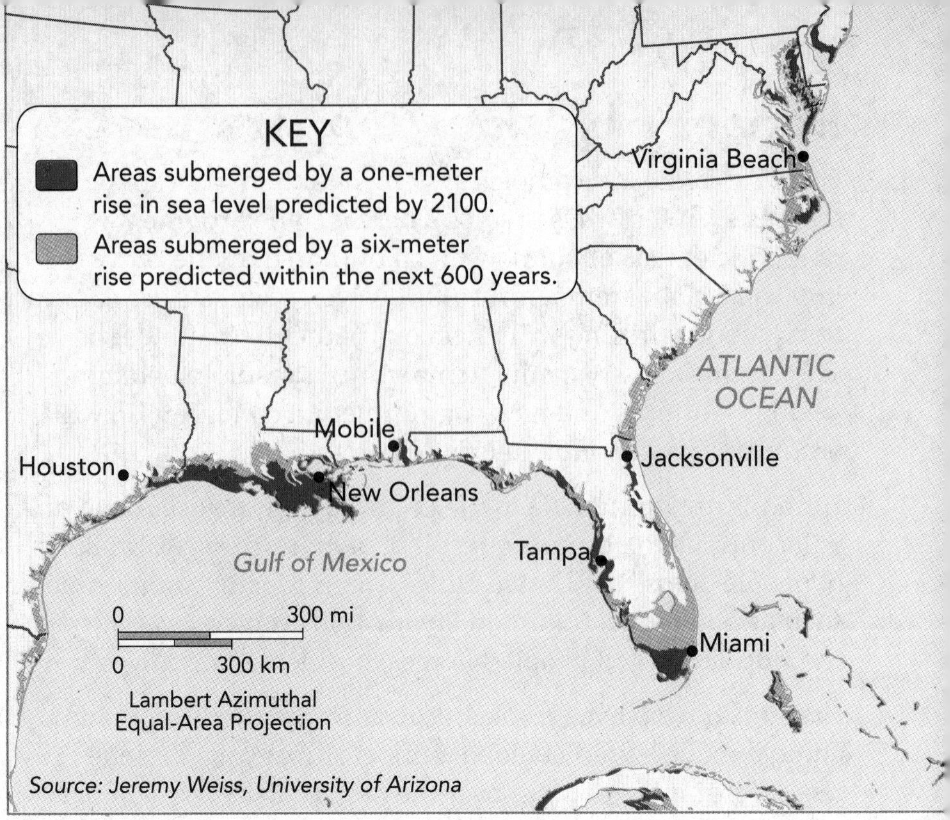

**CCC Cause and Effect** Why is a city like New Orleans especially vulnerable to rising sea levels?

.............................................................

.............................................................

.............................................................

.............................................................

.............................................................

.............................................................

## Literacy Connection

**Support Author's Claim**
As you read, underline evidence in the text that you think supports the author's claim that rising sea levels are a result of global warming.

**KEY**
- Areas submerged by a one-meter rise in sea level predicted by 2100.
- Areas submerged by a six-meter rise predicted within the next 600 years.

Virginia Beach

ATLANTIC OCEAN

Mobile

Houston

New Orleans

Jacksonville

Gulf of Mexico

Tampa

Miami

0       300 mi

0       300 km

Lambert Azimuthal
Equal-Area Projection

Source: Jeremy Weiss, University of Arizona

**Rising Sea Levels** Approximately 71 percent of Earth's surface is covered with water. Most of that water is oceans, but up to two percent of that water is stored as sea ice, glaciers, and permanent snow. The polar regions are particularly vulnerable to global warming because even slight increases in temperature cause huge areas of stored ice to melt and flow into Earth's oceans. As global temperatures rise, so does the global sea level.

Glaciers, huge areas of ice in mountain regions, store fresh water in the form of solid ice. Scientists studying glaciers over the past 50 years observe not only that glaciers are retreating as temperatures rise, but the rate at which they melt is steadily increasing. Melting glaciers carry massive amounts of fresh water and sediment from the land to the ocean. Alaska's glaciers have lost nearly 50 gigatons of ice each year since 2003.

Rising sea levels have devastating effects on coastal areas. In the past century, the global sea level has risen approximately 20 centimeters (8 inches). Low-lying land areas near the coast would be completely submerged in ocean water, resulting in habitat loss for humans and wildlife. The map in **Figure 2** illustrates areas in North America that would be completely submerged by rising sea levels over the next 100 years. Scientists estimate Earth's sea level has risen more than 120 meters (about 394 feet) since the last ice age, and will continue to rise.

**Polar Regions Under Threat** In addition to causing a rise in global sea levels, melting conditions in polar regions appear to have set off a chain reaction of other negative climate effects. Higher temperatures allow the atmosphere above the ice caps to hold more water vapor, which acts as a greenhouse gas. The loss of reflective ice covering the northern ocean also allows solar energy to be absorbed by ocean waters, increasing temperatures even more.

Scientists are now observing unexpected side-effects of global warming in arctic and tundra climates. Near Earth's polar regions, a thin layer of soil supports plant life during the brief summer thaw, while the soil below, called permafrost, is frozen year-round. As rising global temperatures melt permafrost, decomposing plant matter that has been covered for thousands of years releases carbon dioxide and methane gases. The concentration of these greenhouse gases increases in the atmosphere, which further accelerates global warming.

**HANDS-ON LAB**

**Investigate** Model the effects of thermal expansion on water.

## Math Toolbox

### Rising Sea Levels

Since 1993, NASA uses satellites to monitor sea level changes caused by melting land ice and the expansion of sea water as it warms.

| Sea Level Changes Observed By Satellite | |
|---|---|
| **Year** | **Sea Height Variation (mm)** |
| 1995 | 6 mm |
| 2000 | 26 mm |
| 2005 | 42 mm |
| 2010 | 58 mm |
| 2015 | 80 mm |

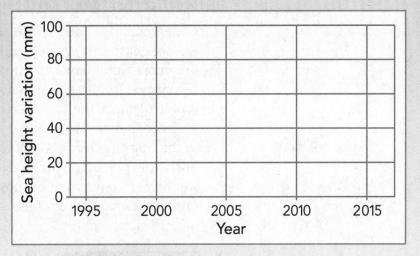

1. **Represent Quantitative Relationships** ✏ Create a line graph of the data in the table.

2. **CCC Cause and Effect** How does your graph provide evidence of rising sea levels? What are some factors that may be causing this phenomenon?

.................................................................................

.................................................................................

.................................................................................

## Adapt or Perish

All living organisms have adaptations to survive in their environments. These adaptations usually develop over very long periods of time as organisms thrive or perish. When conditions in an environment change rapidly, organisms must adapt or move into new locations for food. As global warming accelerates, mass die-offs are predicted.

Global warming has a **cascade effect**, an unforeseen chain of events caused by a disturbance in a system, on Earth's organisms. Scientists estimate 75 percent of the world's coral reefs are under threat due to rising ocean temperatures. Certain types of algae necessary for the survival of reef-building coral are affected by rising temperatures, causing coral to lose all its coloring in a process called bleaching. Entire reefs can die off due to coral bleaching, resulting in the destruction of habitats and many more negative impacts.

## Extreme Weather Change

Global warming refers to the overall warming of Earth's temperatures, but it may not mean all areas of Earth experience warmer conditions. Parts of Earth, such as Europe, could start to experience colder temperatures because of disturbed ocean currents. The world's oceans act as a conveyor belt, circulating cold water from the poles and warm water from the equator. Due to melting ice, that process is gradually being disrupted, and it could prevent ocean currents from stabilizing global climates.

Global climate changes also have cascading effects on regional weather patterns. Warmer temperatures result in more energy and more water vapor in the atmosphere. This can make heat waves hotter, flooding heavier, and severe storms more powerful. Since the 1980s, scientists have measured an increase in both the frequency and intensity of hurricanes in the Atlantic Ocean. If the trend continues, they predict hurricane potential will increase 20 percent by 2100. Extreme weather changes, such as those shown in **Figure 3**, cause property damage, loss of life, and sometimes permanently alter the landscape.

**READING CHECK** **Support Author's Claim** What evidence does the author provide to support the idea that global temperatures and organisms' adaptations are connected?

...................................................................................................

...................................................................................................

...................................................................................................

...................................................................................................

...................................................................................................

## Cascading Effects of Climate Change

**Figure 3** For every change in climate, there are cascading effects for ecosystems and organisms trying to adapt to the changes.

**CCC Cause and Effect** Read each image caption describing a phenomenon caused by climate change. Identify possible cascading effects of each phenomenon.

Disruptions in precipitation patterns cause heat waves and droughts.

Global warming causes atmosphere changes that lead to more extreme storms and flooding.

Effects:
.........................................................................
.........................................................................
.........................................................................

Effects:
.........................................................................
.........................................................................
.........................................................................

Rising ocean temperatures cause coral bleaching when vital algae die off.

Effects:
.........................................................................
.........................................................................
.........................................................................

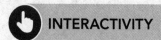

**INTERACTIVITY**

Examine the effects of industrialization on levels of carbon dioxide in the atmosphere.

# Dealing with Climate Change

The effects of climate change may look grim, but there are many ways humans can alter their behaviors to reduce or counteract the increasingly harmful effects of global warming. Scientists, lawmakers, engineers, and other creative minds are working together to find new solutions to reduce the extent of climate change and human vulnerability to its effects. Because these changes have accumulated over time, it will also take time to slow or reverse the effects.

**Alternative Energy** Human activities require energy, and 91 percent of all greenhouse gases emitted by human activities comes from burning fossil fuels. By developing **alternative energy**, or clean energy sources that do not come from fossil fuels, we can reduce the mining and burning of fossil fuels. This will greatly reduce the levels of greenhouse gases being released into the atmosphere. Alternative energy sources such as solar, wind, geothermal, and tidal power do not require fossil fuels and have no greenhouse gas emissions.

**Energy-Efficient Technologies** In addition to developing new sources of energy, we can focus on developing more efficient technologies. In the short term, these technologies might reduce emissions and reliance on traditional forms of energy. And for long-term solutions, engineers might develop technology that changes how we consume energy—from batteries powered by nitrogen in the air to new super-efficient hybrid cars.

# Design it !

### Adapting for Climate Change
Through careful design and consideration of energy use, we can reduce our impact on global climate change, while adapting to the changes already occurring.

**SEP Design Solutions** 🖊
Develop a design for a house that sits on beachfront property. Consider ways to use alternative energy and energy-efficient technologies. The design must also allow for the house to withstand the effects of a rising sea level.

**Engineering New Solutions** Reducing carbon emissions may not be enough to slow climate change. Many scientists think a proactive approach of removing carbon from the atmosphere may be needed. Using nature as a guide, engineers are developing ways to remove carbon dioxide from the atmosphere. This is done through using the natural process of photosynthesis to remove carbon dioxide from the air, or filtering carbon directly and storing it underground. Other engineers are working on solutions to help deal with the effects of climate change by helping communities be less vulnerable to effects such as rising sea levels.

**The Role of Government** Realizing that climate change is a global issue, governments from nations around the world have been coming together to discuss evidence and make plans to wisely counteract global warming. In 2012, the Solomon Islands **(Figure 4)** led the world by passing a comprehensive climate change policy in response to the challenges they are already facing.

Following the example of tiny nations in crisis, over 190 nations joined together in 2016 to commit to controlling greenhouse gas emissions. The Paris Climate Agreement, as it is called, outlines long-term goals and legislation to unite the world in mitigating climate change. By understanding climate science and making informed decisions, people and their governments can reduce human vulnerability to a changing planet.

**Disappearing Islands**
**Figure 4** In recent years, some of the small islands that make up the Solomon Islands have been lost to rising sea levels.

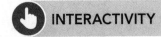

**INTERACTIVITY**

Help a city planner determine how to reduce emissions.

---

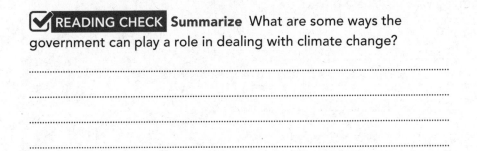 **READING CHECK** **Summarize** What are some ways the government can play a role in dealing with climate change?

.......................................................................................

.......................................................................................

.......................................................................................

.......................................................................................

1. **Identify** What factors are contributing to rising sea levels?

.................................................................

.................................................................

.................................................................

.................................................................

2. **Compare and Contrast** How are localized droughts and increased flooding both related to global warming?

.................................................................

.................................................................

.................................................................

.................................................................

.................................................................

3. **CCC Cause and Effect** What impact does climate change have on organisms that are well-adapted to their environments?

.................................................................

.................................................................

.................................................................

.................................................................

4. **SEP Analyze Systems** What are some possible cascade effects of the melting of sea ice in the Arctic Ocean due to global warming?

.................................................................

.................................................................

.................................................................

5. **Describe** How could using alternative energy sources help slow the process of global warming?

.................................................................

.................................................................

.................................................................

6. **SEP Construct Arguments** How might national governments have a positive impact on the world's climate change crisis?

.................................................................

.................................................................

.................................................................

.................................................................

.................................................................

## Quest CHECK-IN

In this lesson, you learned about the effects of climate change. You explored ways that people and governments are working to reduce greenhouse gas emissions that have caused the rise in global temperatures.

**CCC Stability and Change** Why is it important to consider the cascade effects of global warming when evaluating ways to reduce energy usage at your school?

.................................................................

.................................................................

.................................................................

.................................................................

## 👆 INTERACTIVITY

Make a Difference

**Go online** to record data that will help you evaluate your school's energy use.

# CHANGING
# Climate Change

How do you reduce the amounts of greenhouse gases and lessen severity of climate change? You engineer it!

**The Challenge:** Reduce the level of carbon dioxide in the atmosphere to fight global warming.

**Phenomenon** Efforts are underway to reduce the amount of carbon dioxide released as a result of human activities. Limiting the burning of fossil fuels is one approach. But that method alone is not enough to solve the problem. Another way is to capture the carbon that is released when fuels are burned. The process is known as carbon capture and storage technology, or CCS. The goal is to capture carbon dioxide released during the production and burning of fuels, and then pump it deep underground.

In 2017, one of the country's largest industrial CCS facilities opened in Decatur, Illinois. The company produces ethanol, which is fuel made from corn. Carbon dioxide produced when making ethanol is injected into a saltwater reservoir nearly two kilometers below the surface of the ground. The facility is permitted to run for five years and can bury about one million tons of carbon dioxide each year.

▶ **VIDEO**

Explore how engineers use technology to help reduce levels of carbon dioxide in the atmosphere.

**DESIGN CHALLENGE**

Can you design a house to reduce its carbon footprint? Go to the Engineering Design Notebook to find out!

$CO_2$ source (power plant)

$CO_2$ injection

$CO_2$ transport

$CO_2$ compression unit

$CO_2$ capture & separation plant

$CO_2$ storage

# ☑ TOPIC 10 Review and Assess

## 1 Climate Factors

MS-ESS2-6

**1.** Which of the following terms refers to long-term weather patterns in an area?
- **A.** climate
- **B.** weather
- **C.** altitude
- **D.** prevailing winds

**2.** Why do areas near the equator have warmer climates than areas near the poles?
- **A.** There are fewer mountains near the equator than in areas near the poles.
- **B.** Sunlight strikes Earth's surface more directly at the equator than at the poles.
- **C.** Ocean currents carry warm water from the poles to the equator.
- **D.** Areas near the equator are generally at higher altitudes than areas near the poles.

**3.** Ocean currents traveling from the equator toward the polar zones carry ............................. water, which helps to ............................. air masses at the poles.

**4. CCC Energy and Matter** Why do most tall mountains have cooler climates than the areas at their bases?

........................................................................

........................................................................

........................................................................

........................................................................

**5. SEP Interpret Data** What factors do you think are responsible for the differences in temperatures found in a temperate marine climate and a temperate continental climate?

........................................................................

........................................................................

........................................................................

........................................................................

........................................................................

## 2 Climate Change

MS-ESS3-5

**6.** Why is carbon dioxide considered a greenhouse gas?
- **A.** It is found in high concentrations in greenhouses that contain lots of plants.
- **B.** It is produced as a result of human activity.
- **C.** It traps radiated energy in the atmosphere, which causes air temperatures to rise.
- **D.** It is necessary for plants to survive.

**7.** Which of the following is *not* a natural process that can affect Earth's climate?
- **A.** volcanoes
- **B.** changes in solar radiation
- **C.** lunar eclipses
- **D.** shifting continents

**8. Integrate Information** Why do climate scientists study tree rings and ice cores?

........................................................................

........................................................................

........................................................................

........................................................................

**9. CCC Stability and Change** How has Earth's average global temperature changed in the last 140 years? What is the main cause of this change?

........................................................................

........................................................................

........................................................................

........................................................................

........................................................................

**10. CCC Cause and Effect** How does raising livestock contribute to global warming?

........................................................................

........................................................................

........................................................................

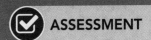
# ③ Effects of a Changing Climate

MS-ESS3-5

**11.** What do most climate models predict about Earth's global temperature in the near future?

A. It will stop rising and remain constant.

B. It will rise several more degrees.

C. It will drop before slowly rising again.

D. It will drop quickly and bring about an ice age.

**12.** As global temperatures rise, the global sea level is expected to rise in part because

A. more precipitation is falling.

B. permafrost is thawing.

C. greenhouse gases cause water to expand.

D. glaciers are melting at a faster rate.

**13.** Which of the following is an effect of the loss of sea ice covering northern oceans?

A. More solar energy is absorbed by ocean water.

B. Sea levels decrease.

C. Earth's global temperature drops.

D. Ocean water becomes saltier.

**14. SEP Engage in Argument** When dealing with climate change, do you think it is more important for us to figure out ways to deal with its effects, figure out ways to reduce climate change, or both? Explain.

..........................................................................

..........................................................................

..........................................................................

..........................................................................

..........................................................................

..........................................................................

..........................................................................

..........................................................................

..........................................................................

**15. SEP Develop Models** ✏ Complete the flow chart to identify cascading effects of global warming.

| Rising temperatures cause glacier ice to melt. |
| --- |

↓

|  |
| --- |

↓

|  |
| --- |

↓

|  |
| --- |

↓

|  |
| --- |

**16. SEP Construct Explanations** Identify one way that technology might be used to mitigate the effects of climate change. Explain how the technology works to reduce the impact of human activity on climate change.

..........................................................................

..........................................................................

..........................................................................

..........................................................................

..........................................................................

..........................................................................

..........................................................................

..........................................................................

MS-ESS3-5C

## Evidence-Based Assessment

A group of students investigates how levels of methane in the atmosphere have changed over time and how this factor contributes to global warming.

From their research, the students learn the following information:

- Methane accounts for about 10 percent of the greenhouse gases in the atmosphere. But its ability to trap heat is 25 times as great as carbon dioxide.

- Some methane is released by natural processes, but over 60 percent of methane emissions are the result of human activities.

- Agricultural activities, such as raising livestock and managing livestock waste, are a major source of methane emissions.

- The production of natural gas and petroleum is another major source of methane emissions.

The students display some of the data collected during research in the graph and tables shown here.

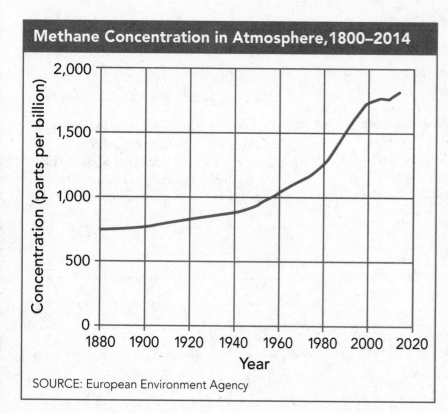

**Methane Concentration in Atmosphere, 1800–2014**

SOURCE: European Environment Agency

### Global Beef Production

| Year | 1,000 Metric Tons |
|------|-------------------|
| 2000 | 49,775 |
| 2005 | 52,374 |
| 2010 | 57,043 |
| 2015 | 60,022 |

Source: USDA

### Global Natural Gas Production

| Year | Billion Cubic Meters |
|------|----------------------|
| 2000 | 2,421,0 |
| 2005 | 2,790.9 |
| 2010 | 3,208.5 |
| 2015 | 3,538.6 |

Source: BP Statistical Review of World Energy, June 2016

1. **SEP Analyze Data** What trend is shown in the data collected by the students?

   A. Methane levels are increasing, as are the levels of beef and natural gas production.

   B. Methane levels are decreasing, as are the levels of beef and natural gas production.

   C. Methane levels are increasing, while the levels of beef and natural gas production are decreasing.

   D. Methane levels are decreasing, while the levels of beef and natural gas production are increasing.

2. **Ask Questions** Which of the following questions are the students attempting to answer in their investigation? Select all that apply.

   ☐ How much do human activities contribute to methane emissions?

   ☐ Why was more natural gas produced in 2005 than in 2000?

   ☐ Why is methane considered a factor in rising global temperatures?

   ☐ How are beef and gas production related to the levels of methane in the atmosphere?

   ☐ How much beef did people consume each year from 2000 to 2015?

3. **SEP Engage in Argument** What is the relationship between the data in the tables and in the graph? Support your answer with evidence.

   ..................................................................................
   ..................................................................................
   ..................................................................................
   ..................................................................................
   ..................................................................................
   ..................................................................................
   ..................................................................................
   ..................................................................................
   ..................................................................................
   ..................................................................................

4. **SEP Engage in Argument** How are recent trends in beef and natural gas production tied to the rise in global temperatures? Use evidence to support your argument.

   ..................................................................................
   ..................................................................................
   ..................................................................................
   ..................................................................................
   ..................................................................................
   ..................................................................................
   ..................................................................................
   ..................................................................................
   ..................................................................................

## Quest FINDINGS

## Complete the Quest!

**Phenomenon** Determine the best way to present your proposals for reducing your school's carbon footprint and to display the supporting data you have collected.

**SEP Evaluate Information** What are some important factors to consider when evaluating the effectiveness of ideas for reducing carbon emissions?

..................................................................................
..................................................................................
..................................................................................
..................................................................................

👆 **INTERACTIVITY**

Reflect on Shrinking Your Carbon Footprint

# An Ocean of a Problem

How can you determine what is responsible for reducing the size of oysters in the ocean?

## Safety

Be sure to follow all safety guidelines provided by your teacher. The Safety Appendix of your textbook provides more details about the safety icons.

## Background

**Phenomenon** As a science expert on an advisory panel, you are charged with examining a complaint from oyster fishers. Oysters caught in the Northwest Pacific and Mid-Atlantic regions of the ocean are smaller than in the past and their numbers are decreasing. The oyster fishers blame the problem on the increased acidity of seawater, which they believe is the result of increased levels of carbon dioxide in the atmosphere. According to the fishers, acidic water prevents the oysters from producing normal shells by dissolving new shell growth. This results in oysters that are smaller and more vulnerable to predators.

In this investigation, you will participate in one of two research teams. Your common goal will be to determine whether ocean acidification could be responsible for the problems with the oysters. You will also investigate whether carbon dioxide in the atmosphere is to blame.

## Materials

(per group)

For Research Team 1
- universal indicator solution or strips
- eggshell from one egg
- 200-mL beaker (2)
- 100 mL vinegar
- 100 mL distilled water

For Research Team 2
- 50 mL universal indicator solution
- small plastic cup (2)
- 300-mL beaker (2)
- 30 mL distilled water
- 30 mL carbonated water
- plastic wrap
- rubber band

According to recent estimates, harvests of oysters in the Chesapeake Bay are less than 1 percent of what they were 100 years ago.

# Design Your Experiment

1. Divide your group into two research teams.

2. 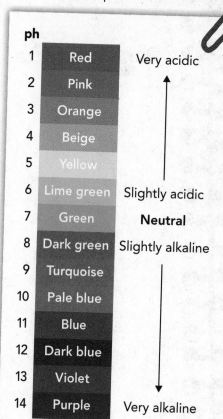 **Research Team 1** should design an experiment using the materials provided to explore the effects of acid on shells. Make sure the experiment you develop uses a control and that you measure and record the pH of the substances you use. Record your team's procedure in the space provided. Include a sketch of your set up. Consider the following questions as you develop and design your experiment:

   • What will the eggshell represent in your tests?

   • How can you model the effects of an acid on the eggshell?

   • How can you use the distilled water as a control in your investigation?

   • What observations will you make? What data will you collect?

   • How can you measure the pH of each substance you use in your experiment? When should you measure the pH?

3. After getting your teacher's approval, carry out your team's experiment. Make a table to record your observations and data in the space provided.

4. **Research Team 2** should design an experiment using the materials provided to determine the effect of carbon dioxide on the acidity of water. Your experiment should use a control to help you analyze your results. Record your team's procedure in the space provided. Include a sketch of your set up. Consider the following questions as you develop your experiment:

   • How can you use the carbonated water to test whether carbon dioxide in the air can change the pH of a substance?

   • How can you design your experiment so that only carbon dioxide in the air—and not the carbonated water—will come into contact with the indicator solution?

   • How can you use the distilled water as a control in your investigation?

   • What observations will you make? What data will you collect?

5. After getting your teacher's approval, carry out your team's experiment. Make a table to record your observations and data in the space provided.

6. When both research teams have completed their experiments, meet as a group to share and discuss the evidence that has been collected.

A pH scale uses both color and number scales to indicate the acidity or alkalinity of a substance. A pH indicator can be used to test the pH of a substance.

| pH | | |
|----|------|------|
| 1 | Red | Very acidic |
| 2 | Pink | |
| 3 | Orange | |
| 4 | Beige | |
| 5 | Yellow | |
| 6 | Lime green | Slightly acidic |
| 7 | Green | **Neutral** |
| 8 | Dark green | Slightly alkaline |
| 9 | Turquoise | |
| 10 | Pale blue | |
| 11 | Blue | |
| 12 | Dark blue | |
| 13 | Violet | |
| 14 | Purple | Very alkaline |

## Observations

## Data Table/Observations

# Analyze and Interpret Data

1. **SEP Communicate Information** Why were there two research teams for this investigation? Why is it important for the two teams to share their results before drawing any conclusions about the complaint?

..................................................................................................................
..................................................................................................................
..................................................................................................................
..................................................................................................................
..................................................................................................................
..................................................................................................................

2. **Claim** What observations did each team make?

..................................................................................................................
..................................................................................................................
..................................................................................................................
..................................................................................................................

3. **Evidence** What evidence can you provide to support the claim that increased levels of carbon dioxide in the atmosphere are responsible for the changes seen in the oysters?

..................................................................................................................
..................................................................................................................
..................................................................................................................
..................................................................................................................
..................................................................................................................
..................................................................................................................

4. **Reasoning** Based on your results and what you know about carbon dioxide levels in the atmosphere and ocean, what recommendations or advice would you give to the oyster fishers?

..................................................................................................................
..................................................................................................................
..................................................................................................................
..................................................................................................................
..................................................................................................................
..................................................................................................................

# Earth-Sun-Moon System

**NGSS PERFORMANCE EXPECTATION**

**MS-ESS1-1** Develop and use a model of the
Earth-sun-moon system to describe the cyclic
patterns of lunar phases, eclipses of the sun and
moon, and seasons.

HANDS-ON LAB

**uConnect** Model systems showing
both Earth and the sun at the center.

**What** is happening to the sun?

**GO ONLINE**
to access your
digital course

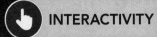 VIDEO

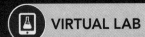 INTERACTIVITY

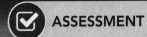 VIRTUAL LAB

 ASSESSMENT

 eTEXT

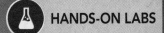 HANDS-ON LABS

## The Essential Question

# How do the sun and the moon affect Earth?

**CCC Patterns** As the moon travels around Earth and Earth travels around the sun, the three objects interact with each other. What are some of the patterns you can observe in the interactions among Earth, the sun, and the moon?

.................................................................................................

.................................................................................................

.................................................................................................

.................................................................................................

.................................................................................................

.................................................................................................

489

# Quest KICKOFF

## How are tides related to our place in space?

**Phenomenon** The ebb and flow of the ocean's tides are as steady and sure as the passage of time. Engineers are investigating how to put the power of the tides to work as an alternative to the burning of fossil fuels. In this Quest activity, you will produce a model to help visitors to a tidal power company understand why tidal power is a reliable source of renewable energy. You will explore how and why our position within the solar system causes tides and their patterns. The model that you produce will demonstrate how tides happen.

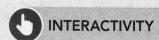 **INTERACTIVITY**

It's as Sure as the Tides

**MS-ESS1-1** Develop and use a model of the Earth-sun-moon system to describe the cyclic patterns of lunar phases, eclipses of the sun and moon, and seasons.

**⚓NBC LEARN** ▶ VIDEO

After watching the Quest Kickoff video about tidal energy, think about this source of energy. Complete the diagram by identifying some benefits and drawbacks of tidal energy.

### Benefits and Drawbacks of Tidal Energy

| Benefits | Drawbacks |
| --- | --- |
|  |  |

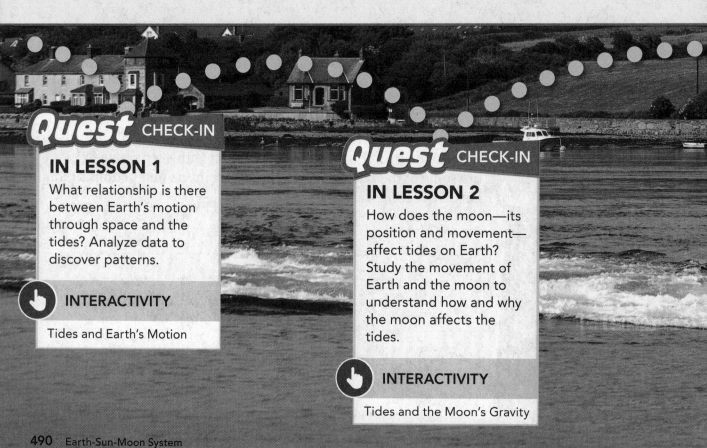

## Quest CHECK-IN

### IN LESSON 1

What relationship is there between Earth's motion through space and the tides? Analyze data to discover patterns.

**INTERACTIVITY**

Tides and Earth's Motion

## Quest CHECK-IN

### IN LESSON 2

How does the moon—its position and movement—affect tides on Earth? Study the movement of Earth and the moon to understand how and why the moon affects the tides.

**INTERACTIVITY**

Tides and the Moon's Gravity

This tidal turbine in Northern Ireland provides enough electricity to power hundreds of homes.

## Quest CHECK-IN

### IN LESSON 3

**STEM** What makes the tides and tidal ranges vary? Investigate how the relative positions of the moon, Earth, and the sun affect the tides.

### HANDS-ON LAB

The Moon's Revolution and Tides

## Quest FINDINGS

## Complete the Quest!

Apply what you've learned to create a model that demonstrates why tides occur and how and why they provide a reliable source of energy.

### 👆 INTERACTIVITY

Reflect on It's as Sure as the Tides

491

# What Is at the Center?

How can you **model** Earth-centered and sun-centered systems?

## Background

**Phenomenon** Early astronomers thought that the sun circled Earth. Astronomers have since determined that Earth circles around the sun. In this activity, you will model the two systems and evaluate whether your models give evidence to support an Earth-centered or sun-centered hypothesis.

## Materials

(per group)
- flashlight
- ball

## Safety

Be sure to follow all safety procedures provided by your teacher. The Safety Appendix of your textbook provides more details about the safety icons.

## Design a Procedure

1. **SEP Develop Models** Use the flashlight and ball to model how the sun would move and how its light would appear to observers on Earth if Earth were at the center of the system. Describe your model in the table. **CAUTION: *Do not shine the flashlight directly into anyone's eyes.***

2. **SEP Use Models** Move the sun and record your observations about when and where sunlight is visible to observers on Earth.

3. **SEP Develop Models** Now model how Earth would move with the sun at the center of the system. Describe your model in the table.

4. **SEP Use Models** Move Earth and record your observations about when and where sunlight is visible to observers on Earth.

# Observations

| Earth-centered model | Sun-centered model |
|---|---|
| | |
| | |

## Analyze and Interpret Data

**HANDS-ON LAB**

**Connect** Go online for a downloadable worksheet of this lab.

1. **SEP Construct Explanations** Based on your observations, what conclusion can you draw about the ability of observers on Earth to see the sun's light in each situation?

........................................................................................................

........................................................................................................

2. **SEP Evaluate Models** Compare your two sets of observations. From these observations, are you able to determine whether Earth or the sun is at the center of the system? What else would you need to evaluate these two viewpoints?

........................................................................................................

........................................................................................................

........................................................................................................

........................................................................................................

# (1) Movement in Space

## Guiding Questions

- What objects can you see in the night sky?
- Why do stars in the night sky seem to move?
- How do objects in the solar system move?

## Connections

**Literacy** Integrate With Visuals

**Math** Create an Equation

MS-ESS1-1

## HANDS-ON LAB

**ⁿInvestigate** Model how stars' positions change relative to a night sky observer on Earth.

### Vocabulary

satellite
star
planet
meteor
comet
constellation
geocentric
heliocentric
ellipse

### Academic Vocabulary

observations

## Connect It !

✏ **Circle the meteors in this photo.**

CCC Energy and Matter  Why do you think meteors leave a trail of light as they move through the sky?

................................................................................................................

................................................................................................................

# The Night Sky

Why do the stars appear to move? What makes the moon shine through the darkness? Aryabhata I (ar yah BAH tah) was an early astronomer who thought about these questions. He was born in 476 CE in what is now India. Aryabhata I wrote that the moon and the planets shine because they reflect light from the sun. He came up with these conclusions based solely on his **observations** of the sky with his naked eye.

**Stars, Planets, and the Moon** You may look up on a clear night, such as the one shown in **Figure 1**, and see stars, the moon, planets, meteors, and comets, much as Aryabhata I did. Earth's moon is the brightest and largest object in our night sky. The moon is Earth's only natural satellite. A **satellite** is a body that orbits a planet. By contrast, stars appear as tiny points of light. However, a **star** is a giant ball of superheated gas, or plasma, composed of hydrogen and helium. As seen from Earth, the positions of stars relative to each other do not seem to change.

Have you ever noticed objects that change position from night to night against the background of the stars? These are planets. A **planet** is an object that orbits the sun, is large enough to have become rounded by its own gravity, and has cleared the area of its orbit of any debris. There are eight planets in our solar system.

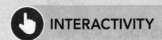
**INTERACTIVITY**

Answer a poll about things you have seen in the night sky.

**Academic Vocabulary**

How does making observations help scientists come up with new ideas?

........................................................

........................................................

........................................................

........................................................

........................................................

**Objects in the Sky**
**Figure 1** On a clear night, you can often see meteors in the night sky.

☐ **Investigate** Model how stars' positions change relative to a night sky observer on Earth.

**Meteors and Comets** Have you ever seen a shooting star? These sudden bright streaks are called meteors. A **meteor** is a streak of light produced when a small piece of rock or ice, known as a meteoroid, burns up as it enters Earth's atmosphere. You can see a meteor on almost any clear night.

Comets are rarer sights than meteors. A **comet** is a cold mixture of dust and ice that develops a long trail of light as it approaches the sun. When a comet is far from the sun, it is frozen. As it gets close to the sun, the cloud trailing behind the comet forms a glowing tail made up of hot dust and gases.

Perhaps the most famous comet is Halley's Comet. This highly visible comet was documented by Edmund Halley, who calculated its orbit and predicted its next appearance in the sky. Sure enough, the comet appeared as he predicted in 1758, although Halley didn't live to see it. It has continued to appear about every 75 years, last appearing in 1986.

## Math Toolbox

### Halley's Comet

In 1910, Halley's Comet traveled close to Earth—about 1/7 of the distance from Earth to the sun. Earth's distance from the sun is 149.6 million kilometers.

1. **SEP Use Computational Thinking** How close was Halley's Comet to Earth in 1910? Create an equation to answer the question.

..............................................................................

2. **Interpret Data** Estimate the next three years when Halley's Comet will appear.

..............................................................................

..............................................................................

3. **SEP Use Mathematics** The core of Halley's comet is oblong in shape, with its longest dimension 16 km long. Earth's diameter is about 12,700 km. How many times larger in diameter is Earth than Halley's comet?

..............................................................................

..............................................................................

## Finding Constellations

**Figure 2** ✏️ Star charts can help you to find constellations in the night sky. This is a summer chart for the Northern Hemisphere. Find these constellations in the star chart. Then write each constellation's name by its picture.

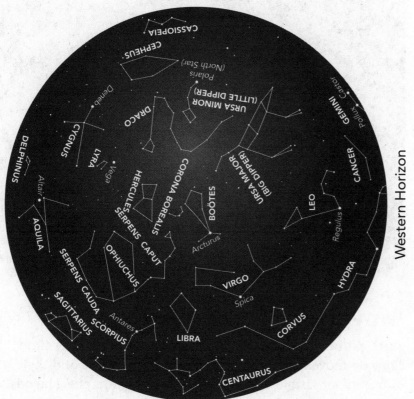

Northern Horizon

Eastern Horizon

Western Horizon

Southern Horizon

...............................................

...............................................

...............................................

...............................................

**Constellations** For thousands of years, human beings in many cultures have seen patterns in groups of stars and given them names. A pattern or group of stars that people imagine represents a figure, animal, or object is a **constellation**. Often, as in the ancient Roman and Greek cultures, constellations supported specific mythologies. Today, scientists divide the sky into 88 constellations. Some constellations are named for people or animals from Greek myths. Pegasus and Perseus, for example, are both mythological characters and constellations. Study the constellations shown in **Figure 2**.

📓 **Reflect** In your science notebook, write about the patterns of stars you see in the night sky.

✅ **READING CHECK** **Integrate With Visuals** How do the pictures in **Figure 2** help you remember the constellations?

...................................................................................

...................................................................................

...................................................................................

...................................................................................

**Star Trails**
**Figure 3** ✏ A time-lapse
photo taken over the course
of minutes or hours captures
the movements of stars. The
North Star happens to be
aligned with the axis of
Earth, directly "above" the
North Pole. Circle the North
Star in the photo.

# Movement in the Sky

Stars, planets, and other objects appear to move over time.
They do move in space, but those actual motions and their
apparent, or visible, motions may be very different. The positions of objects in the sky depend on the motions of Earth.

Stars generally appear to move from east to west through the
night. Toward the poles, stars appear to take a circular path,
as shown in **Figure 3**. As Aryabhata I thought, this apparent
motion is caused by Earth rotating toward the east. The sun's
apparent motion is also caused by Earth's rotation.

**Seasonal Changes** Constellations and star patterns
remain the same from year to year, but the constellations
visible to you vary from season to season. For example,
you can find the constellation Orion in the eastern sky on
winter evenings. But by spring, you'll see Orion in the west,
disappearing below the horizon shortly after sunset.

These seasonal changes are caused by Earth's revolution, or
orbit, around the sun. Each night, the position of most stars
shifts slightly to the west. After a while, you no longer see stars
once visible in the west, and previously unseen stars appear in
the east. After six months, Earth is on the other side of the sun.
Constellations that used to appear in the night sky are now
behind the sun, where the sun's bright light blocks them from
our vision during the day.

**Planets** Planets appear to move against the background of stars. In fact, the word *planet* comes from a Greek word meaning "wanderer." Because the planets all orbit the sun in about the same plane, they appear to move through a narrow band in the sky. This band is called the zodiac.

Some planets are visible all night long. Mars, Jupiter, and Saturn are all farther from the sun than Earth is. When Earth passes between them and the sun, these three planets are visible after sunset, once the sun's bright light no longer blocks the view. You can see Venus and Mercury only in the evening or morning. They are closer to the sun than Earth, and so they always appear close to the sun, as shown in **Figure 4**.

☑️ **READING CHECK** **Cite Textual Evidence** Why would you need two different star charts for finding constellations in the summer and the winter?

........................................................................

........................................................................

........................................................................

........................................................................

........................................................................

**Mercury and Venus**
**Figure 4** The planets Mercury and Venus never appear far from the sun in the sky.

**SEP Use Models**
🖊 Where in this image is Venus farthest from the sun? Place a dot on the image to indicate the spot.

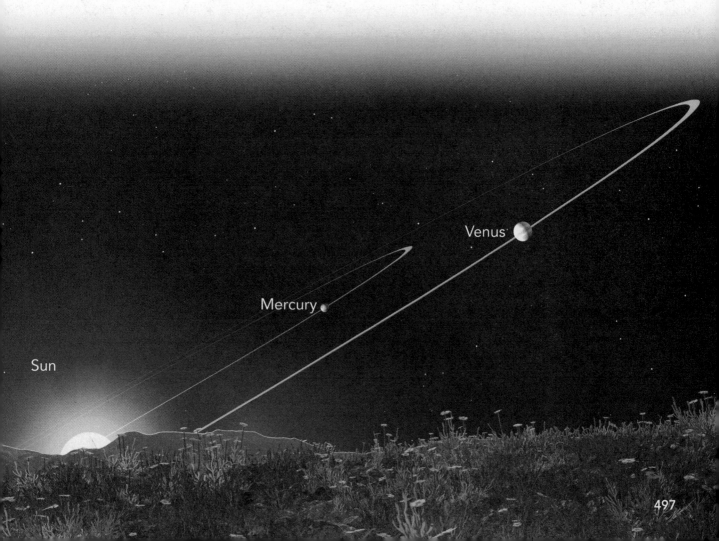

Venus

Mercury

Sun

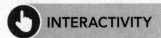
# Models of the Solar System

From here on Earth, it seems as if our planet is stationary and that the sun, moon, and stars are moving around Earth. Ancient peoples such as the Greeks, Chinese, and Mayans noticed that although the stars seemed to move, they stayed in the same position relative to one another.

**Geocentric Model** Many early observers, including the Greek philosopher, Aristotle, thought Earth was the center of the universe, with all the planets and stars circling it, as shown in **Figure 5**. Because *ge* is the Greek word for "Earth," an Earth-centered model is known as a **geocentric** (jee oh SEN trik) model.

In about 140 C.E., the Greek astronomer Ptolemy further developed Aristotle's geocentric model. In Ptolemy's model, the planets made small circles called epicycles as they moved along their orbital paths. This model seemed to explain the motions observed in the sky. As a result, Ptolemy's geocentric model was widely accepted for nearly 1,500 years after his death.

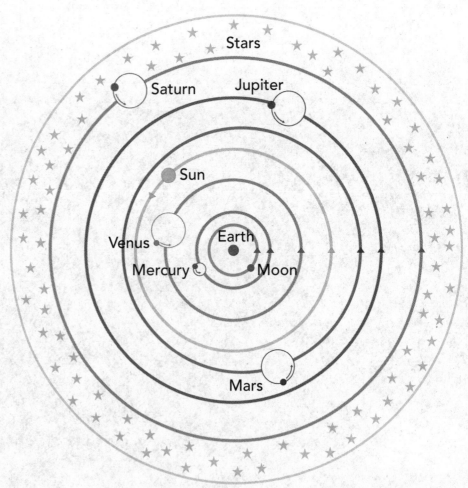

**The Geocentric Model**
**Figure 5** This geocentric model shows our solar system, with Earth in the center. The other planets orbit Earth and move along their epicycles at the same time.

## Heliocentric Model

Not everybody believed in the geocentric system. An ancient Greek scientist named Aristarchus, who lived over 400 years before Ptolemy, developed a sun-centered or **heliocentric** (hee lee oh SEN trik) model. *Helios* is Greek for "sun." In a heliocentric system, Earth and the other planets revolve around the sun. This model was not well received. Many people insisted that Earth had to be at the center of the universe.

**Figure 6** lists four scientists who worked to expand and prove the heliocentric model of the solar system. The Polish astronomer Nicolaus Copernicus further developed the heliocentric model. Copernicus proposed that Earth's rotation and revolution around the sun explained the observed movements of the stars and planets. He published his work in 1543. Copernicus's theory would eventually revolutionize the science of astronomy, the study of space.

Early heliocentric models assumed that planets moved in perfect circles. Their models fit existing observations fairly well. But in the late 1500s, the Danish astronomer Tycho Brahe (TEE koh BRAH huh) made much more accurate observations. Brahe's assistant, Johannes Kepler, used the observations to figure out the shape of the planets' orbits. When he used circular orbits, his calculations did not fit the observations. After years of detailed calculations, Kepler found that the orbit of each planet is actually an **ellipse**, an oval shape, rather than a perfect circle.

## Galileo's Discovery

For many years, people continued to believe the geocentric model. However, evidence collected by the Italian scientist Galileo Galilei gradually convinced others that the heliocentric model was correct. In 1610, Galileo, using a telescope that he constructed himself, discovered moons orbiting Jupiter. These Galilean moons showed that not everything in the sky travels around Earth.

**1500**

**1550**

**1600**

**1650**

### Heliocentric Timeline

**Figure 6** ✎ Explain what each scientist added to our understanding of the heliocentric model of the solar system.

**Copernicus**

..............................................
..............................................
..............................................
..............................................
..............................................
..............................................
..............................................

**Brahe and Kepler**

..............................................
..............................................
..............................................
..............................................
..............................................
..............................................
..............................................

**Galileo**

..............................................
..............................................
..............................................
..............................................
..............................................
..............................................
..............................................

**INTERACTIVITY**

Determine how seasonal changes in our perception of stars support a specific model of the solar system.

## Confirming the Heliocentric Model

Galileo also made other observations that supported Copernicus's theory that the sun was the center of the solar system. For example, Galileo discovered that Venus goes through phases similar to the moon's phases. But, since Venus is never too far away from the sun in the sky, it would not have a full set of phases if both it and the sun circled around Earth. Therefore, Galileo reasoned, the geocentric model did not hold true.

☑ **READING CHECK** **Cite Textual Evidence** How does the development of the heliocentric model show how scientific ideas change over time?

......................................................................................................................

......................................................................................................................

......................................................................................................................

......................................................................................................................

......................................................................................................................

## Model It

### Models of the Universe

SEP Develop Models ✏ Draw Galileo's heliocentric system. Show and label the evidence he produced to support his model.

# ☑ LESSON 1 Check

1. **Predict** Two photographers take time-lapse photos of the night sky. One of them is at the equator. The other is at the South Pole. Which photo will show stars that never rise or set? Explain.

.......................................................................
.......................................................................
.......................................................................
.......................................................................
.......................................................................

2. **CCC System Models** Explain the two theories about how Earth and the sun move in space relative to each other.

.......................................................................
.......................................................................
.......................................................................
.......................................................................
.......................................................................
.......................................................................
.......................................................................

3. **Infer** What observations made by Galileo supported Copernicus's theory about the solar system?

.......................................................................
.......................................................................
.......................................................................
.......................................................................
.......................................................................
.......................................................................
.......................................................................
.......................................................................

4. **SEP Construct Explanations** Which patterns in space are predictable? Why?

.......................................................................
.......................................................................
.......................................................................
.......................................................................

5. **CCC Cause and Effect** What causes the stars to appear to move across the night sky?

.......................................................................
.......................................................................

# Quest CHECK-IN

**In this lesson, you learned why the stars in the night sky seem to move. You learned that various objects move, or seem to move, in space. You also discovered how Earth and the other planets move in relation to the sun.**

Evaluate If the relative positions of the sun and moon affect the ocean's tides, why would it be smart for sailors and other people who work on the ocean to understand patterns in the Earth-sun-moon system?

.......................................................................
.......................................................................
.......................................................................

## 👆 INTERACTIVITY

Tides and Earth's Motion

**Go online** to analyze images and data about tides and look for connections in the patterns you see.

Astronomer Claudius Ptolemaeus, or Ptolemy (100 CE – 170 CE), lived in Alexandria, Egypt.

MS-ESS1-1

# THE PTOLEMAIC MODEL:
# Explaining the Unexplained

**B**efore there were satellites and telescopes, ancient Greek and Roman astronomers relied on their eyes to learn about the solar system. Their observations led them to an understanding of the solar system in which the sun, moon, and planets revolved around Earth.

## Theory from Observation

Believing he was standing at the center of the universe, astronomer Claudius Ptolemy watched planets march across the sky. But he made a few observations that intrigued him. The planets grew brighter or dimmer at times, and they seemed to speed up and slow down. Even more puzzling, some planets—such as Mars—occasionally appeared to move *backward* across the sky. If the planets circled Earth as everyone believed, how could they move so irregularly?

Ptolemy developed a theory to explain this retrograde, or backward, motion of the planets. The planets still revolved around Earth, but he argued that they moved in small circles as they traveled through a circular orbit.

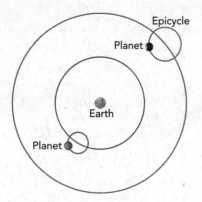

Ptolemy developed the concept of epicycles to explain why some planets appeared to move backward in their orbits. Depending on where a planet was in its epicycle, it would seem to move one way and then the other from Earth.

# Advances in Technology

The Ptolemaic model was the dominant model for centuries. But astronomical instruments improved and provided more accurate measurements. Astronomers began to find errors in Ptolemy's model. In the 1500s, Copernicus proposed a heliocentric model in which the sun was the center of the solar system. Finally, Galileo used newly developed technology—a telescope—to disprove Ptolemy's model. Ptolemy hadn't been standing at the center of the universe after all.

**Use the diagrams to answer the following questions.**

1. **Compare** How does the geocentric model of the solar system differ from the heliocentric model?

2. **Construct Explanations** Explain how our evolving model of the solar system shows why scientists need to keep an open mind as they gather more data.

3. **Connect to Technology** Astronomers continue to refine their understanding of the solar system. How might advances in technology help to add to our knowledge?

**Ptolemaic or geocentric model**

Venus · Earth · Mars · Mercury · Moon · Sun · Jupiter · Saturn

**Copernican or heliocentric model**

Earth · Mercury · Venus · Sun · Mars · Saturn · Jupiter

503

# ② Earth's Movement in Space

## Guiding Questions

- How does Earth's motion affect the amount of daylight and the seasons?
- Why do Earth and the moon remain in orbit?

## Connections

**Literacy** Cite Textual Evidence

**Math** Analyze Quantitative Relationships

MS-ESS1-1

## HANDS-ON LAB

**ᴜInvestigate** Review the differences between mass and weight and how weight is affected by gravity.

## Vocabulary

axis
rotation
revolution
orbit
solstice
equinox
gravity
law of universal
  gravitation
inertia

## Academic Vocabulary

hypothesize

## Connect It !

✏ **Draw an X on the image to indicate the position of the sun.**

**SEP Analyze and Interpret Data** Which part of Earth is experiencing day-time in the image?

......................................................................................................................

......................................................................................................................

......................................................................................................................

# How Earth Moves

The apparent motion of the sun, moon, and stars in the sky is a result of the way Earth itself moves through space. Earth, as well as the other planets, moves around the sun in two separate ways: rotation and revolution.

**Rotation** To help describe Earth's movement, scientists have named an imaginary line that passes from the North Pole, through the Earth's center, to the South Pole. This line is known as Earth's **axis**, and the spinning of Earth on its axis is called **rotation**.

Look at **Figure 1**. You can see that half of Earth is lit and half is in darkness. Earth rotates from west to east (see **Figure 2**.) As it rotates, objects in the sky appear to move in the direction opposite of Earth's rotation.

As Earth rotates eastward, the sun appears to move west across the sky. As Earth continues to turn to the east, the sun appears to set in the west. Because sunlight can't reach the side of Earth facing away from the sun, it is night there. It takes Earth about 24 hours to rotate once. As you know, each of these 24-hour cycles is called a day.

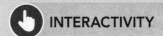

INTERACTIVITY

Investigate the patterns in Earth's rotation and revolution.

**Day and Night**
**Figure 1** Day occurs on the part of Earth that is turned toward the sun. Night occurs on the part of Earth that is turned away from the sun.

## Earth's Axis

**Figure 2**  Earth spins on its axis, rotating from west to east to cause day and night. Shade the part of Earth that is experiencing night.

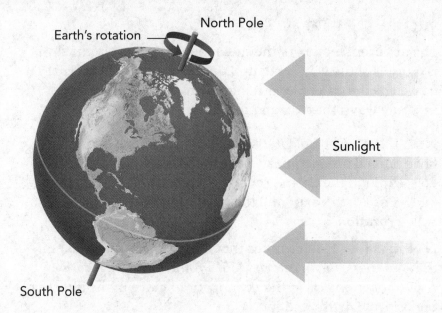

Earth's rotation — North Pole

Sunlight

South Pole

▶ **VIDEO**

Consider the difference between rotating and revolving.

**Revolution**  As you read this page, do you feel as if you are moving? You may not feel it, but as Earth rotates, it is traveling around the sun. **Revolution** is the movement of one object around another. One revolution of Earth around the sun takes one year. Like other planets, Earth's path, or **orbit**, around the sun is an ellipse, an oval shape. The ellipse brings the planet closest to the sun in January.

## Design It!

**SEP Develop Models** ✏ How could you model Earth's movements? Design a model using real objects to represent Earth and the sun. Explain how you could use these objects to illustrate Earth's motions. Include both Earth's rotation and revolution in your design and explanation.

.................................................................................................

.................................................................................................

.................................................................................................

.................................................................................................

# The Seasons

The extent of seasonal change in any given place on Earth depends on how far away that place is from the equator. The farther away a place is from the equator, the more widely its seasonal temperatures vary. This is because of how sunlight hits Earth.

When we look at areas near the equator, we see that sunlight hits Earth's surface very directly. This sunlight is concentrated in the smallest possible area. Near the North and South Poles, sunlight hitting Earth forms a large angle with the local vertical, so the same amount of sunlight spreads over a greater area. That's why it is warmer near the equator than near the poles.

Seasonal differences in temperature are dependent on the tilt of Earth's axis. If the axis were straight up and down relative to Earth's orbit, temperatures in a given area would remain constant year-round, and there would be no seasons. However, Earth's axis is tilted at an angle of 23.5° from the vertical. Therefore, as Earth revolves around the sun, the north end of its axis is tilted away from the sun for part of the year and toward the sun for part of the year. Earth has seasons because its axis is tilted as it revolves around the sun.

**Figure 3** shows how Earth moves during the year. In June, the Northern Hemisphere is tilted toward the sun and we experience summer. The sun's rays fall on a relatively small area and the temperatures are warmer. In December, the Northern Hemisphere is tilted away from the sun and we experience winter. The sun's rays fall on a relatively large area, so temperatures are lower. During March and September, sunlight strikes both hemispheres equally, causing the mild temperatures felt in spring and autumn.

## Literacy Connection

**Cite Textual Evidence**
Reread the second and third paragraphs. Underline the evidence that supports the statement that seasons are caused by the tilt of Earth's axis.

## Seasons

**Figure 3** Earth's tilted axis affects the strength of sunlight in different places throughout the year. Which month labels the part of the diagram showing the South Pole in complete darkness?

....................................................

....................................................

....................................................

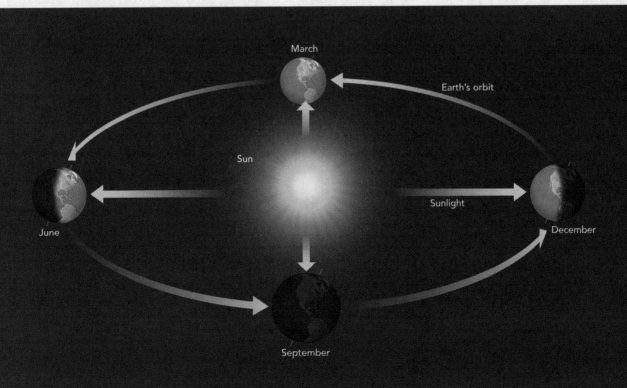

March

Earth's orbit

Sun

Sunlight

June

December

September

HANDS-ON LAB

☑**Investigate** Review the differences between mass and weight and how weight is affected by gravity.

## Day Length

The tilt of Earth's axis also affects day length. The hemisphere that is tilted toward the sun has more hours of day than night. Points on Earth near the poles have the most drastic changes in day length. In Kiruna, Sweden, shown in **Figure 4**, the sun remains below the horizon throughout the day for most of January. However, in June the sun never fully sets.

## Solstices and Equinoxes

In each hemisphere, there is one day per year when the sun appears highest in the sky. Each of these days is called a **solstice**. Solstices occur when either the Northern or Southern Hemisphere is at its strongest tilt towards the sun.

Halfway between the solstices, neither hemisphere is tilted toward the sun. Each of these days is called an **equinox**, which means "equal night." This day occurs when the sun passes directly overhead at the equator at noon, and night and day are both 12 hours long.

The solstices and equinoxes occur at opposite times in the Northern and Southern Hemispheres. In the Northern Hemisphere, the summer solstice occurs around June 21, and the winter solstice occurs around December 22. However, in the Southern Hemisphere, these dates are opposite of what they are in the Northern Hemisphere. Equinoxes occur in both the Northern and Southern Hemispheres around September 22 and March 21.

### Short Days
**Figure 4** At noon in January, the sun is still low in the sky in Sweden.

**Weightlessness**
**Figure 5** Astronauts experience a feeling of weightlessness when they orbit Earth because they are in freefall, with no force countering gravity. However, the inertia of their motion in orbit prevents them from falling to Earth.

# Gravity and Orbits

The force that keeps Earth in orbit around the sun and the moon in orbit around Earth is the same force that prevents you from flying away when you jump. That force is gravity.

**Gravity** In the 1600s, an English scientist named Isaac Newton was curious about why the moon orbits Earth. In his work *Principia,* Newton contended that there must be a force, or a push and pull, acting between Earth and the moon.

Newton **hypothesized** that the same force that pulls the moon toward Earth also pulls apples to the ground when they fall from a tree. This force that attracts all objects toward each other is called **gravity**. Newton's **law of universal gravitation** states that every object in the universe attracts every other object. The strength of the force of gravity between two objects depends on two factors: the masses of the objects and the distance between them. Mass is the amount of matter in an object. Because Earth is so massive, it exerts a much greater force on you than your textbook exerts on you.

The measure of the force of gravity on an object is called weight. Mass doesn't change, but an object's weight can change depending on its location. On the moon, you would weigh about one-sixth as much as on Earth. The moon has less mass than Earth, so the pull of the moon's gravity on you would also be less. In space, as shown in **Figure 5**, you have no weight at all.

Gravity is also affected by the distance between two objects. The force of gravity decreases as distance increases. If the distance between two objects doubles, the force of gravity decreases to one-fourth of its original value.

**Academic Vocabulary**
How have you heard the term *hypothesize* used before?

..................................................

..................................................

..................................................

..................................................

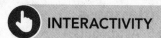
**Inertia** If the sun and Earth are constantly pulling on one another because of gravity, why doesn't Earth fall into the sun? The fact that such a collision has not occurred shows that a factor called inertia is at work.

**Inertia** is the tendency of an object to resist a change in motion. You feel the effects of inertia when you are riding in a car and it stops suddenly, but you keep moving forward. The more mass an object has, the greater its inertia. An object with greater inertia is more difficult to start or stop.

Isaac Newton stated his ideas about inertia as a scientific law. Newton's first law of motion says that an object at rest will stay at rest and an object in motion will stay in motion with a constant speed and direction, unless acted on by a force.

# Math Toolbox
## Gravity vs. Distance

Imagine that a spacecraft is leaving Earth's surface. How does the force of gravity between the rocket and the planet change?

| Distance from Earth's Center (planet's radius = 1) | 1 | 2 | 3 | 4 |
|---|---|---|---|---|
| Force of Gravity on the Spacecraft (million newtons) | 4 | 1 | 0.44 | 0.25 |

1. **Construct Graphs** ✏ Create a line graph of the data above.

2. **SEP Use Mathematics** What is the force of gravity on the spacecraft at twice the planet's radius from its center?

........................................

3. **CCC Scale, Proportion, and Quantity** What would the force of gravity on the spacecraft be at a distance of 8 radii?

........................................

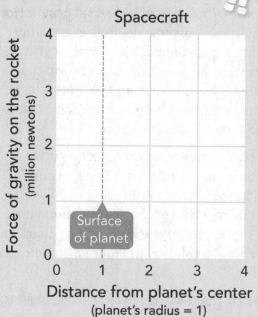

Spacecraft

Force of gravity on the rocket (million newtons)

Surface of planet

Distance from planet's center
(planet's radius = 1)

**Orbital Motion** So, the moon travels through space at the same speed because of its inertia. But, it is constantly changing direction to remain in orbit around Earth. Newton concluded that inertia and gravity combine to keep the moon in orbit around Earth. You can see how this occurs in **Figure 6**.

Without Earth's gravity, the moon would veer away from Earth in a straight line. Earth's gravity pulls the moon inward and prevents it from moving away in a straight line. The combination of these two factors results in a curved orbital path. Similarly, planets are held in their elliptical orbits around the sun by the combined forces of gravity and inertia.

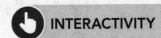

**INTERACTIVITY**

Explore how Earth's tilted axis and revolution influence the seasons.

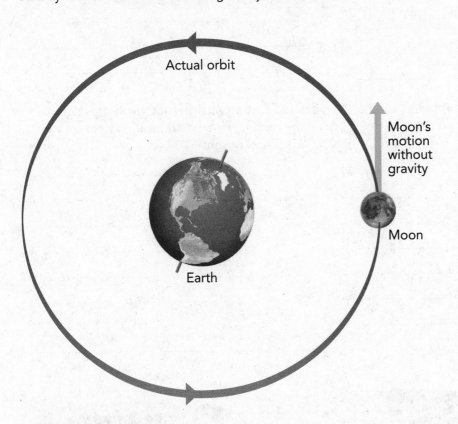

Actual orbit

Moon's motion without gravity

Moon

Earth

**Orbital Motion**

**Figure 6** 🖊 Gravity and inertia keep the moon in orbit around Earth. Complete the diagram by drawing an arrow to indicate the force of gravity Earth exerts on the moon as it orbits Earth.

✔️ **READING CHECK** **Cite Textual Evidence** What factors affect the strength of the pull of gravity between two objects?

..............................................................................................

..............................................................................................

..............................................................................................

..............................................................................................

..............................................................................................

..............................................................................................

..............................................................................................

..............................................................................................

1. **Identify** What are the two ways Earth moves?

............................................................

............................................................

2. **CCC Patterns** What causes the pattern of day and night? What causes the pattern of the seasons?

............................................................

............................................................

............................................................

3. **Draw Conclusions** What happens to the length of the day during the solstices? Why does this occur?

............................................................

............................................................

............................................................

............................................................

............................................................

............................................................

............................................................

4. **SEP Construct Explanations** What parts of Earth generally have the highest temperatures? Which have the lowest? What causes this difference?

............................................................

............................................................

............................................................

............................................................

............................................................

............................................................

5. **CCC Cause and Effect** If you traveled to the moon, what would be the effect on your mass and weight?

............................................................

............................................................

............................................................

............................................................

............................................................

............................................................

## Quest CHECK-IN

**In this lesson, you learned about the way that the sun interacts with Earth to produce day, night, and the seasons. You also discovered how gravity, mass, and inertia affect the movement of Earth and the moon.**

Infer  When the sun, moon, and Earth are aligned, ocean tides are larger—high tide is higher, low tide is lower—than when they are not aligned. How might this relate to gravity?

............................................................

............................................................

............................................................

............................................................

👆 **INTERACTIVITY**

Tides and the Moon's Gravity

**Go online** to study models of the motions of Earth and the moon and observe how these motions affect the tides on Earth's surface.

# Tracking Time in the Sky

**W**ill your birthday fall on a weekend this year? Better check the calendar! A calendar organizes time into days, months, and years. It may seem like a simple grid of squares, but a calendar is actually a measurement of time based on patterns of movement among Earth, the sun, and the moon.

### Egyptian Calendar (3rd Millenium BCE)
The ancient Egyptians created one of the first calendars. They figured out that a year—the time it takes for Earth to orbit the sun—was 365 days long. They used the repeating phases of the moon to divide a year into 12 months of 30 days each and tacked on five extra days at the end of the year.

### Julian Calendar (46 BCE)
The Romans borrowed the Egyptian calendar, but they noticed that it didn't always line up with the first day of spring. It actually takes 365 ¼ days for Earth to orbit the sun. So, Julius Caesar added an extra day every four years to keep the calendar on track. This extra day is inserted into a "leap year," so that February has 29 days instead of 28.

### Gregorian Calendar (1582 CE)
After a few centuries, it became clear that the Roman calendar also wasn't quite right. In fact, it was almost 11 minutes off each year. That may not sound like much, but by the year 1582, the first day of spring was a full ten days too early. To fix the problem, Pope Gregory XIII reset and tweaked the calendar, giving us the one we still use today.

**CONNECT TO YOU**

Divide this year by 4. If the year is evenly divisible by 4, it's a leap year. Years that end in 00 are exceptions. They must be divisible by 400!

The ancient Egyptians created a calendar to keep track of civic events such as festivals. Archeologists discovered this calendar in the Temple of Karnak in Luxor.

#  Phases and Eclipses

## Guiding Questions

- Why does the moon appear to change shape?
- What causes solar and lunar eclipses?
- How do the sun and moon affect the tides?

## Connections

**Literacy** Summarize Text

**Math** Interpret Data

MS-ESS1-1

## HANDS-ON LAB

**ʋInvestigate** Research to find out why we don't see the dark side of the moon from Earth.

## Vocabulary

phase
eclipse
umbra
penumbra
tide
spring tide
neap tide

## Academic Vocabulary

significant

## Connect It !

✏ **Observe the image of the moon in Figure 1. Draw several other shapes that you have seen the moon take.**

SEP Construct Explanations  What might be causing these changes?

...................................................................................................................................

...................................................................................................................................

...................................................................................................................................

CCC Patterns  How is Earth affected by the moon?

...................................................................................................................................

...................................................................................................................................

# The Appearance of the Moon

When the moon is full, it shines so brightly that it makes the night sky significantly brighter. At these times, when viewed from Earth, the moon is round or almost round. Other times, the moon is just a thin crescent in the sky, seeming to emit a small strand of light, as in **Figure 1**. The different shapes of the moon you see are called **phases**. Phases are caused by the motions of the moon around Earth.

**The Two Sides of the Moon** When you look at the moon when it's full, you may see what looks like a face. You are actually seeing some of the most dramatic features of the moon, a pattern of light-colored and dark-colored areas on the moon's surface. The dark-colored areas are low, flat plains of lava called *maria*. You may also be able to detect brighter patterns that indicate highland areas, often dotted with craters.

For observers from Earth these distinctive patterns on the moon never move. The side of the moon that always faces Earth is called the near side. The side of the moon that always faces away from Earth is the far side, or dark side. To find out why the same side of the moon always faces Earth, you must study the motion of the moon around Earth.

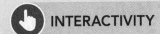
**INTERACTIVITY**

Investigate why the moon is sometimes visible during the day.

**Reflect** Look up at the sky tonight. What phase of the moon do you see? In your science notebook, track the phases of the moon. Based on your observations, what is the position of the moon in relation to the sun and Earth?

**Moon Phases**
**Figure 1** This crescent moon appeared over the horizon shortly before sunrise.

## Lunar Motion

**Figure 2** ✏️ This diagram shows the rotation and revolution of the moon. Add a drawing of a face on the two remaining images of the moon to show how the moon is facing Earth at each phase. How would the moon appear from Earth if the moon did not rotate?

................................................................................................................

................................................................................................................

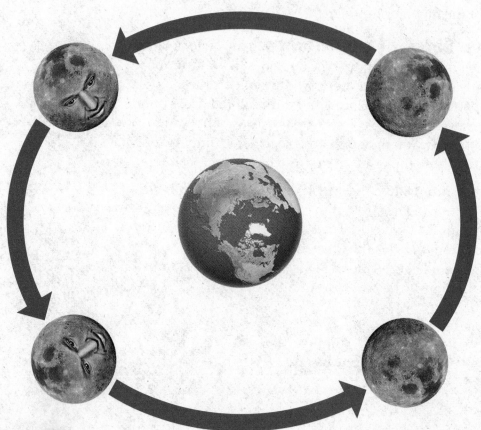

**HANDS-ON LAB**

🔬 **Investigate** Research to find out why we don't see the dark side of the moon from Earth.

## Literacy Connection

**Summarize Text** Underline the sentences that, if gathered together, best summarize how the sun, the moon, and Earth affect one another.

## Motions of the Moon

The moon, like Earth, rotates and revolves. The moon revolves around Earth and also rotates on its own axis. The moon rotates once on its axis in the same time that it takes to revolve once around Earth, as shown in **Figure 2**. Thus, a "day" on the moon is the same length as a "year" on the moon. This also explains why you always see the same side of the moon from Earth.

If you could look at the moon from space, you would see that half of the moon is always lit by the sun. The amount of the moon's surface that is lit is constant. But because the moon orbits Earth, the part of the lit surface that is visible from Earth changes. The phase of the moon you see depends on how much of the sunlit side of the moon faces Earth. These periods of light and darkness occur in predictable patterns, as shown in **Figure 3**.

**Phases of the Moon** During the new moon phase, the moon is between Earth and the sun. The side of the moon facing Earth is dark and the opposite side of the moon is facing the sun. As the moon revolves around Earth, the side of the moon you see gradually becomes more illuminated by direct sunlight.

After about a week, the angle formed by the sun, moon, and Earth is about 90 degrees. This is called the first quarter moon and it is half lit and half dark. About halfway through the moon's revolution, you see the full sunlit side of the moon, called a full moon. About a week later, the sun is shining on the other half of the moon, creating a third quarter moon. At this time you see half of the lit side. After about 29.5 days, the pattern begins again and a new moon occurs.

✔ READING CHECK **Translate Information** Use **Figure 3** to describe what is happening during a waning crescent.

..............................................................................................

..............................................................................................

..............................................................................................

..............................................................................................

INTERACTIVITY

Explore why the moon sometimes appears as a crescent in the sky.

▶ VIDEO

Find out more about the changing appearance of the moon as we see it from Earth.

**Moon Phases**
**Figure 3** ✏ In the empty circle, draw what a waning crescent moon looks like from Earth.

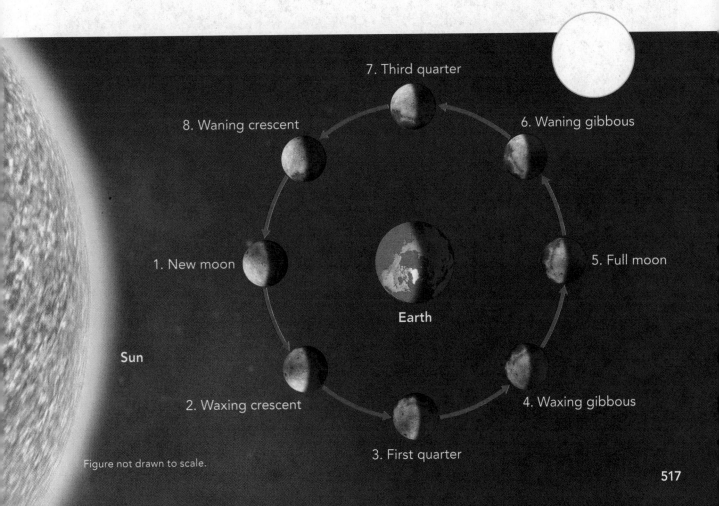

7. Third quarter

8. Waning crescent

6. Waning gibbous

1. New moon

5. Full moon

Earth

Sun

2. Waxing crescent

4. Waxing gibbous

3. First quarter

Figure not drawn to scale.

# Two Types of Eclipses

**Figure 4** ✏️ Draw an X on each diagram to show a spot where each eclipse can be seen. Add labels for the Earth's penumbra and umbra in the lunar eclipse diagram. Mark a *P* to show the places a moon could be during a partial lunar eclipse.

👆 **INTERACTIVITY**

Use a virtual activity to learn more about eclipses.

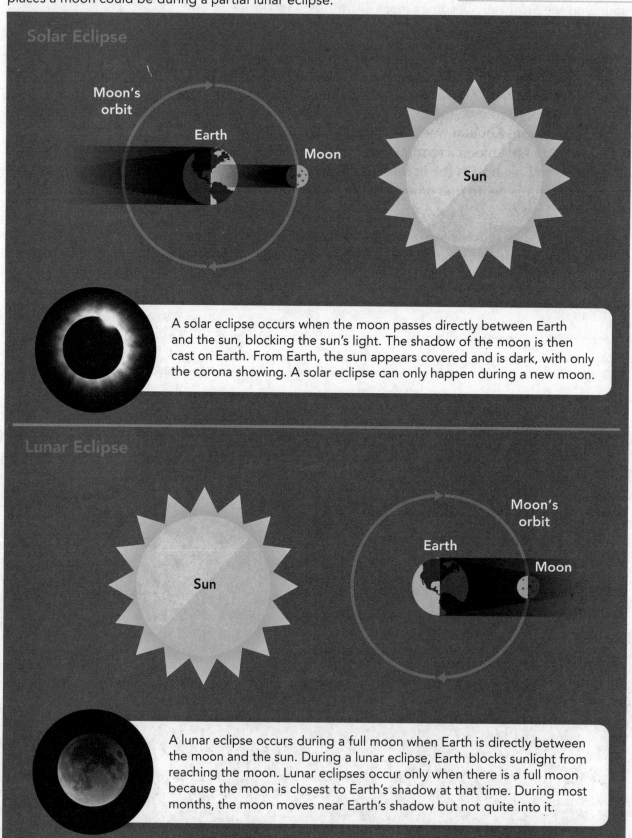

### Solar Eclipse

Moon's orbit

Earth

Moon

Sun

A solar eclipse occurs when the moon passes directly between Earth and the sun, blocking the sun's light. The shadow of the moon is then cast on Earth. From Earth, the sun appears covered and is dark, with only the corona showing. A solar eclipse can only happen during a new moon.

### Lunar Eclipse

Sun

Moon's orbit

Earth

Moon

A lunar eclipse occurs during a full moon when Earth is directly between the moon and the sun. During a lunar eclipse, Earth blocks sunlight from reaching the moon. Lunar eclipses occur only when there is a full moon because the moon is closest to Earth's shadow at that time. During most months, the moon moves near Earth's shadow but not quite into it.

# Eclipses

When an object in space comes between the sun and a third object, it cases a shadow on the third object, causing an **eclipse**. There are two types of eclipses, solar eclipses and lunar eclipses, as shown in **Figure 4**.

Every month there is a new moon and a full moon, but eclipses don't occur every month. The plane of the moon's orbit around Earth is off by about 5 degrees from the plane of Earth's orbit around the sun. During most months, the shadow cast by Earth or the moon misses the other object.

During an eclipse, the very darkest part of the shadow where the light from the sun is completely blocked is the **umbra**. Only people within the umbra experience a total solar eclipse. The moon's umbra is fairly narrow, while Earth's is much broader. Because a lunar eclipse is visible from every point on Earth's night side, more people have a view of a total lunar eclipse than of a total solar eclipse.

The area of the shadow where the sun is only partially blocked is called the **penumbra**. During a solar eclipse, people in the penumbra see only a partial eclipse. A partial lunar eclipse occurs when the moon passes partly into the umbra of Earth's shadow. The edge of the umbra appears blurry, and you can watch it pass across the moon for two or three hours.

☑ READING CHECK **Determine Central Ideas** Why isn't there an eclipse every month?

.......................................................................................

.......................................................................................

.......................................................................................

**INTERACTIVITY**

Learn more about the phases of the moon and eclipses.

**VIDEO**

Discover what it's like to work in a planetarium.

# Model It

### Solar and Lunar Eclipses

Solar and lunar eclipses occur when the sun, moon, and Earth are perfectly aligned.

**SEP Develop Models** ✏ How could you represent Earth, the moon, and the sun during an eclipse? Use real objects to create a model of a solar eclipse and a lunar eclipse. Think about what you could use as a light source to represent the sun. What positions would your objects need to be in to illustrate each type of eclipse? Draw and label the plan for your models.

# Tides

**Tides** are the rise and fall of ocean water that occur approximately every 12.5 hours. Tides result from gravitational differences in how Earth, the moon, and the sun interact at different alignments. The water rises for about 6 hours, then falls for about 6 hours.

**The Moon and Sun** The moon's gravity pulls more strongly on the side of Earth facing the moon. This pull causes the ocean water to bulge on that side of Earth. Another bulge forms on the side of Earth that is farther from the moon, where the moon's pull is weakest. This causes the formation of high tides in both locations and low tides in between. As Earth rotates, the bulges shift to remain oriented with the moon. As a result, a full rotation will result in two high-tides and two low-tides at a given location.

The sun also affects the ocean tides. Even though the sun's gravitational pull on Earth is much stronger than the moon's, the sun is so far away that the differences at the near side and far side of Earth are small. As a result, the sun's effect cannot cancel out the moon's effect, but it does influence it. Changes in the relative positions of the moon and sun affect the changing levels of the tides over the course of a month.

## Math Toolbox

Tides are measured at different locations by choosing a reference height and then determining how far above that height the water rises. The table shows approximate data for high and low tides in Nag's Head, North Carolina, in November 2016.

| High and Low Tides, Nag's Head, NC | | |
|---|---|---|
| Date | High Tide (cm) | Low Tide (cm) |
| Nov. 21 | 99.9 | 20.3 |
| Nov. 23 | 101.6 | 25.4 |
| Nov. 25 | 109.2 | 17.8 |
| Nov. 27 | 116.8 | 10.2 |

1. **SEP Interpret Data** Which tide has the greatest change in centimeters? What was the difference?

........................................................................................................................................

........................................................................................................................................

2. **CCC Patterns** Which of the dates was most likely the closest to a new moon? Explain.

........................................................................................................................................

........................................................................................................................................

**Spring Tide**

Full moon

Earth

New moon

Sun

**Neap Tide**

First quarter moon

Sun

Third quarter moon

Figures not drawn to scale.

**Spring and Neap Tides** The sun, the moon, and Earth line up during the new moon and full moon phases as is shown in **Figure 5**. The gravitational pulls from both the sun and moon combine to produce a tide with the most **significant** difference between consecutive low and high tides, called a **spring tide**.

During the moon's first quarter and third quarter phases, the line between Earth and the sun is at a right angle to the line between Earth and the moon. Because the sun and the moon are pulling in different directions, their gravitational pulls partially cancel each other. This arrangement produces more moderate tides, called neap tides. A **neap tide** is a tide with the least difference between consecutive low and high tides.

✓ **READING CHECK** **Summarize Text** What causes high and low tides?

.........................................................................................

.........................................................................................

.........................................................................................

**Spring and Neap Tides**

**Figure 5** 🖊 Spring and neap tides occur twice a month. Shade in the bulges that occur during the neap tide.

**Academic Vocabulary**

Can you use the word *significant* in a sentence about the weather?

.........................................................

.........................................................

.........................................................

.........................................................

.........................................................

MS-ESS1-1

**1. CCC Patterns** Why does the moon have phases?

.........................................................................

.........................................................................

.........................................................................

.........................................................................

.........................................................................

.........................................................................

**2. SEP Explain Phenomena** In what positions are the sun, moon, and Earth during a full moon?

.........................................................................

.........................................................................

.........................................................................

**3. CCC Cause and Effect** What causes a total lunar eclipse?

.........................................................................

.........................................................................

.........................................................................

.........................................................................

.........................................................................

**4. SEP Construct Explanations** Under what circumstances might you be able to view a partial solar eclipse instead of a full solar eclipse?

.........................................................................

.........................................................................

.........................................................................

.........................................................................

.........................................................................

.........................................................................

**5. Draw Conclusions** What would you expect the tides to be like during a first quarter moon?

.........................................................................

.........................................................................

.........................................................................

.........................................................................

.........................................................................

.........................................................................

# Quest CHECK-IN

In this lesson, you learned about how Earth, the moon, and the sun interact to create the phases of the moon, eclipses, and tides.

**SEP Evaluate Information** What does the pattern among the moon's phases and the cycle of tides suggest about how reliable tidal power would be?

.........................................................................

.........................................................................

.........................................................................

.........................................................................

.........................................................................

## HANDS-ON LAB

The Moon's Revolution and Tides

**Go online** for a downloadable worksheet of this lab. Investigate how the position of the moon relative to Earth and the sun affects tides and to explore why some tidal ranges vary over time.

MS-ESS1-1

# Power From
# THE TIDES

▶ **VIDEO**

Explore the mechanics of a turbine and how it generates usable energy.

**How do you** generate electricity from tides? You engineer it!

**The Challenge:** To harness tidal power to generate electricity.

**Phenomenon** If you've ever had to move your beach towel further up the sand as you notice the tide coming in, you've witnessed one of Earth's greatest renewable resources. Twenty-four hours a day, the tides move millions of gallons of water along coastlines around the world.

Engineers are applying an existing technology—turbines—in a new way to generate power from moving tides. Turbines look like large fans. When placed in shallow water where the tide is strong, moving ocean water turns the turbine's blades. The spinning blades power generators to make electricity. The world's first tidal energy plant, in France, produces enough electricity to power a small city.

Tidal energy doesn't create pollution, and tides are reliable and powerful. But the technology used to harness the tides is expensive. Engineers are looking for ways to make tidal turbines more cost-effective. When that happens, harnessing tidal energy may become the wave of the future.

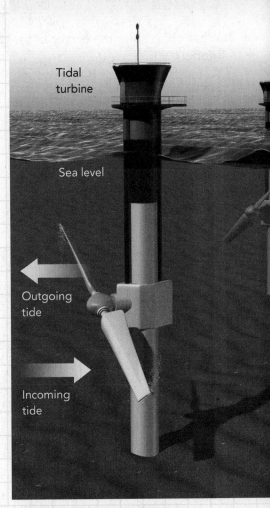

Tidal turbine

Sea level

Outgoing tide

Incoming tide

A tidal turbine generates power both when the tide comes in and when the tide goes out.

**DESIGN CHALLENGE** Can you design a tidal turbine? Go to the Engineering Design Notebook to find out!

# ☑ TOPIC 11 Review and Assess

## 1 Movement in Space

MS-ESS1-1

**1.** Planets appear to move in the sky against the backdrop of
A. other planets.　B. the sun.
C. the stars.　D. the moon.

**2.** What object is at the center of the geocentric model?
A. Earth　B. the moon
C. the sun　D. a star

**3.** What discovery by Galileo supported the heliocentric model?
A. the phases of Venus
B. the elliptical orbits of planets
C. the moon's orbiting of Earth
D. the movement of planets in the night sky

**4.** Objects in the sky appear to move due to Earth's ................................................ and ................................................

**5. CCC Cause and Effect** Why do stars appear to move from east to west in the night sky?

....................................................................
....................................................................
....................................................................
....................................................................

**6. CCC Patterns** The constellation Hercules is visible in the sky in September. Why isn't Hercules visible in the sky in March?

....................................................................
....................................................................
....................................................................
....................................................................

## 2 Earth's Movements in Space

MS-ESS1-1

**7.** The imaginary line that runs through Earth's pole is its
A. axis.　B. orbit.
C. revolution.　D. rotation.

**8.** Which of the following is responsible for the cyclic pattern of day and night on Earth?
A. the tilt of Earth's axis
B. the rotation of Earth on its axis
C. Earth's revolution around the sun
D. the revolution of the moon around Earth

**9.** Earth has seasons because
A. its axis is tilted as it revolves around the sun.
B. it rotates on its axis as it revolves.
C. the moon exerts a gravitational force on it.
D. the relative positions of Earth, the sun, and the moon do not change.

**10.** The two times of the year in which the sun is directly overhead at the equator are the
................................................ and the ................................................

**11. CCC Patterns** How does the distance between two objects affect the force of gravity between them?

....................................................................
....................................................................

**12. CCC Systems** Why is it generally warmer in the Northern Hemisphere in June than it is in December?

....................................................................
....................................................................
....................................................................
....................................................................

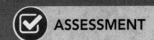
# ③ Phases and Eclipses

MS-ESS1-1

**13.** Which of the following occurs when the moon moves through Earth's shadow?
A. high tide
B. a solar eclipse
C. a lunar eclipse
D. the phases of the moon

**14.** When the sun, the moon, and Earth line up during a new moon, which of the following is produced?
A. low tide
B. high tide
C. spring tide
D. neap tide

**15. SEP Apply Scientific Reasoning** Suppose you traveled to the moon during a lunar eclipse. From your vantage point on the moon, what astronomical event would you be witnessing?

...................................................................

**16. CCC Cause and Effect** Why does the moon have phases?

...................................................................

...................................................................

...................................................................

**17. SEP Use Models** Does the diagram show a solar eclipse or a lunar eclipse? Explain.

...................................................................

...................................................................

...................................................................

...................................................................

**18. Apply Concepts** Which event would be less widely visible from Earth: a partial lunar eclipse or a total lunar eclipse? Explain.

...................................................................

...................................................................

...................................................................

...................................................................

...................................................................

**19. CCC System Models** ✏ Draw a diagram of Earth, the sun, and the moon to demonstrate the phases of the moon: new, first quarter, full, and last quarter. In your diagram, label the four different positions of the moon and sketch what the corresponding phases look like from Earth.

525

MS-ESS1-1

## Evidence-Based Assessment

Gita is constructing a model to help her younger sister in science class. She hopes to use the model to demonstrate how the sun, Earth, and the moon interact so that her sister can describe and explain patterns in the cycles of this system. Gita wants her sister to be able to describe the following phenomena using the model:

- the phases of the moon

- the seasons on Earth

- solar and lunar eclipses

Gita's model is shown here. Gita labels E1, E2, E3, and E4 to show four positions of Earth in its orbit around the sun. She labels M1, M2, M3, and M4 to show four positions of the moon in its orbit around Earth.

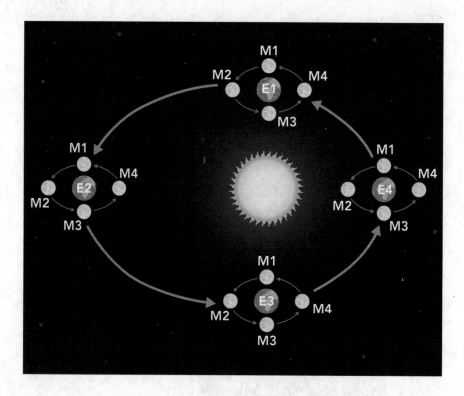

1. **CCC System Models** If Earth is at position E1 on the model and there is a new moon, then what is the moon's position?

   A. M1
   B. M2
   C. M3
   D. M4

2. **CCC Patterns** Complete the table to identify the positions of Earth and the moon in their respective orbits for each phenomenon listed.

| Phenomenon | Earth's Position | Moon's Position |
|---|---|---|
| lunar eclipse | | M4 |
| solar eclipse | E3 | |
| full moon | E1 | |

3. **SEP Use Models** Evaluate Gita's model and explain whether her sister can use it to correctly describe the patterns of the seasons on Earth.

   ......................................................
   ......................................................
   ......................................................
   ......................................................
   ......................................................
   ......................................................
   ......................................................
   ......................................................
   ......................................................
   ......................................................
   ......................................................
   ......................................................
   ......................................................
   ......................................................
   ......................................................

4. **SEP Construct Explanations** Explain how Gita's sister can also use the model to show how patterns in the interactions among the sun, Earth, and the moon allow us to predict when lunar phases and eclipses occur.

   ......................................................
   ......................................................
   ......................................................
   ......................................................
   ......................................................
   ......................................................
   ......................................................
   ......................................................
   ......................................................
   ......................................................
   ......................................................
   ......................................................
   ......................................................

## Quest FINDINGS

## Complete the Quest!

**Phenomenon Think about ways to develop your model to demonstrate how the tides occur.**

**CCC Identify Limitations** What are some of the limitations of your model for the visitor center? How could you make your model more accurate?

......................................................
......................................................
......................................................
......................................................

👆 **INTERACTIVITY**

Reflect on It's as Sure as the Tides

MS-ESS1-1

# Modeling Lunar Phases

Can you **design a model** to describe how the **moon's motion** is related to its **phases**?

## Background

**Phenomenon** One of the greatest achievements of our ancestors was learning to make sense of the repeating patterns in the phases of the moon. People began organizing time and planning major events, such as planting and harvesting crops, according to these cycles, resulting in the earliest stages of human civilization.

In this investigation, you will design a model, using available materials, to show the relationship between the moon's motion around Earth and the moon's phases.

### Materials

(per group)

- bright flashlight
- one small foam ball
- one large foam ball
- sharpened pencils or skewers

| New Moon | First Quarter | Full Moon | Third Quarter |

# Plan Your Investigation

**HANDS-ON LAB**

**Demonstrate** Go online for a downloadable worksheet of this lab.

1. You will model each view of the moon that is shown in the diagram. Look at the images of the moon. What do you think causes the differing amounts of lit moon in each image? Remember that the moon reflects light from the sun. Then think about the materials in the list. What do you think each material could represent in your model?

2. Start by discussing how you could model the view called *First Quarter*. Decide where you could position the flashlight and foam balls to show the sun, Earth, and moon in orbit. Where will you position the moon so an observer on Earth would see the first quarter moon? (Hint: Observe that during the first quarter phase, the right side of the moon is lit and the left side is dark.)

3. The next phase after first quarter is full moon. Based on this information, decide how to model the moon's orbit around Earth. In other words, in which direction does the moon orbit Earth?

4. Decide how to model the full moon, the third quarter, and the new moon. Where in its orbit does the moon take on each shape as seen from Earth?

5. Record your plans for modeling the phases of the moon. Include sketches or drawings that will help you to construct your model. Review your plans with your teacher before building and testing your model.

## Plan

........................................................................

........................................................................

........................................................................

........................................................................

........................................................................

........................................................................

........................................................................

........................................................................

........................................................................

........................................................................

........................................................................

........................................................................

## Sketches

# Analyze and Interpret Data

1. **SEP Develop Models** In your model, where did you place the flashlight, large foam ball, and small foam ball to model the first quarter moon?

......................................................................................................

......................................................................................................

......................................................................................................

......................................................................................................

......................................................................................................

2. **CCC Patterns** Compare and contrast your models of the first quarter moon and the third quarter moon. What causes these shapes to look different to an observer on Earth?

......................................................................................................

......................................................................................................

......................................................................................................

......................................................................................................

......................................................................................................

3. **SEP Apply Scientific Reasoning** At the first and third quarter phases, the moon's shape appears as half a circle. Why do you think these phases are called *quarter* phases and not *half* phases?

......................................................................................................

......................................................................................................

......................................................................................................

......................................................................................................

......................................................................................................

4. **SEP Construct Explanations** One lunar cycle includes all of the lunar phases. One lunar cycle is about one month long. Use evidence from your model to describe how the motions of the moon lead to lunar phases that occur in a lunar cycle.

......................................................................................................

......................................................................................................

......................................................................................................

......................................................................................................

......................................................................................................

**NGSS PERFORMANCE EXPECTATIONS**

**MS-ESS1-2** Develop and use a model to describe
the role of gravity in the motions within galaxies
and the solar system.

**MS-ESS1-3** Analyze and interpret data to
determine scale properties of objects in the solar
system.

**GO ONLINE**
to access your
digital course.

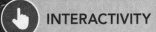 VIDEO

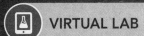 INTERACTIVITY

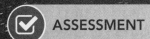 VIRTUAL LAB

 ASSESSMENT

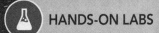 eTEXT

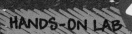 HANDS-ON LABS

**H**ow do astronomers use telescopes and space probes to study the universe?

**HANDS-ON LAB**

⬛**Connect** Develop a model to compare Earth's size to the size of the other planets.

## The Essential Question

# What kind of data and evidence help us to understand the universe?

**SEP Construct Explanations** For thousands of years, people have stared at and studied the sky. Some use tools such as diagrams, telescopes, cameras, and lasers to assist them. Some have even traveled beyond Earth to take a better look. Why do you look at the sky? Why do you think others do?

.................................................................................

.................................................................................

.................................................................................

.................................................................................

# How do we look for things that can't be seen?

**STEM** **Phenomenon** Telescopes and other technology allow astronomers and astrophysicists to collect data on objects in the universe. In this Quest activity, you will help with the hiring of three astronomers for a new observatory. Their specialties include asteroids, extraterrestrial life, and dark matter. In digital activities, you will investigate the work that asteroid, extraterrestrial, and dark matter hunters do. By applying what you have learned, you will develop persuasive advertisements for these positions.

👆 **INTERACTIVITY**

Searching for a Star

**MS-ESS1-2** Develop and use a model to describe the role of gravity in the motions within galaxies and the solar system.

**MS-ESS1-3** Analyze and interpret data to determine scale properties of objects in the solar system.

**NBC LEARN** ▶ VIDEO

After watching the Quest Kickoff video, which examines the work of an astronomer who searches for life on planets outside our solar system, think about the qualities that make for a skilled astronomer. What scientific attitudes are important to the work of an astronomer such as the one in the video? Record your thoughts.

## Qualities of a Skilled Astronomer

**1** .....................................................

**2** .....................................................

**3** .....................................................

**4** .....................................................

### IN LESSON 1

**STEM** How do astronomers study distant objects? Explore how astronomers are able to detect asteroids and the dangers these objects pose to Earth.

👆 **INTERACTIVITY**

Space Invaders

### IN LESSON 2

How do scientists search for extraterrestrial life in the vastness of the universe? Consider the tools they must use to look for signs of life on other planets.

👆 **INTERACTIVITY**

Anybody Out There?

### IN LESSON 3

How do astronomers classify stars? Consider how studying stars helps astronomers in the search for extraterrestrial life.

Telescopes and other equipment in this observatory allow astronomers to learn more about the properties of and relationships among our close neighbors in space as well as distant galaxies.

## Quest FINDINGS

### Complete the Quest!

Apply what you've learned about the work astronomers do by creating a persuasive job advertisement.

 **INTERACTIVITY**

Reflect on Searching for a Star

## Quest CHECK-IN

### IN LESSON 4

**STEM** How do astronomers know that dark matter exists? Explore the ways in which astronomers study something that cannot be seen.

 **INTERACTIVITY**

Searching for the Unseen

535

# Planetary Measures

## Background

**Phenomenon** If you look at the sky at night, you might be able to spot some of the other planets in our solar system. Scientists distinguish between the inner planets, which are planets that are relatively close to the sun, and the outer planets, which are relatively far away. The planets you can see at night appear to be tiny, but that is only because they are so far away from Earth. How big are the other planets compared to Earth? In this activity, you will make a scale model to see how the other planets in our solar system compare in size to Earth.

How can you **analyze data** to compare the sizes of Earth and the other planets?

## Materials

**(per group)**

- quarter
- metric ruler
- butcher paper or poster board
- pencil
- compass
- pushpin
- string

## Safety

Be sure to follow all safety procedures provided by your teacher. The Safety Appendix of your textbook provides more details about the safety icons.

## Design a Model

1. **SEP Analyze and Interpret Data** Find information about the sizes of the planets in the solar system and record it in the table. Be sure to include the name of the dimension that you are recording and its units.

2. **SEP Develop a Model** Choose an object or quantity to represent the size of Earth in your model. Then decide how you will use the materials to represent Earth and the other planets in the model.

3. **CCC Scale, Proportion, and Quantity** Calculate the size of each of the other planets relative to the size of Earth. Then use the relative sizes that you calculated to determine the size that each planet should be in your model. Record the relative sizes and the model sizes in the data table.

4.  Build your model. To create a scale model, make each planet the model size that you have calculated it should be.

# Data

| Inner Planets | Mercury | Venus | Earth | Mars |
|---|---|---|---|---|
| Actual Size | | | | |
| Relative Size Earth = 1 | | | 1.0 | |
| Model Size | | | | |

| Outer Planets | Jupiter | Saturn | Uranus | Neptune |
|---|---|---|---|---|
| Actual Size | | | | |
| Relative Size Earth = 1 | | | | |
| Model Size | | | | |

## HANDS-ON LAB

ыConnect Go online for a downloadable worksheet of this lab.

# Analyze and Interpret Data

1. **SEP Analyze Data** List the planets in order from largest to smallest.

   ......................................................................................................

   ......................................................................................................

2. **SEP Analyze and Interpret Data** What difference do you see between the sizes of the inner planets relative to the sizes of the outer planets?

   ......................................................................................................

   ......................................................................................................

3. **CCC Systems and System Models** What other planetary properties could you investigate with a scale model? Explain how the model would aid in investigating these properties.

   ......................................................................................................

   ......................................................................................................

   ......................................................................................................

   ......................................................................................................

# Solar System Objects

## Guiding Questions

- How do the characteristics of the planets, moons, and smaller objects in the solar system compare?
- What is the role of gravity in the motions of planets, moons, and smaller objects in the solar system?
- What are the relationships between the sun and the planets in the solar system?

## Connections

**Literacy** Integrate With Visuals

**Math** Convert Measurement Units

MS-ESS1-2, MS-ESS1-3

## HANDS-ON LAB

**uInvestigate** Develop a model to describe the role of gravity in the solar system.

### Vocabulary

solar system
astronomical unit
sun
planet
moon
asteroid
meteoroids
comets

### Academic Vocabulary

features

## Connect It !

✏ **Put an X on the object in the center of the solar system. Draw a circle around Earth.**

Use Models List all the objects you can identify.

......................................................................................................

......................................................................................................

SEP Analyze and Interpret Data What do the curved lines in the illustration represent? How can you tell?

......................................................................................................

......................................................................................................

# Understanding the Solar System

Our home, Earth, is a planet. Earth is just one of many objects that make up our solar system. The **solar system** consists of the sun, the planets, their moons, and a variety of smaller objects. Each object in the solar system has a unique set of **features**. The sun is at the center of the solar system, with other objects orbiting around it. The force of the sun's gravitational pull keeps objects in their orbits around it. The strength of the gravitational force between any two objects in the solar system depends on their masses and the distance between them.

**HANDS-ON LAB**

Model the movements of planets around the sun.

## Academic Vocabulary

The term *feature* can be used to mean a trait or characteristic. What are some features of the mode of transportation you use to get to school each day?

.................................................

.................................................

.................................................

.................................................

### Objects in the Solar System

**Figure 1** In the solar system, planets and other objects orbit the sun.

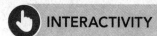

**INTERACTIVITY**

Explore the scale of distances in the solar system.

## Distances in the Solar System

Distances between objects in the solar system are so large that they are not easily measured in meters or kilometers. Instead, scientists frequently use a unit called the **astronomical unit** (AU). One astronomical unit equals the average distance measured from the center of the sun to the center of Earth, which is about 150,000,000 kilometers. The entire solar system extends more than 100,000 AU from the sun.

## Math Toolbox

### Converting Units of Distance

✎ Complete the diagram by drawing a line to represent the distance of 1 AU. Then write the number of kilometers equal to 1 AU.

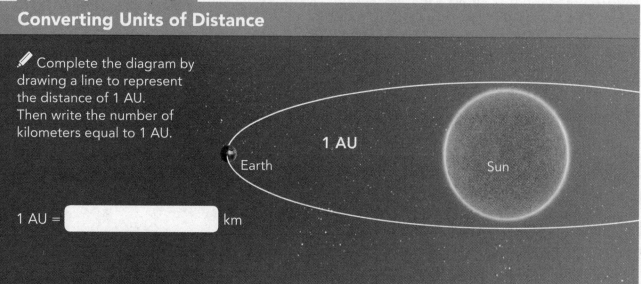

1 AU

Earth

Sun

1 AU = [ ] km

The distances between objects in the solar system are vast. As a result, scientists use the larger value of the astronomical unit to make the numbers easier to work with.

To give you some perspective, the combined length of about 18 football fields is equal to 1 mi. One mile is about 1.6 km. That means 1 AU is equal to 1,650,000,000,000 football fields!

1. **SEP Use Mathematics** Jupiter, the largest planet in our solar system, is about 630,000,000 km from Earth. About how many AU is Jupiter from Earth?

.................................................................................................

2. **SEP Use Computational Thinking** Develop your own conversion between AU and a common distance such as the length of a football field. How many of your common units is equal to 1 AU?

.................................................................................................

.................................................................................................

.................................................................................................

## Comparing the Sun and Planets

Our solar system has the sun at its center. The **sun** is a gaseous body much larger than anything else in the solar system. In fact, the sun accounts for about 99.85 percent of the entire mass of the solar system. Despite being more than a million times the volume of Earth, our sun is actually a very ordinary mid-sized star. Astronomers have used telescopes to observe stars that are a thousand times more massive than the sun. Our ordinary star is expected to continue burning for another five billion years.

A **planet** is round, orbits the sun, and has cleared out the region of the solar system along its orbit. The four inner planets, including Earth, are closer to the sun, small, and made mostly of rock and metal. The four outer planets are farther from the sun, very large, and made mostly of gas and liquid. Like Earth, each planet has a "day" and a "year." A planet's day is the time it takes to rotate on its axis. A planet's year is the time it takes to orbit the sun.

✓ **READING CHECK** **Summarize Text** How do the inner and outer planets differ?

...................................................................................................

...................................................................................................

...................................................................................................

**VIDEO**

Learn about distances in the solar system.

**HANDS-ON LAB**

**Investigate** Develop a model to describe the role of gravity in the solar system.

**Comparing the Sun and Earth**

**Figure 2** 🖊 Circle the word that correctly completes each statement in the table.

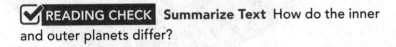

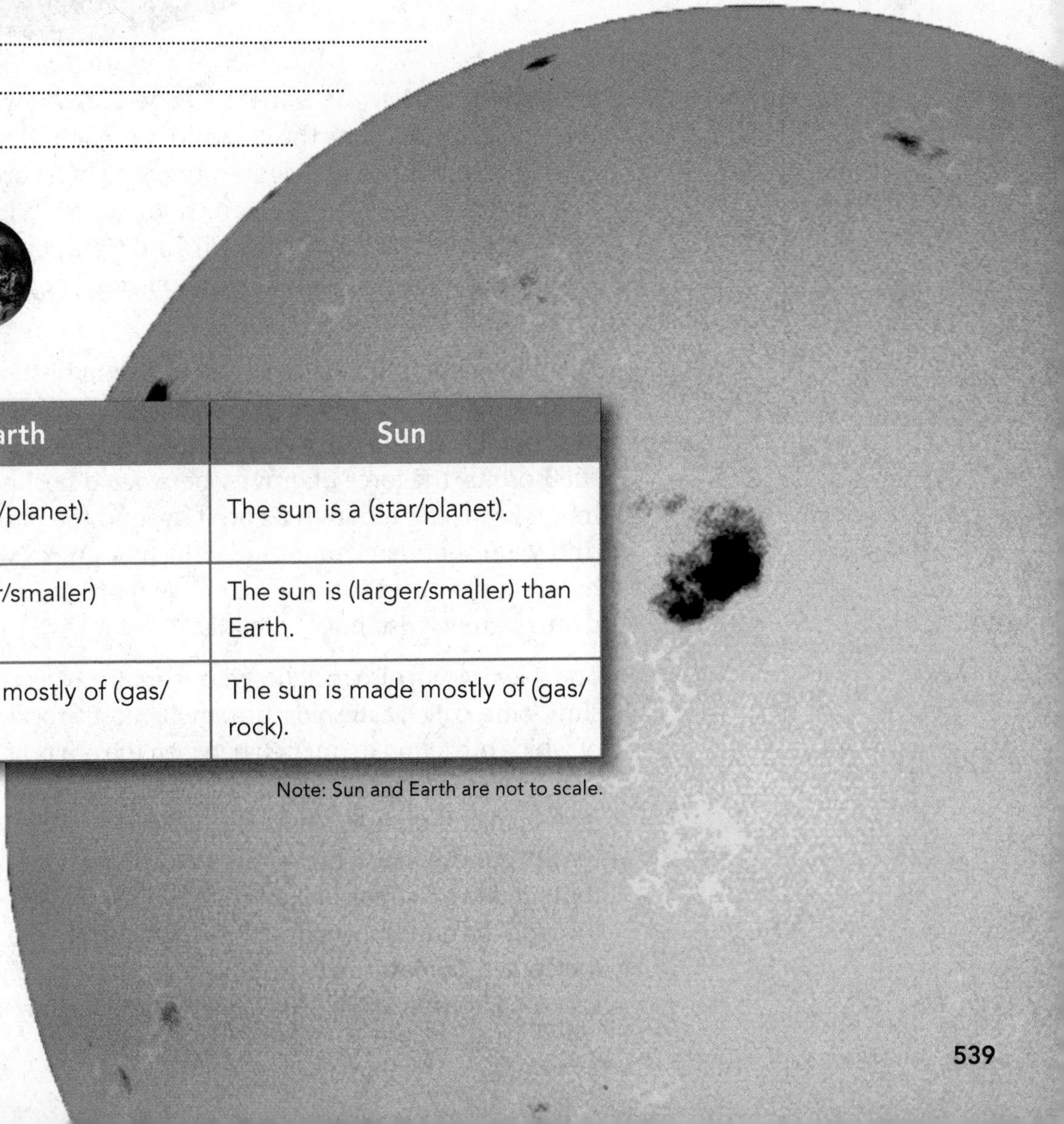

| Earth | Sun |
|---|---|
| Earth is a (star/planet). | The sun is a (star/planet). |
| Earth is (larger/smaller) than the sun. | The sun is (larger/smaller) than Earth. |
| Earth is made mostly of (gas/rock). | The sun is made mostly of (gas/rock). |

Note: Sun and Earth are not to scale.

## Pluto and Ida

**Figure 3** Pluto (right) was considered the ninth planet in our solar system for many years. Astronomers now classify it as a dwarf planet. Asteroid Ida (top), identified in 1884, is the first observed asteroid with a moon.

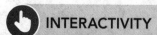

**INTERACTIVITY**

Investigate the factors that affect the interactions of astronomical bodies.

**Smaller Solar System Objects** A dwarf planet is an object that orbits the sun and has enough gravity to be spherical, but it has not cleared the area of its orbit. There are five known dwarf planets in our solar system: Pluto, Eris, Ceres, Makemake (MAH keh MAH keh), and Haumea (how MAY uh). As scientists observe more distant objects, they may identify more dwarf planets.

Six of the eight planets in our solar system host at least one natural satellite, or **moon**. A natural satellite is a celestial body in orbit. Just as the sun's gravitational pull keeps the planets in their orbits, the force of gravity between a host planet and its moon keeps the moon in its orbit around the planet. Mercury and Venus both lack moons. Earth comes next, with just one moon. Jupiter and Saturn each have more than 60! Some dwarf planets also have satellites.

The solar system also includes many smaller objects that orbit the sun. Some, called **asteroids**, are small, mostly rocky bodies, many of which are found in an area between the orbits of Mars and Jupiter. **Figure 3** shows an asteroid named Ida. Chunks of rock or dust smaller than asteroids are called **meteoroids**. When entering Earth's atmosphere, a meteoroid's friction with the air creates heat that produces a streak of light called a meteor. Meteoroids that pass through the atmosphere and hit Earth's surface are called meteorites. **Comets** are loose balls of ice and rock that usually have very long, narrow orbits. They develop tails as they orbit the sun.

# Structure of the Sun

Recall that the sun is a gaseous body much larger than anything else in our solar system. The sun contains no solid surface, unlike our own planet. About three fourths of the sun's mass is hydrogen, and about one fourth is helium. The hydrogen and helium are in the form of plasma, a fourth state of matter. Plasma is a very hot fluid-like gas consisting of electrically-charged particles. However, like Earth, the sun has an interior and an atmosphere.

**The Sun's Interior** The interior of the sun includes the convection zone, the radiative zone, and the core. **Figure 4** shows the sun's interior.

**The Convection Zone** The convection zone is the outermost layer of the sun's interior. Plasma heated by the radiative zone rises up to the surface. The cooling plasma at the surface leads to its contraction, thereby increasing its density and causing it to sink. The heating plasma expands, decreasing its density, causing it to rise, setting up convection loops that move energy toward the surface. Cooler plasma looks darker and hotter plasma looks brighter. This creates the granular appearance of the surface of the convection zone.

**The Radiative Zone** Energy leaves the core primarily as gamma rays, which are a form of electromagnetic radiation. The gamma rays enter and pass through the radiative zone. It is called the radiative zone because most heat flows through here as forms of electromagnetic radiation. Astronomers estimate that it can take up to a million years for energy produced at the core to reach the surface of the sun. This is in part due to the incredibly high density of the plasma in the radiative zone.

**Inside the Sun**

**Figure 4** ✏️ The interior of the sun has three main layers. Draw an arrow to indicate how energy created at the sun's core travels.

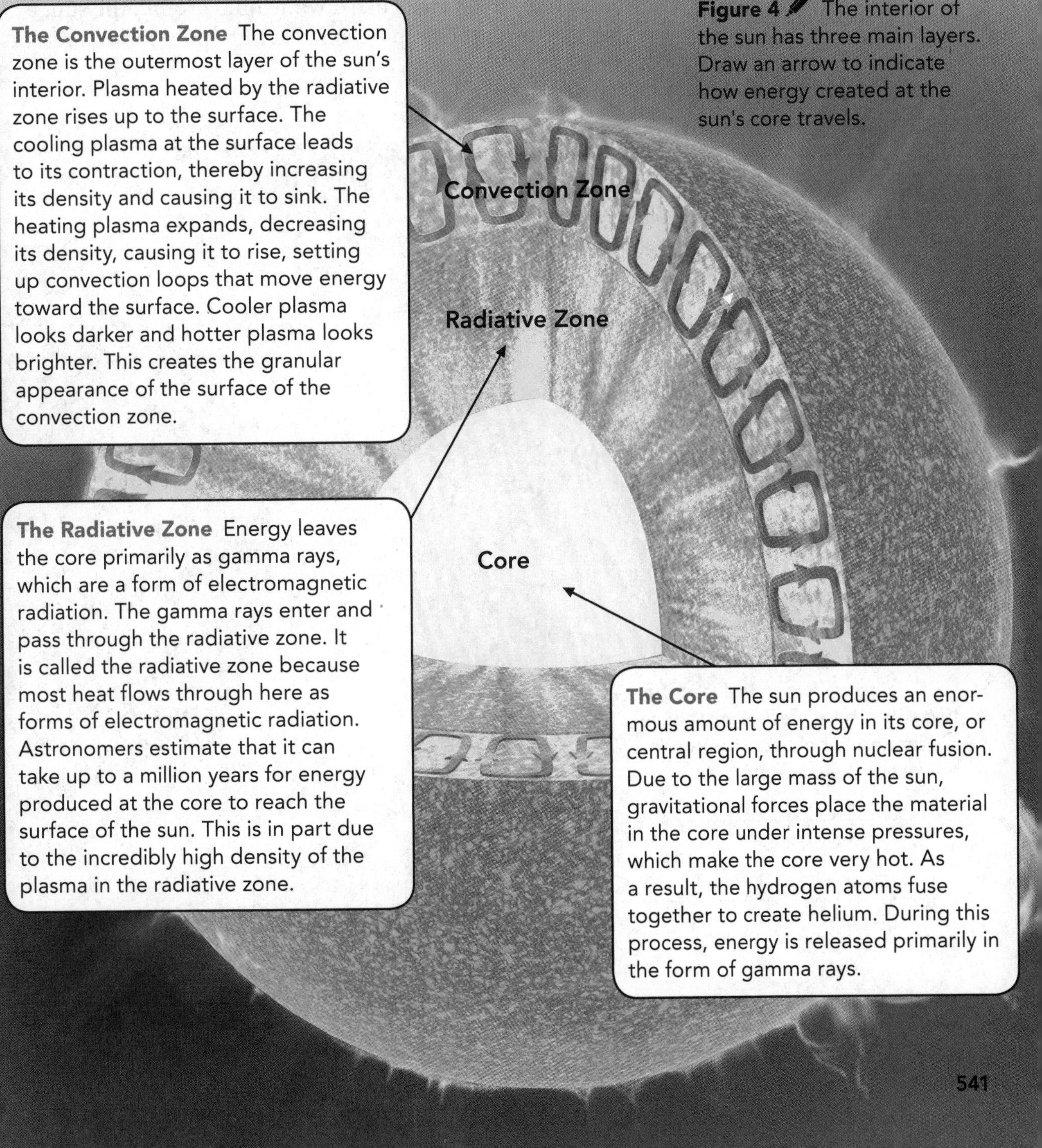

Convection Zone

Radiative Zone

Core

**The Core** The sun produces an enormous amount of energy in its core, or central region, through nuclear fusion. Due to the large mass of the sun, gravitational forces place the material in the core under intense pressures, which make the core very hot. As a result, the hydrogen atoms fuse together to create helium. During this process, energy is released primarily in the form of gamma rays.

**The Sun's Atmosphere** The sun's atmosphere extends far into space, as shown in **Figure 5**. Like the sun's interior, the atmosphere is composed primarily of hydrogen and helium, and consists of three main layers—the photosphere, the chromosphere, and the corona.

The inner layer of the sun's atmosphere is called the photosphere (FOH tuh sfeer). The plasma in this layer is dense enough to be visible and directly observed. A reddish glow is sometimes visible around the edge of the photosphere. Often, this glow can be seen at the beginning and end of a total solar eclipse. This glow comes from the chromosphere, the middle layer of the sun's atmosphere. The Greek word chroma means "color," so this layer is the "color sphere." The outer layer of the atmosphere, which looks like a white halo around the sun, is called the corona. This layer extends into space for millions of kilometers.

## Model It !

### The Sun's Atmosphere

**Figure 5** This image is a combination of two photographs of the sun. One shows the sun's surface and was taken through a special filter that shows the sun's features. The other shows the corona and was taken during an eclipse.

1. SEP Use Models 🖉 On the image, label the photosphere and the corona. Shade in and label the area of the chromosphere.

2. SEP Develop Models 🖉 Think about how you could use commonly available materials to make a model of the sun's atmosphere. Label the layers with the materials you would use to represent them.

3. CCC System Models Describe two ways the materials you chose are limited in how accurately they represent the sun's atmosphere.

........................................................

........................................................

........................................................

........................................................

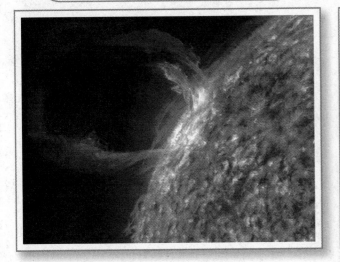

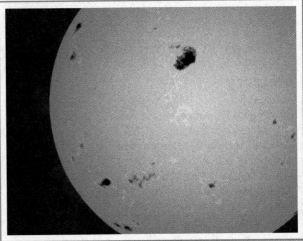

## Features of the Sun

Astronomers have used special telescopes, satellites, and space probes to study the structure and features of the sun. The most visible features are sunspots, prominences, and solar flares.

**Sunspots** Astronomers studying the sun have observed dark areas on the sun's surface. These sunspots are areas of plasma that are cooler than the plasma around them. The cooler plasma gives off less light, resulting in the dark spots. The number of sunspots varies in a regular cycle that peaks every 11 years and corresponds to an increase in the amount of light energy given off by the sun.

Observations of the changing positions of sunspots indicate that the sun rotates, or spins on its axis. Unlike the solid Earth, which has a single rate of rotation, the sun rotates faster at its equator than near its poles.

**Prominences** Sunspots often occur in pairs. Huge loops of plasma that are polarized, called prominences, often link different parts of sunspot regions. Particles following these magnetic forces flow out and back on the sun's surface. You can compare sunspots and prominences in **Figure 6**.

**Solar Flares** Sometimes the loops in sunspot regions suddenly connect, releasing large amounts of magnetic energy. The energy heats plasma on the sun to millions of degrees Celsius, causing it to erupt into space. These eruptions are called solar flares.

✓ **READING CHECK** **Read and Comprehend** When prominences join, they cause (sunspots/solar flares).

### An Active Star
**Figure 6** Different types of photographs show the sun's different features. Label the two images above as either sunspots or prominences.

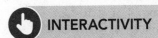 **INTERACTIVITY**

Explore the structure of the sun.

543

**0 AU**                                                    **10 AU**

### Mercury
**Mass:** $0.330 \times 10^{24}$ kg
**Equatorial Diameter:** 4,879 km
**Distance from the sun:** 0.39 AU
**Orbital period:** 88.0 Earth days
**Moons:** 0
**Mean Temperature:** 167°C
**Atmospheric Composition:** None (thin exosphere made up of atoms blasted off surface by solar wind)

During the day, temperatures on Mercury can reach 430°C. But without a real atmosphere, temperatures at night plunge to –170°C.

### Earth
**Mass:** $5.97 \times 10^{24}$ kg
**Equatorial Diameter:** 12,756 km
**Distance from the sun:** 1 AU
**Orbital period:** 365.26 Earth days
**Moons:** 1
**Mean Temperature:** 15°C
**Atmospheric Composition:** nitrogen, oxygen, trace amounts of other gases

Our planet is the only object in the solar system known to harbor life, mainly due to the fact that liquid water exists on its surface.

### Venus
**Mass:** $4.87 \times 10^{24}$ kg
**Equatorial Diameter:** 12,104 km
**Distance from the sun:** 0.72 AU
**Orbital period:** 224.7 Earth days
**Moons:** 0
**Mean Temperature:** 464°C
**Atmospheric Composition:** carbon dioxide (with sulfuric acid clouds)

Most planets and moons in the solar system rotate from west to east. Venus, oddly, rotates from east to west.

### Mars
**Mass:** $0.642 \times 10^{24}$ kg
**Equatorial Diameter:** 6,792 km
**Distance from the sun:** 1.52 AU
**Orbital period:** 687 Earth days
**Moons:** 2
**Mean Temperature:** −63°C
**Atmospheric Composition:** mainly carbon dioxide, with nitrogen and argon

The red planet is home to the largest volcano in the solar system, Olympus Mons.

### The Solar System
**Figure 7** ✏ Mark the position of each planet on the distance scale. (The planets' sizes and distances from the sun are not shown to scale.)

**CCC Patterns** Examine the data about each planet. What patterns do you observe?

..........................................................................................................................

..........................................................................................................................

..........................................................................................................................

..........................................................................................................................

### Jupiter
**Mass:** 1,898 × 10²⁴ kg
**Equatorial Diameter:** 142,984 km
**Distance from the sun:** 5.20 AU
**Orbital period:** 4,331 Earth days
**Moons:** 79
**Mean Temperature:** −110°C
**Atmospheric Composition:** mostly hydrogen with some helium

The Great Red Spot is one of the most noticeable features of Jupiter. This storm is so huge that two to three Earths could fit inside it.

### Uranus
**Mass:** 86.8 × 10²⁴ kg
**Equatorial Diameter:** 51,118 km
**Distance from the sun:** 19.20 AU
**Orbital period:** 30,589 Earth days
**Moons:** 27
**Mean Temperature:** −195°C
**Atmospheric Composition:** hydrogen, helium, and a small amount of methane

Viewed from Earth, Uranus rotates top to bottom instead of side to side. This is because the planet's axis of rotation is tilted at an angle about 90 degrees from vertical.

### Saturn
**Mass:** 568 × 10²⁴ kg
**Equatorial Diameter:** 120,536 km
**Distance from the sun:** 9.55 AU
**Orbital period:** 10,747 Earth days
**Moons:** 82
**Mean Temperature:** −140°C
**Atmospheric Composition:** mostly hydrogen with some helium

The particles that make up Saturn's majestic rings range in size from grains of dust to ice and rock that may measure several meters across.

### Neptune
**Mass:** 102 × 10²⁴ kg
**Equatorial Diameter:** 49,528 km
**Distance from the sun:** 30.05 AU
**Orbital period:** 59,800 Earth days
**Moons:** 14
**Mean Temperature:** −200°C
**Atmospheric Composition:** hydrogen, helium, and a small amount of methane

This planet just might be the windiest place in the solar system. Winds on Neptune can reach speeds of 2,000 kph.

✓ **READING CHECK** **Integrate Visuals** How does the size of the sun compare to the sizes of the planets?

......................................................................

......................................................................

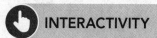
## Literacy Connection

**Integrate With Visuals**
Use the information in the text to write a caption for the top left image in **Figure 8**.

.................................................

.................................................

.................................................

### Forming the Solar System

**Figure 8** ✏️ The solar system formed from a cloud of gas and other materials. Write the numbers 1 through 4 to put the images in order and represent how the solar system formed.

# Solar System Formation

Scientists think the solar system formed at a minimum of 4.6 billion years ago from a cloud of hydrogen, helium, rock, ice, and other materials. The first step in the formation of the solar system occurred as the force of gravity began to pull together materials in the cloud. A rotating disk of gas, ice, and dust formed as the cloud material was drawn toward the central mass. As more material was pulled into the disk's center, it became more dense, pressures increased, and as a result, the center grew hot.

Eventually, temperature and pressures became so high that hydrogen atoms combined to form helium. This process, called nuclear fusion, releases large amounts of energy in the form of electromagnetic radiation, which includes sunlight.

Around the sun, bits of rock, ice, and gas began to pull together first from electrostatic charges, or electrical forces that do not flow. As the objects grew larger, gravity pulled them together. The rock and ice formed small bodies called planetesimals (plan uh TES suh muhllz). These planetesimals collided with each other and eventually created most of the objects that we see in the solar system, shown in **Figure 8**. The inner planets that formed closer to the sun were relatively smaller in size and mass. Their weak gravity, combined with the hot environment, resulted in dry, rocky bodies that were unable to hold onto light gases such as helium and hydrogen. Farther away from the sun, ice combined with rock and metal in the cooler environment. The outer planets that formed were more massive. As a result, gravity exerted a strong pull on hydrogen and helium gases, forming the gas giants we know today.

# ☑ LESSON 1 Check

MS-ESS1-2, MS-ESS1-3

1. **CCC Cause and Effect** What is responsible for the intense heat and pressure in the sun's core?

   ...................................................................
   ...................................................................
   ...................................................................

2. **CCC Systems** Describe the formation of the solar system.

   ...................................................................
   ...................................................................
   ...................................................................
   ...................................................................
   ...................................................................
   ...................................................................
   ...................................................................
   ...................................................................
   ...................................................................
   ...................................................................
   ...................................................................
   ...................................................................

3. **CCC Structure and Function** What is the relationship between a planet's distance from the sun and the length of its year? Explain.

   ...................................................................
   ...................................................................
   ...................................................................
   ...................................................................
   ...................................................................

4. **Compare and Contrast** Compare and contrast asteroids, comets, and meteroids.

   ...................................................................
   ...................................................................
   ...................................................................
   ...................................................................
   ...................................................................

5. **SEP Apply Scientific Reasoning** Explain why you think the solar system could or could not have formed without gravity.

   ...................................................................
   ...................................................................
   ...................................................................
   ...................................................................

# Quest CHECK-IN

**In this lesson, you discovered the characteristics of planets, moons, and smaller solar system objects. You also learned how the sun and other parts of the solar system were formed.**

SEP Evaluate Information How do you think understanding the formation of the solar system can help to explain the presence of smaller solar system objects, such as asteroids?

...................................................................
...................................................................
...................................................................

## ⬇ INTERACTIVITY

Space Invaders

**Go online** to explore more about the characteristics of asteroids and how scientists monitor and predict their possible strikes. Then list experience that an ideal applicant for a job at the observatory would have.

# Comparing
# Solar System Objects

Small solar system objects far from Earth—such as comets, dwarf planets, and asteroids—have been observed for centuries. Only in recent years have astronomers been able to make observations from up close, thanks to technological advances in telescopes and spacecraft.

## Ceres

A dwarf planet in the asteroid belt between Mars and Jupiter, Ceres takes 4.6 Earth years to revolve around the sun. It is about 2.8 AU from the sun. Ceres has a core of water ice and a rocky crust made of different salts. Its crust is marked by numerous impact craters.

## Vesta

An asteroid in the same asteroid belt as Ceres, Vesta is made of hardened lava. About 1 percent of Vesta was blasted into space when another object collided with it, leaving a crater 500 kilometers wide. Vesta is about 530 km wide, though it is not spherical in shape.

## Titan

The largest moon around Saturn, Titan has an icy surface with rivers of liquid methane and ethane. It is 9.54 AU from the sun. With a radius of 2,575 km, it is larger than Earth's moon. Its mass is $1.3455 \times 10^{23}$ kg.

## Hartley 2

A comet that visits the inner solar system every 6.5 years, Hartley 2, also known as 103P, is an icy mass that spins around one axis while tumbling around another. At its closest distance, Hartley 2 is about 1.05 AU from the sun, or 0.05 AU from Earth's orbit. The outer reaches of Hartley 2's orbit takes it about 5.9 AU from the sun. The comet loses some of its icy mass each time it passes near the sun.

Complete the table that summarizes the characteristics of four small objects of the solar system. Then use the information you have gathered to answer the following questions.

|  | Ceres | Vesta | Titan | Hartley 2 |
|---|---|---|---|---|
| Classification | Dwarf planet | Asteroid |  |  |
| Mass (kg) | $9.47 \times 10^{20}$ | $2.67 \times 10^{20}$ |  | $3 \times 10^{11}$ |
| Diameter (km) | 952 |  | 5,150 | 0.16 (nucleus) |
| Distance from Sun (AU) |  | 2.5 |  |  |
| Composition |  |  |  | Ice and carbon dioxide |

1. **SEP Engage in Argument** Why is Vesta considered an asteroid while its "sister" Ceres is classified by astronomers as a dwarf planet?

.................................................................................................................

.................................................................................................................

2. **SEP Construct Explanations** Titan's average distance from the sun is 9.54 AU, which is the same as Saturn's average distance from the Sun. Why doesn't Titan crash into Saturn?

.................................................................................................................

.................................................................................................................

3. **SEP Develop Models** Suppose you are given a diagram that shows the position of the planets from the sun and their relative sizes. You are asked to add the four smaller solar system objects in the chart to the model. Which of the objects' characteristics would be easier to represent in the model? Which characteristics would be difficult to represent?

.................................................................................................................

.................................................................................................................

.................................................................................................................

.................................................................................................................

# 2 Learning About the Universe

## Guiding Questions

- How does the electromagnetic spectrum help scientists learn about the universe?
- How do scientists use technology to learn about the universe?

## Connection

**Literacy** Determine Central Ideas

MS-ESS1-3

## HANDS-ON LAB

**uInvestigate** Design and build a model of a space exploration vehicle.

**Vocabulary**

electromagnetic radiation
visible light
spectrum
wavelength
telescope

**Academic Vocabulary**

complement

## Connect It !

**Study the photo and answer the questions.**

SEP Analyze and Interpret Data  What are some of the objects you see?

......................................................................................................................

SEP Construct Explanations  How do you think astronomers took this image?

......................................................................................................................

......................................................................................................................

# Collecting Space Data

With advances in engineering and technology, humans discover more about the universe every year. Data from telescopes, satellites, and other instruments based both on Earth and in space are opening up the mysteries of the universe to people on Earth.

**The Electromagnetic Spectrum** All objects in space emit, or give off, energy. This energy is known as **electromagnetic radiation**, or energy that can travel in the form of waves. Astronomers use instruments and tools, such as telescopes, that detect electromagnetic radiation to collect data and produce images of objects in space, such as the one in **Figure 1**.

There are many types of electromagnetic radiation, but visible light is the type that is most familiar to you. **Visible light** is the light you can see. If you've ever observed light shining through a prism, then you know that the light separates into different colors with different wavelengths, called a visible light **spectrum**. When you look at the moon or a star with the naked eye or through a telescope, you are observing visible light.

There are many forms of electromagnetic radiation that we cannot see. They include radio waves, infrared radiation, ultraviolet radiation, X-rays, and gamma rays. These waves are classified by **wavelength**, or the distance between the crest of one wave and the crest of the next wave. Radio waves have the longest wavelengths and gamma rays have the shortest wavelengths.

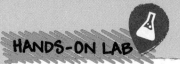

## HANDS-ON LAB

Determine how lenses affect the appearance of objects seen at a distance.

## INTERACTIVITY

Explore how astronomers analyze data collected by telescopes, satellites, and probes.

## Literacy Connection

**Determine Central Ideas**
Underline the sentence that states the central idea of the text.

## A Distant Galaxy

**Figure 1** This image of the distant galaxy NGC 1512 is made up of several images taken by NASA's Hubble Space Telescope. This telescope is able to detect different types of objects in space.

## Optical Telescopes

Objects in space give off all types of electromagnetic radiation. **Telescopes** are instruments that collect and focus light and other forms of electromagnetic radiation. Telescopes make distant objects appear larger and brighter. Some are based on Earth and others can be found floating in space. Optical telescopes use lenses and mirrors to collect and focus visible light. There are two main types of optical telescopes. Reflecting telescopes primarily use mirrors to collect light. Refracting telescopes use multiple lenses to collect light.

## Other Telescopes

Scientists also use non-optical telescopes to **complement** data obtained by other methods. These telescopes collect different types of electromagnetic radiation. Radio telescopes, such as the ones in **Figure 2**, detect radio waves from objects in space. Most radio telescopes have curved, reflecting surfaces. These surfaces focus faint radio waves the way the mirror in a reflecting telescope focuses light waves. Radio telescopes need to be large to collect and focus more radio waves because radio waves have long wavelengths. Other kinds of telescopes produce images in the infrared and X-ray portions of the spectrum.

**Academic Vocabulary**

What does it mean when images in a book complement the text?

...............................................................

**Radio Telescope**

**Figure 2** These radio telescopes are located in Owens Valley, California.

**CCC Structure and function** Why are radio telescopes so large?

...............................................................

...............................................................

☑ READING CHECK **Determine Central Ideas** Why do astronomers rely on different types of telescopes?

...............................................................................................

...............................................................................................

**Space Probes** Since humans first began exploring space, only 27 people have landed on or orbited the moon. Yet, during this period, astronomers have gathered a great deal of information about other parts of the solar system. Most of this information has been collected by space probes. A space probe is a spacecraft that carries scientific instruments to collect and transmit data, but has no human crew.

Each space probe is designed for a specific mission. Some are designed to land on a certain planet, such as the Mars rovers. Others are designed to fly by and collect data about planets and other bodies in the solar system.

**Data from Probes** Each space probe has a power system to produce electricity and a communication system to send and receive signals. Probes often carry scientific instruments to perform experiments. Some probes, called orbiters, are equipped to photograph and analyze the atmosphere of a planet. Other probes, called landers, are equipped to land on a planet and analyze the materials on its surface. Telescopes, satellites, astronauts, and probes have all contributed to our growing knowledge of the solar system and our universe. Space exploration is now limited only by technology, our imaginations, and the availability of funding.

HANDS-ON LAB

**Investigate** Design and build a model of a space exploration vehicle.

✓ READING CHECK **Determine Meaning** Why do you think spacecraft that carry instruments to collect data about objects in space are called probes?

......................................................................................................

......................................................................................................

Plan It

**Space Probe Mission**

SEP Use Models The flowchart shows the stages of a space probe mission to Mars. Write captions to describe the stages of the space probe mission.

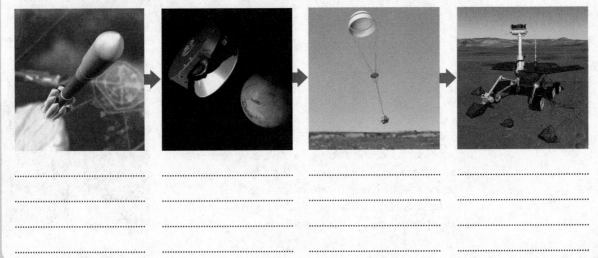

# History of Space Exploration

The advent of rocket technology in the 1940s led to a new era of space exploration, detailed in the timelines in **Figure 3** and **Figure 4**. Astronomers were no longer bound to ground-based observations, as humans, telescopes, and space probes were sent into space.

## 1947 Fruit Flies Launched into Space

Uncertain of the effects of space-travel on organisms, NASA begins experimentation on the effects of space exposure by launching a container of fruit flies into space to see how it affects them. Their container parachutes back to Earth and the fruit flies are recovered alive and in apparent good health.

## 1957 Laika Goes to Space

The Soviet Union also seeks to test the effects of space-travel on living organisms. The Soviets launch a dog named Laika into space on board a small craft called *Sputnik II*. She was the first animal ever to orbit Earth. Sadly, she died in space during the mission.

## 1940s

## 1950s

## 1957 *Sputnik I*

The Soviet Union launches *Sputnik I*, Earth's first artificial satellite, on October 4, 1957. This tiny craft, about the size of a beach ball and weighing little more than 80 kg, orbits Earth in 98 minutes. Its launch marks the start of the space age and a fierce space-race between the United States and the Soviet Union.

## 1958 *Explorer I*

The United States launches its first artificial satellite into space on January 31, 1958. Although the *Sputnik* crafts carried radio technology to signal where they were, *Explorer I* is the first satellite to carry scientific instruments into space. Its instruments help to detect and study the Van Allen Belts, strong belts of charged particles trapped by Earth's magnetic field.

## 1973 Skylab

Long before the International Space Station (ISS), NASA builds America's first space station, Skylab, in 1973. It orbits Earth until 1979 with the objective of helping scientists to develop science-based manned space missions. Weighing more than 77,000 kg, Skylab I includes a workshop, a solar observatory, and systems to allow astronauts to spend up to 84 days in space.

## 1961 First Person to Orbit Earth

On April 12, 1961, Soviet Yuri Gagarin becomes the first person to travel into space and orbit Earth. His 108-minute mission circles the Earth once and reaches a maximum altitude of about 300 kilometers.

## 1977 Voyager 1 & 2

One of the greatest missions to explore our solar system is led by twin space-probes called *Voyager 1* and *Voyager 2*. The two spacecraft are the first human-made objects to visit the planets of the outer solar system. Their instruments help scientists to explore and study Jupiter, Saturn, Uranus, Neptune, and many of their moons.

## 1960s

## 1970s

## 1962 *Mariner 2* to Venus

NASA launches *Mariner 2* toward Venus on August 27, 1962. It is the first human-made object to study another planet from space. As *Mariner 2* flies by Venus, its sensors send back data on the Venusian atmosphere, magnetic field, and mass. Its instruments also take measurements of cosmic dust and solar particles before and after passing the planet.

## 1969 Moon Landing

Three American astronauts travel to the moon aboard *Apollo 11*. As Michael Collins pilots the command module *Columbia* above, Neil Armstrong and Buzz Aldrin land the lunar module *Eagle* on the moon and become the first humans to walk on its surface.

### Space Exploration from the 1940s to the 1970s

**Figure 3** ✏️ Early space exploration involved some missions that carried people and some that did not. In each circle on the timeline, write *U* if the mission was unmanned, or *M* if the mission was manned.

📓 **Write About It** Scientists sent animals into space before they ever considered sending humans. In your science notebook, explain why you think humans were sent only after animals went into space.

## 1981 The Space Shuttles

First lifting off in 1981, the U.S. space shuttle is able to take off like a rocket and land like a plane, making it the first reusable spacecraft. Over the next 30 years, a fleet of five shuttles will be built and fly 135 missions carrying astronauts and cargo into space. Boasting a large cargo bay and lots of room for a crew, the shuttles make it possible for astronauts to launch and repair satellites, conduct research, and assist in the building of the ISS.

## 1998 The International Space Station (ISS)

Construction begins on the ISS, which requires more than 115 space flights to build. With a mass of nearly 420,000 kg, the ISS is almost five times larger than Skylab. About the size of a football field, it is the largest human-made structure ever built in space. A truly international effort, the ISS is a space-based laboratory and observatory used by scientists from around the world to conduct research that requires or focuses on the conditions found in space.

# 1980s

# 1990s

## 1990 Hubble Space Telescope

Carried aboard the space shuttle *Discovery* on April 24, 1990, the Hubble Space Telescope is the first space observatory located in space. Orbiting about 550 km above Earth and its blurry atmosphere, Hubble uses advanced visible-light optical technology to study the most distant objects in our solar system—stars and exoplanets in the Milky Way, as well as the farthest galaxies in the universe.

## 1997 Cassini-Huygens

A joint project between the United States and Europe, the Cassini mission launches on October 15, 1997, on a 3.5-billion-km journey to study Saturn, its ring system, and its many moons. Cassini also carries the Huygens Probe, which captures photos of Saturn's largest moon, Titan, while landing on its surface. The mission's many discoveries include rivers and lakes of liquid hydrocarbons on Titan's surface, making it the only known place in the solar system besides Earth where matter exists as a liquid on the surface.

## 2003 Mars Exploration Rovers

In 2003, NASA launches two rovers—*Spirit* and *Opportunity*—to land on and explore Mars. Their missions are to search for signs of past life. Using wheels to move around, instruments to drill and test rock and soil samples, and several sophisticated cameras, the rovers help scientists find evidence that Mars was once a wet, warm world capable of supporting life.

## 2009 Kepler

Seeking to answer the question of how unique our solar system is, NASA launches the Kepler Space Telescope in 2009, with instruments specially designed to search for planets outside our solar system. The Kepler mission focuses on studying a small part of the sky, counting the number and type of exoplanets it finds, and then using those data to calculate the possible number of exoplanets in our galaxy.

# 2000s

# Present

## 2003 Spitzer Space Telescope

In August of 2003, NASA launches the Spitzer Space Telescope. Spitzer uses an 85-cm infrared telescope capable of seeing heat to peer into regions of space that visible-light telescopes such as the Hubble have difficulty seeing or seeing through. Using Spitzer, scientists can more easily study exoplanets, giant clouds of cool molecular gas and organic molecules, and the formation of new stars.

## Space Exploration from the 1980s to Present

**Figure 4** 🖉 As space exploration evolved, missions changed in focus to studying more distant objects. Continue to write *U* for unmanned missions and *M* for manned missions.

**CCC Patterns** Describe any patterns you observe in the development of space exploration.

...............................................

...............................................

...............................................

...............................................

...............................................

## 2012 *Voyager 1* Leaves the Solar System

On August 25, 2012, *Voyager 1* leaves the area of the sun's influence and enters interstellar space, becoming the first human-made object to leave the solar system. It continues to assist scientists by transmitting data on its location and the density of plasma it encounters at the boundaries of our solar system.

**1. SEP Determine Differences** Contrast the electromagnetic radiation used by radio telescopes and optical telescopes.

.......................................................................................
.......................................................................................
.......................................................................................
.......................................................................................

**2. SEP Communicate Information** Identify a spacecraft operated by human beings and describe how it helped add to our knowledge of space.

.......................................................................................
.......................................................................................
.......................................................................................
.......................................................................................
.......................................................................................

**3. Connect to Technology** Which space technology used today contributes the most to our understanding of distant stars? Explain your answer.

.......................................................................................
.......................................................................................
.......................................................................................
.......................................................................................

**4. CCC Structure and Function** ✏ Choose two tools that astronomers use to learn more about objects in the universe. Draw a Venn diagram to compare and contrast how the tools function and the kinds of data they collect.

## Quest CHECK-IN

**In this lesson, you learned how scientists use technology to study the universe. You also discovered how the electromagnetic spectrum helps scientists to learn about objects in the universe.**

**SEP Engage in Argument** What kinds of technology do you think would be most helpful when looking for signs of extraterrestrial life? Explain your answer.

.......................................................................................
.......................................................................................
.......................................................................................

## 👆 INTERACTIVITY

Anybody Out There?

**Go online** to find out more about what extraterrestrial-life hunters look for and the technology they use. Then identify the technology with which an ideal applicant for a job at the observatory should be familiar.

MS-ESS1-3

# BLAST OFF!

INTERACTIVITY

Launch a Space Probe

## How do you get a
space probe into outer space?
You engineer it! Rocket
technology shows us how.

## The Challenge: To get a
space probe on its way to Pluto
and beyond.

**Phenomenon** In 2006, the *New
Horizons* space probe was launched
from Cape Canaveral, Florida. The
probe was destined for the outer
reaches of our solar system, studying the dwarf planet Pluto in a flyby
encounter from 2015 to 2016. The
Atlas V rocket was used to launch
the probe on its long, 4-billion-km
(2.5-billion-mile), journey. This powerful rocket, like many other rockets
used to launch satellites and probes
into space, is made up of two major
sections called stages.

The payload carries the
*New Horizons* space probe
and the second-stage
Centaur engine.

The Atlas V booster
is the main part of the rocket
that helps thrust the craft upward
and releases it from Earth's
gravitational pull.

The solid booster
rockets provide additional
thrust and then fall away not
long after the launch.

### DESIGN CHALLENGE

Can you design and build a model
of a rocket? Go to the Engineering
Design Notebook to find out!

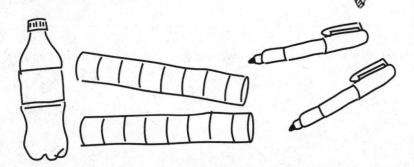

An Atlas V rocket on
the launchpad.

# 3 Stars

## Guiding Questions

- What are the properties of a star?
- How do scientists classify stars?
- What is the role of gravity in the formation of a star?

## Connections

**Literacy** Determine Central Ideas

**Math** Represent Relationships

MS-ESS1-2

## HANDS-ON LAB

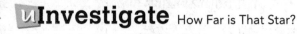

ᵤInvestigate How Far is That Star?

## Vocabulary

nebula
protostar
white dwarf
supernova
apparent
   brightness
absolute brightness

## Academic Vocabulary

analyze

## Connect It !

✏ **Write an X in the circle that points to the location of the brightest stars in the Orion Nebula.**

**SEP Construct Explanations** Why do you think the Orion Nebula is called a stellar nursery?

...................................................................................................................

...................................................................................................................

...................................................................................................................

...................................................................................................................

# Formation and Development of Stars

Stars do not last forever. Each star forms, changes during its life span, and eventually dies. Star formation begins when gravity causes the gas and dust from a nebula to contract and become so dense and hot that nuclear fusion starts. How long a star lives depends on its mass.

All stars start out as parts of nebulas, such as the one in **Figure 1**. A **nebula** is a large cloud of gas and dust containing an immense volume of material. A star, on the other hand, is made up of a large amount of gas in a relatively small volume.

In the densest part of a nebula, gravity pulls gas and dust together. A contracting cloud of gas and dust with enough mass to form a star is called a **protostar**. *Proto-* means "first" in Greek, so a protostar is the first stage of a star's formation. Without gravity to contract the gas and dust, a protostar could not form.

Nuclear fusion is the process by which atoms combine to form heavier atoms. In the sun, for example, gravity causes hydrogen atoms to combine and form helium. During nuclear fusion, an enormous amount of energy is released. Nuclear fusion begins in a protostar.

## Literacy Connection

**Determine Central Ideas**
As you read, look for ways that a nebula and a protostar are similar and different. Write your answers below.

...............................................................

...............................................................

...............................................................

...............................................................

...............................................................

...............................................................

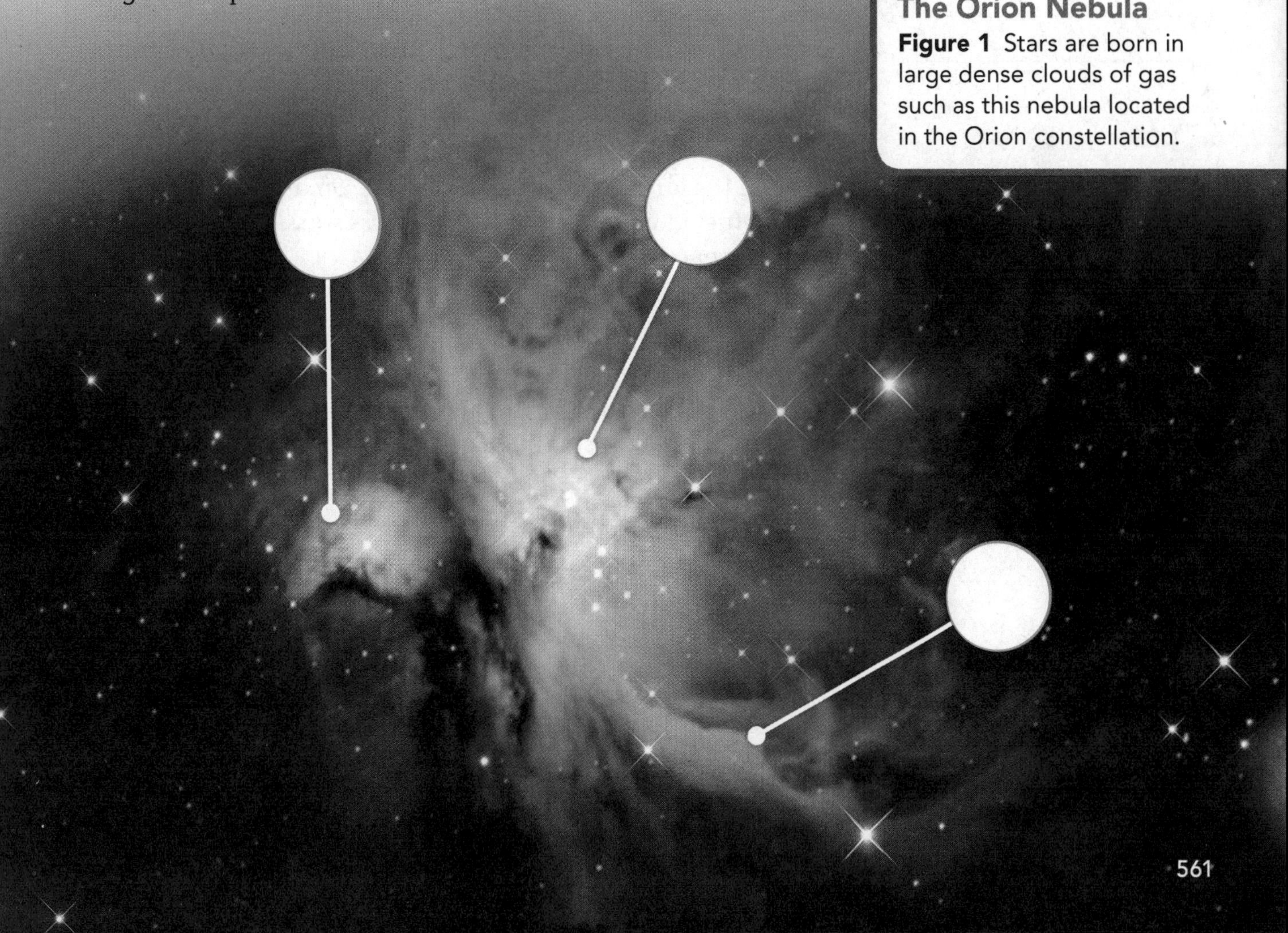

### The Orion Nebula
**Figure 1** Stars are born in large dense clouds of gas such as this nebula located in the Orion constellation.

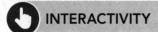
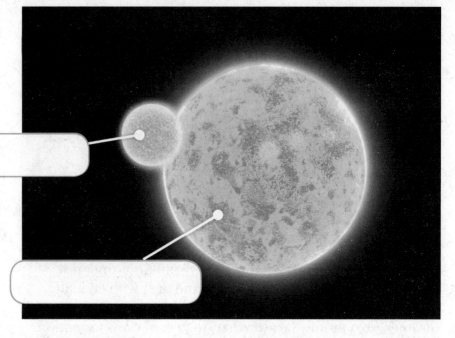

## Star Mass and Life Span

**Figure 2** ✎ How long a star lasts depends on its mass. Look at the yellow and blue stars. Label the star that has more mass and the star that has less mass. Predict which star will last longer by drawing an X on that star.

**SEP Engage in Argument from Evidence** Explain your prediction.

.........................................................

.........................................................

.........................................................

.........................................................

# Life Span

The properties and life span of every star are the result of how massive it is. Each star's mass is determined by how much gas and dust condensed to form its protostar.

How long a star lasts is directly related to its mass and how quickly it uses that mass as fuel. It may seem that stars with more mass would last longer than stars with less mass. But the reverse is true. Stars are like cars. A small car has a small gas tank, but it also has a small engine that burns gas slowly. A large car has a larger gas tank, but its large engine burns gas rapidly. The small car can travel farther on a smaller tank of gas than the larger car with a large tank. Small-mass stars use up their fuel more slowly than large-mass stars, so they last much longer.

Generally, stars that have less mass than our sun use their fuel slowly and can last for up to 200 billion years. A medium-mass star like the sun will last for about 10 billion years. The sun is about 4.6 billion years old, so it is about halfway through its life span. The yellow star in **Figure 2** is similar to the sun.

Stars that have more mass than the sun, such as the blue star shown in **Figure 2**, may last only about 10 million years. That may seem like a very long time, but it is only one-tenth of one percent of the life span of our sun.

✔ **READING CHECK** **Determine Central Ideas** Describe how a star's life span is related to its size.

.........................................................................................................

.........................................................................................................

.........................................................................................................

**White Dwarfs** When a star begins to run out of fuel, its core shrinks and its outer portion expands. Depending on its mass, the star becomes either a red giant or a supergiant. Red giants and supergiants evolve in very different ways.

Low-mass stars and medium-mass stars take billions of years to use up their fuel. As they start to run out of fuel, their outer layers expand, and they become red giants. Eventually, the outer parts grow larger still and drift out into space, forming a glowing cloud of gas called a planetary nebula. The blue-white core that is left behind cools and becomes a **white dwarf**.

White dwarfs are about the size of Earth but about one million times more dense than the sun. White dwarfs have no fuel, but they glow faintly from leftover energy. After billions of years, a white dwarf stops glowing. Then it is a black dwarf.

**Supernovas** The evolution of a high-mass star is quite different. These stars quickly procede into brilliant supergiants. When a supergiant runs out of fuel, it explodes suddenly. Within hours, the star blazes millions of times brighter. The explosion is called a **supernova**. After a supernova, some of the material from the star expands into space. This material may become part of a nebula. This nebula can then contract to form a new, partly recycled star. Nuclear fusion creates heavy elements. A supernova provides enough energy to create the heaviest elements. Astronomers think that the matter in the solar system came from a gigantic supernova. If so, this means that most of the matter around you was created in a star, and all matter on Earth except hydrogen is a form of stardust.

**VIDEO**

Discover how a star begins its life.

**INTERACTIVITY**

Examine the life cycle of a star.

**White Dwarf**

**Figure 3** The Hubble Space Telescope captured this image of a white dwarf. The white dot in the center is the dense remaining core of the star. The glowing cloud of gas surrounds the white dwarf and eventually blows off all its outer layers.

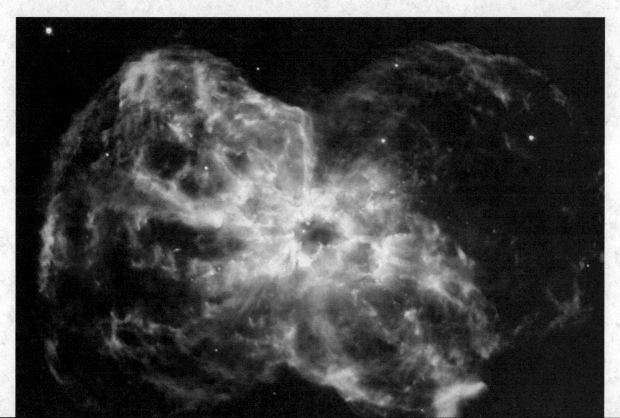

## Neutron Stars, Pulsars, and Black Holes

**Neutron Stars, Pulsars, and Black Holes** After a supergiant explodes, some of the material from the star is left behind. This material may form a neutron star. Neutron stars are even smaller and denser than white dwarfs. A neutron star may contain as much as three times the mass of the sun but be only about 25 kilometers in diameter—the size of a city.

In 1967, Jocelyn Bell, a British astronomy student working with Antony Hewish, detected an object in space that appeared to give off regular pulses of radio waves. Soon, astronomers concluded that the source of the radio waves was a rapidly spinning neutron star. Spinning neutron stars are called pulsars, short for pulsating radio sources. Some pulsars spin hundreds of times per second!

The most massive stars—those that have more than 10 times the mass of the sun—may become black holes when they die. A black hole is an object with gravity so strong that nothing, not even light, can escape. After a very massive star dies in a supernova explosion, the gravity of the remaining mass can be so strong that it pulls the gases inward, packing it into a smaller and smaller space. The star's gas becomes squeezed so hard that the star converts into a black hole. The extreme gravity near a black hole, which is surrounded by large volumes of gas, will turn the gas into super-fast spinning disks around its equator and jets of plasma from its poles.

☑ **READING CHECK**

**Determine Central Ideas**
Will our sun become a black hole? Explain.

..............................................

..............................................

..............................................

**Stages of Star Development**

**Figure 4** ✏ Fill in the missing stages on the diagram.

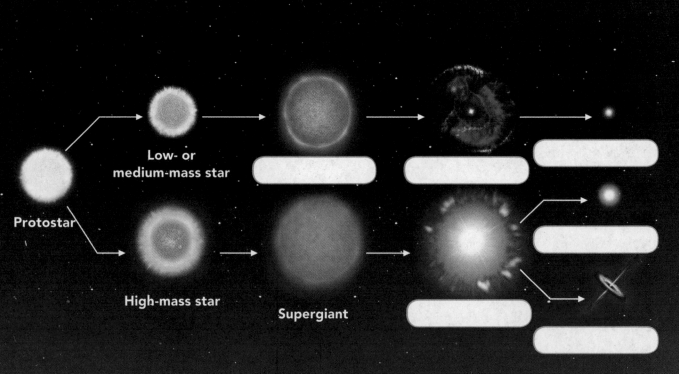

Protostar

Low- or medium-mass star

High-mass star

Supergiant

| Temperature and Star Color | |
|---|---|
| **Approximate surface temperature (Kelvins)** | **Star color** |
| 30,000 – 60,000 K | Blue stars |
| 10,000 – 30,000 K | Blue-white stars |
| 7,500 – 10,000 K | White stars |
| 6,000 – 7,500 K | Yellow-white stars |
| 5,000 – 6,000 K | Yellow stars |
| 3,500 – 5,000 K | Yellow-orange stars |
| <3,500 K | Red stars |

Source: Australia Telescope National Facility

## Star Color and Temperature

**Figure 5** A star's surface temperature determines its color. Look at the two stars in **Figure 2**. Use the information in the table to determine which of those two stars has the greater surface temperature. How much hotter is it than the other star?

................................................................

................................................................

................................................................

................................................................

................................................................

**Write About It** Trace the evolution of a neutron star.

# Star Properties

All stars are huge spheres of super-hot, glowing gas called plasma. The exact composition of this plasma varies from star to star, but it is made mostly of hydrogen. Many stars also contain varying amounts of elements such as helium, oxygen, and carbon. During its life, a star produces energy through the process of nuclear fusion, which generates energy from the process of combining atoms into larger atoms. Most stars do this by combining hydrogen atoms to form helium atoms, slowly changing their compositions over time. A star's size and composition affect its physical characteristics. Astronomers classify stars according to their physical characteristics, including color, temperature, size, composition, and brightness.

**Color and Temperature** If you look at the night sky, you can see slight differences in the colors of the stars. A star's color indicates its surface temperature. The coolest stars—with a surface temperature of less than 3,500 K—appear red. Our yellow sun has an average temperature of about 5,500 K. The hottest stars, with surface temperatures ranging from 30,000 K to 60,000 K, appear bluish.

**Size** Many stars in the sky are about the size of our sun. Some stars—a minority of them—are much, much larger. These very large stars are called giant stars or supergiant stars. Most stars are smaller than the sun. White dwarf stars are about the size of Earth. Neutron stars are even smaller, only about 25 kilometers in diameter.

**Academic Vocabulary**
A scientist is studying an unknown liquid in her lab. Describe a test that she could conduct to analyze a property of the liquid.

**Chemical Composition** Stars vary in their chemical composition. The chemical composition of most stars is about 73 percent hydrogen, 25 percent helium, and 2 percent other elements by mass. Recall that nuclear fusion is the process that powers stars. This process involves the fusing of atoms to form larger atoms. In stars, this process usually involves the fusing of two hydrogen atoms to form one helium atom. As the star uses up its hydrogen, it then begins to fuse helium together, forming carbon when it reaches 100,000,000 K.

Astronomers use spectrographs to determine the elements found in stars. A spectrograph breaks light into colors and produces an image of the resulting spectrum. Today, most large telescopes have spectrographs to **analyze** light.

The gases in a star's atmosphere absorb some wavelengths of light produced within the star. When the star's light is seen through a spectrograph, each absorbed wavelength appears as a dark line on a spectrum. Each chemical element absorbs light at particular wavelengths. Just as each person has a unique set of fingerprints, each element has a unique set of spectral lines for a given temperature.

# Model It

**Star Spectra**

**Figure 6** The spectra below are from four different elements. By comparing a star's spectrum with the spectra of known elements, astronomers can identify the elements in a star. Each star's spectrum is an overlap of the spectra from the individual elements.

**SEP Use Models** Identify the elements with the strongest lines in Stars A and B.

**SEP Develop Models** ✏ Star C is made up of the elements hydrogen and sodium. Draw lines to model the spectrum of a star with this composition.

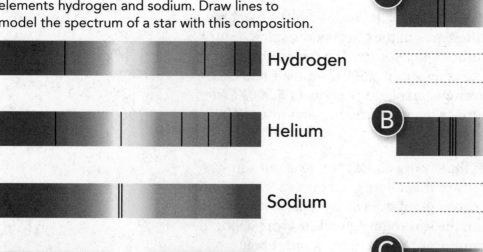

Hydrogen

Helium

Sodium

Calcium

A

B

C

**Brightness** Stars also differ in their brightness, or the amount of light they give off. The brightness of a star depends upon both its size and temperature. A larger star tends to be brighter than a smaller star. A hotter star tends to be brighter than a cooler star.

Astronomers use a unit called the light-year to measure the distances of stars. A light-year is the distance that light travels in one year, or about 9.46 trillion kilometers. How bright a star appears depends on both its distance from Earth and how bright the star truly is. Because of these two factors, the brightness of a star is described in two ways: apparent brightness and absolute brightness.

A star's **apparent brightness** is its brightness as seen from Earth. Astronomers can measure apparent brightness fairly easily using electronic devices. However, astronomers can't tell how much light a star gives off just from the star's apparent brightness. Just as a flashlight looks brighter the closer it is to you, a star looks brighter the closer it is to Earth. For example, the sun looks very bright. Its apparent brightness does not mean that the sun gives off more light than all other stars. The sun looks so bright simply because it is so close to Earth.

A star's **absolute brightness** is the brightness the star would have if it were at a standard distance from Earth. Finding a star's absolute brightness is more complex than finding its apparent brightness. An astronomer must first find out both the star's apparent brightness and its distance from Earth. The astronomer can then calculate the star's absolute brightness.

☑ READING CHECK **Determine Central Ideas** Our sun is a an average-sized star, yet appears brighter than others we can see. Explain why.

......................................................................................

......................................................................................

......................................................................................

......................................................................................

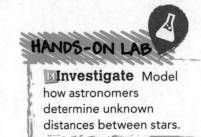
**HANDS-ON LAB**

ᵁ**Investigate** Model how astronomers determine unknown distances between stars.

## Apparent and Absolute Brightness

**Figure 7** 🖉 The three stars Alnitak, Alnilam, and Mintaka in the constellation Orion all seem to have the same apparent brightness from Earth. But Alnilam is actually farther away than the other two stars. Write an asterisk (*) next to the name of the star that has the greatest absolute brightness.

Star: Alnilam
Distance: approximately 1,300 light-years from Earth

Star: Alnitak
Distance: approximately 800 light-years from Earth

Star: Mintaka
Distance: approximately 900 light-years from Earth

567

# Classifying Stars

About 100 years ago, two scientists working independently made the same discovery. Both Ejnar Hertzsprung (EYE nahr HURT sprung) in Denmark and Henry Norris Russell in the United States made graphs to help them to determine whether the temperature and the absolute brightness of stars are related. They plotted the surface temperatures of stars on the x-axis and their absolute brightness on the y-axis. The points formed a pattern. The graph they made is called the Hertzsprung-Russell diagram, or H-R diagram.

Astronomers use H-R diagrams to classify stars and to understand how stars change over time. The diagram in the Math Toolbox shows how most of the stars in the H-R diagram form a diagonal area called the main sequence. More than 90 percent of all stars, including the sun, are main-sequence stars. Within the main sequence, the surface temperature increases as absolute brightness increases. Hot bluish stars occur at the left of an H-R diagram and cooler reddish stars are at the right.

## Math Toolbox

### Classify Stars by Their Properties

The H-R diagram shows the relationship between surface temperature and absolute brightness of stars.

1. **SEP Analyze and Interpret Data** 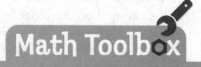 Circle the words that correctly complete the following sentence: Sirius B is a (hot/cool) star with (high/low) brightness.

2. **Represent Relationships** Place the following stars on the H-R diagram and record their classifications below.

   **Star A:** Red-orange, 5,000 K, high brightness

   ..............................................

   **Star B:** Yellow, 6,000 K, medium brightness

   ..............................................

   **Star C:** White, 10,000 K, low brightness

   ..............................................

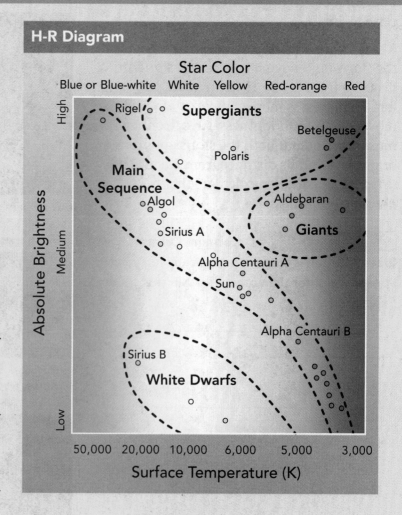

H-R Diagram

# ☑ LESSON 3 Check

1. **Identify** What are three properties astronomers use to describe stars?

.................................................................

.................................................................

.................................................................

.................................................................

.................................................................

2. **Predict** Which of the following will the sun eventually become: a white dwarf, neutron star, or a black hole? Explain your answer.

.................................................................

.................................................................

.................................................................

.................................................................

.................................................................

3. **CCC Energy and Matter** New stars are forming in a part of space known as NGC 346. Explain what is occurring there and the role gravity plays in the formation of these stars.

.................................................................

.................................................................

.................................................................

.................................................................

.................................................................

.................................................................

**Use the H-R diagram in the Math Toolbox activity to help you answer Questions 4 through 6.**

4. **SEP Use Models** The star Procyon B has a surface temperature of 7,500 K and a low absolute brightness. What type of star is it?

.................................................................

.................................................................

.................................................................

5. **SEP Interpret Data** Stars X and Y are both bluish main sequence stars. Star X has a higher absolute brightness than star Y. How do their temperatures compare? Explain your answer.

.................................................................

.................................................................

.................................................................

.................................................................

6. **SEP Develop Models** ✏ Explain why our sun is classified as a main sequence star. Then, in the space below, model the life span of our sun from its birth to its eventual final stage. Include labels that describe its color and size at each stage of your model.

.................................................................

.................................................................

.................................................................

.................................................................

## Guiding Questions

- How can we determine the sizes of and distances between stars and galaxies?
- What makes up galaxies of different sizes and shapes?

## Connections

**Literacy** Summarize Text

**Math** Use Mathematical Representations

MS-ESS1-2

### HANDS-ON LAB

**ʊInvestigate** Develop a model of the Milky Way.

### Vocabulary

galaxy
universe
light-year
big bang

### Academic Vocabulary

determine

## Connect It!

✎ **Place an X on the spiral galaxies you see in this image of deep space.**

**SEP Design Solutions** Based on what you see, how do you think scientists measure the distances between objects in space?

..................................................................................................................

..................................................................................................................

**CCC Scale, Proportion, and Quantity** What are some challenges that you think scientists face when trying to study other galaxies?

..................................................................................................................

..................................................................................................................

..................................................................................................................

# From Stars to Galaxies

The brightest and largest spots of light that you see in **Figure 1** are galaxies. There are estimated to be billions of galaxies, and each of these galaxies is made up of many billions of stars. Measuring the distances between Earth and these objects poses a challenge to astronomers because the distances are so vast.

**Parallax** When trying to determine the distance to nearby stars and other objects, astronomers measure the object's apparent motion in the sky as Earth is on opposite sides of its orbit around the sun. This apparent motion in the object against distant background stars is called parallax.

Parallax is best used to measure the distance to nearby stars. The parallax of objects that are extremely far away is too small to be useful in obtaining an accurate measurement.

**HANDS-ON LAB**

**Investigate** Develop a model of the Milky Way.

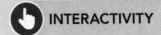
**INTERACTIVITY**

Find out how Hollywood goes to space.

### Deep in Space

**Figure 1** The universe is enormous, almost beyond imagination. This image was captured by the Hubble Space Telescope in 1995 while peering into one of the darkest regions of space as seen from Earth. Astronomers were amazed to see more than 3,000 galaxies in the tiny patch of sky captured by the orbiting observatory.

**Star Systems** Many stars are part of groups of two or more stars, called star systems. Star systems that have two stars are called double stars or binary stars. Groups of three or more stars are called multiple star systems.

Often one star in a binary system is much brighter and more massive than the other. Even if only one star can be seen from Earth, astronomers can often detect its dimmer partner by observing the effects of its gravity. As a dim companion star revolves around a bright star, its gravity causes the bright star to wobble. In 1995, astronomers first discovered an exoplanet—one outside our own solar system—revolving around a star. Again, they detected the planet by observing the effect the planet's gravity had on the star it orbited.

# Model It

### Eclipsing Binary Stars

**Figure 2** A dim star may pass in front of a brighter star and block it. A system in which one dim star eclipses the light from another periodically is called an eclipsing binary. Scientists can measure the brightness of the brighter star and determine when the dim star is eclipsing it.

**SEP Develop Models** ✎ Use the information in the graph to complete the missing panels in the diagram. Indicate the positions of each of the stars in the binary system.

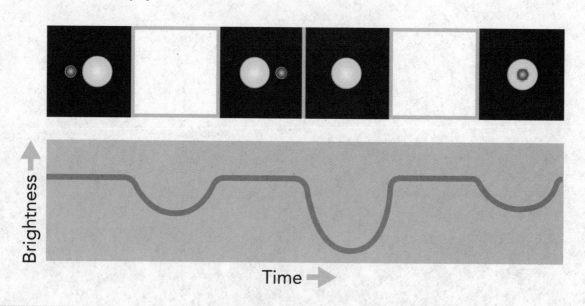

**Star Clusters** Many stars belong to larger groupings called clusters. All of the stars in a particular cluster formed from the same nebula at about the same time. An open cluster looks loose and disorganized. These clusters may contain up to a few thousand stars. They also contain a lot of gas and dust. Globular clusters are large groupings of older stars. They are round and may have more than a million stars.

**Galaxies** A **galaxy** is a group of single stars, star systems, star clusters, dust, and gas bound together by gravity. **Figure 3** shows several common types of galaxies. Spiral galaxies appear to have a bulge in the middle and arms that spiral outward like pinwheels. Our solar system is located in a spiral galaxy that we have named the Milky Way. Elliptical galaxies are rounded but may be elongated and slightly flattened. They contain billions of stars but have little gas or dust between the stars. Stars are no longer forming inside them, so they contain only old stars. Irregular galaxies do not have regular shapes. They are smaller than spiral or elliptical galaxies. They contain young, bright stars and include a lot of gas and dust to form new ones. Quasars are active, young galaxies with black holes at their center. Gas spins around the black hole, heats up, and glows.

**READING CHECK Summarize Text** How are stars, star systems, star clusters, and galaxies related?

.............................................................................................

.............................................................................................

**Kinds of Galaxies**
**Figure 3** From what you know about the shapes of galaxies, label each galaxy.

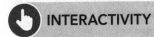 **INTERACTIVITY**

Explore the different types of galaxies.

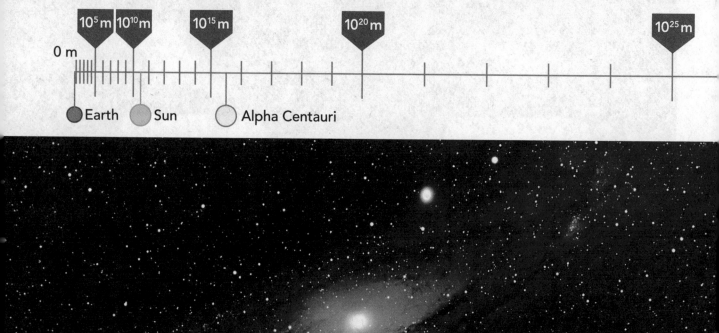

$10^5$ m   $10^{10}$ m   $10^{15}$ m   $10^{20}$ m   $10^{25}$ m

0 m

● Earth   ● Sun   ○ Alpha Centauri

## The Andromeda Galaxy

**Figure 4** 🖉 Our nearest galactic neighbor is a giant spiral galaxy similar to the Milky Way called the Andromeda Galaxy. It is 2.5 × $10^{22}$ meters away. Draw where the Andromeda Galaxy should appear on the distance scale shown.

# The Universe

Astronomers define the **universe** as all of space and everything in it. They study objects as close as the moon and as far away as quasars, the farthest known objects in the universe. Their research also looks at incredibly large objects, such as clusters of galaxies that are millions of light-years across. They also study tiny particles, such as the atoms within stars.

**Light-Years** Distances to the stars are so large that meters are not very practical units. In space, light travels at a speed of about 300,000,000 meters per second. A **light-year** is the distance that light travels in one year, about 9.46 trillion kilometers. The light-year is a unit of distance, not time. Imagine it this way. If you bicycle at a speed of 10 kilometers per hour, it would take you 1 hour to go to a mall 10 kilometers away. You could say that the mall is "1 bicycle-hour" away.

**Scientific Notation** As shown in **Figure 4**, the numbers that astronomers use are often very large or very small, so they frequently use scientific notation to describe sizes and distances in the universe. Scientific notation uses powers of ten to write very large or very small numbers in shorter form. Each number is written as the product of a number between 1 and 10 and a power of 10.

## The Scale of the Universe

Human beings have wondered about the size and distance of the night sky throughout history. Aristarchus of Samos began questioning how far the moon was from Earth as early as the third century BCE. He used the shadow of Earth on the moon during a lunar eclipse to come up with a figure for the distance that was surprisingly accurate.

Edmond Halley is a well-known early astronomer who honed his skills in the 1600s and 1700s. He found a way to measure the distance to the sun and to the planet Venus. He did this by closely observing and measuring the shift of Venus in the sky. His discoveries helped later scientists to **determine** a more accurate scale of the entire solar system.

☑ READING CHECK **Determine Central Ideas** What is the reason astronomers choose to write the measurements of the universe in scientific notation?

..............................................................................................................

..............................................................................................................

### Academic Vocabulary

What difficulties did scientists have when they tried to determine the size of the universe? Explain some ways you can determine the size of something.

..............................................................

..............................................................

..............................................................

..............................................................

..............................................................

..............................................................

# Math Toolbox

## Scientific Notation

One light-year is about 9,460,000,000,000 km. To express this number in scientific notation, first insert a decimal point in the original number to write a number between one and ten. To determine the power of ten, count the number of places that the decimal point moved. Because there are 12 digits after the first digit, the distance be written as $9.46 \times 10^{12}$ km.

**CCC Scale, Proportion, and Quantity** Convert the following numbers from light-years to km. Then express the numbers using scientific notation.

The Andromeda Galaxy is the closest major galaxy to the Milky Way. It is about 2,500,000 light-years from our galaxy, and its diameter is estimated to be 220,000 light-years.

2,500,000 light-years = ............................................................

220,000 light-years = ............................................................

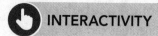
INTERACTIVITY

Design a hierarchical model of a galaxy.

VIDEO

Find out more about the big bang theory.

## Literacy Connection

**Summarize Text** What is dark matter?

...........................................................

...........................................................

...........................................................

...........................................................

# Understanding the Universe

Astronomers theorize that the universe began between 13.77 and 13.82 billion years ago. At that time, the part of the universe we can see was no larger than the period at the end of this sentence.

**The Big Bang** The universe then exploded in what has been called the **big bang**. The big bang theory states that the universe formed in an instant, billions of years ago, in an enormous explosion. New observations lead many astronomers to conclude that the universe is expanding and will likely expand forever.

## The Future of the Universe
In the 1920s, American astronomer Edwin Hubble discovered that almost all galaxies are moving away from Earth and from each other. Hubble's law states that the farther away a galaxy is, the faster it is moving away from us.

Other researchers believe that the force of gravity will begin to pull the galaxies back together into a reverse big bang. The universe would be crushed in an enormous black hole, called the big crunch.

Until recently, astronomers assumed that the universe consisted solely of the matter they could observe directly. But astronomer Vera Rubin discovered that the matter astronomers can see may make up as little as ten percent of the mass in the galaxies. The rest exists in the form of dark matter. Dark matter is matter that does not give off electromagnetic radiation. It cannot be seen directly. However, its presence can be inferred by observing the effect of its gravity on visible objects within a rotating galaxy.

In the late 1990s, astronomers observed that the expansion of the universe appeared to be accelerating. Astronomers infer that a mysterious new force, which they call dark energy, may be causing the expansion of the universe to increase.

☑ READING CHECK **Determine Central Ideas** How does Hubble's law support the big bang theory?

...........................................................................................

...........................................................................................

...........................................................................................

...........................................................................................

**How the Universe Formed**

**Figure 5** This diagram illustrates how astronomers theorize that the universe began and will continue. How does the idea of an expanding universe support the big bang theory?

..............................................................
..............................................................
..............................................................
..............................................................
..............................................................
..............................................................
..............................................................

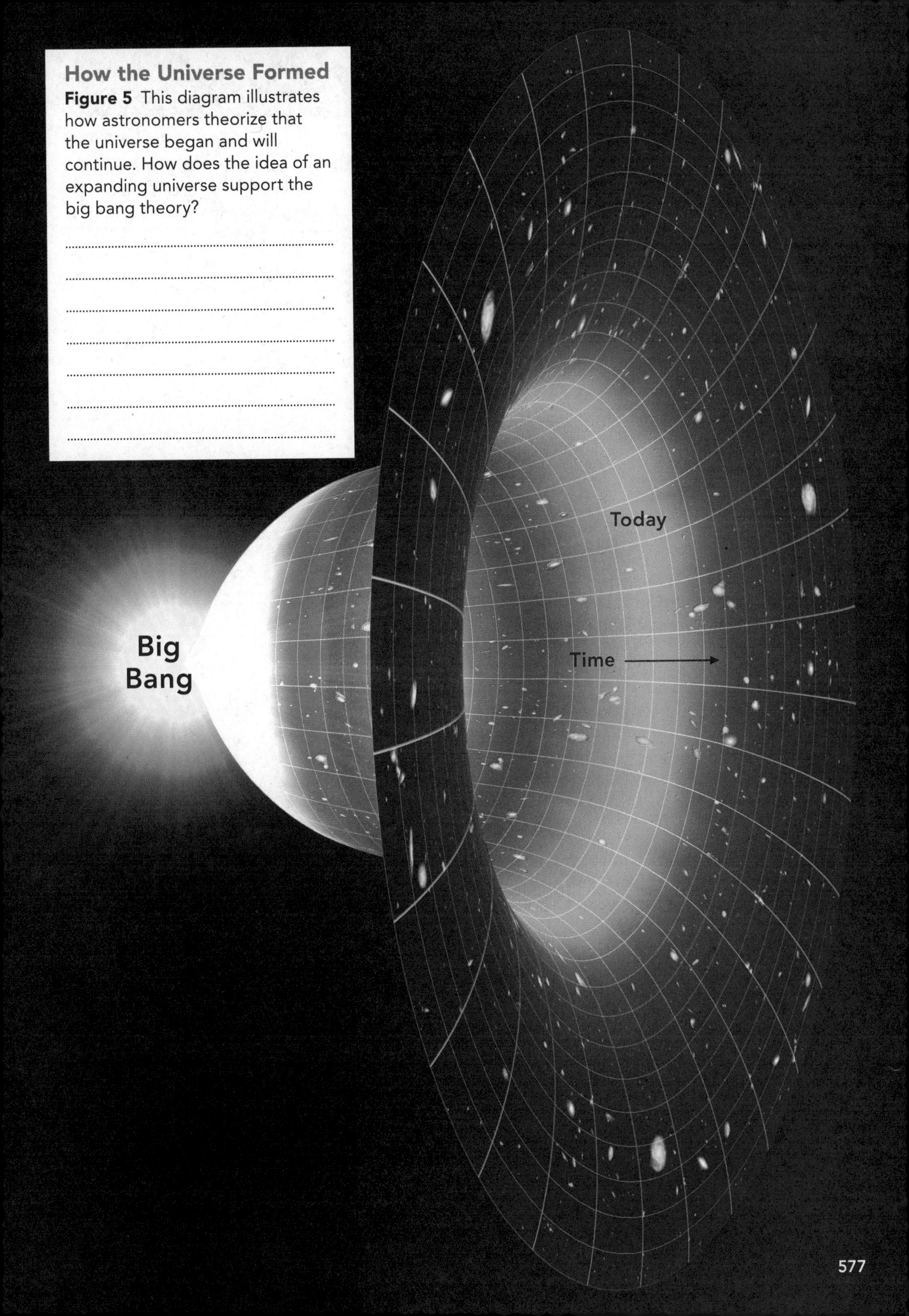

Big Bang

Today

Time ⟶

# ☑ LESSON 4 Check

**1. Identify** What are the four types of galaxies?

........................................................

........................................................

........................................................

........................................................

**2. CCC Cause and Effect** How can astronomers detect a binary star if only one of the two stars is visible from Earth?

........................................................

........................................................

........................................................

........................................................

........................................................

**3. SEP Interpret Data** The speed of light is $3.0 \times 10^8$ m/s when expressed in scientific notation. How would you express this in real numbers?

........................................................

........................................................

........................................................

**4. SEP Evaluate Information** A friend uses an analogy of raisins in rising bread dough to describe galaxies in the expanding universe. Is your friend correct? Explain.

........................................................

........................................................

........................................................

........................................................

........................................................

........................................................

........................................................

**5. Estimate** Based on what astronomers currently know, how old is our universe?

........................................................

........................................................

........................................................

........................................................

........................................................

........................................................

........................................................

## Quest CHECK-IN

**In this lesson, you learned about how astronomers determine the distances between objects. You also learned about how they think the universe began and how it will continue in the future.**

Draw Conclusions Why is it important for astronomers to be able to make inferences when interpreting data about things they cannot observe directly?

........................................................

........................................................

........................................................

........................................................

........................................................

## 👆 INTERACTIVITY

Searching for the Unseen

**Go online** to explore how scientists know dark matter exists even though they cannot see it. Then begin developing the job descriptions for the new positions at the observatory.

MS-ESS1-2

# Traveling Through the
# Milky Way

The Milky Way is a spiral galaxy 100,000 light-years wide. Our solar system is a small speck on one of the arms that spirals out from the center of the galaxy. Just as the planets of our solar system revolve around the sun due to gravity, the entire solar system orbits the center of the Milky Way due to the force of gravity.

Our solar system moves at 240 kilometers per second around the center of the Milky Way. At this speed, it takes 250 million Earth years for our solar system to travel all the way around!

Modern astronomy uses sophisticated tools to measure distances among objects in the Milky Way, and also to identify those objects. The Kepler space telescope, launched into Earth's orbit in 2009, has helped astronomers identify thousands of exoplanets, or planets outside our solar system. The discovery of exoplanets has helped astronomers understand that our solar system is just one of many that travels around the center of the Milky Way. Astronomers have even identified areas and exoplanets of the Milky Way that could have the right conditions to support life.

## MY DISCOVERY

Search for the term *Milky Way* in an online search engine to learn more about our galaxy. What might happen to the solar system without the gravitational force exerted by the center of the galaxy?

The Milky Way is a spiral galaxy like the one shown here.

galactic center

26,100 light years

solar system

240 km/s

579

# ☑TOPIC 12 Review and Assess

## 1 Solar System Objects

MS-ESS1-2, MS-ESS1-3

**1.** What characteristic do all the inner planets have in common?
A. ring system
B. liquid water
C. rocky surface
D. thick atmosphere

**2.** All the gas giants are surrounded by ......................................................... made up of small particles to very large chunks of ice and dust.

**3.** One astronomical unit is equal to the distance from ................................... to ....................................

**4. CCC Cause and Effect** Compare the conditions that led to the formation of the inner planets with those that led to the formation of the outer planets.

...................................................................
...................................................................
...................................................................
...................................................................
...................................................................
...................................................................
...................................................................
...................................................................
...................................................................
...................................................................
...................................................................
...................................................................
...................................................................
...................................................................
...................................................................
...................................................................

## 2 Learning About the Universe

MS-ESS1-3

**5.** Which object is the largest?
A. Earth
B. Saturn
C. Jupiter
D. the sun

**6.** A student is making a model of the sun's interior. Which feature should the student represent in the convection zone?
A. gas erupting into space
B. gases rising and sinking
C. radiation moving outward
D. nuclear fusion producing energy

**7.** Which technology makes it possible for people to live and work in space for long periods?
A. space probe
B. space station
C. radio telescope
D. optical telescope

**8. SEP Analyze Benefits** In 1981, the first space shuttle was launched from Cape Canaveral. Which statement describes an advantage that space shuttles have compared to earlier space probes and capsules?
A. Space shuttles can travel beyond Earth's orbit.
B. Space shuttles are inexpensive to build.
C. Space shuttles can be used more than once.
D. Space shuttles can travel beyond the solar system.

**9. Apply Concepts** Describe one kind of telescope and how you could use it to learn about an object in space.

...................................................................
...................................................................
...................................................................
...................................................................
...................................................................
...................................................................

**10.** Telescopes work by collecting and focusing different forms of ................................... radiation.

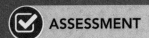

# 3 Stars

MS-ESS1-2

**11.** Using the H-R diagram, astronomers classify stars using which two star properties?

A. color and composition

B. size and surface temperature

C. surface temperature and absolute brightness

D. surface temperature and apparent brightness

**12.** Which property indicates a star's temperature?

A. size  B. color

C. composition  D. brightness

**13.** A ................................................................ forms when ................................................................ pulls together the gas and dust in the densest part of a nebula.

**14. SEP Develop Models** 🖊 Draw a flow chart to model the stages in the life span of a high-mass star.

# 4 Galaxies

MS-ESS1-2

**15.** In what kind of star system does one star sometimes block the light from another?

A. open cluster  B. globular cluster

C. quasar system  D. eclipsing binary

**16.** What is the name of the explosion that began the universe?

A. solar nebula  B. big bang

C. dark matter  D. supernova

**17.** What is dark matter?

A. matter that can be seen directly

B. matter that does not give off electromagnetic radiation

C. matter that makes up about 10 percent of the mass of the universe

D. matter that has no effect on other objects

**18. Compare and Contrast** How do open clusters and globular clusters differ in terms of numbers of stars?

................................................................................................

................................................................................................

**19. CCC Systems** Determine the hierarchy of the universe in a list, starting with stars.

................................................................................................

................................................................................................

................................................................................................

................................................................................................

................................................................................................

................................................................................................

................................................................................................

................................................................................................

................................................................................................

................................................................................................

MS-ESS1-2

## Evidence-Based Assessment

Willa is developing a model to help her study gravity. She wants to understand that role that gravity plays in keeping objects in the solar system in orbit around the sun. She plans on using some household materials to model a gravity well.

A gravity well is a representation of the gravitational field or pull of an object in space. A massive object like the sun has a deep gravity well. A less massive object, such as an asteroid, has a very shallow gravity well.

Willa stretches plastic wrap across a large hoop to represent the "fabric" of space. She has one large clay ball, some small marbles, and tiny ball bearings.

When Willa places the clay ball on the plastic, she observes that it sinks into the plastic and forms a well. When she places a marble or bearing near the ball, Willa observes the marble roll along the surface of the plastic toward the ball.

1. **SEP Develop Models** In Willa's model, which of the following solar system objects does the large clay ball represent?

A. the sun

B. a planet

C. a moon

D. an asteroid

2. **CCC System Models** Willa tests her model by placing the large clay ball, a single marble, and a single ball bearing one at at time on the plastic. Which object creates the deepest well? How can these observations be applied to solar system objects? Explain.

.......................................................................

.......................................................................

.......................................................................

.......................................................................

.......................................................................

.......................................................................

.......................................................................

.......................................................................

.......................................................................

.......................................................................

3. **SEP Identify Limitations** How does Willa's model show that gravity keeps objects in the solar system in orbit around the sun? What are the limitations of her model? Do objects in the solar system behave like they would in the model? Explain.

.......................................................................

.......................................................................

.......................................................................

.......................................................................

.......................................................................

.......................................................................

.......................................................................

4. **SEP Construct Explanations** How can Willa use the materials and her model to explain why objects that are very far from the sun do not orbit it?

.......................................................................

.......................................................................

.......................................................................

.......................................................................

.......................................................................

.......................................................................

.......................................................................

.......................................................................

.......................................................................

.......................................................................

# Quest FINDINGS

## Complete the Quest!

**Phenomenon You learned what it takes to be an asteroid hunter, an extraterrestrial life hunter, and a dark matter hunter. Apply the knowledge you gained to write advertisements to attract great candidates to the new observatory.**

CCC Cause and Effect Think about the three different types of scientists needed. Why might it be important for them to use models in their investigations?

.......................................................................

.......................................................................

.......................................................................

.......................................................................

**INTERACTIVITY**

Reflect on Searching for a Star

MS-ESS1-2, MS-ESS1-3

# Scaling Down the
# Solar System

How can you **build scale models** of **volcanoes** from three **planets** to show which one is largest?

## Background

**Phenomenon** Mauna Loa in Hawaii is currently the largest active volcano on Earth. But is it the largest volcano in the solar system? Sapas Mons on Venus and Olympus Mons on Mars are two other volcanoes that can be viewed from Earth with telescopes. Scientists use scale models to help them answer questions about landforms on other planets. In this investigation, you will make scale models of volcanoes found on different planets in our solar system.

(per group)

- calculator
- graph paper
- a variety of common craft materials, such as construction paper, tape, glue, craft sticks, modeling clay, foam, cotton balls, and markers
- metric ruler

## Safety

Be sure to follow all safety guidelines provided by your teacher. The Safety Appendix of your textbook provides more details about the safety icons.

Mauna Loa, Hawaii

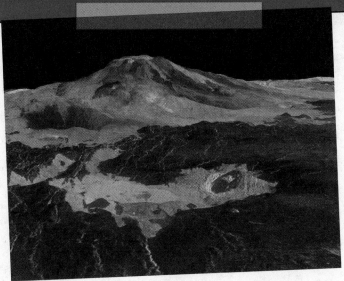

Sapas Mons

Olympus Mons

# Procedure

☐ 1. Examine the images of the three volcanoes that are found on different planets in our solar system. Research the volcanoes to find out about their heights, diameters, and any other distinguishing characteristics. In the space provided on the next page, create a data table to record the names of the volcanoes, their locations, their heights (in km), and their diameters (in km).

☐ 2. Determine an appropriate scale for your models. This decision is affected by two factors: how big an area you need to model and how much detail you want to show. If you need to show a large area, then you would want to choose a smaller scale to avoid the model becoming too big. But at smaller scales, models are limited in the amount of detail they can show. Consider the details you want to show and how large or small you want the models to be. Take into account the greatest and smallest values in your data table. Choose a scale that will allow you to represent these values in the models appropriately.

Record the scale that you will use for your models.

1 km = _____

☐ 3.  You will construct a three-dimensional model of each volcano from construction paper, modeling clay, or other available materials.

☐ 4. Draw a sketch to show your plans. Your sketch should indicate the scale of your models. It also should clearly identify the materials you will use in each part of your models. After obtaining your teacher's approval, follow your plan to construct your models to scale.

**HANDS-ON LAB**

ⁿDemonstrate Go online for a downloadable worksheet of this lab.

## Data Table

## Model Sketch

# Analyze and Interpret Data

1. **SEP Construct Explanations** Could you have used a different scale for each volcano to represent their relative sizes? Explain.

.................................................................................................................

.................................................................................................................

2. **CCC Scale, Proportion, and Quantity** Suppose someone suggested that you add a scale model of a human to your volcano models. Is this a reasonable or unreasonable suggestion? Use the scale of the models to construct your answer. (*Note: The height of a typical adult human is slightly less than 2 m, or 0.002 km.*)

.................................................................................................................

.................................................................................................................

.................................................................................................................

.................................................................................................................

3. **SEP Use Models** When you are studying models of different solar system objects, how does identifying the scale of each model help you to compare and understand their sizes and features?

.................................................................................................................

.................................................................................................................

.................................................................................................................

.................................................................................................................

.................................................................................................................

4. **Identify Limitations** Compare your models to the photographs of each volcano. What are some of the advantages of your models over the photographs? What are some of the disadvantages?

.................................................................................................................

.................................................................................................................

.................................................................................................................

.................................................................................................................

5. **SEP Evaluate Information** Using the scale models created by your class, compare characteristics such as the size and shape of the three different volcanoes found on Venus, Earth, and Mars. What can you infer about the three planets from this analysis?

.................................................................................................................

.................................................................................................................

.................................................................................................................

SEP.1, SEP.8

# The Meaning of Science

## Science Skills

**Reflect** Think about a time you misplaced something and could not find it. Write a sentence defining the problem. What science skills could you use to solve the problem? Explain how you would use at least three of the skills in the table.

Science is a way of learning about the natural world. It involves asking questions, making predictions, and collecting information to see if the answer is right or wrong.

The table lists some of the skills that scientists use. You use some of these skills every day. For example, you may observe and evaluate your lunch options before choosing what to eat.

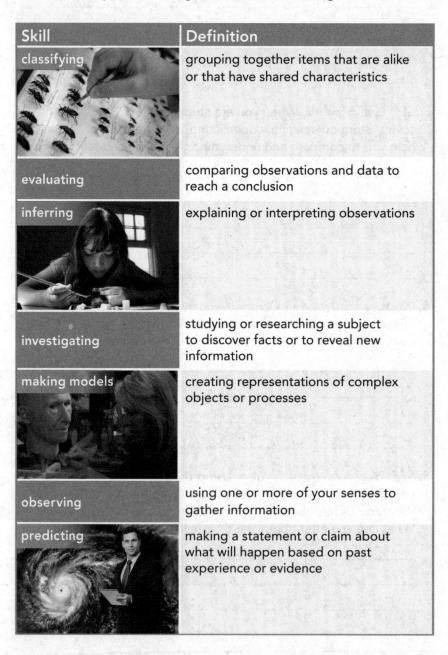

| Skill | Definition |
|---|---|
| classifying | grouping together items that are alike or that have shared characteristics |
| evaluating | comparing observations and data to reach a conclusion |
| inferring | explaining or interpreting observations |
| investigating | studying or researching a subject to discover facts or to reveal new information |
| making models | creating representations of complex objects or processes |
| observing | using one or more of your senses to gather information |
| predicting | making a statement or claim about what will happen based on past experience or evidence |

# Scientific Attitudes

Curiosity often drives scientists to learn about the world around them. Creativity is useful for coming up with inventive ways to solve problems. Such qualities and attitudes, and the ability to keep an open mind, are essential for scientists.

When sharing results or findings, honesty and ethics are also essential. Ethics refers to rules for knowing right from wrong.

Being skeptical is also important. This means having doubts about things based on past experiences and evidence. Skepticism helps to prevent accepting data and results that may not be true.

Scientists must also avoid bias—likes or dislikes of people, ideas, or things. They must avoid experimental bias, which is a mistake that may make an experiment's preferred outcome more likely.

# Scientific Reasoning

Scientific reasoning depends on being logical and objective. When you are objective, you use evidence and apply logic to draw conclusions. Being subjective means basing conclusions on personal feelings, biases, or opinions. Subjective reasoning can interfere with science and skew results. Objective reasoning helps scientists use observations to reach conclusions about the natural world.

Scientists use two types of objective reasoning: deductive and inductive. Deductive reasoning involves starting with a general idea or theory and applying it to a situation. For example, the theory of plate tectonics indicates that earthquakes happen mostly where tectonic plates meet. You could then draw the conclusion, or deduce, that California has many earthquakes because tectonic plates meet there.

In inductive reasoning, you make a generalization from a specific observation. When scientists collect data in an experiment and draw a conclusion based on that data, they use inductive reasoning. For example, if fertilizer causes one set of plants to grow faster than another, you might infer that the fertilizer promotes plant growth.

## Make Meaning
Think about a bias the marine biologist in the photo could show that results in paying more or less attention to one kind of organism over others. Make a prediction about how that bias could affect the biologist's survey of the coral reef.

## Write About It
Suppose it is raining when you go to sleep one night. When you wake up the next morning, you observe frozen puddles on the ground and icicles on tree branches. Use scientific reasoning to draw a conclusion about the air temperature outside. Support your conclusion using deductive or inductive reasoning.

SEP.1, SEP.2, SEP.3, SEP.4, CCC.4

# Science Processes

## Scientific Inquiry

Scientists contribute to scientific knowledge by conducting investigations and drawing conclusions. The process often begins with an observation that leads to a question, which is then followed by the development of a hypothesis. This is known as scientific inquiry.

One of the first steps in scientific inquiry is asking questions. However, it's important to make a question specific with a narrow focus so the investigation will not be too broad. A biologist may want to know all there is to know about wolves, for example. But a good, focused question for a specific inquiry might be "How many offspring does the average female wolf produce in her lifetime?"

A hypothesis is a possible answer to a scientific question. A hypothesis must be testable. For something to be testable, researchers must be able to carry out an investigation and gather evidence that will either support or disprove the hypothesis.

## Scientific Models

Models are tools that scientists use to study phenomena indirectly. A model is any representation of an object or process. Illustrations, dioramas, globes, diagrams, computer programs, and mathematical equations are all examples of scientific models. For example, a diagram of Earth's crust and mantle can help you to picture layers deep below the surface and understand events such as volcanic eruptions.

Models also allow scientists to represent objects that are either very large, such as our solar system, or very small, such as a molecule of DNA. Models can also represent processes that occur over a long period of time, such as the changes that have occurred throughout Earth's history.

Models are helpful, but they have limitations. Physical models are not made of the same materials as the objects they represent. Most models of complex objects or processes show only major parts, stages, or relationships. Many details are left out. Therefore, you may not be able to learn as much from models as you would through direct observation.

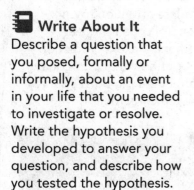

**Write About It**
Describe a question that you posed, formally or informally, about an event in your life that you needed to investigate or resolve. Write the hypothesis you developed to answer your question, and describe how you tested the hypothesis.

**Reflect** Identify the benefits and limitations of using a plastic model of DNA, as shown here.

# Science Experiments

An experiment or investigation must be well planned to produce valid results. In planning an experiment, you must identify the independent and dependent variables. You must also do as much as possible to remove the effects of other variables. A controlled experiment is one in which you test only one variable at a time.

For example, suppose you plan a controlled experiment to learn how the type of material affects the speed at which sound waves travel through it. The only variable that should change is the type of material. This way, if the speed of sound changes, you know that it is a result of a change in the material, not another variable such as the thickness of the material or the type of sound used.

You should also remove bias from any investigation. You may inadvertently introduce bias by selecting subjects you like and avoiding those you don't like. Scientists often conduct investigations by taking random samples to avoid ending up with biased results.

Once you plan your investigation and begin to collect data, it's important to record and organize the data. You may wish to use a graph to display and help you to interpret the data.

Communicating is the sharing of ideas and results with others through writing and speaking. Communicating data and conclusions is a central part of science.

Scientists share knowledge, including new findings, theories, and techniques for collecting data. Conferences, journals, and websites help scientists to communicate with each other. Popular media, including newspapers, magazines, and social media sites, help scientists to share their knowledge with nonscientists. However, before the results of investigations are shared and published, other scientists should review the experiment for possible sources of error, such as bias and unsupported conclusions.

## Write About It

List four ways you could communicate the results of a scientific study about the health of sea turtles in the Pacific Ocean.

SEP.1, SEP.6, SEP.7, SEP.8

# Scientific Knowledge

## Scientific Explanations

Suppose you learn that adult flamingos are pink because of the food they eat. This statement is a scientific explanation— it describes how something in nature works or explains why it happens. Scientists from different fields use methods such as researching information, designing experiments, and making models to form scientific explanations. Scientific explanations often result from many years of work and multiple investigations conducted by many scientists.

## Scientific Theories and Laws

A scientific law is a statement that describes what you can expect to occur every time under a particular set of conditions. A scientific law describes an observed pattern in nature, but it does not attempt to explain it. For example, the law of superposition describes what you can expect to find in terms of the ages of layers of rock. Geologists use this observed pattern to determine the relative ages of sedimentary rock layers. But the law does not explain why the pattern occurs.

By contrast, a scientific theory is a well-tested explanation for a wide range of observations or experimental results. It provides details and describes causes of observed patterns. Something is elevated to a theory only when there is a large body of evidence that supports it. However, a scientific theory can be changed or overturned when new evidence is found.

**Write About It**
Choose two fields of science that interest you. Describe a method used to develop scientific explanations in each field.

SEP Construct Explanations Complete the table to compare and contrast a scientific theory and a scientific law.

|  | Scientific Theory | Scientific Law |
|---|---|---|
| Definition |  |  |
| Does it attempt to explain a pattern observed in nature? |  |  |

## Analyzing Scientific Explanations

To analyze scientific explanations that you hear on the news or read in a book such as this one, you need scientific literacy. Scientific literacy means understanding scientific terms and principles well enough to ask questions, evaluate information, and make decisions. Scientific reasoning gives you a process to apply. This includes looking for bias and errors in the research, evaluating data, and identifying faulty reasoning. For example, by evaluating how a survey was conducted, you may find a serious flaw in the researchers' methods.

## Evidence and Opinions

The basis for scientific explanations is empirical evidence. Empirical evidence includes the data and observations that have been collected through scientific processes. Satellite images, photos, and maps of mountains and volcanoes are all examples of empirical evidence that support a scientific explanation about Earth's tectonic plates. Scientists look for patterns when they analyze this evidence. For example, they might see a pattern that mountains and volcanoes often occur near tectonic plate boundaries.

To evaluate scientific information, you must first distinguish between evidence and opinion. In science, evidence includes objective observations and conclusions that have been repeated. Evidence may or may not support a scientific claim. An opinion is a subjective idea that is formed from evidence, but it cannot be confirmed by evidence.

**Write About It**
Suppose the conservation committee of a town wants to gauge residents' opinions about a proposal to stock the local ponds with fish every spring. The committee pays for a survey to appear on a web site that is popular with people who like to fish. The results of the survey show 78 people in favor of the proposal and two against it. Do you think the survey's results are valid? Explain.

**Make Meaning**
Explain what empirical evidence the photograph reveals.

593

SEP.3, SEP.4

# Tools of Science

## Measurement

Making measurements using standard units is important in all fields of science. This allows scientists to repeat and reproduce other experiments, as well as to understand the precise meaning of the results of others. Scientists use a measurement system called the International System of Units, or SI.

For each type of measurement, there is a series of units that are greater or less than each other. The unit a scientist uses depends on what is being measured. For example, a geophysicist tracking the movements of tectonic plates may use centimeters, as plates tend to move small amounts each year. Meanwhile, a marine biologist might measure the movement of migrating bluefin tuna on the scale of kilometers.

Units for length, mass, volume, and density are based on powers of ten—a meter is equal to 100 centimeters or 1000 millimeters. Units of time do not follow that pattern. There are 60 seconds in a minute, 60 minutes in an hour, and 24 hours in a day. These units are based on patterns that humans perceived in nature. Units of temperature are based on scales that are set according to observations of nature. For example, 0°C is the temperature at which pure water freezes, and 100°C is the temperature at which it boils.

**Write About It**
Suppose you are planning an investigation in which you must measure the dimensions of several small mineral samples that fit in your hand. Which metric unit or units will you most likely use? Explain your answer.

| Measurement | Metric units |
| --- | --- |
| Length or distance | meter (m), kilometer (km), centimeter (cm), millimeter (mm)<br>1 km = 1,000 m    1 cm = 10 mm<br>1 m = 100 cm |
| Mass | kilogram (kg), gram (g), milligram (mg)<br>1 kg = 1,000 g    1 g = 1,000 mg |
| Volume | cubic meter (m³), cubic centimeter (cm³)<br>1 m³ = 1,000,000 cm³ |
| Density | kilogram per cubic meter (kg/m³), gram per cubic centimeter (g/cm³)<br>1,000 kg/m³ = 1 g/cm³ |
| Temperature | degrees Celsius (°C), kelvin (K)<br>1°C = 273 K |
| Time | hour (h), minute (m), second (s) |

# Math Skills

Using numbers to collect and interpret data involves math skills that are essential in science. For example, you use math skills when you estimate the number of birds in an entire forest after counting the actual number of birds in ten trees.

Scientists evaluate measurements and estimates for their precision and accuracy. In science, an accurate measurement is very close to the actual value. Precise measurements are very close, or nearly equal, to each other. Reliable measurements are both accurate and precise. An imprecise value may be a sign of an error in data collection. This kind of anomalous data may be excluded to avoid skewing the data and harming the investigation.

Other math skills include performing specific calculations, such as finding the mean, or average, value in a data set. The mean can be calculated by adding up all of the values in the data set and then dividing that sum by the number of values.

| Hour | Number of Ducks Observed at a Pond |
|------|------------------------------------|
| 1 | 12 |
| 2 | 10 |
| 3 | 2 |
| 4 | 14 |
| 5 | 13 |
| 6 | 10 |
| 7 | 11 |

**SEP Use Mathematics** The data table shows how many ducks were seen at a pond every hour over the course of seven hours. Is there a data point that seems anomalous? If so, cross out that data point. Then, calculate the mean number of ducks on the pond. Round the mean to the nearest whole number.

# Graphs

Graphs help scientists to interpret data by helping them to find trends or patterns in the data. A line graph displays data that show how one variable (the dependent or outcome variable) changes in response to another (the independent or test variable). The slope and shape of a graph line can reveal patterns and help scientists to make predictions. For example, line graphs can help you to spot patterns of change over time.

Scientists use bar graphs to compare data across categories or subjects that may not affect each other. The heights of the bars make it easy to compare those quantities. A circle graph, also known as a pie chart, shows the proportions of different parts of a whole.

**Write About It**
You and a friend record the distance you travel every 15 minutes on a one-hour bike trip. Your friend wants to display the data as a circle graph. Explain whether or not this is the best type of graph to display your data. If not, suggest another graph to use.

SEP.1, SEP.2, SEP.3, SEP.6

# The Engineering Design Process

Engineers are builders and problem solvers. Chemical engineers experiment with new fuels made from algae. Civil engineers design roadways and bridges. Bioengineers develop medical devices and prosthetics. The common trait among engineers is an ability to identify problems and design solutions to solve them. Engineers use a creative process that relies on scientific methods to help guide them from a concept or idea all the way to the final product.

## Define the Problem

To identify or define a problem, different questions need to be asked: *What are the effects of the problem? What are the likely causes? What other factors could be involved?* Sometimes the obvious, immediate cause of a problem may be the result of another problem that may not be immediately apparent. For example, climate change results in different weather patterns, which in turn can affect organisms that live in certain habitats. So engineers must be aware of all the possible effects of potential solutions. Engineers must also take into account how well different solutions deal with the different causes of the problem.

**Reflect** Write about a problem that you encountered in your life that had both immediate, obvious causes as well as less-obvious and less-immediate ones.

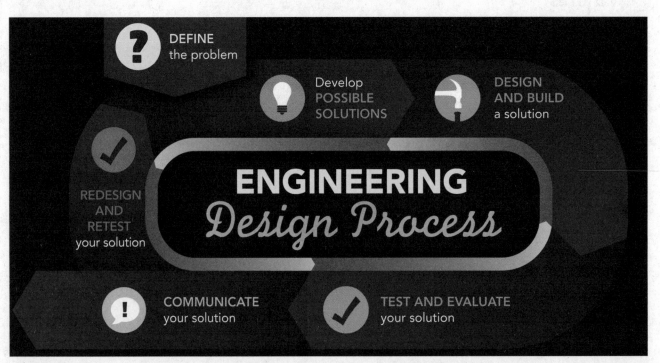

- **DEFINE** the problem
- Develop **POSSIBLE SOLUTIONS**
- **DESIGN AND BUILD** a solution
- **REDESIGN AND RETEST** your solution
- **COMMUNICATE** your solution
- **TEST AND EVALUATE** your solution

**ENGINEERING** *Design Process*

As engineers consider problems and design solutions, they must identify and categorize the criteria and constraints of the project.

Criteria are the factors that must be met or accomplished by the solution. For example, a gardener who wants to protect outdoor plants from deer and rabbits may say that the criteria for the solution are "plants are no longer eaten" and "plant growth is not inhibited in any way." The gardener then knows the plants cannot simply be sealed off from the environment, because the plants will not receive sunlight and water.

The same gardener will likely have constraints on his solution, such as budget for materials and time that is available for working on the project. By setting constraints, a solution can be designed that will be successful without introducing a new set of problems. No one wants to spend $500 on materials to protect $100 worth of tomatoes and cucumbers.

## Develop Possible Solutions

After the problem has been identified, and the criteria and constraints identified, an engineer will consider possible solutions. This often involves working in teams with other engineers and designers to brainstorm ideas and research materials that can be used in the design.

It's important for engineers to think creatively and explore all potential solutions. If you wanted to design a bicycle that was safer and easier to ride than a traditional bicycle, then you would want more than just one or two solutions. Having multiple ideas to choose from increases the likelihood that you will develop a solution that meets the criteria and constraints. In addition, different ideas that result from brainstorming can often lead to new and better solutions to an existing problem.

**Make Meaning**
Using the example of a garden that is vulnerable to wild animals such as deer, make a list of likely constraints on an engineering solution to the problem you identified before. Determine if there are common traits among the constraints, and identify categories for them.

## Design a Solution

Engineers then develop the idea that they feel best solves the problem. Once a solution has been chosen, engineers and designers get to work building a model or prototype of the solution. A model may involve sketching on paper or using computer software to construct a model of the solution. A prototype is a working model of the solution.

Building a model or prototype helps an engineer determine whether a solution meets the criteria and stays within the constraints. During this stage of the process, engineers must often deal with new problems and make any necessary adjustments to the model or prototype.

## Test and Evaluate a Solution

Whether testing a model or a prototype, engineers use scientific processes to evaluate their solutions. Multiple experiments, tests, or trials are conducted, data are evaluated, and results and analyses are communicated. New criteria or constraints may emerge as a result of testing. In most cases, a solution will require some refinement or revision, even if it has been through successful testing. Refining a solution is necessary if there are new constraints, such as less money or available materials. Additional testing may be done to ensure that a solution satisfies local, state, or federal laws or standards.

**Make Meaning** Think about an aluminum beverage can. What would happen if the price or availability of aluminum changed so much that cans needed to be made of a new material? What would the criteria and constraints be on the development of a new can?

A naval architect sets up a model to test how the the hull's design responds to waves.

# Communicate the Solution

Engineers need to communicate the final design to the people who will manufacture the product. This may include sketches, detailed drawings, computer simulations, and written text. Engineers often provide evidence that was collected during the testing stage. This evidence may include graphs and data tables that support the decisions made for the final design.

If there is feedback about the solution, then the engineers and designers must further refine the solution. This might involve making minor adjustments to the design, or it might mean bigger modifications to the design based on new criteria or constraints. Any changes in the design will require additional testing to make sure that the changes work as intended.

# Redesign and Retest the Solution

At different steps in the engineering and design process, a solution usually must be revised and retested. Many designs fail to work perfectly, even after models and prototypes are built, tested, and evaluated. Engineers must be ready to analyze new results and deal with any new problems that arise. Troubleshooting, or fixing design problems, allows engineers to adjust the design to improve on how well the solution meets the need.

SEP Design Solutions Suppose you are an engineer at an aerospace company. Your team is designing a rover to be used on a future NASA space mission. A family member doesn't understand why so much of your team's time is taken up with testing and retesting the rover design. What are three things you would tell your relative to explain why testing and retesting are so important to the engineering and design process?

...............................................................................................

...............................................................................................

...............................................................................................

...............................................................................................

...............................................................................................

...............................................................................................

...............................................................................................

...............................................................................................

# APPENDIX A

## Safety Symbols

These symbols warn of possible dangers in the laboratory and remind you to work carefully.

 **Safety Goggles** Wear safety goggles to protect your eyes in any activity involving chemicals, flames or heating, or glassware.

 **Lab Apron** Wear a laboratory apron to protect your skin and clothing from damage.

 **Breakage** Handle breakable materials, such as glassware, with care. Do not touch broken glassware.

 **Heat-Resistant Gloves** Use an oven mitt or other hand protection when handling hot materials, such as hot plates or hot glassware.

 **Plastic Gloves** Wear disposable plastic gloves when working with harmful chemicals and organisms. Keep your hands away from your face, and dispose of the gloves according to your teacher's instructions.

 **Heating** Use a clamp or tongs to pick up hot glassware. Do not touch hot objects with your bare hands.

 **Flames** Before you work with flames, tie back loose hair and clothing. Follow your teacher's instructions about lighting and extinguishing flames.

 **No Flames** When using flammable materials, make sure there are no flames, sparks, or other exposed heat sources present.

 **Corrosive Chemical** Avoid getting acid or other corrosive chemicals on your skin or clothing or in your eyes. Do not inhale the vapors. Wash your hands after the activity.

 **Poison** Do not let any poisonous chemical come into contact with your skin, and do not inhale its vapors. Wash your hands when you are finished with the activity.

 **Fumes** Work in a well-ventilated area when harmful vapors may be involved. Avoid inhaling vapors directly. Test an odor only when directed to do so by your teacher, and use a wafting motion to direct the vapor toward your nose.

 **Sharp Object** Scissors, scalpels, knives, needles, pins, and tacks can cut your skin. Always direct a sharp edge or point away from yourself and others.

 **Animal Safety** Treat live or preserved animals or animal parts with care to avoid harming the animals or yourself. Wash your hands when you are finished with the activity.

 **Plant Safety** Handle plants only as directed by your teacher. If you are allergic to certain plants, tell your teacher; do not do an activity involving those plants. Avoid touching harmful plants such as poison ivy. Wash your hands when you are finished with the activity.

 **Electric Shock** To avoid electric shock, never use electrical equipment around water, when the equipment is wet, or when your hands are wet. Be sure cords are untangled and cannot trip anyone. Unplug equipment not in use.

 **Physical Safety** When an experiment involves physical activity, avoid injuring yourself or others. Alert your teacher if there is any reason you should not participate.

 **Disposal** Dispose of chemicals and other laboratory materials safely. Follow the instructions from your teacher.

 **Hand Washing** Wash your hands thoroughly when finished with an activity. Use soap and warm water. Rinse well.

 **General Safety Awareness** When this symbol appears, follow the instructions provided. When you are asked to develop your own procedure in a lab, have your teacher approve your plan.

# Using a Laboratory Balance

The laboratory balance is an important tool in scientific investigations. Different kinds of balances are used in the laboratory to determine the masses and weights of objects. You can use a triple-beam balance to determine the masses of materials that you study or experiment with in the laboratory. An electronic balance, unlike a triple-beam balance, is used to measure the weights of materials.

The triple-beam balance that you may use in your science class is probably similar to the balance depicted in this Appendix. To use the balance properly, you should learn the name, location, and function of each part of the balance.

## Triple-Beam Balance

The triple-beam balance is a single-pan balance with three beams calibrated in grams. The back, or 100-gram, beam is divided into ten units of 10 grams each. The middle, or 500-gram, beam is divided into five units of 100 grams each. The front, or 10-gram, beam is divided into ten units of 1 gram each. Each gram on the front beam is further divided into units of 0.1 gram.

**Apply Concepts** What is the greatest mass you could find with the triple-beam balance in the picture?

...............................................

**Calculate** What is the mass of the apple in the picture?

...............................................

**The following procedure can be used to find the mass of an object with a triple-beam balance:**

1. Place the object on the pan.

2. Move the rider on the middle beam notch by notch until the horizontal pointer on the right drops below zero. Move the rider back one notch.

3. Move the rider on the back beam notch by notch until the pointer again drops below zero. Move the rider back one notch.

4. Slowly slide the rider along the front beam until the pointer stops at the zero point.

5. The mass of the object is equal to the sum of the readings on the three beams.

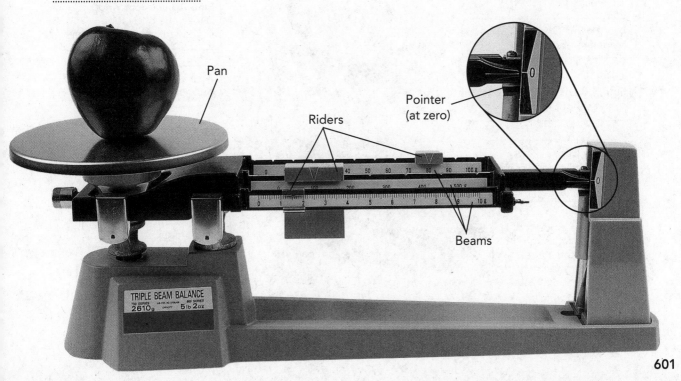

Pan

Riders

Pointer (at zero)

Beams

TRIPLE BEAM BALANCE
700 SERIES
2610g   CAPACITY   5 lb 2 oz

## Using a Microscope

The microscope is an essential tool in the study of life science. It allows you to see things that are too small to be seen with the unaided eye.

You will probably use a compound microscope like the one you see here. The compound microscope has more than one lens that magnifies the object you view.

Typically, a compound microscope has one lens in the eyepiece (the part you look through). The eyepiece lens usually magnifies 10×. Any object you view through this lens will appear 10 times larger than it is.

A compound microscope may contain two or three other lenses called objective lenses. They are called the low-power and high-power objective lenses. The low-power objective lens usually magnifies 10×. The high-power objective lenses usually magnify 40× and 100×.

To calculate the total magnification with which you are viewing an object, multiply the magnification of the eyepiece lens by the magnification of the objective lens you are using. For example, the eyepiece's magnification of 10× multiplied by the low-power objective's magnification of 10× equals a total magnification of 100×.

Use the photo of the compound microscope to become familiar with the parts of the microscope and their functions.

### The Parts of a Microscope

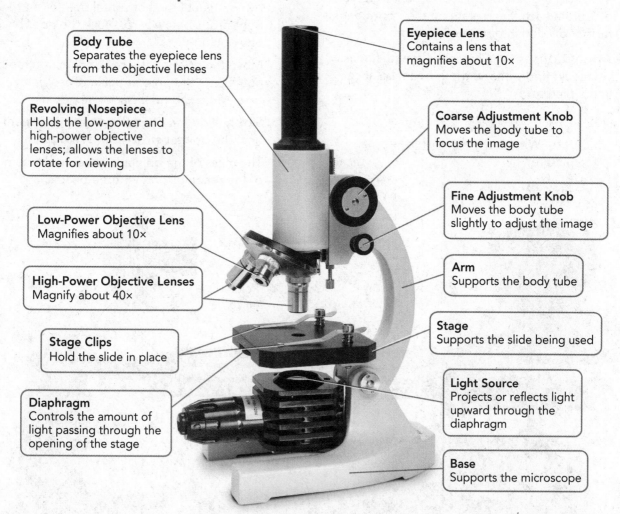

**Body Tube**
Separates the eyepiece lens from the objective lenses

**Revolving Nosepiece**
Holds the low-power and high-power objective lenses; allows the lenses to rotate for viewing

**Low-Power Objective Lens**
Magnifies about 10×

**High-Power Objective Lenses**
Magnify about 40×

**Stage Clips**
Hold the slide in place

**Diaphragm**
Controls the amount of light passing through the opening of the stage

**Eyepiece Lens**
Contains a lens that magnifies about 10×

**Coarse Adjustment Knob**
Moves the body tube to focus the image

**Fine Adjustment Knob**
Moves the body tube slightly to adjust the image

**Arm**
Supports the body tube

**Stage**
Supports the slide being used

**Light Source**
Projects or reflects light upward through the diaphragm

**Base**
Supports the microscope

## Using the Microscope
**Use the following procedures when you are working with a microscope.**

1. To carry the microscope, grasp the microscope's arm with one hand. Place your other hand under the base.

2. Place the microscope on a table with the arm toward you.

3. Turn the coarse adjustment knob to raise the body tube.

4. Revolve the nosepiece until the low-power objective lens clicks into place.

5. Adjust the diaphragm. While looking through the eyepiece, adjust the mirror until you see a bright white circle of light. **CAUTION:** Never use direct sunlight as a light source.

6. Place a slide on the stage. Center the specimen over the opening on the stage. Use the stage clips to hold the slide in place. **CAUTION:** Glass slides are fragile.

7. Look at the stage from the side. Carefully turn the coarse adjustment knob to lower the body tube until the low-power objective almost touches the slide.

8. Looking through the eyepiece, very slowly turn the coarse adjustment knob until the specimen comes into focus.

9. To switch to the high-power objective lens, look at the microscope from the side. Carefully revolve the nosepiece until the high-power objective lens clicks into place. Make sure the lens does not hit the slide.

10. Looking through the eyepiece, turn the fine adjustment knob until the specimen comes into focus.

## Making a Wet-Mount Slide
**Use the following procedures to make a wet-mount slide of a specimen.**

1. Obtain a clean microscope slide and a coverslip. **CAUTION:** Glass slides and coverslips are fragile.

2. Place the specimen on the center of the slide. The specimen must be thin enough for light to pass through it.

3. Using a plastic dropper, place a drop of water on the specimen.

4. Gently place one edge of the coverslip against the slide so that it touches the edge of the water drop at a 45° angle. Slowly lower the coverslip over the specimen. If you see air bubbles trapped beneath the coverslip, tap the coverslip gently with the eraser end of a pencil.

5. Remove any excess water at the edge of the coverslip with a paper towel.

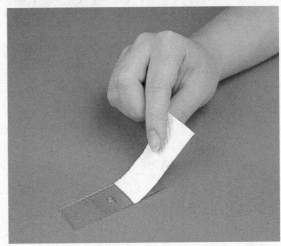

## Periodic Table of Elements

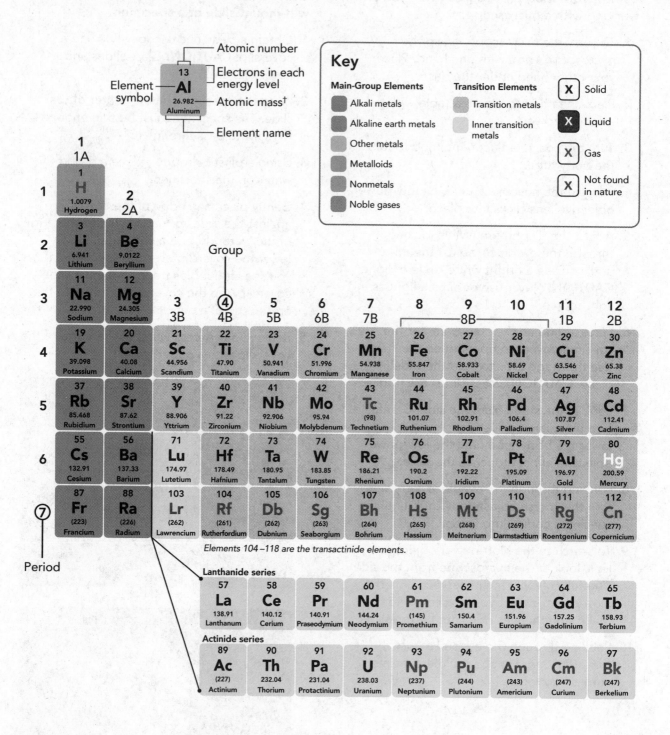

†The atomic masses in parentheses are the mass numbers of the longest-lived isotope of elements for which a standard atomic mass cannot be defined.

| | | | | | 18<br>8A |
|---|---|---|---|---|---|
| | | | | | 2<br>**He**<br>4.0026<br>Helium |
| 13<br>3A | 14<br>4A | 15<br>5A | 16<br>6A | 17<br>7A | |
| 5<br>**B**<br>10.81<br>Boron | 6<br>**C**<br>12.011<br>Carbon | 7<br>**N**<br>14.007<br>Nitrogen | 8<br>**O**<br>15.999<br>Oxygen | 9<br>**F**<br>18.998<br>Fluorine | 10<br>**Ne**<br>20.179<br>Neon |
| 13<br>**Al**<br>26.982<br>Aluminum | 14<br>**Si**<br>28.086<br>Silicon | 15<br>**P**<br>30.974<br>Phosphorus | 16<br>**S**<br>32.06<br>Sulfur | 17<br>**Cl**<br>35.453<br>Chlorine | 18<br>**Ar**<br>39.948<br>Argon |
| 31<br>**Ga**<br>69.72<br>Gallium | 32<br>**Ge**<br>72.59<br>Germanium | 33<br>**As**<br>74.922<br>Arsenic | 34<br>**Se**<br>78.96<br>Selenium | 35<br>**Br**<br>79.904<br>Bromine | 36<br>**Kr**<br>83.80<br>Krypton |
| 49<br>**In**<br>114.82<br>Indium | 50<br>**Sn**<br>118.69<br>Tin | 51<br>**Sb**<br>121.75<br>Antimony | 52<br>**Te**<br>127.60<br>Tellurium | 53<br>**I**<br>126.90<br>Iodine | 54<br>**Xe**<br>131.30<br>Xenon |
| 81<br>**Tl**<br>204.37<br>Thallium | 82<br>**Pb**<br>207.2<br>Lead | 83<br>**Bi**<br>208.98<br>Bismuth | 84<br>**Po**<br>(209)<br>Polonium | 85<br>**At**<br>(210)<br>Astatine | 86<br>**Rn**<br>(222)<br>Radon |
| 113<br>**Nh**<br>(284)<br>Nihonium | 114<br>**Fl**<br>(289)<br>Flerovium | 115<br>**Mc**<br>(288)<br>Moscovium | 116<br>**Lv**<br>(292)<br>Livermorium | 117<br>**Ts**<br>(294)<br>Tennessine | 118<br>**Og**<br>(294)<br>Oganesson |

| 66<br>**Dy**<br>162.50<br>Dysprosium | 67<br>**Ho**<br>164.93<br>Holmium | 68<br>**Er**<br>167.26<br>Erbium | 69<br>**Tm**<br>168.93<br>Thulium | 70<br>**Yb**<br>173.04<br>Ytterbium |
|---|---|---|---|---|
| 98<br>**Cf**<br>(251)<br>Californium | 99<br>**Es**<br>(252)<br>Einsteinium | 100<br>**Fm**<br>(257)<br>Fermium | 101<br>**Md**<br>(258)<br>Mendelevium | 102<br>**No**<br>(259)<br>Nobelium |

# GLOSSARY

**absolute age** The age of a rock given as the number of years since the rock formed. (367)

**absolute brightness** The brightness a star would have if it were at a standard distance from Earth. (567)

**acid rain** Rain or another form of precipitation that is more acidic than normal, caused by the release of molecules of sulfur dioxide and nitrogen oxide into the air. (324)

**air mass** A huge body of air that has similar temperature, humidity, and air pressure at any given height. (67)

**air pressure** The pressure caused by the weight of a column of air pushing down on an area. (51)

**alluvial fan** A wide, sloping deposit of sediment formed where a stream leaves a mountain range. (235)

**alternative energy** Clean energy sources that do not come from fossil fuels. (476)

**altitude** Elevation above sea level. (51)

**amphibian** A vertebrate whose body temperature is determined by the temperature of its environment, and that lives its early life in water and its adult life on land. (386)

**anticyclone** A high-pressure center of dry air. (72)

**apparent brightness** The brightness of a star as seen from Earth. (567)

**aquifer** An underground layer of rock or sediment that holds water. (30)

**asteroid** One of the rocky objects revolving around the sun that is too small and numerous to be considered a planet. (540)

**astronomical unit** A unit of distance equal to the average distance between Earth and the sun, about 150 million kilometers. (538)

**atmosphere** The relatively thin layer of gases that form Earth's outermost layer. (6)

**atmosphere** The relatively thin layer of gases that form Earth's outermost layer. (49)

**axis** An imaginary line that passes through a planet's center and its north and south poles, about which the planet rotates. (505)

**big bang** The initial explosion that resulted in the formation and expansion of the universe. (576)

**biosphere** The parts of Earth that contain living organisms. (6)

**birth rate** The number of people born per 1,000 individuals for a certain period of time. (314)

**cascade effect** An unforeseen chain of events caused by a disturbance in a system. (474)

**chemical weathering** The process that breaks down rock through chemical changes. (214)

**climate** The average annual conditions of temperature, precipitation, winds, and clouds in an area. (449)

**climate change** A sudden or gradual change in Earth's climate. (460)

**coastline** A line that forms the boundary between the land and the ocean or a lake. (17)

**comet** A loose collection of ice and dust that orbits the sun, typically in a long, narrow orbit. (494, 540)

**compression** Stress that squeezes rock until it folds or breaks. (179)

**condensation** The change in state from a gas to a liquid. (26, 58)

**conduction** The transfer of thermal energy from one particle of matter to another. (412)

**conservation** The practice of using less of a resource so that it can last longer. (318)

**constellation** A pattern or grouping of stars that people imagine to represent a figure or object. (495)

**continental glacier** A glacier that covers much of a continent or large island. (244)

**convection** The transfer of thermal energy by the movement of a fluid. (412)

**convergent boundary** A plate boundary where two plates move toward each other. (171)

**Coriolis effect** The effect of Earth's rotation on the direction of winds and currents. (421)

**crust** The layer of rock that forms Earth's outer surface. (110)

**cryosphere** The portion of the hydrosphere that is frozen, including all the ice and snow on land, plus sea and lake ice. (6)

**crystal** A solid in which the atoms are arranged in a pattern that repeats again and again. (119)

**crystallization** The process by which atoms are arranged to form a material with a crystal structure. (123)

**crystallize** To form a crystal structure. (285)

**current** A large stream of moving water that flows through the oceans. (427)

**cyclone** A swirling center of low air pressure. (72)

# D

**death rate** The number of deaths per 1,000 individuals in a certain period of time. (314)

**deflation** The process by which wind removes surface materials. (226)

**deforestation** The removal of forests to use the land for other reasons. (332)

**delta** A landform made of sediment that is deposited where a river flows into an ocean or lake. (17, 235)

**deposition** Process in which sediment is laid down in new locations. (223)

**desalination** A process that removes salt from sea water to make fresh water. (297)

**desertification** The advance of desert-like conditions into areas that previously were fertile; caused by overfarming, overgrazing, drought, and climate change. (335)

**dew point** The temperature at which condensation begins. (58)

**divergent boundary** A plate boundary where two plates move away from each other. (171)

**dormant** Term used to describe a volcano that is not currently acrtive but able to become active in the future. (196)

**drought** A long period of low precipitation. (89)

**dune** A hill of sand piled up by the wind. (17)

# E

**earthquake** The shaking that results from the movement of rock beneath Earth's surface. (183)

**eclipse** The partial or total blocking of one object in space by another. (519)

**El Niño** An abnormal climate event that occurs every two to seven years in the Pacific Ocean, causing changes in winds, currents, and weather patterns for one to two years. (430)

**electromagnetic radiation** The energy transferred through space by electromagnetic waves. (551)

**electromagnetic wave** A wave that can transfer electric and magnetic energy through the vacuum of space. (407)

**ellipse** An oval shape, which may be elongated or nearly circular; the shape of the planets' orbits. (499)

**emissions** Pollutants that are released into the air. (322)

**energy** The ability to do work or cause change. (7)

**equinox** Either of the two days of the year on which neither hemisphere is tilted toward or away from the sun. (508)

**era** One of the three long units of geologic time between the Precambrian and the present. (380)

**erosion** The process by which water, ice, wind, or gravity moves weathered particles of rock and soil. (213, 334)

**evaporation** The process by which molecules at the surface of a liquid absorb enough energy to change to a gas. (25, 57)

**exponential growth** A rate of change that increases more and more rapidly over time. (315)

**extinct** Term used to describe a volcano that is no longer active and unlikely to erupt again. (196)

# F

**fault** A break in Earth's crust along which rocks move. (180)

**flood** An overflowing of water in a normally dry area. (89)

**flood plain** The flat, wide area of land along a river. (233)

**fossil** The preserved remains or traces of an organism that lived in the past. (369)

**fossil fuel** Energy-rich substance formed from the remains of organisms. (266, 464)

**front** The boundary where unlike air masses meet but do not mix. (69)

# G

**galaxy** A huge group of single stars, star systems, star clusters, dust, and gas bound together by gravity. (573)

**geocentric** Term describing a model of the universe in which Earth is at the center of the revolving planets and stars. (498)

**geologic time scale** A record of the geologic events and life forms in Earth's history. (377)

**geosphere** The densest parts of Earth that include the crust, mantle, and core. (6)

**glacier** Any large mass of ice that moves slowly over land. (243)

**global warming** A gradual increase in the Earth's average temperature. (463)

**gravity** The attractive force between objects; the force that moves objects downhill. (509)

**greenhouse effect** The trapping of heat near a planet's surface by certain gases in the planet's atmosphere. (410, 459)

**greenhouse gas** A gas in Earth's atmosphere that absorbs heat leaving Earth's surface. (459)

**groundwater** Water that fills the cracks and spaces in underground soil and rock layers. (237)

# GLOSSARY

## H

**heliocentric** Term describing a model of the solar system in which Earth and the other planets revolve around the sun. (499)

**hot spot** An area where magma from deep within the mantle melts through the crust above it. (193)

**humidity** The amount of water vapor in a given volume of air. (59)

**humus** Dark-colored organic material in soil. (217)

**hurricane** A tropical storm that has winds of about 119 kilometers per hour or higher. (86)

**hydrosphere** The portion of Earth that consists of water in any of its forms, including oceans, glaciers, rivers, lakes, groundwater and water vapor. (6)

## I

**ice age** Time in Earth's history during which glaciers covered large parts of the surface. (244)

**igneous rock** A type of rock that forms from the cooling of molten rock at or below the surface. (131)

**inertia** The tendency of an object to resist a change in motion. (510)

**inner core** A dense sphere of solid iron and nickel at the center of Earth. (112)

**invertebrate** An animal without a backbone. (385)

## J

**jet stream** Band of high-speed winds about 10 kilometers above Earth's surface. (67, 423)

## L

**La Niña** A climate event in the eastern Pacific Ocean in which surface waters are colder than normal. (430)

**land breeze** The flow of air from land to a body of water. (419)

**landform** A feature on the surface of Earth, such as a coastline, dune, or mountain. (13)

**lava** Liquid magma that reaches the surface. (191)

**law of superposition** The geologic principle that states that in horizontal layers of sedimentary rock, each layer is older than the layer above it and younger than the layer below it. (368)

**law of universal gravitation** The scientific law that states that every object in the universe attracts every other object. (509)

**light-year** The distance that light travels in one year, about 9.46 trillion kilometers. (574)

**loess** A wind-formed deposit made of fine particles of clay and silt. (227)

**longshore drift** The movement of water and sediment down a beach caused by waves coming in to shore at an angle. (250)

## M

**magma** A molten mixture of rock-forming substances, gases, and water from the mantle. (191)

**magnitude** The measurement of an earthquake's strength based on seismic waves and movement along faults. (185)

**mammal** A vertebrate whose body temperature is regulated by its internal heat, and that has skin covered with hair or fur and glands that produce milk to feed its young. (388)

**mantle** The layer of hot, solid material between Earth's crust and core. (111)

**mass extinction** When many types of living things become extinct at the same time. (387)

**mass movement** Any one of several processes by which gravity moves sediment downhill. (224)

**mechanical weathering** The type of weathering in which rock is physically broken into smaller pieces. (214)

**metamorphic rock** A type of rock that forms from an existing rock that is changed by heat, pressure, or chemical reactions. (133)

**meteor** A streak of light in the sky produced by the burning of a meteoroid in Earth's atmosphere. (494)

**meteoroid** A chunk of rock or dust in space, generally smaller than an asteroid. (540)

**meteorologist** A scientist who studies the causes of weather and tries to predict it. (75)

**mid-ocean ridge** An undersea mountain chain where new ocean floor is produced; a divergent plate boundary under the ocean. (160)

**mineral** A naturally occurring solid that can form by inorganic processes and that has a crystal structure and a definite chemical composition. (119)

**moon** A natural satellite that orbits a planet. (540)

**mountain** A landform with high elevation and high relief. (16)

## N

**natural resource** Anything naturally occuring in the environment that humans use. (265, 331)

**neap tide** The tide with the least difference between consecutive low and high tides. (521)

**nebula** A large cloud of gas and dust in space. (561)

**nonpoint source** A widely spread source of pollution that is difficult to link to a specific point of origin. (321)

**nonrenewable resource** A natural resource that is not replaced in a useful time frame. (265, 331)

**nuclear fission** The splitting of an atom's nuclues into two nuclei, which releases a great deal of energy. (271)

## O

**ocean trench** An undersea valley that represents one of the deepest parts of the ocean. (162)

**orbit** The path of an object as it revolves around another object in space. (506)

**ore** A mineral deposit large enough and valuable enough for it to be extracted from the ground. (283)

**outer core** A layer of molten iron and nickel that surrounds the inner core of Earth. (112)

**overpopulation** A condition in which the number of humans grows beyond what the available resources can support. (317)

**ozone** A form of oxygen that has three oxygen atoms in each molecule instead of the usual two; toxic to organisms where it forms near Earth's surface. (323)

## P

**penumbra** The part of a shadow surrounding the darkest part. (519)

**period** One of the units of geologic time into which geologists divide eras. (380)

**petroleum** Liquid fossil fuel; oil. (268)

**phase** One of the different apparent shapes of the moon as seen from Earth. (515)

**planet** An object that orbits a star, is large enough to have become rounded by its own gravity, and has cleared the area of its orbit. (493, 539)

**plucking** The process by which a glacier picks up rocks as it flows over the land. (245)

**point source** A specific source of pollution that can be identified. (321)

**pollution** Contamination of Earth's land, water, or air through the release of harmful substances into the environment. (317, 321)

**precipitation** Any form of water that falls from clouds and reaches Earth's surface as rain, snow, sleet, or hail. (26, 60)

**protostar** A contracting cloud of gas and dust with enough mass to form a star. (561)

## R

**radiation** The transfer of energy by electromagnetic waves. (412)

**radioactive dating** The process of determining the age of an object using the half-life of one or more radioactive isotopes. (372)

**radioactive decay** The process in which the nuclei of radioactive elements break down, releasing fastmoving particles and energy. (371)

**relative age** The age of a rock compared to the ages of other rocks. (367)

**relative humidity** The percentage of water vapor in the air compared to the maximum amount of water vapor that air can contain at a particular temperature. (59)

**renewable resource** A resource that is either always available or is naturally replaced in a relatively short time. (275, 331)

**reptile** A vertebrate whose temperature is determined by the temperature of its environment, that has lungs and scaly skin, and that lays eggs on land. (386)

**revolution** The movement of an object around another object. (506)

**river** A natural stream of water that flows into another body of water, such as an ocean, lake, or another river. (17)

**rock cycle** A series of processes on the surface and inside Earth that slowly changes rocks from one kind to another. (137)

**rotation** The spinning motion of a planet on its axis. (505)

**runoff** Water that flows over the ground surface rather than soaking into the ground. (231)

# GLOSSARY

_____ S _____

**sand dune** A deposit of wind-blown sand. (227)

**satellite** An object that orbits a planet. (493)

**sea breeze** The flow of cooler air from over an ocean or lake toward land. (419)

**sea-floor spreading** The process by which molten material adds new oceanic crust to the ocean floor. (161)

**sediment** Small, solid pieces of material that come from rocks or the remains of organisms; earth materials deposited by erosion. (132, 223, 347)

**sedimentary rock** A type of rock that forms when particles from other rocks or the remains of plants and animals are pressed and cemented together. (132)

**seismic wave** Vibrations that travel through Earth carrying the energy released during an earthquake. (108)

**sewage** The water and human wastes that are washed down sinks, toilets, and showers. (346)

**shearing** Stress that pushes masses of rock in opposite directions, in a sideways movement. (179)

**soil** The loose, weathered material on Earth's surface in which plants can grow. (217)

**solar system** The system consisting of the sun and the planets and other objects that revolve around it. (537)

**solstice** Either of the two days of the year on which the sun reaches its greatest distance north or south of the equator. (508)

**spectrum** The range of wavelengths of electromagnetic waves. (551)

**spring tide** The tide with the greatest difference between consecutive low and high tides. (521)

**star** A ball of hot gas, primarily hydrogen and helium, that undergoes nuclear fusion. (493)

**storm** A violent disturbance in the atmosphere. (83)

**storm surge** A "dome" of water that sweeps across the coast where a hurricane lands. (87)

**stream** A channel through which water is continually flowing downhill. (232)

**stress** A force that acts on rock to change its shape or volume. (179)

**subduction** The process by which oceanic crust sinks beneath a deep-ocean trench and back into the mantle at a convergent plate boundary. (162)

**sun** A large, gaseous body at the center of the solar system. (539)

**supernova** The brilliant explosion of a dying supergiant star. (563)

**surveying** A process in which mapmakers determine distances and elevations using instruments and the principles of geometry. (18)

**sustainable** Using a resource in ways that maintain it at a certain quality for a certain period of time. (338)

**sustainable use** The practice of allowing renewable resources time to recover and replenish. (318)

_____ T _____

**telescope** An optical instrument that forms enlarged images of distant objects. (552)

**tension** Stress that stretches rock so that it becomes thinner in the middle. (179)

**thermal energy** The total kinetic and potential energy of all the particles of an object. (411)

**thermal pollution** A type of pollution caused by factories and power plants releasing superheated water into bodies of water. (347)

**thunderstorm** A small storm often accompanied by heavy precipitation and frequent thunder and lightning. (85)

**tide** The periodic rise and fall of the level of water in the ocean. (520)

**till** The sediments deposited directly by a glacier. (246)

**topography** The shape of the land determined by elevation, relief, and landforms. (13)

**tornado** A rapidly whirling, funnel-shaped cloud that reaches down to touch Earth's surface. (88)

**transform boundary** A plate boundary where two plates move past each other in opposite directions. (171)

**transpiration** The process by which water is lost through a plant's leaves. (25)

**tributary** A stream or river that flows into a larger river. (232)

**tsunami** A giant wave usually caused by an earthquake beneath the ocean floor. (187)

_____ U _____

**umbra** The darkest part of a shadow. (519)

**unconformity** A gap in the geologic record that shows where rock layers have been lost due to erosion. (370)

**uniformitarianism** The geologic principle that the same geologic processes that operate today operated in the past to change Earth's surface. (213)

**universe** All of space and everything in it. (574)

# V

**valley glacier** A long, narrow glacier that forms when snow and ice build up in a mountain valley. (244)

**vertebrate** An animal with a backbone. (386)

**visible light** Electromagnetic radiation that can be seen with the unaided eye. (551)

**volcano** A weak spot in the crust where magma has come to the surface. (191)

# W

**water cycle** The continual movement of water among Earth's atmosphere, oceans, and land surface through evaporation, condensation, and precipitation. (25, 57)

**watershed** The land area that supplies water to a river system. (28)

**wavelength** The distance between two corresponding parts of a wave, such as the distance between two crests. (551)

**well** A hole sunk into the ground to reach a supply of water. (30)

**white dwarf** The blue-white hot core of a star that is left behind after its outer layers have expanded and drifted out into space. (563)

**wind** The horizontal movement of air from an area of high pressure to an area of lower pressure. (54, 417)

# INDEX

# INDEX
Page numbers for key terms are printed in boldface type.

## Photographs

Photo locators denoted as follows: Top (T), Center (C), Bottom (B), Left (L), Right (R), Background (Bkgd)
**Front Cover:** Lightphoto/iStock/Getty Images
**Back Cover:** Marinello/DigitalVision Vectors/Getty Images

**Front Matter:**
vi: Mark Whitt Photography/Getty Images; vii: Switas/Getty Images; viii: Demerzel21/Fotolia; x: Robert Harding/Alamy Stock Photo; ix: AFP/Getty Images; xi: Panpilas L/Shutterstock; xii: KPG Payless2/Shutterstock; xiii: Sinclair Stammers/Science Photo Library/Getty Images; xiv: UniversalImagesGroup/Getty Images; xv: Michael Turner/Alamy Stock Photo; xvi: Chris Cook/Science Source; xvii: John A Davis/Shutterstock

**Topic 1**
xx: Mark Whitt Photography/Getty Images; 002 Bkgrd: 123RF; 002 TR: iStockphoto/Getty Images; 004: Samuel BorgesAlamy Stock Photo; 006 BL: Marco Regalia/Alamy Stock Photo; 006 CL: Dorota Wasik/EyeEm/Getty Images; 007 BR: Panther Media GmbH/Alamy Stock Photo; 007 CR: Mario Hoppmann/Shutterstock; 011: seafarer/Shuttesrstock; 014: david pearson/Alamy Stock Photo; 015: Stocktrek Images, Inc./Alamy Stock Photo; 018: Danita Delimont/Alamy Stock Photo; 020 B: UniversalImagesGroup/Getty Images; 020 T: Tetra Images/Alamy Stock Photo; 023 BCR: Songquan Deng/Shutterstock; 023 CR: Everett Collection/Shutterstock; 024: Paul Prescott/Shutterstock; 028: Clint Farlinger/Alamy Stock Photo; 029 CR: Aurora Photos/Alamy Stock Photo; 029 TR: imageBROKER/Alamy Stock Photo; 034: NASA; 037: Westend61/Getty Images; 038: NASA; 040: Sergio Azenha/Alamy Stock Photo; 041: BW Folsom/Shutterstock

**Topic 2**
044: switas/Getty Images; 046: A. T. Willett/Alamy Stock Photo; 048: studio23/Shutterstock; 050: LukaKikina/Shutterstock; 056: alexanderkorotun/Fotolia; 059 C: David J. Green Technology/Alamy Stock Photo; 059 CR: GIPhotoStock/Science Source; 061 B: mario beauregard/Fotolia; 061 CL: georgeion88/Fotolia; 061 CR: Nebojsa/Fotolia; 061 TR: Tatiana Belova/Fotolia; 065: Frans Lemmens/Alamy Stock Photo; 066: ValentinValkov/Fotolia; 069: Galyna Andrushko/Fotolia; 072: harvepino/Fotolia; 074: GIS/Fotolia; 076 Bkgrd: solarseven/Shutterstock; 076 BR: Carolina K. Smith MD/Shutterstock; 076 CR: chanelle/Fotolia; 076 TR: Karim Agabi/Science Source; 077: NOAA; 081 Bkgrd: Pavelk/Shutterstock; 081 BR: Science Source; 081 TR: David R. Frazier/Danita Delimont Photography/Newscom; 082: Smith Collection/Gado/Getty Images; 085: stnazkul/123RF; 088: Carlo Allegri/Reuters; 089: Aram Boghosian/The Boston Globe/Getty Images; 092: Juanmonino/Getty Images; 093: Logan Bowles/AP Images; 098: Paul Aniszewski/Shutterstock; 099: 123RF

**Topic 3**
102: Demerzel21/Fotolia; 104: John Bryson/The LIFE Images Collection/Getty Images; 106: Wead/Shutterstock; 107: John Cancalosi/Getty Images; 115: Paul Silverman/Fundamental Photographs, NYC; 117: ESA/AOES Medialab; 127 B: PerAnders Pettersson/Getty Images; 127 TR: Eric Baccega/AGE Fotostock/Alamy Stock Photo; 128: Brian Jannsen/Alamy Stock Photo; 134: Wead/Shutterstock; 136: Michael Routh/Alamy Stock Photo; 138: kmartin457/Getty Images; 139 C: Mark Yarchoan/Shutterstock; 139 CL: Joel Arem/Science Source; 139 CR: 123RF; 139 TCL: Tom Holt/Alamy Stock Photo; 139 TCR: Trevor Clifford/Pearson Education Ltd; 142 Bkgrd: Brandon B/Shutterstock; 142 CL: Universal Images Group North America LLC/Alamy Stock Photo; 148 : Jon Bilous/Shutterstock; 149 B: MM Studio/Fotolia; 149 CR: Pavlo Burdyak/123RF; 149 TR: image/Shutterstock

**Topic 4**
152: AFP/Getty Images; 154: Christopher Boswell/Shutterstock; 161 TL: Mr. Elliot Lim and Mr. Jesse Varner, CIRES & NOAA/NCEI; 161 TR: OAR/National Undersea Research Program/NOAA; 165: Sueddeutsche Zeitung Photo/Alamy Stock Photo; 166: MarkushaBLR/Fotolia; 172: wildestanimal/Getty Images; 173 B: Vadim Petrakov/Shutterstock; 173 CR: David Burton/Alamy Stock Photo; 176: Travel Pictures/Alamy Stock Photo; 178: The Asahi Shimbun/Getty Images; 187: Jiji Press/AFP/Getty Images; 189: epa european pressphoto agency b.v./Alamy Stock Photo; 190: Pall Gudonsson/Getty Images; 196 TL: Siim Sepp/Alamy Stock Photo; 196 TR: sandatlas/Shutterstock; 197: Hulton Archive/Getty Images; 198 BR: Rosa Irene Betancourt 3/Alamy Stock Photo; 198 TL: Janet Babb, U.S. Geological Survey, Hawaiian Volcano Observatory; 205: space_expert/Fotolia

**Topic 5**
208: Robert Harding/Alamy Stock Photo; 210: Maggie Steber/Getty Images; 211: Xu Jian/Getty Images; 212: Russ Bishop/Alamy Stock Photo; 214 TL: Sean Kaufmann/Getty Images; 214 TR: Thomas Mitchell/Alamy Stock Photo; 215 TC: mironov/Shutterstock; 215 TL: iPics Photography/Alamy Stock Photo; 217: madllen/123RF; 219 TCR: Sean Kaufmann/Getty Images; 219 TR: Vinicius Tupinamba/Shuttertock; 221: Alejandro Zepeda/EPA/Newscom; 222: Macduff Everton/National Geographic Magazines/Getty Images; 229 B: David Weintraub/Science Source; 229 TR: Roman Kadarjan/Alamy Stock Photo; 230: Songquan Deng/Shutterstock; 235 CL: totajla/Shutterstock; 235 TL: Planet Observer/UIG/Getty Images; 237: Macduff Everton/Getty Images; 238: AP Images; 240 B: cobalt88/Shutterstock; 240 BC: Spencer Grant/Getty Images; 242: Design Pics Inc/Alamy Stock Photo; 245: Pavel Svoboda Photography/Shutterstock; 249: Hemis/Alamy Stock Photo; 251: Mick Jack/Alamy Stock Photo

**Topic 6**
260: Panpilas L/Shutterstock; 262: Philipus/Alamy Stock Photo; 266: Aleksandr Pobedimskiy/Shutterstock; 268: Louisiana Governors Office/Alamy Stock Photo; 270: National Geographic Creative/Alamy Stock Photo; 272: Everett Historical/Shutterstock; 274: Raulbaenacasado/Shutterstock; 278: Chris James/Alamy Stock Photo; 282: Henryk Sadura/Shutterstock; 284: WaterFrame/Alamy Stock Photo; 285 B: Siim Sepp/Alamy Stock Photo; 285 T: ShuHung Liu/Shutterstock; 288: The Natural History Museum/Alamy Stock Photo; 290: Pulsar Imagens/Alamy Stock Photo; 294: Larry Geddis/Alamy Stock Photo; 297: Bennyartist/Shutterstock; 299: World History Archive/Alamy Stock Photo; 304: Haizhen Du/Shutterstock; 305 B: Anton Starikov/Alamy Stock Photo; 305 T: iStock/Getty Images

## Topic 7

308: KPG Payless2/Shutterstock; 310: ThavornC/Shutterstock; 312: Justin Lambert/Getty Images; 317: Fotokostic/Shutterstock; 318: Kletr/Shutterstock; 320: Por Nahorski Pavel/Shutterstock; 324: Karol Kozlowski/Shutterstock; 326: Mark Kauzlarich/Bloomberg/Getty Images; 327: Science Source; 329: Vadim Petrakov/Shutterstock; 330: Brian A. Jackson/Shutterstock; 332 BCL: Chad Ehlers/Alamy Stock Photo; 332 BCR: Jiri Foltyn/Shutterstock; 332 BR: Rob Crandall/Alamy Stock Photo; 333: Perytskyy/iStock/Getty Images; 334 CL: Kletr/Shutterstock; 334 CR: Blickwinkel/Alamy Stock Photo; 335: JurgaR/iStock/Getty Images; 338: lowsun/Shutterstock; 340: George Clerk/Getty Images; 344: iStock/Getty Images; 348: Philip Duff/Alamy Stock Photo; 348: Rosanne Tackaberry/Alamy Stock Photo; 350: US Navy Photo/Alamy Stock Photo; 351: ZUMA Press Inc/Alamy Stock Photo; 358: Philipp Dase/Shutterstock

## Topic 8

362: Sinclair Stammers/Science Photo Library/Getty Images; 364: James L. Amos/Science Source; 366: Jim in SC/Shutterstock; 368 BL: Carol Dembinsky/Dembinsky Photo Associates/Alamy Stock Photo; 368 BR: Chris Curtis/Shutterstock; 374: greenfire/Fotolia; 376: Mark Godden/Shutterstock; 378 BL: Chase Studio/Science Source; 378 BR: Ralf Juergen Kraft/Shutterstock; 379 BR: Catmando/Shutterstock; 379 TC: DEA/G. Cigolini/Getty Images; 379 TL: JeanPhilippe Delobelle/Alamy Stock Photo; 379 TR: Kevin Schafer/Alamy Stock Photo; 380: Biophoto Associates/Science Source; 383: James KingHolmes/Science Source; 384: Laurie O'Keefe/Science Source; 386: MarcelClemens/Shutterstock; 387 TL: John Cancalosi/Alamy Stock Photo; 387 TR: Sabena Jane Blackbird/Alamy Stock Photo; 388 BR: Herschel Hoffmeyer/Shutterstock; 388 TL: Stocktrek Images, Inc./Alamy Stock Photo; 390 B: The Natural History Museum/The Image Works; 390 TL: Jerry Young/Dorling Kindersley; 391 BC: Andreas Meyer/123RF; 391 C: Bedrock Studios/Dorling Kindersley; 391 TC: Chase Studio/Science Source; 393 B: Sean Pavone/Alamy Stock Photo; 393 TR: Alan Novelli/Getty Images; 398 : Jonathan Blair/Getty Images; 399: Adwo/Shutterstock

## Topic 9

402: UniversalImagesGroup/Getty Images; 404: dan_prat/Getty Images; 406: Louise Murray/Robert Harding/Getty Images; 413: Iakov Kalinin/Shutterstock; 415: NASA; 416: Ian Brown/Alamy Stock Photo; 418: id1974/123RF; 419 BL: efesenko/Fotolia; 419 BR: Polifoto/Fotolia; 426: Andrey Armyagov/Shutterstock; 430: Stuart Rankin/NOAA; 431: Geraldas Galinauskas/Shutterstock; 434: Kevin Kelley/Getty Images; 440: vermontalm/Fotolia

## Topic 10

444: Michael Turner/Alamy Stock Photo; 446: Paul Prescott/Alamy Stock Photo; 447: K. Arjana/Shutterstock; 448: marcaletourneux/Fotolia; 450 B: Karim Agabi/Science Source; 450 TR: Dorling Kindersley/Getty Images; 454: The Whiteview/Shutterstock; 455: Michael Runkel/Alamy Stock Photo; 457 BR: NASA/Goddard Space Flight Center/Scientific Visualization Studio; 457 TR: NASA/Goddard Space Flight Center/Scientific Visualization Studio; 458: Paulo Nabas/Shutterstock; 461: AFP/Getty Images; 464 BL: David Noton Photography/Alamy Stock Photo; 464 BR: Science Source; 465 BR: Aeropix/Alamy Stock Photo; 465 TL: Blickwinkel/Alamy Stock Photo; 465 TR: Blaize Pascall/Alamy Stock Photo; 470: Westend61/Getty Images; 475 Bkgrd: Volodymyr Goinyk/Shutterstock; 475 CL: Gece33/Getty Images; 475 TR: Ashley Cooper/Getty Images; 477: Lonely Planet Images/Getty Images; 484: Joel Sartore/National Geographic/Getty Images

## Topic 11

488: Chris Cook/Science Source; 490: Paul Lindsay/Alamy Stock Photo; 492: Scott Stulberg/Getty Images; 494: Halley Multicolor Camera Team, Giotto Project, ESA; 496: Alan Dyer/VWPics/Alamy Stock Photo; 502: AF Fotografie/Alamy Stock Photo; 504: Triff/Nasa/Shutterstock; 508: David Clapp/Shutterstock; 509: NASA/Getty Images; 513 Bkgrd: eFesenko/Shutterstock; 513 CR: iStock/Getty Images; 514: David M. Schrader/Shutterstock; 516: Quaoar/Shutterstock; 518 BL: Chris Collins/Shutterstock; 518 CL: Oorka/Shutterstock; 528: Quaoar/Shutterstock; 529: Claudio Divizia/Shutterstock

## Topic 12

532: John A. Davis/Shutterstock; 534: Blickwinkel/Alamy Stock Photo; 539 B: Ivann/Shutterstock; 539 CL: Robert_S/Shutterstock; 540 TL: JPL/NASA; 540 TR: NASA/Shutterstock; 543 TL: NASA; 543 TR: Ivannn/Shutterstock; 548 BL: JPLCaltech/UMD/NASA; 548 CL: JPLCaltech/UCAL/MPS/DLR/IDA/NASA; 548 L: NASA; 548 TL: NASA; 552: Hubble & NASA/S. Smartt/ESA/NASA; 554: European Space Agency; 555: Comstock Images/Getty Images; 556 BR: NASA; 556 CR: Sovfoto/UIG/Getty Images; 556 TR: Sovfoto/UIG/Getty Images; 557 BC: John Baran/Alamy Stock Photo; 557 TR: NASA; 558 BL: NASA & ESA; 558 CL: Everett Historical/Shutterstock; 558 TR: Stocktrek Images, Inc./Alamy Stock Photo; 559 BL: JPL/NASA; 559 CR: Tim Jacobs/NASA; 559 TL: NASA; 564: peresanz/Shutterstock; 567: NASA/S.Dupuis/Alamy Stock Photo; 571: Igordabari/Shutterstock; 574: NASA; ESA; G. Illingworth, D. Magee, and P. Oesch, University of California, Santa Cruz; R. Bouwens, Leiden University; and the HUDF09 Team; 578: Albert Barr/Shutterstock; 583: NASA; 584: Dhoxax/Getty Images; 585 TL: JPL/NASA; 585 TR: Stocktrek Images/Getty Images

## End Matter

588 BCL: Philippe Plailly & Elisabeth Daynes/Science Source; 588 BL: EHStockphoto/Shutterstock; 588 TCL: Cyndi Monaghan/Getty Images; 588 TL: Javier Larrea/AGE Fotostock; 589: WaterFrame/Alamy Stock Photo; 590: Africa Studio/Shutterstock; 591: Jeff Rotman/Alamy Stock Photo; 592: Grant Faint/Getty Images; 593: Ross Armstrong/Alamy Stock Photo; 594: geoz/Alamy Stock Photo; 595: Martin Shields/Alamy Stock Photo; 596: Nicola Tree/Getty Images; 597: Regan Geeseman/NASA; 601: Pearson Education Ltd.; 602: Pearson Education Ltd.; 603 BR: Pearson Education Ltd.; 603 CR: Pearson Education Ltd.

## Program graphics

ArtMari/Shutterstock; BeatWalk/Shutterstock; Irmun/Shutterstock; LHF Graphics/Shutterstock; Multigon/Shutterstock; Nikolaeva/Shutterstock; silm/Shutterstock; Undrey/Shutterstock

# Take Notes